3124300 597 5304

Lake Forest Library
360 E. Deerpath
Lake Forest, IL 60045
847-234-0636
www.lakeforestlibrary.org

2018
Guidebook to
ILLINOIS
TAXES

Library Use Only

Marilyn A. Wethekam

Fred O. Marcus

Jordan M. Goodman

David A. Hughes

Breen M. Schiller

David S. Ruskin

Christopher T. Lutz

David W. Machemer

Justin B. Stone

Samantha K. Breslow

Contributing Editors

D1366295

. Wolters Kluwer

Wolters Kluwer Editorial Staff Publication

Editors . . . . Tim Bjur, Lisa Lopata, Glenn Wesley

Production Coordinator . . . . Govardhan. L

Production . . . . Jadunath Panigrahi, Balaraju.T

This publication is designed to provide accurate and authoritative information in regard to the subject matter covered. It is sold with the understanding that the publisher is not engaged in rendering legal, accounting, or other professional service. If legal advice or other expert assistance is required, the services of a competent professional person should be sought.

ISBN 978-0-8080-4712-4

©2017 CCH Incorporated and its affiliates. All rights reserved.

2700 Lake Cook Road
Riverwoods, IL 60015
800 344 3734
CCHGroup.com

No claim is made to original government works; however, within this Product or Publication, the following are subject to CCH Incorporated's copyright: (1) the gathering, compilation, and arrangement of such government materials; (2) the magnetic translation and digital conversion of data, if applicable; (3) the historical, statutory, and other notes and references; and (4) the commentary and other materials.

Printed in the United States of America

PREFACE

This *Guidebook* gives a general picture of the taxes imposed by the state of Illinois and the general property tax levied by the local governments. All 2017 legislative amendments received as of press time are reflected, and references to Illinois and federal laws are to the laws as of the date of publication of this book.

The emphasis is on the law applicable to the filing of income tax returns in 2018 for the 2017 tax year. However, if legislation has made changes effective after 2017, we have tried to note this also, with an indication of the effective date to avoid confusion.

The taxes of major interest—income and sales and use—are discussed in detail. Other Illinois taxes, including estate taxes, are summarized, with particular emphasis on application, exemptions, returns, and payment.

Throughout the *Guidebook,* tax tips are highlighted to help practitioners avoid pitfalls and use the tax laws to their best advantage.

The *Guidebook* is designed as a quick reference work, describing the general provisions of the various tax laws, regulations, and administrative practices. It is useful to tax practitioners, businesspersons, and others who prepare or file Illinois returns or who are required to deal with Illinois taxes.

The *Guidebook* is not designed to eliminate the necessity of referring to the law and regulations for answers to complicated problems, nor is it intended to take the place of detailed reference works such as the CCH ILLINOIS TAX REPORTS. With this in mind, specific references to the publisher's Illinois and federal tax products are inserted in most paragraphs. By assuming some knowledge of federal taxes, the *Guidebook* is able to provide a concise, readable treatment of Illinois taxes that will supply a complete answer to most questions and will serve as a time-saving aid where it does not provide the complete answer.

SCOPE OF THE BOOK

This *Guidebook* is designed to do three things:

1. Give a general picture of the impact and pattern of all taxes levied by the state of Illinois and the general property tax levied by local governmental units.

2. Provide a readable quick-reference work for the personal income tax and the tax on corporate income. As such, it explains briefly what the Illinois law provides and indicates whether the Illinois provision is the same as federal law.

3. Analyze and explain the differences, in most cases, between Illinois and federal law.

HIGHLIGHTS OF 2017 ILLINOIS TAX CHANGES

The most important 2017 Illinois tax changes received by press time are noted in the "Highlights of 2017 Illinois Tax Changes" section of the *Guidebook*, beginning on page 13. This useful reference gives the practitioner up-to-the-minute information on changes in tax legislation.

LOCAL TAXES

The Illinois *Guidebook* also features a chapter on Chicago taxes. The scope of the chapter includes discussions on the employers' expense tax, the sales and use taxes, the transaction taxes, the use tax on titled and nontitled property, the amusement tax, soft drink taxes, the telecommunications tax, the motor vehicle lessor tax, the parking lot and garage operations tax, and the airport departure and ground transportation taxes. The discussions can be found at Chapter 23, "Chicago Taxes."

4

FINDERS

The practitioner may find the information wanted by consulting the general Table of Contents at the beginning of the *Guidebook*, the Table of Contents at the beginning of each chapter, the Topical Index, or the Law and Regulation Locator.

The Topical Index is a useful tool. Specific taxes and information on rates, allocation, credits, exemptions, returns, payments, collection, penalties, and remedies are thoroughly indexed and cross-referenced to paragraph numbers in the *Guidebook*.

The Law and Regulation Locator is an equally useful finders tool. Beginning on page 487, this finding list shows where sections of Illinois statutory law and administrative regulations referred to in the *Guidebook* are discussed.

October 2017

ABOUT THE EDITORS

Marilyn A. Wethekam

Marilyn A. Wethekam is a partner at Horwood Marcus & Berk, Chartered in Chicago. Ms. Wethekam co-chairs the firm's nationally recognized multistate State and Local Tax practice. She has a national SALT practice representing multistate and multinational corporations in all areas of state tax. In 2010 she was named as the second recipient of the Council on State Taxation's Paul Frankel Excellence in State Taxation Award. She received the 2012 Bloomberg BNA, Frank Latcham Award for Distinguished Service in State and Local Tax Law and in 2013 was named one of the Illinois's Leading Female Attorneys.

Ms. Wethekam advises her clients on multistate tax issues that involve income, franchise and transaction taxes. Her eighteen years of corporate tax experience with Mobil Oil Corporation and Montgomery Ward & Co. provide her with an understanding of the complex issues encountered by multistate and multinational corporations. This understanding allows her to develop innovative solutions for multistate tax issues as well as the practical resolution of multi-jurisdictional tax disputes. She has formulated multistate audit strategies, drafted legislation, and represented multistate and multinational corporations in income, franchise, transactional tax matters in more than thirty five states. In addition, she has worked with clients to develop organizational structures that incorporate both an understanding of the business needs and address tax burdens.

Ms. Wethekam is a frequent speaker before such groups as the Council on State Taxation (COST), Georgetown University Institute on State and Local Taxation; The Paul J. Hartman State Tax Forum; Tax Executives Institute; and the Institute for Professionals in Taxation (IPT). She is on the Steering Committee for IPT's State Business Income Taxation book.

Marilyn received her B.A. in Political Science from Loyola University of Chicago, her law degree from Illinois Institute of Technology Chicago-Kent College of Law and an L.L.M. in Taxation from John Marshall Law School. She is licensed to practice in the states of Illinois and Texas.

Fred O. Marcus

Fred O. Marcus is a principal in the Chicago law firm of Horwood Marcus & Berk Chartered where he co-chairs the firm's state and local tax practice group. Mr. Marcus concentrates his practice in state and local tax planning and the resolution of state and local tax disputes on a nationwide basis for multistate and multinational corporations. He has appeared before the United States Supreme Court, the California Supreme Court, and the California Appellate Court, has argued before the Illinois and Missouri Supreme Courts and the Illinois and New Jersey Appellate Courts and has tried cases before the courts and administrative tribunals of numerous other states. He is a frequent lecturer before such groups as the Council on State Taxation, the Tax Executives Institute, the Chicago Tax Club, New York University's Conference on State and Local Taxation, Vanderbilt University's School of Law's Paul J. Hartman State and Local Tax Forum and Georgetown University School of Law's Institute on State and Local Taxation. He is also an Adjunct Professor of Law at Northwestern University's School of Law's Graduate Tax Program where he teaches state and local taxation.

Mr. Marcus is a member of the American Bar Association's Section of Taxation's State and Local Tax Committee; a member of the Illinois Taxpayers' Federation Board of Trustees and Advisory Board; a member of Tax Management's State Tax Advisory Board; and a member of New York University's School of Continuing Legal Education's State and Local Tax Advisory Board and a member of the Illinois Department of Revenue's Director's Practitioner Advisory Group. He is the author of a Bloomberg/BNA Tax Management Multistate Tax Portfolio, entitled "Limitations on the States' Jurisdiction to Impose Net Income Based Taxes," has co-authored three additional Tax Management portfolios entitled "Sales and Use Taxes: The Machinery and Equipment Exemption," "Illinois Net Income Taxes," and "Illinois Sales and Use Taxes" and is a Contributing Editor to Commerce Clearing House's State Tax Report. He is also the author of a chapter on Illinois Franchise Taxes for the Illinois Institute of Continuing Legal Education and numerous other articles on various aspects of state and local taxation. Mr. Marcus received his B.S. degree (Accounting) from the University of Illinois at Chicago (1970) and his J.D. degree from DePaul University's College of Law (1974).

Mr. Marcus is the 2015 recipient of the Council on State Taxation's Paul H. Frankel Excellence in State Taxation Award and has been annually recognized as an Illinois Super Lawyer. He can be reached at 312.606.3210 or by e-mail at fmarcus@saltlawyers.com.

Jordan M. Goodman

Jordan M. Goodman is a shareholder at the law firm of Horwood Marcus & Berk Chartered, where he co-chairs the firm's state and local tax practice. Jordan plans for and resolves state and local tax controversies for multistate and multinational corporations. He advises businesses in various industries on the tax ramifications and benefits of certain organizational structures. He has also successfully resolved state tax controversies in virtually every state. Jordan has lectured on numerous state and local tax topics before business and professional associations, including the Council on State Taxation, the Tax Executives Institute, the Chicago Tax Club, Georgetown University Institute on State and Local Taxation, the National Institute Symposium, and annual meetings for CPAmerica and AGN International. In addition, Mr. Goodman has created and presented accredited state and local tax seminars throughout the country. Mr. Goodman has also been recognized as an "Illinois Super Lawyer" by his clients and peers.

Mr. Goodman is a member of the Editorial Boards for *The Journal of Multistate Taxation* and *CCH State Tax Income Alert*. Jordan is also a contributing editor to Commerce Clearing House's *State Tax Report*. Mr. Goodman is author of the chapter entitled "Other State Taxes and Unclaimed Property" in Illinois Institute of Continued Legal Education's Illinois Taxes and co-author of the chapter entitled "Illinois Income Tax Considerations" for the publication *Organizing and Advising Illinois Businesses*. He is also co-author of the Tax Management Multistate Tax portfolios entitled "Sales and Use Taxes: The Machinery and Equipment Exemption," "Illinois Income Tax," and "Illinois Sales and Use Tax." Mr. Goodman has also authored the chapter entitled "Illinois Sales and Use Tax" in the American Bar Association's *Sales and Use Tax Handbook* and multiple articles on the unitary business principle, nonbusiness income, apportionment irregularities, and situsing of services for income and sales tax purposes. He received his B.S. in Accounting with high honors from Indiana University and his J.D. from the University of Illinois. Mr. Goodman is also a Certified Public Accountant.

David A. Hughes

David A. Hughes is a partner in Horwood Marcus & Berk's State and Local Tax (SALT) Group. David's clients, who range from multinational corporations to individuals, all have one thing in common: the need to limit their state and local tax exposure either through planning or litigation. David advises clients on how to structure their business to reduce their state tax liabilities and he also defends clients in audits, administrative proceedings and court against tax assessments.

David has represented clients in over 30 states and has advised clients on income tax, sales/use tax, franchise tax, and unclaimed property matters, including matters involving nexus, apportionment, business income, unitary business groups, credits, losses, exemptions, and the tax base. David has argued cases at the Illinois Supreme Court, the Illinois Appellate Court and the New York Supreme Court (Appellate Division).

In addition to representing clients on a national basis, David is also very active in the SALT community. He is the former Chair of the SALT committee for the Illinois CPA Society and the former chair of the Chicago Bar Association's committee on state and local taxation. David also speaks and writes regularly on SALT matters. He is a co-author of the chapter entitled "Illinois Sales and Use Tax" in the American Bar Association's Sales and Use Tax Handbook and was previously on the Editorial Board of the Journal of Multistate Taxation and Incentives. In addition, he has spoken on behalf of NYU's School of Continuing and Professional Studies, the Council on State Taxation (COST), Tax Executives Institute (TEI), the American Bar Association, the Institute of Professionals in Taxation (IPT), the Illinois CPA Society, the Unclaimed Property Professionals Organization (UPPO), the Chicago Tax Club, the Association of Consumer Vehicle Lessors (ACVL) and Telestrategies.

David graduated magna cum laude with a degree in English from the University of Notre Dame and received his law degree from Columbia University.

Breen M. Schiller

Breen M. Schiller is a partner with Horwood Marcus & Berk Chartered where she concentrates her practice in state and local tax planning and the resolution of state and local tax controversies for multi-state and multi-national corporations. She advises Fortune 500 companies as well as mid-size and closely-held businesses and start-up companies on issues related to all types of state and local tax, including income tax, sales/use tax, franchise tax, public utility and motor fuel taxes, transaction taxes, andgross receipts-based taxes. Breen has represented clients across the country on diverse income tax engagements such as nexus, business/nonbusiness income, apportionment, unitary business principle, combined reporting, federal change reporting and credits and deductions and various sales and use tax engagements such as nexus, exemptions, and inclusions and exclusions from the tax base, in addition to e-commerce, sharing economy and cloud-computing issues and hotel occupancy tax related issues. This experience helps Breen assist her clients in developing innovative solutions for multistate tax issues as well as the practical resolution of disputes.

Breen has spoken on state and local tax matters for the Chicago Tax Club, the Center for Professional Education (CPE), the Illinois CPA Society, the Council on State Taxation (COST), Taxpayers' Federation of Illinois (TFI), the Interstate Tax Corporation, The National Business Institute, The Institute for Professionals in Taxation (IPT) and The Paul J. Hartman State Tax Forum and Tax Executives Institute. Breen is a co-author of CCH's Annual Guidebook to Illinois Taxes, and on the board of the Journal of State Taxation. She has had articles published in The Journal of State Taxation, Tax Analysts the IPT Insider, State Tax Notes and The Journal of Multistate Taxation. Breen currently serves as one of the co-chairs of TFI's local taxes committee as well as the chair of the Tax Administration Committee for the Chicago Tax Club and Chair of IPT's 2017 Annual Conference Income Tax Section. In 2016, Breen received the Article of the Year Award for Special Tax Topics from IPT discussing state taxation of Airbnb.

Breen received her J.D. from DePaul University College of Law and also received her B.A. in English Literature and Political Science from Illinois Wesleyan University.

David S. Ruskin

David S. Ruskin is a partner within both Horwood Marcus & Berk Chartered's Litigation Group and State & Local Tax (SALT) Group. He focuses his practice on State and Local Tax litigation and regularly represents his clients before state courts and administrative tax tribunals in numerous states across the country. David also litigates on behalf of his clients in appellate and federal courts, and in audit disputes and informal dispute resolution with departments of revenue. David's tax litigation has covered a broad range of taxes and issues, including income, sales/use, franchise, telecommunications and utility taxes. David has also successfully tried numerous cases across the country and is consistently engaged in various stages of tax litigation. He speaks regularly on the tips and traps of litigation procedure and strategies in the state and local tax context.

David began his career litigating commercial and business disputes. Over the years, his extensive litigation experience has included a broad array of contractual disputes, business torts, employment related matters, real estate and construction matters. David has successfully obtained and defended against injunctive relief, motions for summary judgment and jury trials in both state and federal courts. His primary focus is always to resolve clients' disputes in the most efficient and satisfactory manner possible.

David received his B.A. in Political Science from the University of Wisconsin-Madison and obtained his J.D. from Loyola University of Chicago Law School, where he was the recipient of the American Jurisprudence Award in Secured Transactions and Creditors' Rights.

Christopher T. Lutz

Christopher T. Lutz is an attorney at Horwood Marcus & Berk Chartered who concentrates his practice on representing clients with respect to multistate tax issues. The primary component of Chris's practice is litigating in courts and administrative forums with respect to contested state and local tax liabilities for multinational corporations as well as mid-size businesses. Chris uses that litigation experience to advise clients on a range of issues including corporate income tax, financial institutions taxes, sales and use tax, local taxes, gross receipts taxes, telecommunications taxes, and motor fuel taxes.

Chris is an author and frequent speaker before such groups as Georgetown University Institute on State and Local Taxation, the Council on State Taxation (COST), National Business Institute, the Interstate Tax Corporation, and The Institute for Professionals in Taxation. Chris has published articles in Bloomberg BNA, State Tax Notes, the Journal of Multistate Taxation and Incentives, and the National Litigation Consultants' Review.

Chris received his J.D. from the George Washington University Law School with honors and received his B.A. from Vassar College. Prior to HMB, he worked at the Council on State Taxation, where he was active in drafting amicus briefs and state tax policy advocacy.

David W. Machemer

David W. Machemer is an associate at the law firm of Horwood Marcus & Berk Chartered and concentrates his practice in state and local tax matters. David advises multistate and multinational taxpayers on state and local tax planning and resolution of tax controversies in the arenas of sales and use, income, franchise, motor fuel, real property and employment taxes.

David brings a unique and practical approach to solving clients' problems. This is a result of his prior experiences working for a Fortune 15 multinational company with a financial and leasing arm and also having litigated state tax cases at the Illinois Attorney General's Office. He understands the challenges and complexities of compliance in today's marketplace, and the significant risks and costs associated with noncompliance. At the leasing company, David counseled business units engaged in the manufacturing, aeronautics, marine, motor vehicle and trucking industries on state and local tax laws in 45+ states. He also defended sales and use tax audits in 15+

state and local jurisdictions. Prior to that, David served as an Illinois Assistant Attorney General where he represented the Illinois Department of Revenue in state tax litigation matters.

David received his B.A. from Michigan State University and his law degree from The John Marshall Law School.

Justin B. Stone

Justin B. Stone concentrates his practice in state and local tax matters. Justin advises multistate and multinational taxpayers on state and local tax planning, transactions and resolution of tax controversies for an extensive range of clients and industries. He advises clients on a range of state and local tax topics, including sales and use tax, franchise tax, corporate income tax, gross receipts tax and ad valorem property tax.

Justin is a 2012 graduate of the Georgetown University Law Center where he received his Master of Laws in Taxation and Certificate in State and Local Taxation. He received his juris doctor degree from Wake Forest University School of Law in 2011 and his undergraduate degree in Economics and Political Science from Clemson University in 2008. Prior to joining Horwood Marcus & Berk Chartered, Justin practiced state and local tax at Jones Walker LLP in the New Orleans, Louisiana office with an emphasis in tax controversies and advising clients in the manufacturing and energy industries.

Justin is a member of the American Bar Association State and Local Tax Executive Committee and a liaison to the American Bar Association Diversity Committee.

Samantha K. Breslow

Samantha K. Breslow is an associate with Horwood Marcus & Berk Chartered where she focuses her practice on multistate tax litigation and planning. Samantha resolves state and local tax controversies for a wide array of clients, including Fortune 500 corporations, investment partnerships, and high net worth individuals. She advises clients on a range of state and local tax topics, including sales and use tax, franchise tax, corporate income tax, personal income tax, gross receipts tax, and unclaimed property.

Samantha received her J.D. from the University of Illinois College of Law and her B.A. in English and Spanish from The University of Texas at Austin. She previously served as a multistate tax consultant at Deloitte Tax LLP, where she was active in state tax compliance and planning for high-yield investment partnerships, large law firms, and prominent corporations in most states and jurisdictions.

CONTENTS

HIGHLIGHTS OF 2017 ILLINOIS TAX CHANGES

The most important 2017 tax changes and new developments are noted below.

Sales and Use Taxes

• *Rental Purchase Agreement Occupation and Use Tax Act*

Illinois has enacted two 6.25% taxes on transactions involving merchandise rented or used by consumers. The rental purchase agreement occupation tax (rental sales tax) is imposed on transactions where a consumer rents merchandise. And the rental purchase agreement use tax (rental use tax) is imposed on a consumer's use of rented merchandise. Both taxes go into effect on January 1, 2018. (¶1521)

• *Exemption for graphic arts machinery and equipment*

Sales of graphic arts machinery and equipment are included under the manufacturing exemptions for sales tax, service occupation tax, use tax, and service use tax, effective July 1, 2017. (P.A. 100-22 (S.B. 9), Laws 2017) (¶1702)

• *Gasohol*

Sales of gasohol are subject to 100% sales tax, service occupation tax, use tax, and service use tax, effective July 1, 2017. (P.A. 100-22 (S.B. 9), Laws 2017) (¶1702)

• *Blended Ethanol, Biodiesel and Biodiesel Blends*

The sales tax, service occupation tax, use tax, and service use tax exemptions for majority blended ethanol, biodiesel and certain biodiesel blends are extended to December 31, 2023 (P.A. 100-22 (S.B. 9), Laws 2017) (¶1702)

Income Taxes

• *Tax rate increase, domestic production activities addback, and other changes enacted*

Illinois budget legislation has been enacted that increases corporate (¶903) and personal income tax rates (¶102), creates an income tax addback for the federal domestic production activities deduction under IRC §199 (¶205, ¶1026), expands the definition of "unitary business group" (¶1103) and eliminates the noncombination rule for unitary group members that must use different apportionment formulas (¶1104), extends the sunset date for the research and development income tax credit (¶407, ¶1211), increases the education expense (¶411) and earned income tax credits (¶414), eliminates the educational expense credit (¶411), the property tax credit (¶402), and personal income tax exemptions for certain taxpayers (¶213), and establishes a new income tax credit for teachers, instructors, counselors, principals, or aides who purchase school instructional materials and supplies (¶424). (P.A. 100-22 (S.B. 9), Laws 2017)

• *EDGE credit reinstated and modified*

Legislation has been enacted that reinstates and modifies the corporate (¶1207) and personal income tax credit (¶413) that may be claimed under the Economic Development for a Growing Economy Tax Credit Act (EDGE credit) by new or existing businesses that create or retain jobs in Illinois. (P.A. 100-0511 (H.B. 162), Laws 2017)

• *Invest in Kids Credit created*

Legislation has been enacted that creates the Invest in Kids credit that may be claimed against Illinois corporate (¶1223) and personal income tax liability (¶425) for contributions to scholarship granting organizations. (P.A. 100-0465 (S.B. 1947), Laws 2017)

- *Sunset date for new markets credit extended, recapture provision revised*

Legislation has been enacted that extends the sunset date and revises the recapture provision for the credit that may be claimed against Illinois corporate income, personal income, and insurance gross premiums tax liability by taxpayers who invest in long-term debt securities issued by a qualified community development entity (CDE) that participates in the federal new markets tax credit program and provides financing to businesses in Illinois low-income communities. (P.A. 100-0408 (S.B. 652), Laws 2017) (¶418, ¶1217)

- *Sunset date established for live theater production credit*

Legislation has been enacted that establishes a sunset date for the credit that may be claimed against Illinois corporate and personal income tax liability for certain live theater production and labor expenses. (P.A. 100-0415 (S.B. 852), Laws 2017) (¶417, ¶1214)

- *Angel investment credit reinstated and modified*

The angel investment credit that may be claimed against Illinois corporate and personal income tax liability by taxpayers that make direct equity investments in certain Illinois businesses has been reinstated until taxable years ending on or before December 31, 2021. Among other modifications to the credit program, angel investors must make a minimum investment to qualify for the credit. (P.A. 100-0328 (S.B. 2012), Laws 2017) (¶421, ¶1220)

- *Sunset date extended for River Edge Historic Preservation Credit*

The sunset date for the River Edge Historic Preservation Credit that taxpayers may claim against Illinois corporate and personal income tax liability has been extended from January 1, 2017 to January 1, 2022. (P.A. 99-0914 (S.B. 1488), Laws 2016; P.A. 100-236 (S.B. 1783), Laws 2017) (¶420, ¶1219)

- *Sunset date for Affordable Housing Tax Credit extended*

The sunset date for the Illinois Affordable Housing Tax Credit (IAHTC) has been extended from December 31, 2016 to December 31, 2021. (P.A. 99-0915 (S.B. 2921), Laws 2016) (¶415, ¶1213)

- *Regulation implements State Tax Preparer Oversight Act*

The Illinois Department of Revenue has adopted a regulation implementing a requirement under the State Tax Preparer Oversight Act that preparers of Illinois corporate and individual income tax returns include their preparer tax identification number (PTIN) on any return or claim for a tax refund prepared by the preparer, effective for taxable years beginning on or after January 1, 2017. (P.A. 99-0925 (S.B. 513), Laws 2017) (¶501, ¶1201)

Property Taxes

- *Senior citizens homestead exemption*

Certain Illinois property tax homestead exemption amounts and maximum income levels for eligibility have been increased. The exemptions involved are the senior citizens homestead exemption, the senior citizens assessment freeze homestead exemption, and the general homestead exemption. (P.A. 100-401 (S.B. 473), Laws 2017) (¶2003)

- *Local rebate ordinance repeal not unconstitutional*

An Illinois city's repeal of a property tax rebate ordinance did not result in either an unlawful taking of property or a denial of due process in violation of the federal Constitution. A right derived from a remedial statute is not a vested right, and the Legislature has ongoing authority to repeal or amend the statute. (*Bell v. City of*

Country Club Hills, U.S. Court of Appeals, Seventh Circuit, Nos. 16-1245, 16-1448, November 8, 2016, CCH ILLINOIS TAX REPORTS, ¶ 403-151) (¶ 2004)

- *Taxpayer liable for erroneous homestead exemption arrearage*

An Illinois taxpayer was liable for unpaid taxes and interest due to an erroneously granted homestead exemption on a property she inherited because the taxpayer had improperly taken simultaneous homestead exemptions on two different properties. The General Assembly had clearly and unequivocally expressed its intention that the newly enacted section of the statute applied to exemptions erroneously taken in "any of the three collection years immediately prior to the current collection year." (*Mulry v. Berrios*, Appellate Court of Illinois, First District, No. 2017 IL App (1st) 152563, March 16, 2017, CCH ILLINOIS TAX REPORTS, ¶ 403-204) (¶ 2004)

- *Six-year collection period for erroneous exemption permissible*

A taxpayer who had claimed homestead exemptions on 11 different properties, of which only one property was his principal residence, unsuccessfully challenged the erroneous homestead exemption law with claims that the law (1) had an unconstitutionally retroactive effect, (2) violated state and federal constitutional guarantees of uniform taxation, equal protection, and due process, and (3) was vague, ambiguous, and arbitrary. (*Cuevas v. Berrios*, Appellate Court of Illinois, First District, No. 1-15-1318, 1-16-0602 cons, March 31, 2017, CCH ILLINOIS TAX REPORTS, ¶ 403-218) (¶ 2004)

- *New law not applicable to mobile home despite noncompliance with old law*

In light of a "grandfather clause" in a new law generally requiring mobile and manufactured homes installed outside a mobile home park to be taxed as real property, the requirement did not apply to a manufactured home whose owner failed to register the home and pay a privilege tax after its installment outside a mobile home park just months before the effective date of the new law where the county did not conduct a new assessment of the property before the law was enacted. (*Jones v. State of Illinois Property Tax Appeal Board*, Appellate Court of Illinois, Fifth District, No. 5-16-0199, August 1, 2017, CCH ILLINOIS TAX REPORTS, ¶ 403-258) (¶ 2003)

Unclaimed Property

- *Revised Uniform Unclaimed Property Act adopted*

Effective January 1, 2018, the state enacted the Revised Uniform Unclaimed Property Act to replace the current unclaimed property law. New types of property were specified, generally with a three-year dormancy period from some event related to the property. Examples include tax-deferred retirement accounts and custodial accounts for minors. In addition, from the time a property is presumed abandoned, any other property right or interest accrued or accruing from the property and not previously presumed abandoned is also presumed to be abandoned. The current law is repealed on January 1, 2018. (P.A. 100-22 (S.B. 9), Laws 2017) (¶ 2901)

- *Interagency agreement would facilitate return of properties*

Effective August 11, 2017, the Illinois Department of Revenue (DOR) is authorized to exchange personal income tax return information with the State Treasurer's office for the purpose of administering the Uniform Disposition of Unclaimed Property Act. The agencies also may enter into an interagency agreement concerning protection of confidential information, data match rules, and other issues. (P.A. 100-47 (H.B. 1808), Laws 2017) (¶ 2901)

Miscellaneous Taxes

• *CNG, LNG, and propane rates set*

For Illinois motor fuel tax purposes, rates have been set for compressed natural gas (CNG), liquefied natural gas (LNG), and propane. Effective July 1, 2017, the rate for CNG is $0.19 per gasoline gallon equivalent, and the rate for LNG and propane is $0.215 per diesel gallon equivalent. The definition of "gallon" is amended to include gasoline gallon equivalent and diesel gallon equivalent. (P.A. 100-9 (H.B. 2801), Laws 2017) (¶2203)

• *Telphone laws, rates reenacted and extended*

Provisions of the Illinois Emergency Telephone System Act, the Prepaid Wireless 9-1-1 Surcharge Act, and the telecommunication provisions of the Public Utilities Act, all of which were set to expire July 1, 2017, have been reenacted or extended.

The Emergency Telephone System Act is reenacted, extending the application of existing provisions for local wireless and non-wireless surcharges to December 31, 2017. Effective January 1, 2018, to December 31, 2020, either surcharge, when imposed by a city with a population exceeding 500,000, may not exceed $5.

The Prepaid Wireless 9-1-1 Surcharge Act is amended to extend the time period during which a city with a population exceeding 500,000 may impose a 9% prepaid wireless 9-1-1 surcharge to end on December 31, 2020. Beginning January 1, 2021, such a city may not impose more than a 7% prepaid wireless 9-1-1 surcharge.

Article XIII Telecommunications of the Public Utilities Act is reenacted, effective July 1, 2017. The legislation expressly provides that the law has been in continuous effect since July 1, 2017. The new repeal date is December 31, 2020. (P.A. 100-20 (H.B. 1811), Laws 2017, effective July 1, 2017) (¶2207)

TAX CALENDAR

The following table lists significant dates of interest to Illinois taxpayers and tax practitioners.

Annually Recurring Dates

January
1st—Real property tax assessment date for real property
    Real property tax lien attaches in the year tax levied
10th—Estimated annual gross revenue returns for utility administration tax due
20th—Sales and use tax return due for annual filers (monthly average tax not over $50)
    Live adult entertainment surcharge returns for prior year due
31st—Withholding information statement (W-2s) must be furnished to employees
    Most property tax exemption affidavits due
    Deadline for filing open-space exemption applications in Cook County

February
1st—Surplus line brokers' tax due

March
1st—Insurance companies' reports due and payments due if preceding year's taxes less than $5,000
    First installment of real property taxes in Cook County due
15th—Annual insurance companies' reports and payments due
31st—Annual insurance companies' fire marshal tax returns due

April
15th—Annual income tax returns for corporations, individuals, partnerships, and fiduciaries due
    Special fuel bulk users' returns due

May
1st—Deadline for application for senior citizens' homestead exemptions

June
1st (or the day after the date specified on the real estate tax bill)—Real property taxes (first installment) due
15th—Motor vehicle registration fee reduced one-half if applicant became owner after this date
3rd Monday—Meeting of Board of Review
30th—Mailing of second installment of preceding year's property taxes by counties using accelerated payment system
    Deadline for filing open-space exemption applications (except January 31st in Cook County)

August
1st—Surplus line brokers' semiannual tax and return due
    Second installment of real property taxes in Cook County due
15th—Annual tax returns and annualization schedule due for specified city of Chicago taxes

September
1st (or the day after the date specified on the real estate tax bill as the second installment due date)—Real property taxes (second installment) due

December
31st—Property tax relief applications due from senior citizens and disabled persons

Quarterly Recurring Dates
15th day of April, June, Sept., Jan.—Income tax installments of estimated tax due for individuals with liability estimate over $500
15th day of April, June, Sept., Dec.—Income tax installments of estimated tax due for corporations with liability estimate over $400
    Quarterly installments of insurers with annual liability greater than $5,000
    Specific Chicago tax payments due for previous quarter
20th day of April, July, Oct., Jan.—Quarterly returns of sales and use tax due for quarterly filers (monthly average tax not over $200)
Last day of April, July, Oct., Jan.—Quarterly report of income tax withheld by employers
    Quarterly income tax withholding tax returns

Monthly Recurring Dates
5th—Cigarette manufacturers qualifying as distributors pay occupation and use taxes
15th—Alcoholic beverage reports due
    Cigarette and tobacco product distributors' reports due
    Monthly payment of withheld income taxes by employers not required to make semi-weekly payments
    Utility gross receipts tax returns due
    Oil and gas production assessment due
    Specific Chicago tax payments due for previous month

20th—Taxes and returns due from gasoline distributors and unlicensed purchasers of motor fuel thereafter used on public highways

Special fuel suppliers' tax and returns due

Sales and use taxes and returns due for monthly filers

Tire user fee returns due

Medical cannabis (marijuana) privilege tax returns due

30th—Gasoline transporters' reports due

Last Day—Hotel occupancy tax and returns due

Hydraulic fracturing tax returns due from purchasers and operators

Weekly and Semi-weekly Recurring Dates

7th, 15th, 22nd, and Last Day of Month—Sales and use (ROT, UT, SOT, SUT) payment due quarter-monthly if the average liability was $20,000 or more during the preceding four calendar quarters

Every Wednesday and Friday Employers who withheld or were required to withhold more than $12,000 in any calendar quarter or in the previous calendar year ending on June 30 must make semi-weekly payments.

PART I

TABLES

TAX RATES

¶1 Income Tax

Individual: The income tax rate for individuals, estates, and trusts is increased from 3.75% to 4.95% of net income for taxable years beginning on or after July 1, 2017 (¶102).

Corporate: The corporate income tax rate is increased from 5.25% to 7% of net income for taxable years beginning on or after July 1, 2017 (¶903).

• *Personal property replacement income tax*

In addition to the income tax, corporations, partnerships, limited liability companies, and trusts are subject to the personal property replacement income tax. The rate for C corporations is 2.5%, and the rate for S corporations, partnerships, LLCs, and trusts is 1.5%.

• *Standard exemptions*

The standard exemption allowed to resident individuals is $2,175 for 2016, multiplied by the number of exemptions that were taken on the federal returns (¶213). An additional $1,000 exemption is granted to taxpayers who are 65 years of age or older and to blind taxpayers.

Partnerships, estates, and trusts are allowed a standard exemption of $1,000 (¶213, 1021).

¶5 Franchise Tax

The initial franchise tax is payable at the annual rate of $^{15}/_{100}$ of 1% of paid-in capital for the first year of incorporation (¶1404). The annual franchise tax is payable at the rate of $^1/_{10}$ of 1% thereafter.

¶10 Sales and Use Taxes

The rate of the state retailers' occupation (sales), use, service occupation, and service use taxes is 6.25% (¶1601). A rate of 1% applies to certain food, medicine (including medical cannabis), and medical equipment. A privilege tax on the cultivation of medical cannabis (marijuana) is imposed at the rate of 7% of the sales price per ounce (¶1520).

In addition to the 6.25% state tax, home-rule counties and municipalities are authorized to levy local taxes in increments of ¼ of 1% (¶1518, 1601). The Regional Transportation Authority and the Metro East Mass Transit District are also authorized to levy taxes at various rates (¶1518).

In lieu of the retailers' occupation and use taxes, a 5% state automobile renting occupation and use tax is imposed on persons engaged in the business of renting or leasing automobiles, and a 5% tax is imposed on the privilege of using a rented automobile (¶1517, 1601). In addition to the 5% state automobile rental taxes, cities, Cook County, the Regional Transportation Authority, and the Metro East Mass Transit District are authorized to impose automobile rental taxes of up to 1%. The Chicago Metropolitan Pier and Exposition Authority imposes a 6% occupation tax on the gross receipts of all persons engaged in the business of renting automobiles.

Local tax rates: A link to the local tax rate finder is available on the Department of Revenue's website at **https://mytax.illinois.gov/_/** (¶1601).

FEDERAL/STATE COMPARISON OF KEY FEATURES

¶40 Personal Income Tax Comparison

The following is a comparison of key features of federal income tax laws that have been enacted as of December 18, 2015, and the Illinois personal income tax laws. The starting point for computing Illinois personal income tax liability is federal adjusted gross income (see ¶201). Illinois incorporates by reference the Internal Revenue Code as amended, as well as other federal provisions relating to federal income tax laws applicable for the taxable year (¶202). State modifications to federal adjusted gross income required by law differences are discussed beginning at ¶205.

Nonresidents and part-year residents: Nonresidents are taxed only on income as specifically modified and allocated or apportioned to Illinois. Part-year residents are taxed on all income received while a resident of Illinois and income attributable to Illinois sources while a nonresident. Allocation and apportionment of income provisions applying to nonresidents and part-year residents are discussed in Chapter 3.

The taxable income base and computation of income tax for partnerships and estates and trusts is discussed beginning at ¶207 and ¶208.

Alternative minimum tax (IRC Sec. 55—IRC Sec. 59).—There is no Illinois equivalent to the federal alternative minimum tax on tax preference items.

Asset expense election (IRC Sec. 179 and IRC Sec. 1400N).—The same as federal because the starting point for computing Illinois personal income tax liability is federal adjusted gross income (see ¶202).

Bad debts (IRC Sec. 166).—The same as federal because the starting point for computing Illinois personal income tax liability is federal adjusted gross income (see ¶202).

Capital gains and capital losses (IRC Sec. 1(h), IRC Sec. 1211, IRC Sec. 1212, and IRC Sec. 1221).—Generally, the same as federal because the starting point for computing Illinois personal income tax liability is federal adjusted gross income (see ¶202). An Illinois subtraction adjustment from federal adjusted gross income is allowed for certain capital gains on employer securities received in a lump-sum distribution and capital gain resulting from appreciation of certain property acquired before August 1, 1969 (¶205).

Charitable contributions (IRC Sec. 170 and IRC Sec. 1400S).—Illinois does not allow itemized deductions (see ¶205) and therefore, Illinois does not incorporate the federal charitable contribution deduction (IRC Sec. 170 and IRC Sec. 1400S). Illinois also does not allow an equivalent state subtraction for charitable contributions (see ¶205).

Child care credit (IRC Sec. 45F).—Illinois has no equivalent to the federal employer-provided child care credit.

Civil rights deductions (IRC Sec. 62).—The same as federal because the starting point for computing Illinois personal income tax liability is federal adjusted gross income (see ¶202).

Dependents (IRC Sec. 152).—The same as federal because Illinois adopts the federal definition of "dependent" by incorporation of IRC provisions as amended (¶202) and allows the same exemptions allowed on the federal return (see ¶213).

Depreciation (IRC Sec. 167, IRC Sec. 168 and IRC Sec. 1400N).—The same as federal because the starting point for computing Illinois personal income tax liability is federal adjusted gross income (see ¶202). However, Illinois requires an addition to federal taxable income for IRC Sec. 168(k) bonus depreciation, except the 100% federal bonus depreciation deduction allowed for property placed in service before January 1, 2012. A subtraction from taxable income is allowed for a portion of bonus depreciation. (¶205).

Earned Income Credit (IRC Sec. 32).—Illinois taxpayers are entitled to a refundable earned income tax credit that may be claimed against Illinois personal income tax liability equal to a portion of the federal EITC (IRC Sec. 32). The amount of the credit for nonresidents or part-year residents is based on the proportion of taxable income attributable to Illinois sources (see ¶414).

Educational benefits and deductions (IRC Sec. 62(a)(2)(D), IRC Sec. 127, IRC Sec. 221, IRC Sec. 222, IRC Sec. 529).—The same as federal because the starting point for computing Illinois personal income tax liability is federal adjusted gross income (see ¶202).

Foreign earned income (IRC Sec. 911 and IRC Sec. 912).—The same as federal because the starting point for computing Illinois personal income tax liability is federal adjusted gross income (see ¶202).

Health insurance and health savings accounts (HSAs) (IRC Sec. 106(e), IRC Sec. 162(l), IRC Sec. 223, IRC Sec. 139C, IRC Sec. 139D).—The same as federal because the starting point for computing Illinois personal income tax liability is federal adjusted gross income (see ¶202). However, unlike federal law (IRC Sec. 213(a)), Illinois does not allow an itemized deduction for unreimbursed medical expenses (¶205).

Indebtedness (IRC Sec. 108 and IRC Sec. 163).—The same as federal because the starting point for computing Illinois personal income tax liability is federal adjusted gross income (see ¶202).

Interest on federal obligations (IRC Sec. 61).—Interest on federal obligations which is exempt from Illinois personal income tax may be subtracted from federal adjusted gross income for purposes of computing state income tax liability. In addition, Illinois allows a subtraction from federal adjusted gross income for distributions from mutual funds investing exclusively in U.S. government obligations (¶211).

Interest on state and local obligations (IRC Sec. 103).—Interest on state and local obligations, except those exempt under Illinois law, must be added to federal adjusted gross income for purposes of computing Illinois personal income tax liability (¶205). Expenses related to the federally-exempt interest income, which are disallowed as deductions for federal purposes, may be subtracted from federal adjusted gross income for Illinois tax purposes (¶205).

Losses not otherwise compensated (IRC Sec. 165 and IRC Sec. 1400S).—The same as federal because the starting point for computing Illinois personal income tax liability is federal adjusted gross income (see ¶202), except Illinois does not allow itemized deductions for personal casualty and theft losses.

Net operating loss (IRC Sec. 172 and IRC Sec. 1400N).—The same as federal because the starting point for computing Illinois personal income tax liability is federal adjusted gross income and the state does not require any adjustment to the federal deduction or carryback/carryfoward periods. (see ¶204)

Personal residence (IRC Sec. 121 and IRC Sec. 1033).—The same as federal because the starting point for computing Illinois personal income tax liability is federal adjusted gross income (see ¶202).

Retirement plans (IRC Secs. 401—IRC Sec. 424, IRC Sec. 457A, and IRC Sec. 1400Q).—Illinois generally conforms to federal provisions regarding retirement plans (see ¶202). Illinois allows a subtraction from federal adjusted gross income for distributions from a self-employed retirement or qualified employee benefit plan to the extent the amount is included in federal adjusted gross income (¶205).

Start-up expenses (IRC Sec. 195).—The same as federal because the starting point for computing Illinois personal income tax liability is federal adjusted gross income (see ¶202).

Taxes paid (IRC Sec. 164).—Illinois does not allow personal income taxpayers to claim itemized deductions for state income taxes, sales and use taxes, property taxes, or other taxes (see ¶205). A credit may be claimed against Illinois personal income tax liability by resident taxpayers for real property taxes paid during the taxable year on a principal residence located in Illinois (see ¶402). In addition, residents and part-year residents may claim a credit against Illinois personal income tax liability for income tax paid to another state (see ¶403).

Unemployment compensation (IRC Sec. 85).—The same as federal because the starting point for computing Illinois personal income tax liability is federal adjusted gross income (see ¶202).

¶45 Corporate Income Tax Comparison

The following is a comparison of key features of federal income tax laws that have been enacted as of December 18, 2015, and the Illinois corporate income tax law. The starting point for computing Illinois corporation income and replacement tax liability is federal taxable income after the net operating loss and special deductions, which is modified by Illinois addition and subtraction adjustments. (see ¶1001). Federal conformity for purposes of computing the Illinois corporation income tax is based on the Internal Revenue Code as amended to date. State modifications to taxable income required by law differences are discussed beginning at ¶1010.

IRC Sec. 27 foreign tax credit.—Illinois has no equivalent to the federal foreign tax credit and does not allow a deduction for foreign income, franchise, or capital stock taxes regardless of whether the federal foreign tax credit was taken (¶1012).

IRC Sec. 40 alcohol fuels credit.—Illinois has no equivalent to the federal alcohol fuel credit. However, Illinois allows a subtraction from federal taxable income for amount of the credit that must be included in federal gross income if the federal credit was taken (¶1010).

IRC Sec. 41 incremental research expenditures credit.—Illinois provides a credit for expenditures that were used for increasing research activities in Illinois that is similar to the federal credit (¶1211). In addition, Illinois allows a deduction for expenses associated with the federal credit for increasing research activities that are disallowed as federal deductions under IRC 280C (¶1022).

IRC Sec. 42 low-income housing credit.—Illinois has no equivalent to the federal low-income housing credit. However, Illinois provides a credit for donations to sponsors of affordable housing projects (¶1201).

IRC Sec. 44 disabled access credit.—Illinois has no equivalent to the federal disabled access credit.

IRC Sec. 45A Indian employment credit.—Illinois has no equivalent to the federal Indian employment credit. However, Illinois allows a deduction for the portion of wages or salaries paid during the taxable year that was disallowed as a federal deduction when the Indian employment credit was taken (¶1022).

IRC Sec. 45B employer social security credit.—Illinois has no equivalent to the federal employer social security credit.

IRC Sec. 45C orphan drug credit.—Illinois has no equivalent to the federal orphan drug credit. However, Illinois allows a deduction for expenses associated with the federal credit for qualified clinical testing expenses (¶1022).

IRC Sec. 45D new markets credit.—Illinois has an equivalent to the federal new markets credit (see ¶1217).

IRC Sec. 45E small employer pension plan start-up costs.—Illinois has no equivalent to the federal small employer pension plan start-up costs credit.

IRC Sec. 45F employer-provided child care credit.—Although it has no direct equivalent to the federal employer-provided child care credit, Illinois allows employers to claim a credit for a percentage of the start-up costs associated in opening an employee child care facility and for a percentage of the costs associated in operating the facility.

IRC Sec. 45K fuel from nonconventional source credit.—Illinois has no equivalent to the federal fuel from nonconventional source credit.

IRC Sec. 45L new energy efficient homes credit.—Illinois has no equivalent to the federal new energy efficient homes credit.

IRC Sec. 45M energy efficient appliances credit for manufacturers.—Illinois has no equivalent to the federal energy efficient appliances credit for manufacturers.

IRC Sec. 46—IRC Sec. 49 investment credit (former law).—Illinois has no equivalent to the former federal investment or reforestation credits. Illinois also has no equivalent to the federal energy credit or the federal advanced energy project credit. However, Illinois provides a credit similar to the federal rehabilitation credit for expenditures in the rehabilitation of certified historic property located in a River Edge Redevelopment Zone. (¶1219) Illinois also provides credits that are similar to the current federal investment credit to encourage investments in new gasification facilities and new coal based energy generating facilities that generate a specified amount of electricity (see ¶1205).

IRC Sec. 51—Sec. 52 (and IRC Sec. 1396) wage credits.—Illinois has no equivalent to the federal work opportunity credit or the empowerment zone employment credit. However, Illinois allows a deduction for wages disallowed under IRC Sec. 280C when the credits are claimed (see ¶1022). Illinois also allows credits for hiring ex-felons (¶1215).

IRC Sec. 55—IRC Sec. 59 alternative minimum tax.—There is no Illinois equivalent to the federal alternative minimum tax on tax preference items.

IRC Sec. 78 deemed dividends.—Foreign dividend gross-up income may be subtracted from Illinois taxable income (see ¶1014).

Interest on federal obligations.—Illinois allows a subtraction from federal taxable income for interest on federal obligations that is exempt from state taxation. A subtraction is also allowed for mutual fund distributions attributable to federal obligations (see ¶1011).

IRC Sec. 103 interest on state obligations.—Illinois requires an addition to federal taxable income for interest income received on state or local obligations, including those of Illinois and its political subdivisions (¶1011).

IRC Sec. 108 discharge of indebtedness.—The same as federal because the starting point for computing Illinois corporation income and replacement tax liability is federal taxable income after the net operating loss and special deductions (see ¶1001), except a reduction may be required to any net operating loss (NOL) incurred in the taxable or loss carryover year for income from the discharge of indebtedness that was excluded from federal taxable income. (¶1013)

IRC Sec. 163 interest on indebtedness.—The same as federal because the starting point for computing Illinois corporation and replacement tax liability is federal taxable income after the net operating loss and special deductions (see ¶1001).

IRC Sec. 164 income and franchise tax deductions.—An addition to federal taxable income is required for any amount of Illinois income or replacement taxes that were deducted on the taxpayer's federal return (see ¶1012).

IRC Sec. 165 losses.—The same as federal because the starting point for computing Illinois corporation and replacement tax liability is federal taxable income after the net operating loss and special deductions (see ¶1001).

IRC Sec. 166 bad debts.—The same as federal because the starting point for computing Illinois corporation and replacement tax liability is federal taxable income after the net operating loss and special deductions (see ¶1001).

IRC Sec. 167 and IRC Sec. 168 (and IRC Sec. 1400N) depreciation.—Generally the same as federal because the starting point for computing Illinois corporation and replacement tax liability is federal taxable income after the net operating loss and special deductions (see ¶1001). However, Illinois requires an addition to federal taxable income for IRC Sec. 168(k) bonus depreciation, except the 100% federal bonus depreciation deduction allowed for property placed in service before January 1, 2012. A subtraction from taxable income is allowed for a portion of bonus depreciation. Illinois also requires certain adjustments if a taxpayer sells, transfers, abandons, or otherwise disposes of property for which it claimed depreciation (¶1024).

IRC Sec. 168(f) safe harbor leasing (pre-1984 leases).—Illinois recognized safe harbor leases under former IRC Sec. 168(f)(8).

IRC Sec. 169 pollution control facilities amortization.—The same as federal because the starting point for computing Illinois corporation and replacement tax liability is federal taxable income after the net operating loss and special deductions (see ¶1001).

IRC Sec. 170 (and IRC Sec. 1400S) charitable contributions.—Generally the same as federal because the starting point for computing Illinois corporation and replacement tax liability is federal taxable income after the net operating loss and special deductions (see ¶1001). In addition, corporations are allowed a subtraction from federal taxable income for certain charitable contributions to designated enterprise zone organizations (¶1017).

IRC Sec. 171 amortizable bond premium.—Generally the same as federal because the starting point for computing Illinois corporation and replacement tax liability is federal taxable income after the net operating loss and special deductions (see ¶1001), except that Illinois allows a deduction for amortizable bond premiums attributable to tax-exempt bonds, which are disallowed under IRC Sec. 171(a)(2) (see ¶1015).

¶45

IRC Sec. 172 net operating loss.—Illinois requires an addition modification to federal taxable income for the amount of any net operating loss (NOL) (Sec. 172) claimed for federal taxable income purposes. A subtraction from adjusted and apportioned Illinois base income is allowed for NOL carryforward from a loss year return (¶1013).

IRC Sec. 174 research and experimental expenditures.—The same as federal because the starting point for computing Illinois corporation and replacement tax liability is federal taxable income after the net operating loss and special deductions (see ¶1001).

IRC Sec. 179 (and IRC Sec. 1400N) asset expense election.—The same as federal because the starting point for computing Illinois corporation and replacement tax liability is federal taxable income after the net operating loss and special deductions (see ¶1001).

IRC Sec. 179D energy efficient commercial building deduction.—The same as federal because the starting point for computing Illinois corporation and replacement tax liability is federal taxable income after the net operating loss and special deductions (see ¶1001).

IRC Sec. 190 deduction for barriers removal.—The same as federal because the starting point for computing Illinois corporation and replacement tax liability is federal taxable income after the net operating loss and special deductions (see ¶1001).

IRC Sec. 195 start-up expenditures.—The same as federal because the starting point for computing Illinois corporation and replacement tax liability is federal taxable income after the net operating loss and special deductions (see ¶1001).

IRC Sec. 197 amortization of intangibles.—The same as federal because the starting point for computing Illinois corporation and replacement tax liability is federal taxable income after the net operating loss and special deductions (see ¶1001).

IRC Sec. 199 domestic production activities.—llinois requires an addition to federal taxable income for an amount equal to any federal deduction claimed by a taxpayer under IRC Sec. 199 for domestic production activities. (see ¶1026).

IRC Sec. 243—IRC Sec. 245 dividends received deduction.—The same as federal because the starting point for computing Illinois corporation and replacement tax liability is federal taxable income after the net operating loss and special deductions (see ¶1001). Illinois allows a subtraction from federal taxable income for a portion of dividends received from foreign corporations, including both actual and deemed dividends under the IRC (¶1018).

IRC Sec. 248 organizational expenditures.—The same as federal because the starting point for computing Illinois corporation and replacement tax liability is federal taxable income after the net operating loss and special deductions (see ¶1001).

IRC Sec. 301—IRC Sec. 385 corporate distributions and adjustments.—The same as federal because the starting point for computing Illinois corporation and replacement tax liability is federal taxable income after the net operating loss and special deductions (see ¶1001).

IRC Sec. 401—IRC Sec. 424 deferred compensation plans.—The same as federal because the starting point for computing Illinois corporation and replacement tax liability is federal taxable income after the net operating loss and special deductions (see ¶1001).

IRC Sec. 441—IRC Sec. 483 accounting periods and methods.—The same as federal. Illinois has adopted a provision similar to IRC Sec. 482 that gives the state tax agency the authority to allocate income and deductions among related taxpayers to clearly reflect income (see ¶1001).

¶45

IRC Sec. 501—IRC Sec. 530 exempt organizations.—Organizations that are exempt from the federal income tax under IRC Sec. 501(a) are also exempt from the Illinois income and replacement taxes. Exempt organizations are subject to corporation income and replacement tax liability on unrelated business income (¶ 905).

IRC Sec. 531—IRC Sec. 547 corporations used to avoid shareholder taxation.— Illinois has no provisions regarding corporations used to avoid shareholder taxation; Illinois does not impose a tax on accumulated earnings or an additional tax on the undistributed income of personal holding companies (IRC Sec. 541).

IRC Sec. 581—IRC Sec. 597 banking institutions.—Illinois has no equivalent to the federal provisions regarding financial institutions. All banks, investment companies, and savings and loan associations are subject to tax to the same extent as corporations (¶ 904).

IRC Sec. 611—IRC Sec. 638 natural resources.—The same as federal because the starting point for computing Illinois corporation and replacement tax liability is federal taxable income after the net operating loss and special deductions (see ¶ 1001).

IRC Sec. 801—IRC Sec. 848 insurance companies.—Illinois generally follows the federal income tax treatment of insurance companies. Insurance companies are subject to Illinois corporation and replacement tax liability in the same manner as other corporations, except the starting point for computing tax liability is generally tied to the federal provisions applicable to insurance companies (see ¶ 1004). Insurance companies doing business in Illinois also must pay a privilege tax on net premiums written (see ¶ 2206).

IRC Sec. 851—IRC Sec. 860L RICs, REITs, REMICs, and FASITs.—Generally, the same as federal, except Illinois requires an addition to taxable income for dividends paid by captive REITs (¶ 1007) and undistributed capital gains that are not included in the taxable income of RICs for federal income tax purposes (¶ 1006). Federal provisions on the tax treatment of FASITs were generally repealed after 2004.

IRC Sec. 861—IRC Sec. 865 foreign source income.—Illinois does not follow the federal foreign sourcing rules (IRC Sec. 861—IRC Sec. 865). Multistate and international businesses that conduct business both inside and outside Illinois utilize the state's allocation and apportionment rules for determining whether income is attributable to state sources (see ¶ 1101).

IRC Sec. 901—IRC Sec. 908 foreign tax credit.—Illinois has no equivalent to the federal foreign tax credit and does not allow a deduction for foreign income, franchise, or capital stock taxes regardless of whether the federal foreign tax credit was taken.

IRC Sec. 1001—IRC Sec. 1092 gain or loss on disposition of property.— Generally, the same as federal because the starting point for computing Illinois corporation and replacement tax liability is federal taxable income after the net operating loss and special deductions (see ¶ 1001).

IRC Sec. 1201 alternative capital gains tax.—Illinois does not provide for an alternative tax on capital gains.

IRC Sec. 1211 and Sec. 1212 capital losses.—The same as federal because the starting point for computing Illinois corporation and replacement tax liability is federal taxable income after the net operating loss and special deductions (see ¶ 1001).

IRC Sec. 1221—IRC Sec. 1260 determining capital gains and losses.—The same as federal because the starting point for computing Illinois corporation and replacement tax liability is federal taxable income after the net operating loss and special deductions (see ¶ 1001).

IRC Sec. 1361—IRC Sec. 1379 S corporations.—Generally, Illinois adopts the federal income tax treatment of S corporations (IRC Sec. 1361—IRC Sec. 1379), but S corporations are subject to the Illinois personal property replacement tax (see ¶906).

IRC Sec. 1391, IRC Sec. 1397F and IRC Sec. 1400E—IRC Sec. 1400J empowerment zones and renewal communities.—Illinois has no equivalent to the federal provisions regarding empowerment zones and renewal communities. However, Illinois allows a credit for investments in qualified property placed in service in an enterprise zone (¶1201).

IRC Sec. 1501—IRC Sec. 1504 consolidated returns.—Illinois does not allow the filing of consolidated returns, but requires corporations that are members of the same unitary group to file a combined return (¶1104).

BUSINESS INCENTIVES AND CREDITS

¶50 Introduction

Illinois has created a number of tax incentives designed to attract business to the state, stimulate expansion, and/or encourage certain economic activity. These incentives are listed below, by tax, with a brief description and a cross reference to the paragraph at which they are discussed in greater detail. Exemptions and deductions, which are too numerous to be fully included below, are discussed under the taxes to which they apply (see the Table of Contents or the Topical Index).

¶55 Corporate Income Tax

• *Replacement tax investment credit*

A taxpayer primarily engaged in manufacturing, mining coal or fluorite, or retailing is allowed a credit against the personal property replacement income tax (PPRIT—see ¶902) for investments in tangible property, including structural components of a building. An additional credit is available if the taxpayer's base employment in Illinois increases over the prior year. [35 ILCS 5/201(e)] (¶1203)

• *High impact business investment credit*

Taxpayers engaged in a certified high-impact business not located in an enterprise zone are allowed a credit for investments in qualified property placed in service during the tax year. [35 ILCS 5/201(h)](¶1205)

• *River edge redevelopment zone investment credit*

An income tax credit is available for investments in qualified property that is placed in service in an enterprise zone or river edge redevelopment zone. The credit may be passed through to partners, LLC members, and S corporation shareholders. [35 ILCS 5/201(f)](¶1204)

• *River edge redevelopment zone remediation credit*

A taxpayer is allowed a credit for a portion of certain unreimbursed environmental remediation costs incurred at a Site Remediation Program that is located in a River Edge Redevelopment Zone (RERZ). [35 ILCS 5/201(n)] (¶1212)

• *Economic Development for a Growing Economy Act (EDGE) credit*

The EDGE credit is intended to help Illinois compete with its neighboring states for the location of large job creation projects. The credit is directed toward manufacturers; retailers do not qualify. The amount of the credit is equal to the incremental personal income tax generated by jobs created in Illinois under the EDGE tax credit incentive program. [35 ILCS 5/211](¶1201)

- *Ex-felons jobs credit*

A credit may be claimed for a portion of the qualified wages paid by the taxpayer during the taxable year to one or more Illinois residents who are qualified ex-felons. [35 ILCS 5/216] (¶1215)

- *Tech-prep youth vocational program credit*

Taxpayers primarily engaged in manufacturing are allowed a credit for cooperative secondary school youth vocational programs in Illinois that are certified as qualifying TECH-PREP programs by the State Board of Education. [35 ILCS 5/209] (¶1208)

- *Dependent care assistance credit*

A credit may be claimed by employers that are primarily engaged in manufacturing for expenditures to provide an on-site dependent care assistance program at the employer's Illinois workplace. [35 ILCS 5/210] (¶1209)

- *Research and development credit*

Taxpayers may take a credit for qualified expenditures used for increasing research activities in Illinois. [35 ILCS 5/201(k)](¶1211)

- *Affordable housing donation credit*

A tax credit is available to a taxpayer who makes a minimum donation in connection with the acquisition, construction, rehabilitation, and financing of an affordable housing project. [20 ILCS 3805/7.28; 35 ILCS 5/214] (¶1213)

- *Film production services and live theater production credits*

Film and digital media producers are allowed a nonrefundable credit generally equal to a portion of the salary or wages paid to employees for services on an accredited production in Illinois. Also, taxpayers who are theater producers, owners, licensees, or operators, or who otherwise present live stage presentations, are entitled to a nonrefundable credit against their income tax liability for a portion of the Illinois labor expenditures for each tax year, a portion of the Illinois production spending for each tax year, and a portion of the Illinois labor expenditures generated by the employment of Illinois residents in geographic areas of high poverty or high unemployment in each tax year. [35 ILCS 5/213; 35 ILCS 15/10] (¶1214)

- *New markets credit*

The New Markets Development Program Act includes a credit for taxpayers who make qualified cash equity investments in a qualified community development entity. [20 ILCS 663/1 *et seq.*] (¶1217)

- *Student-assistance contribution credit*

A credit is available for employers who make matching contributions to a College Savings Pool Account (pool) or to the Illinois Prepaid Tuition Trust Fund (trust) in the same year that a contribution is made by an employee of the taxpayer. [35 ILCS 5/218] (¶1218)

- *Credits for historic structure rehabilitation*

A credit is available for the renovation of qualified historic structures in the city of Peoria (namely, the Hotel Pere Marquette). In addition, an historic preservation credit is allowed for a portion of the rehabilitation expenditures incurred pursuant to an approved rehabilitation plan in the restoration and preservation of a certified historic structure located in a River Edge Redevelopment Zone. [35 ILCS 5/219; 35 ILCS 5/221] (¶1219)

¶55

- *Angel investment credit*

A nonrefundable and nontransferable tax credit may be claimed for a portion of the taxpayer's investment made directly in a qualified new business venture. [35 ILCS 5/220] (¶ 1220)

- *Hospital credit*

A credit is available to owners of for-profit hospitals for the lesser of the cost of free or discounted services provided during the tax year or the hospital's property taxes paid during the tax year on real property used for hospital purposes during the prior tax year. [35 ILCS 5/223] (¶ 1222)

- *Invest in Kids credit*

A credit is available to taxpayers who have been awarded a tax credit certificate by the Illinois Department of Revenue for making a qualified contribution to non-profit organizations that use the contribution received during a taxable year for scholarships to low-income elementary or high school students. [35 ILCS 5/224] (¶ 1223)

- *Targeted business activity or zone deductions*

Enterprise zones businesses are also eligible for the following:

— Individuals, corporations, trusts and estates may deduct from their taxable income an amount equal to those dividends that were paid to them by a corporation that conducts substantially all of its operations in an enterprise zone or zones; and

— Corporations may make take a double deduction for donations to designated organizations for projects approved by the Illinois Department of Commerce and Economic Opportunity [35 ILCS 5/203](¶ 1017).

¶60 Sales and Use Taxes

- *Agriculture*

Various exemptions apply to farm machinery and equipment, livestock, feed, seeds, fertilizer, and chemicals (¶ 1702).

- *Enterprise zones, River Edge redevelopment zones, and high-impact businesses*

Building materials: A retailer located within an enterprise zone who makes a sale of building materials to be incorporated into that enterprise zone may deduct the receipts from those sales on the retailer's sales tax return. The retailer does not charge sales tax on these sales. The building materials must be items that are permanently affixed to real property. Similar provisions apply to sales to high-impact businesses and sales for use in a River Edge redevelopment zone [35 ILCS 120/2-54, 120/5k, 120/5l](¶ 1702, 1808).

Manufacturing: A certified enterprise zone business may qualify for a 6.25% sales tax exemption on all tangible personal property, used or consumed within an enterprise zone in the process of manufacturing or assembly of tangible personal property for wholesale or retail sale or lease [35 ILCS 120/1d, 120/1f](¶ 1702).

- *Manufacturing*

The general manufacturers' exemption from the ROT, the UT, the SOT, and the SUT applies to purchases of machinery, equipment, and material that are primarily (more than 50%) used in a manufacturing process or an assembling process that results in the production of tangible personal property for sale or lease. Machinery and equipment used to repair or maintain other exempt machinery or equipment, or to manufacture exempt machinery and equipment for in-house use are exempt.

Lessors of qualified machinery and equipment qualify for the exemption [35 ILCS 105/3-50, 120/2-45, 110/2, 115/2, 105/3-85, and 110/3-70] (¶ 1702).

Sales of graphic arts machinery and equipment are included under the manufacturing exemptions for sales tax, service occupation tax, use tax, and service use tax, effective July 1, 2017.

¶65 Property Tax

• *Property tax abatement*

Enterprise zone property, River Edge redevelopment zone property, and property of a commercial or industrial firm are given preferred treatment through property tax abatements. The effect of an abatement is to reduce or eliminate property tax on a particular piece of property. The abatement for a commercial or industrial firm is 10 years and $4 million. With regard to enterprise zone or River Edge redevelopment zone property, the amount of taxes that may be abated cannot exceed the amount attributable to new construction, renovation or rehabilitation [35 ILCS 200/18-165, 200/18-170; 55 ILCS 5/5-30004](¶ 2003).

• *Pollution control equipment*

A certified water or air pollution control facility is assessed at $33^1/3\%$ of the fair cash value of its economic productivity to the owner. Certified property is removed from the local tax assessment rolls [35 ILCS 200/11-5](¶ 2005).

¶70 Utility Tax

• *Enterprise zone exemption*

A business that makes an enterprise zone investment that either creates a minimum of 200 full-time equivalent jobs in Illinois or retains a minimum of 1,000 full-time jobs in Illinois is entitled to a 5% state tax exemption on gas, electricity, and the Illinois Commerce Commission 0.1% administrative charge [35 ILCS 630/2(a)(5); 220 ILCS 5/9-222.1].

Local units of government may also exempt their taxes on gas, electricity, and water.

¶75 Insurance Tax

• *New markets credit*

The New Markets Development Program Act includes a credit for taxpayers who make qualified cash equity investments in a qualified community development entity. This credit is scheduled to expire after 2017. [20 ILCS 663/1 *et seq.*] (¶ 2206)

PART II
PERSONAL INCOME TAX
CHAPTER 1
RATES, PERSONS SUBJECT TO TAX

¶101 Overview

Illinois has two taxes measured by net income: the income tax and the personal property replacement income tax (the Replacement Tax or PPRIT). Both taxes are imposed for the privilege of earning or receiving income in Illinois, but individuals are subject only to the income tax.

The income tax was enacted in 1969 to apply to individuals, estates, trusts, and corporations and closely follows federal law. The tax was held to be constitutional by the Illinois Supreme Court in *Thorpe v. Mahin* (1969, SCt), 43 Ill2d 36; CCH ILLINOIS TAX REPORTS, ¶200-500. The replacement tax was enacted in 1979 to apply to partnerships, trusts, and corporations and was held constitutional by the Illinois Supreme Court in *Continental Illinois National Bank and Trust Co. of Chicago et al. v. Zagel, Director of Revenue et al.* (1979, SCt), 78 Ill2d 387, 410 NE2d 491; CCH ILLINOIS TAX REPORTS, ¶201-059.

The basis of the tax and various modifications to the tax base are discussed in Chapter 2. Allocation and apportionment of income of nonresidents, part-year residents, estates, and trusts is treated in Chapter 3. The various credits against tax are discussed in Chapter 4. Information on returns, forms, estimated tax requirements, payments, and due dates is found in Chapter 5. Requirements for withholding tax are set forth in Chapter 6. Administration of tax, including refunds, deficiencies, penalties, interest, and taxpayers' rights is discussed in Chapter 8 and in Chapter 24, which also includes information on recordkeeping requirements and audits.

¶102 Rates of Tax

Law: Income Tax Act, Sec. 201 [35 ILCS 5/201]; Compassionate Use of Medical Cannabis Pilot Program Act [410 ILCS 130]; 86 Ill. Adm. Code Sec. 100.2060 (CCH ILLINOIS TAX REPORTS, ¶15-355).

The Illinois personal income tax is imposed on individuals, trusts, and estates at a flat rate of 4.95%, effective for taxable years beginning on or after July 1, 2017 (35 ILCS 5/201(b)(5.3) and (5.4)). The Illinois personal income tax was imposed at a rate of:

— 3.75% for taxable years beginning on or after January 1, 2015 and before July 1, 2017 (35 ILCS 5/201(b)(5.2) and (5.3)); and

— 5% for tax years 2011-2014 (35 ILCS 5/201(b)(5)).

The rate of the personal property replacement tax, which is applicable to partnerships, trusts, and S corporations (see ¶902), but not to individuals, is 1.5% of net income for the taxable year (35 ILCS 5/201(d)).

Local rates: The legislature has not authorized the levy of any local income taxes, but a portion of the revenue from the state income tax is allocated among the cities of Illinois (35 ILCS 5/901(b)).

• *Surcharge on income from medical marijuana*

For each of the taxable years during the Compassionate Use of Medical Cannabis pilot program (2014 through 2017), a surcharge is imposed on all taxpayers on income arising from the sale or exchange of capital assets, depreciable business property, real property used in the trade or business, and Section 197 intangibles of any registrant organization. The amount of the surcharge is equal to the amount of federal income tax liability for the taxable year attributable to those sales and exchanges. (410 ILCS 130/190; 86 Ill. Adm. Code Sec. 100.2060)

The surcharge does not apply if the medical cannabis cultivation center registrant, medical cannabis dispensary registrant or the property of a registrant is transferred as a result of any of the following: bankruptcy, a receivership, or a debt adjustment initiated by or against the initial registration or the substantial owners of the initial registration; cancellation, revocation, or termination of any registration by the Illinois Department of Public Health; a determination by the Department of Public Health that transfer of the registration is in the best interests of Illinois qualifying patients as defined by the Medical Cannabis Pilot Program Act; the death of an owner of the equity interest in a registrant; the acquisition of a controlling interest in the stock or substantially all of the assets of a publicly traded company; a transfer by a parent company to a wholly owned subsidiary; or the transfer or sale to or by one person to another person where both persons were initial owners of the registration when the registration was issued.

In addition, the surcharge does not apply if the cannabis cultivation center registration, medical cannabis dispensary registration, or the controlling interest in a registrant's property is transferred to lineal descendants in which no gain or loss is recognized or to a controlled corporation in which no gain or loss is recognized. (410 ILCS 130/190)

¶103 Persons Subject to Tax—Individuals, Estates and Trusts, Partnerships

Law: Income Tax Act, Sec. 201 [35 ILCS 5/201]; Income Tax Act, Sec. 1501 [35 ILCS 5/1501] (CCH ILLINOIS TAX REPORTS, ¶ 15-005, 15-105, 15-205, 15-505).

Comparable Federal: Secs. 1—5, 112, 641—685, 701—704, 1361—1378 (U.S. MASTER TAX GUIDE, ¶ 109—116, 301—335, 401—482, 501—590).

The Illinois income tax is imposed on every individual, estate, and trust on the privilege of earning or receiving income in or as a resident of Illinois. In addition to the income tax, partnerships and trusts are subject to the personal property replacement income tax.

A partnership as an entity is not subject to the regular income tax but is subject to the personal property tax replacement income tax (¶ 105).

The personal income tax and the personal property replacement income tax provisions are applicable to limited liability companies. A limited liability company will be treated as a corporation, partnership, or person if it is so classified for federal tax purposes.

All income of resident individuals, estates, and trusts is taxable by Illinois, regardless of its source. Allocation and apportionment of income provisions applying to nonresidents and part-year residents are discussed in Chapter 3.

Printing: A person not subject to the income tax will not become liable for the tax by reason of his or her ownership of tangible personal property located at the premises of a printer in Illinois with whom the person has contracted for printing or by reason of the activities of the person's employees or agents who are located at the printer's premises solely to perform services related to quality control, distribution, or printing.

- *"Resident," "nonresident," and "part-year resident" defined*

A "resident" is (35 ILCS 5/1501(a)(20)):

(1) an individual who is in the state for other than a temporary or transitory purpose during the taxable year;

(2) an individual who is domiciled in Illinois but is absent from the state for a temporary or transitory purpose during the taxable year;

(3) the estate of a decedent who was domiciled in Illinois at the time of his or her death;

(4) a trust created by the will of a decedent who was domiciled in Illinois at the time of his or her death; and

(5) an irrevocable trust, the grantor of which was domiciled in Illinois at the time the trust became irrevocable. A trust is considered irrevocable, for purposes of determining residence, to the extent that the grantor is not treated as the owner under IRC Secs. 671—678.

Effective April 19, 2013, the following create rebuttable presumptions of Illinois residence (86 Ill. Admin. Code Sec. 100.3020):

— an individual who is receiving a homestead exemption for Illinois property; or

— an individual who is an Illinois resident in one year and who in the following year is present in Illinois more days than he or she is present in any other state.

Previously, a presumption of Illinois residence existed if an individual spent an aggregate of more than nine months of any taxable year in Illinois. A presumption of nonresidence existed if an individual was absent from Illinois for one year or more.

The rule includes several examples and types of evidence that may be submitted by an individual to rebut the presumption of residence or nonresidence. (86 Ill. Admin. Code Sec. 100.3020)

An Illinois Appellate Court ruled that a taxpayer who was employed for a three-year term in Hong Kong was not precluded, as a matter of law, from asserting nonresident status for Illinois personal income purposes, even though he claimed a homestead exemption on property taxes and filed a joint Illinois income tax return with his wife during the tax years coinciding with his employment contract. (*Grede v. Illinois Department of Revenue*, Appellate Court of Illinois, Second District, No. 2-12-0731, April 22, 2013, CCH ILLINOIS TAX REPORTS, ¶402-650)

Practitioner Comment: Taxpayer's Intent is Key to Residency

The Illinois Court of Appeals, First District, affirmed a Circuit Court grant of summary judgment in favor of taxpayers on their complaint for a declaration that they were not required to pay resident Illinois income taxes for years during which they split their time between Illinois and Florida. For almost fifty years, the plaintiffs lived and worked in Illinois. However, for the years 1996 through 2005, they spent 1,700 days in Florida, 1,666 in Illinois, and 284 elsewhere. According to Illinois law, "individuals are considered Illinois residents if they are present in the state for other than a 'temporary or transitory purpose' or are 'domiciled' in Illinois but leave for a temporary or transitory purpose." As a result, the Department contended that the plaintiffs were domiciled in Illinois for purposes of the personal income tax. The Court disagreed, however, noting that a taxpayer may only be a domiciliary of one state. Moreover, "[i]f individuals leave the state for other than a temporary or transitory purpose, or establish domicile elsewhere, they cease to be Illinois residents." Plaintiffs had physically left their Illinois home, renounced their Illinois residency, physically moved to Florida, and declared Florida their domicile. The Court found that the plaintiffs' intent controlled, and that they "wished to establish Florida as their permanent residence in 1995, even though they planned to keep ties in Illinois and have regular seasonal visits. That is, Plaintiffs intended to live in Florida for half the year and visit Illinois, not the other way around." Consequently, Plaintiffs were not required to pay Illinois income taxes for the years at issue. (*Cain v. Hamer*, Ill. App. Ct. (1st Dist.), No. 112833, 7/16/2012; CCH ILLINOIS TAX REPORTS, ¶402-518)

The question of residency continues to be an issue in Illinois, particularly in light of Illinois' recent increases in the personal income tax rate. As reflected in the Cain decision above, determining a person's intent is the key to determining residency. Intent is determined by examining the specific facts and circumstances in a case-by-case basis. In this case and most other residency cases, days in the state versus days out of the state is a key factual component. However, it is not the only component. Courts also look to community involvement. The key to be successful in any residency case is the ability to prove up these components. Illinois residents looking to change their residency should make extra efforts to document each of the steps taken to establish residency outside of Illinois.

Marilyn A. Wethekam, Horwood Marcus & Berk, Chartered

Residence of trust grantor: The Illinois Appellate Court held that a trust whose grantor was an Illinois resident, but otherwise had no connections with the State, could not be subject to the Illinois income tax, as assertion of such jurisdiction violated the Due Process Clause of the United States Constitution. The Illinois Appellate Court found that the trust had nothing in and sought nothing from Illinois since all of the trust's business was conducted in Texas; the trustee, protector, and the noncontingent beneficiary resided outside Illinois; and none of the trust's property was in Illinois. Moreover, the trust possessed none of the factors that would give Illinois personal jurisdiction over the trust. Neither the provisions of the trust instrument, the residence of the trustees, the residence of its beneficiaries, the location of the trust assets, nor the location where the business of the trust was conducted indicated any contact with Illinois. Therefore, the court held that insufficient contacts existed between Illinois and the trust to satisfy the requirements of the Due Process Clause, thus rendering the income tax imposed on the trust for the tax year 2006 unconstitutional. (*Linn v. Dep't of Revenue*, 2013 IL App (4th) 121055, CCH ILLINOIS TAX REPORTS, ¶402-751)

Practitioner Comment: Minimizing Trust Exposure to Illinois Tax

The Appellate Court's decision in *Linn* was decided based on the specific set of facts at issue, but there may be other instances in which it is arguable that an irrevocable *inter vivos* trust established by Illinois resident(s) should not remain subject to Illinois' taxing jurisdiction. Illinois resident trusts should also be reviewed to determine if any steps, such as those taken in Linn, can be taken to minimize or possibly eliminate their exposure to Illinois' taxing jurisdiction.

Breen M. Schiller, Esq., Horwood Marcus & Berk, Chartered

Nonresidents: A "nonresident" is any person who is not a resident (35 ILCS 5/1501(a)(17)). See ¶106, concerning reciprocal agreements among states on taxation of compensation paid to nonresidents.

Part-year residents: A "part-year resident" is an individual who became a resident during the taxable year or ceased to be a resident during the taxable year (35 ILCS 5/1501(a)(14)). Under (1) above, residence begins with presence in the state for other than a temporary or transitory purpose and ceases with absence from the state for other than a temporary or transitory purpose. Under (2) above, residence begins with the establishment of domicile in Illinois and ceases with the establishment of domicile in another state. Part-year residents are entitled to allocate and apportion their income for that part of the year they were not Illinois residents (¶303).

Practitioner Comment: Edmund Sweeney v. Dep't of Revenue, Case No. 10 L 050514

The Illinois Circuit Court of Cook County reversed the Department of Revenue's conclusion that the taxpayer was an Illinois resident for years 2002 and 2003 for state income tax purposes. Although the court concluded that the Department had met its burden of establishing its prima facie case demonstrating that the taxpayer was in fact an Illinois resident, the court concluded that the plaintiff successfully rebutted the Department's argument. Noting that to establish domicile, a person must physically go to the new location and live there with the intention of making it their permanent home [,] the court found that a variety of factors indicated the plaintiff had in fact intended to make Florida his new domicile. Specifically, the plaintiff (1) moved to Florida, (2) actually abandoned his Illinois residence, (3) intended not to return to his Illinois domicile, and (4) intended to make Florida his permanent home. To support these findings, the court referenced the fact that the plaintiff owned no property in Illinois, obtained Florida driver's license and voter registration, established phone service in Florida, he closed his Illinois bank accounts and opened a Florida bank account, and received mail in Florida. As a result of these objective and subjective factors indicating that the plaintiff intended to move from Illinois to Florida, the court concluded that the plaintiff was not a resident for the years 2002 and 2003.

Breen M. Schiller, Esq., Horwood Marcus & Berk, Chartered

Time-splitting between homes: The Illinois Independent Tax Tribunal considered whether the Illinois Department of Revenue correctly determined that a couple had abandoned their Florida residence and established Illinois residency such that they were required to file returns as part year residents as of May 1, 2001. Whereas the Petitioners contended they maintained a Florida residence for all of 2001, the Department admitted Florida residency for the beginning of 2001, but claimed that beginning May 1, Petitioners were in Illinois from for more than a "temporary or transitory purpose." The Tribunal determined the Petitioners were residents of Florida for the entire year, as the Department failed to demonstrate that anything changed on May 1, 2001 other than the time the couple spent in Illinois. The Court determined a change in residency rests on the disparity of connections with Florida and Illinois, rather than on "the level of time-splitting" in each state. Therefore, the amount of time spent in Illinois was not determinative of residency, because travelling between two states is not indicative of intent to abandon a person's residence. Further, even though the Petitioners spent far more money in Illinois than Florida to repair, remodel and refurnish their house and on their country club membership, the Tribunal determined this behavior does not demonstrate relocation. (*Corbin v. Dep't of Revenue*, July 15, 2015, 14 TT 9, CCH ILLINOIS TAX REPORTS, ¶402-980)

Practitioner Comment: Ample living space

In *Corbin*, the Tribunal also commented that comparative house size may be relevant in considering questions of domicile. Here, the Tribunal ultimately determined the difference in size between the Illinois home (5,300 square feet on a 2 acre lot) and the Florida home (3200 square feet on a quarter acre lot) was not material, because both were adequate to provide ample living space for a couple. This application could provide a dangerous and notable precedent for areas of the country where homes are generally larger in square feet. Also, the Tribunal does not clarify its coinage of the term "ample living space."

Samantha K. Breslow, Esq., Horwood Marcus & Berk, Chartered

CCH Advisory: Exemption for foreign-earned income

Income earned by an Illinois resident while working in Germany was exempt from Illinois personal income tax to the same extent that it was exempt from federal income tax. Under IRC Sec. 911, up to $80,000 of foreign earned income is exempt from federal personal income tax. Because the computation of Illinois personal income tax begins with federal adjusted gross income and Illinois does not require federally excluded foreign earned income to be added back to federal adjusted gross income for Illinois purposes, the first $80,000 of the taxpayer's foreign earned income is also exempt from Illinois personal income tax. (*General Information Letter IT 05-0044-GIL*, Illinois Department of Revenue, September 14, 2005; CCH ILLINOIS TAX REPORTS, ¶ 401-593)

• *Domicile*

The question of whether an individual is a resident or a nonresident depends in part on whether he or she is "domiciled" in Illinois. The question of domicile is determined on the basis of the particular facts and circumstances of each case. An individual's domicile is the place where he or she lives, the place to which, whenever absent, intends to return—his or her true, permanent home. Once domicile is established, it continues until a new domicile is established. A change of domicile involves a physical moving coupled with an intent to establish a new domicile. For a discussion of abandonment of Illinois domicile, see *Sweeney v. State of Illinois*, Department of Revenue, Circuit Court, Cook County Judicial Circuit (Illinois), 10 L 050524, June 26, 2013, CCH ILLINOIS TAX REPORTS, ¶ 402-685.

• *Interstate carriers*

Compensation paid by rail, rail-water, express, pipeline, and motor carriers operating under the jurisdiction of the Interstate Commerce Commission and by private carriers to employees who regularly perform duties in more than one state is subject to the income tax laws of the state in which the employee resides (Amtrak Reauthorization and Improvement Act of 1990, P.L. 101-322; CCH ILLINOIS TAX REPORTS, ¶ 400-459).

Also, the compensaton of the pilot, master, officer, or crew member of a vessel operating on the navigable water of more than one state may be taxed only by the person's state of residence.

¶104 Military Personnel

Law: Income Tax Act, Sec. 203(a)(2)(E) [35 ILCS 5/203] (CCH ILLINOIS TAX REPORTS, ¶ 15-175, 16-308).

Comparable Federal: Secs. 112, 121(9), 132(n), 134, 692 (U.S. MASTER TAX GUIDE, ¶ 889—896, 1078, 2609, 2533).

Pay received for active duty in the U.S. Armed Forces and any compensation paid to a member of the National Guard of any state is exempt from Illinois income tax and is subtracted to the extent that it is included in federal adjusted gross income (35 ILCS 5/203(a)(2)(e)). The exemption also applies to pay for duty as a cadet at the U.S. Military, Air Force, and Coast Guard academies, as a midshipman at the U.S. Naval Academy, or in ROTC.

The exemption for military pay does not apply to the following (*Publication 102, Illinois Filing Requirements for Military Personnel* Department of Revenue, April, 2011, CCH ILLINOIS TAX REPORTS, ¶ 402-315):

— military income (such as combat pay) that is excluded from AGI on Form IL-1040, Line 1;

— pay received under the Voluntary Separation Incentive Program;

— pay received from the military as a civilian;

— payments made under the Ready Reserve Mobilization Income Insurance Program; or

— pay for duty as an officer in the Public Health Service.

• *Residency and domicile*

Under the provisions of the Soldiers' and Sailors' Civil Relief Act of 1940, a member of the Armed Forces retains, while in service, the same domicile as when entering military service. Military personnel (usually career personnel) may change their domicile from Illinois to another state just as any other individual. Conclusive evidence must be submitted showing that their Illinois domicile has been abandoned and a new domicile established in another state.

Military personnel temporarily assigned and living in Illinois are not subject to tax on their income or compensation for military service even if they have changed their domicile with intent to establish an Illinois residence (50 U.S.C. § 574). Income from nonmilitary Illinois sources is subject to Illinois income tax and must be reported on a nonresident or part-year resident return.

Family members: Civilian spouses and dependents of military personnel who are living in Illinois temporarily because of assignment of the military spouse are subject to tax as nonresidents. Taxpayers who are nonresidents of Illinois who marry military personnel who are Illinois residents living outside Illinois are not subject to Illinois income tax merely because the military spouse is a resident.

Military Spouses Residency Relief Act: Under this 2009 federal law (P.L. 111-97 (S. 475)), a spouse of a servicemember will neither lose nor acquire a residence or domicile for personal income or personal property tax purposes by reason of being absent or present in any tax jurisdiction of the United States solely to be with the servicemember in compliance with the latter's military orders if the residence or domicile, as the case may be, is the same for the servicemember and the spouse. Income for services performed by the spouse will not be deemed to be income for services performed or from sources within a tax jurisdiction of the United States if the spouse is not a resident or domiciliary of the jurisdiction in which the income is earned because the spouse is in the jurisdiction solely to be with the servicemember serving in compliance with military orders. For additional information, see *Publication 102, Illinois Filing Requirements for Military Personnel*, Illinois Department of Revenue, April 2011, CCH ILLINOIS TAX REPORTS, ¶ 402-315.

• *Combat pay exclusion*

For federal income tax purposes, members of the Armed Forces may exclude combat pay and hostile fire pay for any month for which such pay is received. However, the exclusion for a commissioned officer is limited to the highest rate of enlisted pay for each month.

Hospitalization: The monthly exclusion also applies if the service member is hospitalized anywhere as the result of wounds, disease, or injury sustained while serving in a combat zone, but is limited to two years after the termination of combatant activities in the combat zone. Payments for leave accrued during service in a combat zone are also excluded.

• *Tax forgiveness for decedents*

Federal income tax is forgiven for members of the Armed Forces who die as the result of wounds, disease, or injury incurred in a combat zone or as a result of wounds or injuries sustained in terroristic or military action. Forgiveness includes the entire taxable year in which the death occurs, not just the shortened tax year, and extends to any earlier year ending on or after the first day of service in a combat zone. Taxes for those years are abated, credited, or refunded. However, refunds are subject to the statute of limitations. All income of a person whose federal income tax

¶104

on that income is forgiven because the person died in a combat zone or due to wounds, disease, or injury incurred in a combat zone is exempt from Illinois personal income tax.

CCH Advisory: Spouse of Deceased Member

The federal tax forgiveness applies only to the deceased person, not to the spouse.

The federal forgiveness provisions also include astronauts who die in the line of duty.

• *Combat zones and hazardous duty areas*

There are three designated (by Executive Order of the President) combat zones, which include the airspace above, as follows:

— **Arabian Peninsula.** Beginning January 17, 1991: Bahrain, Iraq, Kuwait, Oman, Qatar, Saudi Arabia, the United Arab Emirates, Gulf of Aden, Gulf of Oman, Persian Gulf, Red Sea, and part of the Arabian Sea. Beginning January 1, 2003: Israel and Turkey. Beginning April 11, 2003: part of the Mediterranean Sea.

— **Kosovo.** Beginning March 24, 1999: Yugoslavia (Serbia and Montenegro), Albania, the Adriatic Sea, and the northern Ionian Sea. Additional areas have been designated in support of Operation Enduring Freedom, including Pakistan, Tajikistan, and Jordan (beginning September 19, 2001); Incirlik Air Base, Turkey (beginning September 21, 2001); Kyrgyzstan and Uzbekistan (beginning October 1, 2001); Phillipines (beginning January 9, 2002); Yemen (beginning April 10, 2002); and Djibouti (beginning July 1, 2002).

— **Afghanistan.** Beginning September 19, 2001. Separately, the Department of Defense (DOD) has certified that military personnel in Uzbekistan, Kyrgystan, Pakistan, Tajikistan, and Jordan are eligible for all combat zone related tax benefits due to their service in direct support of military operations in the Afghanistan combat zone.

A "qualified hazardous duty area" is treated as if it were a combat zone. Bosnia, Herzegovina, Croatia, and Macedonia have been designated as hazardous duty areas.

The Department of Defense has certified several additional locations for combat zone tax benefits due to their direct support of military operations; see **http://www.irs.gov/uac/Combat-Zones**.

• *Other nontaxable items*

Miscellaneous items of income received by service members are nontaxable, as follows:

— living allowances, including Basic Allowance for Quarters (BAQ), Basic Allowance for Subsistence (BAS), Variable housing Allowance (VHA), and housing and cost-of-living allowances abroad;

— family allowances, including those for emergencies, evacuation, separation, and certain educational expenses for dependents;

— death allowances, including those for burial services, travel of dependents, and the death gratuity payment to eligible survivors;

— moving allowances for dislocation, moving household and personal items, moving trailers or mobile homes, storage, and temporary lodging;

— other benefits, including dependent care, disability, medical benefits, group-term life insurance, professional education, defense counseling, ROTC allowances, survivor and retirement protection plan premiums, uniform allowances for offices, and uniforms furnished to enlisted personnel.

¶104

- *Sale of residence*

Two important federal income tax benefits are available to members of the military who sell their homes.

Homeowner's Assistance Program (HAP): The HAP reimburses military homeowners for losses incurred on the private sale of their homes after a base closure or reduction in operations. The HAP payment is the difference between 95% of the home's fair market value before the closure or reduction announcement and the greater of the home's fair market value at the time of sale or the actual sale price.

HAP payments made after November 11, 2003, are excludable from gross income.

Capital gains: All homeowners may exclude up to $250,000 ($500,000 on a joint return) of gain on the sale of a home if they have owned and used the home as their personal residence for two of the five years preceding the date of sale. Because members of the military, Public Health Service officers, and Foreign Service officers may be required to move frequently, the Military Family Tax Relief Act of 2003 provided for these personnel by suspending the five-year testing period for up to 10 years. The suspension applies whenever the person is on qualified official extended duty for more than 90 days and is stationed at least 50 miles from the person's residence or is under orders to reside in government quarters.

- *Moving expenses*

Armed forces members, their spouses and dependents may deduct moving expenses without regard to the distance and time requirements that otherwise would apply. The move must be pursuant to a military order that results in a permanent change of station.

- *Filing requirements*

Members of the military are generally subject to the same filing requirements as other taxpayers (¶501). Illinois usually grants tax return extensions that correspond to federal extensions for military personnel. For additional information, see *Publication 102, Illinois Filing Requirements for Military Personnel,* Illinois Department of Revenue, April 2011, CCH Illinois Tax Reports, ¶402-315.

Members in combat zones: For service members in designated combat zones, hazardous duty areas, hospitalized outside the U.S. due to a combat injury, or deployed in contingency operations, the federal due date is postponed without interest or penalties until 180 days after the member's return to the U.S. The extended due date also applies to filing amended returns.

- *Veterans*

Payments to veterans for benefits administered by the Veterans Administration are tax-free for federal income tax purposes. Such items include education, training, or subsistence allowances; veterans' pensions, insurance proceeds, and dividends paid to veterans or their families or beneficiaries; grants to disabled veterans for motor vehicles or homes with disability accommodations; and disability compensation.

¶105 Taxation of Partnerships

Law: Income Tax Act, Sec. 201(c) [35 ILCS 5/201]; Income Tax Act, Sec. 205 [35 ILCS 5/205]; Income Tax Act, Sec. 502(d) [35 ILCS 5/502]; Income Tax Act, Sec. 1501(a)(16) [35 ILCS 5/1501] (CCH Illinois Tax Reports, ¶15-505).

Comparable Federal: Secs. 701, 761 (U.S. Master Tax Guide, ¶63, 401—481).

A partnership as an entity is not subject to the regular income tax but is subject to the personal property tax replacement income tax (35 ILCS 5/201(c), 35 ILCS

5/205). Partnerships are required to compute base income and file information returns (¶511). A partnership may claim the credit for personal property tax replacement income tax, discussed at ¶1201.

A "partnership" includes a syndicate, group, pool, joint venture, or other unincorporated organization, through or by means of which any business, financial operation, or venture is carried on, and which is not a trust, estate, or corporation. "Partner" includes a member in a syndicate, group, pool, joint venture, or organization (35 ILCS 5/1501(a)(16)).

Practitioner Comment: Investment Partnerships

For tax years ending on or after December 31, 2004, Illinois no longer subjects investment partnerships to Illinois' replacement tax, and they are not required to file Form IL-1065. The term "investment partnership" is defined at 35 ILCS 5/1501(a)(11.5). Illinois' law change was intended to encourage investment partnerships to locate in Illinois without subjecting its nonresident partners to Illinois tax. The laws of New York, California and Massachusetts also encourage nonresident limited partners to invest in those states without triggering state income taxes.

Horwood Marcus & Berk Chartered

For additional information on taxation of partnerships, see ¶852.

• *Other pass-through entities*

Any entity, including a limited liability company formed under the Illinois Limited Liability Company Act, must be treated as a partnership if it is so classified for federal income tax purposes (35 ILCS 5/1501(a)(16)).

Limited partnership: Imposition of Illinois personal property replacement income tax on the distributable income received by a Delaware limited partner of a limited partnership that operated in Illinois was not in violation of the Due Process and Commerce Clauses of the U.S. Constitution. Although the limited partner asserted that it could not be taxed because it had no connection with Illinois other than the investment in a partnership that operated in Illinois, the limited partnership availed itself of the laws of Illinois and the limited partner received distributable income earned in Illinois and, thus, imposition of the tax did not violate the Due Process Clause of the U.S. Constitution.

Further, the Commerce Clause of the U.S. Constitution was not violated, because the limited partnership had substantial nexus with Illinois. The limited partner agreed that there was substantial nexus between Illinois and the limited partnership but argued that substantial nexus had to exist between it and Illinois. The limited partner asserted that because it had no physical presence in Illinois, substantial nexus did not exist and it could not be taxed. However, physical presence was not required to establish substantial nexus between the limited partner and Illinois because the limited partnership was physically present in Illinois and operated in Illinois and served only as a conduit to shift the incidence of the tax to the partners (*Borden Chemicals and Plastics, L.P.,* Illinois Appellate Court, First District, No.1-98-4456, February 14, 2000; CCH ILLINOIS TAX REPORTS, ¶401-120).

¶106 Reciprocal Agreements on Exemption of Nonresidents

Law: Income Tax Act, Sec. 701(d) [35 ILCS 5/701] (CCH ILLINOIS TAX REPORTS, ¶16-610).

The Director of the Department of Revenue is authorized to enter into agreements with other states imposing income taxes to exempt from taxation compensation paid a resident of one state for services performed in the other state (35 ILCS 5/701(d)). Illinois has entered into agreements with Iowa, Kentucky, Michigan and Wisconsin. Details of the agreements regarding returns are covered at ¶305 and regarding withholding at ¶604 and 605.

PERSONAL INCOME TAX
CHAPTER 2
COMPUTATION OF INCOME

¶201 In General

Law: Income Tax Act, Sec. 250 [35 ILCS 5/250].

Illinois net income is based on federal adjusted gross income, with adjustments for individuals and on federal taxable income, with adjustments for estates and trusts (35 ILCS 5/203(a)). For the personal property replacement income tax, the taxable amount is federal taxable income as defined in the Internal Revenue Code, with adjustments, for partnerships and trusts (35 ILCS 5/203(c), (d)). Taxpayers should not compute or fill out their Illinois returns until after they have completed the federal returns, since some figures needed for the Illinois return are taken from the federal return.

Because Illinois takes federal adjusted or federal taxable income as the starting point for determining Illinois taxable income, federal changes are automatically adopted by Illinois unless specifically rejected by the legislature (¶202). Federal itemized deductions are not deductible by Illinois taxpayers (¶205).

Sunset date for deductions enacted after September 16, 1994: The application of every deduction against the income tax that is enacted after September 16, 1994, must be limited by a sunset date. If a "reasonable and appropriate" sunset date is not specified, the deduction will expire five years after the effective date of the enacting law (35 ILCS 5/250).

The sunset date is extended by five years for all tax exemptions, credits, or deductions that would have expired in 2011-2013 (35 ILCS 5/250).

CCH Advisory: Same-sex Marriages; Civil Unions

Since same-sex marriages are legal in the State of Illinois, same-sex couples who married in Illinois or converted their civil union to an official marriage on or before December 31,2014, are considered married for federal and state tax purposes when filing their tax returns. Taxpayers in a civil union are no longer considered married for Illinois Income Tax purposes. Civil Union partners must file their Illinois Income Tax return using the same filing status as on their federal return. (http://tax.illinois.gov/News/2014CivilUnionInfo.htm)

The Internal Revenue Service (IRS) now considers same-sex couples married if they were lawfully married in a state (or foreign country) whose laws authorize the marriage of two individuals of the same sex. However, individuals who have entered into a registered domestic partnership, civil union, or other similar relationship that is not considered a marriage under state (or foreign) law are not considered married for federal tax purposes.

¶202 Tax Based on Federal Law—"Internal Revenue Code" Defined

Law: Income Tax Act, Sec. 102 [35 ILCS 5/102]; Income Tax Act, Sec. 203(a)(2)(Z) [35 ILCS 5/203(a)(2)(Z)]; Income Tax Act, Sec. 1501(a)(11) [35 ILCS 5/1501](CCH ILLINOIS TAX REPORTS, ¶ 15-510, 15-670).

Comparable Federal: Secs. 61, 62 (U.S. MASTER TAX GUIDE, ¶ 61, 1401).

The Illinois income tax is based on the federal law as currently amended. Except as expressly provided otherwise or clearly appearing from the context, terms used in the Illinois law have the same meaning as when used in a comparable context in the Internal Revenue Code and other provisions of the U.S. statutes relating to federal income taxes (35 ILCS 5/102).

"Internal Revenue Code" is defined to mean the code as in effect for the taxable year (35 ILCS 5/1501(a)(11)).

Bonus depreciation: Illinois does not allow the 30% or 50% "bonus" depreciation under IRC Sec. 168(k) (*Information Bulletin FY 2004-21*, Illinois Department of Revenue, December 2003, CCH ILLINOIS TAX REPORTS, ¶ 401-450). For taxable years 2001 and thereafter, in determining base income, a taxpayer must add to the taxpayer's federal adjusted gross income or taxable income an amount equal to the IRC Sec. 168(k) bonus depreciation deduction (30% or 50% of the adjusted basis of qualified property) taken on the taxpayer's federal income tax return for the taxable year. The special depreciation addition is entered on Form IL-1040, Schedule M, line 6.

For taxable years ending on or before December 31, 2005, the taxpayer's Illinois depreciation deduction on such property in the year the federal bonus depreciation is taken and for each year thereafter is the amount of the taxpayer's federal depreciation deduction, excluding the bonus depreciation deduction, multiplied by 0.429. For taxable years ending after December 31, 2005, for property on which a bonus depreciation deduction of 30% of the adjusted basis was taken, the depreciation deduction equals the amount of the taxpayer's federal depreciation deduction, excluding the bonus depreciation, multiplied by 0.429. For property on which a bonus depreciation deduction of 50% of the adjusted basis was taken, the depreciation deduction equals the amount of the taxpayer's federal depreciation deduction, excluding the bonus depreciation (35 ILCS 5/203(b)(2)(E-10), (T)). The aggregate amount deducted in all taxable years for any one piece of property may not exceed the amount of the bonus depreciation deduction taken on that property on the taxpayer's federal income tax return. The depreciation calculation is made on Form IL-4562, and the subtraction is entered on Form IL-1040, Schedule M, step 3, line 17.

If the taxpayer sells, transfers, abandons, or otherwise disposes of property for which a bonus depreciation addition modification was required in any year, the taxpayer may deduct the amount of the addition modification (35 ILCS 5/203(b)(2)(E-11), (U)).

CCH Advisory: Gulf Opportunity Zone and Liberty Zone "bonus" depreciation

No addback is required for the additional 50% bonus depreciation for Gulf Opportunity Zone or Liberty Zone property. (Form IL-4562, Special Depreciation)

Sales tax deduction: Illinois does not allow the itemized deductions allowed on the federal income tax return. Therefore, Illinois does not allow taxpayers to elect to deduct general sales taxes in lieu of personal income taxes, under IRC Sec. 164(b).

¶203 Tax Imposed on Net Income—"Net Income" Defined

Law: Income Tax Act, Sec. 202 [35 ILCS 5/202] (CCH ILLINOIS TAX REPORTS, ¶15-505).

Comparable Federal: Secs. 62, 63 (U.S. MASTER TAX GUIDE, ¶61, 124, 126, 1005).

A taxpayer's "net income," which is the base for computation of the tax, is that portion of the "base income" that is attributable to Illinois under the allocation and apportionment provisions (Chapter 3) of the law, minus the standard exemption allowed (¶213) (35 ILCS 5/202). "Base income" means federal adjusted gross income, with modifications, for individuals (¶205) and federal taxable income, with modifications, for estates and trusts (¶209).

¶204 Base Income—In General

Law: Income Tax Act, Sec. 203(a)(1) [35 ILCS 5/203]; Income Tax Act, Sec. 207 [35 ILCS 5/207]; 86 Ill. Adm. Code 100.2410 (CCH ILLINOIS TAX REPORTS, ¶15-510, 16-310).

Comparable Federal: Secs. 62, 63, 172 (U.S. MASTER TAX GUIDE, ¶61, 124, 126, 1005, 1173).

Under the Illinois law, a taxpayer's net income, which is the figure to which the tax rate is applied, is computed by applying the allocation and apportionment provisions (Chapter 3) to "base income" and then subtracting the standard exemption (¶213). "Base income" for individuals (¶205) is federal adjusted gross income, with modifications, and for estates and trusts (¶209) is federal taxable income, with modifications.

Practitioner Comment: Federal Income

Illinois defines the terms "gross income," "adjusted gross income," and "taxable income" to mean the amount of gross income, adjusted gross income or taxable income properly reportable for federal income tax purposes. Taxpayers are generally bound, for Illinois tax reporting purposes, to reporting positions taken for federal income tax purposes. For example, taxpayers who elect to take a tax credit on their federal tax return for foreign taxes paid, as opposed to claiming a deduction from taxable income, may not claim a deduction for foreign tax payments from the amount of federal taxable income reported on the Illinois income tax return. (*Caterpillar Tractor Co. v. Lenckos,* 84 Ill.2d 102 (1981), CCH ILLINOIS TAX REPORTS, ¶201-154)

Horwood Marcus & Berk Chartered

• *Net operating losses*

If, after applying all applicable addition modifications, an individual taxpayer's net income results in a loss, the taxpayer is entitled to the NOL carryback or carryforward deduction properly allowed on the federal return. For all other taxpayers, the following carryover and carryback provisions apply (35 ILCS 5/207(a)):

— for taxable years ending prior to December 31, 1999, the loss is allowed as a carryover or carryback deduction in the manner allowed under Section 172 of the Internal Revenue Code;

— for taxable years ending on or after December 31, 1999, and prior to December 31, 2003, the loss may be carried back two taxable years and carried forward 20 taxable years; and

— for taxable years ending on or after December 31, 2003, the loss may be allowed as a net operating carryover to each of the 12 taxable years following the taxable year of the loss; no carryback is allowed.

When computing a net operating loss, taxpayers who are required to reduce their federal net operating loss and carryovers by the amount of any discharge of indebtedness income that was excluded from taxation because the taxpayer is insolvent or in bankruptcy are also required to reduce any Illinois net loss and carryover to a taxable year by an equal amount. See 86 Ill. Adm. Code 100.2410.

The suspension of the net loss carryover deduction for tax years 2011-2014 that applied to corporations (see ¶ 1013) did not apply for personal income tax purposes.

CCH Advisory: Double Deductions Prohibited

The Illinois Income Tax Act (IITA) does not provide for any Illinois net operating loss deduction (NOLD), but relies upon the federal NOLD in computing federal adjusted gross income (AGI), which is the starting point for determining a taxpayer's Illinois base income. However, the federal AGI reported on a taxpayer's Illinois income tax return cannot be less than zero. This is to prevent the double benefit that would occur if an individual carried back a current net operating loss federally, thereby reducing the amount reported as AGI during the carryback year and thereby also reducing the amount calculated as Illinois base income for the carryback year, while at the same time reporting the same loss as current negative AGI on its Illinois return for a subsequent loss carry back or a loss carry forward year.

Illinois law specifically prohibits double deductions and authorizes the modification of a taxpayer's adjusted gross income to prevent them. In this case, the taxpayer had applied the NOLD, as shown on his federal transcript, and reduced his previously reported AGI to a negative number on his amended Illinois tax return. Further, the taxpayer failed to provide a completed U.S. Form 1045, Application for Tentative Refund, which is used by federal taxpayers to apply for a refund resulting from an NOL carryback. The Illinois amended return instructions expressly state that a pro-form Form 1045, must be prepared and submitted even if the taxpayer is not required to prepare and file one by the IRS. Therefore, the taxpayer failed to show what portion of his federal net operating loss he was allowed to carry forward to the tax year at issue. (*Administrative Hearing Decision No. IT 16-01*, Illinois Department of Revenue, January 13, 2016, CCH ILLINOIS TAX REPORTS, ¶ 403-092)

¶205 Base Income of Individuals—Modifications

Law: Income Tax Act, Sec. 203(a)(2), (f) [35 ILCS 5/203]; Prepaid Tuition Act, Sec. 55 [110 ILCS 979/55]; Homelessness Prevention Act, Sec. 12 [310 ILCS 70/12]; State Treasury Act, Sec. 16.6 [15 ILCS 505/16.6]; 86 Ill. Adm. Code Secs. 100.2450, 100.2455 (CCH ILLINOIS TAX REPORTS, ¶ 15-505—16-370).

The sunset date is extended by five years for all tax exemptions, credits, or deductions that would have expired in 2011-2013 (35 ILCS 5/250).

Individuals are not allowed the itemized deductions allowed under federal law (*e.g.*, medical expenses, taxes, mortgage interest payments, charitable contributions) in computing the Illinois income tax.

For individuals, Illinois base income means federal adjusted gross income with the following listed modifications:

- *Addition modifications*

(1) *Interest and dividends:* Amounts received as interest or dividends must be added back to federal adjusted gross income to the extent excluded on the federal return (35 ILCS 5/203(a)(2)(A)). (Dividends are not subject to exclusion under current federal law)

Also, any interest from state or local obligations (including those of Illinois and its political subdivisions), which is exempt from federal taxation, must be added back. The amount exempted is the interest net of bond premium amortization.

(2) *Illinois income tax:* Any Illinois income tax deducted from gross income in the computation of federal adjusted gross income must be added back in computing Illinois base income (35 ILCS 5/203(a)(2)(B)). However, for individuals, generally, no adjustment will be necessary, since, under the federal law, deductions for state personal income taxes are allowed *from* adjusted gross income, as itemized deductions, rather than from gross income in the computation of adjusted gross income. For the same reason, no adjustment is necessary if the taxpayer elects to deduct state sales and use taxes.

Personal Property Replacement Income Tax (PPRIT) deducted because it is passed through from a partnership, S corporation, or trust must be added back (35 ILCS 5/203(a)(2)(B)), but it can also be deducted (35 ILCS 5/203(a)(2)(H)). This is to make the payment of PPRIT neutral in the computation of adjusted gross income. See 86 Ill. Adm. Code Sec. 100.2450.

(3) *Capital gain deduction:* Any deduction of capital gains permitted under federal law is added back to the federal base (35 ILCS 5/203(a)(2)(D)).

(4) *Medical care savings accounts:* Money withdrawn from a medical care savings account (MCSA) for any other purpose than to pay the employee's or a dependent's medical expenses or to purchase a health coverage policy is income subject to state income tax in the taxable year of the withdrawal (35 ILCS 5/203(a)(2)(D-5)).

(5) *Remediation costs claimed as credit:* An amount equal to any eligible remediation costs that the individual deducted in computing adjusted gross income and for which the individual claims an environmental remediation credit (¶408) (35 ILCS 5/203(a)(2)(D-10)).

(6) *Bonus depreciation:* For taxable years 2001 and thereafter, an amount equal to the 30% or 50% bonus depreciation deduction (IRC Sec. 168(k)) taken on the taxpayer's federal income tax return for the taxable year (35 ILCS 5/203(a)(2)(D-15)). However, no addback is required for the additional 50% bonus depreciation for Gulf Opportunity Zone or Liberty Zone property (see Form IL-4562, Special Depreciation). See also the discussion of bonus depreciation at ¶202.

Practitioner Comment: Luxury Autos and Bonus Depreciation

Under federal law, when bonus depreciation exceeds the "cap" on depreciation expense allowed for luxury automobiles, the taxpayer is allowed to deduct only the bonus depreciation in an amount equal to the cap for federal income tax purposes; no regular depreciation deduction is allowed.

The Department maintains that taxpayers are not entitled to any depreciation deduction in the year a luxury automobile is placed in service when the bonus depreciation exceeds the cap on depreciation allowed. Indeed, the taxpayer is not allowed any regular depreciation deduction for federal tax purposes, and Illinois requires all bonus depreciation to be added back. See Ill. Dep't of Revenue 2002 Tax Practitioner Meeting Questions and Answers.

Marilyn A. Wethekam, Horwood Marcus & Berk Chartered

---

(7) *College tuition programs:* Amounts excluded from federal gross income for distributions received from qualified federal tuition programs other than the college savings pool ("Bright Start") or the Illinois Prepaid Tuition Trust Fund ("College Illinois!") (35 ILCS 5/203(a)(2)(D-20)). An addback also is required for distributions from certain out-of-state tuition programs.

An addback is required in the amount of any funds transferred from an Illinois-administered qualified tuition program to an out-of-state program, to the extent that the transferred funds were previously deducted from base income (35 ILCS 5/203(a)(2)(D-21)).

For taxable years beginning on or after January 1, 2009, an addition modification is required in an amount equal to the contribution component of any nonqualified withdrawal or refund from a tuition savings program that was previously deducted from base income and was not used for qualified education expenses at an eligible education institution, if it did not result from the death or disability of the beneficiary. (35 ILCS 5/203(a)(2)(D-22); see also *General Information Letter IT 12-0004-GIL,* Department of Revenue, March 13, 2012, CCH ILLINOIS TAX REPORTS, ¶ 402-473)

(8) *Sale of bonus-depreciation property:* If the taxpayer sells, transfers, abandons, or otherwise disposes of property for which a bonus depreciation addition modification was required in any year, the taxpayer may deduct the amount of the addition modification (35 ILCS 5/203(a)(2)(Z)).

(9) *Net operating losses:* see ¶ 204.

(10) *Interest and intangible expenses:* Interest and intangible expenses and costs otherwise allowed as a deduction but paid directly or indirectly (1) to a person who would be a member of the same unitary business group but for the fact that the person's business activity outside the U.S. is 80% or more of the person's total business activity, or (2) interest and intangible expenses and costs otherwise allowed as a deduction, but paid directly or indirectly, to a person who would be a member of the same unitary business group but for the fact the person is prohibited from being included in the unitary business group because he or she is ordinarily required to apportion business income under a different apportionment formula must be added back to compute Illinois taxable income/base income (35 ILCS 5/203(a)(2)(D-17, D-18)). See also ¶ 1025.

The addback requirements do not apply if the taxpayer can establish that (1) the person paid, accrued, or incurred the interest or intangible expense or cost to a person who is not a related member and (2) the transaction between the taxpayer and the person did not have as a principal purpose the avoidance of Illinois income tax. Also, an add-back is not required if the taxpayer can establish that the adjustment regarding an item of interest or intangible expense or cost from a transaction with a person would be unreasonable.

(11) *Insurance premiums:* Taxpayers must add back any amount of insurance premium expenses and costs otherwise allowed as a deduction, but paid directly or

indirectly, to an insurance company that would be a member of the same unitary business group but for the fact the company is ordinarily required to apportion business income under a different apportionment formula (35 ILCS 5/203(a)(2)(D-9)).

For taxable years ending on or after December 31, 2011, a taxpayer that was required to add back any insurance premium may elect to subtract that part of a reimbursement received from the insurance company equal to the amount of the expense or loss (including expenses incurred by the insurance company) that would have been taken into account as a deduction for federal income tax purposes if the expense or loss had been uninsured. If a taxpayer makes this election, the insurer must add back to income the amount subtracted by the taxpayer. (35 ILCS 5/203(a)(2)(GG))

(12) *Domestic production activities:* Effective for taxable years ending on or after December 31, 2017, Illinois requires an addition adjustment by personal income taxpayers for the amount of any federal deduction under IRC § 199 for domestic production activities (35 ILCS 5/203(a)(2)(D-24)).

• *Subtraction modifications*

(1) *Constitutionally exempt items:* Income received by residents that is exempted from state taxation by the Illinois Constitution or federal law is subtracted from federal adjusted gross income (35 ILCS 5/203(a)(2)(N)). The following are the most common exempt items: interest on federal obligations, supplemental annuity payments under the Railroad Retirement Act, and interest from Illinois Housing Development Authority bonds and notes. Details are covered at ¶211.

(2) *Refunds of Illinois income tax:* Under the federal law, any state income tax previously deducted in computing federal taxable income must be included in adjusted gross income when refunded. Any Illinois income tax that is refunded to the taxpayer and included in federal adjusted gross income must be subtracted from federal adjusted gross income in computing Illinois base income (35 ILCS 5/203(a)(2)(H); see also 86 Ill. Adm. Code Sec. 100.2450).

(3) *Military pay:* Pay received for active duty in the U.S. Armed Forces and any compensation paid to a member of the National Guard of any state are exempt from Illinois income tax and may be subtracted from federal adjusted gross income (35 ILCS 5/203(a)(2)(E)). See ¶104.

(4) *Distributions from pension, profit-sharing, and retirement plans:* Income received from the following sources is subtracted to the extent that it has been included in federal adjusted gross income (and excluded in computing net earnings from self-employment under IRC Sec. 1402) (35 ILCS 5/203(a)(2)(F)): qualified private and public retirement plans; individual retirement accounts; payments to retired partners; and advance payments received from a life insurance policy, an endowment, or an annuity that are used as an indemnity for a terminal illness. An individual may subtract any withdrawal from an IRC Sec. 401(k) plan that is included in federal adjusted gross income (see *General Information Letter IT 10-0025-GIL*, Illinois Department of Revenue, October 18, 2010, CCH ILLINOIS TAX REPORTS, ¶402-230). Ordinary income from a qualified retirement plan for which the special federal ten-year averaging method is elected on the federal return does not require subtraction because it has not been included in federal taxable income.

CCH Advisory: Roth IRA Rollovers

If a taxpayer's profit-sharing plan qualifies under IRC Sec. 401(a), the distributions from the plan must be included in the taxpayer's federal adjusted gross income, whether or not the distribution is rolled over into a Roth IRA, and therefore may be subtracted under the Illinois Income Tax Act. (*General Information Letter IT 15-0008-GIL*, Illinois Department of Revenue, August 4, 2015, CCH ILLINOIS TAX REPORTS, ¶ 403-023)

All income from pension plans of a governmental agency or unit may be subtracted, whether or not the pension qualifies under IRC Sec. 457. The deduction allowed for distributions from government retirement plans does not depend on whether the plan is a qualified plan under federal income tax law. A government plan that qualifies as an eligible deferred compensation plan as defined in IRC Sec. 457(b), is eligible for the Illinois deduction because the plan constitutes "a retirement or disability plan for employees of any governmental agency or unit." Similarly, a plan that is taxable under IRC Sec. 457(f), because the plan is not an eligible deferred compensation plan, may still qualify for the state deduction provided that the deferred compensation arrangement is a retirement or disability plan for government employees. (*General Information Letter IT 09-0031-GIL*, Illinois Department of Revenue, September 17, 2009, CCH ILLINOIS TAX REPORTS, ¶ 402-033)

CCH Advisory: Foreign Country Pension Plans

Pension paid by an Italian corporation and social security payments by the Italian government did not qualify for an Illinois personal income tax subtraction. The Department of Revenue noted that upon review of the U.S.-Italy Income Tax Treaty referred to in the taxpayer's letter, the Treaty provides that U.S. and Italian pensions are taxable only in the country of residence of the recipient. Thus, as a resident of Illinois, the taxpayer was required to pay tax on its Italian pension and social security payments received while a resident of Illinois. (*General Information Letter IT 12-0013-GIL*, Illinois Department of Revenue, May 24, 2012, CCH ILLINOIS TAX REPORTS, ¶ 402-504; see also *General Information Letter IT 13-0003-GIL*, Illinois Department of Revenue, March 26, 2013, CCH ILLINOIS TAX REPORTS, ¶ 402-647 and *General Information Letter IT 13-0004-GIL*, Illinois Department of Revenue, March 26, 2013, CCH ILLINOIS TAX REPORTS, ¶ 402-648)

(5) *Recovery of items previously deducted:* Amounts included federally as a recovery of expenses previously deducted as an itemized deduction, such as insurance reimbursements of medical expenses deducted in a previous year, are subtracted from federal adjusted gross income (35 ILCS 5/203(a)(2)(I)).

(6) *Ridesharing benefits:* Money and other benefits, other than salary, received by a resident driver of a motor vehicle in a ridesharing arrangement and included in federal gross income are subtracted from federal adjusted gross income (35 ILCS 5/203(a)(2)(BB)). Reimbursements for car-pooling expenses are not included in federal income, so that generally an adjustment is not necessary.

(7) *Amortizable bond premiums, expenses, and interest related to tax exempt income:* The following paid expenses are subtracted from federal adjusted gross income: amortizable bond premium not deducted federally because it is attributable to tax-free bonds; interest not deducted federally because the underlying liability has been incurred or continued to purchase or carry tax-free obligations; and all other expenses not deducted federally because they are attributable to tax-free income. (35 ILCS 5/203(a)(2)(M), (N))

¶205

(8) *Social security and railroad retirement benefits:* Social security and railroad retirement benefits to the extent taxed under federal law are subtracted from federal adjusted gross income (35 ILCS 5/203(a)(2)(L); *General Information Letter IT 12-0026-GIL,* Illinois Department of Revenue, September 13, 2012, CCH ILLINOIS TAX REPORTS, ¶ 402-572).

(9) *Enterprise zone/foreign trade zone/redevelopment zone dividends:* Dividends from corporations that conduct substantially all of their operations in River Edge redevelopment zones are subtracted from federal adjusted gross income if they have earlier been included on the federal return (35 ILCS 5/203(a)(2)(J)). Similarly, dividends from high-impact businesses located in Illinois that conduct business operations in federally designated foreign trade zones or sub-zones are also subtracted if they have been included on the federal return (35 ILCS 5/203(a)(2)(K)). Dividends from corporations in enterprise zones are not eligible for subtraction as dividends (P.A. 97-905 (S.B. 3616), Laws 2012, effective August 7, 2012).

(10) *Job training contributions:* Contributions made by individuals to a job training project established pursuant to the Tax Increment Allocation Redevelopment Act are subtracted from federal adjusted gross income (35 ILCS 5/203(a)(2)(O)).

(11) *Repayment to another of items previously included in income:* Individuals who take the federal income tax credit under IRC Sec. 1341 for repayment to another of income items previously included in gross income as being held under a claim of right may subtract from federal taxable income, for Illinois income tax purposes, an amount equal to the deduction used to compute the federal income tax credit (35 ILCS 5/203(a)(2)(P)).

(12) *Valuation limitation amount:* Capital gain attributable to pre-August 1, 1969, asset appreciation is subtracted as computed and reported on Form F, Gains from Sales or Exchanges of Property Acquired Before August 1, 1969 (35 ILCS 5/203(f)).

(13) *Amounts received under the Homelessness Prevention Act:* Amounts included federally under the Homelessness Prevention Act for rental arrearages or for payments of a rent deposit are not income for state tax purposes and may be subtracted from federal adjusted gross income (310 ILCS 70/12).

(14) *Medical care savings accounts:* Principal contributed to, and interest earned on, a medical care savings account (MCSA) program, as well as reimbursements to an employee for eligible medical expenses, are exempt from tax. (35 ILCS 5/203(a)(2)(S), (T))

(15) *Conversion to Roth IRA:* The amount included in an individual's federal gross income from a conversion of a regular individual retirement account (IRA) to a Roth IRA is subtracted from the individual's federal adjusted gross income in computing base income for Illinois personal income tax (35 ILCS 5/203(a)(2)(W)).

(16) *Prepaid tuition contract earnings:* Any undistributed earnings of the Illinois Prepaid Tuition Trust (¶ 411) that are included in a taxpayer's federal taxable income or adjusted gross income because a prepaid tuition contract does not qualify under IRC Sec. 529 may be subtracted in computing the taxpayer's base income, and all disbursements included in a beneficiary's adjusted gross income may be subtracted to the extent they are used in accordance with the Illinois prepaid tuition contract under which the disbursements are made, regardless of whether the prepaid tuition contract qualifies under IRC Sec. 529 (110 ILCS 979/55).

(17) *Expenses for producing tax-exempt income:* Taxpayers may subtract from adjusted gross income those interest and expenses related to producing tax exempt income that are disallowed as federal deductions under IRC Sec. 265 (35 ILCS 5/203(a)(2)(M)).

(18) *Expenses related to credits:* Expenses associated with federal employment credits, the credit for qualified clinical testing expenses, and the credit for increasing research activities, which are disallowed as federal deductions under IRC Sec. 280C, may be subtracted from adjusted gross income (35 ILCS 5/203(a)(2)(M)). Also, a deduction is allowed for amounts disallowed by IRC Sec. 45G (railroad track maintenance credit) and for amounts included in the taxpayer's federal adjusted gross income under IRC Sec. 87 (alcohol and biodiesel fuel credit). (35 ILCS 5/203(a)(2)(M))

(19) *Payments to Holocaust victims:* Holocaust victims may deduct settlement payments from their income subject to Illinois personal income tax to the extent such amounts are includible in their federal adjusted gross income (35 ILCS 5/203(a)(2)(X)). The deduction applies to distributions or income received by individuals, trusts, and estates as a result of their status as a victim or descendant or a victim of Nazi persecution. Such payments are excluded from consideration for eligibility under the public aid provisions. A "victim of Nazi persecution" is defined as an individual persecuted for racial or religious reasons by Nazi Germany or any other Axis regime.

(20) *College savings:* A maximum of $10,000 per taxable year may be deducted from a taxpayer's adjusted gross income for amounts contributed to a college savings pool account ("Bright Start") or the Illinois Prepaid Tuition Trust Fund (College Illinois!). Rollovers to Bright Start from another IRC Sec. 529 college savings plan are not deductible (35 ILCS 5/203(a)(2)(Y)). Contributions made by an employer are treated as made by the employee. However, contributions made by an employer who matches an employee's contribution and claims the credit (discussed at ¶419) for that contribution must add back the amount of the credit (35 ILCS 5/203(a)(2)(D-22)). For an explanation of the required addback, see *General Information Letter IT 09-0043-GIL,* Illinois Department of Revenue, October 28, 2009, CCH ILLINOIS TAX REPORTS, ¶402-049.

Practitoner Comment: Educational Deductions

For 2002, 2003, and 2004, Illinois allowed a tax deduction for all amounts contributed to Bright Start, which is Illinois' college savings pool, excluding rollovers. For 2005 and forward, Illinois allows a deduction up to $10,000 per year for amounts contributed to Bright Start or College Illinois, which is Illinois' Prepaid Tuition Trust Fund, excluding rollovers (35 ILCS 5/203(a)(2)(Y)); see also ¶205.

Horwood Marcus & Berk, Chartered

---

(21) *Income earned on investments under the Home Ownership Made Easy Act:* Income earned on investments made under the Home Ownership Made Easy Act may be subtracted from federal adjusted gross income for purposes of determining Illinois base income (86 Ill. Adm. Code Sec. 100.2470).

(22) *Bonus depreciation:* A portion of the federal depreciation deduction, which Illinois requires to be added back, may be claimed as a deduction (35 ILCS 5/203(a)(2)(Z)). See the discussion at ¶202.

(23) *Sale of bonus-depreciation property:* If the taxpayer sells, transfers, abandons, or otherwise disposes of property for which a bonus depreciation addition modification was required in any year, the taxpayer may deduct the amount of the addition modification (35 ILCS 5/203(a)(2)(Z)).

¶205

(24) *ABLE accounts:* Accrued earnings on investments in Achieving a Better Life Experience (ABLE) savings accounts are exempt when disbursed on behalf of a designated beneficiary for qualified disability expenses related to the blindness or disability of the designated beneficiary. The exemption applies to all Illinois state and local income taxation to the extent that such income is exempt from federal income taxation. (15 ILCS 505/16.6(d))

Subtraction of federally nondeductible expenses: A regulation (86 Ill. Admin. Code Sec. 100-2455) provides guidance for taxpayers in determining the subtractions they are allowed for expenses that are not deductible for federal purposes because they are incurred in connection with income that is exempt from federal income tax, but not from Illinois income tax, or with credits allowed for federal income tax purposes, but not for Illinois income tax purposes.

Specifically, individual Illinois taxpayers are entitled to subtract from adjusted gross income an amount equal to the sum of all amounts disallowed as deductions by IRC Secs. 171(a)(2) and 265(a)(2), and all amounts of expenses allocable to interest and disallowed as deductions by IRC Sec. 265(a)(1), and, for taxable years ending on or after August 13, 1999, IRC Secs. 171(a)(2), 265, 280C, 291(a)(3) and 832(b)(5)(B)(i). (86 Ill. Admin. Code Sec. 100-2455)

Unjust prison time served: A taxpayer may deduct any amount awarded by the Court of Claims for time unjustly served in a State prison (35 ILCS 5/203(a)(2)(FF)).

• *Computation of income*

After computing "base income," a nonresident individual allocates and apportions (Chapter 3) income within and without the state (all income of residents is taxable) and all taxpayers subtract their standard exemptions (¶ 213).

Individuals are not allowed either a standard deduction or itemized deductions.

For additional information on exemptions, see *Publication 101, Income Exempt from Tax,* Illinois Department of Revenue, March 2010, CCH ILLINOIS TAX REPORTS, ¶ 402-087.

CCH Advisory: Double Taxed Income

The Illinois Department of Revenue explains how to compute a taxpayer's taxable income when part of the income was double taxed for personal income tax purposes by another state. Illinois adjusts income using the foreign tax credit. See the current version of *Publication 111, Illinois Schedule CR for Individuals,* available at **http:// www.revenue.state.il.us/Publications/Pubs/index.htm.**

¶206   Chart of Illinois Individual Income Tax

On the following pages are two charts illustrating briefly the items that go into federal adjusted gross income and the adjustments necessary to obtain Illinois net income. The charts indicate only the general computations and adjustments, and do not include any special adjustments that may be necessary for particular taxpayers.

The chart relating to the computation of Illinois net income includes references to paragraphs in the *Guidebook* where items listed in the chart are discussed in detail.

COMPUTATION OF FEDERAL TAXABLE INCOME—INDIVIDUALS

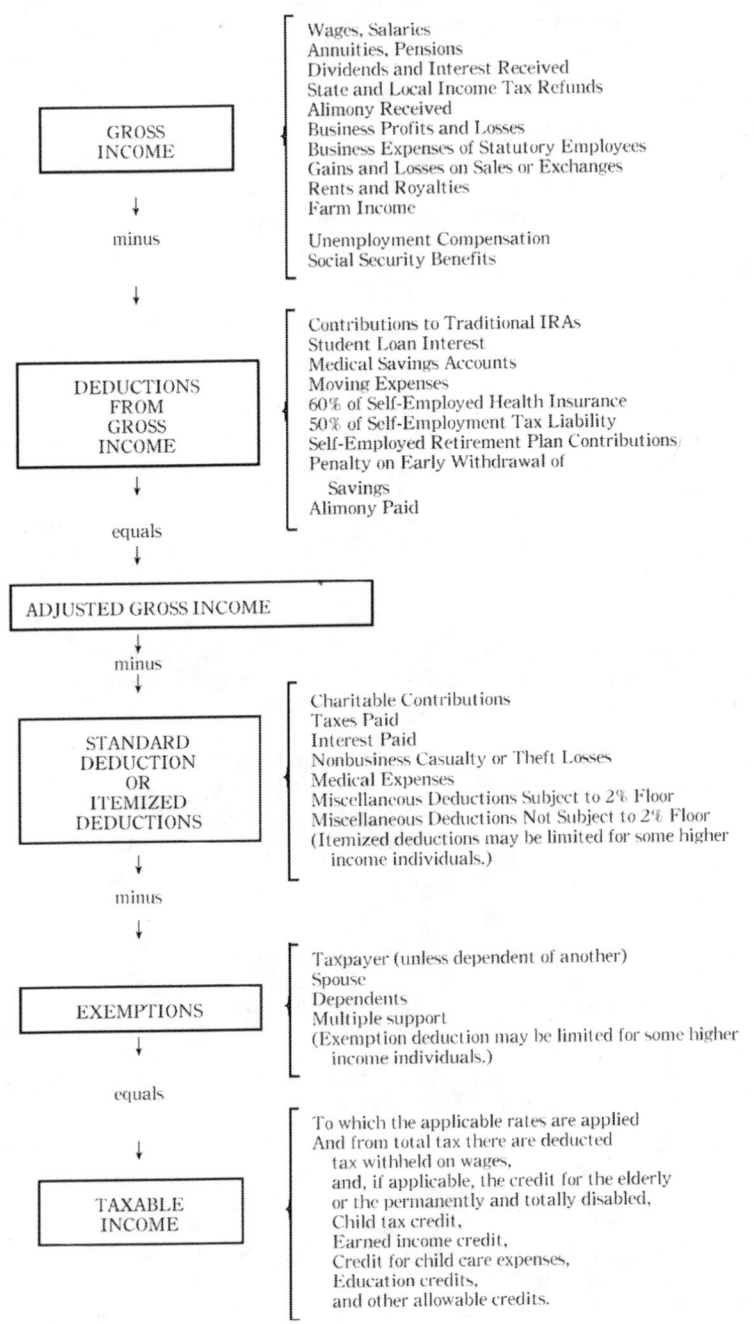

GROSS
INCOME

Wages, Salaries
Annuities, Pensions
Dividends and Interest Received
State and Local Income Tax Refunds
Alimony Received
Business Profits and Losses
Business Expenses of Statutory Employees
Gains and Losses on Sales or Exchanges
Rents and Royalties
Farm Income

minus

Unemployment Compensation
Social Security Benefits

DEDUCTIONS
FROM
GROSS
INCOME

Contributions to Traditional IRAs
Student Loan Interest
Medical Savings Accounts
Moving Expenses
60% of Self-Employed Health Insurance
50% of Self-Employment Tax Liability
Self-Employed Retirement Plan Contributions
Penalty on Early Withdrawal of
    Savings
Alimony Paid

equals

ADJUSTED GROSS INCOME

minus

STANDARD
DEDUCTION
OR
ITEMIZED
DEDUCTIONS

Charitable Contributions
Taxes Paid
Interest Paid
Nonbusiness Casualty or Theft Losses
Medical Expenses
Miscellaneous Deductions Subject to 2% Floor
Miscellaneous Deductions Not Subject to 2% Floor
(Itemized deductions may be limited for some higher
    income individuals.)

minus

EXEMPTIONS

Taxpayer (unless dependent of another)
Spouse
Dependents
Multiple support
(Exemption deduction may be limited for some higher
    income individuals.)

equals

TAXABLE
INCOME

To which the applicable rates are applied
And from total tax there are deducted
    tax withheld on wages,
    and, if applicable, the credit for the elderly
    or the permanently and totally disabled,
    Child tax credit,
    Earned income credit,
    Credit for child care expenses,
    Education credits,
    and other allowable credits.

COMPUTATION OF ILLINOIS NET INCOME—INDIVIDUALS

	FEDERAL ADJUSTED GROSS INCOME	
PLUS (¶205) State and Local Bond Interest Illinois Income Tax Dividend Exclusion Capital Gains Medical Care Savings Accounts "Bonus" Depreciation	with	**MINUS (¶205)** Military Pay of Residents Federal Bond Interest Illinois Income Tax Refunds

	ILLINOIS MODIFICATIONS	Pension and Retirement Benefits
		Social Security and Railroad
		   Retirement Benefits
		"IRC. Sec. 111 Recoveries"
		Amounts Exempt Under Illinois
		   and Federal Constitutions
		Ridesharing Benefits
		Dividends Paid by Enterprise
		   Zone Corporations and
		   Certain Foreign Trade Zone
		   High-impact Businesses
		Disallowed Deductions Under
		   Sections 171(a)(2), 265(a)(1),
		   and 265(a)(2):
		   Certain Tax-Exempt Income
		Medical Care Savings Accounts
		Job Training Expenses
		College Savings/Earnings
		Expenses Related to Credits

	equals	
	ILLINOIS BASE INCOME	
	subject to	
	ALLOCATION AND APPORTIONMENT	Applies to Nonresidents and Part-year Residents Only
	minus	
	ILLINOIS EXEMPTION	Taxpayer, Spouse, Dependents (¶213)
	equals	

	ILLINOIS NET INCOME	To Which is Applied the
		   the 3.75% Rate (¶102)
		And from the Resulting
		   Tax is Deducted:
		Withheld Tax (¶409)
		Estimated Tax Payments (¶410)
		Tax Paid Another State
		   (¶403)
		Credits Against Tax (Ch. 4)

¶207 Base Income of Partnerships

Law: Income Tax Act, Sec. 201 [35 ILCS 5/201]; Income Tax Act, Sec. 203 [35 ILCS 5/203]; 86 Ill. Adm. Code Sec. 100.2450 (CCH ILLINOIS TAX REPORTS, ¶15-510, 16-005).

Comparable Federal: Secs. 701—763 (U.S. MASTER TAX GUIDE, ¶63, 401—481).

The computation for the personal property replacement income tax (Replacement Tax or PPRIT) basis begins with ordinary income or loss from the federal partnership return (35 ILCS 5/203(e)(2)(H)). The following income, loss, and deduction items that are required to be separately stated for federal purposes (Form 1065, Schedule K) are added to, or subtracted from, ordinary income or loss for replacement tax purposes.

Additions include:

— income from rental real estate;

— income from rental activities;

— portfolio income;

— net IRC Sec. 1231 gain from involuntary conversions or casualties; and

— gains from sales or exchanges.

Subtractions include:

— charitable contributions;

— IRC Sec. 179 expense deductions;

— payments for partners to an IRA, Keough, or SEP;

— oil and gas depletion; and

— interest on investment indebtedness.

The resulting "unmodified base income" is then adjusted by Illinois addition and subtraction modifications to determine Illinois base income. If the partnership derives all of its income from Illinois sources, the standard exemption (¶213) is subtracted and the resulting net income is subject to the 1.5% tax. Partnerships that derive income from inside and outside Illinois allocate and apportion base income to determine base income allocable to Illinois (¶321). Then an apportioned standard exemption is subtracted (¶213) to determine net income.

Investment partnerships: Investment partnerships are not subject to personal property replacement income tax. For additional information, see ¶105 or ¶852.

• *Illinois modifications*

Partnership modifications of the following items are the same as those of individuals (¶205): interest; dividends; bonus depreciation; net operating losses; constitutionally exempt obligations; capital gains; bond premiums; contributions to job-training projects and river edge redevelopment zone organizations; and repayment to another of items previously included in income.

In addition, the following modifications apply specifically to partnerships.

Modifications from other entities: A partnership must take into account the partnership's share of Illinois addition and subtraction modifications from other partnerships, trusts, or estates of which the partnership is a partner or beneficiary.

Federal jobs tax credit: See ¶854 for a subtraction that may be claimed by partners.

CCH Advisory: Merger or Consolidation

Illinois has adopted the provisions of IRC Sec. 708, concerning continuation of a partnership. Thus, an acquiring partnership may claim the personal income tax credits and net operating losses of a partnership that is acquired. The adoption of these federal provisions concerning successor organizations is applicable retroactively to all acquisitions occurring in tax years ending after 1986. However, transitional rules apply concerning a taxpayer's eligibility for refunds and assessment reductions for pre-1999 tax liabilities.

Income distributed to other entities: Partnership income distributed to an entity (*i.e.,* another partnership, trust, or estate) subject to the replacement tax is subtracted from income (35 ILCS 5/203(d)(2)(I)).

Guaranteed payments: No addition is required for deductions allowed for guaranteed payments to an individual partner for personal services by that partner. For taxable years ending before December 31, 2009, amounts deducted on the federal return as guaranteed payments under IRC Sec. 707(c) were added to base income. (35 ILCS 5/203(d)(2)(C)) "Guaranteed payments" are fixed amounts paid for services or the use of capital without regard to the income of the partnership.

¶207

Replacement tax: The amount of personal property replacement tax deducted for federal purposes is added to income (35 ILCS 5/203(d)(2)(B)).

The amount of replacement tax refunds that were included in the partnership's federal taxable income is subtracted (35 ILCS 5/203(d)(2)(F)). This is to make the payment of replacement tax neutral in the computation of adjusted gross income. See 86 Ill. Adm. Code Sec. 100.2450.

Personal service income: Partnership income that constitutes personal service income is subtracted from income. The amount of the subtraction is the greater of (1) the amount of "personal service income" under IRC Sec. 1348(b)(1) as in effect December 31, 1981; or (2) a reasonable allowance for compensation paid or accrued for service rendered by the partners to the partnership (35 ILCS 5/203(d)(2)(H)).

Practitioner Comment: Extra Tax on Personal Service Partnerships Eliminated

P.A. 96-0835 (HB 2239), Laws 2009, was signed into law on December 16, 2009. The law reverses earlier legislation that would have increased taxes for personal service partnerships starting December 31, 2009. The earlier legislation limited partnerships' deductions to "guaranteed payments" rather than "reasonable compensation," and ultimately would have amounted to an additional 1.5% tax on partnership profits. HB 2239 restores the original tax treatment by amending subsection 203(d) of the Illinois Income Tax Act (35 ILCS 5). Personal services income may now be deducted when calculating the base income of a partnership.

Marilyn A. Wethekam, Esq., Horwood Marcus & Berk Chartered

Practitioner Comment: Compensation for Services

The Department has stated that one method of computing the reasonable allowance for compensation for services is to "determine the number of hours worked in performing personal services for the partnership during the particular year, and multiply that amount by a fair hourly wage." GIL 98-IT-0036 (April 3, 1998). The effect of the subtraction modification is to "greatly reduce or eliminate the replacement tax liability of partnerships of doctors, lawyers, accountants, architects and other professional practitioners." PLR 91-IT-0339 (Dec. 24, 1991). The Department has indicated that it will not contest deductions for compensation paid to partners unless the amount subtracted is patently unreasonable.

Horwood Marcus & Berk Chartered

¶208 How Estates and Trusts Are Taxed

Law: Income Tax Act, Sec. 301(a) [35 ILCS 5/301(a)]; Income Tax Act, Sec. 307 [35 ILCS 5/307]; Income Tax Act, Sec. 1501(a)(20) [35 ILCS 5/1501](CCH ILLINOIS TAX REPORTS, ¶15-205).

Comparable Federal: Secs. 641—683, 7701(a)(3) (U.S. MASTER TAX GUIDE, ¶64, 501—585).

Both estates and trusts are liable for the Illinois income tax; however, only trusts are also liable for the Illinois personal property replacement income tax (¶103).

Estates and trusts may be either residents or nonresidents (¶103). Resident estates and trusts are taxed on federal taxable income modified by Illinois additions and subtractions (¶205). Nonresident estates and trusts allocate and apportion modified fiduciary income and are taxed on the amount attributable to Illinois (¶322).

• *Beneficiaries*

Beneficiaries of estates and trusts are taxed for Illinois income tax purposes on their pro rata share, if any, of fiduciary income that is deemed to have been paid, credited, or distributed by the entity (35 ILCS 301(a)). The trust or estate furnishes a schedule detailing information reportable by the beneficiaries on their individual income tax returns. A resident beneficiary's entire pro rata share of fiduciary base income is attributed to Illinois. Nonresident beneficiaries take into account their share of estate and trust income allocated and apportioned to Illinois (35 ILCS 307).

• *What is a resident estate or trust?*

The following estates and trusts are treated as residents for purposes of the Illinois income tax: (1) the estate of a decedent who was domiciled in Illinois at the date of death; (2) a trust created by the will of a decedent who at death was domiciled in the state; and (3) an irrevocable trust, if the grantor was domiciled in Illinois at the time the trust became irrevocable. A trust is considered irrevocable to the extent that the grantor is not considered the owner of the trust under the grantor trust provisions of IRC Secs. 671—678. (35 ILCS 1501(a)(20))

¶209 Base Income of Estates and Trusts

> *Law:* Income Tax Act, Sec. 203(c)(2), (e) [35 ILCS 5/203] (CCH ILLINOIS TAX REPORTS, ¶15-210, 15-215).

> *Comparable Federal:* Secs. 641—683, 7701(a)(3); 86 Ill. Adm. Code Sec. 100.2450 (U.S. MASTER TAX GUIDE, ¶64, 501—585).

Resident trusts and estates begin computation of the income tax basis with taxable income from the federal fiduciary return (35 ILCS 203(e)). Illinois addition and subtraction modifications (see below) are made in order to arrive at Illinois fiduciary "base income."

The standard exemption is deducted (¶213) in order to arrive at net income that is subject to tax. See ¶102 for the current tax rate. Credits (see Chapter 4) are subtracted in order to determine the amount due.

There is a deduction in an amount equal to all amounts included pursuant to the provisions of IRC Sec. 111 as a recovery of items previously deducted by the decedent from adjusted gross income in the computation of taxable income (Sec. 203(c)(2)(W)). There is also a deduction for an amount equal to the refund included in such total of any tax deducted for federal income tax purposes, to the extent that the deduction was added back (Sec. 203(c)(2)(X)).

• *Nonresident trusts and estates*

Nonresidents trusts and estates determine fiduciary "base income" in the same way as do resident trusts above.

Next, the amount of base income attributable to Illinois is determined on Schedule NR. The standard exemption, apportioned in the ratio of Illinois income to base income is subtracted to arrive at net income subject to tax. See ¶102 for the current tax rate. Credits are subtracted to determine the amount due or refundable (see Chapter 4).

• *Illinois modifications*

Estate and trust modifications are generally the same as those of individuals (¶205).

In addition, the following modifications apply specifically to estates and trusts (35 ILCS 203(c)(2)).

Modifications from other entities: Estates and trusts must take into account their share of Illinois addition and subtraction modifications from other estates, trusts, or partnerships of which the estates or trusts are beneficiaries or partners.

Charitable contributions: Modifications otherwise required are adjusted by amounts included in the modifications that would qualify as charitable deductions under federal rules.

Federal exemption: The amount of standard exemption deducted on the federal return, if any, is added to income.

Net operating loss: The amount of net operating loss deduction in arriving at federal taxable income carried forward for tax years ending on or after December 31, 1986, is added to income. The suspension of the net loss carryover deduction for tax years 2011-2014 that applies to corporations (see ¶1013) does not apply for personal income tax purposes.

Foreign tax credit: The tax deducted federally that is claimed for purposes of the Illinois foreign tax credit is added to income.

• *Replacement tax basis for trusts*

Basis for the replacement tax to which trusts are subject is the same as for the income tax, as described above.

A trust must add back any Personal Property Tax Replacement Income Tax that is deducted in computing adjusted gross income because it is passed through from a partnership, S corporation, or trust (35 ILCS 5/203(c)(2)(C)). Another provision (35 ILCS 5/203(c)(2)(J)) allows a trust to subtract any such refund included in adjusted gross income. The purpose of the subtraction and addition is to render the payment of Illinois income tax and replacement income tax neutral in the computation of adjusted gross income. See 86 Ill. Adm. Code Sec. 100.2450.

¶210 S Corporation Shareholders

Law: Income Tax Act, Sec. 201(c) [35 ILCS 5/201]; Income Tax Act, Sec. 205(c) [35 ILCS 5/205]; Income Tax Act, Sec. 308(a), (b) [35 ILCS 5/308]; 86 Ill. Adm. Code Sec. 100.2450 (CCH Illinois Tax Reports, ¶15-115, 15-505).

Comparable Federal: Secs. 1361—1379 (U.S. Master Tax Guide, ¶309—333).

S corporation shareholders who are Illinois residents are subject to tax on all income received from the S corporation. This income is reflected in the federal adjusted gross income figure from which Illinois taxable income is derived.

An Illinois statute (35 ILCS 5/203(b)(2)(B)) requires corporations to add back any Personal Property Tax Replacement Income Tax that is deducted in computing adjusted gross income because it is passed through from a partnership, S corporation, or trust. Another provision (35 ILCS 5/203(b)(2)(F)) allows corporations to subtract any such refund included in adjusted gross income. The purpose of the subtraction and addition is to render the payment of Illinois income tax and replacement income tax neutral in the computation of adjusted gross income. See 86 Ill. Adm. Code Sec. 100.2450.

• *Part-year residents*

Part-year residents are taxed as residents for the residential period and as nonresidents (see below) for the nonresidential period. The time at which S corporation income is earned and loss sustained is determined under federal rules. Under federal rules, income is considered earned as of the close of the taxable year.

Part-year residents may take a credit for any tax paid to other states on S corporation income also taxed by Illinois. If another state taxes an S corporation directly instead of passing the income through to shareholders (and such income is also taxed by Illinois), the part-year resident does not qualify for the credit, which applies only to taxes directly paid by the part-year resident.

• *Nonresidents*

The shares of nonresident shareholders in S corporation business income allocated or apportioned to Illinois are attributed to such shareholders under federal rules (35 ILCS 308(a)). That is, Illinois-source income is deemed received by shareholders on a pro-rata basis. Such income is taken into account by shareholders individually and allocated to Illinois. The shares of nonresident shareholders in S corporation nonbusiness income and deductions are also attributed under federal rules; however, such income is taken into account by the shareholders individually and allocated as if such items had been paid, incurred, or accrued directly to such shareholders in their separate or individual capacities (35 ILCS 308(b)). For example, portfolio income follows the residence of the investor and is not taxable by Illinois. Nonbusiness income derived from property held in Illinois, on the other hand, would be taxable to the nonresident.

There is no credit for taxes paid to other states by nonresidents.

¶211 Exempt Income from Governmental Obligations

Law: Income Tax Act, Sec. 203 [35 ILCS 5/203]; 86 Ill. Adm. Code 100.2470(c) (CCH ILLINOIS TAX REPORTS, ¶ 16-075, 16-280).

Comparable Federal: Sec. 103 (U.S. MASTER TAX GUIDE, ¶731).

In computing "base income," taxpayers may subtract amounts that are exempt for Illinois purposes by reason of Illinois law, the Illinois or U.S. Constitution, or U.S. treaties or statutes (35 ILCS 203(a)(2)(N)). A federal statute (31 U.S.C. §3124(a)) exempts interest on federal stocks and obligations from Illinois taxation. "Obligations of the United States," within the meaning of the federal statute, are obligations issued "to secure credit to carry on the necessary functions of government." A rule provides an extensive list of federal and state obligations whose interest income is deemed to be exempt (86 Ill. Adm. Code Sec. 100.2470, CCH ILLINOIS TAX REPORTS, ¶ 17-625).

- *Interest on obligations of the United States*

The following types of income are currently recognized as exempt under 31 U.S.C.A. Sec. 3124(a):

— interest on U.S. Treasury bonds, bills, certificates, and savings bonds; and

— income from GSA Public Building Trust Participation Certificates: First Series; Series A through E; Second Series, Series F; Third Series; Series G, Fourth Series H and I.

- *Other income exempt under federal statutes*

Other federal statutes provide exemption from state income taxation for various types of income. The following is a list of exempt income and related statutes (86 Ill. Adm. Code 100.2470(c)):

— *Banks for Cooperatives:* income from notes, debentures, and other obligations issued by Banks for Cooperatives (12 U.S.C.A. Sec. 2134);

— *Commodity Credit Corporation:* interest derived from bonds, notes, debentures, and other similar obligations issued by the Commodity Credit Corporation (15 U.S.C.A. Sec. 713a-5);

— *Farm Credit System Financial Assistance Corporation (Financial Assistance Corporation):* income from notes, bonds, debentures, and other obligations issued by the Financial Assistance Corporation (12 U.S.C.A. Sec. 2278b-10(b));

— *Federal Deposit Insurance Corporation:* interest derived from notes, debentures, bonds, or other such obligations issued by the Federal Deposit Insurance Corporation (12 U.S.C.A. Sec. 1825);

— *Federal Farm Credit Banks:* income from consolidated system-wide notes, bonds, debentures, and other obligations issued jointly and severally under 12 U.S.C.A. Sec. 2153 by Banks of the Federal Farm Credit System (12 U.S.C.A. Sec. 2023; 12 U.S.C.A. Sec. 207; 12 U.S.C.A. Sec. 2098; and 12 U.S.C.A. Sec. 2134);

— *Federal Home Loan Banks:* interest derived from notes, debentures, bonds, and other obligations issued by Federal Home Loan Banks and from consolidated Federal Home Loan Bank bonds and debentures (12 U.S.C.A. Sec. 1433);

— *Federal Intermediate Credit Banks:* income from notes, bonds, debentures, and other obligations issued by Federal Intermediate Credit Banks (12 U.S.C.A. Sec. 2023);

— *Federal Land Banks and Federal Land Bank Associations:* income from notes, bonds, debentures, and other obligations issued by Federal Land Banks and Federal Land Bank Associations (12 U.S.C.A. Sec. 2055);

— *Federal Savings and Loan Insurance Corporation:* income from notes, bonds, debentures, and other obligations issued by the Federal Savings and Loan Insurance Corporation (12 U.S.C.A. Sec. 1725(e));

— *Financing Corporation (FICO):* income from obligations issued by the Financing Corporation (12 U.S.C.A. Sec. 1441(e)(8));

— *General Insurance Fund:*

a. interest derived from debentures issued by the General Insurance Fund under War Housing Insurance Law (12 U.S.C.A. Sec. 1739(d));

b. interest derived from debentures issued by the General Insurance Fund to acquire rental housing projects (12 U.S.C.A. Sec. 1747g(g));

c. interest derived from Armed Services Housing Mortgage Insurance Debentures issued by the General Insurance Fund (12 U.S.C.A. Sec. 1748b(f));

— *Guam:* interest derived from bonds issued by the government of Guam (48 U.S.C.A. Sec. 1423a). Note that this income is not presently included in federal taxable income;

— *Mutual Mortgage Insurance Fund:* income from such debentures as are issued in exchange for property covered by mortgages insured after February 3, 1988 (12 U.S.C.A. Sec. 1710(d)). Note that this income is not presently included in federal taxable income;

— *National Credit Union Administration Central Liquidity Facility:* income from the notes, bonds, debentures, and other obligations issued on behalf of the Central Liquidity Facility (12 U.S.C.A. Sec. 1795K(b));

— *Production Credit Associations:* income from notes, debentures, and other obligations issued by Production Credit Associations (12 U.S.C.A. Sec. 2098);

— *Puerto Rico:* interest derived from bonds issued by the Government of Puerto Rico (48 U.S.C.A. Sec. 745). Note that this income is not presently included in federal taxable income;

— *Railroad Retirement Act:* annuity and supplemental annuity payments as qualified under the Railroad Retirement Act of 1974 (45 U.S.C.A. Sec. 231m);

— *Railroad Unemployment Insurance Act:* unemployment benefits paid pursuant to the Railroad Unemployment Insurance Act (45 U.S.C.A. Sec. 352(e));

— *Resolution Funding Corporation:* interest from obligations issued by the Resolution Funding Corporation (12 U.S.C.A. Sec. 1441b(f)(7)(A));

— *Special Food Service Program:* assistance to children under the Special Food Service Program (42 U.S.C.A. Sec. 1760(e));

— *Student Loan Marketing Association:* interest derived from obligations issued by the Student Loan Marketing Association (20 U.S.C.A. Sec. 1087-2(h)(221));

— *Tennessee Valley Authority:* interest derived from bonds issued by the Tennessee Valley Authority (16 U.S.C.A. Sec. 831n-4(d));

¶211

— *United States Postal Service:* interest derived from obligations issued by the United States Postal Service (39 U.S.C.A. Sec. 2005(d)(4));

— *Virgin Islands:* interest derived from bonds issued by the Government of the Virgin Islands (48 U.S.C.A. Sec. 1574(b)(ii)(A)). Note that this income is not presently included in federal income;

—· *American Samoa:* interest on bonds issued by the Government of American Samoa (48 USCA 1670(b));

— Northern Mariana Islands: interest on bonds issued by the Government of the Northern Mariana Islands (48 USCA 1801 note).

Flow-through tax-exempt treatment applies to interest that is earned by mutual funds from all the U.S. obligations listed above (see CCH ILLINOIS TAX REPORTS, ¶ 400-298).

• *Interest on obligations of state and local governments*

Income from state or local obligations issued in Illinois is subject to the income tax except where authorizing legislation adopted after August 1, 1969, specifically provides for an exemption from state taxes. Exempt obligations are listed in a regulation (86 Ill. Adm. Code 100.2470). Income from these bonds is not exempt if the bonds are owned indirectly through a mutual fund.

• *Other income exempt from Illinois taxation*

Income earned on funds held in a trust fund suspense account until the final determination is made regarding the payee of the account under the Illinois Pre-Need Cemetery Sales Act [815 ILCS 390/1—815 ILCS 390/27] or the Illinois Funeral or Burial Funds Act [225 ILCS 45/4a(c)].

Income in the form of education loan repayments made for primary care physicians who agree to practice in designated shortage areas for a specified period of time under the terms of the Family Practice Residency Act [110 ILCS 935/4.10].

Income earned by nuclear decommissioning trusts established pursuant to Section 8-508.1 of the Public Utilities Act [220 ILCS 5/8-508.1].

• *Nonexempt income*

The following types of income are not exempt from Illinois income taxation (86 Ill. Adm. Code 100.2470(h)):

— income from securities commonly known as GNMA "Pass-Through Securities" and also known as "GNMA Mortgage-Backed Securities" issued by approved issuers under 12 U.S.C.A. Sec. 1721(g) and guaranteed by GNMA under 12 U.S.C.A. Sec. 1721(g) (*Rockford Life Insurance Co. v. Department of Revenue* (1987, US SCt), 482 US 182, 107 SCt 2312; CCH ILLINOIS TAX REPORTS, ¶ 400-221); and income from debentures, notes, and bonds issued by the Federal National Mortgage Association including mortgage-backed bonds issued under authority of 12 U.S.C.A. Sec. 1719(d) and guaranteed by GNMA under 12 U.S.C.A. Sec. 1721(g);

— accumulated interest on IRS tax refunds. Illinois Department of Revenue Income Tax Letter Ruling No. IT 86-0640, dated July 11, 1986, citing *Glidden Co. v. Glander* (1949, Ohio SCt), 151 OS 344, 86 NE2d 1, 9 ALR2d 515; and

— income from U.S. securities acquired by a taxpayer under a repurchase agreement ("repo") with a bank or similar financial organization. The Department takes the position that, for income tax purposes, such agreements are generally to be treated as loans. That is, the taxpayer "loans" money to the bank and receives interest in return. The securities subject to repurchase by the bank serve as collateral for the loan. The bank remains legally entitled to receive the interest payments from the issuing authority and remains the actual owner of

¶211

the securities. Therefore, any tax benefit attributable to the "exempt" income paid by the issuing authority accrues to the bank and not to the investor.

The Department of Revenue has emphasized that before a taxpayer may subtract an item of exempt income, the taxpayer must be sure that he or she has included the item in Illinois base income. Some tax-exempt items are "automatically" included in base income because they are included in federal adjusted gross income, which is a part of base income. Interest on U.S. Treasury notes is in this category. Other exempt items must be included as an addition on the Illinois tax return in figuring base income.

¶212 No Deduction Allowed for Federal Income Tax

Under the Illinois law, no deduction is allowed for federal income taxes paid or accrued. Since the base for computation of Illinois net income is federal adjusted gross income (individuals) or federal taxable income (estates, trusts, and corporations) and no adjustment is provided for a deduction for federal taxes, no deduction is allowed.

¶213 Standard Exemption

Law: Income Tax Act, Sec. 204 [35 ILCS 5/204] (CCH Illinois Tax Reports, ¶15-535).

Comparable Federal: Secs. 151—153 (U.S. Master Tax Guide, ¶133—149).

For the 2016 tax year, the standard exemption for individuals is $2,175, including a cost-of-living adjustment based on the increase in the federal Consumer Price Index, and multiplied by the number of exemptions that were properly taken on the federal return.

For the 2015 tax year, the standard exemption was $2,150 (previously, $2,125). (35 ILCS 5/204(b); 35 ILCS 5/204(d-5)).

Taxpayers who are 65 years of age or older and people who are blind are entitled to an additional exemption of $1,000 (35 ILCS 5/204(d)).

Effective for taxable years beginning on or after January 1, 2017, taxpayers who have adjusted gross income for the taxable year exceeding $500,000 for taxpayers filing a joint federal return or $250,000 for all other taxpayers may not claim personal exemptions (35 ILCS 5/204(g)).

Partnerships, subject to the replacement tax, are allowed a standard exemption equal to $1,000 multiplied by the amount of base income allocable to Illinois and divided by total base income.

• *Nonresidents and part-year residents*

For nonresidents, the standard exemption or exemptions allowed must be apportioned to Illinois by multiplying them by a fraction, the numerator of which is the amount of the taxpayer's base income allocated and apportioned to Illinois (Chapter 3) and the denominator of which is the taxpayer's total base income.

For a taxable period of fewer than 12 months, the standard exemption allowed must be prorated on the basis of the ratio of the number of days in the taxable period to 365.

¶214 "Taxable Year" Defined

Law: Income Tax Act, Sec. 1501(a)(9), (23) [35 ILCS 5/1501].

Comparable Federal: Secs. 441, 7701 (U.S. Master Tax Guide, ¶416, 1501).

"Taxable year" means the calendar year, or the fiscal year ending during such calendar year, upon the basis of which the base income is computed. In the case of a return made for a fractional part of a year, "taxable year" means the period for which the return is made [35 ILCS 5/1501(a)(23)].

"Fiscal year" means an accounting period of 12 months ending on the last day of any month other than December [35 ILCS 5/1501(a)(9)].

PERSONAL INCOME TAX

CHAPTER 3

ALLOCATION AND APPORTIONMENT

¶301 Allocation or Apportionment of Income Required

Law: Income Tax Act, Sec. 301(a)—(c) [35 ILCS 5/301] (CCH ILLINOIS TAX REPORTS, ¶15-105, 15-110, 15-120, 16-505).

Comparable Federal: Secs. 861—877.

All income of resident individuals, estates, and trusts is allocated to, and taxable by, Illinois. Income of nonresident individuals, estates, and trusts is allocated and apportioned within and without Illinois, as is income of a partnership (replacement tax) that is derived from inside and outside Illinois (35 ILCS 5/301(a) (c)).

Income of part-year residents is allocated to Illinois for that part of the year that the part-year resident was an Illinois resident, and is allocated and apportioned to Illinois in the same manner as income of nonresidents for the remainder of the year (35 ILCS 5/301(b)).

The Illinois provisions for the allocation and apportionment of income within and without the state are substantially the same as those of the Uniform Division of Income for Tax Purposes Act, promulgated by the National Conference of Commissioners on Uniform State Laws, and designed to provide uniformity among the states in the division of income of multistate businesses. Illinois is not a member of the Multistate Tax Compact.

Compensation paid to nonresident individuals is allocated (¶304) on the basis of whether or not it was "paid in this state" (¶318). Nonbusiness income (capital gains, interest, dividends, *etc.*) of partnerships and of nonresident individuals, estates, and trusts is directly allocated (¶312—314). Business income is apportioned by means of a three-factor apportionment formula (¶315).

Special provisions apply for the allocation of income of partnerships (¶321) and estates and trusts (¶322, ¶323).

¶302 All Income of Residents Allocated to Illinois

Law: Income Tax Act, Sec. 301(a) [35 ILCS 5/301]; Income Tax Act, Sec. 1501(a)(20) [35 ILCS 5/1501]; 86 Ill. Adm. Code Sec. 100.3020 (CCH Illinois Tax Reports, ¶15-105, 15-110).

All items of income of an Illinois resident are allocated to Illinois (35 ILCS 5/301(a)). "Resident" includes (35 ILCS 5/1501(a)(20)):

— an individual who is in the state for other than a temporary or transitory purpose during the taxable year;

— an individual who is domiciled in Illinois but is absent from the state for a temporary or transitory purpose during the taxable year;

— the estate of a decedent who at the time of his death was domiciled in Illinois;

— a trust created by a will of a decedent who at the time of his death was domiciled in Illinois; and

— an irrevocable trust, the grantor of which was domiciled in Illinois at the time the trust became irrevocable.

(86 Ill. Adm. Code Sec. 100.3020)

¶303 Income of Part-year Residents

Law: Income Tax Act, Sec. 301(b) [35 ILCS 5/301] (CCH Illinois Tax Reports, ¶15-120).

Income of a part-year resident is allocated to Illinois for that part of the year that the individual was a resident of Illinois (35 ILCS 5/301(b)). For the remainder of the year, the individual's income is allocated and apportioned under the same provisions that apply to nonresidents.

¶304 Compensation of Nonresident Individuals

Law: Income Tax Act, Sec. 301(c)(1) [35 ILCS 5/301]; Income Tax Act, Sec. 302(a) [35 ILCS 5/302], Income Tax Act, Sec. 304(a)(2) [35 ILCS 5/302](CCH Illinois Tax Reports, ¶15-115).

All items of compensation "paid in this state" to an individual who is a nonresident at the time of payment, and all deductions directly allocable thereto, are allocated to Illinois (35 ILCS 5/301(c)(1)). However, compensation paid to persons employed by certain interstate carriers may be taxed only by the person's state of residence (¶103).

"Compensation" is defined at ¶318 and "nonresident" at ¶103. Payments that qualify as made in Illinois are discussed at ¶318.

• *Sourcing provisions for nonresident professional athletes*

The Illinois source income of a nonresident individual who is a member of a professional baseball, basketball, football, soccer, or hockey team includes a portion of the individual's total compensation for services performed as a member of the professional athletic team during the taxable year. The portion to be included is a ratio, which the number of duty days spent within Illinois performing services for the team in any manner during the taxable year bears to the total number of duty days spent both within and without Illinois during the taxable year (35 ILCS 304(a)(2)(B)(iv)).

Members of a professional athletic team include all employees who are active players, players on the disabled list, and any other persons who are required to travel and who actually travel with and perform services on behalf of the team on a regular basis. This includes, but is not limited to, coaches, managers, and trainers. Previously, the Department of Revenue maintained that all compensation paid to a member of an Illinois-based team was taxable by Illinois.

Practitioner Comment: Professional Athletes

In July 2005, the Illinois Governor signed a law (P.A. 247 (H.B. 310), Laws 2005) that changed Illinois' income tax treatment of compensation earned by nonresident professional athletes. The law change came after an Illinois circuit court declared the prior law unconstitutional. With the law change, Illinois now taxes nonresident professional athletes' compensation based on a duty-days formula (35 ILCS 304(a)(2)(B)(iv)).

The Department had maintained that under the prior law, the entire compensation paid to a professional sports athlete who is employed by an Illinois-based team is "'compensation paid in Illinois" because some of the athlete's service is performed in Illinois and the employer's base of operations is located in Illinois. The Circuit Court of Cook County held that Illinois' compensation-sourcing rule, as applied to nonresidents for individual income tax purposes, was unconstitutional as a violation of the Due Process Clause and the Commerce Clause of the U.S. Constitution. (*Radinsky v. Zehnder*, Doc. No. 96 L 51192 (Ill. Cir. Ct. Jan. 24, 2003), appeal filed, No. 95818 (Illinois Supreme Court, March 4, 2003.))

The 2005 law change does not overturn a 2001 Illinois administrative decision in which the Department held that Illinois could not tax a nonresident professional athlete on his signing bonus or his option-year buy-out payment received from his Illinois-based employer when neither payment was compensation by reason that neither payment represented remuneration for services performed. (*Smith v. Department of Revenue*, Admin. Hearings IT 01-6) It is questionable whether the *Smith* case has continuing application after January 13, 2005, as a result of Internal Revenue Ruling 2004-109, in which the Internal Revenue Service held that a signing bonus is considered compensation for purposes of federal income tax withholding. See ¶ 601.

Horwood Marcus & Berk Chartered

"Duty days" defined: "Duty days" means all days during the taxable year from the beginning of the team's official preseason training period through the last game in which the team competes or is scheduled to compete (35 ILCS 304(a)(2)(B)(iv)(c)(3)). Duty days are counted for the year in which they occur, even if they occur during more than one taxable year. Duty days include game days (including postseason game days), practice days, days spent at team meetings, and days spent at preseason training camps. Duty days also include days on which a team member performs services for the team outside of the period from the beginning of the team's official preseason training through the team's last game, such as days spent participating in instructional leagues, all-star games, promotional caravans, and training and rehabilitation activities conducted at team facilities.

Travel days that do not involve a game, practice, team meeting, or other similar team event are not considered duty days spent within Illinois. However, such travel days are considered in the total duty days spent both within and without Illinois. Duty days for any person who joins a team after the start of the team's official preseason training period will begin on the day that the person joins the team, and duty days for any person who leaves a team before the team's last game will end on the day that the person leaves the team. If a person switches teams during a taxable year, separate duty-day calculations will be made for the periods during which the person was with each team. Days for which a team member is not compensated and is not performing services for the team in any manner, including days when such member has been suspended without pay and prohibited from performing any services for the team, will not be treated as duty days. Days for which a team member is on the disabled list and is not conducting rehabilitation activities at team facilities, or otherwise performing services for the team in Illinois, will not be considered duty days spent within Illinois. However, all days on the disabled list will be considered in the total duty days spent both within and without Illinois. (35 ILCS 304(a)(2)(B)(iv)(c)(3))

"Total compensation" defined: "Total compensation for services performed as a member of a professional athletic team" means the total compensation received during the taxable year for services performed (1) from the beginning of the official preseason training period through the last game in which the team competes or is scheduled to compete during that taxable year; and (2) during the taxable year on a date that does not fall within the foregoing period (e.g., during participation in instructional leagues, all-star games, or promotional caravans). This compensation includes, but is not limited to, salaries, wages, performance bonuses, signing bonuses contingent upon the performance of services, and any other type of compensation paid during the taxable year to the team member for services performed in that year. It does not include strike benefits, severance pay, termination pay, contract or option year buy-out payments, expansion or relocation payments, or any other payments not related to services performed for the team (35 ILCS 304(a)(2)(B)(iv)(c)(4)).

CCH Advisory: Compensation to British Consulate Employees

Compensation paid to British citizens and to dual U.S.-U.K. citizens employed by the British consulate in Illinois is exempt from Illinois personal income tax. Under the 1951 Consular Officers Convention between the United States and Great Britain, no consular employee is subject to either federal or state income tax on his or her compensation received for consular services unless he or she is a citizen of the U.S. and not also a citizen of the U.K. (*Private Letter Ruling, IT 05-0008-PLR*, Illinois Department of Revenue, November 8, 2005; CCH ILLINOIS TAX REPORTS, ¶401–662)

¶305 Reciprocal Agreements for Exemption of Compensation of Nonresidents

Law: Income Tax Act, Sec. 302(b) [35 ILCS 5/302]; Income Tax Act, Sec. 701(d) [35 ILCS 5/701]; 86 Ill. Adm. Code Sec. 100.7090 (CCH ILLINOIS TAX REPORTS, ¶16-610).

The Director of the Illinois Department of Revenue may enter into an agreement with the taxing authorities of any state that imposes an income tax to provide that compensation paid in that state to residents of Illinois will be exempt from withholding of that state's income tax and that any compensation paid in Illinois to residents of the other state will be exempt from withholding of Illinois income tax. Pursuant to such reciprocal agreements, the employer in Illinois should, upon request by an employee residing in the other state, withhold tax on his or her compensation for the state of the employee's residence. (35 ILCS 5/302(b); 86 Ill. Adm. Code Sec. 100.7090)

Illinois has reciprocal agreements with Iowa, Kentucky, Michigan, and Wisconsin to exempt from Illinois taxation and withholding the compensation paid to a resident of the other state who is working in Illinois (35 ILCS 5/302(b); 35 ILCS 5/701(d)). Residents of Iowa, Kentucky, Michigan, and Wisconsin must file with their employer a copy of Form IL-1W-5, Employee's Statement of Non-Residence in Illinois. A reciprocal agreement with Indiana expired January 1, 1998.

CCH Advisory: Indiana Employees

Illinois residents who are Indiana employees must first complete an Indiana return. Then an Illinois Schedule CR (Credit for Taxes Paid to Other States) is filled out to determine whether the resident is eligible for credit for the taxes withheld by Indiana.

• *Reciprocal agreements with Iowa, Kentucky, Michigan, and Wisconsin*

Employers of persons who reside in those states may, but are not required by Illinois law, to withhold income tax for the other state (*Publication 130, Who is Required to Withhold Illinois Income Tax*, February 2015, available on the Department of Revenue's website at **http://www.revenue.state.il.us/Publications/Pubs/index.htm**).

For provisions relating to withholding under the reciprocal agreements, see ¶604 and ¶605.

CCH Advisory: Reciprocity in Action

An Illinois resident was not entitled to a personal income tax credit for taxes paid to another state, because the taxpayer was exempt from Wisconsin income tax due to a reciprocal agreement entered into between Illinois and Wisconsin. Illinois and Wisconsin entered a "reciprocal agreement" effective January 1, 1974, pursuant to which neither state taxes, or requires withholding from, wages earned in the state by a resident of the other state. Specifically, instructions to the credit form state that taxpayers who earned wages, salaries, tips, or other employee compensation from an employer in Iowa, Kentucky, Michigan, or Wisconsin while a resident of Illinois are covered by a reciprocal agreement between that state and Illinois and are not taxed by that state on compensation. If the taxpayer's employer withheld taxes or if the taxpayer paid tax to these states on compensation, the taxpayer must claim a refund from that state and may not claim a credit on Schedule CR for that tax. (*General Information Letter IT 10-0021-GIL*, Illinois Department of Revenue, August 17, 2010, CCH ILLINOIS TAX REPORTS, ¶402-202)

However, an Illinois resident who worked part time in Kentucky was allowed to claim an Illinois credit for foreign taxes paid on *local* income taxes withheld by the Kentucky county. (*General Information Letter IT 12-0020-GIL*, Illinois Department of Revenue, July 31, 2012, CCH ILLINOIS TAX REPORTS, ¶402-534)

¶306 Direct Allocation of Nonbusiness Income—In General

Law: Income Tax Act, Sec. 303(a) [35 ILCS 5/303]; Income Tax Act, Sec. 304(a) [35 ILCS 5/304] (CCH ILLINOIS TAX REPORTS, ¶15-115).

Because all income of Illinois residents is allocated to Illinois (¶302), the provisions relating to direct allocation of nonbusiness income apply to nonresident individuals, estates, and trusts, and to partnerships (replacement tax) that derive income from inside and outside Illinois. Generally, nonbusiness income is allocated to Illinois on the basis of the situs of the property giving rise to the income or the commercial domicile of the taxpayer (35 ILCS 5/303(a)). "Commercial domicile" is defined at ¶307.

"Nonbusiness income" means all income other than "business income" (defined at ¶316) or "compensation" (defined at ¶318). A taxpayer may make an irrevocable election to treat all nonbusiness income as business income (35 ILCS 5/1501(a)(1); 86 Ill. Adm. Code Sec. 100.3015).

Liquidation of partnership: A nonresident partner's distributive share of liquidation gain, interest income, and dividend income, earned as a result of the partnership's sale of intangible trading technology in connection with the liquidation of the partnership, was nonbusiness income and therefore, not subject to Illinois personal income tax. Because the sale of the trading technology constituted a cessation of the partnership's business activities, and the proceeds from the sale were distributed to the partners and not used to acquire business assets or generate income for use in future business operations, gain from the sale was nonbusiness income under an exception to the functional test recognized by the Illinois Appellate Court in *Blessing/White, Inc. v. Zehnder*, 329 Ill. App. 3d 714 (1st Dist. 2002, CCH ILLINOIS TAX REPORTS, ¶ 401-337). Although the trading technology was used in and essential to the partnership's business operations, the disposition of the trading technology was not essential to the business, and thus, the income generated was nonbusiness income (*Shakkour v. Bower*, Illinois Appellate Court, First District, No. 1-04-1646, September 1, 2006, CCH ILLINOIS TAX REPORTS, ¶ 401-715).

Practitioner Comment: Taxation of Liquidation Gain

In *Comark, Inc. v. Hamer*, Docket No. 06-L-51067, Circuit Court of Cook County (November 19, 2009), the court held that gain from the complete liquidation of assets was nonbusiness income pursuant to the Illinois Appellate Court decisions in *Blessing/White Inc. v. Zehnder*, 329 Ill. App. 3d 714 (2002), and *Nicor Corp. v. Dep't of Revenue*, Dkt Nos. 1-07-1359 and 1-07-1591 (Ill. App. Ct. December. 5, 2008).

Comark argued that the Department should be estopped from claiming that the liquidation gain was "nonbusiness income" because under the Department's regulations the gain would constitute "business income," and the Department continued to advocate "business income" in similar cases. The circuit court rejected these arguments and held that a taxpayer may not enforce a regulation that conflicts with the judicial interpretation of the statute. Comark also alleged that under Illinois' constitutional definition of "business income," statutorily adopted effective July 30, 2004, its liquidation gain should be classified as such because that was the definition in effect when the Department issued its Notice of Deficiency in 2006. The court also rejected this argument, holding that the amendment to the "business income" definition did not apply retroactively. Therefore, the court applied the UDIPTA definition that was in existence in 2002 and which had consistently been interpreted as including a so-called "liquidation exception."

Comark filed income tax returns in other states, which taxed the gain on an apportioned basis. As such, Illinois' taxation of the gain on an allocated basis, rather than on an apportioned basis, may result in "multiple taxation." Even though Comark's liquidation gain was held to be statutory "nonbusiness income," an argument may be made that 100% of the gain, is inconsistent with the Due Process and Commerce Clauses of the United States Constitution. The United States Supreme Court has held: "Taxation by apportionment and taxation by allocation to a single situs are theoretically incommensurate, and if the latter method is constitutionally preferred, a tax based on the former cannot be sustained." Consistent with the Court's reasoning, it may be unconstitutional for one state to tax a gain on an allocated basis if another state may constitutionally tax the liquidation gain on an apportioned basis.

Horwood Marcus & Berk Chartered

¶307 "Commercial Domicile" Defined

Law: Income Tax Act, Sec. 1501(a)(2) [35 ILCS 5/1501]; 86 Ill. Adm. Code Sec. 100.3210 (CCH ILLINOIS TAX REPORTS, ¶ 16-505, 16-515).

"Commercial domicile" means the principal place from which the trade or business of the taxpayer is directed or managed (35 ILCS 5/1501(a)(2)). Generally, this is the place at which the offices of the principal executives are located. If executive authority is scattered, the place of daily operational decision-making controls (86 Ill. Adm. Code Sec. 100.3210).

¶308 Allocation of Nonbusiness Income—Taxpayer Taxable in Another State

Law: Income Tax Act, Sec. 303(f) [35 ILCS 5/303]; Income Tax Act, Sec. 1501(a)(22) [35 ILCS 5/1501]; 86 Ill. Adm. Code Sec. 100.3200; 86 Ill. Adm. Code Sec. 100.3110 (CCH ILLINOIS TAX REPORTS, ¶16-505, 16-515).

In determining the allocation of certain items of nonbusiness income, it is necessary to determine whether or not the taxpayer is taxable in another state. A taxpayer is taxable in another state if (35 ILCS 5/303(f)):

— the taxpayer is subject to a net income tax, a franchise tax measured by net income, a franchise tax for the privilege of doing business, or a corporate stock tax in the other state; or

— the other state has jurisdiction to subject the taxpayer to a net income tax, regardless of whether the other state actually subjects the taxpayer to the tax.

(86 Ill. Adm. Code Sec. 100.3200 sets out examples of taxability in another state.)

"State" means any state of the United States, the District of Columbia, Puerto Rico, any territory or possession of the United States, and any foreign country, or any political subdivision of any of the foregoing (86 Ill. Adm. Code Sec. 100.3110).

CCH Advisory: Alimony

An Illinois personal income tax ruling discusses the decision of the U.S. Supreme Court in *Lunding v. N.Y. Tax Appeals Tribunal,* 522 U.S. 287 (1998), which requires a state to allow nonresidents to allocate to the state deductions for alimony paid. Accordingly, Illinois allows nonresidents to allocate the full amount of the federal deduction for alimony paid to Illinois in determining their Illinois net income. The limit on the credit for taxes paid to other states must be computed by allocating the deduction for alimony paid to other states as if they followed the same allocation principles as Illinois. (*General Information Letter IT 11-0014-GIL,* Illinois Department of Revenue, July 12, 2011, CCH ILLINOIS TAX REPORTS, ¶402-388)

¶309 Allocation of Nonbusiness Income—Rents and Royalties

Law: Income Tax Act, Sec. 303 [35 ILCS 5/303]; 86 Ill. Adm. Code Sec. 100.3220 (CCH ILLINOIS TAX REPORTS, ¶16-530, ¶16-550).

Because all income of residents is allocated to Illinois (¶302), the following provisions relating to allocation of nonbusiness income apply to nonresident individuals, estates, and trusts, and to partnerships (replacement tax) that derive income from inside and outside Illinois.

• *Real property*

Rents and royalties from *real property* (if nonbusiness income) are allocated on the basis of the situs of the property (35 ILCS 5/303(c)(1)). Thus, income from real property located in Illinois is allocated to Illinois and income from property located outside Illinois is allocated outside Illinois.

• *Tangible personal property*

Rents and royalties from *tangible personal property* are allocated to Illinois (35 ILCS 5/303(c)(2)):

— if and to the extent that the property is utilized in Illinois; or

— in their entirety if, at the time such rents or royalties were paid or accrued, the taxpayer had its commerical domicile in Illinois and was not organized under the laws of, or taxable with respect to the rents and royalties in, the state in which the property was utilized.

The extent of utilization in Illinois is determined by multiplying the rents or royalties by a fraction, the numerator of which is the number of days of physical location of the property in Illinois during the rental or royalty period in the taxable year, and the denominator of which is the number of days of physical location of the property everywhere during all rental or royalty periods in the taxable year. If the physical location of the property during the rental or royalty period is unknown or unascertainable, the property is considered to have been utilized in the state in which located at the time the rental or royalty payer obtained possession.

Any income from rents or royalties not allocated to Illinois under the above provisions is allocated outside the state. See 86 Ill. Adm Code Sec. 100.3220, which includes examples of allocation of rents and royalties from tangible personal property.

"Resident" is defined at ¶302, "commercial domicile" at ¶307, and "taxable in another state" at ¶308.

• *Intangible property*

A nonresident's nonbusiness income from patent and copyright royalties is allocable to Illinois to the extent that the patent or copyright is used by the payer in Illinois (35 ILCS 5/303(d)). For additional information, see ¶312.

¶310 Allocation of Nonbusiness Income—Capital Gains and Losses

Law: Income Tax Act, Sec. 303(b) [35 ILCS 5/303] (CCH ILLINOIS TAX REPORTS, ¶16-555).

Because all income of Illinois residents is allocated to Illinois (¶302), the following provisions relating to allocation of nonbusiness income apply only to corporations and nonresident individuals, estates, and trusts.

• *Real property*

Capital gains and losses from sales or exchanges of *real property* are allocated according to the situs of the property (35 ILCS 5/303(b)(1)). Thus, gains and losses from sales of property located in Illinois are allocated to Illinois, and gains or losses from sales of property located outside Illinois are allocated outside Illinois.

• *Tangible personal property*

Capital gains and losses from sales or exchanges of *tangible personal property* are allocated to Illinois if, when sold or exchanged (35 ILCS 5/303(b)(2)):

— the property had its situs in Illinois; or

— the taxpayer had its commercial domicile in Illinois and was not taxable in the state in which the property had its situs.

• *Intangible property*

Capital gains and losses from sales or exchanges of *intangible personal property* are allocated to Illinois if the taxpayer had its commercial domicile in Illinois at the time of the sale or exchange (35 ILCS 5/303(b)(3)).

Any capital gains or losses not allocated to Illinois under the above provisions are allocated outside the state.

"Resident" is defined at ¶302, "commercial domicile" at ¶307, and "taxable in another state" at ¶308.

¶311 Allocation of Nonbusiness Income—Interest and Dividends

Law: Income Tax Act, Sec. 301 [35 ILCS 5/301] (CCH ILLINOIS TAX REPORTS, ¶16-530, 16-565).

All income of residents, including interest and dividends, is allocated to Illinois (¶302). Interest and dividends received by corporations and nonresident individuals, estates, and trusts are allocated outside Illinois (35 ILCS 5/301(c)(2)(A)). Interest and dividends received by partnerships are allocated to the state in which the partnership had its commercial domicile at the time the income was received (35 ILCS 5/301(c)(2)(B)).

"Resident" is defined at ¶302 and "commercial domicile" at ¶307.

¶312 Allocation of Nonbusiness Income—Patent and Copyright Royalties

Law: Income Tax Act, Sec. 303(d) [35 ILCS 5/303]; 86 Ill. Adm. Code Sec. 100.3220 (CCH ILLINOIS TAX REPORTS, ¶16-530).

Because all income of residents is allocated to Illinois (¶302), the following provisions relating to allocation of income from patents and copyrights apply only to corporations and nonresident individuals, estates, and trusts, and to partnerships (replacement tax) that derive income from inside and outside Illinois.

Patent and copyright royalties are allocated to Illinois (35 ILCS 5/303(d)(1)):

— if and to the extent the patent or copyright is utilized by the payer in Illinois; or

— if and to the extent the patent or copyright is utilized by the payer in a state in which the taxpayer is not taxable with respect to the royalties and, at the time the royalties are paid or accrued, the taxpayer has its commercial domicile in Illinois.

Any patent or copyright income not allocated to Illinois under the above provisions is allocated outside the state.

• *Utilization of patent or copyright*

A patent is utilized in Illinois to the extent that it is employed in production, fabrication, manufacturing, or other processing in the state or to the extent that a patented product is produced in the state (35 ILCS 5/303(d)(2)(A)). A copyright is utilized in Illinois to the extent that printing or other publication originates in the state (35 ILCS 5/303(d)(2)(B))D. If the basis of receipts from patent or copyright royalties does not permit allocation to states or if the accounting procedures do not reflect states of utilization, the patent or copyright is utilized in Illinois if the taxpayer has its commercial domicile in Illinois (35 ILCS 5/303(d)(2)).

(86 Ill. Adm. Code Sec. 100.3220 sets out an example of allocation of nonbusiness royalty income.)

"Resident" is defined at ¶302, "commercial domicile" at ¶307, and "taxable in another state" at ¶308.

¶313 Allocation of Nonbusiness Income—Lottery Prizes

Law: Income Tax Act, Sec. 303(e) [35 ILCS 5/303].

Prizes awarded under the Illinois lottery law are allocated to Illinois by residents and nonresidents (35 ILCS 5/303(e)).

¶314 Allocation of Nonbusiness Income—Items Not Specifically Allocated or Apportioned

Law: Income Tax Act, Sec. 301(c) [35 ILCS 5/301] (CCH ILLINOIS TAX REPORTS, ¶ 15–115, 16-505, 16-515).

All income of residents is allocated to Illinois (¶ 302). Any item of income or deduction that was taken into account in determining base income for the taxable year by a nonresident that is not specifically allocated or apportioned is allocated as follows (35 ILCS 5/301(c)):

In the case of a nonresident individual, estate, or trust, the income or deductions are allocated outside the state.

In the case of a partnership, such items are allocated to the state in which the taxpayer had its commercial domicile at the time such item was paid, incurred, or accrued.

Specifically included in these "unspecified items" to be so allocated are interest, dividends (¶ 311), income taken into account under the provisions of IRC Secs. 401—425, benefit payments received by a beneficiary of a supplemental unemployment benefit trust referred to in IRC Sec. 501(c)(17), and royalties from intangible personal property (other than patent and copyright royalties).

"Resident" is defined at ¶ 302 and "commercial domicile" at ¶ 307.

¶315 Apportionment of Business Income

Law: Income Tax Act, Sec. 203(e)(3) [35 ILCS5/203], Sec. 304(a) [35 ILCS 5/304](CCH ILLINOIS TAX REPORTS, ¶ 16-505, 16-515).

All income of resident individuals, estates, and trusts is allocated to Illinois (¶ 302). Therefore, the apportionment provisions covered below apply only to business income of corporations and nonresident individuals, estates, and trusts, and of partnerships (replacement tax) deriving income within and outside of Illinois.

Business income, other than business income of certain industries (¶ 1108), is apportioned to Illinois by means of a single-factor apportionment formula that consists of the sales factor (¶ 319).

• *Reclassification of income*

If income from an asset or business has been classified as business income but in a later year is deemed nonbusiness income, all related expenses deducted in that later year and the two immediately preceding taxable years have to be recaptured as business income in the year of disposition of the asset (35 ILCS 5/203(e)(3)).

¶316 "Business Income" Defined

Law: Income Tax Act, Sec. 1501(a)(1) [35 ILCS 5/1501]; 86 Ill. Admin. Code Secs. 100.3010, 100.3015 (CCH ILLINOIS TAX REPORTS, ¶ 16-515).

"Business income" is defined as all income that may be treated as apportionable business income under the U.S. Constitution and is net of allocable deductions (35 ILCS 5/1501(a)(1); 86 Ill. Admin. Code Sec. 100.3010). All other income is nonbusiness income and is allocable to a single state.

"Prior to July 30, 2004, the business income definition read 'business income is income arising from transactions and activity in the regular course of a trade or business and includes income from tangible and intangible property constituting integral parts of a person's regular trade or business operations.' By creating the new definition above, the General Assembly was specifically overruling certain court decisions such as *Blessing/White, Inc. V. Zehnder*, 329 Ill. App. 3d 714 (Third Div. 2002) (gain on a liquidating sale was nonbusiness income)." (*General Information Letter IT 09-0033-GIL*, Illinois Department of Revenue, September 28, 2009, CCH ILLINOIS TAX REPORTS, ¶ 402-035)

A taxpayer may make an irrevocable election to treat all income other than compensation as business income (35 ILCS 5/1501(a)(1); 86 Ill. Adm. Code Sec. 100.3015).

Practitioner Comment: Constitutional Standard of Business Income

Income is "business income" under Illinois law if it may be treated as apportionable business income under the United States Constitution. Income is apportionable under the U.S. Constitution if either (1) there exists a unitary relation between the payee and payor, or (2) the capital transaction serves an operational, rather than an investment, function (*Allied-Signal, Inc. v. Dir., Div. of Tax'n*, 504 U.S. 768 (1992), CCH ILLINOIS TAX REPORTS, ¶ 400-577).

The constitutional test for a unitary business focuses on functional integration, centralization of management, and economies of scale (*Container Corp. v. Franchise Tax Bd.*, 463 U.S. 159 (1983)). A unitary business may exist without a flow of goods between a parent and subsidiary if, instead, there is a flow of value between the entities.

The operational test focuses on the objective characteristics of the asset's use and its relation to the taxpayer and its activities within the taxing state. The inquiry is whether the taxpayer's managers treated an asset as serving an operational function, as opposed to an investment function. For example, income earned on short-term deposits in a bank located in another state is apportionable income if that income forms part of the company's working capital (See *Allied-Signal*). Yet, income from short-term deposits is not apportionable to the extent the income is not actually used as working capital (*Home Interiors and Gifts, Inc. v. Dep't of Revenue*, 318 Ill. App. 3d 205 (2000), CCH ILLINOIS TAX REPORTS, ¶ 401-173).

Horwood Marcus & Berk Chartered

The holding for investment purposes of stock, securities, land, or other property, or the making of casual sales, does not normally constitute a trade or business. Therefore, investment income will generally be presumed to be nonbusiness income. However, if a taxpayer is engaged in a trade or business, and if the regular trade or business operations include the acquisition, management, and disposition of tangible or intangible property, income from such property will be business income, even though such income is a type of investment income (for specific rules, presumptions, and examples with respect to certain types of income in the hands of specified taxpayers, see 86 Ill. Adm. Code Sec. 100.3010).

Practitioner Comment: Business Income Election

Taxpayers may make an annual, irrevocable election to treat all income other than compensation as business income. (35 ILCS 5/1501(a)(1))

Taxpayers with an Illinois commercial domicile may benefit by making the election because items of interest income, dividend income, and capital gains from sales or exchanges of intangible personal property that could otherwise be classified as nonbusiness income and sourced entirely to Illinois, may now be classified as apportionable business income.

Horwood Marcus & Berk Chartered

¶317 Apportionment of Business Income—Property Factor

Law: Income Tax Act, Sec. 304(a)(1) [35 ILCS 5/304]; 86 Ill. Adm. Code Sec. 100.3350 (CCH ILLINOIS TAX REPORTS, ¶ 16-505, 16-515).

The property factor is not a part of the normal apportionment formula, although it may be included in an alternate method (¶ 320).

The property factor is a fraction, the numerator of which is the average value of the taxpayer's real and tangible personal property owned or rented and used in the trade or business in Illinois during the taxable year and the denominator of which is the average value of all the taxpayer's real and tangible personal property owned or rented and used in the trade or business everywhere during the taxable year (35 ILCS 5/304(a)(1)). Property giving rise to nonbusiness income—rents, royalties, capital gains, *etc.*—that is directly allocated within or without Illinois (¶ 308—314) should not be included in the property factor.

Property owned by the taxpayer is valued at its original cost. Property rented by the taxpayer is valued at eight times the net annual rental rate. The net annual rental rate is the annual rental rate paid by the taxpayer less any amounts received from subrentals.

The average value of property is determined by averaging the values at the beginning and end of the taxable year. However, the Director of Revenue may require the averaging of monthly values during the taxable year if necessary to properly reflect the average value of the taxpayer's property (86 Ill. Adm. Code Sec. 100.3350contains examples pertaining to apportionment of business income under the property factor).

When valuing property owned by a person for purposes of determining the property factor used in the formula for calculating nonresident business income, a taxpayer must include capitalized intangible drilling and development costs, whether or not they have been expensed for federal or state tax purposes (86 Ill. Adm. Code Sec. 100.3350).

¶318 Apportionment of Business Income—Payroll Factor

Law: Income Tax Act, Sec. 304(a)(2) [35 ILCS 5/304]; 86 Ill. Adm. Code Sec. 100.3100; 86 Ill. Adm. Code Sec. 100.3120; 86 Ill. Adm. Code Sec. 100.3360; 86 Ill. Adm. Code Sec. 100.7010 (CCH ILLINOIS TAX REPORTS, ¶ 16-505, ¶ 16-515).

The payroll factor is not a part of the normal apportionment formula, although it may be included in an alternate method (¶ 320).

The payroll factor is a fraction, the numerator of which is the total compensation paid in Illinois during the taxable year and the denominator of which is the total compensation paid everywhere during the taxable year (35 ILCS 5/304(a)(2)). "Compensation" means wages, salaries, commissions, and any other form of remuneration paid employees for personal services.

An "employee" is any individual performing services if the relationship between the employee and the person for whom the employee performs such services is the legal relationship of employer and employee (details of the definitions of "compensation" and "employee" for purposes of apportionment appear in 86 Ill. Adm. Code Sec. 100.3360).

Sourcing: Compensation is paid in Illinois if:

— the individual's service is performed entirely within Illinois;

— the individual's service is performed both within and without Illinois, but the service performed without Illinois is incidental to the service performed within Illinois, or

— some of the service is performed in Illinois and either the base of operations or, if there is no base of operations, the place from which the service is directed or controlled is within Illinois, or the base of operations or place from which the service is directed or controlled is not in any state in which some of the service is performed, but the individual's residence is in Illinois (86 Ill. Adm. Code Sec. 100.3120contains examples of apportionment of business income under the payroll factor).

For personal income tax purposes, an employer is required to source compensation paid to an employee who has performed services in multiple states entirely to Illinois if the employee's base of operations is located in Illinois. According to the Illinois Income Tax Act, employee compensation is allocable to Illinois if the employee performs some of the service within Illinois and the base of operations is located within Illinois. Under these allocation provisions, 100% of taxable wage income is sourced to Illinois even if, for example, the employee performs 75% of his or her work in Illinois and 25% of his or her work in Ohio and, under Ohio law, the employee is taxed on 25% of his or her wages. (*General Information Letter IT 15-0007-GIL*, Illinois Department of Revenue, July 14, 2015, CCH ILLINOIS TAX REPORTS, ¶403-022)

These allocation provisions also affect residents in the computation of the credit allowed for taxes paid to other states (¶403).

Deferred compensation: Compensation paid to a nonresident for past services is presumed to have been earned ratably over the employee's last five years of service with the employer (or any predecessor, successor, parent, or subsidiary of the employer) in the absence of clear and convincing evidence that such compensation is properly attributable to a different period of employment, or was not earned ratably over the five years (86 Ill. Adm. Code Sec. 100.3120; *General Information Letter IT 12-0031-GIL*, Illinois Department of Revenue, November 13, 2012, CCH ILLINOIS TAX REPORTS, ¶402-602). Compensation paid for past service includes amounts paid under deferred compensation plans when the amount of compensation is unrelated to the amount of service currently rendered.

Compensation of athletes: For residents of states that impose a comparable tax liability on Illinois residents, compensation is paid in Illinois if the person performs personal services under a personal service contract for a sports performance. Such services performed at a sporting event taking place in Illinois are deemed to be a performance entirely within Illinois. The income from such performance is allocated to Illinois on the basis of "duty days," as defined at ¶304. The amount of income constituting compensation paid in Illinois to such a person is determined by multiplying the person's total compensation for performing personal services by a fraction, the denominator of which is the total number of duty days and the numerator of which is the number of duty days in Illinois during the taxable year (86 Ill. Adm. Code Secs. 100.3100, 100.3120, and 100.7010).

Stock options and stock appreciation rights: Generally, the taxation of stock options depends upon whether the option is a statutory or a nonstatutory option. Statutory options consist of employee stock purchase plans (ESPs) and incentive stock option plans (ISOs). Plans that fail to meet the statutory qualifications for ESPs and ISOs are called nonstatutory options (NSOs).

For statutory plans structured as an ESP or ISO, employees recognize income on the grant or exercise of the option when the stock is sold. Gain or loss on the sale is normally capital gain or loss. For NSOs, compensation income is recognized either when the option is exercised or later when any substantial risk of forfeiture lapses. When the stock is sold, any income is taxed at capital gain.

Tax treatment of stock options depends upon whether the option is an ESP, an ISO, or an NSO. Thus, careful attention must be directed toward whether or not the option complies with specific statutory requirements. Failure to meet any of the requirements means that ESPs and ISOs are governed by NSO rules.

In an administrative decision, a taxpayer's request for a refund of overpaid Illinois personal income taxes was denied because the taxpayer failed to prove that his gain on the value of stock options and stock appreciation rights was improperly determined to be compensation. The taxpayer argued that the gain he received in connection with the stock options and stock appreciation rights was not "compensa-

¶318

tion" within the meaning of Illinois statutes and was not allocable to Illinois. Specifically, the taxpayer admitted that the value of the stock options and stock appreciation rights upon vesting was allocable to Illinois as compensation, but argued that the increase in value after they vested was investment income and not compensation from employment.

However, the administrative law judge (ALJ) held that the taxpayer failed to meet his burden of proving that a portion of the income that he received when he sold his stock appreciation rights in 2008 was investment income that was not allocable to Illinois. The ALJ reasoned that if any of the income had actually been investment income, such as interest, dividends, or capital gains, then the taxpayer should have reported it as investment income on his federal Form 1040. Because the Department of Revenue's determination was *prima facie* correct and the taxpayer bore the burden of proving that he is entitled to a deduction, the fact that the stipulations were confusing and did not clearly present the taxpayer's case warranted a finding in favor of the department with respect to the stock options. (*Administrative Hearing Decision No. IT 12-09*, Illinois Department of Revenue, December 7, 2012, CCH ILLINOIS TAX REPORTS, ¶ 402-604)

Items of income taken into account as "compensation" by a nonresident employee under the provisions of IRC Secs. 401-425 (such as, for example, amounts received by a beneficiary of an employee's trust for which the employee is taxable) are not "paid in Illinois" for purposes of the payroll factor (86 Ill. Adm. Code Sec. 100.3120).

In cases in which the Director of Revenue has entered into an agreement with the taxing authorities of another state providing that compensation paid in the other state to residents of Illinois is exempt from such state's tax, compensation paid in Illinois to residents of the other state is not allocated to Illinois (86 Ill. Adm. Code Sec. 100.3120).

¶319 Apportionment of Business Income—Sales Factor

Law: Income Tax Act, Sec. 304(a)(3) [35 ILCS 5/304]; 86 Ill. Adm. Code Sec. 100.3370; 86 Ill. Adm. Code Sec. 100.3380 (CCH ILLINOIS TAX REPORTS, ¶ 16-505, 16-515).

For tax years ending after 2000, the normal apportionment formula consists solely of the sales factor (¶ 315).

The sales factor is a fraction, the numerator of which is the total sales of the taxpayer in Illinois during the taxable year, and the denominator of which is the total sales of the taxpayer everywhere during the taxable year (35 ILCS 5/304(a)(3)). Only sales that produce business income are included in the factor. Sales that produce capital gains or losses are directly allocated under the provisions relating to nonbusiness income (¶ 310).

Dividends, amounts included under IRC Sec. 78 (dividends received from certain foreign corporations), and Subpart F income, as defined in IRC Sec. 952, are not included in the numerator or denominator of the sales factor for taxable years ending on or after 1995.

"Sales" means all gross receipts of the taxpayer other than compensation and nonbusiness income (86 Ill. Adm. Code Sec. 100.3370 contains examples of apportionment of business income under the sales factor).

• *Basis of allocating sales*

Tangible personal property: Sales of tangible personal property are in Illinois if:

— the property is delivered or shipped to a purchaser (other than the U.S. government) within Illinois, regardless of the f.o.b. point or other conditions of the sale; or

— the property is shipped from an office, store, warehouse, factory, or other place of storage in Illinois and either the purchaser is the U.S. government or the taxpayer is not taxable in the state of the purchaser.

An Illinois regulation specifies that premises owned or leased by a person who has independently contracted with the taxpayer for the printing of newspapers, periodicals, or books is not deemed to be an office, store, warehouse, factory, or other place of storage for purposes of determining which state gives rise to receipts from sales of tangible personal property (86 Ill. Adm. Code Sec. 100.3370).

Intangible property in general: For taxable years ending on or after December 31, 2008, in the case of interest, net gains, and other items of income from intangible personal property, the sale of the intangible property is considered to be in Illinois if (35 ILCS 5/304(a)(3)(C-5)(iii)):

(1) in the case of a taxpayer who is a dealer in the intangible property (IRC Sec. 375), the income or gain is received from a customer in Illinois; or

(2) in all other cases, the income-producing activity of the taxpayer is performed in Illinois or proportionally greater in Illinois than in any other state based on performance costs.

Apportionment of services: Sales of services are in Illinois if the services are received in the state (35 ILCS 5/304(a)(3)(C-5)(iv)). Gross receipts from the performance of services provided to a corporation, partnership, or trust may only be attributed to a state where that corporation, partnership, or trust has a fixed place of business. If the state where the services are received is not readily determinable or is a state where the business does not have a fixed place of business, the services will be deemed to be received at the location of the office of the customer from which the services were ordered in the regular course of the customer's trade or business. If the ordering office cannot be determined, the services will be deemed to be received at the office of the customer to which the services are billed. If the taxpayer is not taxable in the state in which the services are received, the sale must be excluded from both the numerator and the denominator of the sales factor (35 ILCS 5/304(a)(3)(C-5)(iv); see also *General Information Letter IT 08-0022-GIL*, Illinois Department of Revenue, July 16, 2008, CCH Illinois Tax Reports, ¶ 401-897, and *General Information Letter IT 08-0034-GIL*, Illinois Department of Revenue, October 15, 2008, CCH Illinois Tax Reports, ¶ 401-934).

Practitioner Comment: Sales of Publishing and Advertising Services

The Department has amended its regulations on Net Income in 86 Ill. Adm. Code 100.3373 to include a "circulation factor" for calculating where income from publishing services should be apportioned. The circulation factor is the ratio between the taxpayer's in-state circulation to purchasers to total circulation. The regulation also provides that if the taxpayer is not taxable in the state in which the publishing services are received, the sale must be excluded from both the numerator and the denominator.

Illinois adopted market-based sourcing for services for tax years ending on or after December 31, 2008 (35 ILCS 5/304(a)(3)(C-5)). The Department was granted the authority to adopt regulations to determine where certain types of services are received. The Department has yet to adopt regulations on where general services are received, but this guidance on sourcing of sales for publishing and advertising service, including Internet publishing, gives taxpayers doing business in Illinois a lot to think about. First, this regulation introduces concepts that may not have been considered when a taxpayer filed returns in prior years. Second, the new regulation is considered the Department's "interpretation" of the law changes that are applicable to all tax years on or after December 31, 2008. As a result, depending on how returns were previously filed, this provides for potential refund opportunities for taxpayers or potential understatement of tax liabilities. It will be imperative for taxpayers to review prior and current year methodologies employed to determine if either situation exists. Further, the Department has yet to offer guidance on how this election should be made, but has made clear that once it is made, it must be applied consistently from year to year.

Breen M. Schiller, Esq., Horwood Marcus & Berk, Chartered

Patents, copyrights, trademarks: See ¶312.

• *Throwback rule*

An Illinois regulation adds a throwback rule for the attribution of sales of tangible or intangible personal property to the state when neither the origin nor the destination of the sale is within Illinois (86 Ill. Adm. Code Sec. 100.3380). In such a case, if the taxpayer is not taxable in either the state of origin or the state of destination and it has activities in Illinois in connection with the sale that are not protected by the provisions of P.L. 86-272, the sale is attributed or "thrown back" to Illinois. Although the limitation on state taxing power in P.L. 86-272 applies solely to sales of tangible personal property, the Illinois regulation applies the limitation to sales of intangible property for purposes of this attribution rule.

¶320 Alternate Methods

Law: Income Tax Act, Sec. 304(f) [35 ILCS 5/304] (CCH ILLINOIS TAX REPORTS, ¶16-515).

If the single sales factor apportionment method does not fairly represent the extent of the taxpayer's business activity in Illinois, the taxpayer may petition for, or the Director of Revenue may require, the following, in respect of all or any part of the taxpayer's business activity, if reasonable (35 ILCS 5/304(f)):

— separate accounting;

— the exclusion of any one or more apportionment factors, or the inclusion of one or more additional factors that will fairly represent the taxpayer's business activities in Illinois; or

— the employment of any other method to effectuate an equitable allocation and apportionment of the taxpayer's business income.

Practitioner Comment: Illinois Changes the Standard for Alternative Allocation

For taxable years ending on or after December 31, 2008, the General Assembly changed when a taxpayer may receive the benefit of alternative allocation or apportionment. Whereas the prior standard required a taxpayer to show that the standard approach in the Income Tax Act does not fairly represent the extent of the taxpayer's business activity in the State, now a taxpayer must demonstrate that the requirements under the Act do not fairly represent the market for the person's goods, services, or other sources of business income. (P.A. 98-0478).

Marilyn A. Wethekam, Esq., Horwood Marcus & Berk, Chartered

¶321 Allocation of Partnership Income

Law: Income Tax Act, Sec. 301(c) [35 ILCS 5/301]; Income Tax Act, Sec. 305 [35 ILCS 5/305]; 86 Ill. Adm. Code Sec. 100.3380 (CCH ILLINOIS TAX REPORTS, ¶16-505, ¶16-515).

Resident partners: All income of Illinois residents is allocated to Illinois (¶302). Therefore, any partnership income received by a resident is allocated to Illinois.

Nonresident partners—Business income: The respective shares of nonresident partners in partnership business income allocated or apportioned to Illinois in the hands of the partnership is taken into account by the partners *pro rata* in accordance with their respective distributive shares of the partnership income for the partnership's taxable year and allocated to Illinois (35 ILCS 5/305(a)).

Practitioner Comment: Unitary Business

As a general rule, a partnership's business income is apportioned at the partnership level using the partnership's apportionment factors, and each partner takes into account his pro-rata share of the partnership's Illinois-apportioned business income in determining the partner's Illinois taxable income. However, when a partner and the partnership are engaged in a unitary business (see ¶1103), the partnership's business income is apportioned at the partner level. Specifically, each partner includes within his business income and apportionment factors his distributive share of the partnership's business income and apportionment factors (86 Ill. Admin. Code Sec. 100.3380(d)).

When a partnership and one of its partners are engaged in a unitary business and the partnership is itself a partner in a second partnership, the following rules apply: (1) if the partner is engaged in a unitary business with the second partnership, the partner's share of the first partnership's share of the business income and apportionment factors of the second partnership shall be included in the partner's business income and apportionment factors; and (2) if the partner is not engaged in a unitary business with the second partner's share of the first partnership's share of the business income and apportionment factors of the second partnership shall not be included in the partner's business income and apportionment factors. Instead, the partner's share of the first partnership's share of the base income apportioned to Illinois by the second partnership will be included in the partner's Illinois net income.

It is unclear whether the rules regarding tiered partnerships apply retroactively to periods prior to June 20, 2002, the date the regulation was amended. Indeed, the Department has previously issued private letter rulings that suggest that the income and factors of a second tier partnership cannot be combined with the income and factors of a first tier partnership for apportionment purposes.

Moreover, taxpayers are currently challenging whether the Department, by combining shares of a partnership's income and factors with the income and factors of its partners, is violating the Illinois Income Tax Act. (*Exxon Corp. v. Bower*, Doc. No. 1-01-3302 (Ill. App. Ct. May 21, 2004) (unpublished decision) CCH ILLINOIS TAX REPORTS, ¶401-477; *BP Oil Pipeline Co. v. Zehnder*, Doc. No. 1-01-2364 (Ill. App. Ct. May 21, 2004) (unpublished decision), CCH ILLINOIS TAX REPORTS, ¶401-476)

David Hughes, Esq., Horwood Marcus & Berk Chartered

If substantially all of the interests in a partnership are owned or controlled by members of the same unitary business group, the partnership is treated as a member of the unitary business group for all purposes, and, for purposes of allocating income to any nonresident partner who is not a member of the same unitary business group, the business income of the partnership apportioned to Illinois is determined using the combined apportionment method (35 ILCS 5/304(e)). For this purpose, substantially all of the interests in a partnership are owned or controlled by members of the same unitary business group if more than 90% of the federal taxable income of the partnership is allocable to one or more of the following persons (86 Ill. Admin. Code Sec. 100.3380(d)):

— any member of the unitary business group;

— any person who would be a member of the unitary business group if not for the fact that 80% or more of such person's business activities are conducted outside the United States;

— any person who would be a member of the unitary business group except for the fact that such person and the partnership apportion their business incomes under different subsections of (35 ILCS 5/304); or

— any person who would be disallowed a federal deduction for losses by virtue of being related to any person described above, as well as any partnership in which a person listed above is a partner.

Nonresident partners—Nonbusiness income: The respective shares of nonresident partners in items of partnership income and deduction not taken into account in computing the business income of a partnership are taken into account by the partners pro rata in accordance with their respective distributive shares of the partnership income for the partnership's taxable year and are allocated as if paid, incurred, or accrued directly to the partners in their separate capacities (35 ILCS 5/305(b)).

Guaranteed payments: The Illinois Department of Revenue stated in a general information letter that the guaranteed payment the taxpayer received from an LLP was ordinary income of the partnership, which was characterized by the partnership as business income. Accordingly, the amount of the taxpayer's guaranteed payment that was apportioned to Illinois by the partnership was taxable and also subject to withholding. The DOR also noted that although the matter has never been raised before an Illinois court, courts in other states have held that guaranteed payments received by a nonresident partner from a partnership doing business in the state are subject to the state's income tax, even when the partner has no other connection with the state. (*General Information Letter IT 12-0028-GIL,* Illinois Department of Revenue, September 27, 2012, CCH ILLINOIS TAX REPORTS, ¶ 402-574)

Apportionment of business income by partnership (replacement tax): Business income of a partnership is apportioned to Illinois under the apportionment provisions relating to business income discussed in the preceding paragraphs of this chapter.

Base income of nonresident partnership: The base income of a nonresident partnership must be allocated or apportioned to Illinois in the same manner as it is allocated or apportioned for any other nonresidents (35 ILCS 5/305(c)).

Any item of income or deduction that was taken into account in the computation of base income for the tax year by a nonresident partnership and that is not otherwise specifically allocated or apportioned must be allocated to Illinois if the taxpayer had its commercial domicile in Illinois at the time the item was paid, incurred, or accrued.

• *Taxable income of an investment partnership*

Taxable income of an investment partnership that is distributable to a nonresident partner is treated as nonbusiness income and allocated to the partner's state of residence, unless the partner has made an election to treat all such income as business income or the income is from investment activity (35 ILCS 5/305(c-5)):

— that is directly related to any other business activity conducted in Illinois by the nonresident partner;

— that serves an operational function to any other business activity of the nonresident partner; or

— where assets of the investment partnership were acquired with working capital from a trade or business in Illinois in which the nonresident partner owns an interest.

¶322 Allocation of Estate or Trust Income

Law: Income Tax Act, Sec. 306 [35 ILCS 5/306] (CCH ILLINOIS TAX REPORTS, ¶ 15-215).

If an estate or trust is an Illinois resident (¶302), all Illinois base income (federal income adjusted by Illinois modifications) is attributed to Illinois (35 ILCS 5/306). Nonresident estates or trust are taxed only on income allocated and apportioned to Illinois. The allocation rules for nonbusiness income are discussed at ¶ 308—314, and the apportionment of business income is covered at ¶ 315—319.

Items of income and deduction taken into account by an estate or trust in computing base income to the extent properly paid, credited, or required to be distributed to beneficiaries for the taxable year, are deemed to have been so paid, credited, or distributed pro rata.

A trust may not succeed to an Illinois net loss carryover of another trust for Illinois corporate income tax purposes. Federal rules did not apply for Illinois income tax purposes unless state law applied them. There was no provision in state law that either incorporated or provided for a transfer similar to federal trust and estate loss carryover rules in the case of Illinois net operating loss carryovers upon termination of a trust; therefore, no such rule applied. (*General Information Letter IT 09-0038-GIL*, Illinois Department of Revenue, October 19, 2009, CCH ILLINOIS TAX REPORTS, ¶402-044)

¶323 Allocation of Income to Estate or Trust Beneficiaries

Law: Income Tax Act, Sec. 307 [35 ILCS 5/307] (CCH ILLINOIS TAX REPORTS, ¶15-235).

Illinois residents: All income of residents is allocated to Illinois (¶302) regardless of its source. Therefore, any income received by an estate or trust beneficiary who is a resident would be allocated to Illinois.

Nonresident beneficiaries—Business income: To the extent the business income of an estate or trust, allocated or apportioned to Illinois in the hands of the estate or trust, is deemed to have been paid, credited, or distributed by the estate or trust (¶322), the respective shares of nonresident beneficiaries of the estate or trust in the business income are taken into account, in proportion to the beneficiaries' respective shares of the distributable net income of the estate or trust for its taxable year, and allocated to Illinois (35 ILCS 5/307(a)).

Nonresident beneficiaries—Nonbusiness income: To the extent that items of estate or trust income and deduction not taken into account in computing business income are deemed to have been paid, credited, or distributed by the estate or trust (¶322), the respective shares of nonresident beneficiaries of the estate, in such items are taken into account in proportion to the beneficiaries' respective shares of the distributable net income of the estate or trust for its taxable year and allocated as if paid, incurred, or accrued directly to the beneficiaries in their separate capacities (35 ILCS 5/307(b)).

Accumulation and capital gains distributions: If a trust makes an accumulation distribution or a capital gain distribution (both as defined in IRC Sec. 665), the total of the amounts included in the income of each beneficiary of the trust, other than a resident, under IRC Secs. 668 and 669 is allocated to Illinois to the extent that the items of income included in the distribution were allocated or apportioned to Illinois in the hands of the trust (35 ILCS 5/305(c)).

Both resident and nonresident trust beneficiaries are allowed a credit for Illinois taxes paid by the trust in past years on income currently included in the federal gross income of the beneficiary as an accumulation distribution.

PERSONAL INCOME TAX
CHAPTER 4
EXEMPTIONS AND CREDITS

¶401 In General

Law: Corporate Accountability for Tax Expenditures Act, Sec. 5 [20 ILCS 715/5]; Corporate Accountability for Tax Expenditures Act, Sec. 25 [20 ILCS 715/25]; Civil Administrative Code, Sec. 605 [20 ILCS 605/605-320]; Income Tax Act, Sec. 250 [35 ILCS 5/250] (CCH ILLINOIS TAX REPORTS, ¶16-805).

Every income tax exemption or credit enacted after September 16, 1994, must be limited by a sunset date (35 ILCS 5/250). If a "reasonable and appropriate" sunset date is not specified, then the exemption or credit will expire five years after the effective date of the enacting law.

The sunset date is extended by five years for all tax exemptions, credits, or deductions that would have expired in 2011-2013 (35 ILCS 5/250).

A Department of Revenue publication explains what income is exempt from Illinois personal income tax. This document identifies who is entitled to a subtraction of income exempt from state income tax, defines income that is exempt from state income tax, identifies exceptions, and explains how to claim a subtraction of exempt income on Illinois tax returns (*Publication 101, Income Exempt From Tax,* Illinois Department of Revenue, March 2010, CCH ILLINOIS TAX REPORTS, ¶402-087).

• *Requirements for development assistance*

The Corporate Accountability for Tax Expenditures Act imposes minimum recapture requirements for credits against Illinois personal income taxes (20 ILCS 715/25).

Recapture requirements: All development assistance agreements must contain, at a minimum, the following recapture provisions (20 ILCS 715/25):

(1) incentive recipients must make the level of capital investment in the economic development project specified in the development assistance agreement, create and/or retain the requisite number of jobs, paying at least the wages specified for the jobs, for the duration of time specified in the authorizing legislation or the implementing administrative rules;

(2) incentive recipients that fail to create or retain the requisite number of jobs for the specified time period will no longer qualify for the economic assistance and the applicable recapture provisions will take effect;

(3) taxpayers operating in Illinois enterprise zones that qualify for the Illinois retailers' occupation (sales) tax exemption for building materials incorporated into a high impact business location that fail to create or retain the requisite number of jobs within the requisite period of time must pay to Illinois the full amount of the exemption they received as a result of the high impact business designation;

(4) recipients of Large Business Development Program or Business Development Public Infrastructure Program, or Industrial Training Program grants or loans that fail to create or retain the requisite number of jobs for the requisite time period must repay to Illinois the pro rata amount of the grant or loan reflecting the percentage of the deficiency between the number of jobs required to be created or maintained and the actual number of jobs in existence on the date the Department of Commerce and Economic Opportunity determines that the recipients are in breach of the job creation or retention covenants;

(5) recipients of Large Business Development Program or Business Development Public Infrastructure Program, or Industrial Training Program grants or loans that cease operations at the specific project site within five years of the date they received the grant or loan will be required to repay the entire amount of the grant or to accelerate repayment of the loan back to Illinois; and

(6) in the case of taxpayers receiving Economic Development for a Growing Economy (EDGE) credits against Illinois corporate or personal income tax, development assistance agreements must provide that (a) if the number of new or retained employees falls below the requisite number, the credit will be automatically suspended until the number of new or retained employees equals or exceeds the requisite number, (b) if the credit recipient discontinues operations at the specific project site during the first five years of the 10- year term of the development assistance agreement, the recipient will forfeit all the credits it took during the five-year period, and (c) if a credit is revoked or suspended, the Department of Commerce and Economic Opportunity must contact the Director of Revenue to initiate proceedings against the recipient to recover the income tax credited and the recipient must promptly repay that amount to the Illinois Department of Revenue.

Waiver: The Director of Revenue may waive enforcement of any contractual provision of a development assistance agreement if the waiver is necessary to avert a hardship to a recipient that may result in the recipient's insolvency or in the discharge of workers (20 ILCS 715/25(a)(5)(b)). If the Director grants a waiver, the recipient must agree to contractual modifications, including recapture provisions, to the development assistance agreement.

¶401

"Development assistance" defined: "Development assistance" means (20 ILCS 715/5):

(1) tax credits and tax exemptions (other than those given under tax increment financing (TIF)) given as an incentive to a recipient business organization pursuant to an initial certification or an initial designation made by the Department under the Economic Development for a Growing Economy Tax Credit Act and the Illinois Enterprise Zone Act, including the High Impact Business program;

(2) grants or loans given to a recipient as an incentive to a business organization pursuant to the Large Business Development Program, the Business Development Public Infrastructure Program, or the Industrial Training Program;

(3) the State Treasurer's Economic Program Loans;

(4) the Illinois Department of Transportation Economic Development Program; and

(5) all successor and subsequent programs and tax credits designed to promote large business relocations and expansions.

The term "development assistance" does not include tax increment financing, assistance provided under the Illinois Enterprise Zone Act pursuant to local ordinance, participation loans, or financial transactions through statutorily authorized financial intermediaries in support of small business loans and investments or given in connection with the development of affordable housing.

• *Reporting requirements for recipients of tax incentives*

An annual reporting requirement is imposed on Illinois taxpayers that receive corporate income tax credits, personal income tax credits, sales tax exemptions, or the abatement of property tax under the Economic Development for a Growing Economy Tax Credit Act, the River Edge Redevelopment Zone Act, or the Enterprise Zone Act, including the High Impact Business program (20 ILCS 605/605-320). Recipients of such incentives must provide the Department of Commerce and Economic Opportunity the following:

— a detailed list of the occupation or job classifications and number of new employees or retained employees to be hired in full-time, permanent jobs;

— a schedule of anticipated starting dates of the new hires and the actual average wage by occupation or job classification; and

— total payroll to be created as a result of the incentives.

• *Enterprise zones and river edge redevelopment zones defined*

Enterprise zone: A contiguous area within a municipality and/or an unincorporated area in which pervasive poverty, unemployment, and economic distress exits. Enterprise zones range from a half square mile to 15 square miles (20 ILCS 655/4). An enterprise zone will exist for 30 years or for a lesser number of years as specified in the zone designation (20 ILCS 655/5.3).

River edge redevelopment zone: A contiguous area adjacent to or surrounding a river that (65 ILCS 115/10-4):

(1) comprises a minimum of one half square mile and not more than 12 square miles, exclusive of lakes and waterways;

(2) satisfies any additional criteria established by the Department of Commerce and Economic Opportunity;

(3) is entirely within a single home rule municipality; and

(4) has at least 100 acres of environmentally challenged land within 1500 yards of the riverfront.

Designation: A home-rule municipality may designate a river edge redevelopment zone (65 ILCS 115/10-5).

Extension: Enterprise zone credits may be extended by municipal or county ordinance for an additional 10 years. In addition, any credit that is scheduled to expire before July 1, 2016, may be extended by municipal or county ordinance until July 1, 2016. Applications for an extension to July 1, 2016, must be submitted by December 31, 2014. (20 ILCS 655/5.3(c))

¶402 Homestead Realty Tax Credit

Law: Income Tax Act, Sec. 208 [35 ILCS 5/208] (CCH Illinois Tax Reports, ¶ 16-950).

Illinois residents are allowed an income tax credit equal to 5% of the real property taxes they paid during the tax year on their principal residence. In the case of multi-unit or multi-use structures and farm dwellings, the taxes on the taxpayer's principal residence are that portion of the total taxes that is attributable to the principal residence (35 ILCS 5/208).

Effective for taxable years beginning on or after January 1, 2017, taxpayers who have adjusted gross income for the taxable year exceeding $500,000 for taxpayers filing a joint federal return or $250,000 for all other taxpayers may not claim the credit.

The credit may be claimed only for:

— property tax paid on a taxpayer's principal residence (whether or not for the current year) and tax paid on an adjoining lot to the principal residence if it is used for residential purposes;

— prorated property tax paid in the year a taxpayer sells his or her principal residence; and

— village taxes paid during the current year.

The credit may not be claimed for late-payment interest; the current year's property tax if it has not yet been paid; accountant fees or attorney fees paid in association with the property tax; homeowner's association fees; or property tax paid on an out-of-state home (*Publication 108,* Illinois Department of Revenue, January 2011, CCH Illinois Tax Reports, ¶ 402-275).

A taxpayer that purchases a home may not claim the credit for the year of purchase because his or her tax for the year of purchase is not assessed and paid until the following year. However, the seller may claim the credit for the prorated portion that he or she pays at closing. If a portion of a taxpayer's residence is used for a business or if the residence is located on a farm, the amount deducted as a business expense on the taxpayer's federal return must be deducted from the property tax before the credit is computed.

Spouses filing joint returns, but who maintain separate Illinois residences, may each claim a personal income tax credit for property taxes paid on his or her own residence. *Publication 108, Illinois Property Tax Credit,*(CCH Illinois Tax Reports, ¶ 402-275; also available at **http://tax.illinois.gov/Publications/Pubs/**) states that "if you and your spouse each have a principal residence or if you had two principal residences during the tax year due to the sale of your home, you may claim the tax paid on both residences when figuring this credit." Additionally, the revenue department does not require taxpayers to file separately when claiming the property tax credit for two different residences. (*General Information Letter IT 10-0027-GIL,* Illinois Department of Revenue, October 26, 2010, CCH Illinois Tax Reports, ¶ 402-232)

Taxpayers who participate in the state's senior citizens real estate tax deferral program (see ¶ 2003) may not claim this credit (*General Information Letter IT 11-0020-GIL,* Illinois Department of Revenue, October 20, 2011, CCH Illinois Tax Reports, ¶ 402-424).

¶403 Credit for Tax Paid Another State—Residents

Law: Income Tax Act, Sec. 601(b)(3) [35 ILCS 5/601]; 86 Ill. Adm. Code Sec. 100.2197 (CCH ILLINOIS TAX REPORTS, ¶ 16-825).

Comparable Federal: Secs. 33, 901—906 (U.S. MASTER TAX GUIDE, ¶ 1311).

Forms: Schedule CR.

Resident individuals are allowed a credit for taxes imposed upon or measured by income paid to another "state" on income subject to the Illinois income tax (35 ILCS 5/601(b)(3); 86 Ill. Adm. Code Sec. 100.2197). The term "state" means any state of the United States, the District of Columbia, the Commonwealth of Puerto Rico, and any territory or possession of the United States, and any political subdivision of the foregoing.

The credit may not exceed that amount that bears the same ratio to the Illinois income tax that would otherwise be due as the taxpayer's base income that would be allocated or apportioned to other states if all other states had adopted this credit bears to the taxpayer's total base income subject to tax by Illinois for the taxable year. (35 ILCS 5/601(b)(3); 86 Ill. Adm. Code Sec. 100.2197(e))

If a resident's only income is from wages sourced to Illinois (¶ 318), then the total credit for taxes paid to other states is zero because, if they followed Illinois's allocation provisions, no other state would tax those wages (*General Information Letter IT 15-0007-GIL*, Illinois Department of Revenue, July 14, 2015, CCH ILLINOIS TAX REPORTS, ¶ 403-022).

CCH Example: Computation of Credit

The taxpayer, a resident of Illinois, has a computation for the taxable year as follows: Illinois income tax due (before credits) in the amount of $950; Illinois base income of $40,000; $20,000 of Illinois base income taxed by another state; and tax of $800 paid to the other state on the income taxed by both states. The taxpayer's Illinois credit for state income taxes is $475, computed as follows:

(1)	Illinois base income	$40,000
(2)	Illinois base income taxed by other state	$20,000
(3)	Illinois tax before credits	$950
(4)	Other state tax on items of Illinois base income	$800
(5)	Divide (2) by (1)	.50000
(6)	Multiply (3) by (5)	$475
(7)	Credit: lesser of (4) or (6)	$475

In computing the credit, compensation that would be attributable to Illinois if the taxpayer apportioned income (¶ 318) is not considered income subject to tax by another state. However, see ¶ 305 regarding a credit for local Kentucky income taxes withheld from wages paid to an Illinois resident.

The credit is elected by filing Schedule CR with the income tax return. Taxpayers taking the credit must notify the Director of any refund or reduction in the amount of tax paid to another state that has been claimed as a credit. The manner of notification is provided in the regulations. Further information on the credit may be found in Illinois *Publication 111*, December 2009, CCH ILLINOIS TAX REPORTS, ¶ 402-057; see also *CR Equivalency Chart*, Illinois Revenue Department, February 3, 2016, CCH ILLINOIS TAX REPORTS, ¶ 403-079.

Practitioner Comment: Double Taxation

In July 2005, the Illinois Governor signed a law (P.A. 247 (H.B. 310), Laws 2005) that deletes a provision in Sec. 601(b)(3) of the Illinois Income Tax Act that denied Illinois residents a credit for taxes paid to other states on compensation from out-of-state services. The law change was prompted by litigation over whether the former law was constitutional.

The Department had construed the former law to deny Illinois residents a credit for out-of-state taxes paid on their compensation that is deemed "paid in this State" (see ¶318). Under the prior law, compensation was deemed "paid in this State" when: (1) the employee performs some service in Illinois and some service without Illinois; and (2) the employee maintains his base of operations within Illinois. Thus, when an Illinois resident maintained his base of operations in Illinois, but the resident's employment required him or her to work in Illinois and for a substantial period of time in State X, the Illinois resident's entire compensation was deemed "paid in this State," and none of that compensation could be included in double-taxed income, even if State X actually taxed the compensation earned for periods during which the resident was working in State X (86 Ill. Admin. Code Sec. 100.2197).

In 2003, an Illinois circuit court upheld the constitutionality of Illinois' disallowance of a credit for out-of-state taxes paid an Illinois resident professional athlete on his compensation from performing professional sports services outside of Illinois on behalf of his Illinois-based employer (*Sosa v. Bower*, Doc. No. 02 L 050670 (June 26, 2003), on appeal, Ill. App. Ct. Doc. No. 03-1992).

Horwood Marcus & Berk Chartered

See also *Administrative Hearing Decision No. IT 15-02*, Illinois Department of Revenue, January 14, 2015, CCH ILLINOIS TAX REPORTS, ¶402-929.

Allocation of alimony payments: The decision of the U.S. Supreme Court in *Lunding v. N.Y. Tax Appeals Tribunal*, 522 U.S. 287 (1998), requires a state to allow nonresidents to allocate to the state deductions for alimony paid. Accordingly, Illinois allows nonresidents to allocate the full amount of the federal deduction for alimony paid to Illinois in determining their Illinois net income. The limit on the credit for taxes paid to other states must be computed by allocating the deduction for alimony paid to other states as if they followed the same allocation principles as Illinois. (*General Information Letter IT 11-0014-GIL*, Illinois Department of Revenue, July 12, 2011, CCH ILLINOIS TAX REPORTS, ¶402-388)

¶404 Investment and Enterprise Zone Credits

Law: Income Tax Act, Sec. 201(e), (f), (g) [35 ILCS 5/201]; 14 Ill. Adm. Code Sec. 520; 86 Ill. Adm. Code Secs. 100.2100—2120 (CCH ILLINOIS TAX REPORTS, ¶ 16-830, 16-845, 16-850, 16-855).

There is an investment credit that may be taken with respect to businesses operating in an enterprise zone. Also, an investment credit against the personal property replacement income tax is available to partnerships and trusts, regardless of enterprise zone operation. A jobs credit for enterprise zone businesses was eliminated by 2012 legislation (see below).

• *Investment credit against income tax*

Taxpayers are allowed a credit against the income tax for investments in qualified property that is placed in service in an enterprise zone or, for property placed in service on or after July 1, 2006, a River Edge redevelopment zone (35 ILCS 5/201(f)). In the case of S corporations, partnerships and owners of LLCs treated as partnerships, the credit is allocated to the owners or partners.

"Qualified property" is tangible property, new or used, including buildings and structural components of buildings and signs that are real property, but not including land or improvements to real property that are not a structural component of a building, such as landscaping, sewer lines, local access roads, fencing, parking lots, and other appurtenances, depreciable for federal purposes, having a class life of four years or more as of the date placed in service, acquired by purchase as defined by IRC Sec. 179(d), used in an enterprise zone by the corporation, and not previously used in Illinois.

Credit amount: The amount of the credit is 0.5% of the basis of the property. The "basis of qualified property" is the basis used to compute the depreciation deduction for federal income tax purposes. The credit may be carried forward five taxable years.

Bonus credit: An additional credit of 0.5% is allowed for qualified property placed in service during the taxable year in a River Edge redevelopment zone, provided the property is placed in service on or after July 1, 2006, and the taxpayer's base employment in Illinois has increased by 1% or more over the preceding year. A taxpayer who is new to Illinois is presumed to meet the 1% increase in base employment for the first year. If the increase in Illinois base employment is less than 1% in any year, the additional credit is limited to the percentange of increase times a fraction the numerator of which is 0.5% and the denominator of which is 1%. The additional credit may not, however, exceed 0.5%.

Limitations: If, within 48 months after being placed in service, the property is moved outside the enterprise zone, the income tax is increased by the amount of the credit allowed with respect to the property.

- *Investment credit against replacement tax*

An investment credit is available to partnerships and trusts to be applied against replacement tax at the entity level (35 ILCS 5/201(e)). Qualifications for the credit are similar to that for the income tax credit (see also ¶1201). The basis of qualified property may not include costs incurred after December 31, 2018, except for costs incurred pursuant to a binding contract entered into on or before December 31, 2018 (35 ILCS 5/201(e)(8)). Qualifying property need not be used in an enterprise zone. Additional credit is available provided certain employment level criteria are met. Excess credits may be carried forward for five years.

A partner that is subject to personal property replacement tax (PPRIT) (¶207) and that qualifies its partnership for a subtraction of income allocable to the partner is allowed a credit against PPRIT equal to its share of the investment credit earned during the taxable year by the partnership. Similarly, a shareholder that qualifies an S corporation for a subtraction of income allocable to the shareholder subject to PPRIT (¶1009) is allowed a credit against PPRIT equal to its share of the investment credit earned during the taxable year by the S corporation.

Practitioner Comment: Investment Credits

The Illinois Appellate Court has held that a nonresident partner was entitled to claim the investment credit allocated to it from the operating partnership against its own 1988 and 1989 replacement tax liability, even though the statute was not amended until 1997 to explicitly provide for the flow through of the credit to the partnership's partners (*Borden Chemicals and Plastics, L.P. v. Zehnder,* 312 Ill. App. 3d 35 (Feb. 14, 2000), CCH ILLINOIS TAX REPORTS, ¶401-120).

Horwood Marcus & Berk Chartered

- *Jobs credit (expired)*

This jobs credit was eliminated for high-impact and other enterprise zone businesses by P.A. 97-905 (S.B. 3616), Laws 2012, effective August 7, 2012. The $500 corporation and personal income tax credit for each job created in a river edge redevelopment zone and foreign trade zone or subzone was repealed, effective July 25, 2013 (P.A. 98-0109 (S.B. 20), Laws 2013).

The credit was allowed for the tax year immediately following the one in which the eligible employees were hired, or if the credit exceeds the tax liability for that year, the excess may be carried forward and applied to the tax liability for five taxable years following the excess credit year.

¶405 High-Impact Business Credit

Law: Income Tax Act, Sec. 201(g), (h) [35 ILCS 5/201]; 86 Ill. Adm. Code Sec. 100.2130 (CCH ILLINOIS TAX REPORTS, ¶ 16-830, 16-845).

Individuals are allowed an investment credit of 0.5% of the basis of property placed into service in Illinois by a business designated as a "high-impact business" by the Illinois Department of Commerce and Economic Opportunity (DCEO) (35 ILCS 5/201(g)). Except for energy-related businesses, the credit is claimed in the year the property is placed in service. Unused credit may be carried forward for five years. If the basis is increased federally after it is placed in service, the increase is deemed property placed in service on the date of the increase. Credit may not be claimed for property eligible for the enterprise zone investment credit (¶ 404).

For additional information about the credit, see the discussion at ¶ 1201.

Recapture of credit: A taxpayer that has received the credit and that later relocates its entire facility in violation of its contract with a local taxing authority, will have its income tax increased for the taxable year in which the facility was relocated by an amount equal to the credit received.

Jobs credit (expired): The enterprise zone jobs credit is no longer available to high-impact businesses; see ¶ 404. However, eligibility for high impact business credits was extended to a business that invests a minimum of $500 million and creates 125 jobs at a newly constructed or upgraded fertilizer plant. Applications for the credit had to be submitted to the Department of Revenue within 60 days after July 25, 2013 (P.A. 98-0109 (S.B. 20), Laws 2013).

¶406 Credit for Tax Paid by Trust

Law: Income Tax Act, Sec. 201(i) [35 ILCS 5/201]; Income Tax Act, Sec. 601(b)(4) [35 ILCS 5/601] (CCH ILLINOIS TAX REPORTS, ¶ 15-230, 15-235).

Comparable Federal: Sec. 665.

Both resident and nonresident trust beneficiaries are allowed a credit for Illinois taxes paid by the trust in past years on income currently included in the federal gross income of the beneficiary as an accumulation distribution (35 ILCS 5/601(b)(4)).

¶407 Credit for Research Expenditures

Law: Income Tax Act, Sec. 201(k) [35 ILCS 5/201] (CCH ILLINOIS TAX REPORTS, ¶ 16-870).

Comparable Federal: Sec. 41 (U.S. MASTER TAX GUIDE, ¶ 1330).

For tax years ending before January 1, 2022, taxpayers may take a credit against personal income taxes for qualified expenditures used for increasing research activities in Illinois (35 ILCS 5/201(k)). The credit equals $6^1/2$% of the qualifying expenditures.

For purposes of claiming a research expenditure credit, the term "qualifying expenditures" means expenditures in Illinois as defined in the similar federal credit provisions of IRC Sec. 41.

Practitioner Comment: Pass-Through of R & D Credit

In 1999, the Illinois General Assembly amended the research and development credit to provide that the credit may be passed through by a partnership, subchapter S corporation, and limited liability company to its partners, shareholders, and owners, respectively. The law change stated that "no inference shall be drawn from this amendatory Act of the 91st General Assembly in construing this Section for taxable years beginning before January 1, 1999."

The Illinois Supreme Court held that the R&D credit law change in 1999 was prospective only, and the court upheld the pre-amended law as constitutional, even though without the pass-through provision, an S corporation could not benefit from the credit because S corporations do not pay Illinois income taxes, while a regular "C" corporation could benefit by claiming the credit against its income tax liability (*Caveney v. Bower*, Doc. No. 92963, Illinois Supreme Court, May 8, 2003).

Horwood Marcus & Berk Chartered

Extension of credit: The research and development credit, which was scheduled to expire on December 31, 2010, has been extended through tax years ending on or before December 31, 2015. Eligible taxpayers that are fiscal year filers that did not claim any research and development credit on their return for a tax year ending in 2011 may amend their return for that tax year to claim the credit as if the credit never expired. (*Information Bulletin FY 2012-05*, Department of Revenue, January 2012)

¶408 River Edge Redevelopment Zone Site Remediation Credit

Law: Income Tax Act, Sec. 201(n) [35 ILCS 5/201(n)] (CCH ILLINOIS TAX REPORTS, ¶16-885).

A taxpayer is allowed a credit for certain amounts paid for unreimbursed eligible remediation costs at a site in a River Edge Redevelopment Zone (35 ILCS 5/201(n)).

"Unreimbursed eligible remediation costs" means costs approved by the Illinois Environmental Protection Agency that were paid in performing environmental remediation at a site within a River Edge redevelopment zone for which a no further remediation letter was issued and recorded by the Agency. "Related party" includes the persons disallowed a deduction under IRC Sec. 267(b), (c), and (f)(1) by virtue of being a related taxpayer, as well as any of its partners. "Taxpayer" includes a person whose tax attributes the taxpayer has succeeded to under IRC Sec. 381 (35 ILCS 5/201(n)).

Credit amount: The credit equals 25% of the unreimbursed eligible remediation costs in excess of $100,000 per site (35 ILCS 5/201(n)).

Planning considerations: The credit must be claimed for the taxable year in which Agency approval of the eligible remediation costs is granted. The credit is not available if the taxpayer or any related party caused or contributed to a release of regulated substances on, in, or under the site that was identified and addressed by the remedial action pursuant to the Site Remediation Program of the Environmental Protection Act. This credit is not subject to the automatic sunset provision that applies to most other income tax credits.

Jobs credit: The $500 corporation and personal income tax credit for each job created in a river edge redevelopment zone and foreign trade zone or subzone was repealed, effective July 25, 2013; see ¶404.

Carryover: Unused credit amounts may be carried forward for five tax years.

Credit transfers: A credit may be sold to a buyer as part of a sale of all or part of the remediation site for which the credit was granted. To perfect the transfer, the assignor must record the transfer in the chain of title for the site and provide written notice to the Director of the Illinois Department of Revenue of the assignor's intent to sell the remediation site and the amount of the tax credit to be transferred as a portion of the sale.

¶409 Credit for Withheld Taxes

Law: Income Tax Act, Sec. 601(b)(1) [35 ILCS 5/601].

Comparable Federal: Sec. 31 (U.S. MASTER TAX GUIDE, ¶ 1372).

Illinois income tax withheld from wages by an Illinois employer is allowed as a credit against the tax due (35 ILCS 5/601(b)(1)). The amount withheld during any calendar year is allowed as a credit against the tax due for the taxable year beginning in the calendar year. If more than one taxable year begins in a calendar year, the withheld tax will be allowed against the tax due for the last taxable year.

For treatment of withholding on wages of Illinois residents working out-of-state, see ¶ 305.

¶410 Credit for Estimated Taxes

Law: Income Tax Act, Sec. 601(b)(2) [35 ILCS 5/601].

Comparable Federal: Sec. 6315 (U.S. MASTER TAX GUIDE, ¶ 105).

Amounts of estimated tax paid are allowed as credits against the Illinois income tax due (35 ILCS 601(b)(2)). See Chapter 5 for provisions relating to declarations and payments of estimated tax.

¶411 Credit for School Expenses

Law: Income Tax Act, Sec. 201(m) [35 ILCS 5/201(m)]; Income Tax Act, Sec. 203(a), (e), [35 ILCS 5/203] (CCH ILLINOIS TAX REPORTS, ¶ 16-915).

Comparable Federal: Secs. 25A, 222, 529 (U.S. MASTER TAX GUIDE, ¶ 697, 1082, 1303).

Forms: Schedule ED.

A taxpayer who is the parent or custodian of a qualified pupil is allowed a personal income tax credit for qualified education expenses, defined as those costs in excess of $250 that are incurred on behalf of a pupil for tuition, book fees, and lab fees at a school in which the pupil is enrolled during the regular school year (35 ILCS 5/201(m)). A "school" means any public or nonpublic elementary or secondary school in Illinois that is in compliance with Title VI of the Civil Rights Act of 1964 and the School Code. See *Publication 132, Education Expense Credit General Rules and Requirements for Parent and Guardians,* Illinois Department of Revenue, February 2015; CCH ILLINOIS TAX REPORTS, ¶ 402-920 and *General Information Letter IT 13-0005-GIL,* Illinois Department of Revenue, April 9, 2013, CCH ILLINOIS TAX REPORTS, ¶ 402-662.

The credit also applies to qualifying home schools (*Publication 119,* Illinois Department of Revenue, February 2015; CCH ILLINOIS TAX REPORTS, ¶ 402-919).

Effective for taxable years beginning on or after January 1, 2017, taxpayers who have adjusted gross income for the taxable year exceeding $500,000 for taxpayers filing a joint federal return or $250,000 for all other taxpayers may not claim the credit. (35 ILCS 5/201(m))

Calculation of credit: The tax credit is equal to 25% of the qualified expenses, with a maximum credit of $750 ($500 for tax years before 2017) per family per year. The tax credit is allowed for full-time pupils enrolled in a kindergarten through grade 12 education program who are residents of Illinois and under the age of 21 at the close of the school year for which a credit is sought.

CCH Advisory: School Supplies Must Be Consumable

Amounts spent to purchase books and other items that are not consumed during the year do not qualify for the education expense credit. A taxpayer was denied the credit because her purchases of books and laboratory equipment could not be classified as "qualified education expenses" because the items did not appear to be the kind that could be consumed during the school year, as required by the credit. (*General Information Letter IT 12-0015-GIL,* Department of Revenue, July 10, 2012, CCH ILLINOIS TAX REPORTS, ¶402-529)

¶412 Credit for Wages Paid to Ex-Offenders

Law: Income Tax Act, Sec. 216 [35 ILCS 5/216] (CCH ILLINOIS TAX REPORTS, ¶16-875).

A credit may be taken for wages paid to qualified ex-offenders (35 ILCS 5/216). "Qualified ex-offender" means any person who (1) is an eligible offender, as defined under Sec. 5-5.5-5 of the Unified Code of Corrections; (2) was sentenced to a period of incarceration in an Illinois adult correctional center; and (3) was hired by the taxpayer within three years after being released from an Illinois correctional center. An offender required to register under the Sex Offenders Registration Act is not qualified. (35 ILCS 5/216(c))

Qualified wages (1) include only wages that are subject to federal unemployment tax under IRC Sec. 3306, without regard to any dollar limitation contained in the section; (2) do not include any amounts paid or incurred by an employer for any period to any qualified ex-offender for whom the employer receives federally funded payments for on-the-job training of that qualified ex-offender for that period; and (3) include only wages attributable to service rendered during the one-year period beginning with the day the qualified ex-offender begins work for the employer.

Credit amount: The credit equals 5% of the qualified wages paid by the taxpayer during the taxable year to one or more Illinois residents who are qualified ex-offenders. The total credit allowed to each taxpayer with respect to each qualified ex-offender may not exceed $1500 for all taxable years.

Planning considerations: If the taxpayer has received any payment from a program established under Sec. 482(e)(1) of the federal Social Security Act with respect to a qualified ex-offender, the amount of the qualified wages must be reduced by the payment amount.

Carryover: If the amount of the credit exceeds the tax liability for the tax year, the excess may be carried forward and applied to the tax liability of the five taxable years following the excess credit year. If there are credits for more than one year that are available to offset a liability, the earlier credit must be applied first.

¶413 EDGE Job Creation Credit

Law: Income Tax Act, Sec. 211 [35 ILCS 5/211]; Economic Development for a Growing Economy Tax Credit Act, Sec. 5-5 [35 ILCS 10/5-5]; 14 Ill. Adm. Code 527.30 (CCH ILLINOIS TAX REPORTS, ¶16-875).

Eligible businesses that enter into an agreement before June 30, 2022, with the Illinois Department of Commerce and Economic Opportunity (DCEO) to expand operations or relocate in Illinois resulting in job creation or retention may be awarded a credit against Illinois personal income tax liability under the Economic Development for a Growing Economy Credit Act (EDGE credit) (35 ILCS 5/211). Eligible entities include individuals, corporations, partnerships, or other entities with Illinois income tax liability, including shareholders or partners of a pass-through entity (35 ILCS 5/211; 35 ILCS 10/5-5).

Qualifications: Effective beginning September 18, 2017, credit applicants with more than 100 employees must invest at least $2.5 million in capital improvements that are placed in service in the state. There is no capital investment requirement for businesses with 100 or fewer employees. (35 ILCS 10/5-20). New jobs created in the state on the date a credit application is filed with the Department of Commerce and Economic Opportunity (DCEO) must be equal to the lesser of 50 new employees or:

— 10% of the full-time employees employed world-wide by businesses with more than 100 employees; or

— 5% of the full-time employees employed world-wide by businesses with 100 or fewer employees. (35 ILCS 10/5-20)

A "full-time employee" is an individual who is employed for consideration for at least 35 hours each week or who renders any other standard of service generally accepted by industry custom or practice as full-time employment (35 ILCS 10/5-5). An employee of a professional employer organization is a full-time employee if employed in the service of the applicant for at least 35 hours each week or who renders any other standard of service generally accepted by industry custom or practice as full-time employment to applicant.

Amount of credit: The credit is equal to the lesser of:

— 50% of the income tax withheld from new employees, plus 10% of their training costs; or

— 100% of the income tax withheld from new employees (35 ILCS 10/5-5).

If the business is located in an underserved area that meets certain poverty, unemployement, and federal assistance rates, then the amount of the credit may not exceed the lesser of:

— 75% of the income tax withheld from new employees, plus 10% of their training costs; or

— 100% of the income tax withheld from new employees (35 ILCS 10/5-5).

Businesses that agree to hire the required number of new employees may claim an additional credit of 25% of the income tax withheld for employees that are retained at the same location as the new employees (35 ILCS 10/5-5).

Carryover: Unused credits may be carried forward and applied to the tax liability of the five tax years following the excess credit year.

A taxpayer may not generally claim the credit for jobs relocated from one site in Illinois to another, although there are exceptions.

Eligible costs: The aggregate amount of costs include the following: (1) capital investment including, but not limited to, equipment, buildings, and land; (2) infrastructure development; (3) debt service, except refinancing of current debt; (4) research and development; (5) job training and education; (6) lease costs; or (7) relocation costs.

Loss of credit: The agreement that taxpayers must enter into with the DCEO must provide that if the taxpayer does not meet either the investment requirement or the job creation and retention requirement specified in the agreement during the five-year period beginning on the first day of the first taxable year in which the agreement is executed and ending on the last day of the fifth taxable year after the agreement is executed, then (1) the agreement is automatically terminated on the last day of the fifth taxable year after the agreement is executed and (2) the taxpayer is not entitled to the award of any credits for any of that five-year period. Effective beginning September 18, 2017, the agreement must also include a provision specifying that, if the taxpayer ceases principal operations with the intent to shut down the project in the state permanently during the term of the agreement, then the entire credit

¶413

amount awarded to the taxpayer before the date the taxpayer ceases principal operations must be returned to the DCEO and reallocated to the local workforce investment area in which the project was located. (35 ILCS 10/5-50)

Pass-through entities: Pass-through entities that are awarded a credit may treat the credit as a tax payment. The term "tax payment" is also defined as a composite payment made by a pass-through entity on behalf of any of its shareholders or partners to satisfy such shareholders' or partners' taxes. (35 ILCS 10/5-15(g))

¶414 Earned Income Tax Credit

Law: Income Tax Act, Sec. 212 [34 ILCS 5/212] (CCH ILLINOIS TAX REPORTS, ¶ 16-820).

Comparable Federal: Sec. 32 (U.S. MASTER TAX GUIDE, ¶ 1375).

Individual taxpayers are entitled to an earned income tax credit (EITC) against personal income tax (35 ILCS 5/212). The Illinois EITC is equal to:

— 5% of the federal EITC for taxable years ending before December 31, 2012;

— 7.5% of the federal EITC for taxable years beginning on or after January 1, 2012 and ending before December 31, 2013;

— 10% of the federal EITC for taxable years beginning on or after January 1, 2013 and ending before 2017;

— 14% of the federal EITC for taxable years beginning on or after January 1, 2017 and ending before 2018; and

— 18% of the federal EITC for taxable years beginning on or after January 1, 2018.

The credit is refundable, and may not be included in the taxpayer's income. For a nonresident or part-year resident, the amount of the credit is in proportion to the amount of income attributable to Illinois.

The credit is exempt from sunset provisions that apply to credits generally (35 ILCS 5/212).

Practitioner Comment: Earned Income Tax Credit and the Standard Exemption Expanded

Illinois Public Act 97-0652 (SB 400), Laws 2010, increased Illinois's earned income credit to 7.5% of the federal credit for tax year 2012 and 10% for tax year 2013 and beyond. The law also provides that the standard exemption is $2,050 for taxable years ending on or after December 31, 2012 and prior to December 31, 2013, and $2,050 plus a cost-of-living adjustment for taxable years ending on or after December 31, 2013. (35 ILCS 130/5).

Both the Taxpayer's Federation of Illinois and the Illinois Chamber of Commerce were successful in lobbying for a rollback of the decoupling from bonus depreciation. The decoupling from the bonus depreciation was the "funding" needed for other items in SB 397 such as the Sears/CME tax relief and the limiting of the NOL suspension. Further, the key to passage of both bills was separating the large omnibus bill into two parts: Tax changes for employers and tax changes for individuals.

Jennifer A. Zimmerman, Esq., Horwood Marcus & Berk, Chartered

---

When an individual files an amended federal return claiming an earned income credit, an amended Illinois return claiming the credit cannot be filed until after the federal amendment is agreed to by the IRS. The amended Illinois return then must be filed within 120 days after the IRS has reached such a conclusion. See *Administrative Hearing Decision No. IT 13-07,* Illinois Department of Revenue, October 18, 2013, CCH ILLINOIS TAX REPORTS, ¶ 402-725.

¶415   Affordable Housing Credit

Law: Income Tax Act, Sec. 214 [35 ILCS 5/214]; Housing Development Act, Sec. 7.28 [20 ILCS 3805/7.28]; 47 Ill. Adm. Code Sec. 355.103 et seq. (CCH ILLINOIS TAX REPORTS, ¶16-905).

Comparable Federal: Sec. 42 (U.S. MASTER TAX GUIDE, ¶1334).

An affordable housing tax credit is available in connection with the acquisition, construction, rehabilitation, and financing of an affordable housing project to a taxpayer who makes a donation between January 1, 2002, and December 31, 2021 (35 ILCS 5/214).

An affordable housing project is either (1) a rental project in which at least 25% of the units have rents not exceeding 30% of the gross monthly income of a household earning the maximum income for a low income household or (2) a unit for sale to low income households who will pay no more than 30% of their gross household income for mortgage principal, interest, property taxes, and property insurance upon the purchase of the unit (20 ILCS 3805/7.28).

A donation includes money, securities, or real or personal property that is donated to a not-for-profit sponsor and that is used solely for costs associated with either the purchasing, constructing, or rehabilitating an affordable housing project, an employer-assisted housing project, general operating support, or technical assistance.

A low income household is a household whose adjusted income is less than or equal to 60% of the median income of the geographical area of the household's affordable housing project, adjusted for family size.

Credit amount: The amount of the credit is 50% of the value of the donation. The minimum amount of a donation is $10,000 (20 ILCS 3805/7.28).

Planning considerations: A taxpayer must complete and remit an application to the Illinois Housing Development Authority indicating the taxpayer's ability to meet the requirements imposed by the Act, the financial feasibility of the project, the chance of successful construction, evidence of site control, the amount of the proposed donation, and the location of the project. The agency will issue of certificate of approval to qualifying taxpayers.

Funds used by a donor to acquire an ownership interest in an affordable housing project will not qualify as a donation.

If the amount of the credit exceeds the tax liability for the year, the excess may be carried forward for five taxable years following the excess credit year.

Transfer provisions: A donor, including persons or entities not subject to income tax, may transfer the tax credit to another individual or entity if the transfer is made to an individual or entity that has purchased land for the affordable housing project or another donor that has made a donation to the affordable housing project for which a certificate was issued. The certificate must indicate the name of the original donor and the name of the entity to which the certificate is transferred. (20 ILCS 3805/7.28)

¶416   Credit for Hiring Post-9/11 Veterans

Law: Income Tax Act, Sec. 217.1 [35 ILCS 5/217.1] (CCH ILLINOIS TAX REPORTS, ¶16-875a).

An income tax credit is available for employing qualified veterans initially hired by the taxpayer on or after June 1, 2012. A "qualified veteran" is a person who was an honorably-discharged member of the Armed Forces of the United States, the Illinois National Guard, or any reserve component of the Armed Forces of the United States who served on active duty on or after September 11, 2001. Additionally, the veteran must have been unemployed for an aggregate period of four weeks or more during the six-week period ending on the Saturday immediately preceding the date he or she was hired by the taxpayer. (35 ILCS 5/217.1)

Credit amount: The credit is equal to 20% of the gross wages paid to the qualified veteran, but may not exceed $5,000 (35 ILCS 5/217.1).

Planning considerations: The sunset date for claiming a veterans jobs credit for qualified veterans was tax years beginning on or after January 1, 2015 (35 ILCS 5/217(a); 35 ILCS 5/250(a)). However, the Illinois jobs credit for qualified unemployed veterans is scheduled to sunset for tax years after 2016 (35 ILCS 5/217.1(a)).

The credit may be carried forward for five years, and taxpayers claiming this credit may not claim a different credit for the same veteran for that taxable year. (35 ILCS 5/217.1)

Prior law: For taxable years beginning after 2006 and ending before 2011, a credit could be taken for wages paid to qualified veterans. (35 ILCS 5/217)

The credit was equal to 10%, but could not exceed $1200 of the gross wages paid by the taxpayer to a qualified veteran in the course of that veteran's sustained employment during the taxable year.

If the amount of the credit exceeds the tax liability for the tax year, the excess may be carried forward and applied to the tax liability of the five taxable years following the excess credit year. If there are credits for more than one year that are available to offset a liability, the earlier credits must be applied first.

¶417 Film and Live Theater Production Services Credits

Law: Film Production Services Tax Credit Act, Sec. 10 [35 ILCS 16/1 *et seq.*]; Live Theater Production Tax Credit Act, Secs. 30 and 45 [35 ILCS 17/30; 35 ILCS 17/45]; Income Tax Act, Secs. 213 and 222 [35 ILCS 5/213; 35 ILCS 5/222]; 14 Ill. Adm. Code Sec. 528.10 *et seq.*; 14 Ill. Adm. Code 532.10 *et seq.* (CCH ILLINOIS TAX REPORTS, ¶16-875b).

Film producers are allowed a nonrefundable credit against Illinois corporate income tax and personal income tax for a portion of the salary or wages paid to employees for services on an accredited production in Illinois (35 ILCS 5/213). A credit for live theater productions, discussed separately below, is also available (35 ILCS 5/222).

"Accredited production" means a film, video, or television production in which the Illinois production spending (for productions beginning before May 1, 2006, aggregate Illinois labor expenditures) exceed $100,000 for productions of 30 minutes or longer, or $50,000 for productions of less than 30 minutes (35 ILCS 15/10). An accredited production must be certified by the Department of Commerce and Economic Opportunity (DCEO) and excludes certain types of programming, such as news or current events, talk shows, game and awards shows, sports events, and productions produced primarily for industrial, corporate, or institutional purposes. An applicant proposing a film or television production in Illinois may apply to the DCEO for an accredited production certificate, which would certify that the production meets credit guidelines.

The credit includes an "accredited animated production," which is defined as an accredited production in which movement and characters' performances are created using a frame-by-frame technique and a significant number of major characters are animated. Motion capture by itself is not an animation technique. (35 ILCS 16/10)

Credit amount: For an accredited production beginning on or after January 1, 2009, the credit equals (1) 30% (formerly, 20%) of the Illinois production spending for the taxable year plus (2) 15% of the Illinois labor expenditures generated by the employment of residents of geographic areas of high poverty or high unemployment (as determined by the DCEO). A taxpayer's Illinois labor expenditures are limited to the first $100,000 of wages paid or incurred to each employee of a production beginning on or after May 1, 2006. (35 ILCS 16/10)

Planning considerations: A film producer must file an application with the DCEO for the credit. If the application is approved, the DCEO will issue a certificate stating the amount of the tax credit to which the applicant is entitled. The credit may be passed through partnerships to partners and through subchapter S corporations to shareholders. The credit may not reduce the taxpayer's liability to less than zero.

Applicants requesting credits for an accredited animated production commencing on or after July 1, 2010, may make an application to the DCEO in each taxable year beginning with the taxable year in which the production commences and ending with the taxable year in which production is complete (35 ILCS 16/44).

The film production services credit may not be claimed for tax years beginning on or after May 6, 2021 (35 ILCS 16/42). The General Assembly may extend the sunset date by five-year intervals.

Carryover: If the amount of the credit exceeds the film producer's tax liability for the year, the excess may be carried forward for up to five taxable years (35 ILCS 5/213). The credit may not be carried back. The credit must be applied to the earliest year for which there is a tax liability. If there are credits from more than one taxable year that are available to offset a tax liability, the earliest credit must be applied first.

Credit transfers: A film producer earning the credit is specifically allowed to transfer the credit within one year after the credit is awarded, in accordance with rules adopted by the Department of Commerce and Economic Opportunity (35 ILCS 5/213; 14 Ill. Adm. Code Sec. 528.10 *et seq.*).

Live theater production credit: Certain taxpayers who are theater producers, owners, licensees, or operators, or who otherwise present live stage presentations, may claim a nonrefundable credit against their income tax liability, effective for tax years beginning on or after January 1, 2012 and before January 1, 2022, equal to 20% of the Illinois labor expenditures for each tax year, plus 20% of the Illinois production spending for each tax year, plus 15% of the Illinois labor expenditures generated by the employment of Illinois residents in geographic areas of high poverty or high unemployment in each tax year. (35 ILCS 5/222; 35 ILCS 17/10-45; 14 Ill. Adm. Code Sec. 532.10–532.120)

Eligibility for the credit is determined by the Department of Commerce and Economic Opportunity (35 ILCS 17/10-30). A total of $2 million in credits are to be awarded each year on a first come, first served basis. The tax credit award may not be carried back and can be carried forward five years (35 ILCS 5/222(e)).

¶418 New Markets Credit

Law: New Markets Development Program Act, Sec. 663 [20 ILCS 663/1 *et seq.*](CCH ILLINOIS TAX REPORTS, ¶16-830a).

The New Markets Development Program includes a credit against the corporate and personal income, franchise, and the insurance and gross premiums taxes for taxpayers who make qualified cash equity investments in a qualified community development entity. This credit is set to expire after the 2021 fiscal year. (20 ILCS 663/1, 20 ILCS 663/50)

A "qualified equity investment" is any equity investment in, or long-term debt security issued by, a qualified community development entity that (1) is acquired after the effective date of this legislation at its original issuance solely in exchange for cash; (2) has at least 100% (85% for investments made before January 1, 2017) of its cash purchase price used by the issuer to make qualified low-income community investments in the state; and (3) is designated by the issuer as a qualified equity investment under IRC §45D and is certified by the Department of Commerce and

Economic Opportunity as not exceeding the annual cap. This term includes any qualified equity investment that does not meet the provisions of item (1) of this definition if the investment was a qualified equity investment in the hands of a prior holder. (20 ILCS 663/5)

Credit amount: Upon certification, taxpayers who make qualified equity investments earn a vested right to tax credits, as follows (20 ILCS 663/10):

— on each credit allowance date of the investment, the purchaser of the investment, or subsequent holder of the investment, is entitled to a tax credit during the taxable year including that credit allowance date;

— the tax credit amount is equal to the applicable percentage (0% for each of the first two credit allowance dates, 7% for the third, and 8% for the next four credit allowance dates) for such credit allowance date multiplied by the purchase price paid to the issuer of the qualified equity investment; and

— the amount of the tax credit claimed can not exceed the amount of the state tax liability of the holder, or the person or entity to whom the credit is allocated for use, for the tax year for which the tax credit is claimed.

The total amount of credits allowed under this program is capped at $20 million per year (20 ILCS 663/20). Unused credits may be carried forward up to 5 years. (20 ILCS 663/15)

Credits received under the program are not refundable or saleable on the open market. Credits earned by a pass-through entity are to be allocated to the partners, members, or shareholders of that entity according to their agreement. (20 ILCS 663/15)

For additional details about this credit, see ¶1217.

¶419 Credit for Employers Who Match Employees' College Savings Contributions

Law: Income Tax Act, Sec. 203 [35 ILCS 5/203.], Income Tax Act, Sec. 218 [35 ILCS 5/218.] (CCH ILLINOIS TAX REPORTS, ¶16-915).

Applicable to tax years 2009 through 2020, a credit is available for employers who make matching contributions to a College Savings Pool Account (pool) or to the Illinois Prepaid Tuition Trust Fund (trust) in the same year that a contribution is made by an employee of the taxpayer. (35 ILCS 5/203(a)(2)(D-22); 35 ILCS 5/218)

Credit amount: The credit is in the amount of 25% of the employer's contribution up to $500 per employee (35 ILCS 5/218(a)).

Planning considerations: The credit may not be carried back and may be carried forward up to five years (35 ILCS 5/218(c)).

An addition modification to the taxpayer's base income is required in the amount of the credit.

For purposes of the personal income subtraction modification for contributions made to the pool and trust, matching contributions are treated as made by the employee.

¶420 Credits for Historic Structure Rehabilitation

Law: Income Tax Act, Sec. 219 [35 ILCS 5/219.], Income Tax Act, Sec. 221 [35 ILCS 5/221] (CCH ILLINOIS TAX REPORTS, ¶12-090).

Instead of a general credit for rehabilitation or restoration of historic structures, Illinois has enacted credits for specific rehabilitation projects, as follows:

• *River Edge Redevelopment Zone projects*

For tax years beginning after 2011 and ending before 2022, an historic preservation income tax credit is allowed for a portion of the qualified expenditures incurred pursuant to a qualified rehabilitation plan by a qualified taxpayer during the taxable year in the restoration and preservation of a qualified historic structure located in a River Edge Redevelopment Zone (35 ILCS 5/221). The total amount of expenditures must equal at least $5,000 and must exceed 50% of the purchase price of the property.

A "qualified historic structure" means a certified historic structure as defined under IRC Sec. 47(c)(3). A "qualified rehabilitation plan "means a project that is approved by the Historic Preservation Agency as being consistent with the standards in effect on July 28, 2011, for rehabilitation as adopted by the U.S. Secretary of the Interior. (35 ILCS 5/221(d))

A "qualified taxpayer" means the owner of the qualified historic structure or any other person who qualifies for the federal rehabilitation credit that is allowed by IRC Sec. 47 with respect to the qualified historic structure. A "qualified expenditure" means all the costs and expenses that are defined as qualified rehabilitation expenditures under IRC Sec. 47 that were incurred in connection with a qualified historic structure. (35 ILCS 5/221(d))

Credit amount: The credit is allowed in an amount equal to 25% of the qualified expenditures incurred (35 ILCS 5/221(a)), but may not reduce a taxpayer's liability to less than zero (35 ILCS 5/221(c)).

Planning considerations: In order to obtain the credit, a taxpayer must apply with the Department of Commerce and Economic Opportunity, and the department, in consultation with the Historic Preservation Agency, must determine the amount of eligible rehabilitation costs and expenses. The Historic Preservation Agency must also determine whether the rehabilitation is consistent with the standards of the U.S. Secretary of the Interior for rehabilitation. (35 ILCS 5/221(b))

River Edge Redevelopment Zones are authorized in Aurora, East St. Louis, Elgin, Rockford, and Peoria (65 ILCS 115/10-5.3).

• *Peoria project*

An income tax credit is available for the renovation of qualified historic structures in the city of Peoria (namely, the Hotel Pere Marquette). A "qualified taxpayer" is the owner of the qualified historic structure or any other person who may qualify for the federal rehabilitation credit allowed by IRC Sec. 47. "Qualified expenditures" means all the costs and expenses defined as qualified rehabilitation expenditures under IRC Sec. 47 that were incurred in connection with a qualified historic structure. (35 ILCS 5/219)

Credit amount: The credit is allowed in an amount equal to 25% of the qualified expenditures incurred by a qualified taxpayer during the taxable year in the restoration and preservation of the structure pursuant to a qualified rehabilitation plan, provided that the total amount of such expenditures is at least $5,000 and it exceeds 50% of the purchase price of the property.

Planning considerations: The credit may be claimed for taxable years beginning on or after January 1, 2010, and ending on or before December 31, 2015. The project must be approved by the Historic Preservation Agency as being consistent with the standards in effect for rehabilitation as adopted by the federal Secretary of the Interior. Unused credit can be carried forward for up to 10 years and may be transferred. The total amount of credits that can be awarded to one qualified rehabilitation plan is $10 million.

If the taxpayer is a corporation having a federal Subchapter S election, a partnership, or a limited liability company, the credit may be claimed by the shareholders of the corporation, the partners of the partnership, or the members of the limited liability company in the same manner as those shareholders, partners, or members account for their proportionate shares of the income or losses of the corporation, partnership, or limited liability company, or as provided in the bylaws or other executed agreement of the corporation, partnership, or limited liability company. Credits granted to a partnership, a limited liability company taxed as a partnership, or other multiple owners of property will be passed through to the partners, members, or owners respectively on a pro rata basis or pursuant to an executed agreement among the partners, members, or owners documenting any alternate distribution method. (P.A. 96-0933 (S.B. 2534), Laws 2010)

¶421 Angel Investor Credit

Law: Income Tax Act, Sec. 220 [35 ILCS 5/220.]; 14 Ill. Adm. Code Sec. 531.10 through 531.90 (CCH ILLINOIS TAX REPORTS, ¶16-830b).

Effective for taxable years 2011 through 2021, a nonrefundable and nontransferable tax credit may be claimed for a portion of a taxpayer's equity investment of at least $10,000 made directly in a qualified new business venture. Taxpayers eligible to apply for the credit include a corporation, partnership, limited liability company, or a natural person that makes an investment in a qualified new business venture. The term "applicant" does not include a corporation, partnership, limited liability company, or a natural person who has a direct or indirect ownership interest of at least 51% in the profits, capital, or value of the investment or a related member. (35 ILCS 5/220)

Credit amount: The credit may be claimed in an amount equal to 25% of the taxpayer's investment made directly in a qualified new business venture. (35 ILCS 5/220(b)) The maximum amount of a taxpayer's investment that may be used as the basis for a credit is $2 million for each investment. (35 ILCS 5/220(c)) The annual cap on credits is $10 million of which:

— $500,000 is reserved for businesses owned by minorities, women, and individuals with a disability; and

— $500,000 is reserved for businesses that are located in counties with a population of 250,000 or less.

Planning considerations: A business venture must satisfy the following conditions before it can be registered as a qualified business (35 ILCS 5/220(e)):

— it has its headquarters in Illinois;

— at least 51% of its employees are employed in Illinois;

— it has the potential for increasing jobs or capital investments, or both, in Illinois and either, (1) it is principally engaged in innovation in manufacturing, biotechnology, nanotechnology, communications, agricultural sciences, clean energy creation or storage technology, processing or assembling products (including medical devices, pharmaceuticals, computer software or hardware, semiconductors, other innovative technology products, or other products that are produced using manufacturing methods that are enabled by applying proprietary technology), or providing services that are enabled by applying proprietary technology, or (2) it is undertaking pre-commercialization activity related to proprietary technology that includes conducting research, developing a new product or business process, or developing a service that is principally reliant on applying proprietary technology;

— it is not principally engaged in real estate development, insurance, banking, lending, lobbying, political consulting, professional services provided by attorneys, accountants, business consultants, physicians, or health care consultants, wholesale or retail trade, leisure, hospitality, transportation, or construction, except construction of power production plants that derive energy from a renewable energy resource, as defined in the Illinois Power Agency Act;

— it has fewer than 100 employees;

— it has been in operation in Illinois for not more than 10 consecutive years prior to the year of certification; and

— it has received not more than $10 million in aggregate private equity investment in cash and not more than $4 million in investments that qualified for tax credits under this section.

The businesses must have applied for and received certification for the taxable year in which the investment was made prior to the date on which the investment was made (35 ILCS 5/220(b)).

Unused credit may be carried forward for five years.

Practitioner Comment: Importance of Angel Investor Credit

Angel investment tax credits are a win-win-win proposition. New business ventures benefit from an infusion of capital from the angel investors. The investors/taxpayers benefit from the tax credit, which effectively serves as an immediate return on their investments. Lastly, states benefit because the creation of new businesses increases employment and innovation, which ultimately enhances the local economy.

David A. Hughes, Esq., Horwood Marcus & Berk Chartered

¶422 Small Business Job Creation Credit (closed)

Law: Income Tax Act, Sec. 25 [35 ILCS 25/25]; 14 Ill. Adm. Code Sec. 529.80; 86 Ill. Adm. Code Sec. 100.7380 (CCH Illinois Tax Reports, ¶16-875d).

The small business job creation credit is available for eligible businesses, but the credit is closed to new applicants. Eligible businesses are entitled to a credit against withholding taxes in connection with the hiring of new full-time employees during an incentive period beginning on July 1 and ending on June 30 of the following year. The first incentive period began on July 1, 2010 and the last incentive period ended on June 30, 2016. The required net increase in the number of employees is based on the employer's number of Illinois employees as of June 30 of the incentive period. (35 ILCS 25/25(a), (e), and (f)) This credit must be claimed in the first year ending on or after the day commerce department issues a tax credit certificate to the taxpayer. (35 ILCS 25/25(c); 86 Ill. Adm. Code Sec. 100.7380(b))

Credit amount: For small businesses with less than 50 employees, the credit is $2,500 per job on withholding tax for employers who hire new, full-time Illinois employees during an incentive period if the net increase in the employer's full-time Illinois employees is maintained for at least 12 months (35 ILCS 25/25(a)(2)).

Businesses that hired "Put Illinois to Work" worker-trainees between July 1, 2010, and June 30, 2011, are entitled to 1/2 of the credit, $1,250, allowable if that employee is employed for at least 6 months after the date of hire. The employer is entitled to the other half of the credit, $1,250, if that employee is employed for at least 12 months after the date of hire. (35 ILCS 25/25(d); 14 Ill. Adm. Code Sec. 529.80; 86 Ill. Adm. Code Sec. 100.7380(b))

Planning considerations: An individual for whom a W-2 is issued by a professional employer organization (PEO) is a full-time employee if he or she is employed in the service of the taxpayer for a basic wage for at least 35 hours each week or renders any other standard of service generally accepted by industry custom or practice as full-time employment (35 ILCS 25/10). A PEO does not include a regulated day and temporary labor service agency.

¶422

The state has created a website that allows taxpayers to register, keep abreast of any announcements, as well as obtain general information concerning the credit: http://jobstaxcredit.illinois.gov/. For more information on the credit, see ¶1221.

¶423 Credit for Hospital Owners

Law: Income Tax Act, Sec. 223 [35 ILCS 5/223] (CCH ILLINOIS TAX REPORTS, ¶16-950b).

For tax years ending on or after December 31, 2012, a credit against personal and corporate income taxes is available for qualified hospital owners (35 ILCS 5/223). The credit applies to owners of hospitals licensed under the Hospital Licensing Act, but not to organizations that are exempt from federal income taxes.

Credit amount: The credit is equal to the lesser of (35 ILCS 5/223):

— the amount of real property taxes paid during the tax year on real property used for hospital purposes during the prior tax year; or

— the cost of free or discounted services provided during the tax year pursuant to the hospital's charitable financial assistance policy, measured at cost.

Planning considerations: The credit may be passed through to partners of partnerships and shareholders of S corporations (35 ILCS 5/223(b)).

Unused credit may be carried forward for five years. The credit will be applied to the earliest year for which there is a tax liability. If there are credits from more than one tax year that are available to offset a liability, the earlier credit will be applied first. (35 ILCS 5/223(b))

¶424 School Instructional Materials and Supplies Credit

Law: Income Tax Act, Sec. 223 [35 ILCS 5/225] (CCH ILLINOIS TAX REPORTS, ¶16-915b).

Effective for taxable years beginning on or after January 1, 2017, teachers, instructors, counselors, principals, or aides who work at least 900 hours in a public or non-public school during the school year may claim a credit against personal income tax liability for the purchase of classroom instructional materials and supplies (35 ILCS 5/225).

Credit amount: The credit is equal to the amount paid for classroom instructional materials and supplies or $250, whichever is less. The credit may not reduce the taxpayer's liability to less than zero (35 ILCS 5/225).

Planning considerations: Unused classroom instructional material and supply credits may be carried forward up to 5 years (35 ILCS 5/225)

¶425 School Instructional Materials and Supplies Credit

Law: Income Tax Act, Sec. 224 [35 ILCS 5/224] (CCH ILLINOIS TAX REPORTS, ¶16-915c).

Effective for taxable years beginning on or after January 1, 2018 and ending before January 1, 2023, taxpayers who have been awarded a tax credit certificate by the Illinois Department of Revenue (DOR) for making a qualified contribution to nonprofit organizations that use at least 95% of the contribution received during a taxable year for scholarships to low-income elementary or high school students may claim a credit against Illinois personal income tax liability. (35 ILCS 5/224)

Credit amount: The credit is equal to 75% of the total amount of qualified contributions made by the taxpayer during a taxable year up to a maximum of $1 million. The total amount of all credits the DOR may award in any calendar year may not exceed $75 million. If the annual cap is not reached by June 1 of a given year, remaining credits will be awarded on a first-come, first-served basis. (Uncodified §10, (S.B. 1947) Laws 2017)

Planning considerations: The credit may be passed through to partners of partnerships and shareholders of S corporations (35 ILCS 5/224).

Unused credits may be carried forward and applied to a taxpayer's tax liability for up to 5 taxable years following the excess credit year. (35 ILCS 5/224)

PERSONAL INCOME TAX
CHAPTER 5
RETURNS AND PAYMENT

¶501 Annual Returns and Payments Required

Law: Income Tax Act, Sec. 501 [35 ILCS 5/501]; Income Tax Act, Sec. 502(a), (f) [35 ILCS 5/502]; Income Tax Act, Sec. 505(a) [35 ILCS 5/505]; Income Tax Act, Sec. 601(a) [35 ILCS 5/601]; 86 Ill. Adm. Code Sec. 100.5130 (CCH ILLINOIS TAX REPORTS, ¶ 15-105, 15-205, 15-255, 17-155).

Comparable Federal: Secs. 6001—6012 (U.S. MASTER TAX GUIDE, ¶ 124).

Forms: IL-1040, IL-1041, IL-1065.

An Illinois income tax return must be filed by every person (individual, estate, trust) for any taxable year (35 ILCS 5/502):

— for which the person is liable for the Illinois income tax; or

— in the case of a resident, for which such person is required to make a federal return, regardless of whether the person is liable for the Illinois income tax, unless the person has an Illinois base income of $2,000 or less and is claimed as a dependent on another's federal or Illinois tax return.

Annual returns for an individual, partnership, or fiduciary are due on or before April 15 of the year following the taxable year (35 ILCS 5/505). Any tax due must be paid at the time of filing the annual return.

• *Replacement tax*

A personal property replacement income tax return must be filed by every trust or partnership (except investment partnerships—see ¶ 852) for each taxable year (35 ILCS 5/505(a)(2)). The replacement tax is reported with the income tax by trusts filing Form IL-1041. Partnerships report replacement tax on Form IL-1065. Payment of any tax is due with the return. Partnerships and trusts replacement income tax returns are due on or before the 15th day of the fourth month following the close of the taxable year (35 ILCS 5/505(a)(2)). Any tax due must be paid at the time of filing the annual return.

• *Composite returns*

Effective for tax years before 2015, nonresident individual partners of the same partnership, nonresident shareholders of the same S corporation, and nonresident individuals operating an insurance business in Illinois under a Lloyd's plan of operation could elect to file composite individual income tax returns showing the individuals' composite income allocable to Illinois. Taxpayers who made this election must also make composite payments (35 ILCS 5/502(f); 86 Ill. Adm. Code Sec. 100.5130).

Composite returns may include the income tax owed by Illinois residents from their income from partnerships, S corporations, and insurance businesses operating under a Lloyd's plan. These Illinois residents may also claim credits on their individual returns for their shares of the composite tax payments (86 Ill. Adm. Code Secs. 100.5100—100.5170). For additional information, see ¶859.

Residents may be included in a composite return if the Department of Revenue determines from a partnership's petition that no other method of filing would achieve the same degree of compliance and administrative ease for both the DOR and the taxpayer. The factors to be considered in allowing resident partners to be included in a composite partnership return include the number of partners involved, the inability of the partnership's authorized agent to file a composite return in another manner, and the availability of a reliable method for claiming credit on the separate individual returns (*General Information Letter IT 05-0045-GIL*, Illinois Department of Revenue, September 21, 2005; CCH ILLINOIS TAX REPORTS, ¶401–590).

• *Payments*

There are several payment methods available to taxpayers. Individual taxpayers can pay tax using, credit cards, direct debit, check, or money order (IL-1040 Instructions). Taxpayers who owe withholding tax can remit the amount due with the withholding form or may be required to use the electronic funds transfer method of payment. For additional information on payments, see ¶2402.

• *Abusive tax shelters*

Any material advisor required to make a return under IRC Sec. 6111 with respect to a reportable transaction must send a duplicate of the return to the Department of Revenue not later than the federal filing date. Any person required to maintain an investors list under IRC Sec. 6112 regarding federal abusive tax shelters must furnish a duplicate of such list to the Department of Revenue not later than the earlier of the time such list is required to be furnished to the Internal Revenue Service for inspection under IRC Sec. 6112 or the date of written request by the Department (35 ILCS 5/1007).

The above requirements apply to any reportable transaction having a nexus with Illinois. A reportable transaction has nexus with Illinois if, at the time the transaction is entered into, the transaction has one or more investors that is an Illinois taxpayer. A penalty is imposed on any taxpayer who fails to include on a return or statement any information with respect to a reportable transaction that is required by state or federal law to be included with such return or statement. For additional information on penalties, see ¶2503.

• *Tax Preparers*

Effective for taxable years beginning on or after January 1, 2017, preparers of Illinois personal income tax returns must include their preparer tax identification number (PTIN) on any return or claim for a tax refund prepared by the preparer. (35 ILCS 35/10; 86 Ill. Adm. Code 9910).

The term "income tax return preparer" means any person who prepares for compensation, or who employs one or more persons to prepare for compensation, any Illinois income tax return or refund claim. The preparation of a substantial portion of a return or claim for refund will be treated as the preparation of that return or claim for refund. (35 ILCS 5/1501(a)(26); 86 Ill. Adm. Code 9910) The PTIN requirement applies only to a preparer who would be considered the "signing tax return preparer" under federal regulations and only to an income tax return preparer who holds an active PTIN at the time of filing the Illinois return or claim for refund. If there is an employment relationship or association between the individual required to sign a return and another person, the name, Employer Identification Number (EIN), and signature of that other person must be included on the filed return or claim for refund when required by department forms (86 Ill. Adm. Code 9910).

The PTIN information allows the department to identify preparers who prepare fraudulent or otherwise erroneous returns, and returns reflecting unsubstantiated tax positions. The department will share and exchange PTIN information with the Internal Revenue Service (IRS) on income tax return preparers who are suspected of fraud, disciplined, or barred from filing tax returns with the department or the IRS. The department will share similar enforcement or discipline information with other states (86 Ill. Adm. Code 9910).

The department may investigate the actions of any income tax return preparer doing business in Illinois and may bar or suspend an income tax return preparer from filing returns for good cause. A penalty of $50 for each offense, up to $25,000, may be imposed against any preparer for failing to provide his or her PTIN, unless it is shown that the failure is due to reasonable cause and not due to willful neglect. (35 ILCS 35/15, Laws 2016; 86 Ill. Adm. Code 9910)

Practitioner Comment: Tax Preparer Oversight Act

The DOR's objective in instituting the Tax Preparer Oversight Act (35 ILCS 35/1) is to recognize and document questionable return practices by income tax return preparers. The DOR is also required to establish communications protocols with the Commissioner of the Internal Revenue Service to exchange PTIN information of income tax preparers suspected of fraud or barred from filing returns. As a result, tax preparers should be aware that the Department and IRS will be dually monitoring the tax positions of income tax preparers in search of potential patterns of errors.

Samantha K. Breslow, Esq., Horwood Marcus & Berk, Chartered

¶502 Annual Returns—Extension of Time for Filing

Law: Income Tax Act, Sec. 505(b) [35 ILCS 5/505]; Income Tax Act, Sec. 602 [35 ILCS 5/602](CCH ILLINOIS TAX REPORTS, ¶ 17-155).

Comparable Federal: Sec. 6081 (U.S. MASTER TAX GUIDE, ¶ 120).

Forms: IL-505-I, Automatic Extension Payment for Individuals.

An extension for filing the return does not extend the time for paying the tax (35 ILCS 5/602(a)).

• *Extension on the basis of federal extension*

Taxpayers with extensions of time to file their federal income tax returns are granted equal extensions for their Illinois returns (35 ILCS 5/505(b)). To qualify for the extension, a taxpayer with tax due must file Form IL-505-I, "Application for Extension of Time to File Form IL-1040" with payment of the amount estimated as the tax for the year. The application and payment are due by the due date for filing the return (without regard to extensions). Taxpayers with federal extensions and no Illinois tax due for the year are granted an automatic extension to file the Illinois return without having to file the application. A copy of the approved federal extension must be attached to the Illinois return.

If an Illinois extension based on a federal extension is for longer than six months, the taxpayer must attach to the Illinois income tax return when filed a copy of the approved federal extension or the application for an automatic federal extension.

• *Military personnel*

U.S. military personnel serving in combat zones are usually granted Illinois individual income tax return extensions that conform to the maximum time extensions allowed for federal tax purposes (see ¶ 104).

• *Foreign travelers' extension*

The return of a separately filing individual living or traveling outside the United States on April 15 is due June 15, and the joint return of a husband and wife is also due June 15 if at least one spouse is living or traveling outside the country on April 15 (35 ILCS 5/505(c)).

• *Illinois-only extensions*

Taxpayers who do not have an extension to file their federal returns and who do not qualify for the foreign travel extension may be granted an extension of six months, by filing Form IL-505-I. Taxpayers with no Illinois tax due for the year are granted an extension without having to file an application.

If there is tax due, the taxpayer should transmit the payment with Form IL-505-I by the original filing due date in order to avoid an underpayment penalty and interest.

¶503 Copies of Federal Return May Be Required

Law: Income Tax Act, Sec. 506(a) [35 ILCS 5/506]; 86 Ill. Adm. Code Sec. 100.5080.

Taxpayers required to file Illinois tax returns may be required, at the request of the Department, to furnish a copy of any return filed under the Internal Revenue Code (35 ILCS 5/506(a)).

Practitioner Comment: Tax Shelter Disclosure Requirements

Following California's lead in enacting tax shelter legislation in October 2003, the Illinois General Assembly in July 2004 also enacted tax shelter legislation. Illinois taxpayers are now required to file with the Department a copy of their federal disclosure statement with respect to reportable transactions. See 86 Ill. Adm. Code Sec. 100.5080.

See ¶ 2503 for penalties that are imposed for failure to disclose a reportable transaction.

Horwood Marcus & Berk Chartered

¶504 Filing Status

Law: Income Tax Act, Sec. 502(c) [35 ILCS 5/502]; 86 Ill. Adm. Code Sec. 760.100 (CCH ILLINOIS TAX REPORTS, ¶ 15-125).

Comparable Federal: Sec. 6013 (U.S. MASTER TAX GUIDE, ¶ 152—175).

For tax years ending on or after December 31, 2009, spouses who file federal joint returns are authorized to file separate returns for state personal income tax purposes. The election to file separately must be made on or before the due date of the return, including applicable extensions. (35 ILCS 5/502(c)(1)(B)) Effective for taxable years beginning after 2013, any taxpayer who is required to file a joint Illinois personal income tax return and who is not included on that return and does not file a separate return is deemed to have failed to file a return; see ¶ 2503.

Individuals: Taxpayers filing as single, head of household, or qualifying widow(er) for federal purposes must do so for Illinois also, according to form instructions.

Same-sex couples: Marital status as of Dec. 31, 2014, or later will determine the status for tax filing purposes (**http://tax.illinois.gov/News/2014CivilUnionInfo.htm**).

For prior treatment of same-sex couples, see *General Information Letter IT 12-0003-GIL*, Department of Revenue, February 7, 2012, CCH ILLINOIS TAX REPORTS, ¶ 402-463; *Important Tax Information for Civil Union Couples Filing 2013 Illinois Income Tax Returns*, Illinois Department of Revenue, February 28, 2014, CCH ILLINOIS TAX REPORTS, ¶ 402-774.

¶505 Annual Return Forms

Prescribed annual return forms include:

Individual Income Tax Return	IL-1040
Fiduciary Income and Replacement Tax Return	IL-1041
Partnership Information and Replacement Income Tax Return	IL-1065

The Department of Revenue accepts approved substitutions and reproductions of the state's income tax return forms. Requirements are set out in the Illinois Department of Revenue's *Guidelines for Substitute and Reproduced Tax Forms*.

For information on obtaining forms, see **http://tax.illinois.gov/TaxForms/**.

• *Electronic filing*

The Department of Revenue authorizes the electronic filing of the following individual income tax returns: IL-1040, Schedule NR (Nonresident and Part-Year Resident Computation of Tax), IL-1040-X, W-2, W-2G (Statement of Certain Gambling Winnings), 1099-R (Total Distributions from Profit-Sharing, Retirement Plans, Individual Retirement Arrangements), US 1040, US 1040A, US Schedule B, or US Schedule I (Interest and Dividend Income).

Each income tax return preparer who is required to file any federal income tax return electronically and who prepared more than 10 Illinois personal income tax returns during the preceding calendar year is required to file electronically. This does not require electronic filing of amended returns or of returns of trusts or estates, or of any return the department has announced cannot be filed by electronic means. (86 Ill. Adm. Code Sec. 760.100)

• *Internet returns*

An Internet return consists of data transmitted to the Department of Revenue electronically via the Internet, and includes an electronic signature. An Internet return may also contain paper documents that are mailed to the Department or retained by the taxpayer for verification. Only those taxpayers who receive an access code from the Department of Revenue are eligible to file over the Internet.

Taxpayers can choose to pay any balance due by credit card but will be responsible for any discount fee charged by the credit card issuer. Also, qualifying taxpayers may authorize their refunds to be directly deposited into their bank accounts rather than receive paper refund checks.

PIN requirement: Illinois personal income tax returns filed via the Internet are required to include a personal identification number (PIN) issued to the taxpayer by the Illinois Department of Revenue. Married taxpayers filing a joint return online must include the PINs assigned to each spouse.

Electronic return originators (EROs) transmitting on-line returns are required to include the taxpayer PIN in the return, notify the taxpayer of the acceptance or rejection by the Department of an on-line return, and retain copies of transmitted material until December 31 of the filing year.

Confirmation: An Internet return must be confirmed by the Department of Revenue before it is considered to have been filed, and the date of confirmation is the filing date. Additional information is contained in regulations (86 Ill. Adm. Code Secs. 106.100—106.400).

¶506 Estimated Tax Required

Law: Income Tax Act, Sec. 601.1 [35 ILCS 5/601.1]; Income Tax Act, Sec. 704A [35 ILCS 5/704A]; Income Tax Act, Sec. 803(a), (b) [35 ILCS 5/803]; Income Tax Act, Sec. 806 [35 ILCS 5/806] (CCH ILLINOIS TAX REPORTS, ¶ 17-155).

Comparable Federal: Sec. 6654 (U.S. MASTER TAX GUIDE, ¶ 101—107).

Forms: IL-1040-ES.

Individuals must pay estimated tax if the estimate can reasonably be expected to be more than $500. Individuals earning at least two-thirds of their total estimated gross income for the taxable year from farming are excluded from paying estimated tax (35 ILCS 5/803(a)).

A taxpayer is not subject to a penalty for failing to pay estimated tax if the taxpayer is 65 years old or older and is a permanent resident of a nursing home, including skilled nursing or intermediate long term care facilities subject to licensure under the MR/DD Community Care Act (¶ 802).

Required annual payment: For installments of estimated taxes due after January 31, 2012, the required annual payment is (35 ILCS 5/804(c)):

— 90% of the tax shown on the return (or if no return is filed, 90% of the tax for that year), or

— 100% of the tax shown on the return of the previous year if the taxpayer filed a return for a taxable year of 12 months.

Annualized payments: A taxpayer who receives unpredictable nonwage income mostly in the last two quarters of the year must still make quarterly estimated Illinois personal income tax payments, but may use the annualization of income method outlined in Form 2210, Computation of Penalties for Individuals, to calculate the amount of payment required to avoid a penalty for underpayment of estimated taxes (*General Information Letter IT 05-0048-GIL*, Illinois Department of Revenue, November 8, 2005; CCH ILLINOIS TAX REPORTS, ¶ 401–623).

Electronic funds transfer: Individual taxpayers with a tax liability of $200,000 or more or quarterly withholding tax liability of $12,000 or more must make all payments by electronic funds transfer (35 ILCS 5/601.1; 35 ILCS 5/704A(c)).

¶507 Due Dates for Payments of Estimated Tax

Law: Income Tax Act, Sec. 803(d) [35 ILCS 5/803]; 86 Ill. Adm. Code Sec. 100.8010(c) (CCH ILLINOIS TAX REPORTS, ¶ 17-155).

Estimated tax payments are reported on Form IL-1040-ES and paid in four equal installments (35 ILCS 5/803; 86 Ill. Adm. Code Sec. 100.8010(c)). Installment payments of estimated tax are due as follows (35 ILCS 5/803(d)):

Installment:	Due Date:
1st	April 15
2nd	June 15
3rd	September 15
4th	January 15 of the following taxable year

¶508 Joint Payments

Law: Income Tax Act, Sec. 803(c) [35 ILCS 5/803] (CCH ILLINOIS TAX REPORTS, ¶ 17-155).

A husband and wife eligible to file a joint federal return may pay estimated tax as one taxpayer (35 ILCS 5/803(c)). If they elect to determine their tax separately, the estimated tax may be treated as the estimated tax of either husband or wife or may be divided between them, as they elect.

¶509 Estimated Tax—Not Required of Estates and Trusts, Partnerships, S Corporations, and Farmers

Law: Income Tax Act, Sec. 803(a) [35 ILCS 5/803] (CCH Illinois Tax Reports, ¶17-155).

Estates, trusts, partnerships, S corporations, and farmers are not required to make payments of estimated tax under the regular income tax act or the personal property replacement income tax act (35 ILCS 5/803(a)).

¶510 Notice of Change in Federal Return

Law: Income Tax Act, Sec. 506(b) [35 ILCS 5/506] (CCH Illinois Tax Reports, ¶17-155).

Taxpayers must notify the Department of any recomputation of federal income tax liability, any change in any item of income or deduction on the federal return that changes any item entering into the taxpayer's Illinois base income (specifically including net income, net loss, or any income tax credit), or any change in the number of personal exemptions allowed for federal purposes. Notification must be made within 120 days after the alteration is agreed to or finally determined or any deficiency or refund, tentative carryback adjustment, abatement or credit resulting therefrom has been assessed or paid, whichever occurs first (35 ILCS 5/506(b)).

¶511 Information Returns—Partnerships

Law: Income Tax Act, Sec. 502(d) [35 ILCS 5/502] (CCH Illinois Tax Reports, ¶15-510, 17-155).

Comparable Federal: Secs. 6031—6049.

Comparable Federal: Sec. 6013 (U.S. Master Tax Guide, ¶406, 2501, 2509).

Forms: IL-1065.

Every partnership having base income allocable to Illinois must make an information return setting forth all items of income, gain, loss, and deduction; names and addresses of all partners or persons entitled to share in the base income if distributed, and members of a limited liability company; distributive shares of all partners or other persons; and other pertinent information required by the Department. Form IL-1065 is used as both the partnership information return and as a return of personal property replacement income tax liability of a partnership. (35 ILCS 5/502(d))

Practitioner Comment: Investment Partnerships

For tax years ending on or after December 31, 2004, Illinois no longer subjects investment partnerships to Illinois' replacement tax, and they are not required to file Form IL-1065. The term "investment partnership" is defined at 35 ILCS 5/1501(a)(11.5). Illinois' law change was intended to encourage investment partnerships to locate in Illinois without subjecting its nonresident partners to Illinois tax. The laws of New York, California and Massachusetts also encourage nonresident limited partners to invest in those states without triggering state income taxes.

Horwood Marcus & Berk Chartered

PERSONAL INCOME TAX
CHAPTER 6
WITHHOLDING

¶601 Employers Required to Withhold

Law: Income Tax Act, Sec. 701(a) [35 ILCS 5/701]; 86 Ill. Adm. Code Sec. 100.7000 *et. seq.* (CCH ILLINOIS TAX REPORTS, ¶16-605).

Comparable Federal: Secs. 3401—3403 (U.S. MASTER TAX GUIDE, ¶2601—2663).

Every employer maintaining an office or transacting business in Illinois and required to withhold federal income tax on compensation paid in Illinois to an individual must deduct and withhold from wages an amount equal to 3% of the amount by which an individual's compensation exceeds the withholding exemption (35 ILCS 5/701). "Compensation" means wages, salaries, commissions, and any other form of remuneration paid to employees for personal services. Every employer required to deduct and withhold Illinois personal income tax must register with the Department of Revenue (86 Ill. Adm. Code Sec. 100.7040).

Payments, including compensation, that are (1) made to Illinois residents by payors maintaining offices or transacting business in the state and (2) subject to federal withholding are subject to Illinois withholding to the extent included in the recipient's base income and not subject to withholding by another state. Certain income of nonresidents is subject to withholding regardless of whether or not federal tax is withheld (¶603).

The Illinois Department of Revenue has published two documents explaining who is required to withhold Illinois income tax, as well as the filing and payment requirements. *Publication 130, Who is Required to Withhold Illinois Income Tax,* December 19, 2016, CCH ILLINOIS TAX REPORTS,¶403-184, also available on the Department of Revenue's website at **http://www.revenue.state.il.us/Publications/Pubs/index.htm**, discusses the following withholding tax issues:

— who is an employer;

— who is an employee;

— when withholding must occur;

— other withholding requirements for payments of lottery or gambling winners;

— what forms are required; and

— what records are required.

Publication 131, Withholding Income Tax Payment and Filing Requirements, December 19, 2016, CCH Illinois Tax Reports,¶403-185), also available at **http://www.revenue.state.il.us/Publications/Pubs/index.htm**, discusses the following withholding tax issues:

— which returns must be filed and when are they due;

— when payment is due; and

— how one files or pays.

Practitioner Comment: A Nonresident's Compensation

Illinois' rule of when "compensation" is "paid in this State" is virtually the same for income tax purposes and unemployment tax purposes. For unemployment purposes, wages are allocated entirely to one state, rather than being apportioned among the various states where services are rendered. Thus, for income tax purposes, as a general rule, if a nonresident's wages are not sourced to Illinois for unemployment tax purposes, then there is no withholding tax requirement on the income from services performed in Illinois. Likewise, as a general rule, such compensation is not subject to Illinois income tax. However, special sourcing rules exist for compensation paid to nonresident professional athletes (see ¶304, 602).

Jennifer A Zimmerman, Esq., Horwood Marcus & Berk Chartered

• *Withholding tables*

Withholding tables are published in *Booklet IL-700-T, Illinois Withholding Tax Tables*, Illinois Department of Revenue, December 2016, CCH Illinois Tax Reports,¶16-620, and are also available on the Department of Revenue's website at **http://tax.illinois.gov/TaxForms/Withholding/IL-700-T.pdf**.

• *Supplemental wages*

Supplemental wages, *i.e.,* bonuses, commissions, and overtime pay, are subject to withholding when paid. The amount of tax to be withheld on such wages may be determined in accordance with the methods provided for withholding such wages under the Internal Revenue Code and regulations, or the employer may elect to compute the amount of tax to be withheld using a flat rate of 3% (86 Ill. Adm. Code Sec. 100.7050).

• *Pension benefits*

Pension or annuity payments to residents from qualified pension plans are not subject to withholding because, generally, distributions from such plans are excluded from the computation of IL income (86 ILCS 5/701(e); 86 Ill. Adm. Code 7030(c)(1)). However, IL does require withholding on nonqualified pension plans (*General Information Letter IT00-0092-GIL*, Illinois Department of Revenue, November 27, 2000, CCH Illinois Tax Reports, ¶401-193).

Pension and annuity payments from qualified employee benefit plans made to nonresidents of Illinois are not taxable by Illinois, and, therefore, are not subject to withholding. The same applies to income received by nonresidents from private annuity or life insurance contracts. Also, pension and annuity payments made to nonresidents from nonqualified plans are not subject to withholding if they constitute deferred compensation (86 Ill. Adm. Code Sec. 100-7010).

¶601

CCH Advisory: Deferred Compensation of Nonresidents for Past Service in Illinois

Deferred compensation received by a nonresident for past services performed in Illinois is subject to withholding tax. The amounts paid to the nonresident were reported on federal Form W-2. Illinois withholding is required with respect to any item of compensation paid in Illinois for which federal withholding is required. (*General Information Letter IT 12-0031-GIL*, Illinois Department of Revenue, November 13, 2012, CCH ILLINOIS TAX REPORTS, ¶ 402-602)

• *Military spouses*

Employers are not required to withhold Illinois income tax from wages earned in Illinois by a nonresident spouse who is present in Illinois only to accompany the service member who is stationed in Illinois, is a resident of the same state as the service member, other than Illinois, and who completes Form IL-W-5-NR and checks the box to indicate that he or she is exempt from Illinois withholding. However, employers must withhold for:

— the spouse who earns wages in Illinois and lives in another state;

— an employee who is an Illinois resident working in another state and whose wages are exempt from tax and withholding in that other state under the new act, for employers conducting business in Illinois; and

— a service member who takes a civilian job. For the service members, the Servicemembers Civil Relief Act only exempts military pay from tax by any state other than the state of residence.

The spouse will no longer be eligible for this treatment if the servicemember leaves the service, they are divorced, they are physically separated due to duty changes, or the spouse performs some action that clearly establishes Illinois as his or her state of residence. (*Informational Bulletin FY 2010-12*, Illinois Department of Revenue, January 2010, CCH ILLINOIS TAX REPORTS, ¶ 402-078)

• *Unemployment insurance benefits*

Illinois unemployment insurance benefit payments made to an individual are not subject to Illinois personal income tax withholding unless the individual has voluntarily elected the withholding (35 ILCS 5/701(b)).

• *Employer liability*

Employers required to withhold tax are liable for the withheld tax. Amounts withheld are considered to be held in trust for the state.

The phrase "employer transacting business within Illinois" includes any employer having or maintaining within Illinois, directly or by a subsidiary, an office, distribution house, sales house, warehouse or other place of business, or any agent or representative operating in the state under the authority of the employer or its subsidiary, regardless of whether the place of business or representative is located in the state temporarily or whether the employer or subsidiary is licensed to do business in Illinois (86 Ill. Adm. Code Sec. 100.7020).

Vacation payments are subject to withholding as though they were regular wage payments made for the period covered by the vacation. If the vacation allowance is paid in addition to the regular wage payment for such period, the allowance is subjected to withholding in the same manner as supplemental wages (86 Ill. Adm. Code Sec. 100.7050).

Practitioner Comment: Employer and Responsible Employee Liability

Employers are required to hold the funds "actually deducted and withheld" from an employee's paycheck in a special fund in trust for the Department of Revenue. Illinois courts have found that a trust is established whenever money is withheld from an employee's paycheck. The trust arises when the paycheck is issued in an amount that reflects a deduction for taxes. An Illinois employer does not actually need to establish a formal trust account, separate bank account, or segregated cash flow for this trust to occur.

In light of the fact that withheld taxes are deemed property of the state and not property of the employer or employee, the failure to pay these taxes to the state carries potentially onerous penalties. These penalties may be civil and/or criminal and they apply to the employer or any responsible employee. For example, any taxpayer who "accepts money" that is due to the Department of Revenue as an agent for another, but who willfully fails to remit this money, is guilty of a Class A misdemeanor. In addition, the civil penalty provisions provide that the failure to pay withholding taxes could potentially create personal liability for responsible officers and employees of the company.

Jennifer A Zimmerman, Esq., Horwood Marcus & Berk Chartered

Household employees: The Department of Revenue has published an explanation of personal income tax withholding requirements for household employees *Publication 121*, Illinois Department of Revenue, April 2015, available on the DOR's website at **http://www.revenue.state.il.us/Publications/Pubs/index.htm**. The objectives of the publication are to identify:

— who is a household employee;

— who is an employer;

— if withholding Illinois Income Tax is required;

— how to figure, pay and report Illinois income tax that is withheld for a household employee;

— what records must be kept; and

— what forms must be given to the employee.

A taxpayer who has household employees may report withholding income tax on Line 22 of Form IL-1040 (Illinois Individual Income Tax Return) if the taxpayer is eligible to file federal Schedule H of Form 1040 (Household Employment Taxes). A taxpayer who reports on Form IL-1040 does not need to register with the department. If a taxpayer does not qualify to use Form IL-1040, the taxpayer must register and report the tax on Form IL-941 (Illinois Withholding Income Tax Return).

Practitioner Comment: Illinois' "Employee Classification Act"

Illinois' "Employee Classification Act" carries stiff civil and criminal penalties for misclassifying employees as independent contractors. Directed only at the construction business, the law is designed to make sure that employees in the construction trade are properly classified, thus entitling them to protections under numerous labor laws.

First time violators may face penalties up to $1,500 per violation (for "each person and for each day the violation continues"), and a willful violation of the law carries double penalties, punitive damages, and jail time. Repeat offenders are subject to civil penalties up to $2,500 per violation and may be barred from being awarded state contracts. Parties cannot waive the provisions of the Act. Moreover, it is a Class C misdemeanor for an employer to attempt to induce any individual to waive any provision of the Act.

The Act does not impact the classification of workers as independent contractors or employees for federal tax purposes. Because the Illinois' income tax withholding classification rules are modeled after the federal rules, contractors and subcontractors may question whether this Act trumps the current classification rules for Illinois income tax withholding purposes. Likewise, it is unclear, in cases where a worker really is an "independent contractor" for federal tax purposes, if the Act trumps that classification for Illinois labor law purposes. There is also a question whether the law is unconstitutional insofar as it applies only to the construction industry.

Horwood Marcus & Berk Chartered

¶602 Compensation Subject to Withholding— "Paid in This State" Defined

Law: Income Tax Act, Sec. 302 [35 ILCS 5/302]; Income Tax Act, Sec. 304(a)(2) [35 ILCS 5/304]; Income Tax Act, Sec. 701(b) [35 ILCS 5/701]; 86 Ill. Adm. Code Sec. 100-7010 (CCH ILLINOIS TAX REPORTS, ¶ 16-605, 16-615).

Compensation is paid in Illinois, and, therefore, subject to withholding, if (86 Ill. Adm. Code Sec. 100-7010):

— the individual's service is entirely performed within Illinois;

— the individual's service is performed both within and without Illinois, but the service performed without Illinois is incidental to the individual's service performed within Illinois; or

— some of the service is performed within Illinois and either the base of operations or, if there is no base of operations, the place from which the service is directed or controlled is within Illinois, or the base of operations or the place from which the service is directed or controlled is not in any state in which some part of the service is performed, but the individual's residence is in Illinois.

CCH Advisory: When is Compensation "Paid in This State?"

An Illinois personal income tax withholding ruling discusses the application of law regarding when compensation is "paid in this State." In the examples, given the services performed in Illinois are incidental to the services performed in another state, the wages would be paid in the other state and would not be treated as "paid in this State" and withholding would not be required. Assuming the wages were not paid in another state under state law, if the employee's "base of operations" is outside Illinois, the employee's wages would not be "paid in this State."

In each of the examples, the employee would have a "permanent job location" in another state. From these descriptions, the permanent job location would be the "base of operations" of the employee, and none of the wages paid to an employee would be "paid in this State." Accordingly, none of the wages paid to an employee would be subject to Illinois income tax withholding under 35 ILCS 5/701(a)(1). Under 35 ILCS 5/701(b), however, wages paid to an Illinois resident employee are subject to Illinois income tax withholding if the wages are subject to federal income tax withholding but are not subject to withholding of another state's income taxes. Under this provision, in each of the examples involving an Illinois resident whose permanent job location is in a state that does not impose an income tax, the employee's wages would be subject to Illinois income tax withholding. (*General Information Letter IT 11-0009-GIL,* Illinois Department of Revenue, May 13, 2010, CCH ILLINOIS TAX REPORTS, ¶ 402-350)

Another ruling provides general explanations on determining when compensation paid to an employee providing services within and without Illinois is subject to withholding. Specifically, the ruling states that the localization test included in regulations is not the only thing to consider when making this determination. Taxpayers must also be aware of bases of operation and places of direct control Additionally, an example is giving showing that a nonresident whose base of operations is in Illinois is subject to Illinois withholding on all compensation despite working in various states. A taxpayer would also be subject to Illinois withholding when Illinois is the permanent place of direction or control of a nonresident employee working in multiple states (*General Information Letter IT 10-0015-GIL*, Illinois Department of Revenue, June 28, 2010, CCH ILLINOIS TAX REPORTS, ¶402-159).

It should be noted that, if withholding is required, all compensation paid is subject to withholding; there is no allocation of compensation partly to Illinois and partly to other states.

The Department has issued a regulation (86 Ill. Adm. Code Sec. 100.7010) setting out examples showing how the rules given above apply in specific circumstances.

Agricultural employers are not exempt from withholding requirements.

Household employees: Employers must withhold Illinois taxes from wages paid to household employees if such employees are not exempt from federal withholding *Publication 121*, Illinois Department of Revenue, April, 2015; available at http://www.revenue.state.il.us/Publications/Pubs/index.htm.

Internet services: An Illinois college was not required to withhold Illinois personal income tax from compensation paid to a nonresident professor who taught courses over the Internet, because none of the teaching services were actually performed in Illinois. The professor was not physically present in Illinois at any time in the performance of his duties and did not maintain a base of operations within Illinois from which to direct or control his teaching services (*General Information Letter IT 00-0025-GIL*, Illinois Department of Revenue, March 14, 2000, CCH ILLINOIS TAX REPORTS, ¶401-138).

Professional athletes: The Illinois source income of a nonresident individual who is a member of a professional baseball, basketball, football, soccer, or hockey team includes a portion of the individual's total compensation for services performed as a member of the professional athletic team during the taxable year. The portion to be included is a ratio, which the number of duty days spent within Illinois performing services for the team in any manner during the taxable year bears to the total number of duty days spent both within and without Illinois during the taxable year (35 ILCS 304(a)(2)(B)(iv)). For additional information, see ¶304.

CCH Advisory: Illinois Residents Employed in Missouri

No withholding of Illinois personal income tax is required from compensation paid to Illinois residents for employment in Missouri when Missouri taxes are withheld and the compensation is not paid in Illinois. The taxpayer had operations in both Missouri and Illinois and had employees who reside in Illinois, but work in Missouri. Because a reciprocal agreement does not exist between Missouri and Illinois, the taxpayer requested guidance on withholding.

Under 35 ILCS 5/701(a), employers maintaining an office or transacting business in the state who are required under federal law to withhold tax on compensation paid in Illinois must withhold Illinois tax. Another provision, 35 ILCS 5/701(b), states that payment to a resident by an employer maintaining an office or transacting business in Illinois is considered compensation paid in Illinois to the extent the payment is not subject to withholding by another state. Thus, Illinois tax does not need to be withheld if compensation paid to an Illinois resident does not qualify as being paid in Illinois under 35 ILCS 5/701(a) and is subject to Missouri withholding under 35 ILCS 5/701(b). Conversely, compensation paid in Illinois by an employer meeting the conditions of 35 ILCS 5/701(a) is subject to Illinois withholding even though the same compensation is subject to another state's withholding under a different test. *General Information Letter IT 06-0016-GIL*, Illinois Department of Revenue, June 19, 2006, CCH ILLINOIS TAX REPORTS, ¶401-689.

¶602

¶603 Payments Other Than Compensation Subject to Withholding

Law: Income Tax Act, Sec. 710 [35 ILCS 5/710] (CCH ILLINOIS TAX REPORTS, ¶16-655).

Comparable Federal: Sec. 3402(q) (U.S. MASTER TAX GUIDE, ¶2607).

Persons making payments of Illinois lottery winnings of $1,000 or more to a resident or nonresident must withhold Illinois income tax from such payments (35 ILCS 5/710).

Gambling winnings paid to an Illinois resident are subject to Illinois income tax withholding if they are subject to federal income tax withholding.

See also ¶606.

¶604 Reciprocal Withholding Exemption Agreements

Law: Income Tax Act, Sec. 701(d) [35 ILCS 5/701] (CCH ILLINOIS TAX REPORTS, ¶16-605).

The Director of the Department of Revenue is authorized to enter into agreements with the taxing authorities of other states imposing income taxes to provide for exemption from withholding on compensation paid to residents of one state for the performance of services in the other state (35 ILCS 5/701(d)). The agreements may also provide that residents of one state working in the other state be liable for income tax only to their state of residence.

Illinois has entered into reciprocal agreements with Iowa, Kentucky, Michigan, and Wisconsin. For details of the agreements as they apply to withholding, see ¶605. The coverage of the agreements as regards exemption from tax is discussed at ¶305.

¶605 Implementation of Reciprocal Withholding Agreements

Law: Income Tax Act, Sec. 302(b) [35 ILCS 5/302]; Income Tax Act, Sec. 304(a)(2) [35 ILCS 5/304]; Income Tax Act, Sec. 701(d) [35 ILCS 5/701](CCH ILLINOIS TAX REPORTS, ¶16-605).

Illinois has entered into agreements with Iowa, Kentucky, Michigan, and Wisconsin to exempt from taxation and withholding the compensation paid to a resident of the other state who is working in Illinois. Residents of Iowa, Kentucky, Michigan, and Wisconsin must file with their employer a copy of Form IL-1W-5, Employee's Statement of Nonresidence in Illinois. Employers of persons who reside in those states may, but are not required by Illinois law, to withhold income tax for the other state (*Publication 130, Who is Required to Withhold Illinois Income Tax*, December 19, 2016, available on the Department of Revenue's website at **http://www.revenue.state.il.us/Publications/Pubs/index.htm**).

Declaration of residence required: In order to be entitled to the exemption, the employees must file with their employers a declaration of their residence in Iowa, Kentucky, Michigan, or Wisconsin. The form used is Form IL-1W-5.

Withholding of Local Income Taxes

Income taxes imposed by local authorities are generally not covered by the reciprocal agreements. However, an Illinois resident who worked part time in Kentucky was allowed to claim an Illinois credit for foreign taxes paid on local income taxes withheld by the Kentucky county. (*General Information Letter IT 12-0020-GIL*, Illinois Department of Revenue, July 31, 2012, CCH ILLINOIS TAX REPORTS, ¶402-534)

¶606 Withholding Exemptions

Law: Income Tax Act, Sec. 702 [35 ILCS 5/702] (CCH ILLINOIS TAX REPORTS, ¶16-660).

Comparable Federal: Sec. 3401 (U.S. MASTER TAX GUIDE, ¶2601—2663).

An employee subject to withholding is entitled to an exemption of $2,000 multiplied by the number of personal exemptions to which he or she is entitled for federal income tax withholding purposes, except that an employee is not entitled to the extra federal withholding allowances based on large amounts of itemized deductions (35 ILCS 5/702). An employee may elect to forego all or part of the exemptions for withholding tax purposes.

¶607 Methods of Withholding

Law: Income Tax Act, Sec. 701(a) [35 ILCS 5/701]; 86 Ill. Adm. Code Sec. 100.7050 (CCH ILLINOIS TAX REPORTS, ¶16-605, 16-620).

Comparable Federal: Sec. 3402 (U.S. MASTER TAX GUIDE, ¶2614, 2616).

The amount of tax withheld may be determined by automated payroll computation, or by use of withholding tables prescribed by the state (*Withholding Tax Guide,* CCH ILLINOIS TAX REPORTS, ¶16-620).

• *Automated payroll computation*

Employers that have an automated payroll system may use a formula for computing income tax withholding, using the following number of pay periods in a year:

Daily	365
Weekly	52
Bi-weekly	26
Semi-monthly	24
Monthly	12
Bi-monthly	6
Quarterly	4
Semi-annually	2
Annually	1

After selecting the proper number of pay periods and determining the employee's wages and withholding exemptions, the tax is computed as follows to determine the amount of tax to be withheld for each period:

$$3\% \times (\text{Wages} - \frac{\text{Exemptions} \times 2000}{\text{No. of Pay Periods}})$$

NOTE: When the result is a negative number, you do not need to withhold.

¶608 Withholding on a Bonus

Law: 86 Ill. Adm. Code Sec. 100.7050(c) (CCH ILLINOIS TAX REPORTS, ¶16-605).

Comparable Federal: (U.S. MASTER TAX GUIDE, ¶2639).

Supplemental wages, such as bonuses, commissions and overtime pay may be paid for the same period as payment of wages paid for the regular payroll period or for a different period or without regard to any particular period. The amount of tax to be withheld on such supplemental wages may be determined in accordance with the same methods provided for withholding on such wages under the Internal Revenue Code and the federal regulations or the employer may elect to compute the amount of tax to be withheld using a flat rate.

Detailed instructions are provided in the current withholding booklet, available at **http://tax.illinois.gov/TaxForms/Withholding/IL-700-T.pdf.**

¶609 Returns and Remittance of Withheld Taxes

Law: Income Tax Act, Sec. 704 [35 ILCS 5/704]; Income Tax Act, Sec. 704A [35 ILCS 5/704A]; Income Tax Act, Sec. 601.1 [35 ILCS 5/601.1]; 86 Ill. Adm. Code Sec. 100.7300; 86 Ill. Adm. Code Sec. 100.7310, 86 Ill. Adm. Code 100.7350 (CCH ILLINOIS TAX REPORTS, ¶16-665).

Comparable Federal: Sec. 3501 (U.S. MASTER TAX GUIDE, ¶2650).

Forms: IL-W-3, Annual Withholding Income Tax Return; IL-941, Quarterly Withholding Income Tax Return; IL-501, Withholding Income Tax Payment Form.

Effective January 1, 2017, all withholding taxpayers must pay withholding income tax on a monthly or semi-weekly schedule. The annual filing and payment option is no longer available. In addition, all withholding taxpayers must file quarterly returns on Form IL-941, which has been updated for the 2017 tax year, including a line to verify compliance with the Illinois Secure Choice Savings Program Act, a section for entering required withholding information for each month of the quarter, and entry lines for the amount of income tax withheld based on payroll dates. A new line has been added for preparers to enter their Internal Revenue Service (IRS) preparer tax identification number (PTIN). Beginning on or after January 1, 2017, all paid income tax return preparers must include their PTIN on any tax returns they prepare and file or on any refund claim. Failure to comply may result in assessment of a penalty on the preparer. (35 ILCS 5/704A(b); 86 Ill. Adm. Code Sec. 100.7310; *Informational Bulletin FY 2017-07*, Illinois Department of Revenue, September 26, 2016, CCH ILLINOIS TAX REPORTS, ¶ 403-132)

Semi-weekly payments: Employers who withheld or were required to withhold more than $12,000 in any calendar quarter or in the previous calendar year ending on June 30 must make semi-weekly payments (35 ILCS 5/704A(c)). Payments are required on Fridays to cover withholding for the previous Saturday, Sunday, Monday, and Tuesday. Payments are required on Wednesdays to cover withholding for the previous Wednesday, Thursday, and Friday. If any of the three weekdays following the close of a semi-weekly period is a holiday on which banks are closed, the employer has an additional banking day by which to make the required deposit (86 Ill. Adm. Code 100.7325).

The regulation covers the due dates for filing quarterly and annual returns and for making monthly and semi-weekly payments of withheld taxes. With respect to semi-weekly payments, employers who make electronic payments of withheld taxes may use the due dates prescribed in 26 CFR 31.63021(c)(2)(iii), which allows semi-weekly depositors at least three banking days following the close of the semi-weekly period by which to deposit taxes during the semi-weekly period. Thus, if any of the three weekdays following the close of a semi-weekly period is a holiday on which banks are closed, the employer has an additional banking day by which to make the required deposit. (86 Ill. Adm. Code 100.7325)

Monthly payments: Employers not required to make semi-weekly payments must make monthly payments by the 15th of the month following the month for which witholding is required.

Annual payments: Timely filers of returns who previously have reported a tax liability of $12,000 or less may file a single annual return provided the tax due in the return's calendar year does not exceed $12,000. If the tax due exceeds $12,000, returns must be filed quarterly. If the tax liability for the calendar year is $1,000 or less, the tax payment is due with the annual return. (35 ILCS 5/704A(d); 86 Ill. Adm. Code Sec. 100.7310)

An employer of persons in domestic service may make an annual report and payment on or before the 15th day of the fourth month following the close of the employer's taxable year (35 ILCS 5/704A(e); 86 Ill. Adm. Code 100.7350).

Annual reconciliation form required: An annual reconciliation of payments of withheld taxes is required of all employers (¶ 613).

Domestic services: Every employer who deducts and withholds tax from a domestic service employee may file an annual return and pay the taxes required to be deducted and withheld on or before the 15th day of the fourth month following the close of the employer's taxable year. Withheld taxes may be paid and reported in the above manner regardless of the amount of taxes withheld and regardless of whether the employer has other employees who are subject to other withholding provisions. Employers who wish to pay and report taxes withheld from domestic service employees on an annual basis must register to do so with the Illinois Department of Employment Security and use the form required by that Department to report Illinois withholding taxes and unemployment insurance contributions. (86 Ill. Adm. Code 100.7350)

Federal deposit rules: Illinois does not follow the federal income tax deposit rules. The requirements for the payment of tax by Illinois employers are found in Section 704 of the Illinois Income Tax Act.

Electronic funds transfer: Employers who are required to file their federal withholding returns electronically are also required to file their Illinois withholding returns electronically (86 Ill. Adm. Code Sec. 100.7300).

CCH Advisory: Federal Payment System Available for Illinois Payers

The electronic federal tax payment system (EFTPS) is available to pay Illinois withholding taxes. EFTPS is free and may be used to make payments weekly, monthly, or quarterly. Existing EFTPS users will need to modify their enrollment to allow for Illinois payments. New users may simultaneously enroll for both Illinois withholding tax payments and federal tax payments. For more information and future announcements, see **www.eftps.gov**.

¶610 Lottery and Gambling Winnings

Law: Income Tax Act, Sec. 701 [35 ILCS 5/701]; Income Tax Act, Sec. 710 [35 ILCS 5/710] (CCH ILLINOIS TAX REPORTS, ¶16-655).

Comparable Federal: Sec. 3501 (U.S. MASTER TAX GUIDE, ¶2607).

Forms: IL-5754, Statement by Person Receiving Gambling Winnings; IL-W-4G, Gambling Withholding Exemption Certificate.

Any person making a payment of Illinois lottery winnings of $1,000 or more, whether to a resident or a nonresident, must withhold Illinois income tax and report the amount withheld in the same manner as employers (35 ILCS 5/710(a)(1)). Gambling winnings paid to Illinois residents are subject to Illinois withholding if they are subject to federal withholding (35 ILCS 5/701).

Assignments: For taxable years beginning after 2013, in the case of an assignment of a lottery prize, any person making a payment of the purchase price must withhold from the amount of each payment at a rate equal to the individual income tax rate (35 ILCS 5/710(a)(2)).

¶611 Withholding Certificates

Law: Income Tax Act, Sec. 702 [35 ILCS 5/702] (CCH ILLINOIS TAX REPORTS, ¶16-660).

Comparable Federal: Sec. 3402 (U.S. MASTER TAX GUIDE, ¶2655).

Forms: IL-W-4, Employee's Illinois Withholding Allowance Certificate.

Employees are required to furnish their employers with information needed to make an accurate withholding. The employer may rely on this information for withholding purposes. If an employee fails to furnish the required information (Form IL-W-4), the employer must withhold the full rate of tax from the employee's total compensation.

An employer may use any software application that will allow employees to prepare the IL-W-4 electronically, provided that any such electronic system meets the federal requirements of 26 CFR 31.3402(f)(5)-1(c) and requires the production and retention of the same information required on the written Form IL-W-4 (86 Ill. Admin. Code Sec. 100.7110).

Employers who are residents of a state with a reciprocal agreement exempting residents of that state (¶ 604) from Illinois withholding must file a signed certificate of residency to receive the exemption.

¶612 Annual Statements of Wages Paid

Law: Income Tax Act, Sec. 703 [35 ILCS 5/703] (CCH Illinois Tax Reports, ¶ 16-665).

Comparable Federal: Sec. 6051.

By January 31 of the succeeding year, employers must provide employees with a statement, in duplicate, of the total compensation paid during the preceding year and the amount of tax deducted or withheld. Illinois does not issue a state Form W-2, but, instead, authorizes use of the six-part federal form, Form W-2, Wage and Tax Statement, which may be used for both federal and state purposes. If any employee permanently terminates employment before the end of a calendar year, or a federal voluntary withholding agreement is terminated, the employer must furnish the employee with a completed copy of Form W-2 within 30 days of the last payment of wages on which compensation was required.

Employers are required to include on the Illinois personal income tax withholding information statement (W-2) provided to employees the tax-exempt amount contributed to a medical savings account.

An employer may not file multiple Form W-2's even though an employee works in more than one branch office of the same corporation or is paid a bonus or incentive under a corporation's executive bonus plan (86 Ill. Adm. Code Sec. 100-7200; CCH Illinois Tax Reports, ¶ 18-200).

Beginning in 2015, taxpayers that must submit Form W-2s electronically must submit the forms to the Illinois Department of Revenue by February 15 of the year following the year of withholding. The deadline was previously March 31; see (*Publication 110, Form W-2 Electronic Transmittal Requirements,* Illinois Department of Revenue, December 22, 2014, CCH Illinois Tax Reports, ¶ 402-898, also available on the Department of Revenue's website at **http://www.revenue.state.il.us/Publications/Pubs/index.htm**).

¶613 Annual Reconciliation of Tax Withheld Required

Law: Income Tax Act, Sec. 704 [35 ILCS 5/704] (CCH Illinois Tax Reports, ¶ 16-6659).

Comparable Federal: Sec. 6011 (U.S. Master Tax Guide, ¶ 2650).

Forms: IL-W-3, Annual Withholding Income Tax Return.

An annual reconciliation of income tax withheld (Form IL-W-3) must be filed by employers by February 15 of the succeeding calendar year for the preceding year (*Publication 110, W-2, W-2G, and 1099 Filing and Storage Requirements for Employers and Payers,* Illinois Department of Revenue, March, 2015, available on the Department of Revenue's website at **http://www.revenue.state.il.us/Publications/Pubs/index.htm**).

¶614 Employers and Payroll Providers Required to Keep Records of Withholding

Every employer subject to Illinois withholding is required to maintain a current, accurate record of all persons from whom tax is withheld. The records must include amounts and dates of all compensation paid subject to withholding, names, addresses and social security numbers of employees, periods of employment, amount of compensation paid by pay period (including sick pay), copies of annual, quarterly and monthly returns filed, federal Employee's Withholding Allowance Certificates (Form IL-W-4) if applicable, Gambling Withholding Exemption Certificate (Form IL-W-4-G), Employee Statement of Nonresidence in Illinois (Form IL-W-5NR), and Certificate of Residence in Illinois (Form IL-W-5). Records must be kept for at least three years.

Employers required to report and pay withheld taxes on an annual basis must retain a copy of each wage and tax statement on a combined W-2 form and must maintain copies of the combined W-2 forms until January 31 of the fourth year following the calendar year. If an employer issues a corrected copy of a combined W-2 to an employee for a prior calendar year, a copy must be retained for a period of four years from the date fixed for filing the employer's return of tax withheld for the period ending December 31 of the year in which the correction is made, or for any period in the year for which the return is made as a final return. A statement explaining the corrections must also be retained. (86 Ill. Adm. Code 100.7300)

Payroll providers: Payroll providers who withhold Illinois income tax for employers during the year and who are required to file copies of W-2s on magnetic media under 26 CFR 301.6011-2 must file copies of the W-2's with the Illinois Department of Revenue using the same magnetic media used for their federal filing no later than March 31 of the year following the year of the withholding, unless a later due date is prescribed under federal law. (86 Ill. Adm. Code 100.7300)

PERSONAL INCOME TAX
CHAPTER 7
ADMINISTRATION, ASSESSMENT, COLLECTION

¶701 Overview

Illinois statutory provisions relating to delinquencies and deficiencies are equally applicable to individual and to corporate taxpayers and are covered in detail in the corporate division at Chapter 13.

Consult Part X, "Administration and Procedure," beginning at Chapter 24, for information on returns, payments, recordkeeping requirements, audits, penalties, interest, and taxpayer remedies.

PERSONAL INCOME TAX
CHAPTER 8
REFUNDS, PENALTIES, RECORDS

¶801 Refunds and Deficiencies

Law: Income Tax Act, Secs. 905, 909, 911 [35 ILCS 5/905, 909, 911]; 20 ILCS 2505/2505-275 (CCH ILLINOIS TAX REPORTS, ¶17-155).

Comparable Federal: Secs. 6401—6404, 6511, 6611 (U.S. MASTER TAX GUIDE, ¶1173, 2759).

Generally, claims for refund must be filed not later than three years after the date the return was filed, or one year after the date the tax was paid, whichever is later (35 ILCS 5/911(a)).

Financial disability: Effective January 1, 2015, the limitations period for claiming an Illinois corporate or personal income tax refund is suspended while the taxpayer is unable to manage financial affairs due to disability including, in the case of an individual, financial disability. An individual is "financially disabled" if the individual is unable to manage financial affairs by reason of a medically determinable physical or mental impairment of the individual that can be expected to result in death or that has lasted or can be expected to last for a period of not less than 12 months. An individual cannot be treated as financially disabled during any period in which the individual's spouse or any other person is authorized to act on behalf of the individual with respect to financial matters. (35 ILCS 5/911(i))

NOL carrybacks: For claims relating to overpayments resulting from net operating loss carrybacks, the limitations period extends to three years after the time prescribed (including extensions) for filing the return for the loss year. However, no claim for refund is allowed to the extent the refund is the result of an amount of net loss incurred in any taxable year ending prior to December 31, 2002, that was not reported to the Department within three years of the due date (including extensions) of the return for the loss year on either the original return filed by the taxpayer or an amended return. Also, no claim for refund is allowed to the extent that the refund is the result of an amount of net loss incurred in any taxable year for which no return was filed within three years of the due date (including extensions) of the return for the loss year (35 ILCS 5/911(h)). The statute of limitations period for filing a claim for refund relating to a change in a credit carryover resulting from the carryback of an NOL incurred in a tax year beginning after 1999 is three years from the due date of the return, including extensions, for the subsequent tax year. Refund claims relating to a carryover of a credit or a NOL earned or incurred in a tax year beginning after 1999 or used in a year for which a notification of change affecting federal taxable income must be filed are required to be filed within two years from the date on which the notification was due.

Withholding tax: Claims for refund in the case of returns required under the withholding provisions of the act must be filed not later than three years after the fifteenth day of the fourth month following the close of the calendar year in which the withholding was made, or one year after the date the tax was paid, whichever is later (35 ILCS 5/911(a)).

Federal change: If notification of a change in the federal return is required (¶510), a claim for refund may be filed within two years after the date on which the notice was due, but the amount recoverable is limited to the amount of overpayment resulting from recomputation of the taxpayer's net income for the year after giving effect to the item or items reflected in the alteration required to be reported (35 ILCS 5/911(b)).

A corporate income tax or personal income tax deficiency notice resulting from a taxpayer's failure to report a federal change to the Department may be issued at any time for the tax year for which the notification is required or for any tax year to which the taxpayer may carry a personal income tax or corporate income tax credit or a NOL earned, incurred, or used in the tax year for which the notification is required. If a taxpayer notifies the Department of a federal change, the Department must issue a deficiency notice within two years after the date of notification for the tax year for which the notification is given or for any tax year for which the taxpayer may carry a credit or NOL earned, incurred, or used in the year for which the notification is given. The deficiency assessed is limited to the amount of deficiency resulting from the federal changes (35 ILCS 5/905(e)).

Offsets: The Department may credit overpayments against any income tax liability of the taxpayer and refund the balance of the overpayment to the taxpayer, regardless of whether other collection remedies are closed to the Department. Overpayments of tax may be credited against estimated tax for the succeeding year (35 ILCS 5/911.2).

If an Illinois taxpayer is owed an income tax refund by the state of Illinois, but is identified by another state as owing taxes, the Illinois Department of Revenue may withhold any refund to which the taxpayer is entitled upon certification of the Illinois taxpayer's delinquent income tax liability in the claimant state and a request by a tax officer of the claimant state to the Illinois Director of Revenue that the refund be withheld (35 ILCS 5/911.2).

Additionally, in the case of overpayment by an Illinois taxpayer, the Department of Revenue, may credit the amount of the overpayment and interest against any of the taxpayer's federal tax liability (20 ILCS 2505/2505-275).

CCH Advisory: Spousal Relief

When the Department withholds a refund on a joint return because one spouse has another state tax liability, the other spouse is entitled to his or her portion of the refund and may not be unfairly penalized. See also ¶802.

Interest is paid on overpayments at the same rate as on underpayments (¶2503). However, if an overpayment is refunded within three months after the last date prescribed for filing the return or within three months after the return was filed, whichever is later, no interest is allowed.

CCH Advisory: Refund Anticipation Loans

Persons engaged in the business of making or facilitating tax refund anticipation loans must disclose the following to borrowers on a document separate from the loan application (815 ILCS 177/10):

— the fee for the refund anticipation loan or refund anticipation check;

— the refund anticipation loan interest rate;

— the total cost to the consumer for utilizing a refund anticipation loan;

— that the consumer borrower is responsible for repayment of the loan and related fees in the event the tax refund is not paid or not paid in full; and

— the availability of electronic filing for the income tax return of the consumer and the average time announced by the IRS within which the consumer can expect to receive a refund if the consumer's return is filed electronically and the consumer does not obtain a refund anticipation loan.

Facilitators are required to display a schedule showing the current fees for refund anticipation loans and/or refund anticipation checks depending on what services are offered (815 ILCS 177/15).

Prohibited activities include charging or imposing fees or other forms of consideration in the making or facilitating of a refund anticipation loan or refund anticipation check apart from the fee charged by the creditor or financial institution that provides the loan or check (815 ILCS 177/25). The making or facilitating of a nonbank refund anticipation loan with an interest rate higher than 36% per annum is prohibited (815 ILCS 177/30).

¶802 Penalties and Interest

Law: Income Tax Act, Sec. 502(c)(4) [35 ILCS 5/502(c)(4)]; Income Tax Act, Sec. 602(b) [35 ILCS 5/602]; Income Tax Act, Sec. 804 [35 ILCS 5/804]; Income Tax Act Sec. 806 [35 ILCS 5/806]; Income Tax Act, Secs. 1001—1006 [35 ILCS 5/1001—5/1006]; Uniform Penalty and Interest Act, Secs. 3-1—3-6 [35 ILCS 735/3-1—735/3-6]; 86 Ill. Adm. Code Sec. 100.5040 (CCH ILLINOIS TAX REPORTS, ¶ 17-155, 89-204).

Comparable Federal: Secs. 6015, 6601, *et seq.* (U.S. MASTER TAX GUIDE, ¶ 2838—2845)

Forms: IL-8857, Claim for Innocent Spouse Relief.

Interest: If any tax due, excluding estimated tax due, is not paid on time, interest is charged for the period from the due date to the date of payment. Interest must also be paid on tax due and unpaid for the period of any extension. The rate of interest is determined semiannually under the Uniform Penalty and Interest Act (see CCH ILLINOIS TAX REPORTS, ¶ 89-204). See ¶ 2503 for the current rate of interest.

If a waiver of restrictions under 35 ILCS 5/907 on the assessment and collection of the tax has been filed, and if notice and demand for the tax is not made within 30 days after the filing of the waiver, interest is not imposed for the period beginning immediately after the 30th day and ending with the date of notice and demand.

Employers: Employers who fail to file a return or pay withholding tax are subject to interest for the delinquent period. The interest, and any penalty, is paid by the employer and may not be passed through to employees. If a business is not solvent, or if a responsible corporate officer or employee willfully fails to collect or remit withholding tax, the responsible officer is held personally liable for the unpaid tax, plus penalties and interest (35 ILCS 5/1002).

Penalties: See ¶ 2503 for discussion of penalties, including abatement provisions.

Waiver for certain military personnel: Taxpayers who are members, or, in the case of joint returns, spouses of members, of the United States Armed Forces serving in a combat zone and granted a filing extension by Presidential Proclamation under IRC Sec. 7508 are exempt from the penalty and interest provisions (35 ILCS 5/602(b)).

Waiver for certain senior citizens: A taxpayer is not subject to a penalty for failing to pay estimated tax if the taxpayer is 65 years old or older and is a permanent resident of a nursing home (35 ILCS 5/806). For purposes of the waiver, "nursing home" is defined as a skilled nursing or immediate long-term care facility that is subject to licensure by the Illinois Department of Public Health.

• *Innocent spouse relief*

An individual may elect that any tax liability arising from a joint return be limited to his or her separate return liability and the portion of the deficiency appropriately allocable to the individual (35 ILCS 5/502(c)(4)). This election is similar to that provided for under IRC Sec. 6015, and any determination made by the Secretary of the Treasury concerning an individual's eligibility and allocation of liability will be followed by Illinois.

A federal IRC Sec. 6015 election will constitute an Illinois election. However, the election will not be effective for Illinois tax purposes until the individual has notified the Illinois Department of Revenue. A separate Illinois election filed with the Department is allowed, but will be denied if the Department determines that assets were transferred between individuals filing a joint return as part of a tax evasion scheme. An election applies to all years for which the individual and the spouse named in the election filed a joint return.

In determining the separate tax liability of a spouse seeking innocent spouse relief, an estimated tax payment or overpayment refund or credit is allocated in proportion to the separate return amount of each spouse for the taxable year as determined without regard to the estimated tax payment or credited or refunded overpayment (86 Ill. Adm. Code Sec. 100.5040).

No collection action may be commenced against an electing individual for any tax liability arising from a joint return covered by the election until the Department notifies the individual in writing that the election is invalid or of the portion of the liability the Department has allocated to the electing individual. An individual has 60 days to appeal the notification, or 150 days if the individual is outside the United States (35 ILCS 5/502(c)(4)(B)(vi)).

For additional information, see *Publication 125, Injured and Innocent Spouse Relief*, Illinois Department of Revenue, April 2010, CCH ILLINOIS TAX REPORTS, ¶ 402-115, also available at **http://tax.illinois.gov/Publications/Pubs/**.

• *Amnesty*

A general tax amnesty period ran from October 1, 2010, through November 8, 2010. Under the terms of the amnesty, upon payment by a taxpayer of all taxes due for any taxable period ending after June 30, 2002, and prior to July 1, 2009 (taxable period), the department would abate and not seek to collect any interest or penalties that might apply and would not seek civil or criminal prosecution for any taxpayer for the period of time for which the amnesty was granted.

Practitioner Comment: Amnesty

In May 2008, the Illinois Appellate Court (First District) issued an unpublished order upholding the constitutionality of the Illinois Tax Delinquency Amnesty Act over statutory and constitutional challenges.

In upholding the amnesty act over a uniformity clause challenge, the appellate court found that the tax classification drawn by the amnesty act was reasonable and passed constitutional muster. To survive scrutiny under the uniformity clause, a tax classification must: (1) be based on a real and substantial difference between the persons taxed and those not taxed; and (2) bear some reasonable relationship to the object of the legislation or to public policy.

In this case, there were two types of taxpayers: (1) taxpayers with outstanding tax liabilities who paid their liabilities during the amnesty window and therefore were given amnesty from interest and penalties that otherwise would have accrued on the outstanding tax liability; and (2) taxpayers with outstanding tax liabilities who did not pay their liability during the amnesty window and therefore are subject to doubled interest and penalties on the outstanding tax liabilities.

The court found that these classifications did not run afoul of the uniformity clause because there was a real and substantial difference between the two classes of taxpayers. Furthermore, the court reasoned that the tax classifications set forth in the Amnesty Act were reasonably related to the undisputed goals of the legislation. The court held that the Amnesty Act did not arbitrarily discriminate against a narrow class, but rather set forth rational classifications that bear a reasonable relationship to a valid State objective. Accordingly, the court found no violation of the uniformity, equal protection or due process clauses. The court also rejected the Plaintiff's argument that the Amnesty Act violated Section 4 of the Illinois Statute on Statutes (5 ILCS 70/4) by retroactively doubling interest and penalties on tax liabilities. Section 4 prohibits new laws that repeal a former law as to any penalty. The court found that Section 4 of the Statute on Statutes is implicated only if the General Assembly has not indicated whether the statute should be applied retroactively. In this case, the court found that the Amnesty Act imposed double interest and penalties on taxpayers who failed to take advantage of the Amnesty window, and that the window was prospective at the time of the statute's enactment. Accordingly, the court held that it was the plaintiff's "contemporaneous failure" to avail itself of amnesty that subjected it to double interest and penalties under the Amnesty Act.

Jennifer A. Zimmerman, Esq., Horwood Marcus & Berk, Chartered

¶803 Criminal Penalties

Law: Income Tax Act, Sec. 1301 [35 ILCS 5/1301]; Income Tax Act, Sec. 1302 [35 ILCS 5/1302](CCH ILLINOIS TAX REPORTS, ¶17-155).

Comparable Federal: Secs. 7201 *et seq.*

Criminal penalties are discussed at ¶2503.

¶804 Records

Law: Civil Administrative Code, Sec. 39b12 [20 ILCS 2505/39b12]; Income Tax Act, Sec. 501 [35 ILCS 5/501]; Income Tax Act, Secs. 913—917 [35 ILCS 5/913—5/917]; Income Tax Act, Sec. 1301 [35 ILCS 5/1301] (CCH ILLINOIS TAX REPORTS, ¶17-155, 89-134).

Comparable Federal: Sec. 6001 (U.S. MASTER TAX GUIDE, ¶2523).

Every person liable for any income tax must keep records, render statements, make returns and notices and comply with the rules and regulations of the Department (35 ILCS 5/501(a)). If necessary, the Department may require any person to make returns and notices, render statements or keep records sufficient to show whether or not the person is liable for tax. All books and records required to be kept must be available for inspection by the Department at all times during business hours of the day (35 ILCS 5/913).

The Department may exchange tax information with federal and state officials. The Department may also exchange taxpayer information with the Illinois Department of Public Aid that may be necessary for the enforcement of a child support order. The Director of Revenue may divulge taxpayer information to any person pursuant to a request or authorization made by the taxpayer, by an authorized representative of the taxpayer, or where information from a joint return is requested, by the spouse filing the joint return with the taxpayer.

For additional information, see ¶2403.

¶805 Reallocation of Items of Income or Deduction

Law: Income Tax Act, Sec. 404 [35 ILCS 5/404] (CCH ILLINOIS TAX REPORTS, ¶11-505).

If it appears to the Director that any agreement or understanding exists between any persons to cause any person's base income allocable to Illinois to be improperly or inaccurately reflected, the Director may adjust the items of income and deduction and any factor taken into account in allocating income to Illinois in order to determine the base income properly allocable to Illinois (35 ILCS 5/404).

¶806 Taxpayers' Bill of Rights

Law: Taxpayer's Bill of Rights Act, Secs. 2520/1—2520/7 [20 ILCS 2520/1—2520/7](CCH ILLINOIS TAX REPORTS, ¶89-136, ¶89-222).

The Taxpayers' Bill of Rights guarantees that Illinois taxpayers' rights are protected during the assessment and collection of taxes. For a comprehensive discussion of taxpayers' rights, see ¶2601.

Practitioner Comment: Expenses and Attorney's Fees

Attorney-fee awards are authorized under the Taxpayer's Bill of Rights Act as well as under the Illinois Administrative Procedure Act ("APA"). The APA provides for recovery of reasonable expenses, including attorney's fees, when an agency makes an untrue allegation without reasonable cause and the case does not proceed to court for judicial review. The APA also provides for recovery of reasonable expenses, including attorney's fees, when a party has an administrative rule invalidated by a court for any reason.

Horwood Marcus & Berk Chartered

PART II.5
PASS-THROUGH ENTITIES
Chapter 8.5
INCOME TAX TREATMENT OF PASS-THROUGH ENTITIES

¶850 Introduction

This chapter covers the various types of pass-through entities, the treatment of the pass-through entity at the entity level, the tax treatment of pass-through entity owners, reporting requirements, unified reporting options for nonresidents, and penalties.

¶851 Limited Liability Companies

Law: 35 ILCS 5/201, 35 ILCS 5/1501 (CCH ILLINOIS TAX REPORTS, ¶10-240).

Comparable Federal: Treas. Reg. Secs. 301.7701-1 through 301.7701-3 (U.S. MASTER TAX GUIDE, ¶402B).

An LLC that is treated as a partnership for federal income tax purposes is also treated as a partnership for Illinois tax purposes (35 ILCS 5/1501(a)(4) and (16)). Since Illinois adopts the federal income tax treatment of limited liability companies (LLCs) and their members, as set out in the federal "check-the-box" regulations, income and losses, including net losses, of the LLC flow to its members.

An LLC that is treated as a partnership is not subject to corporate income tax but is subject to the personal property replacement income tax at the entity level (see ¶105) (35 ILCS 5/201(c)).

LLC organizational provisions are found in the Limited Liability Company Act, located at 805 ILCS 180/1-1 *et seq.*

¶852 Partnerships

Law 35 ILCS 5/201(c), 35 ILCS 5/205(b), 35 ILCS 5/1501(a), 805 ILCS 210/201; 86 Ill. Adm. Code 100.4500, 86 Ill. Adm. Code 100.9750 (CCH ILLINOIS TAX REPORTS, ¶10-220 through 10-235, 16-005 through 16-380).

Comparable Federal: Secs. 701–761, 7704 (U.S. MASTER TAX GUIDE, ¶401–481).

A "partnership" includes a syndicate, group, pool, joint venture, or other unincorporated organization that carries on a business, financial operation, or venture and that is not a corporation, trust, or estate (35 ILCS 5/1501(a)(16)). The term includes a limited liability company treated as a partnership for federal income tax purposes, but does not include an unincorporated organization established for the sole purpose of playing the Illinois lottery.

Partnerships are not subject to corporate income tax but are subject to the personal property replacement income tax (PPRIT) at the entity level equal to 1.5% of net income (35 ILCS 5/201(c); 35 ILCS 5/205(b); 35 ILCS 5/1501(16)). Since Illinois generally follows the federal income tax treatment of general partnerships and their partners, as set out in IRC Secs. 701 through 761, income and losses, including net losses, of the partnership flow to its partners (86 Ill. Adm. Code 100.9750).

Partnerships compute base income for two purposes:

—to determine the partnership's replacement income tax; and

—to determine partnership income passing through to partners.

The base income of partnerships is discussed at ¶207.

Investment partnerships: Investment partnerships are not subject to personal property replacement income tax (35 ILCS 5/205(b)).

The term "investment partnership" means any entity treated as a partnership for federal income tax purposes and that meets the following requirements (35 ILCS 5/1501(a)):

(1) no less than 90% of the investment partnership's cost of its total assets consists of qualifying investment securities, deposits at banks or other financial institutions, and office space and equipment reasonably necessary to carry on its activities as an investment partnership;

(2) no less than 90% of its gross income consists of interest, dividends, and gains from the sale or exchange of qualifying investment securities; and

(3) the partnership is not a dealer in qualifying investment securities.

The term "investment securities" means (35 ILCS 5/1501(a)):

—common and preferred stock;

—bonds, debentures, and other debt securities;

—foreign and domestic currency deposits;

—mortgage or asset-backed securities;

—repurchase agreements and loan participation;

—forward currency exchange contracts and forward and futures contracts on foreign currencies;

—stock and bond index securities and futures contracts and other similar financial securities and futures contracts on those securities;

—options for the purchase or sale of the foregoing securities, currencies, or contracts;

—regulated futures contracts;

—commodities or futures, forwards, or options with respect to such commodities;

—derivatives; and

—a partnership interest in another partnership that is an investment partnership.

• *Interaction of federal and state provisions*

The Illinois definition of "partnership," which includes limited liability companies that are classified as partnerships for federal income tax purposes, syndicates, groups, or other unincorporated organizations, parallels the federal definition found in IRC Sec. 761. However, the term "partnership" does not include a syndicate, group, pool, joint venture, or other unincorporated organization that is established for the sole purpose of playing the Illinois lottery. Illinois regulations provide

¶852

guidance as to when a partnership ceases to be a partnership for Illinois income tax purposes and how reorganization or transfer of shares of the partnership will effect taxation (35 ILCS 5/1501(a)(16); 86 Ill. Adm. Code 100.4500; 86 Ill. Adm. Code 100.9750).

A general information letter states that a partnership that derives income from both lottery winnings and investment income is not excluded, for Illinois income tax purposes, from partnership treatment as an entity formed for the sole purpose of playing the lottery. Also, if a partnership derives more than 10% of its gross income from lottery winnings, it is not an investment partnership.

In this instance the taxpayers formed a partnership for the purpose of collecting and distributing Illinois lottery winnings as well as for investing their lottery winnings. The taxes were paid on the winnings and investment income on an individual level. More than 10% of the partnership's gross income was derived from lottery winnings. The DOR noted that 35 ILCS 5/205 provides that partnerships are not subject to the regular Illinois income tax, but that partnerships other than "investment partnerships" u are subject to the personal property tax replacement income tax.

The DOR stated that because more than 10% of the partnership's income was comprised of lottery winnings, the partnership did not qualify as an investment partnership. Furthermore, there is nothing in the Illinois Income Tax Act that could be read to exempt lottery winnings or income from "qualifying investment securities" received by a partnership that is otherwise subject to Illinois tax, so the partnership would be subject to Illinois's personal property tax replacement income tax on all such income. (*General Information Letter IT 12-0032-GIL,* Illinois Department of Revenue, December 3, 2012, CCH ILLINOIS TAX REPORTS, ¶ 402-618)

Practitioner Comment: Income of Limited Partners

In *Borden Chemicals and Plastics, L.P. v. Zehnder,* February 14, 2000, 312 Ill. App. 3d 35, 726 N.E. 2d 73, CCH ILLINOIS TAX REPORTS, ¶ 401-120, the Illinois Appellate Court, in a case of first impression, held that the imposition of Illinois personal property replacement income tax on the distributable income received by a Delaware limited partner of a limited partnership that operated in Illinois was not in violation of the Due Process and Commerce Clauses of the U.S. Constitution. Although the limited partner asserted that it could not be taxed because it had no connection with Illinois other than the investment in a partnership that operated in Illinois, the limited partnership availed itself of the laws of Illinois and the limited partner received distributable income earned in Illinois and, thus, imposition of the tax did not violate the Due Process Clause of the U.S. Constitution.

Further, the Commerce Clause of the U.S. Constitution was not violated because the limited partnership had substantial nexus with Illinois. The limited partner agreed that there was substantial nexus between Illinois and the limited partnership but argued that substantial nexus had to exist between it and Illinois. The limited partner asserted that because it had no physical presence in Illinois, substantial nexus did not exist and it could not be taxed. However, physical presence was not required to establish substantial nexus between the limited partner and Illinois because the limited partnership was physically present in Illinois and operated in Illinois and served only as a conduit to shift the incidence of the tax to the partners.

Horwood Marcus & Berk Chartered

• *Limited partnerships and limited liability partnerships*

In order to form a limited partnership, a partnership must file a certificate of limited partnership with the Illinois Secretary of State (805 ILCS 210/201). A partnership may convert to an LLP by filing an application with the Secretary of State.

An LLP is not subject to corporate income tax, but is subject to personal property replacement income tax at the entity level equal to 1.5% of net income.

¶853 S Corporations

Law: 35 ILCS 5/201(c); 35 ILCS 5/204(b); 35 ILCS 5/205(c), 35 ILCS 5/1501; 86 Ill. Adm. Code 100.2330, 86 Ill. Adm. Code 100.4500, 86 Ill. Adm. Code 100.9750 (CCH ILLINOIS TAX REPORTS, ¶10-215).

Comparable Federal: Secs. 1361–1379 (U.S. MASTER TAX GUIDE, ¶305–349).

S corporations are exempt from the Illinois corporate income tax but are subject to the personal property replacement income tax (PPRIT) equal to 1.5% of net income (35 ILCS 5/201(c); 35 ILCS 5/205(c)). Since Illinois adopts the federal income tax treatment of S corporations, as set out in IRC Secs. 1361 through 1379, income and losses, including net losses, of the S corporation flows to its shareholders (86 Ill. Adm. Code 100.9750). See also ¶1009.

• *Interaction of federal and state provisions*

"S corporations" are defined to include not only corporations having an election in effect under IRC Sec. 1362, but also certain corporations producing oil and gas that elect federally to "opt out" of the provisions of the Subchapter S Revision Act of 1982. These latter corporations may, for state purposes, apply the prior Subchapter S rules as they were in effect on July 1, 1982, under former IRC Secs. 1371 *et seq.*

Illinois Department of Revenue regulations provide guidance as to when the transfer of ownership of an S corporation causes the entity to cease to exist or continue as the same entity for Illinois income tax purposes (35 ILCS 5/1501; 86 Ill. Adm. Code 100.4500; 86 Ill. Adm. Code 100.9750).

Base income and taxable income: Corporations that do business entirely within Illinois compute a hypothetical federal base income, "unmodified base income," from information reported on federal Form 1120-S. Illinois addition and subtraction modifications are then made to arrive at "base income." Taxable income is then determined by deducting a standard exemption of $1,000 (35 ILCS 5/204(b)).

Modifications to base income: Multistate S corporations subtract nonbusiness income from the modified hypothetical federal base income figure. After the remainder is apportioned, nonbusiness income allocable to Illinois is added to arrive at "base income allocable to Illinois." A standard exemption, computed by dividing the base income allocable to Illinois by the total base income and multiplying the result by $1,000, is then subtracted to arrive at taxable income (35 ILCS 5/204(a)).

Regulations provide special carryover periods allowed under IRC Sec. 172(b) for specific kinds of losses or taxpayers (86 Ill. Adm. Code 100.2330). For example, "specified liability losses" may be carried back to each of the ten taxable years preceding the taxable year in which the loss was incurred (86 Ill. Adm. Code 100.2330(b)(2)(C)(i)). Similarly, bad debt losses of commercial banks may be carried back to each of the ten taxable years preceding the taxable year in which the loss was incurred, and to each of the five taxable years following the taxable year in which the loss was incurred (86 Ill. Adm. Code 100.2330(b)(2)(C)(ii)).

In order to avoid the recognition of a federal net operating loss in more than one taxable year, the amount of any federal NOL deduction taken in arriving at federal taxable income must be added back in the computation of Illinois base income for corporations, trusts and estates. Partnerships and S corporation are allowed to carry over deductions for losses incurred (86 Ill. Adm. Code 100.2330(f)(4)(A)). A loss incurred in a taxable year in which a corporation is an S corporation must be carried to and deducted in any taxable year in which it is not an S corporation in the same manner as if the corporation were an S corporation in that year; a loss incurred in a taxable year in which a corporation is not an S corporation is to be carried to and deducted in any taxable year in which it is an S corporation (86 Ill. Adm. Code 100.2330(f)(4)(B)). The deduction of losses that result when the taxpayer's own taxable income is less than zero, and no loss carried over and deducted by a partnership or an S corporation, may reduce the taxable income of any partner or shareholder of the taxpayer in that taxable year (86 Ill. Adm. Code 100.2330(f)(4)(C)).

Valuation elimination deduction: Although individuals, estates, and trusts are permitted to deduct the appreciation to capital assets that occurred prior to the 1969 enactment of the income tax in determining income, corporations—including S corporations—are not entitled to do so (35 ILCS 5/203(f)(1); *Brown v. Department of Revenue* (1980, App Ct) 89 IllApp3d 238, 411 NE2d 882, CCH ILLINOIS TAX REPORTS, ¶ 201-113).

¶854 Investment Pass-Through Entities

Law: (CCH ILLINOIS TAX REPORTS, ¶ 10-355–10-370).

Comparable Federal: Secs. 851–860, 860A–860L, 1361–1379 (U.S. MASTER TAX GUIDE, ¶ 2301–2369).

This paragraph discusses the tax treatment of investment pass-through entities and their shareholders. Such entities include:

— regulated investment companies (RICs);

— real estate investment trusts (REITs);

— real estate mortgage investment conduits (REMICs); and

— financial asset securitization trusts (FASITs).

Investment partnerships are discussed at ¶ 852.

• *Regulated investment companies (RICs)*

A regulated investment company (RIC) (commonly known as a "mutual fund") is a corporation that acts as an investment agent for its shareholders, typically investing in government and corporate securities. On behalf of its shareholders, the RIC makes and manages various investments, earning dividends and interest on these investments, passing them on as dividends to the shareholders, and ideally retaining nothing after accounting for expenses.

Illinois adopts the federal income tax treatment of regulated investment companies, as set out in IRC Secs. 851 through 855 (*Illinois Response to CCH Corporate Income Tax Multistate Survey*, Illinois Department of Revenue, June 27, 2003).

Federal treatment: As a type of pass-through entity, a RIC may entirely avoid federal income taxation at the entity level if all of its income is annually distributed to its shareholders as dividends. Even if less than all of its income is distributed, but a minimum distribution threshold is satisfied (i.e., 90%), only the undistributed investment company income and net undistributed capital gains will be subject to tax. However, if this 90%-threshold is not met, then all of the RIC's income is subject to tax (IRC Sec. 852(a)(1)).

Qualifications: To qualify as a RIC for federal income tax purposes, an entity must generally be a domestic corporation that is also registered with the Securities and Exchange Commission in compliance with the Investment Company Act of 1940 (15 U.S.C. Sec. 80a-1 to 80b-2) (IRC Sec. 851(a)). In addition, the corporation must affirmatively elect to be a RIC, which it may do so simply by computing its income on Form 1120-RIC (IRC Sec. 851(b)(1)). This election is irrevocable, although the beneficial federal RIC income tax rules will not apply unless certain mechanical asset composition and income distribution requirements continue to be met.

- *Real estate investment trusts (REITs)*

In many ways, a real estate investment trust (REIT) resembles a regulated investment company (RIC), except that a REIT is utilized for passive real estate, rather than for stock, investments. A REIT calculates its income as if it were a regular C corporation, except that certain adjustments apply, the most important of which is the deduction for dividends paid. As with a RIC, if a REIT distributes 90% or more of its ordinary income as dividends, and meets certain requirements as to ownership, management, purpose, and asset diversification, then the REIT is entitled to a deduction for all dividends paid that may be used to offset its income. If applicable, then, similar to other pass-through entities, there is only one level of federal income tax, and that is at the shareholder level. If an entity qualifies as a REIT, income that is distributed to its investors is taxed directly to them without first being taxed at the REIT level. Any retained earnings, of course, are taxed at the regular corporate rates (i.e., the highest corporate tax rate under IRC Sec. 11). A REIT is also subject to tax at the highest corporate rate on its net income from foreclosure property. Furthermore, a 4% excise tax is imposed on any undistributed income (IRC Sec. 857).

Illinois adopts the federal income tax treatment of a REIT, as set out in IRC Secs. 856 through 860 (*Illinois Response to CCH Corporate Income Tax Multistate Survey*, Illinois Department of Revenue, June 27, 2003).

Qualifications: To qualify for REIT status for federal income tax purposes, an entity generally must satisfy detailed organizational requirements, source of income tests, asset holding tests, distribution requirements, and recordkeeping requirements.

- *Real estate mortgage investment conduits (REMICs)*

A real estate mortgage investment conduit (REMIC) is an entity that holds a fixed pool of mortgages and issues multiple classes of interests in itself to investors (IRC Sec. 860D). Under federal income tax law, a REMIC is generally not taxed on its income, but rather its income is taxable to the holders of its interests. In general, it is treated as a partnership, with its interests allocated to, and taken into account by, the holders of the interests in the REMIC (IRC Sec. 860A—IRC Sec. 860C).

Illinois generally adopts the federal income tax treatment of a REMIC, as set out in IRC Secs. 860A through 860G (*Illinois Response to CCH Corporate Income Tax Multistate Survey*, Illinois Department of Revenue, June 27, 2003). However, in the case of a residual interest holder in a REMIC, the net loss is equal to: (1) the amount computed normally or, if that amount is positive, zero; (2) minus an amount equal to the amount computed normally, minus the amount that would be normally computed if the taxpayer's federal taxable income were computed without regard to IRC Sec. 860E.

Qualifications: A C corporation, an association taxable as a C corporation, a trust, or a partnership can all qualify to be a REMIC for federal income tax purposes if it satisfies certain requirements and elects REMIC status (using federal Form 1066) for its first and all subsequent tax years. An entity can qualify as a REMIC if substantially all of its assets consist of qualified mortgages and permitted investments within three months after the entity's startup date (IRC Sec. 860D).

- *Financial asset securitization investment trusts (FASITs)*

A financial asset securitization investment trust (FASIT) is used to secure debt obligations, such as credit card receivables, home equity loans, and auto loans (former IRC Secs. 860H—860L).

Illinois adopts the federal income tax treatment of a FASIT, as set out in IRC Secs. 860H through 860L (*Illinois Department of Revenue General Information Letter, IT 98-0019-GIL*, February 20, 1998, CCH ILLINOIS TAX REPORTS, ¶ 401-439).

¶854

Qualifications: The American Jobs Creation Act of 2004 (P.L. 108-357) repealed IRC Secs. 860H through 860L, which permitted the establishment of FASITs for federal income tax purposes. However, the repeal does not apply to any FASIT in existence on October 22, 2004, to the extent that any regular interests already issued by the FASIT remain outstanding in accordance with their original terms (AJCA Sec. 835(c)(2)).

¶855 Tax Treatment of Pass-Through Entities

Law: 35 ILCS 5/401, 35 ILCS 5/402 (CCH Illinois Tax Reports, ¶ 10-520, 11-520).

Comparable Federal: Secs. 701–761, 1361–1379 (U.S. Master Tax Guide, ¶ 305–349, 401–481).

As discussed in previous paragraphs, Illinois generally adopts the federal treatment of pass-through entities, except that S corporations, partnerships, and trusts are subject to the personal property tax replacement income tax at the entity level (see ¶ 902, ¶ 903).

Federal law treats pass-through entities as separate entities, but requires that the entities' income, gain, losses, deductions and credits be passed-through to the entity's owners, generally in proportion to their ownership interests.

• *Allocation and apportionment*

Partnerships, LLPs, LLCs treated as partnerships, and S corporations apportion their income to Illinois in the same manner as C corporations by using a single-sales factor to determine Illinois source income (see ¶ 315 and ¶ 1107).

• *Accounting periods and methods*

Except to the extent required by differences between Illinois and federal tax law, pass-through entities must use the same accounting periods and methods used on their federal returns (35 ILCS 5/401, 35 ILCS 5/402).

• *Taxable income computation*

The base income of partnerships is discussed at ¶ 207. The base income of S corporations is discussed at ¶ 1009. See ¶ 1006 and ¶ 1007 for discussion of the base income of RICs and REITs, respectively.

Practitioner Comment: EDGE Credit Treated as Tax Payment for Pass-through Entities

The Economic Development for a Growing Economy (EDGE) Tax Credit Act was amended to allow pass-through entities that are awarded an EDGE credit to treat the credit as a tax payment for purposes of the Illinois income tax (HB 2414 Signed into law as Public Act 96-0836; codified at 35 ILCS 10/5-15(f)).

Marilyn Wethekam, Esq., Horwood Marcus & Berk Chartered

¶856 Treatment of Owners' Income

Law: 35 ILCS 5/1501(a)(16); 86 Ill. Adm. Code 100.9750 (CCH Illinois Tax Reports, ¶ 15-115, 15-185, 16-826).

Comparable Federal : Secs. 701–761, 1366, 1367 (U.S. Master Tax Guide, ¶ 309–322, 401–488).

• *Partnerships*

As under federal law, items of income, gain, deductions, and loss are passed through to the partners (86 Ill. Adm. Code 100.9750) (see also ¶ 105). A "partnership" includes a syndicate, group, pool, joint venture, or other unincorporated organization that carries on a business, financial operation, or venture and that is not a corporation, trust, or estate (35 ILCS 5/1501(a)(16)). The term includes a limited liability company treated as a partnership for federal income tax purposes, but does not include an unincorporated organization established for the sole purpose of playing the Illinois lottery.

Guaranteed payments: Although the matter has never been raised before an Illinois court, courts in other states have held that guaranteed payments received by a nonresident partner from a partnership doing business in the state are subject to the state's income tax, even when the partner has no other connection with the state (*General Information Letter IT 12-0028-GIL,* Illinois Department of Revenue, September 27, 2012, CCH ILLINOIS TAX REPORTS, ¶ 402-574).

Allocation of partnership income is discussed at ¶ 321.

See also *Publication 129, Pass-Through Entity Income,* Illinois Department of Revenue, available at **http://tax.illinois.gov/Publications/Pubs/**.

Subtraction for certain wages: Partners are allowed to subtract wages for which the federal Jobs Tax Credit (nondeductible under IRC Sec. 280C) has been claimed (35 ILCS 5/203(d)(2)(J)).

- *S corporation shareholders*

Since Illinois adopts the federal income tax treatment of S corporations, as set out in IRC Secs. 1361 through 1379, income and losses, including net losses, of the S corporation flows to its shareholders (86 Ill. Adm. Code 100.9750). An S corporation is entitled to a subtraction modification for Illinois income allocable to shareholders who are themselves subject to the Illinois Personal Property Tax Replacement Income Tax (35 ILCS 5/203(b)(2)(S)). Taxation of resident and nonresident shareholders is discussed at ¶ 210.

- *Limited liability companies*

An LLC that elects to be taxed as a partnership is a pass-through entity in which profits and losses are passed through to members (35 ILCS 5/1501(a)(16)).

¶857 Nonresident Owners

Law: 35 ILCS 5/308 (CCH ILLINOIS TAX REPORTS, ¶ 15-115).

As discussed at ¶ 321, special allocation rules apply to nonresident partners because the Illinois nonresident federal taxable income of a nonresident partner includes only those items of income, gain, loss, deduction, or credit that are derived from Illinois sources.

S corporation shareholders: The shares of nonresident shareholders in S corporation business income allocated or apportioned to Illinois are attributed to such shareholders under federal rules. Such income is taken into account by the shareholders individually and allocated to Illinois. The shares of nonresident shareholders in S corporation nonbusiness income and deductions are also attributed under federal rules; however, such income is taken into account by the shareholders individually and allocated as if such items had been paid, incurred, or accrued directly to such shareholders in their separate or individual capacities (35 ILCS 5/308(a), (b)).

¶858 Withholding

Law: 35 ILCS 5/709.5; 36 Ill. Adm. Code Sec. 100.5130 (CCH ILLINOIS TAX REPORTS, ¶ 17-155, 89-104).

Comparable Federal : Secs. 701-761, 1366, 1367 (U.S. MASTER TAX GUIDE, ¶ 2447).

Partnerships, S corporations, and trusts are required to withhold income tax from each nonresident partner, shareholder, or beneficiary amounts equal to the sum of:

(1) the nonresident's distributive share of business income that is apportionable to Illinois, plus

(2) for taxable years ending on or after December 31, 2014, the share of nonbusiness income of the partnership, S corporation, or trust allocated to Illinois (other than an amount allocated to the commercial domicile of the taxpayer) that is distributable to that partner, shareholder, or beneficiary under IRC Secs. 702, 704, and Subchapter S.

The total is multiplied by the applicable rates of tax for that partner or shareholder, net of the share of any credit that is distributable by the partnership, S corporation, or trust and allowable against the tax liability of that partner, shareholder, or beneficiary for a taxable year ending on or after December 31, 2014. (35 ILCS 5/709.5(a))

This amount must be withheld and reported even if it is not actually distributed (35 ILCS 5/709.5; *Informational Bulletin FY 2009-02*, Illinois Department of Revenue, October 2008, CCH ILLINOIS TAX REPORTS, ¶ 401-915).

Although this is referred to as "pass-through entity withholding," it is not true withholding. Instead, the pass-through entity is required:

(1) to make a payment based on its nonresident owners' share of apportioned Illinois business income; and

(2) to notify the nonresident owner of the amount of pass-through entity payment made on his or her behalf.

Form tax years ending on or after December 31, 2014, Form IL-1023-C and Form IL-1000 have been eliminated. Amounts that would have been reported on behalf of pass-through entity shareholders or members must be reported on Form IL-1120-ST, Form IL-1065, or Form IL-1041 and Schedule B or Schedule D, and paid with the return, using Form IL-505-B, *Automatic Extension Payment*, or voluntarily prepaid with Form IL-516-I or Form IL-516-B, *Pass-through Prepayment Vouchers*.

The calculation of the amount of pass-through withholding to be reported and paid also has changed. Some nonbusiness income and income tax credits are now included in this calculation.

New forms include (*Informational Bulletin FY 2015-10*, Illinois Department of Revenue, January 2015, CCH ILLINOIS TAX REPORTS, ¶ 402-907):

— Schedule K-1-P(3), *Pass-through Withholding Calculation for Nonresident Members;*

— Schedule K-1-P(3)-FY, *Pass-through Withholding Calculation for Nonresident Members (for Fiscal-year filers);*

— Schedule K-1-T(3), *Pass-through Withholding Calculation for Nonresident Members;* and

— Schedule K-1-T(3)-FY, *Pass-through Withholding Calculation for Nonresident Members (for Fiscal-year filers).*

The applicable schedule must be filed and retained for each of the nonresident members who have not submitted to the pass-through entity Form IL-1000-E, *Certificate of Exemption for Pass-through Withholding Payments.*

Form IL-516-I and Form IL-516-B. Form IL-516-I and Form IL-516-B allow the entity to prepay its own tax liability and to make voluntary pass-through withholding prepayments on behalf of nonresident members for tax years ending on or after December 31, 2014.

Due to the elimination of Form IL-1023-C, Lloyd's plan of operation filers now must file on Form IL-1065. See 36 Ill. Adm. Code Sec. 100.5130 and the Form IL-1065

Instructions for more information. (*Informational Bulletin FY 2015-10*, Illinois Department of Revenue, January 2015, CCH ILLINOIS TAX REPORTS, ¶ 402-907)

If the pass-through entity's payment covers the nonresident owner's Illinois Individual Income Tax obligation, that owner need not file an Illinois individual income tax return. The nonresident owner who does file an Illinois tax return must report the income and is allowed to take a credit for the pass-through entity payment (*Informational Bulletin FY 2009-02*, Illinois Department of Revenue, October 2008, CCH ILLINOIS TAX REPORTS, ¶ 401-915).

¶859 Returns

Law: 35 ILCS 5/502, 35 ILCS 5/505, 35 ILCS 5/602(a); 86 Ill. Adm. Code 100.5100–5170; 86 Ill Adm Code 39-22-116.2 (CCH ILLINOIS TAX REPORTS, ¶ 17-155, 89-102).

Effective for taxable years beginning after 2014, nonresident S corporation shareholders, members of pass-through entities classified as partnerships for federal purposes, trust beneficiaries, and certain Lloyds plan insurance underwriters are no longer permitted to file composite income and replacement tax returns (35 ILCS 5/502(f)). See ¶ 858 for withholding and payment requirements and forms.

Through taxable year 2014, composite returns could be filed on behalf of nonresident and resident individuals, trusts, and estates who derived income from Illinois and who were partners or S corporation shareholders or who transacted insurance business under a Lloyds plan of operation (35 ILCS 5/502(f); 86 Ill. Adm. Code 100.5100–5170).

Additional changes effective after 2014 include (*Informational Bulletin FY 2015-10*, Illinois Department of Revenue, January 2015, CCH ILLINOIS TAX REPORTS, ¶ 402-907):

— elimination of separate composite and withholding income tax returns (Form IL-1023-C and Form IL-1000) for S corporations, partnerships, and fiduciaries (withholding for owners or beneficiaries now must be reported on the return filed by the S corporation, partnership, or fiduciary);

— replacement of the composite return estimated tax payment form (Form IL-1023-CES) and prepayment voucher for pass-through entity payments (Form IL-1000-P) with new payment vouchers (Form IL-516-I and Form IL-505-B);

— new schedules (Schedule K-1-P(3), Schedule K-1-P(3)-FY, Schedule K-1-T(3), and Schedule K-1-T(3)-FY) to assist S corporations, partnerships, or fiduciaries with the calculation of the amount of pass-through withholding, which now includes nonbusiness income and income tax credits.

The following discussion details the return requirements for various types of pass-through entities.

• *S corporations*

S corporations that have net income or loss, as defined under the Illinois Income Tax Act, or are qualified to do business in Illinois and are required to file federal Form 1120S must file an Illinois tax return, Form IL-1120-ST, Small Business Corporation Replacement Tax Return, including Schedule B, Partners' or Shareholders' Identification (35 ILCS 5/505(a)(1)).

Illinois S corporations must also give a completed copy of Illinois Schedule K-1-P, Partner's or Shareholder's Share of Income, Deductions, Credits, and Recapture, and a copy of Illinois Schedule K-1-P(2), Instructions for Schedule K-1-P (For Partners and Shareholders), to each shareholder. (Instructions, Form IL-1120-ST, Small Business Corporation Replacement Tax Return)

Due dates: The due date for filing the Illinois S corporation return is the same as the due date for filing the federal form; thus, Form IL-1120-ST is due on or before the

15th day of the third month following the close of the S corporation's tax year (35 ILCS 5/505(a)(1); 86 Ill. Admin. Code 100.5000).

Extensions: If the S corporation has been granted an extension or extension of time within which to file its federal income tax return for any taxable year, a seven-month extension to file the Illinois return will be granted automatically (35 ILCS 5/505(b)). If no tax is expected to be due, the extension will be granted without the filing of Form IL-505-B, Automatic Extension Payment; if tax is expected to be due, Form IL-505-B must be filed in order to avoid interest and penalty on tax not paid by the original due date (35 ILCS 5/602(a); 86 Ill. Adm. Code 100.5020).

The Director of Revenue may grant an additional extension of more than seven months for filing an Illinois S corporation return if the IRS has granted an extension in excess of six months. A copy of the approved federal extension must be attached to Form IL-1120-ST (86 Ill. Adm. Code 100.5020).

Attachments: There are no specific provisions regarding items that must be attached to Form IL-1120-ST. However, S corporations are specifically instructed not to attach a copy of Schedule K-1-P to their Form IL-1120-ST (Instructions, Form IL-1120-ST, Small Business Corporation Replacement Tax Return).

Further, S corporations that are members of a unitary business group must include a copy of Schedule UB, Combined Apportionment for Unitary Business Group, with their tax returns (Instructions, Form IL-1120-ST, Small Business Corporation Replacement Tax Return; Instructions, Schedule UB, Combined Apportionment for Unitary Business Group).

Composite returns (prior law): Effective for tax years before 2015, an S corporation could file Form IL-1023-C, Composite Income and Replacement Tax Return, on behalf of certain members (35 ILCS 5/502(f); 86 Ill. Admin. Code 100.5130). Generally, the composite return was filed on behalf of S corporation shareholders that are nonresidents of Illinois and had no Illinois income other than that from the S corporation.

Form IL-1023-CES, Composite Estimated Tax Payments for Partners and Shareholders, was used to make estimated tax payments for a composite filing (Instructions, Form IL-1023-CES, Composite Estimated Tax Payments for Partners and Shareholders).

Corrected returns: If the S corporation needs to correct or change its return after it has been filed but before the automatic extension due date has passed, a corrected Form IL-1120-ST must be filed. "CORRECTED" must be written at the top of the return and the changes must be shown (Instructions, Form IL-1120-ST, Small Business Corporation Replacement Tax Return; Instructions, Form IL-843, Amended Return or Notice of Change in Income).

Amended returns: If the S corporation needs to correct or change its return after filing and the automatic extension due date has passed, Form IL-843, Amended Return or Notice of Change in Income, must be filed (Instructions, Form IL-843, Amended Return or Notice of Change in Income).

If an error is discovered on the Illinois return that does not relate to an error on the federal return but was caused by:

—a mistake in transferring information from the federal return to the Illinois return;

—failing to report to Illinois an item that has no effect on the federal return; or

—a mistake in another state's tax return that affects the computation of Illinois tax liability.

The S corporation must file Form IL-843. To claim a refund, Form IL-843 must be filed within three years after the extended due date or the date the return was filed or within one year after the tax giving rise to the refund was paid, whichever is latest. (Instructions, Form IL-1120-ST, Small Business Corporation Replacement Tax Return)

If an amended federal return is filed or if the S corporation is notified by the IRS that it has made changes to the federal return, Form IL-843 must be filed no later than 120 days after the changes have been agreed to or finally determined (35 ILCS 5/506(b)) If the S corporation is claiming a refund, Form IL-843 must be filed within two years after the date of notification by the IRS (regardless of whether notice was given).

- *Partnerships and LLPs*

Partnerships with base income or loss, as defined in the Illinois Income Tax Act, must file an Illinois replacement tax return, Form IL-1065, Partnership Replacement Tax Return (35 ILCS5/505 (a)(2)).

Illinois partnerships and LLPs must also give a completed copy of Illinois Schedule K-1-P, Partner's or Shareholder's Share of Income, Deductions, Credits, and Recapture, and a copy of Illinois Schedule K-1-P(2), Instructions for Schedule K-1-P (For Partners and Shareholders), to each partner (Instructions, Form IL-1065, Partnership Replacement Tax Return).

Illinois Schedule B, Partners' or Shareholders' Identification, must also be filed with Form IL-1065 (Instructions, Form IL-1065, Partnership Replacement Tax Return).

Due dates: The due date for filing the Illinois partnership replacement tax return is the same as the due date for filing the federal form; thus, Form IL-1065 is due on or before the 15th day of the fourth month following the close of the partnership or LLP's tax year (35 ILCS5/505 (a)(2); 86 Ill. Admin. Code 100.5000).

Extensions: A six-month extension to file the Illinois return will be granted automatically (Instructions, Form IL-1065, Partnership Replacement Tax Return). If no tax is expected to be due, the extension will be granted without the filing of Form IL-505-B, Automatic Extension Payment.; if tax is expected to be due, Form IL-505-B must be filed in order to avoid interest and penalty on tax not paid by the original due date (35 ILCS 5/602(a); 86 Ill. Adm. Code 100.5020).

The Director of Revenue may grant an additional extension of more than six months for filing an Illinois partnership replacement tax return if the IRS has granted an extension in excess of six months. A copy of the approved federal extension must be attached to Form IL-1065 (35 ILCS 5/505).

Attachments: There are no specific provisions regarding items that must be attached to Form IL-1065. However, partnerships and LLPs are specifically instructed not to attach a copy of Schedule K-1-P to their Form IL-1065 (Instructions, Form IL-1065, Partnership Replacement Tax Return).

Composite returns: See information under "S corporations," above.

Corrected returns: If the partnership or LLP needs to correct or change its return after it has been filed but before the automatic extension due date has passed, a corrected Form IL-1065 must be filed. "CORRECTED" must be written at the top of the return and the changes must be shown (Instructions, Form IL-843, Amended Return or Notice of Change in Income).

Amended returns: See information under "S corporations," above.

- *Limited liability companies*

Because Illinois treats limited liability companies (LLCs) as either partnerships or corporations and has no LLC-specific provisions or forms, see the specific discussions above for those entity types.

¶860 Penalties

Penalties are discussed at ¶802 and ¶2503.

PART III
CORPORATE INCOME TAX
CHAPTER 9
RATES, TAXPAYERS SUBJECT TO TAX

¶901 Overview

Illinois has two taxes measured by net income: the income tax and the personal property replacement income tax (Replacement Tax). Both taxes are imposed for the privilege of earning or receiving income in Illinois, but only corporations, trusts, and partnerships are subject to the replacement tax. Federal taxable income is the starting point in determining Illinois income (¶1001).

The income tax was enacted in 1969 to apply to individuals, estates, trusts, and corporations, and was held to be constitutional by the Illinois Supreme Court in *Thorpe v. Mahin* (1969, SCt), 43 Ill2d 36; CCH ILLINOIS TAX REPORTS, ¶200-500. The replacement tax was enacted in 1979 to apply to partnerships, trusts, and corporations and was held constitutional by the Illinois Supreme Court in *Continental Illinois National Bank and Trust Co. of Chicago et al. v. Zagel, Director of Revenue et al.* (1979, SCt), 78 Ill2d 387, 410 NE2d 491, CCH ILLINOIS TAX REPORTS, ¶201-059.

Computation of tax, including the base income of various entities, is discussed in Chapter 10. Allocation and apportionment of income is the subject of Chapter 11. Credits against tax, returns, and estimated tax requirements are found in Chapter 12. Information on administration of the tax and collection is located in Chapters 13 and 24.

¶902 Personal Property Replacement Income Tax

Law: Income Tax Act, Sec. 201 [35 ILCS 5/201], Income Tax Act, Sec. 205 [35 ILCS 5/205]; 86 Ill. Adm. Code Sec. 100.9730.

The personal property replacement income tax (PPRIT) was enacted in 1979 to replace the corporate personal property tax abolished by the Illinois Constitution of 1970. Article IX, Sec. 5(c), mandated the General Assembly to abolish all *ad valorem* personal property taxes and, by imposing statewide taxes, to replace revenue lost after January 2, 1971, by local government and school districts. A replacement tax was not required for the personal property taxes of individuals, because individual personal property taxes had been abolished prior to the January 2, 1971, date. Individuals had been exempt from personal property taxation under the former 1870 Illinois Constitution.

The PPRIT consists of additional income taxes for corporations and trusts, new income taxes for S corporations and partnerships, and a new tax on the invested capital of utilities. Because partnerships and trusts are covered in the Personal Income Tax Division, application of the replacement taxes for these entities is discussed at ¶103.

The Section 5 mandate specified that the replacement taxes would not violate the Section 3 Constitutional provision limiting to one the taxes that could be imposed on corporate income. Thus, in practice, the replacement tax, although a specific tax, is treated as part of the corporate income tax. It is measured by the same net income as is the income tax and is reported on the same form.

Practitioner Comment: Anti-Pyramiding Rules

The Income Tax Act (35 ILCS 5/203(d)(2)(I)) provides that, in computing "base income," a partnership subtracts from its income amounts distributed to partners subject to the replacement tax. Thus, to the extent that the partners of a partnership are themselves subject to replacement tax, the incidence of the tax is shifted from the partnership to the partners.

Brian L. Browdy, Esq., Horwood Marcus & Berk Chartered

Investment partnerships are not subject to personal property replacement income tax (35 ILCS 5/205(b); 86 Ill. Adm. Code Sec. 100.9730).

¶903 Rates of Tax

Law: Income Tax Act, Sec. 201 [35 ILCS 5/201]; Compassionate Use of Medical Cannabis Pilot Program Act [410 ILCS 130]; 86 Ill. Adm. Code Sec. 100.2060 (CCH ILLINOIS TAX REPORTS, ¶ 10-380).

Comparable Federal: Secs. 1—5, 11, 12.

The Illinois corporation income tax rate is 7% of a corporation's net income, effective beginning July 1, 2017 (35 ILCS 5/201(b)(13) and (14)). The tax was imposed at rate of:

— 5.25% for taxable years beginning on or after January 1, 2015 and before July 1, 2017 (35 ILCS 5/201(b)(12) and (13); *Informational Bulletin FY 2015-09*, Illinois Department of Revenue, January 2015); and

— 7% for taxable years before 2015 (35 ILCS 5/201(b)(10)).

Practitioner Comment: Senate Bill 9 (Budget Bill)

While Senate Bill 9 (Budget Bill) included a number of substantive changes to tax laws and policies, the headliner was the increase in individual and corporate tax rates. The increase brings the rates back to the level they were at during 2011 to 2014.

David W. Machemer, Esq., Horwood Marcus & Berk Chartered

S corporations, partnerships, and trusts are subject to the personal property tax replacement income tax at a rate of 1.5% (35 ILCS 5/201(d)). Corporations other than S corporations are subject to the personal property tax replacement tax at a rate of 2.5%, which is in addition to the tax rate on corporate income.

Local rates: The legislature has not authorized the levy of any local income taxes, but a portion of the revenue from the state income tax is allocated among the cities of the state (35 ILCS 5/901(b)).

• *Foreign insurance companies*

A foreign insurer's Illinois corporate income tax and personal property tax replacement income tax may not be reduced below the amount of tax needed to produce 1.75% of the insurer's net taxable premiums for a tax year after being added to the insurer's Illinois insurance privilege tax, Illinois fire insurance company tax, and Illinois fire department tax. A tax reduction must be applied first against the corporate income tax rate, minus all credits except the credit for payment of personal property tax replacement income tax. No reduction may be claimed by foreign insurers whose assumed insurance premiums, other than assumed premiums from interaffiliate reinsurance arrangements, are 50% or more of their total insurance premiums. (35 ILCS 5/201(d-1))

• *Surcharge on income from medical marijuana*

For each of the taxable years during the Compassionate Use of Medical Cannabis pilot program (2014 through 2017), a surcharge is imposed on all taxpayers on income arising from the sale or exchange of capital assets, depreciable business property, real property used in the trade or business, and Section 197 intangibles of any registrant organization. The amount of the surcharge is equal to the amount of federal income tax liability for the taxable year attributable to those sales and exchanges. (410 ILCS 130; 86 Ill. Adm. Code Sec. 100.2060)

The surcharge does not apply if the medical cannabis cultivation center registrant, medical cannabis dispensary registrant or the property of a registrant is transferred as a result of any of the following: bankruptcy, a receivership, or a debt adjustment initiated by or against the initial registration or the substantial owners of the initial registration; cancellation, revocation, or termination of any registration by the Illinois Department of Public Health; a determination by the Department of Public Health that transfer of the registration is in the best interests of Illinois qualifying patients as defined by the Medical Cannabis Pilot Program Act; the death of an owner of the equity interest in a registrant; the acquisition of a controlling interest in the stock or substantially all of the assets of a publicly traded company; a transfer by a parent company to a wholly owned subsidiary; or the transfer or sale to or by one person to another person where both persons were initial owners of the registration when the registration was issued.

In addition, the surcharge does not apply if the cannabis cultivation center registration, medical cannabis dispensary registration, or the controlling interest in a registrant's property is transferred to lineal descendants in which no gain or loss is recognized or to a controlled corporation in which no gain or loss is recognized. (410 ILCS 130)

¶904 Businesses Subject to the Tax

Law: Income Tax Act, Sec. 201 [35 ILCS 5/201]; Income Tax Act, Sec. 203 [35 ILCS 5/203]; Income Tax Act, Sec. 205 [35 ILCS 5/205]; Income Tax Act, Sec. 1501 [35 ILCS 5/1501]; 86 Ill. Admin. Code Sec. 100.9720 (CCH Illinois Tax Reports, ¶10-205—10-265).

The Illinois income tax is imposed on corporations for the privilege of earning or receiving income in Illinois (35 ILCS 5/201(a); 86 Ill. Admin. Code Sec. 100.9720). An additional personal property replacement income tax is applicable to all corporations subject to the regular income tax (¶902).

Specially treated entities are discussed in the paragraphs that follow. Corporations that are exempt from the income tax are discussed at ¶905. Included as exempt corporations are such entities as political organizations and homeowners' associations that, although generally tax-exempt, are subject to tax on certain specified categories of income. S corporations, which are exempt from the regular income tax but are subject to the replacement income tax, are discussed at ¶906. DISCs (domestic international sales corporations) and FSCs (foreign sales corporations) are discussed at ¶907. Insurance companies are included in the definition of "corporation" and as such are subject to the tax. Special rules affecting these companies are discussed at ¶1004 and 1005.

Financial organizations and public utilities are subject to the income tax and the replacement income tax in the same manner as other corporations. Determination of the taxable income of financial organizations is discussed at ¶1003. There are, in addition, special rules for the apportionment of the business income of financial organizations and pipeline companies that are discussed at ¶ 1108. The determination of taxable income of regulated investment companies, real estate investment trusts, and cooperatives, together with relevant definitions, is discussed at ¶ 1006, 1007, and 1008.

The corporate income tax and the personal property replacement income tax provisions apply to limited liability companies (35 ILCS 5/1501(a)(4)). A limited liability company will be treated as a corporation, partnership, or person if it so classified for federal tax purposes.

A corporation that is not subject to the Illinois income tax will not become liable for the tax by reason of its ownership of tangible personal property located at the premises of a printer in Illinois with which the corporation has contracted for printing or by reason of the activities of its employees or agents who are located on the printer's premises solely for performing services related to quality control, distribution, or printing (35 ILCS 5/205(f)).

• *Nexus*

The nexus rules for the sales and use tax and the corporate income tax are generally the same: the physical presence of the taxpayers' employees, agents, or property usually creates a taxable connection with the state. However, the U.S. Supreme Court has ruled that some form of physical presence is needed to establish nexus with regard to sales and use taxes (*Quill Corp. v. North Dakota* (US SCt 1992) 504 US 298). There is no such rule with respect to corporate income tax; therefore, intangible property and economic presence could be sufficient to create a filing responsibility for income tax but not for the sales and use tax.

Public Law 86-272, the Interstate Income Tax Act, protects a foreign corporation from state income tax if its only business activities in the state are the solicitation of orders for sales of tangible personal property. Solicitation activity related to the sale of services or intangible property, including electronic commerce, is not protected. Consequently, a software company may lose the protection of P.L. 86-272 if it solicits sales in the state and it distributes some of its products electronically. Mere "solicitation" is not protected if sales involve both tangible and intangible property.

Nexus-creating activities: The following activities have been held to create nexus in Illinois for corporate income tax purposes:

— **Approval of orders.**—A corporate income tax ruling discusses activities that are considered to be beyond "mere solicitation" and are therefore not protected by P.L. 86-272., One such activity is the approval of orders. According to the facts of the ruling request, the taxpayer "approves" the distributor's customers. If the distributor is unable to sell products without authorization from the taxpayer, then the taxpayer's activities are likely unprotected and will be considered beyond "mere solicitation" for purposes of P.L. 86-272. Further, if the approval is not done by an Illinois employee, there would be no nexus. If the approval is done by an Illinois employee, the taxpayer is not entitled to immunity under the federal statute unless the activity is *"de minimis "* considering the taxpayer's entire business activity. The department further stated that, for example, if the taxpayer does a one-time approval for each customer (perhaps for creditworthiness reasons) and those approved customers become regular customers of the distributor so that all sales after the initial approval are handled by the distributor only, the one-time involvement by the taxpayer may be considered *de minimis*. A factual determination must be made taking into account all of the taxpayer's business activities. (*General Information Letter IT 10-0018-GIL*, Illinois Department of Revenue, July 23, 2010, CCH ILLINOIS TAX REPORTS, ¶ 402-177)

— **Sales through distributors.**—The U.S. of affiliate of a global network marketing company purposefully directed regular sales of the parent company's products to thousands of distributors, who contractually agreed to promote and sell the products, at retail, in Illinois and who were required to act as the affiliate's agents for purposes of fulfilling its refund guarantee to retail customers. Rather than merely selling the parent company's products to distributors and being done with them, the U.S. affiliate also agreed to pay distributors for increasing the levels at which they purchased more products to resell to others. Although the products were not sold at a physical retail store in Illinois, the marketplace for the products in the state was in the private homes of distributors, the homes of retail purchasers, or other non-traditional retail settings. The physical presence and activities of the distributors in Illinois were necessary to fulfill the affiliate's guarantee, to maintain its market in Illinois, and to protect its interests. The company's U.S. affiliate had nexus with Illinois and the gross receipts that the affiliate derived from selling the global parent company's products to distributors who lived and/or worked in Illinois should have been included in the combined unitary group's Illinois sales factor for the tax years at issue. Those activities created sufficient minimum contacts between the affiliate and Illinois to satisfy the Due Process Clause under the U.S. Constitution and for the state to impose a tax on the affiliate for the privilege of earning income in the state. Public Law 86-272 did not preclude Illinois from imposing income and replacement tax on the affiliate. There was no credible evidence produced to show that the Illinois distributors were independent contractors or that their activities exceeded mere solicitation of sales. The distributors were not engaged in selling tangible personal property for more than one principal. Retail orders did not have to be sent outside of Illinois for approval. Possession of the parent company's products was physically transferred to retail purchasers from inventory the distributors kept in Illinois. The distributors collected payment for such sales from customers in Illinois. Product returns, replacement products, and refunds were processed by the distributors in Illinois. (*Administrative Hearing Decision No. IT 13-05*, Illinois Department of Revenue, August 2, 2013, CCH ILLINOIS TAX REPORTS, ¶ 402-723)

— **Telecommuting.**—The presence of a single full-time employee working in a state generally meets the substantial nexus standard set forth by the U.S. Supreme Court in *Quill*. The fact that the employee was not required to be located in Illinois, was not located in Illinois for the convenience of the company, and was able to work in Illinois only because the Internet made telecommuting possible did not protect the company from taxation under the federal law. Any taxpayer with an employee working in Illinois, regardless of the reason, would be subject to Illinois taxation (*General Information Letter IT 99-0058-GIL*, Department of Revenue, May 24, 1999; CCH ILLINOIS TAX REPORTS, ¶ 401-091).

An Illinois regulation (86 Ill. Adm. Code 100.9720) provides guidance on when corporate income tax cannot be imposed on nonresidents due to the protections found in federal P.L. 86-272 or statutory provisions. The regulation points out that P.L. 86-272 only prohibits the imposition of tax on those soliciting for sales of tangible personal property and does not apply to efforts to sell intangibles, such as services, franchises, and copyrights. Further, if a nonresident engages in both protected and unprotected activities in a tax year, none of the income earned or received in Illinois in that year will be protected from taxation by P.L. 86-272. For additional information, see *General Information Letter IT 07-0002-GIL*, Illinois Department of Revenue, February 02, 2007, CCH ILLINOIS TAX REPORTS, ¶ 401-773, and *General Information Letter IT 08-0020-GIL*, Illinois Department of Revenue, July 3, 2008, CCH ILLINOIS TAX REPORTS, ¶ 401-895.

Practitioner Comment: Foreign Corporate Partners

A foreign corporate partner of a limited partnership doing business in Illinois is subject to tax in the state, regardless of whether the corporate partner has a physical presence in Illinois, and regardless of whether the partner is a general partner or a limited partner. *Borden Chemicals and Plastics, L.P. v. Dep't of Revenue,* 312 Ill. App. 3d 35 (1st Dist. 2000), CCH ILLINOIS TAX REPORTS, ¶ 401-120.

Brian L. Browdy, Esq., Horwood Marcus & Berk Chartered

Nexus issues are not generally suitable for resolution by letter ruling (*General Information Letter IT 10-0020-GIL,* Illinois Department of Revenue, August 5, 2010, CCH ILLINOIS TAX REPORTS, ¶ 402-201; to the same effect: *General Information Letter IT 12-0007-GIL,* Department of Revenue, March 15, 2012, CCH ILLINOIS TAX REPORTS, ¶ 402-476).

Call centers: A taxpayer asked whether it would owe Illinois income taxes as a result of operating a 24/7 call center for national retailers with multi-site locations. The taxpayer's business consists of coordinating contracted labor on an as-needed basis for its national customers, some of them located in Illinois. The contracted work is done by independent contractors and the taxpayer does not have payroll, inventory, personal property, or a physical presence in Illinois.

The DOR noted that a regulation (86 Ill. Adm. Code Section 110.9720(c)(6)) states that the use of independent contractors may only afford a nonresident immunity from taxation for "limited activities." The fact that the taxpayer's business is entirely set up around using independent contractors on a regular basis may jeopardize the protections afforded in the Illinois regulation.

The DOR stated that it does not issue rulings regarding whether a taxpayer has nexus with Illinois, because such a determination can only be made in the context of an audit where a DOR auditor has access to all relevant facts and circumstances. However, based on the limited facts presented, the DOR conceded that it seems likely that contracting sales of services in Illinois on a regular basis will subject the taxpayer to Illinois income taxation. (*General Information Letter IT 12-0001-GIL,* Department of Revenue, January 12, 2012, CCH ILLINOIS TAX REPORTS, ¶ 402-451)

¶905 Exempt Corporations

Law: Income Tax Act, Sec. 205(a) [35 ILCS 5/205] (CCH ILLINOIS TAX REPORTS, ¶ 10-245).

Comparable Federal: Sec. 501 (U.S. MASTER TAX GUIDE, ¶ 601—608).

Illinois generally follows the federal income tax provisions relating to exempt organizations, as set out in IRC Secs. 501 through 503. Organizations that are exempt from the federal income tax under IRC Sec. 501(a) are also exempt from the Illinois income and replacement taxes and are not required to file Form IL-1120. However, such organizations are subject to income and replacement taxes on any unrelated business income that is determined under IRC Sec. 512 (35 ILCS 5/205(a); see also *General Information Letter IT 10-0019-GIL,* Illinois Department of Revenue, August 3, 2010, CCH ILLINOIS TAX REPORTS, ¶ 402-199 and *General Information Letter IT 15-0011-GIL,* Illinois Department of Revenue, September 8, 2015, CCH ILLINOIS TAX REPORTS, ¶ 403-027).

Exempt organizations report unrelated business income on Form IL-990T. To the unrelated business income computed and reported for federal purposes is added any Illinois income and replacement taxes deducted as an unrelated income expense. The standard exemption is not applicable. Similarly, "political organizations," as defined under IRC Sec. 527, although treated as tax-exempt organizations for tax purposes, are subject to tax on certain investment income that must be reported on federal Form 1120-POL. This nonexempt income is reported on Form IL-1120.

• *Homeowners' associations*

Homeowners' associations that elect federal tax-exempt treatment under IRC Sec. 528 are subject to Illinois income and replacement taxes on the taxable income (nonexempt function income) that is reported on federal Form 1120-H. Both political organizations and homeowners' associations add back any Illinois income taxes that have been deducted for federal purposes.

• *Nonprofit risk organizations*

A nonprofit risk organization that holds a certificate of authority pursuant to Illinois Insurance Code, Art. VIID, is exempt from corporate income tax. A "nonprofit risk organization" is a nonprofit company organized to do business solely with nonprofit organizations as a qualified charitable risk pool under IRC Sec. 501(n) (35 ILCS 5/205).

¶906 S Corporations

Law: Income Tax Act, Sec. 205 [35 ILCS 5/205]; Income Tax Act, Sec. 1501(a)(28) [35 ILCS 5/1501] (CCH Illinois Tax Reports, ¶10-215).

Comparable Federal: Secs. 1371—1379 (U.S. Master Tax Guide, ¶301—345).

S corporations are exempt from the Illinois income tax, but subject to the personal property replacement income tax (¶902). As under federal law, S corporation taxable income or loss is allocated directly to the shareholders in proportion to their respective interests (¶210, ¶856).

For Illinois purposes, an S corporation is a corporation for which there is in effect an election under IRC Sec. 1362 or for which there is a federal election to opt out of the provisions of the Subchapter S Revision Act of 1982 and that may apply the prior federal Subchapter S rules in effect on July 1, 1982 (35 ILCS 5/1501(a)(28)). (For federal purposes, only qualified casualty insurance companies and certain corporations with oil and gas production may elect to have the law on July 1, 1982, apply rather than the current law.)

Computation of base income for S corporations is discussed at ¶1009; see also ¶853.

¶907 DISCs and FSCs

(CCH Illinois Tax Reports, ¶10-255)

(U.S. Master Tax Guide, ¶211, 2468—2471.)

The system of Domestic International Sales Corporations (DISCs) has been replaced by Foreign Sales Corporations (FSCs) as the primary tax-favored vehicle for U.S. exporters. The changes resulted from a dispute between the U.S. and European Economic Community countries over whether the pre-1985 DISC system constituted an illegal export subsidy in violation of the General Agreement on Tariffs and Trade (GATT). Although DISCs were not abolished by the Tax Reform Act of 1984 (P.L. 98-369), their tax benefits were limited and an interest charge for tax-deferred amounts was imposed on DISC shareholders. In addition, their accumulated income was treated as previously taxed income for federal (and Illinois) purposes and, therefore, exempt from income tax if certain conditions were met.

• *Foreign sales corporations*

Under the FSC Repeal and Extraterritorial Income Exclusion Act of 2000 (P.L. 106-519), a corporation may not elect to be a FSC after September 30, 2000. If a FSC has no foreign trade income, as defined in Former IRC Sec. 923(b)(l), for any period of five consecutive tax years beginning after 2001 it will no longer be treated as a FSC for any tax year beginning after that period.

Foreign Sales Corporations or FSCs are organized under the laws of a foreign country or a U.S. possession and must conform to certain arm's-length pricing standards, which are mandated by GATT. Complex rules determine the taxation of FSC income. However, generally, (1) there is no corporate income tax on exempt foreign trade income (at either the FSC or corporate shareholder level), (2) there is a single corporate income tax (at the FSC level) on nonexempt foreign trade income (other than nonexempt foreign trade income under the arm's-length pricing rules), and (3) other FSC income (such as investment and carrying charge income) will be taxed at both the FSC and corporate shareholder level. Distributions to noncorporate shareholders constitute income to the shareholders; noncorporate shareholders are not allowed the 100% deduction generally allowed corporate shareholders for FSC dividends distributed from earnings and profits attributable to foreign trade income.

Like DISCs before them, FSCs have been held to illegally subsidize American exports. Special provisions govern the computation of income for federal income tax purposes (see IRC Secs. 114 and 941—943).

Illinois law contains no special provisions relating to the taxation of FSCs, but if an FSC has an Illinois nexus it must file Form IL-1120. The inclusion of FSC income and expense (to the extent the FSC is taxable) in a combined report with its parent depends on the same factors as the inclusion of ordinary business corporations (*Letters*, Department of Revenue, April 2 and September 3, 1986).

CORPORATE INCOME TAX

CHAPTER 10

COMPUTATION OF INCOME

¶1001 Starting Point for Computation of Taxable Income

Law: Income Tax Act, Sec. 102 [35 ILCS 5/102]; Income Tax Act, Sec. 203 [35 ILCS 5/203]; Income Tax Act, Sec. 250 [35 ILCS 5/250] (CCH ILLINOIS TAX REPORTS, ¶10-505, 10-510).

Illinois, a tie-in state, has adopted federal law as currently amended as the starting point for computing the Illinois taxable income of corporations (35 ILCS 5/203(b)). Income tax terms are defined in relation to the Internal Revenue Code (35 ILCS 5/1501(a)(11)). Taxpayers are required to use the same taxable year and accounting methods as are used for federal reporting. Therefore, most corporations begin computation of Illinois net income with federal taxable income from federal Form 1120, adjusted on the Illinois form worksheet to arrive at Illinois base income. The federal loss carryover deduction may not be used to reduce Illinois income to less than zero. Generally, special entities that file a federal return other than Form 1120 derive federal taxable income from the alternate federal form filed. The starting point for partnerships, for example, is the federal taxable income reported on federal Form 1065.

Bonus depreciation not allowed: Illinois does not allow the 30% or 50% "bonus" depreciation under IRC Sec. 168(k) (35 ILCS 5/203(b)(2)(E-10)). Illinois requires an addition to federal taxable income for the amount of "special depreciation" computed on Form IL-4562. Special depreciation includes bonus depreciation claimed on the federal return, less any IRC Sec. 179 expense deduction, plus any Illinois depreciation subtractions previously claimed on property sold or transferred during the tax year in a transaction for which capital gain or loss was reported for federal purposes. The special depreciation addition is entered on Schedule M of Form IL-1120.

Illinois allows a subtraction from federal taxable income for 42.9% of regular depreciation claimed on the federal return plus the amount of Illinois special depreciation addition reported on any prior year Form IL-4562 for property sold or transferred during the tax year in a transaction for which capital gain or loss was reported for federal purposes (Instructions, Form IL-4562). The depreciation subtraction is entered on the Schedule M of Form IL-1120.

For additional information, see ¶ 1024.

CCH Comment: Gulf Opportunity Zone and Liberty Zone "bonus" depreciation

No addback is required for the additional 50% bonus depreciation for Gulf Opportunity Zone or Liberty Zone property. (Form IL-4562, Special Depreciation)

Corporations may subtract from federal taxable income dividends received from a corporation qualified as a "high-impact business" within a federally designated foreign trade zone or subzone (35 ILCS 5/203(b)(2)(L)).

Dividends eligible for the enterprise zone deduction explained above do not qualify for this deduction.

Corporations may subtract from federal taxable income twice the amount of charitable contributions made to a designated enterprise zone organization if the contributions are used for a project approved by the Department of Commerce and Community Affairs under Section 12 of the Illinois Enterprise Zone Act (35 ILCS 5/203(b)(2)(N)). Certified Enterprise Zones are listed at ¶ 11-166 of the CCH ILLINOIS TAX REPORTS.

Extended NOL carryback not allowed: Illinois law requires federal NOLs to be added back in the computation of Illinois taxable income. A separate Illinois NOL deduction is then taken, as discussed at ¶ 1013.

S corporations: The starting point for S corporations is discussed at ¶ 1009.

Sunset date for deductions: Every deduction against the corporate income tax enacted after September 16, 1994, must be limited by a sunset date. If a "reasonable and appropriate" sunset date is not specified, then the deduction will expire five years after the effective date of the enacting law.

The sunset date is extended by five years for all tax exemptions, credits, or deductions that would have expired in 2011-2013 (35 ILCS 5/250).

• *Exempt income*

A publication identifies who is entitled to a subtraction for exempt income, defines income that is exempt from tax and provides exceptions to those rules, and explains how to claim a subtraction on the taxpayer's tax return. (Publication 101, *Income Exempt from Tax,* Illinois Department of Revenue, March 2010, CCH ILLINOIS TAX REPORTS, ¶ 402-087)

¶1001

¶1002 Chart of Illinois Corporate Tax

On the following pages are two charts illustrating briefly the items that go into federal taxable income and the adjustments necessary to obtain Illinois net income. The charts indicate only the general computations and adjustments, and do not include any special adjustments that may be necessary for taxpayers such as insurance companies, regulated investment companies, *etc.*

COMPUTATION OF FEDERAL TAXABLE INCOME — CORPORATIONS

GROSS INCOME	Gross Profit: Gross Sales, plus Gross Receipts from Services less Cost of Goods Sold Dividends 100% Includible in Gross Income Interest Rents and Royalties Net Gain on Sales or Exchanges Other Income

minus

DEDUCTIONS FROM GROSS INCOME	Compensation of Officers Salaries and Wages Repairs Bad Debts Rents Taxes Interest Ordinary Losses on Sales or Exchanges Contributions Amortization, Depreciation and Depletion Advertising

and minus

	Pension and Profit-sharing Plans; Employee Benefit Programs Other, including Casualty Losses and Research and Experimental Costs

SPECIAL DEDUCTIONS	Net Operating Loss Deduction Dividends-received Deduction (100% Deduction in case of Certain Corporate Groups) Organizational Expense Amortization, Elective

equals

TAXABLE INCOME	To which rates are applied And from total tax there are deducted estimated tax payments for the year, any Foreign Tax Credit, any Credit for Federal Excise Tax on Gasoline, Special Fuels, and Lubricating Oil Used for Nontaxable Purposes and the Combined General Business Credit And there is added any tax from recomputing a Prior Year's Investment Credit and any Alternative Minimum Tax on Tax Preferences

COMPUTATION OF ILLINOIS NET INCOME—CORPORATIONS

PLUS	FEDERAL TAXABLE INCOME BEFORE NOL DEDUCTION	MINUS
State and Local Bond Interest (¶1011) Illinois Income Tax and Replacement Tax (¶1012)	with ILLINOIS MODIFICATIONS	Interest on Federal Obligations (¶1016) Illinois Income Tax Refunds (¶1012) "Section 78 Dividends" (¶1014) Expenses Related to Tax- exempt Income (¶1015) Dividends from Foreign Subsidiaries (¶1018) Dividends Paid by Enter- prise Zone Corporation (¶1017) Dividends Paid by Foreign

Trade Zone Corporation
Designated as High-
impact Business (¶1017)
Contributions to Enter-
prise Zone Projects (¶1017)
Contributions to Job
Training Project (¶1019)
Illinois Apportioned
NOL (¶1013)

equals	
ILLINOIS BASE INCOME	
subject to	
ALLOCATION AND APPORTIONMENT	
minus	
ILLINOIS EXEMPTION (¶1021)	
equals	To Which Is Applied the 7% and 1¹/₂% or 2¹/₂% Rates (¶903)
ILLINOIS NET INCOME	And from the Resulting Tax Deduct: Estimated Tax Payments (¶1203) Credits Against Tax (¶1201)

¶1003 Base Income of Financial Organizations

Law: Income Tax Act, Sec. 201(f) [35 ILCS 5/201(f)]; Sec. 203(b)(2) [35 ILCS 5/203]; Income Tax Act, Sec. 1501(a)(8) [35 ILCS 5/1501]; 86 Ill. Admin. Code Sec. 100.2655 (CCH ILLINOIS TAX REPORTS, ¶10-340).

Comparable Federal: Sec. 291.

Financial organizations, as corporations subject to income and replacement taxes, determine taxable income from federal taxable income as do other corporations and make the same modifications. In addition, financial organizations are entitled to certain interest-related subtractions that are discussed below.

Special rules for apportioning the business income of multistate financial organizations are discussed at ¶1108.

Financial organizations are broadly defined by statute to include any bank, bank holding company, trust company, savings bank, industrial bank, land bank, safe deposit company, private banker, savings and loan association, building and loan association, credit union, currency exchange, cooperative bank, small loan company, sales finance company, investment company, or any person owned by a bank or bank holding company under provisions of the federal 1956 Bank Holding Company Act.

• *Special subtraction adjustments*

In addition to the modifications made by all corporations, financial corporations may subtract:

(1) interest income received on loans made to taxpayers eligible to claim an investment tax credit for property placed in service in a river edge development zone (35 ILCS 5/203(b)(2)(M); 35 ILCS 201(f); 86 Ill. Admin. Code Sec. 100.2655);

(2) interest income on loans for property qualified for the high impact business investment credit (35 ILCS 5/203(b)(2)(M-1)) (see ¶1201 for discussion of the credit); and

(3) the amount disallowed as interest expense under IRC Sec. 291(a)(3), which requires a 20% reduction in the deduction for the financial institution preference items set forth at IRC Sec. 291(e) (35 ILCS 5/203(b)(2)(I)).

The deduction for the interest income on the qualified loans explained at (2) above may be taken only to the extent that the loan is secured by the qualified property. The deductible portion of the interest is computed by multiplying the total amount of interest paid by a fraction whose numerator is the original basis of the property at the time it was placed in service in either the enterprise zone or the federally designated foreign trade zone and whose denominator is the entire principal amount of the loan or loans. The deduction of interest income from high impact business loans may not be taken by a taxpayer eligible for the former deduction of interest on enterprise zone loans; see ¶1017.

¶1004 Base Income of Life Insurance Companies

Law: Income Tax Act, Sec. 203(e)(2)(A) [35 ILCS 5/203] (CCH ILLINOIS TAX REPORTS, ¶10-525).

Comparable Federal: Sec. 801 (U.S. MASTER TAX GUIDE, ¶2370).

The federal taxable income used as the starting point in computing Illinois base income (¶1010) of life insurance companies subject to the tax imposed by IRC Sec. 801 is life insurance company taxable income plus the amount of a distribution from pre-1984 policyholder surplus accounts as calculated under IRC Sec. 815a (35 ILCS 5/203(e)(2)(A)).

"Gross income" from life insurance, for tax years after 2011, means all amounts included in life insurance gross income under IRC Sec. 803(a)(3). (35 ILCS 5/203(b)(3))

When computing Illinois base income, life insurance companies make the same adjustments to federal life insurance company taxable income as do ordinary corporations (¶1010).

Other taxes imposed on insurance companies are discussed at ¶2206.

• *Tax limitation*

Foreign insurers are subject to a limit on the amount of tax they may be required to pay (¶903).

¶1005 Base Income of Mutual Insurance Companies

Law: Income Tax Act, Sec. 203(e)(2)(B) [35 ILCS 5/203] (CCH ILLINOIS TAX REPORTS, ¶10-525).

Comparable Federal: Secs. 831, 834 (U.S. MASTER TAX GUIDE, ¶2378).

The federal taxable income used as the starting point in computing Illinois base income of mutual insurance companies subject to the tax imposed by IRC Sec. 831 is mutual insurance company taxable income or taxable investment income, as the case may be (35 ILCS 5/203(e)(2)(B)).

When computing Illinois base income, mutual insurance companies make the same adjustments to federal mutual insurance company taxable income or taxable investment income as do ordinary corporations (¶1010). Once Illinois base income is computed, net income, which is the base of the tax, is computed by application of the allocation and apportionment provisions (Chapter 11) and subtraction of the standard exemption (¶1021).

Adjustment: If a mutual insurance company that is an interinsurer or reciprocal insurer has made an election under IRC Sec. 835 to take into account the income of an attorney-in-fact that results from the insurance company's payment of commissions to the attorney-in-fact, the insurance company may take an adjustment for that income in calculating its base income for Illinois corporate income tax purposes. An insurance company makes the adjustment in calculating base income by adding to federal taxable income any excess of the amounts the insurance company paid to the attorney-in-fact during the taxable year over the deduction allowed to the insurance company under IRC Sec. 835(b) for the attorney-in-fact's deductions allocable to the income received from the insurance company.

Other taxes imposed on insurance companies are discussed at ¶2206.

• *Tax limitation*

Foreign insurers are subject to a limit on the amount of tax they may be required to pay (¶903).

¶1006 Base Income of Regulated Investment Companies— Adjustment

Law: Income Tax Act, Sec. 203(b)(2)(C), (b)(2)(H), and (e)(2)(C) [35 ILCS 5/203](CCH ILLINOIS TAX REPORTS, ¶10-525).

Comparable Federal: Sec. 852 (U.S. MASTER TAX GUIDE, ¶2301—2323).

The federal taxable income used as the starting point in computing Illinois base income of a regulated investment company subject to the tax imposed by IRC Sec. 852 is investment company taxable income (35 ILCS 5/203(e)(2)(C)).

Although a regulated investment company makes the same modifications to investment company taxable income as an ordinary corporation does to federal taxable income (¶1010), it must also add the excess of net long-term capital gain over capital gain dividends and deduct the amount of exempt interest dividends, as defined in IRC Sec. 852(b)(5), paid to shareholders for the taxable year (35 ILCS 5/203(b)(2)(C), (H)). Once base income is computed, net income, which is the base of the Illinois income tax, is computed by application of the allocation and apportionment provisions (Chapter 11) and subtraction of the standard exemption (¶1021).

¶1007 Base Income of Real Estate Investment Trusts

Law: Income Tax Act, Sec. 203(e)(2)(D) [35 ILCS 5/203] (CCH ILLINOIS TAX REPORTS, ¶10-525).

Comparable Federal: Secs. 857, 858 (U.S. MASTER TAX GUIDE, ¶2326—2340).

The federal taxable income used as the starting point in computing Illinois base income of a real estate investment trust subject to the tax imposed by IRC Sec. 857 is real estate investment trust taxable income (35 ILCS 5/203(e)(2)(D)).

Once base income is computed, net income, which is the base of the Illinois income tax, is computed by application of the allocation and apportionment provisions (Chapter 11) and subtraction of the standard exemption (¶1021).

• *Captive REITs*

Any deduction for dividends paid to a corporation by a REIT that is allowed a real estate investment trust under IRC Sec. 857(b)(2)(B) for dividends paid must be added back. This serves to eliminate the deduction for dividends paid by captive REITs to corporate shareholders. (35 ILCS 5/203(E-15)) The attribution rules in IRC Sec. 318 are used to determine ownership for purposes of determining whether a REIT is a captive REIT (*General Information Letter IT 10-0009-GIL*, Illinois Department of Revenue, April 8, 2010, CCH ILLINOIS TAX REPORTS, ¶402-127).

The definition of a "captive REIT" provides that at least 50% of the voting power or value of the beneficial interest must be controlled by a single corporation (35 ILCS 5/1501) However, certain entities that are organized outside the U.S. are not considered to be captive REITs. Specifically, captive REITs do not include REITs with more than 50% of the voting power or value of the beneficial interest or shares owned by an entity that is organized outside the laws of the U. S. and satisfies the following:

¶1006

— at least 75% of the entity's total asset value at the close of its year is represented by real estate assets (including shares or certificates of beneficial interest in any real estate investment trust), cash and cash equivalents, and U.S. Government securities;

— the entity is not subject to tax on amounts that are distributed to its beneficial owners or is exempt from entity-level taxation;

— the entity distributes at least 85% of its taxable income to the holders of its shares or certificates of beneficial interest on an annual basis;

— either the shares or beneficial interests of the entity are regularly traded on an established securities market or not more than 10% of the voting power or value in the entity is held by a single entity or individual; and

— the entity is organized in a country that has entered into a tax treaty with the U.S.

Effective for taxable years ending on or after August 16, 2007, the voting power or value of the beneficial interest or shares of a REIT does not include any voting power or value of beneficial interest or shares held directly or indirectly in a segregated asset account by a life insurance company to the extent that such voting power or value is for the benefit of entities or persons who are either immune from taxation or exempt from taxation for federal income tax purposes. (35 ILCS 5/1501(1.5))

¶1008 Base Income of Cooperatives

Law: Income Tax Act, Sec. 203(e)(2)(F) [35 ILCS 5/203] (CCH ILLINOIS TAX REPORTS, ¶10-525).

Comparable Federal: Secs. 1381—1388.

The federal taxable income used as the starting point in computing Illinois base income of a cooperative corporation or association is the taxable income determined in accordance with IRC Secs. 1381—1388 (35 ILCS 5/203(e)(2)(F)).

Cooperatives make the same adjustments to federal taxable income as do ordinary corporations (¶1010). Once Illinois base income is computed, net income, which is the base of the tax, is computed by application of the allocation and apportionment provisions (Chapter 11) and subtraction of the standard exemption (¶1021).

For a cooperative corporation or association, the taxable income is determined in accordance with the provisions of IRC Secs. 1381—1388, but without regard to the prohibition against offsetting losses from patronage activities against income from nonpatronage activities, except that a cooperative corporation or association may make an election to follow its federal income tax treatment of patronage losses and nonpatronage losses. If the election is made, the losses are computed and carried over according to state net loss law and apportioned by the apportionment factor reported by the cooperative on its Illinois income tax return filed for the year in which the losses are incurred. The election is effective for all taxable years with original returns due on or after the date of the election. In addition, the cooperative may file an amended return to provide that the election shall be effective for losses incurred or carried forward for previous years. Once made, the election may only be revoked upon approval of the director of the revenue department. (35 ILCS 203(e)(2)(F))

¶1009 Base Income of S Corporations

Law: Income Tax Act, Sec. 203(e)(2)(G) [35 ILCS 5/203] (CCH ILLINOIS TAX REPORTS, ¶10-215, 10-525).

Comparable Federal: Secs. 1361—1379 (U.S. MASTER TAX GUIDE, ¶301—349).

S corporations that do business entirely within Illinois compute a hypothetical federal base income, "unmodified base income," from information reported on federal Form 1120-S (35 ILCS 5/203(e)(2)(G)). Illinois addition and subtraction modifications are then made to arrive at "base income." Taxable income is then determined by deducting a standard exemption of $1,000.

Subtraction for certain shareholders: An S corporation may subtract from unmodified base income an amount equal to income allocable to a shareholder that is subject to the personal property tax replacement income tax (*e.g.,* a corporation, partnership, or another S corporation), including amounts allocable to organizations exempt from federal income tax under IRC Sec. 501(a) (35 ILCS 5/203(b)(2)(S)).

Allocation and apportionment: Multistate S corporations subtract nonbusiness income from the modified hypothetical federal base income figure. After the remainder is apportioned, nonbusiness income allocable to Illinois is added to arrive at "base income allocable to Illinois." A standard exemption, computed by dividing the base income allocable to Illinois by the total base income and multiplying the result by $1,000, is then subtracted to arrive at taxable income.

Practitioner Comment: S Corporations Operating a Unitary Business

If an individual owns all the shares of stock of two S corporations, and the two S corporations are unitary (see ¶1103), then the two S corporations are required to file separate Illinois unitary returns. If both S corporations operate solely in Illinois and one S corporation is profitable and the other S corporation has losses, the S corporations will collectively pay less replacement tax if they are unitary (rather than non-unitary) because the income and losses will be netted in the unitary computation.

Horwood Marcus & Berk Chartered

The reporting of dividend income and pro rata credits from S corporations by resident or nonresident shareholders is discussed under the personal income tax at ¶210.

• *Valuation elimination deduction*

Although individuals, estates, and trusts are permitted to deduct the appreciation to capital assets that occurred prior to the 1969 enactment of the income tax in determining income, corporations—including S corporations—are not entitled to do so. Because the realization of gain is considered to occur at the corporate level, the valuation elimination deduction may not be passed through to shareholders (*Brown v. Department of Revenue* (1980, Ill AppCt), 89 IllApp3d 238, 411 NE2d 882; CCH ILLINOIS TAX REPORTS, ¶10-215.15).

¶1010　Modifications to Federal Taxable Income

Law: Income Tax Act, Sec. 203 [35 ILCS 5/203]; Sec. 1501 [35 ILCS 5/1501]; 86 Ill. Admin. Code Sec. 100-2455 (CCH ILLINOIS TAX REPORTS, ¶10-505, 10-510, 10-600, 10-800).

"Base income," the measure of both the Illinois income tax and the property replacement income tax, is determined by reference to current federal taxable income as computed under the Internal Revenue Code. The statute defines taxable income as that "properly reportable for federal income tax purposes" (35 ILCS 5/203(e)(1)) Throughout the history of the tax, the Department of Revenue has strictly interpreted the statute, permitting adjustments to federal taxable income only when there are express statutory sanctions. The issue has rarely been litigated. However, in one appellate court case, the taxpayer challenged the Department's position that fictitious income reported federally could not be deducted on the Illinois return, pointing out that the statute stipulated "reportable," rather than "reported," income (*Caterpillar Tractor Co. v. Department of Revenue* (1979, Ill AppCt), 77 Ill App3d 90, 395 NE2d 1167; CCH ILLINOIS TAX REPORTS, ¶201–058). The court held that the statute expresses a legislative intent that taxable income for Illinois tax purposes is that taxable income reported for federal income tax purposes.

¶1010

The starting point for computing Illinois taxable income is federal taxable income adjusted on the Illinois form worksheet to arrive at line 30 of federal Form 1120. This figure is modified by mandatory statutory adjustments to arrive at Illinois taxable income. The statutory adjustments are discussed in the following paragraphs.

• *Miscellaneous modifications*

Subtraction of federally nondeductible expenses: A regulation (86 Ill. Admin. Code Sec. 100-2455) provides guidance for taxpayers in determining the subtractions they are allowed for expenses that are not deductible for federal purposes because they are incurred in connection with income that is exempt from federal income tax, but not from Illinois income tax, or with credits allowed for federal income tax purposes, but not for Illinois income tax purposes.

Specifically, corporate taxpayers are entitled to subtract from taxable income an amount equal to the sum of all amounts disallowed as deductions by IRC Secs. 171(a)(2) and 265(a)(2), and all amounts of expenses allocable to interest and disallowed as deductions by IRC Sec. 265(a)(1), and, for taxable years ending on or after August 13, 1999, IRC Secs. 171(a)(2), 265, 280C, 291(a)(3) and 832(b)(5)(B)(i). (86 Ill. Admin. Code Sec. 100-2455). Also, a deduction is allowed for (35 ILCS 5/203(b)(2)(I)):

(1) amounts disallowed by IRC Sec. 45G(e)(3) (railroad track maintenance credit);

(2) for taxable years ending on or after December 31, 2008, for amounts included in the taxpayer's federal adjusted gross income under IRC Sec. 87 (alcohol and biodiesel fuel credit); and

(3) for amounts disallowed by IRC Sec. 807(a)(2)(B) or (b)(1)(B) (reserves included in gross income).

Dividends from captive REITs: An addback is required in the amount of any deduction for dividends paid to a corporation by a captive real estate trust (35 ILCS 5/203(b)(2)(E-15)). A captive real estate investment trust includes privately held REITs, provided more than 50% of the voting power or value is owned or controlled by a single C corporation. A REIT that is not a captive REIT, preparing to go public, a tax-exempt entity, or a listed Australian property trust is not included in the definition. (35 ILCS 5/1501) See also ¶1107.

College contributions claimed as a credit: An addition is required for amounts claimed as a credit by an employer who matched an employee's contribution to certain college savings plans (¶1218) (35 ILCS 5/203(c)(2)(G-15)). For an explanation of the required addback, see *General Information Letter IT 09-0043-GIL*, Illinois Department of Revenue, October 28, 2009, CCH ILLINOIS TAX REPORTS, ¶402-049.

Extension of sunset dates: The sunset date is extended by five years for all tax exemptions, credits, or deductions that would have expired in 2011-2013 (35 ILCS 5/250).

¶1011 Interest on State Obligations

Law: Income Tax Act, Sec. 203(b)(2)(A) [35 ILCS 5/203] (CCH ILLINOIS TAX REPORTS, ¶10-610).

Interest on state and local obligations, including those of Illinois and its political subdivisions, is generally taxable in Illinois. Therefore, such interest, which is exempt from federal taxation, must be added back to taxable income for Illinois purposes, including any such exempt interest that is distributed by a regulated investment company (35 ILCS 5/203(b)(2)(A)).

Exempt interest: Income from bonds, notes, and other obligations of the Illinois Sports Facilities Authority, the Financially Distressed City Assistance Program, the Land Bank Fund, the Quad Cities Regional Economic Development Authority, and the Will-Kankakee Regional Development Authority is specifically exempted from Illinois taxation, as is income from College Savings Bonds. For additional information, see ¶211.

Corporations may subtract interest amounts that are exempt from corporate income tax under Illinois law, the Illinois or U.S. Constitutions, or U.S. treaties or statutes. The exempt amount of income derived from bonds or other obligations is the interest net of bond premium amortization. (35 ILCS 5/203(b)(2)(J); Ill. Adm. Code 100.2470(a)) The subtraction for interest income derived from state and local obligations that are exempt from Illinois taxation is entered on Form IL-1120, Schedule M, line 12. (Instructions, Form IL-1120, Illinois Corporation Income and Replacement Tax Return)

The amount of interest on exempt bonds that represents amortized bond premium is not subject to tax (*Continental Illinois National Bank and Trust Company of Chicago v. Department of Revenue* (1984, SCt), 102 Ill2d 210, 464 NE2d 1064; CCH ILLINOIS TAX REPORTS, ¶400–010).

¶1012 Income and Franchise Tax Deductions

Law: Income Tax Act, Sec. 203(b)(2)(B), (b)(2)(F) [35 ILCS 5/203]; 86 Ill. Adm. Code Sec. 100.2450 (CCH ILLINOIS TAX REPORTS, ¶10-615).

The Illinois income tax and replacement tax deducted from federal gross income to compute federal taxable income are added back for Illinois purposes (35 ILCS 5/203(b)(2)(B)). Illinois income tax that is refunded to the corporation and was therefore included in federal taxable income is subtracted for Illinois purposes because it has previously been included in the measure of tax (35 ILCS 5/203(b)(2)(F)). Because these taxpayers receive no Illinois income tax benefit from these deductions, any refund of Illinois regular income tax or replacement tax that is included in the taxpayer's federal taxable income may be subtracted (86 Ill. Adm. Code Sec. 100.2450).

• *Other states' taxes*

Taxes imposed by other states are deductible for Illinois corporate income tax purposes to the same extent they are deductible for federal income tax purposes.

Tax refunds: A general information letter discusses the corporate income tax treatment of tax refunds that taxpayers receive from other jurisdictions. Illinois does not allow a subtraction modification for a refund of state taxes included in a corporation's federal taxable income. Under 35 ILCS 5/1501(a)(1), a federal income tax deduction for state or local income taxes imposed on the business income of an out-of-state corporation is a deduction allocable to business income, and any taxable refund of that tax should be characterized as business income. As business income, the refund must be apportioned to Illinois in the same manner and to the same extent as the taxpayer's other business income for the taxable year. Taxpayers that claim a tax refund that is not taxable by Illinois may file a petition to be allowed to use an alternative apportionment method ¶1107or to separately account for that refund. (*General Information Letter IT 15-0009-GIL,* Illinois Department of Revenue, August 31, 2015, CCH ILLINOIS TAX REPORTS,¶403-020)

CCH Advisory: Foreign Income Taxes

Foreign income taxes are deductible for Illinois income tax purposes to the extent they are deducted by the taxpayer in the computation of federal taxable income. No Illinois deduction is permitted if the taxpayer claims a foreign tax credit on the federal return instead of taking the corresponding deduction. However, if a gross-up dividend was included in federal taxable income under IRC Sec. 78 because a foreign tax credit was claimed, the gross-up dividend may be subtracted for Illinois corporate income tax purposes. (*Response to CCH Survey,* Illinois Department of Revenue, June 27, 2003.)

¶1013 Net Operating Loss Deduction

Law: Income Tax Act, Sec. 203(b)(2)(D), (b)(2)(E), and (e)(1) [35 ILCS 5/203]; Income Tax Act, Sec. 207 [35 ILCS 5/207]; Income Tax Act, Sec. 405 [35 ILCS 5/405]; 86 Ill. Adm. Code 100.2410 (CCH ILLINOIS TAX REPORTS, ¶10-540, 10-805).

Comparable Federal: Sec. 172.

An Illinois net operating loss is determined on the basis of federal taxable income to which all appropriate addition and subtraction modifications have been made, and allocating and apportioning the result to determine how much of the loss is attributable to Illinois (35 ILCS 5/203(b)(2)(D), (E); 35 ILCS 5/203(e)(1); 86 Ill. Adm. Code Sec. 100.2410). With the adoption of this formula, the determination of Illinois net operating loss for corporations (including S corporations), trusts, estates, and partnerships has been made independent of federal change provisions.

Taxpayers who are required to reduce their federal net operating loss and carryovers by the amount of any discharge of indebtedness income that was excluded from taxation because the taxpayer is insolvent or in bankruptcy are also required to reduce any Illinois net loss and carryover to a taxable year by an equal amount (86 Ill. Adm. Code 100.2310). The regulation clarifies attribution and ordering rules for calculating the loss and carryover, and specific examples are provided. See also *General Information Letter IT 09-0028-GIL*, Illinois Department of Revenue, September 9, 2009, CCH ILLINOIS TAX REPORTS, ¶402-031.

Federal carryback: The federal Job Creation and Worker Assistance Act of 2002 (JCWAA), P.L. 107-147, temporarily extended the federal carryback period for net operating losses from two years to five years for losses incurred in 2001 and 2002; however, this provision does not apply to Illinois corporate income taxpayers, and losses may be carried back two years. Illinois law requires federal NOLs to be added back in the computation of Illinois taxable income. A separate NOL deduction is then taken, calculated as discussed below.

• *Net loss carryover and carryback periods*

CAUTION: The net loss carryover deduction was suspended for tax years 2011-2012, and the carryover deduction is limited $100,000 for any taxable year ending on or after December 31, 2012 and prior to December 31, 2014. For purposes of determining the taxable years to which a net loss may be carried, no taxable year for which a deduction is disallowed may be counted. (35 ILCS 5/207(d)).

After the suspension period, full deductions again are allowed. For additional information, see *Informational Bulletin FY 2011-09*, Illinois Department of Revenue, February 10, 2011, CCH ILLINOIS TAX REPORTS, ¶402-281; see also *General Information Letter IT 12-0017-GIL*, Department of Revenue, July 19, 2012, CCH ILLINOIS TAX REPORTS, ¶402-531.

In addition, the law suspending net loss deductions for C corporations contains no exception or special provision for taxpayers that cease operations during the period in which net loss deductions are suspended; see *General Information Letter IT 11-0013-GIL*, Illinois Department of Revenue, July 8, 2011, CCH ILLINOIS TAX REPORTS, ¶402-387.

If, after applying all applicable addition modifications, the taxpayer's net income results in a loss, the following carryover and carryback provisions apply (35 ILCS 5/207):

— for taxable years ending prior to December 31, 1999, the loss is allowed as a carryover or carryback deduction in the manner allowed under Section 172 of the Internal Revenue Code;

— for taxable years ending on or after December 31, 1999, and prior to December 31, 2003, the loss may be carried back two taxable years and carried forward 20 taxable years; and

— for taxable years ending on or after December 31, 2003, the loss may be allowed as a net operating carryover to each of the 12 taxable years following the taxable year of the loss; no carryback is allowed (except as affected by the suspension and limitation discussed above).

For NOL carryforward and carryback issues relating to individual taxpayers, see ¶204.

• *Computation of deduction*

Except as provided above, the amount of the Illinois net loss deduction for any taxable year is the aggregate of the Illinois net loss carryovers and Illinois net loss carrybacks to such taxable year. The following steps are to be taken in computing the amount of the Illinois net loss deduction:

(1) compute the Illinois net loss in accordance with 86 Ill. Adm. Code Sec. 100.2320, for any preceding or succeeding taxable year from which a net loss may be carried;

(2) compute the Illinois net loss carryovers and carrybacks from preceding or succeeding taxable years in accordance with 86 Ill. Adm. Code Sec. 100.2330; and

(3) add the Illinois net loss carryovers and carrybacks (86 Ill. Adm. Code Sec. 100.2310).

In order to avoid the recognition of a federal net operating loss in more than one taxable year, the amount of any federal NOL deduction taken in arriving at federal taxable income must be added back in the computation of Illinois base income for corporations, trusts, and estates. Since partnerships and S corporations are not allowed a net operating loss deduction for federal purposes, the addback does not apply.

A corporation that incurred Illinois net losses and then ceased conducting business in Illinois is not barred from carrying the losses forward and deducting them in subsequent years when it is again conducting business in Illinois, subject to the same limitations as if it had continuously conducted business in Illinois. A taxpayer that ceases to do business in Illinois does not, on such account, lose any tax attributes it may have acquired under the state NOL provision. Assuming that a loss is otherwise carried under that provision to a taxable year when the taxpayer resumes carrying on business in Illinois, the taxpayer is allowed any Illinois net loss deduction as specified under that provision. (*General Information Letter IT 05-0007-GIL*, Illinois Department of Revenue, May 7, 2013, CCH ILLINOIS TAX REPORTS, ¶402-666)

• *Mergers and acquisitions*

Applicable to all acquisitions described in IRC Sec. 381(a) regarding carryovers in certain corporate acquisitions, all of an acquired corporation's corporate income tax credits (¶1201) and NOLs may be claimed by the acquiring corporation without consideration of the limitations imposed under the IRC Sec. 382 limitation on NOL carryforwards or the federal separate return limitation year regulations (35 ILCS 5/405). Similarly, the IRC Sec. 381(c) limitations on the use of net loss carryover deductions of an acquired corporation are not incorporated into the Illinois corporate income tax law (*General Information Letter IT 09-0032-GIL*, Illinois Department of Revenue, September 23, 2009, CCH ILLINOIS TAX REPORTS, ¶ 402-034).

An acquiring partnership may also claim the personal income tax credits and NOLs of a partnership that is acquired in an IRC Sec. 708 continuation of a partnership. The adoption of these federal provisions concerning successor organizations is applicable retroactively to all acquisitions occurring in tax years ending after 1986. However, transitional rules apply concerning a taxpayer's eligibility for refunds and assessment reductions for pre-1999 tax liabilities.

¶1014 Section 78 Dividends Deemed Paid

Law: Income Tax Act, Sec. 203(b)(2)(G) [35 ILCS 5/203] (CCH ILLINOIS TAX REPORTS, ¶ 10-810).

Comparable Federal: Sec. 78 (U.S. MASTER TAX GUIDE, ¶ 241).

Illinois does not allow a foreign tax credit and has no provision for the inclusion in income of a dividend in the amount deemed paid from a corporation 10% or more of which is owned by a foreign national. Any such amount included in federal taxable income under IRC Sec. 78 is subtracted for Illinois purposes (35 ILCS 5/203(b)(2)(G)).

¶1015 Tax-Exempt Income, Attributable Expense

Law: Income Tax Act, Sec. 203(b)(2)(I) [35 ILCS 5/203] (CCH ILLINOIS TAX REPORTS, ¶ 10-855).

Comparable Federal: Secs. 171, 265, 291 (U.S. MASTER TAX GUIDE, ¶ 970).

Corporations may deduct expenses and interest related to federally tax-exempt income that is taxable in Illinois and is added back on the Illinois return. "Deductible expenses" are defined as those amounts disallowed under the following (35 ILCS 5/203(b)(2)(I)):

IRC Sec. 171(a)(2) (amortizable bond premium);

IRC Sec. 265 (expenses and interest related to tax-exempt income);

IRC Sec. 280C (expenses associated with federal employment credits, the credit for qualified clinical testing expenses, and the credit for increasing research activities);

IRC Sec. 291(a)(3) (certain financial institution preference items);

IRC Sec. 832(b)(5)(B)(i) (reduction of the deduction in computing insurance company taxable income).

For additional information, see Publication 101, *Income Exempt from Tax*, Illinois Department of Revenue, March 2010, CCH ILLINOIS TAX REPORTS, ¶ 402-087.

¶1016 Interest on Federal Obligations

Law: Income Tax Act, Sec. 203(b)(2)(J) [35 ILCS 5/203]; 86 Ill. Adm. Code 100.2470 (CCH ILLINOIS TAX REPORTS, ¶ 10-815).

In computing Illinois taxable income, corporations may subtract amounts that would otherwise be included but that are exempt for Illinois purposes by reason of the Illinois Constitution or the U.S. Constitution, treaties, or statutes (35 ILCS 5/203(b)(2)(J)). The exempt amount of income derived from bonds or other obligations is the interest net of bond premium amortization (35 ILCS 5/203(b)(2)(J); 86 Ill. Adm. Code 100.2470(a)) The subtraction for interest income derived from federal obligations that are exempt from Illinois taxation is entered on Form IL-1120, line 12. (*Instructions*, Form IL-1120, Illinois Corporation Income and Replacement Tax Return)

A federal statute (31 U.S.C. §3124(a)) exempts interest on federal stocks, bonds, treasury notes, and other U.S. obligations from Illinois taxation (86 Ill. Adm. Code Sec. 100.2470)."Obligations of the United States," within the meaning of the federal statute, are obligations issued "to secure credit to carry on the necessary functions of government." A list of such obligations is provided at ¶211.

Practitioner Comment: U.S. Interest

Income from the U.S. Treasury and exempt federal obligations is not taxable by Illinois. However, the amount that is not taxable by Illinois is reduced by both bond premium amortization (existing law), as well as "interest expense incurred on indebtedness to carry the bond or other obligation, expenses incurred in producing the income to be deducted, and all other related expenses" (new provisions).

Horwood Marcus & Berk Chartered

¶1017 River Edge Redevelopment Zone and High-Impact Business Dividends

Law: Income Tax Act, Sec. 203(b)(2)(J), Sec. 203(b)(2)(K) [35 ILCS 5/203]; P.A. 94-1021 (S.B. 17), Sec. 10-10, Laws 2006; 86 Ill. Adm. Code 100.2490 (CCH ILLINOIS TAX REPORTS, ¶10-845).

Corporations may subtract from federal taxable income dividends received from corporations that conduct substantially all of their business in a River Edge redevelopment zone (35 ILCS 5/203(b)(2)(J)) or by a high-impact business in a foreign trade zone or subzone (35 ILCS 5/203(b)(2)(K)).

CCH Advisory: Eligibility for Deduction

Even though a single sales factor is used to apportion business income under Sec. 304(a) of the Illinois Income Tax Act (see ¶1107), the property and payroll factors also must be computed to determine whether a taxpayer conducts "substantially" all of its business within a zone in order to qualify for a zone dividend subtraction. (86 Ill. Adm. Code 100.2480 and 100.9720, Illinois Department of Revenue, effective November 18, 2002.)

Corporations may subtract from federal taxable income dividends received from a corporation qualified as a "high-impact business" within a federally designated foreign trade zone or subzone (35 ILCS 5/203(b)(2)(K)).

CAUTION: Enterprise zone businesses are no longer eligible for this dividend deduction (P.A. 97-905 (S.B. 3616), Laws 2012, effective August 7, 2012).

¶1018 Dividends Received from Foreign Corporations

Law: Income Tax Act, Sec. 203(b)(2)(O) [35 ILCS 5/203] (CCH ILLINOIS TAX REPORTS, ¶10-810).

Comparable Federal: Sec. 245 (U.S. MASTER TAX GUIDE, ¶241).

Illinois does not allow a foreign tax credit and has no provision for the inclusion in income of a dividend in the amount deemed paid under IRC Sec. 78. (35 ILCS 5/203(b)(2)(G)) Any such amount included in federal taxable income on Form 1120, Schedule C, line 15 is subtracted for Illinois purposes.

A corporation may deduct from federal taxable income a percentage of the amount by which dividends received from a foreign corporation exceed the "deemed paid" subtraction related to the dividends (¶1014), plus 100% of the amount by which dividends received from an affiliated foreign corporation exceed the amount of the "deemed paid" subtraction (35 ILCS 5/203(b)(2)(O)).

Illinois allows a percentage of foreign dividends to be subtracted from federal taxable income on the basis of percentage of ownership. The percentages are 70%, 80%, or 100%, depending on the ownership percentage of the receiving corporation. (Form IL-1120, Schedule J, Illinois Corporation Income and Replacement Tax Return) Amounts claimed on federal Form 1120, Schedule C are entered on Form IL-1120, Schedule J and the net federal amount is then multiplied by the allowable Illinois percentage.

"Affiliated," for this purpose, includes those corporations so defined under IRC 1504(a), except that the exclusion for foreign corporations in IRC Sec. 1504(b)(3) does not apply. The amount of dividends subtracted must be reduced by the amount of any federal special deduction allowed with respect to the same dividends.

There is also a deduction for the difference between the nondeductible controlled foreign corporation dividends under IRC Sec. 965(e)(3) (temporary dividends received deduction) over the taxable income of the taxpayer, computed without regard to IRC Sec. 965(e)(2)(A) and without regard to any net operating loss deduction.

¶1019 Contributions to Employee Training Programs

Law: Income Tax Act, Sec. 203(b)(2)(P) [35 ILCS 5/203] (CCH ILLINOIS TAX REPORTS, ¶10-890).

Corporations may subtract amounts contributed to job training projects established under the Tax Increment Allocation Redevelopment Act (35 ILCS 5/203(b)(2)(P)). These projects, funded by municipalities so that contributing corporations may have employees vocationally trained, do not qualify for the federal IRC Sec. 170 charitable deduction.

¶1020 Claim of Right Repayments

Law: Income Tax Act, Sec. 203(b)(2)(Q) [35 ILCS 5/203] (CCH ILLINOIS TAX REPORTS, ¶10-855).

Corporations that take the federal credit under IRC Sec. 1341 may deduct the amount that would have been deducted from federal income had the credit not been claimed (35 ILCS 5/203(b)(2)(Q)). IRC Sec. 1341 allows a credit, in lieu of a deduction, for amounts held under a claim of right that were previously included in federal gross income but were subsequently repaid to others.

¶1021 Standard Exemption (expired)

Law: Income Tax Act, Sec. 204(a) [35 ILCS 5/204]; Income Tax Act, Sec. 205(a) [35 ILCS 5/205] (CCH ILLINOIS TAX REPORTS, ¶10-800).

For tax years ending before December 31, 2003, for both the income tax and the property replacement tax, corporations (other than exempt corporations paying the tax on unrelated business income) were allowed an exemption equal to $1,000, multiplied by the amount of base income allocable to Illinois divided by total base income.

Exemption eliminated: The amount of this exemption is zero for tax years ending on or after December 31, 2003 (35 ILCS 5/204(b); 35 ILCS 5/205(a)).

¶1022 Expenses Related to Credits

Law: Income Tax Act, Sec. 203(b)(2)(I) [35 ILCS 5/203(b)(2)(I)] (CCH ILLINOIS TAX REPORTS, ¶10-855).

Expenses associated with federal employment credits (IRC Secs. 45A, 51, 51A, 1396), the credit for qualified clinical testing expenses (IRC Sec. 45C), and the credit for increasing research activities (IRC Sec. 41) that are disallowed as federal deductions under IRC Sec. 280C may be subtracted from federal taxable income (35 ILCS 5/203(b)(2)(I)).

Partners: Effective for tax years ending on or after August 13, 1999, partners are allowed to subtract wages for which the federal Jobs Tax Credit (nondeductible under IRC Sec. 280C) has been claimed (35 ILCS 5/203(d)(2)(J)).

¶1023 Environmental Remediation Costs

Law: Income Tax Act, Sec. 203(b)(2)(E-5) [35 ILCS 5/203(b)(2)(E-5)](CCH ILLINOIS TAX REPORTS, ¶10-701).

The amount of eligible remediation costs federally deducted by a corporation and claimed as part of the former state environmental remediation tax credit (¶1201) must be added back to the corporation's federal taxable income in computing base income (35 ILCS 5/203(b)(2)(E-5)).

¶1024 Depreciation

Law: Income Tax Act, Sec. 203(b)(2)(E-10), (E-11), (T), (U) [35 ILCS 5/203(b)(2)(E-10), (E-11), (T), (U)] (CCH ILLINOIS TAX REPORTS, ¶10-670).

In determining base income, a taxpayer must add to the taxpayer's federal adjusted gross income or taxable income an amount equal to any IRC Sec. 168(k) bonus depreciation deduction taken on the taxpayer's federal income tax return for the taxable year.

For taxable years ending on or before December 31, 2005, the taxpayer's Illinois depreciation deduction on such property in the year the federal bonus depreciation was taken and for each year thereafter is the amount of the taxpayer's federal depreciation deduction, excluding the bonus depreciation deduction, multiplied by 0.429. For taxable years ending after December 31, 2005, for property on which a bonus depreciation deduction of 30% of the adjusted basis was taken, the depreciation deduction equals the amount of the taxpayer's federal depreciation deduction, excluding the bonus depreciation, multiplied by 0.429. For property on which a bonus depreciation deduction of 50% of the adjusted basis was taken, the depreciation deduction equals the amount of the taxpayer's federal depreciation deduction, excluding the bonus depreciation (35 ILCS 5/203(b)(2)(E-10), (T)). The aggregate amount deducted in all taxable years for any one piece of property may not exceed the amount of the bonus depreciation deduction taken on that property on the taxpayer's federal income tax return.

CCH Comment: Gulf Opportunity Zone and Liberty Zone "bonus" depreciation

No addback is required for the additional 50% bonus depreciation for Gulf Opportunity Zone or Liberty Zone property. (Form IL-4562, Special Depreciation)

Sale of property: If the taxpayer sells, transfers, abandons, or otherwise disposes of property for which a bonus depreciation addition modification was required in any year, the taxpayer may deduct the amount of the addition modification (35 ILCS 5/203(b)(2)(E-11), (U)).

¶1025 Interest and Intangible Expenses

Law: Income Tax Act, Sec. 203(b)(2)(E-12) [35 ILCS 5/203(b)(2)(E-12)]; 86 Ill. Adm. Code Sec. 100.2430 (CCH ILLINOIS TAX REPORTS, ¶10-702).

Foreign interest and intangible expenses: An addition is required for interest and intangible expenses and costs otherwise allowed as a deduction but paid directly or indirectly to a person who would be a member of the same unitary business group but for the fact that the person's business activity outside the U.S. is 80% or more of the foreign person's total business activity (35 ILCS 5/203(b)(2)(E-12); 86 Ill. Adm. Code Sec. 100.2430). The addition must be reduced to the extent that dividends were included in the taxable income/base income of the unitary group for the same taxable year and received by the taxpayer or by a member of the taxpayer's unitary business group with respect to the stock of the same person to whom the interest and intangible expenses and cost were paid, accrued, or incurred.

The deduction will be allowed, however, if the item was paid to a person who is subject to a net income tax with respect to such payment by a foreign country or state (other than a state that requires mandatory unitary reporting).

Also, the deduction will be allowed if the taxpayer can establish that:

— during the same year, the person paid, accrued, or incurred the interest, expense, or cost to an unrelated person and that the transaction giving rise to the interest, expense, or cost did not have the principal purpose of Illinois tax avoidance;

— the interest, expense, or cost paid relates to an arm's length contract and was not paid to avoid Illinois or federal tax; or

— the adjustments made are unreasonable.

"Intangible expenses and costs" include:

— expenses, losses, and costs for, or related to, the direct or indirect acquisition, use, maintenance or management, ownership, sale, exchange, or any other disposition of intangible property;

— losses incurred, directly or indirectly, from factoring transactions or discounting transactions;

— royalty, patent, technical, and copyright fees;

— licensing fees; and

— other similar expenses and costs.

"Intangible property" means patents, patent applications, trade names, trademarks, service marks, copyrights, mask works, trade secrets, and similar types of intangible assets.

Practitioner Comment: Interest and Royalty Expense Limitations

Since 1999, an increasing number of separate-company filing states (*e.g.,* Connecticut, Maryland, Massachusetts) have enacted laws that limit or disallow any tax benefit from paying or accruing royalties to an affiliate, including an affiliated intangible holding company. These laws are intended to close an alleged "loophole" by which an in-state taxpayer reduces its taxable income for royalty expenses paid to an affiliate that may limit its physical presence to only its state of incorporation, which is commonly Delaware or Nevada because those states do not tax that income. Specifically, a number of separate-company filing states have enacted laws that require taxpayers to addback certain intangible expenses and costs paid or accrued to an affiliate in determining their taxable income. In addition, a number of separate-company filing states also require taxpayers to add-back interest paid or accrued to an affiliate.

In 2004, the Illinois General Assembly added a similar provision to the Illinois Income Tax Act applicable for tax years ending on or after December 31, 2004. Illinois' addback rule applies to interest, intangible expenses and costs that a taxpayer pays, accrues, or incurs, directly or indirectly, to a "foreign person." The term "foreign person" is a newly defined term in the Act and it includes a corporation, regardless of where created or organized, whose business activity outside the United States is 80% or more of the entity's total business activity (See P.A. 93-0840). Under Illinois law, a corporation that is a "foreign person" may not be included in the composition of a unitary business group (See ¶ 1103).

Illinois' add-back law is intended to close the "loophole" whereby Illinois taxpayers had been deducting royalties and interest paid to an affiliate that is a so-called 80/20 company that is excluded from the composition of the unitary group. Now, certain intercompany royalty and interest payments that are not eliminated in combination are required to be added back. For tax years prior to 2004, the Department has challenged whether the affiliated payee is actually an 80/20 company; see *Zebra Technologies Corp. v. Dep't of Revenue*, 344 Ill. App. 3d 474 (2003), CCH ILLINOIS TAX REPORTS, ¶401-431.

Horwood Marcus & Berk Chartered

Affiliated businesses: Interest and intangible expenses and costs otherwise allowed as a deduction, but paid directly or indirectly, to a person who would be a member of the same unitary business group but for the fact the person is prohibited from being included in the unitary business group because he or she is ordinarily required to apportion business income under a different apportionment formula (*e.g.,* financial organizations, transportation companies) must be added back to compute Illinois taxable income/base income (35 ILCS 5/203(b)(2)(E-12, E-13; 86 Ill. Adm. Code Sec. 100.2430)).

Additionally, taxpayers must add back any amount of insurance premium expenses and costs otherwise allowed as a deduction, but paid directly or indirectly, to an insurance company that would be a member of the same unitary business group but for the fact the company is ordinarily required to apportion business income under a different apportionment formula. (35 ILCS 5/203(b)(2)(E-14; 86 Ill. Adm. Code Sec. 100.2430))

For taxable years ending on or after December 31, 2011, a taxpayer that was required to add back any insurance premium may elect to subtract that part of a reimbursement received from the insurance company equal to the amount of the expense or loss (including expenses incurred by the insurance company) that would have been taken into account as a deduction for federal income tax purposes if the expense or loss had been uninsured. If a taxpayer makes this election, the insurer must add back to income the amount subtracted by the taxpayer. (35 ILCS 5/203(b)(2)(Y))

Practitioner Comment: Interest and Intangible Expenses

Since 2004, Illinois has had both an interest addback provision and an intangible expenses and costs addback provision. Those addback provisions applied only to amounts payable to an 8/20 company. Beginning with the 2008 tax year, the addback provisions also apply to amounts "paid, accrued, or incurred, directly or indirectly," to unitary members that are excluded from the composition of the unitary return by reason of using a different formulary apportionment method (*i.e.,* insurance, transportation, and financial organizations). There are exceptions to the add-back provisions.

Horwood Marcus & Berk Chartered

¶1026 Domestic Production Activities

Law: Income Tax Act, Sec. 203(b)(2)(E-17) [35 ILCS 5/203(b)(2)(E-17)](CCH ILLINOIS TAX REPORTS, ¶10-660).

Effective for taxable years ending on or after December 31, 2017, an addition to federal taxable income is required by taxpayers computing Illinois corporate income and replacement tax liability equal to the amount of any federal deduction claimed under IRC §199 for domestic production activities (35 ILCS 5/203(b)(2)(E-17)).

CORPORATE INCOME TAX
CHAPTER 11
ALLOCATION AND APPORTIONMENT

¶1101 Allocation and Apportionment—Overview

(CCH ILLINOIS TAX REPORTS, ¶11-505—11-550)

Assigning the income of a multi-jurisdictional corporation among states that already have the right to tax the corporation is generally accomplished by a process known as allocation and apportionment.

CCH Advisory: Determination of Nexus Issues

A regulation discusses the scope of the P.L. 86-272 nexus standards for purposes of the income and replacement taxes (86 Ill. Adm. Code, Sec. 100.9720). The regulation lists specific "protected" and "unprotected" activities, and offers detailed guidance for when a taxpayer may or may not invoke the immunity provided by this federal statute. In addition, the regulation states that Illinois will apply the provisions of the federal law to business activities conducted not only in interstate, but international commerce.

Nexus is discussed at ¶904.

• *Allocation*

Allocation refers to assigning certain types of income, which are usually designated nonbusiness income, to a state on the basis of rules varying according to the type of property that gave rise to the income. "Business" and "nonbusiness" income are distinguished at ¶1106. Rental income from real property, for instance, is commonly assigned to the state in which the property is located. Allocation rules purport to assign income to the state that is its source. When the source of the income is intangible property, *e.g.*, patents or investments, the location of which may be difficult to ascertain, however, allocation rules may adopt an objective criterion for assignment, such as the taxpayer's commercial domicile. Allocation rules are discussed at ¶1109.

• *Apportionment*

Apportionment refers to assigning business income to a state by means of a formula based on such objective factors as sales, property, or payroll. Formula apportionment is used because the source of the income is difficult to determine. Formula apportionment, discussed at ¶1107, is an attempt to measure, if imprecisely, the taxing state's contribution to the environment that permitted the corporation to earn an income.

• *Unitary business*

The complexity of business relationships contributes to the difficulty of determining the source of a corporation's income. This situation led to creation of the concept known as the "unitary business." The U.S. Supreme Court, after questioning the propriety of assigning income to a state on the basis of formal geographical or transactional accounting, explained the unitary business/formula apportionment approach in *Container Corporation of America v. Franchise Tax Board* (1983, US SCt), 103 SCt 2933 (CCH Illinois Tax Reports, ¶ 201-301). In *Container Corp.*, the Court noted that the unitary business/formula apportionment method is a very different approach to the problem of taxing businesses operating in more than one jurisdiction in that it rejects geographical or transactional accounting, and instead calculates the local tax base by first defining the scope of the "unitary business" of which the taxed enterprise's activities in the taxing jurisdiction form one part, and then apportioning the total income of that "unitary business" between the taxing jurisdiction and the rest of the world on the basis of a formula taking into account objective measures of the corporation's activities within and without the jurisdiction. See also *Hans Rees' Sons, Inc. v. North Carolina ex rel. Maxwell* (1931), 283 US 123; *Bass, Ratcliff & Gretton, Ltd. v. State Tax Comm.* (1924, US SCt), 266 US 271, 45 SCt 82 [1—2 N.Y. Tax Cases] ¶ 312; *Underwood Typewriter Co. v. Chamberlain* (1920), 254 US 113, 41 SCt 45. The method has now gained wide acceptance, and is in one of its forms the basis for the Uniform Division of Income for Tax Purposes Act (UDITPA), which has been substantially adopted by a number of states, including Illinois.

The unitary business principle is discussed at ¶ 1103.

¶1102 Illinois as UDITPA State

Law: Income Tax Act, Sec. 303 [35 ILCS 5/303]; Income Tax Act, Sec. 304 [35 ILCS 5/304]; Income Tax Act, Sec. 1501 [35 ILCS 5/1501] (CCH Illinois Tax Reports, ¶ 11-505).

Illinois provisions have been adopted that are substantially similar to the Uniform Division of Income for Tax Purposes Act, except that Illinois now uses a single-factor apportionment formula instead of the three-factor formula of UDITPA (¶ 1107) (35 ILCS 5/303, 35 ILCS 5/304).

Illinois was a member of the Multistate Tax Compact from 1967 to 1975. Although Illinois withdrew its membership in 1975, it became an associate member in 1996. The principles of the Multistate Tax Compact are embodied in the statutory provisions of the income tax law. An overview of UDITPA and the MTC follows.

CCH Advisory: MTC Regulations

The Illinois DOR has issued a comparison table listing the MTC regulations that have been adopted by Illinois (*General Information Letter IT 00-0096-GIL*, Illinois Department of Revenue, December 28, 2000, CCH Illinois Tax Reports, ¶ 401-205).

• *Uniform Division of Income for Tax Purposes Act (UDITPA)*

The Uniform Division of Income for Tax Purposes Act (UDITPA) is a model act for the allocation and apportionment of income among states. UDITPA was drafted to remedy the diversity that existed among the states for determining their respective shares of a corporation's income. UDITPA had been adopted, in whole or in part, by the majority of states.

UDITPA divides income into "business income," which is apportioned by means of a three-factor formula, and "nonbusiness income," which is allocated according to the type of income and property giving rise to the income. Business and nonbusiness income are distinguished at ¶ 1106.

• *Multistate Tax Compact*

The Multistate Tax Compact is a document to which states may subscribe in the interest of uniform taxation of multistate corporate income. The Compact created the Multistate Tax Commission and established for member states a joint audit program for multistate taxpayers. The Compact adopts UDITPA as an optional method of apportionment in member states. The option is not significant in such states as Illinois that have adopted UDITPA as their apportionment law.

¶1103 Unitary Business

Law: Income Tax Act, Sec. 1501(a)(27) [35 ILCS 5/1501]; 86 Ill. Adm. Code Sec. 100.9700; 86 Ill. Adm. Code Sec. 100.3010; 86 Ill. Adm. Code Sec. 100.3380 (CCH ILLINOIS TAX REPORTS, ¶11-520).

The unitary business principle, a case law doctrine (see ¶1101) that predated enactment of the Illinois income tax law, was adopted by the income tax law provisions. Under this doctrine, businesses operating in several jurisdictions that qualify as a "unitary business" are required to apportion income (*Underwood Typewriter Co. v. Chamberlain* (1920), 254 US 113, 41 SCt 45). The income of such a unitary business is attributed not to geographical segments through separate accounting of the specific transactions in a particular state but rather to all the states where business is conducted on the basis of such measuring factors as sales or property (see ¶1107 for current Illinois measuring factors). The unitary business concept also provides the rationale for combined reporting, permitted or required in several states. Combined reporting is required by Illinois (¶1104).

• *Statutory definition of "unitary business"*

The term "unitary business group" means a group of entities related through common ownership whose business activities are integrated with, dependent upon, and contribute to, each other (35 ILCS 5/1501(a)(27)). The unitary business group does not include members whose business activity outside the United States is 80% or more of any member's total business activity; "United States" means only the 50 states and the District of Columbia, and does not include any territory or possession of the U.S. Effective for taxable years ending on or after December 31, 2017, the definition also includes any area over which the U.S. has asserted jurisdiction or claimed exclusive rights over natural resource exploration or exploitation. While a unitary business group must generally be composed exclusively of business corporations, a special rule permits the inclusion of corporate partners and partnerships for tax years ending prior to April 24, 1984 (86 Ill. Adm. Code Sec. 100.9700; 86 Ill. Adm. Code Sec. 100.3380).

Practitioner Comment: Impact of Definitional Changes

Illinois in 1982 adopted a water's-edge combined filing method. Specifically, excluded were companies that had 80 percent or more of their property or payroll outside the United States. The statue defines the term "states" to include the 50 states, the District of Columbia, the Commonwealth of Puerto Rico and any territory or possession of the United States. The term "United States," as it is used for purposes of determining the water's edge group was limited to the 50 states, the District of Columbia and specifically excluded the outer continental shelf (OCS) that was used for mineral exploration. Thus, there is an inconsistency in the two definitions. Arguably, OCS would fall within the definition of a state as it is technically a territory of the United States. The exclusion of the OCS was perceived to be a loophole for corporate income tax purposes. It should be noted, that a very limited group of corporations could have used the exclusion. Effective July 6, 2017 the term "United States" includes OCS. As a result of the amendment the definition of states and United States are more aligned.

Marilyn A. Wethekam, Esq., Horwood Marcus & Berk Chartered

"Common ownership" means the direct or indirect control or ownership of more than 50% of the outstanding voting stock of the corporations carrying on unitary business activity. One corporation has direct ownership of the outstanding voting stock of another to the extent that it owns such stock; it has indirect control to the extent that it owns the voting stock of a third corporation that owns such stock. Any combination of direct and indirect control or ownership aggregating more than 50% qualifies the corporation whose stock is owned for membership in the group. The standards of IRC Sec. 318(a)(1) are used to determine the indirect ownership by an individual.

Passive ownership of as much as 100% of related corporations will not, in the absence of any other indicia of unitary operations, lead to a conclusion that the operations of the group are unitary in nature (86 Ill. Adm. Code Sec. 100.3010). A regulation provides examples of common ownership and rules for determining common ownership in the case of partnerships (86 Ill. Adm. Code Sec. 100.97000).

Business activity is ordinarily unitary when activities of the members are (1) in the same general line, such as manufacturing, wholesaling, retailing of tangible personal property, insurance, transportation, or finance; or (2) steps in a vertically structured enterprise or process. A regulation provides guidelines for determining whether entities are deemed vertically structured enterprises or are in the same general line of business (86 Ill. Adm. Code Sec. 100.3010). In either case, the corporate members must be functionally integrated through the exercise of strong centralized management with authority over such matters as purchasing, financing, tax compliance, product line, personnel, marketing, and capital investment. A regulation provides guidelines for determining whether strong centralized management exists (86 Ill. Adm. Code Sec. 100.9700).

The presence of any one of the above indicia of ownership creates a strong indication that the activities of the corporations constitute a single trade or business (86 Ill. Adm. Code Sec. 100.3010). Examples of unitary businesses are contained in the regulation.

A taxpayer, Clarcor, Inc., sought judicial review of a decision by the Administrative Law Judge finding that its filtration subsidiary and its packaging subsidiary were engaged in a unitary business for purposes of the Illinois Income Tax Act. The analysis engaged in by the Circuit Court focused on the applicability and viability of the 7th Circuit decision *In Re: Envirodyne Industries, Inc.,* U.S. Ct. of Appeals (7th Cir.), Dkt. No. 02-1632, 1/6/2004, where the 7th Circuit considered the requirements governing composition of a unitary group and found that the requirements had not been met on the facts before it. However, according to the Circuit Court, the opinion in *Envirodyne* "ignored [the fact] that functional integration can be demonstrated through a strong centralized management," when it stated that, "[t]he statute, however, says that the members of a unitary business group must depend on and contribute to each other. It cannot be enough that each depends on and contributes to its parent." (no citation provided). The Circuit Court narrowed the issue before it to whether the Clarcor subsidiaries were sufficiently functionally integrated through the exercise of their parent's strong centralized management so as to constitute a unitary business group.

In answering this question, the Circuit Court found factually that the Clarcor subsidiaries were engaged in the same general line of business: manufacturing. Further, the court adopted the ALJ's finding that "a pervasive functional integration existed within the CLARCOR organization during the tax periods in controversy." Following its delineation of the ALJ's factual findings in support of this conclusion, the court stated, "the facts in this matter support functionally integrated enterprise through the exercise of strong centralized management [sic]," and ultimately held that the evidence presented was sufficient to allow the ALJ to conclude that Clarcor's subsidiaries constituted a single, unitary business group for purposes of the Illinois Income Tax Act.

Practitioner Comment: Functional Integration

The legal position taken by Clarcor in this case—that otherwise independent operating subsidiaries cannot be included in the same unitary business group merely because of the presence of a common parent—was the exact same position taken by the Department in the *Envirodyne* litigation. In *Envirodyne,* Judge Posner of the 7th Circuit Court of Appeals referred to the Department's position as "shortsighted" because it would make it harder for the Department to tax affiliates operating outside Illinois. In *Clarcor*, the Department circumvented Judge Posner's warning by changing its legal position, a strategy endorsed by the Circuit Court.

David A. Hughes, Esq., Horwood Marcus & Berk Chartered

Practitioner Comment: Composition of the Unitary Group

Illinois law provides that a unitary business activity can ordinarily be illustrated where (1) the activities of the members are either horizontally or vertically integrated, and (2) the members are functionally integrated through the exercise of strong centralized management. The question has arisen whether a unitary business group may include a parent company and all its subsidiaries over which it exercises strong centralized management, even though the subsidiaries are not functionally integrated with each other. A federal court held that to comprise a unitary business group under Illinois law, all members must be functionally integrated with each other (*In re Envirodyne Industries, Inc.*, 354 F.3d 646 (7th Cir. 2004), CCH ILLINOIS TAX REPORTS, ¶ 401-448).

The Department has historically taken unitary positions contrary to *Envirodyne*. It is uncertain whether the Department will follow the *Envirodyne* decision. The *Envirodyne* case is not binding precedent in Illinois state courts. The *Envirodyne* court acknowledged that Illinois state courts decisions appear to be in conflict with its decision (See *A.B.Dick Co. v. McGaw*, 287 Ill. App. 3d 230 (1997), CCH ILLINOIS TAX REPORTS, ¶ 400-850; *Borden, Inc. v. Dep't of Revenue*, 295 Ill. App. 3d 1001 (1998), CCH ILLINOIS TAX REPORTS, ¶ 400-900).

Horwood Marcus & Berk Chartered

Practitioner Comment: Clarcor, Inc. v. Hamer

The Illinois Court of Appeals, First Division, affirmed the Circuit Court's finding that Clarcor, Inc's filtration subsidiary and its packaging subsidiary were engaged in a unitary business for purposes of the Illinois Income Tax Act (*Clarcor, Inc. v. Hamer*, Dkt. No. 09-L-51291, (Ill. App. Ct. 6th Dist.) 111674 (5/11/12); CCH ILLINOIS TAX REPORTS, ¶ 402-483).

Relying on *In Re: Envirodyne Industries, Inc.*, cited above, the plaintiffs argued that for the Department to treat the subsidiaries as a unitary business, the members of the group must "depend on and contribute to each other. It cannot be enough that each depends on and contributes to the parent." Clarcor argued, there was insufficient horizontal integration between the two subsidiaries to justify treating them as a unitary business. The Court of Appeals, however, focused on Envirodyne's characterization of a unitary business group as "an enterprise that generates income which can't confidently be ascribed to a particular state in which the enterprise operates." "If cash and incomes are intermingled in a cash sharing system," the court concluded, "then it becomes difficult to confidently ascribe them to a particular subsidiary or state." Based on the fact that subsidiaries' shared cash and stock option compensation for senior management was based on both subsidiaries' performances, the court held that the groups were part of a unitary business group for purposes of the Illinois Income Tax Act. Unlike the Circuit Court and the administrative law judge, the Appellate Court at least applied the holding of *Envirodyne* and analyzed the relationship (or lack thereof) between the operating subsidiaries themselves. The Court's application of the *Envirodyne* test, however, is highly questionable. Despite the overwhelming evidence establishing a lack of horizontal integration between the Clarcor subsidiaries, this Court, relying almost exclusively on the centralized cash management system, found that a single unitary business group existed. The *Clarcor* decision suggests that a unitary business determination will turn on the presence or absence of a centralized cash management system. No other Illinois unitary business decision places such heavy emphasis on any one factor.

David A. Hughes, Horwood Marcus & Berk, Chartered

• *Partnerships*

If substantially all of the interests in a partnership are owned or controlled by members of the same unitary business group, the partnership is treated as a member of the unitary business group for all purposes, and, for purposes of allocating income to any nonresident partner who is not a member of the same unitary business group, the business income of the partnership apportioned to Illinois is determined using the combined apportionment method prescribed by 35 ILCS 5/304(e). For this purpose, substantially all of the interests in a partnership are owned or controlled by members of the same unitary business group if more than 90% of the federal taxable income of the partnership is allocable to one or more of the following persons (86 Ill. Adm. Code Sec. 100.3380(d)):

— any member of the unitary business group;

— any person who would be a member of the unitary business group if not for the fact that 80% or more of such person's business activities are conducted outside the United States;

— any person who would be a member of the unitary business group except for the fact that such person and the partnership apportion their business incomes under different subsections of 35 ILCS 5/304; or

— any person who would be disallowed a federal deduction for losses by virtue of being related to any person described above, as well as any partnership in which a person listed above is a partner.

• *Worldwide combinations*

A member of a unitary group is excluded from the combined reporting requirement if the member's business activity outside the United States is 80% or more of the member's total business activity. To determine the percentage of activity within the United States, corporations other than transportation, insurance, and financial companies compute a special apportionment formula consisting of a payroll factor and a property factor. The sum of the two factors is divided by two (or one, if either factor has a denominator of zero). The special factors are computed by dividing the United States amounts by the worldwide amounts (35 ILCS 5/1501(a)(27); 86 Ill. Adm. Code Sec. 100.9700).

Transportation services divide U.S. revenue miles by worldwide revenue miles to determine the percentage of U.S. business activity.

Insurance companies divide premiums on property or risk in the United States by worldwide premiums to determine the percentage of U.S. business activity.

Financial organizations divide financial organization business income from U.S. sources by the worldwide income to determine the percentage of U.S. business activity.

A regulation provides guidelines for determining the portion of an entity's income within and without the United States (86 Ill. Adm. Code Sec. 100.9700).

An Illinois appellate court held that Illinois' combined water's-edge method of apportioning the income of worldwide combinations does not discriminate against foreign commerce (*Caterpillar Financial Services Corporation*, Illinois Appellate Court, Third District, No. 3-94-0830, May 19, 1997; CCH ILLINOIS TAX REPORTS, ¶ 400-855).

¶1104 Combined Reporting

Law: Income Tax Act, Sec. 304(e) [35 ILCS 5/304]; Income Tax Act, Sec. 502(e) [35 ILCS 5/502]; Income Tax Act, Sec. 1401(c) [35 ILCS 5/1401]; Income Tax Act, Sec. 1501(a)(27) [35 ILCS 5/1501]; 86 Ill. Adm. Code Sec. 2310—2350; 86 Ill. Adm. Code Sec. 3010; 86 Ill. Adm. Code Sec. 3310; 86 Ill. Adm. Code Sec. 3320; 86 Ill. Adm. Code Sec. 5270 (CCH ILLINOIS TAX REPORTS, ¶ 11-550).

In utilizing the combined method of apportionment, members of a unitary group filing Illinois income tax returns are required to disclose, in columnar form, all items of income, credit, deduction, or exclusion that would enter into the computation of Illinois base income if each member of the unitary group were required to file an Illinois return (86 Ill. Adm. Code Sec. 100.3320). Schedule UB, Combined Apportionment for Unitary Business Group, is provided for this purpose.

• *Computation of income of unitary member*

The business income of a member of a unitary group is apportioned to Illinois by the applicable apportionment formula (¶ 1107, ¶ 1108). The factors are determined by dividing the Illinois factors for each member filing an Illinois return by the total factor figures of all the members of the unitary group. The appropriate amount of allocable nonbusiness income is then added to each member's share of apportioned Illinois business income to arrive at "base income" allocable to Illinois.

If activities of a corporation with regard to sales of tangible personal property do not give rise to sufficient nexus for taxation under P.L. 86-272 (¶ 1105), those sales will not be included in the numerator of the sales factor for that member. However, such sales are included in the denominator to the extent that they arise out of the group's unitary business activity (86 Ill. Adm. Code Sec. 100.3320).

• *Differing accounting periods*

Unitary income of a group filing a combined report is determined generally on the same accounting periods for all members (86 Ill. Adm. Code Sec. 100.3320). If the member's accounting periods for federal purposes differ, the common parent's accounting period is used. If there is no common parent, the income of the group's members is determined generally on the basis of the accounting period of the member filing an Illinois return that is expected to have, on a recurring basis, the greatest liability for Illinois income tax.

To determine the correct amount of income allocable to the common accounting period, a member may either determine income on the basis of the actual book or accounting entries of the member for the relevant period, or a proration of income based on the number of months falling within the required common accounting period. Estimates of income may be necessary if the proration method involves a member's year that ends subsequent to the common accounting period.

• *Intercompany eliminations*

Income and deductions arising from transactions between members of a unitary group are eliminated whenever necessary to avoid distortion of the group's income or apportionment factors (86 Ill. Adm. Code Sec. 100.3320).

Some intercompany transactions that may distort income if not eliminated are fees received from other members of the group for management and other services, rents, royalties, interest, and dividends. See also ¶ 1025.

Transactions may also result in charges to expense, asset, surplus, or other accounts that must be eliminated if they cause a distortion of income.

The unrealized profit in a member's ending inventory as a result of intercompany sales of merchandise is eliminated unless it tends to remain constant from year to year. If such unrealized profit remains constant from year to year, it will not cause a substantial distortion of income.

CCH Note: Schedule UB

The Illinois Department of Revenue has determined that a significant number of unitary taxpayers are incorrectly adding an eliminations column to Schedule UB, *Combined Apportionment for Unitary Business Groups,* when calculating their apportionment factor for corporate income tax purposes. The DOR provides the following guidance:

— Unitary groups filing Schedule UB may not "add" an eliminations column to Schedule UB, Step 4. Nor may a unitary group use a member's column (Columns A, B, or C) as an eliminations column. Unitary groups that are using a canned software program and forms that were approved by the Illinois DOR may not alter that product.

— The amounts claimed for each member's everywhere and Illinois sales amounts must be net of intercompany eliminations.

Additionally, the DOR recommends that taxpayers review the appropriate tax law provisions before filing Schedule UB. (*Compliance Alert,* Illinois Department of Revenue, January 2012)

- *Unitary groups that include special industries*

Effective for taxable years ending before December 31, 2017, all members of a unitary business group were required to use the same apportionment formula (35 ILCS 5/1501(a)(27)(B); 86 Ill. Adm. Code Sec. 100.9700). For example, insurance companies, financial organizations, and transportation services, which must use special one-factor formulas, could not form a unitary group with a corporation required to use the regular one-factor formula. However, insurance companies could form unitary business groups with holding companies of insurance companies, and transportation service companies could form unitary business groups with holding companies of transportation service companies. Also, corporations that would have formed a unitary group except for the prohibition against varying apportionment formulas could form smaller unitary groups, each of which used the same apportionment formula, as long as there were two or more of each type of corporation in each smaller group. Effective for taxable years ending on or after December 31, 2017, the noncombination rule no longer applies and unitary business groups may include members that must use different apportionment formulas (35 ILCS 5/1501(a)(27)(A)).

Practitioner Comment: Impact of Noncombination Rule Elimination

In 1982, when the water's-edge combined filing method was adopted, the General Assembly adopted provisions which prohibited the inclusion of members in a unitary group who apportioned their income using different formulas. Insurance companies, transportation companies and financial entities each used a distinct apportionment method which related to the manner in which the entities generated income. The methods also mirrored the Uniform Division of Income for Tax Purposes approaches for these industries. For more than 30 years Illinois has followed this method for determining members of a unitary group. An amendment enacted by 2017 budget legislation (Public Act 100-0022 (S.B. 9), Laws 2017) removes the prohibition but fails to address how these 3 distinct industries will be included and apportion their income in a single unitary. It will be up to the Department of Revenue to promulgate regulations that specifically address the inclusion and apportionment of the income of insurance, transportation and financial companies.

Marilyn A. Wethekam, Esq., Horwood Marcus & Berk Chartered

The proper method for determining unitary business group memberships is to identify all entities that are related through common ownership and engaged in either horizontally or vertically integrated enterprises with the requisite exercise of strong centralized management, and to create from the population of entities thus identified, unitary business groups required to use the same apportionment formula (86 Ill. Adm. Code Sec. 100.3010).

CCH Advisory: Captive Insurance Company Excluded from Combined Return

The Ohio parent company of an affiliated group of corporations in the business of operating fast food restaurants throughout the U.S., including Illinois, was not required to include income from an affiliated captive insurance company in the unitary business group's Illinois combined corporation income tax return. Under Illinois law, insurance companies cannot be included in a combined return with noninsurance affiliates because insurance companies are required to apportion business income using a different single-factor apportionment formula based on direct premiums written. Although a significant amount of the insurance company's income for the tax years in question was generated from intercompany trademark royalty payments and interest, rather than from insurance premiums paid by affiliates, the facts showed that it was a *bona fide* insurance company that should have been excluded from the combined return.

The company was licensed as an insurance company under Vermont law. The Internal Revenue Service (IRS) treated it as an insurance company under separate federal audits and did not dispute its status, even making adjustments to the company's loss reserves deductions consistent with that treatment. The company was formed for the purpose of providing insurance to the parent and its affiliates, including business interruption insurance to protect against catastrophic losses from various contingencies, such as an outbreak of mad cow disease, for which the parent had been unable to obtain insurance coverage. Coverage provided by the insurance company also included workers' compensation, general liability, auto liability, auto physical damage, property, crime liability, excess liability insurance, product recall, terrorism coverage, strike insurance, pollution wraparound, and price volatility coverage. Consequently, the insurance arrangements with the affiliated companies met the requirements of risk shifting and risk distribution. Furthermore, there was no evidence indicating the insurance company was formed as a sham business or lacked a valid business purpose.

Given these facts, along with Illinois conformity to federal law, the company constituted an insurance company for federal income tax purposes and should have been treated in a similar fashion for purposes of the Illinois tax law. Thus, the trial court erred in granting summary judgment in favor of the Illinois Department of Revenue and denying the parent company's motion for summary judgment seeking to enjoin the department from collecting deficient taxes, penalties, and interest. (*Wendy's International, Inc. v. Hamer,* Appellate Court of Illinois, Fourth District, No. 4-11-0678, October 7, 2013, CCH ILLINOIS TAX REPORTS, ¶ 402-714)

Holding companies: Within the definition of a unitary business group, the legislation defines holding companies (35 ILCS 5/1501(a)(27)(C));. A "holding company" is a "corporation (other than a bank holding company or a company owned by a bank or a bank holding company) that owns a controlling interest in one or more other taxpayers (controlled taxpayers) that, during the period that includes the taxable year and the two immediately preceding taxable years or, if the corporation was formed during the current or immediately preceding taxable year, the taxable years in which the corporation has been in existence, derived substantially all its gross income from dividends, interest, rents, royalties, fees or other charges received from controlled taxpayers for the provision of services, and gains on the sale or other disposition of interests in controlled taxpayers or in property leased or licensed to controlled taxpayers or used by the taxpayer in providing services to controlled taxpayers; and that incurs no substantial expenses other than expenses (including interest and other costs of borrowing) incurred in connection with the acquisition and holding of interests in controlled taxpayers and in the provision of services to controlled taxpayers or in the leasing or licensing of property to controlled taxpayers." (35 ILCS 5/1501(a)(27)(C)(i))

The income of a holding company that is a member of more than one unitary business group must be included in each unitary business group of which it is a member on a *pro rata* basis, by including in each unitary business group that portion of the base income of the holding company that bears the same proportion to the total base income of the holding company as the gross receipts of the unitary business group bear to the combined gross receipts of all unitary business groups (in both cases without regard to the holding company) or on any other reasonable basis, consistently applied. (35 ILCS 5/1501(a)(27)(C)(ii))

A holding company must apportion its business income in the same manner used by the other members of its unitary business group. The apportionment factors of a holding company that would be a member of more than one unitary business group must be included with the apportionment factors of each unitary business group of which it is a member on a *pro rata* basis using the same method used above. (35 ILCS 5/1501(a)(27)(C)(iii))

If including the base income and factors of a holding company in more than one unitary business group does not fairly reflect the degree of integration between the holding company and one or more of the unitary business groups, the dependence of the holding company and one or more of the unitary business groups upon each other, or the contributions between the holding company and one or more of the unitary business groups, the holding company may petition for permission to include all base income and factors of the holding company only with members of a unitary business group apportioning their business income under one subsection of 35 ILCS 5/304(a), (b), (c), or (d). (35 ILCS 5/1501(a)(27)(D))

- *Combined return requirement*

Corporations, other than S corporations, that are members of the same unitary business group must be treated as one taxpayer for purposes of any original return, amended return, extension, claim for refund, assessment, collection and payment, and determination of the group's income tax liability (35 ILCS 5/502(e)).

- *Part-year unitary members*

If a corporation becomes a member of a group during the group's common accounting period or loses its status as a member during the period, other members, in computing their tax liabilities, must take into account the appropriate portion of the applicable sales factor data of the part-year member in computing their tax liabilities (86 Ill. Adm. Code Sec. 100.3320; 86 Ill. Adm. Code Sec. 100.2350).

The corporation that is a part-year unitary member computes its liability as follows (86 Ill. Adm. Code Sec. 100.3320): (1) business income attributable to the portion of the year it was a member of the group is combined with business income that other members of the group had for the same part year, and the total is apportioned to Illinois on a combined apportionment basis; and (2) business income attributable to the portion of its year during which it was not a unitary member is apportioned to Illinois on the basis of its own Illinois sales for the part year as a respective fraction of its own total sales for that part year. The corporation is required to file a separate return for this portion of its income.

A part-year unitary member, or a corporation that is a member of two different unitary groups during the year, may attribute its taxable income or loss, modifications, business income or loss, apportionment factors, nonbusiness or partnership income or loss, and credits to the different portions of its taxable year using either a proration or specific accounting method. A proration must be done on the basis of the number of months falling within the respective periods. The specific accounting method must be an assignment of specific amounts based on generally accepted accounting principles applied as though the respective periods were separate and distinct for financial reporting purposes. Whichever method is used by the part-year member, the group must use the same method for each portion of the combined return year (86 Ill. Adm. Code Sec. 100.2350; 86 Ill. Adm. Code Sec. 100.3320; 86 Ill. Adm. Code Sec. 100.5270).

- *Net operating losses*

The rules for determining a net loss or net loss deduction are the same as those set forth in 86 Ill. Adm. Code Sec. 100.2310—100.2330. They apply whether or not an election for combined reporting is in effect. If an election is in effect, any Illinois net loss and Illinois net loss deduction of the unitary business group must be determined as if the group were one taxpayer. If such an election is not in effect, any Illinois net loss and Illinois net loss deduction must be determined separately on the basis of the separate corporate returns of each member of the group.

Although the amount of the loss will be the same whether or not a combined return is filed, an election to file a combined return may affect whether or not an Illinois net loss is incurred by particular members of the unitary business group if some members have nonunitary income or loss. If a combined return is not filed, any such loss will be apportioned among all members of the group on the basis of each member's apportionment factors in Illinois as compared to their combined apportionment factors everywhere.

¶1104

Practitioner Comment: AT&T Teleholdings, Inc. v. Dep't of Revenue, 1-11-0493

The Illinois Appellate Court affirmed the lower court's approval of the Department of Revenue's use of a separate accounting method when calculating the portion of a net loss that can be carried back by a recently acquired subsidiary. In 1999, SBC Teleholdings, Inc. acquired all of Ameritech Corp.'s stock, which became part of SBC's federal consolidated group. However, under Illinois law, the companies remained separate and distinct businesses until December 31, 1999. SBC's unitary group reported a net combined capital loss for 2002. Subsequently, Ameritech filed an amended tax return attempting to carry back some of the SBC loss to offset a 1999 capital gain. The Department of Revenue partially denied the amended return finding that the separate company accounting method governed the amount that could be carried back. Ameritech appealed, arguing that the Illinois Income Tax Act requires the combined apportionment method. The administrative law judge ruled that separate company accounting is the proper valuation method. The circuit court affirmed the ALJ. On appeal, Ameritech made a number of arguments. First, the ALJ's interpretation conflicted with other sections of the Illinois Income Tax Act that treat unitary businesses as one taxpayer. The court acknowledged the presence of this language in the Act; however, the court found that the Act merely requires a unitary group be treated as a single taxpayer to permit the filing of a single return and because it is silent on the allocation of capital losses to members of a unitary group, no inconsistency existed. Moreover, the separate accounting method is specifically authorized by the Income Tax Act. Ameritech also contended that the valuation method utilized by the Department distorted its business in Illinois. Rejecting this argument, the court held the taxpayer did not meet their burden of proving the department's method caused a gross distortion of income attributable to Illinois as is necessary for an alternative valuation. Finally, Ameritech argued that the Department's regulation was invalid, as federal regulations govern the allocation of capital losses. The court rejected this argument as well, finding that capital losses, which continue to be governed by federal provisions, are separate from rules governing Illinois net losses. In affirming the lower court's decision, this court confirmed that separate accounting is the proper method for valuing the portion of a parent company's capital loss that can be carried back by a recently acquired. Consequently, Ameritech was entitled to only a fraction of the return they claimed. The decision upholds the Department's long-standing rule, reflected in its regulations, that capital losses are determined prior to apportionment. Although a unitary group is characterized as a single taxpayer, for purposes of utilizing capital losses, a separate company accounting method must be applied.

Marilyn A. Wethekam, Esq., Horwood Marcus & Berk, Chartered

• *Carryback and carryforward of net operating losses*

Except for the suspension and limitations discussed at ¶ 1013, the law imposes no limitation on the amount of Illinois net loss that is available as a carryback or carryover. However, the election of whether or not to adopt combined reporting may affect the amount of Illinois net loss deduction that can be absorbed in a particular year. If a combined return is filed, any Illinois net loss deductions are combined and subtracted from combined Illinois net income, whereas if a separate return is filed, the Illinois net loss deduction of that member only would be deducted from that member's separate Illinois net income.

Practitioner Comment: FSCs in Unitary Groups

Over the past years, the Department has made inconsistent public statements as to whether a foreign sales corporation (FSC) may be excluded from a unitary business group under the so-called 80/20 rule. Under the 80/20 rule, a corporation may not be included as a member of a unitary business group if the corporation's business activity outside the United States is 80% or more of the member's total business activity. A corporation's U.S. business activity percentage is generally based upon its U.S. property and payroll, as compared to its property and payroll everywhere.

The Department had issued a letter ruling in July 1991 that stated that the 80/20 rule should not be applied or considered in determining whether an FSC should be included as a member of a unitary business group. The Department had presumed that, to the extent that an FSC had foreign payroll and property, those factors were related solely to income not taxable by Illinois, and as such, should not be considered in determining an FSC's U.S. business activity percentage.

The Department rescinded its July 1991 letter ruling in an October 1997 letter ruling. Then, in May 2001, the Department issued a regulation that provided that an FSC shall use all its worldwide property and payroll factors in determining whether the FSC meets the 80/20 test, and all of its factors in apportioning its business income.

The Department has offered to settle any disputes involving the issue of whether an FSC may be excluded under the 80/20 test for open taxable years ending after December 31, 1989, and beginning prior to January 1, 1998. The Department has offered to concede 70% of the tax liability and abate penalties in full.

Marilyn A. Wethekam, Esq., Horwood Marcus & Berk Chartered

¶1105 Corporations Subject to Illinois Allocation and Apportionment Provisions

Law: Income Tax Act, Sec. 303 [35 ILCS 5/303]; Income Tax Act, Sec. 304 [35 ILCS 5/304]; 86 Ill. Adm. Code Sec. 100.3110; 86 Ill. Adm. Code Sec. 100.3200 (CCH ILLINOIS TAX REPORTS, ¶ 11-520).

Illinois has adopted UDITPA and substantially all of the MTC regulations (35 ILCS 5/303, 35 ILCS 5/304). Therefore, the Illinois allocation and apportionment provisions are applicable to taxpayers who are "taxable in another state" (see below). MTC Reg. IV.2(b)(3) permits allocation of nonbusiness income regardless of whether the corporation is taxable in another state. Although Illinois has not adopted this rule, a taxpayer may make an irrevocable election to treat all nonbusiness income as business income (35 ILCS 5/1501(a)(1); 86 Ill. Adm. Code Sec. 100.3015). Insurance and transportation companies are subject to the Illinois allocation and apportionment rules. These companies are required to use special formulas to apportion income (¶1108).

• *Right to allocate and apportion under UDITPA*

The Uniform Division of Income for Tax Purposes Act draws a distinction between business and nonbusiness income. To the extent the income is business income as defined by UDITPA and the taxpayer is taxable both within and without a state, the taxpayer has the right to apportion that income. Although the MTC Regulations embody the UDITPA concepts and draw a distinction between business and nonbusiness income, the concept is construed as favoring business income.

For purposes of the UDITPA provision, a taxpayer is taxable in another State if (1) in that State the taxpayer is subject to a net income tax, a franchise tax measured by income, a franchise tax for the privilege of doing business, or a corporate stock tax, or (2) that State has jurisdiction to subject the taxpayer to a net income tax regardless of whether, in fact, the State does or does not. The UDITPA comments explain that the Act establishes two tests of taxability, one actual and one hypothetical. Thus, a taxpayer may apportion if it is actually subjected to one of the four taxes listed or if its activities in another state were such that the state could constitutionally impose an income tax on the taxpayer, regardless of whether, in fact, it does so.

CCH Advisory: Apportionment Without Nexus

The Illinois DOR allowed a financial institution and a bank holding company that were chartered and doing business in Illinois but that lacked nexus with any other state to apportion interest income earned from customers in other states. Corporations are considered nonresidents because they do not meet the statutory definition of "residents." Consequently, they may apportion income as long as it is not derived solely from Illinois. Further, a regulation (86 Ill. Adm. Code Sec. 100.3200), which states that a nonresident who is "taxable in another state" may apportion its income, could not be read to imply that a nonresident must actually be taxable in another state to apportion income, because such a reading would be contrary to the statute (35 ILCS 5/101) (*General Information Letter IT 01-003-GIL*, Department of Revenue, January 8, 2001, CCH ILLINOIS TAX REPORTS, ¶401-228).

- *Type of tax that will satisfy the UDITPA tests*

Regulations issued by the Multistate Tax Commission explain that the list of taxes that may make a taxpayer "subject to" a tax in another state (test one) is directed at income taxes or "other types of taxes [that] may be imposed as a substitute for an income tax." In determining, therefore, whether a taxpayer is "subject to" a tax in another state, the regulations call for consideration of only those taxes listed that "may be considered as basically revenue raising rather than regulatory measures . . . ." Illinois, like UDITPA, has adopted a two-part test to determine when a taxpayer is taxable in another state. In accordance with 35 ILCS 5/303, a taxpayer is taxable in another state if subject to that state's net income tax, a franchise tax measured by net income, a franchise tax for the privilege of doing business, or a capital stock tax. In addition, a taxpayer is taxable if the state has jurisdiction to subject the taxpayer to a net income tax regardless of whether such a tax is imposed.

- *Test One: Proof of taxability; voluntary payments*

In explaining the first UDITPA test of apportionability—whether a taxpayer is "subject to" one of the specified taxes in another state—the regulations issued by the Multistate Tax Commission establish two conditions: (1) the taxpayer must carry on business activities in the other state, and (2) the other state must impose one of the specified taxes on those activities.

Upon a taxpayer's assertion that it is subject to one of the types of taxes listed, the MTC regulations provide that the state taxing administrator may require the taxpayer to furnish evidence to support its assertion. The taxpayer's failure to furnish proof may be taken into account in determining whether the taxpayer is subject to one of the specified taxes.

If a taxpayer voluntarily pays one of the enumerated taxes when not required to do so by the laws of the state, or pays a minimal fee for the qualification or for the privilege of doing business in the state, but is not actually engaged in business in the state, then the taxpayer is not "subject to" a tax to qualify for apportionment.

Illinois has adopted a similar position. A corporation that pays a minimum franchise tax for the privilege of doing business in a state is not taxable in the state for apportionment purposes if the minimum amount paid bears no relation to the business activities within the state. Unlike UDITPA and the MTC Rules, 86 Ill. Adm. Code Sec. 100.3200(2) requires that tax actually be paid.

- *Test Two: Standards of P.L. 86-272*

The second UDITPA test of taxability—whether a state has "jurisdiction" to tax—applies, according to the MTC Regulations, if the taxpayer's business activity is sufficient to give the state jurisdiction to impose a net income tax by reason of such business activity under the Constitution and statutes of the United States.

Shortly after the 1959 U.S. Supreme Court decision permitting states to tax the income of an out-of-state seller with salesmen and a stock of goods in the state (*Portland Cement Co. v. Minnesota* (1959, US SCt), 358 US 450, 79 SCt 357), Congress enacted P.L. 86-272. Under P.L. 86-272, income derived by a corporation from interstate sales of tangible personal property can be taxed only if the minimum standards of P.L. 86-272 have been met by the corporation's activity in the state. P.L. 86-272 prohibits a state from imposing a net income tax on income derived from interstate commerce when the only business activity in the state consists of soliciting orders for the purchase of tangible personal property, which orders are filled from out of state.

The MTC regulations adopt the standards of P.L. 86-272 for purposes of determining a state's jurisdiction to tax. Thus, the regulation states that jurisdiction to tax is not present when the state is prohibited from imposing the tax by reason of the provisions of P.L. 86-272. For this purpose, "state" includes a foreign country (86 Ill. Adm. Code Sec. 100.3110); the determination of whether the foreign country has jurisdiction to subject the taxpayer to a net income tax is made as though the jurisdictional standards applicable to a state apply in the foreign country (86 Ill. Adm. Code Sec. 100.3200).

Public Law 86-272 applies only to the sale of tangible personal property; the taxability of other types of income, such as service income, is governed by general U.S. Constitutional principles.

¶1106 Business/Nonbusiness Income Distinguished

Law: Income Tax Act, Sec. 203(e)(3) [35 ILCS5/203]; Income Tax Act, Sec. 301 [35 ILCS 5/301]; Income Tax Act, Sec. 1501 [35 ILCS5/1501]; 86 Ill. Adm. Code Sec. 100.3010; 86 Ill. Adm. Code Sec. 100.3015 (CCH ILLINOIS TAX REPORTS, ¶11-510).

The Supreme Court's Commerce Clause and Due Process Clause decisions have held that a state may not tax the income of a nondomiciliary multistate taxpayer unless there is some nexus between the taxpayer and its income and the state seeking to tax the taxpayer's income (*Allied Signal, Inc. v. Director, Division of Taxation,* 504 US 768 (1992) and *Mobil Oil Corporation v. Commissioner of Taxes,* 445 US 425 (1980)). The nexus required by the Court will be established either by the existence of a unitary relationship between the income and the taxpayer's business activity, or if the capital transaction generating the item of income served as an operational rather than investment function in the taxpayer's business.

Operational function: The operational function concept is not a separate ground for apportionment in the absence of a unitary business, according to a unanimous U.S. Supreme Court ruling in an Illinois corporate income tax dispute. The Illinois courts misinterpreted references to "operational function" in previous Court decisions, and erred in considering whether a business division served an operation function in its out-of-state parent's business without first finding that the two were unitary. Therefore, the Court vacated the Illinois court's judgment and remanded the case so that the state court may take up the question of the existence of a unitary relationship.

Mead argued that the exception for apportionment of income from nonunitary businesses serving an operational function was narrow and did not apply to a purely passive investment such as Lexis. However, the Court identified "a more fundamental error" in vacating the judgment below. The Illinois courts erred in interpreting the references to "operational function" in *Container Corp.,* 463 U.S. 159 (1983), and *Allied-Signal, Inc.,* 504 U.S. 768 (1992), as modifying the unitary business principle to add a new ground for apportionment. Instead, the operational function concept described in those two decisions merely recognized that an asset can be part of a taxpayer's unitary business even if there is no unitary relationship between a payor and payee. For example, the interest earned on out-of-state bank deposits may be apportioned if it is part of the working capital of a unitary business, even though there is no unitary relationship between the taxpayer and the bank. The taxpayer's bank deposits, as working capital, would be operational assets and unitary with the taxpayer's business.

The finding in previous U.S. Supreme Court opinions that an asset served an operational function merely meant that it was a unitary part of the business, rather than a discrete asset to which a nondomiciliary state had no claim. Because the Illinois courts misinterpreted these statements as creating a basis for apportioning the income of nonunitary businesses, the judgment was vacated. Without expressing its own opinion, the Court stated that on remand the Illinois Appellate Court may consider if, contrary to the trial court's conclusion, Mead and Lexis formed a unitary business.

¶1106

The Court declined to consider an alternative theory that it described as a new ground for apportioning intangibles based on a state's contact with the capital asset rather than the taxpayer. According to this theory, advanced by Illinois and its amici, Lexis' own contacts with Illinois justified apportionment of Mead's capital gain. This alternative theory was raised for the first time in Illinois' brief on the merits. Ohio and New York have both adopted this alternative rationale, but neither state appeared as an amicus or was on notice that the constitutionality of its tax scheme was at issue. Therefore, the Court chose not to rule on the viability of this theory, saying that it was "best left for another day." Furthermore, the Court noted, even if it adopted this theory the case would have to be remanded because the apportionment formula presumably would have to be applied to Lexis rather than to Mead to determine the tax base (*MeadWestvaco Corp. v. Illinois Department of Revenue*, U.S. Supreme Court, Dkt. 06-1413, vacating the Illinois Appellate Court, April 15, 2008, CCH Illinois Tax Reports, ¶ 401-877).

Practitioner Comment: Operational Test

On April 15, 2008, The United States Supreme Court unanimously vacated and remanded the decision of the Illinois Appellate Court in *Meadwestvaco Corp. v. Illinois Department of Revenue*. The Illinois Appellate Court had permitted the Department of Revenue to tax an apportioned share of the Mead Corporation's gain on the sale of its Lexis/Nexis division. In its ruling, the Supreme Court reaffirmed that the unitary business principle is the linchpin of apportionability, but cast serious doubt on the continuing relevance of the operational function test in the context of certain corporate dispositions.

Under the *Meadwestvaco* decision, an asset – whether it is short-term deposits at a bank, a futures contract, or another business – will produce apportionable income as long as that asset is part of or used in a taxpayer's unitary business. While the *Meadwestvaco* Court did not discard the operational function test, it explained that the test simply recognizes that an asset can be part of a taxpayer's unitary business even if a unitary relationship does not exist between the payor and the payee. However, the *Meadwestvaco* Court, unlike the Illinois courts below, did not apply the operational function test to Mead's gain on the sale of Lexis/Nexis. The *Meadwestvaco* Court specifically stated that when the asset in question is another business, the only test to be applied is the traditional unitary criteria of functional integration, centralized management and economies of scale. In light of the fact that the Illinois Appellate Court never addressed the unitary issue, the Supreme Court remanded the case to give the Appellate Court that opportunity.

The *Meadwestvaco* decision could have significant ramifications for corporate dispositions. The Supreme Court made it clear that gain on the sale of a business is to be evaluated solely by reference to the unitary criteria of functional integration, centralized management and economies of scale. As evidenced by the *Meadwestvaco* case itself, many taxing authorities and taxpayers assumed that *Allied-Signal* created an independent, alternative basis for apportionment, including apportionment of the gain on the sale of a business. The *Meadwestvaco* decision refutes that notion and suggests that the operational function test is really just a proxy for the unitary business principle, which is to be applied when the asset in question is something other than a separate business (such as short-term deposits or futures contracts). The *Meadwestvaco* Court's clarification of the *Allied-Signal* test is especially important in light of the number of states that have abandoned the UDITPA definition of business income in favor of a constitutional standard.

David Hughes, Esq., Horwood Marcus & Berk Chartered

• *Illinois' definition of business income*

"Business income" is defined as all income that may be treated as apportionable business income under the U.S. Constitution and is net of allocable deductions (35 ILCS 5/1501(a)(1); 86 Ill. Adm. Code Sec. 100.3010). Business income is subject to apportionment (¶1107). All other income is nonbusiness income and is allocable to a single state (¶1109). A taxpayer may make an irrevocable election to treat all nonbusiness income as business income (35 ILCS 5/1501(a)(1); 86 Ill. Adm. Code Sec. 100.3015).

Practitioner Comment: Constitutional Standard of Business Income

Effective July 30, 2004, income is "business income" under Illinois law if it may be treated as apportionable business income under the United States Constitution. Income is apportionable under the U.S. Constitution if either (1) there exists a unitary relation between the payee and payor, or (2) the capital transaction serves an operational, rather than an investment, function (*Allied-Signal, Inc. v. Dir., Div. of Tax'n*, 504 U.S. 768 (1992), CCH ILLINOIS TAX REPORTS, ¶400-577).

The constitutional test for a unitary business focuses on functional integration, centralization of management, and economies of scale (*Container Corp. v. Franchise Tax Bd.*, 463 U.S. 159 (1983)). A unitary business may exist without a flow of goods between a parent and subsidiary if, instead, there is a flow of value between the entities.

The operational test focuses on the objective characteristics of the asset's use and its relation to the taxpayer and its activities within the taxing state. The inquiry is whether the taxpayer's managers treated an asset as serving an operational function, as opposed to an investment function. For example, income earned on short-term deposits in a bank located in another state is apportionable income if that income forms part of the company's working capital. (See *Allied-Signal*). Yet, income from short-term deposits is not apportionable to the extent the income is not actually used as working capital (*Home Interiors and Gifts, Inc. v. Dep't of Revenue*, 318 Ill. App. 3d 205 (2000), CCH ILLINOIS TAX REPORTS, ¶401-173).

Horwood Marcus & Berk Chartered

Practitioner Comment: Effect of Amended Definition of "Business Income"

In response to Illinois' 2004 amendment to the Illinois Income Tax Act's definition of business income, the Illinois Department of Revenue amended Illinois Income Tax Regulation Section 100.3010. The rule now provides as follows: "By adopting the business income definition, the General Assembly overruled the decisions in *Blessing White v. Zehnder*, 329 Ill. App. 3d 714 (Third. Div. 2002) (CCH ILLINOIS TAX REPORTS, ¶401-337), *American States Insurance Co. v. Hamer*, 352 Ill. App. 3d 521 (First Div. 2004) (CCH ILLINOIS TAX REPORTS, ¶401-493), and *Hercules v. Zehnder*, 324 Ill. App. 3d 329 (First Div. 2001) (CCH ILLINOIS TAX REPORTS, ¶401-273)."

In regard to *Blessing White* and *American States*, the Department stated that the liquidating sale exclusion was based on the courts' statutory construction of the former definition of business income and not on any principle of the United States Constitution. In regard to *Hercules*, the Department states that Hercules' gain realized from the sale of Himont stock received in exchange for assets of Hercules is subject to apportionment under *Allied Signal* because the gain was attributable in part to Hercules' use of those assets in its business before the exchange. Further, the investment that produced the gain had an operational function to the business.

Unitary business: In addition, rule now provides that there is no common ownership requirement, and that a unitary business may exist with less than 50% common ownership. The Department's position is misleading because Illinois law provides that a corporation must be owned more than 50% in order to be engaged in a unitary business and the Department conceded that the unitary relationship test was not met in *Hercules* because Hercules did not own or control more than 50% of Himont's stock.

Furthermore, the rule provides that if, in prior years, income from an asset or business has been classified as business income and in a later year is demonstrated to be nonbusiness income, all expenses deducted in the later tax year and in the two immediately preceding tax years related to the asset or business that generated the nonbusiness income, must be added back and recaptured as business income in the year of the disposition of the asset or business.

Jennifer A. Zimmerman, Esq., Horwood Marcus & Berk Chartered

¶1106

• *UDITPA definition of "business income"*

"Business income" is defined by UDITPA as income arising from transactions and activity in the regular course of the taxpayer's trade or business and includes income from tangible and intangible property if the acquisition, management, and disposition of the property constitute integral parts of the taxpayer's regular trade or business operations.

UDITPA establishes alternative tests for apportionable business income. The transactional test requires the transaction to have taken place as a regular part of the taxpayer's regular trade or business. The analysis focuses on the frequency and regularity of an income-producing transaction. The alternative functional test requires an analysis of the relationship between the income-producing asset and the taxpayer's regular business operations.

Under the functional test, the focus is on the "acquisition, management, and disposition" of the property producing the income, rather than the scope of the taxpayer's trade or business, evaluated by the first test. If such "acquisition, management, and disposition" constitute "integral parts" of the taxpayer's trade or business, the income in question is apportionable business income.

Practitioner Comment: Business Income Election

The "business income" definition has been amended to provide an annual, irrevocable election to treat income (other than compensation) as business income, effective for taxable years beginning on or after January 1, 2003.

For multistate corporations domiciled in Illinois, the election is a potential boon because items of interest, dividends, and capital gains that might otherwise be allocated in their entirety to Illinois as nonbusiness income may now be apportioned as business income. Nondomiciliary corporations may benefit from making the election as well, since certain nonbusiness items (*e.g.,* capital gains from the sale of a plant located in Illinois) may now be apportioned, instead of being allocated entirely to Illinois (35 ILCS 5/1501(a)(1), as added by P.A. 92-0846 (S.B. 2212), Laws 2002).

Brian L. Browdy, Esq., Horwood Marcus & Berk Chartered

CCH Advisory: Interest Paid by Subsidiary Was Business Income

Interest on a loan made by a corporation taxable in Illinois to its Danish subsidiary was business income apportionable to Illinois under both the transactional and functional tests. The interest income arose from a loan used to acquire a subsidiary in furtherance of an overall corporate plan of expansion, satisfying the transactional test. The interest income satisfied the functional test because the loan was an integral part of the corporation's regular business operations and the corporation exercised centralized management and control over the subsidiary, engaged in intercompany transactions with the subsidiary, and used excess interest from dividends for its regular business operations (*A.L. Laboratories v. Director of Revenue,* Illinois Circuit Court, Cook County, No. 96 L 50934, December 23, 1998; CCH ILLINOIS TAX REPORTS, ¶401-001).

• *Liquidation or sale of subsidiary*

Practitioner Comment: Gains from Asset Sales

In Illinois, as well as across the nation, taxpayers are litigating the issue of whether the gain from a stock sale transaction that is deemed to be an asset sale under IRC Sec. 338(h)(10) may be characterized as nonbusiness income. With a regular asset sale, a gain will be classified as nonbusiness income in Illinois under the so-called "liquidation exception" when the taxpayer sells all its business assets and distributes the proceeds to its owners (*Blessing/White, Inc. v. Zehnder,* 329 Ill. App. 3d 714 (2002), CCH ILLINOIS TAX REPORTS, ¶401-337) (interpreting the "business income" definition that existed prior to July 30, 2004).

Taxpayers have argued that the "liquidation exception" applies to IRC Sec. 338(h)(10) transactions as well because, under the fiction of Sec. 338(h)(10), there is a complete sale of assets followed by a distribution of the proceeds. The Illinois Appellate Court held that Illinois recognizes a Sec. 338(h)(10) election and found that Illinois could not tax a taxpayer, on an apportioned basis, on its gain from selling stock in a Sec. 338(h)(10) transaction (*American States Ins. Co. v. Hamer*, 352 Ill. App. 3d 521 (2004), CCH Illinois Tax Reports, ¶401-493). The Illinois Supreme Court denied the DOR's petition to appeal.

In *NICOR, Inc. v. Illinois Dep't of Revenue*, No. 05-L-01306, Circuit Court of Cook County, April 19, 2007, the Circuit Court granted the taxpayer's Motion for Summary Judgment and held that the gain recognized on a Section 338(h)(10) transaction must be characterized as nonbusiness income as a matter of law. The court reaffirmed that there was a liquidation exception to the functional test. In addition the court held that an election under Section 338(h)(10) fails squarely within that exception, as there is a cessation of business by the "target" and there is a distribution of the proceeds to the shareholders. The decision was affirmed on appeal, and the First District court noted for the record that, effective July 30, 2004, Illinois radically amended, prospectively, the definition of "business income" that applied to this case. As a result, the functional test, which also applied here, no longer exists. Essentially, then, the arguments raised in this appeal would have no relevance in a similar situation occurring today (*Nicor v. Illinois Department of Revenue*, Illinois Appellate Court, First District, Nos. 1-07-1359 & 1-07-1591, December 5, 2008, CCH Illinois Tax Reports, ¶401-942).

Marilyn A. Wethekam, Esq., Fred O. Marcus, Esq., Horwood Marcus & Berk Chartered

---

A Delaware holding company was not liable for Illinois corporate income tax plus interest on gain from the liquidation of subsidiaries that were engaged in the retail grocery business, including 15 stores in Illinois, because the trial court correctly concluded that the gain was nonbusiness income and was not apportionable Illinois business income. In affirming the trial court's judgment, the Illinois Appellate Court for the Fourth District joined the First District in recognizing a business-liquidation exception to the "functional test" for determining business and nonbusiness income. The business-liquidation exception was applicable in this case, the Fourth District concluded, because all of the liquidation proceeds were distributed to the parent company and were never reinvested in the ongoing retail grocery business. (*National Holdings, Inc. v. Zehnder*, Illinois Appellate Court, Fourth District, No. 4-06-0148, January 19, 2007, CCH Illinois Tax Reports, ¶401-743)

A private letter ruling held that a company's gain on the sale of a unitary subsidiary was business income, but receipts would be excluded from the sales factor numerator and denominator for apportionment purposes. In this instance, the company requested guidance regarding the sale of stock in its subsidiary. The Department ruled that the company could treat the gains from this sale as business income. However, the gross receipts from the stock sale had to be excluded from the numerator and denominator of the sales factor when apportioning its income because the stock sales were not part of the company's usual and ordinary course of business. The stock was sold as part of a merger. (*Private Letter Ruling, IT 07-0001-PLR*, Illinois Department of Revenue, March 23, 2007, CCH Illinois Tax Reports, ¶401-779)

CCH Advisory: Noncompetition Agreement Was Not Business Income

In reconsidering an earlier private letter ruling, the Illinois Department of Revenue held that income received under a covenant not to compete in connection with the sale of a partnership interest did not constitute business income, because the income did not arise in the regular course of the taxpayer's trade or business. Rather, the income arose from the liquidation of the taxpayer's interest in the business.

In *Texaco-Cities Service Pipeline Co. v. McGaw* (1998, SCt), 182 Ill2d 262, the Illinois Supreme Court rejected the taxpayer's argument that a transaction must occur in the "regular course" of its business in order to produce business income. The Supreme Court also declined to hold that gain realized upon a sale made in liquidation of a taxpayer's business was nonbusiness income as a matter of law. To the contrary, the Supreme Court held that a sale of nearly 90% of the business of the taxpayer in that case generated business income.

¶1106

A regulation (86 Ill. Adm. Code Sec. 100.3010(a)(3)(C)) provides that all income "is business income unless clearly classifiable as nonbusiness income." Because the ruling request did not state any facts with regard to the transaction except that it involved the sale of a partnership interest, there was no basis for ruling that the income from the covenant not to compete was nonbusiness income. Accordingly, the portion of the earlier private letter ruling (No. IT 92-145, dated May 11, 1992) stating that the income was nonbusiness income is revoked. In the absence of any facts indicating the contrary, the income should have been characterized as business income (*Private Letter Ruling IT 99-0005*, Department of Revenue, July 12, 1999; CCH ILLINOIS TAX REPORTS, ¶401-093).

• *Reclassification of income*

If income from an asset or business has been classified as business income but in a later year is deemed nonbusiness income, all related expenses deducted in that later year and the two immediately preceding taxable years have to be recaptured as business income in the year of disposition of the asset (86 Ill. Adm. Code Sec. 100.3010).

¶1107 Formula Apportionment of Business Income

Law: Income Tax Act, Sec. 304 [35 ILCS 5/304]; 86 Ill. Adm. Code Secs 100.3120; 86 Ill. Adm. Code Sec. 100.3200; 86 Ill. Adm. Code Sec. 100.3360; 86 Ill. Adm. Code Sec. 100.3370; 86 Ill. Adm. Code 100.3371; 86 Ill. Adm. Code 100.3373; 86 Ill. Adm. Code Sec. 100.3380; 86 Ill. Adm. Code Section 100.3390 (CCH ILLINOIS TAX REPORTS, ¶11-520—11-535).

Business income, other than business income of certain industries (¶1108), is apportioned to Illinois by means of a single-factor apportionment formula that is the sales factor (35 ILCS 5/304(h)(3)).

• *Alternative methods*

If the single sales factor apportionment method does not fairly represent the extent of the taxpayer's business activity in Illinois or fairly represent the market for the person's goods, services, or other sources of business income, the taxpayer may petition for, or the Director of Revenue may require, the following, in respect of all or any part of the taxpayer's business activity, if reasonable (35 ILCS 5/304(f)):

— separate accounting;

— the exclusion of any one or more apportionment factors, or the inclusion of one or more additional factors that will fairly represent the taxpayer's business activities in Illinois; or

— the employment of any other method to effectuate an equitable allocation and apportionment of the taxpayer's business income.

A petition to use an alternative apportionment method must be filed at least 120 days prior to the due date, including extensions, of the first return for which the taxpayer wants to use an alternative method (86 Ill. Adm. Code Section 100.3390(c)).

Practitioner Comment: *Alternative Apportionment —No Petition Filed*

Illinois has an alternative apportionment provision that is analogous to UDITPA Section 18. Illinois' alternative apportionment statute has been amended to provide that "the person may petition for, or the Director may, without a petition, permit or require [alternative apportionment]" (35 ILCS 5/304(f)). Under prior law, the Department could deny a taxpayer's use of an alternative apportionment method on procedural grounds if a petition was not filed. This amendment appears to allow the Director to accept a taxpayer's use of an alternative apportionment method even though the taxpayer may not have filed a petition.

Horwood Marcus & Berk Chartered

- *Sales factor—Items included*

"Sales" means all gross receipts of the taxpayer other than compensation and nonbusiness income. A regulation (86 Ill. Adm. Code Sec. 100.3370) contains examples of apportionment of business income under the sales factor.

Gross receipts includible in the sales factor encompass income from sales of goods, less returns and allowances, and interest on accounts receivable. The sales factor also includes business income from interest and dividends, royalties, sales of capital assets, rents from tangible personal property, rents from real estate, and income from personal services.

Dividends, amounts included under IRC Sec. 78 (dividends received from certain foreign corporations), and Subpart F income, as defined in IRC Sec. 952, are not included in the numerator or denominator of the sales factor.

Effective January 1, 2014, gross receipts from the assignment of Illinois lottery prize winnings are received in Illinois for purposes of computing the single sales factor apportionment formula (35 ILCS 5/304(a)(3)(B-1)).

Wagering: The Illinois Circuit Court held that the calculation of gross receipts for purposes of determining the taxpayer's Illinois apportionment factor should include only the gross commission from bets placed and not the entire handle. The Court reasoned that since the taxpayer did not have legal right to the total handle and only controlled the handle momentarily, the handle was not a proper reflection of the taxpayer's business activity in Illinois. Whereas a handle is comprised of the total amounts wagered by each bettor, the commission is a predetermined maximum percentage of the total amount wagered and set by statute. Also, any item excluded from gross income for federal taxable purposes cannot be included in Illinois gross income and the sales factor. Therefore, the Court determined that due to the taxpayer's lack of complete dominion over the handle and its exclusion from federal taxable income, inclusion of the entire handle in the sale factor was inappropriate. (*Churchill Downs Inc. v. Illinois Department of Revenue*, Cook County Circuit Court, No. 2012 L 51385, May 14, 2015, CCH Illinois Tax Reports, ¶403-014)

Practitioner Comment: Gross Receipts from Wagering

While the connection between Illinois base income and federal taxable income is well established, the *Churchill Downs* decision underscores that same connection between the Illinois sales factor and federal taxable income. It was undisputed that Churchill Downs reported only its gross commission on line 1 of its federal income tax return as part of its gross receipts or sales. Nevertheless, the Illinois Department of Revenue sought to include the entire handle – an amount that could be found nowhere in the taxpayer's federal return – in its Illinois sales factor, which would have significantly increased the factor due to the presence of a Churchill Downs racetrack in Illinois. By rejecting this approach, the Circuit Court confirmed that "gross receipts" for Illinois sales factor purposes begins – and probably ends – with gross receipts or sales for federal income tax purposes.

David A. Hughes, Esq., Horwood Marcus & Berk, Chartered

- *Sales factor—Numerator tests*

Under UDITPA, there are two separate tests for assigning receipts to the taxing state's sales factor numerator: the destination test and the income-producing activity test. The former applies to sales of tangible personal property, while the latter applies to all other types of gross receipts.

Destination test: Under the destination test, which applies to sales of goods in the ordinary course of business, receipts are assigned to the state to which the goods are shipped if the seller is taxable there. Sales are generally assigned to Illinois under the "throwback rule" when the property is shipped from an office, store, warehouse, factory, or other place of storage in Illinois and the taxpayer is not taxable in the destination state. However, premises owned or leased by a person who had independently contracted with the seller for the printing of newspapers, periodicals, or books are not deemed to be an office, store, warehouse, factory, or place of storage. Sales to the U.S. Government are assigned to the state from which shipment is made, even if the seller is taxable in the destination state.

CCH Advisory: "Throwback Rule" Applied

Sales by a corporation's subsidiaries shipped from Illinois to customers in other states where the subsidiaries were not subject to tax, but where other members of the corporation's unitary business group were taxable, were thrown back to Illinois for inclusion in the corporation's combined Illinois sales factor. Although the group elected to be treated as a single taxpayer for purposes of determining its tax liability (¶1104), business income attributable to Illinois by any group member doing business in Illinois must be apportioned using the combined apportionment method. The method required the calculation of each group member's Illinois sales, including sales shipped to states where the member was not taxable (*Hartmarx Corporation and Subsidiaries*, Illinois Appellate Court, First District, No. 1-98-2309, December 23, 1999; CCH ILLINOIS TAX REPORTS, ¶401-105. See also *Follett Corp. v. Illinois Department of Revenue*, Illinois Appellate Court, Fourth District, No. 4-02-0938, November 13, 2003, CCH ILLINOIS TAX REPORTS, ¶401-442, and *General Information Letter IT 08-0023-GIL*, Illinois Department of Revenue, July 21, 2008, CCH ILLINOIS TAX REPORTS, ¶401-898).

Although an Illinois statute adopts the UDITPA definition of "taxable in another state" (35 ILCS 5/303(f)), a regulation provides that in order to be taxable in another state, a taxpayer must not only be subject to tax but must also pay the tax (86 Ill. Adm. Code Sec. 100.3200(a)(2)). This regulation was upheld in *Dover Corporation et al. v. Department of Revenue* (1995, App Ct), 271 IllApp3d 700, 648 NE2d 1089; CCH ILLINOIS TAX REPORTS, ¶400-718.

Practitioner Comment: Foreign Sales

An Illinois court held that the throwback rule did not apply to sales shipped from Illinois to purchasers located in foreign countries where the taxpayer paid income taxes to those foreign countries by virtue of having income taxes withheld on foreign-source dividends and royalties. The court disagreed with the Department's position that the throwback rule applied because the taxpayer did not pay income taxes to the foreign countries on the sales at issue. The court acknowledged that its holding would result in "nowhere sales" (*Morton Int'l, Inc. v. Dep't of Revenue*, No. 01 L 50752 (Ill. Cir. Ct. July 8, 2004); CCH ILLINOIS TAX REPORTS, ¶401-498).

Horwood Marcus & Berk Chartered

Interunitary-group sales: Sales of tangible personal property between members of a unitary group are not attributed to Illinois if either the seller or the purchaser is excluded from joining in the combined report of the group, because (1) the volume of its sales outside the United States exceeds 80% and (2) the purchase is for resale (35 ILCS 5/304(a)(3)(B)).

Drop shipments: Neither UDITPA provisions nor Illinois statutes specifically cover "drop shipments," those sales in which property is shipped by a taxpayer from an out-of-state supplier to an out-of-state destination. In a case of first impression, the Illinois Supreme Court relied upon UDITPA Section 18, the provision allowing use of "any other method" to reach a fair result, to include drop shipment sales in the numerator of the sales factor. A regulation attributes sales of tangible or intangible personal property to Illinois when neither the origin nor the destination of the sale is within Illinois in the following circumstances: (1) the taxpayer is not taxable either in the state of origin or the state of destination; and (2) the taxpayer has activities in Illinois in connection with the sale that are not protected by the provisions of P.L. 86-272 (discussed at ¶1105) (86 Ill. Adm. Code Sec. 100.3380).

Practitioner Comment: Dock Sales

.Illinois' sales factor sources sales of tangible personal property to Illinois if the property is "delivered or shipped to a purchaser . . . within this State regardless of the f.o.b. point." The Department has interpreted that provision to source a sale to Illinois when the destination of the property is Illinois, even though a customer receives physical possession of the property outside Illinois. Thus, dock sales are sourced to the state in which the buyer is located, even when the buyer itself picks up the property.

Horwood Marcus & Berk Chartered

Income-producing activity test: Under UDITPA, assignment of receipts arising from sales other than sales of tangible personal property is accomplished under the income-producing activity test. Because "sales" is defined by UDITPA to include all business income, this category covers all types of income, not just what are commonly thought of as sales. In this context, "sales" includes interest, dividends, capital gains and losses, rents, royalties, and all other types of miscellaneous income.

Receipts are assigned to a taxing state when the income-producing activity that gave rise to the receipts was performed in the state. A special rule is applied to income-producing activities performed in two or more states: receipts arising from income-producing activities performed both within and outside the state are assigned to the taxing state if a greater proportion of the activity is performed in the state, based on cost of performance. "Cost of performance," not defined by UDITPA, is defined by the Multistate Tax Commission as direct costs consistent with generally accepted accounting principles.

The following three rules are prescribed by MTC regulations for determining when receipts from income-producing activities are in the taxing state:

(1) For real property, activity is located in the state in which the property is located;

(2) Similarly, for personal property, activity is located in the state in which the property is located; and

(3) Activity from services is located in the state in which the services are performed.

Practitioner Comment: Marketplace Rule

The income-producing activity rule is repealed for sales other than tangible personal property. "Beginning with the 2008 tax year, a sale of a service is sourced to Illinois if 'the purchaser is in this State or the sale is otherwise attributable to this State's marketplace.' Pursuant to this rule, a sale of a service is sourced to Illinois if 'the benefit of the service is realized in this State'. Further, if such benefit were realized in more than one state, 'the gross receipts from the sale shall be divided among those states in which the taxpayer is taxable in proportion to the benefit of service realized in each state'" (35 ILCS 5/305(a)(3)(C-5)).

Horwood Marcus & Berk Chartered

Royalties from intangibles: Net losses from sales of business intangibles may be included in the sales factor of the income apportionment formula only to the extent of net gains from such sales (*General Information Letter IT 00-0061-GIL*, modifying *General Information Letter IT 00-0049-GIL*, Department of Revenue, August 15, 2000; CCH ILLINOIS TAX REPORTS, ¶ 401-172).

Apportionment of interest, gain, and income from intangibles: For taxable years ending on or after December 31, 2008, in the case of interest, net gains, and other items of income from intangible personal property, the sale of the intangible property is considered to be in Illinois if (35 ILCS 5/304(a)(3)(C-5)(iii)):

(1) in the case of a taxpayer who is a dealer in the intangible property (IRC Sec. 475), the income or gain is received from a customer in Illinois; or

(2) in all other cases, the income-producing activity of the taxpayer is performed in Illinois or proportionally greater in Illinois than in any other state based on performance costs.

Apportionment of services: Sales of services are in Illinois if the services are received in the state. Gross receipts from the performance of services provided to a corporation, partnership, or trust may only be attributed to a state where that corporation, partnership, or trust has a fixed place of business. If the state where the services are received is not readily determinable or is a state where the business does not have a fixed place of business, the services will be deemed to be received at the location of the office of the customer from which the services were ordered in the regular course of the customer's trade or business. If the ordering office cannot be determined, the services will be deemed to be received at the office of the customer to which the services are billed. If the taxpayer is not taxable in the state in which the services are received, the sale must be excluded from both the numerator and the denominator of the sales factor (35 ILCS 5/304(a)(3)(C-5)(iv)); see also *General Information Letter IT 08-0022-GIL,* Illinois Department of Revenue, July 16, 2008, CCH ILLINOIS TAX REPORTS, ¶401-897, and *General Information Letter IT 08-0034-GIL,* Illinois Department of Revenue, October 15, 2008, CCH ILLINOIS TAX REPORTS, ¶401-934.

Telecommunications services and mobile telecommunications services: Receipts from the sale of telecommunications service or mobile telecommunications service are in Illinois if the customer's service address is in the state, with certain noted exceptions. (35 ILCS 5/304(a)(3)(B-5); 86 Ill. Adm. Code 100.3371)

Publishing: Sales within Illinois from publishing include the sum of gross receipts derived from the sale of published materials in the form of tangible personal property, as provided in 86 Ill. Adm. Code 100.3370(c) and 86 Ill. Adm. Code 100.3380(c); and the portion of gross receipts derived from sales of published materials in a form other than tangible personal property, from advertising and from the sale, rental or other use of the taxpayer's customer lists for a particular publication or any portion thereof attributed to Illinois using the taxpayer's circulation factor for that publication during the applicable tax period. (86 Ill. Adm. Code 100.3373)

Practitioner Comment: Regulation for Apportioning Sales of Publishing and Advertising Services

The Department has amended its regulations on Net Income in 86 Ill. Adm. Code 100.3373 to include a "circulation factor" for calculating where income from publishing services should be apportioned. The circulation factor is the ratio between the taxpayer's in-state circulation to purchasers to total circulation. The regulation also provides that if the taxpayer is not taxable in the state in which the publishing services are received, the sale must be excluded from both the numerator and the denominator.

Illinois adopted market-based sourcing for services for tax years ending on or after December 31, 2008 (35 ILCS 5/304(a)(3)(C-5)). The Department was granted the authority to adopt regulations to determine where certain types of services are received. The Department has yet to adopt regulations on where general services are received, but this guidance on sourcing of sales for publishing and advertising service, including Internet publishing, gives taxpayers doing business in Illinois a lot to think about. First, this regulation introduces concepts that may not have been considered when a taxpayer filed returns in prior years. Second, the new regulation is considered the Department's "interpretation" of the law changes that are applicable to all tax years on or after December 31, 2008. As a result, depending on how returns were previously filed, this provides for potential refund opportunities for taxpayers or potential understatement of tax liabilities. It will be imperative for taxpayers to review prior and current year methodologies employed to determine if either situation exists. Further, the Department has yet to offer guidance on how this election should be made, but has made clear that once it is made, it must be applied consistently from year to year.

Breen M. Schiller, Esq., Horwood Marcus & Berk, Chartered

• *Property factor*

The property factor is not a part of the normal apportionment formula, although it may be included in an alternate method (see above).

Illinois has adopted without change UDITPA provisions and MTC regulations on the property factor. The denominator of the property factor is the average value of all the taxpayer's real and tangible personal property owned or rented and used during the tax period. The numerator of the property factor is the average value of the taxpayer's real and tangible personal property owned or rented and used in Illinois during the tax period. Property owned by the taxpayer is valued at its original cost. Property rented by the taxpayer is valued at eight times the net annual rental rate.

• *Payroll factor*

Like the property factor, the payroll factor is not a part of the normal apportionment formula, although it may be included in an alternate method (see above).

Illinois has adopted UDITPA provisions and MTC regulations on the payroll factor. The denominator of the payroll factor is the total compensation paid everywhere during the tax period. The numerator of the payroll factor is the total amount paid in this state. The following UDITPA tests for determining whether compensation has been "paid in this state" were taken from the Model Unemployment Compensation Act:

— All the individual's services are performed in the taxing state, or only incidental services are performed outside the taxing state;

— Some of the individual's services are performed in the taxing state, and the individual's base of operations is in the taxing state;

— If there is no base of operations, some of the individual's activities are performed in the state, and the state is the place from which his or her work is directed or controlled; or

— If there is no base of operations or place where the work is directed and controlled, some of the individual's services are performed in the taxing state, and the individual is a resident of the taxing state.

In addition, an Illinois regulation explains how to allocate compensation paid to nonresidents for past services (86 Ill. Adm. Code Sec. 100.3120). The standards for whether such compensation is paid in Illinois is the same as for other compensation. However, such compensation is considered to have been earned ratably over the employee's last five years of service with the employer (or any predecessor, successor, parent, or subsidiary of the employer) in the absence of convincing evidence that it is not attributable to a different period of employment or was not earned ratably. Compensation paid for past service includes amounts paid under deferred compensation plans when the amount paid is unrelated to the amount of service rendered.

Items of income taken into account as compensation by nonresident employees under the provisions of IRC Secs. 401—425 are not allocated to the Illinois payroll factor (86 Ill. Adm. Code Sec. 100.3120).

Reciprocal agreements: The compensation of nonresidents of states with which Illinois has reciprocal agreements exempting nonresident compensation is not allocated to the Illinois payroll factor (86 Ill. Adm. Code Sec. 100.3120). Such agreements are in effect for the states of Iowa, Kentucky, Michigan, and Wisconsin.

Cash reporting: An Illinois regulation omits an election of MTC regulation IV.13(a) that allows a corporation to report compensation by the cash rather than the accrual method if the taxpayer is required to report unemployment compensation by wages reported under the cash method (86 Ill. Adm. Code Sec. 100.3360). The regulation omits, as well, the MTC presumption that wages reported under the cash method for unemployment compensation purposes may be equated with the numerator of the payroll factor.

¶1107

¶1108 Apportionment Factors for Special Industries

Law: Income Tax Act, Sec. 304 [35 ILCS 5/304]; Income Tax Act, Sec. 1501(a)(8), (26) [35 ILCS 5/1501]; 86 Ill. Adm. Code Sec. 100.3400; 86 Ill. Adm. Code Sec. 100.3405; 86 Ill. Adm. Code Sec. 100.3450; 86 Ill. Adm. Code Sec. 100.9710 (CCH Illinois Tax Reports, ¶11-540).

Illinois has not adopted the MTC regulations on construction contractors, airlines, and railroads, or the UDITPA provision that precludes apportionment of the business income of financial organizations and public utilities. Illinois has adopted special provisions relating to apportionment factors for broadcasters, insurance companies, financial organizations, international banking facilities, railroads, and transportation services other than railroads. Additionally, Illinois has added certain organizations to the MTC definition of "financial organization."

• *Broadcasting*

In determining the sales factor for nonresidents, receipts from the sale of broadcasting services are in Illinois if the broadcasting services are received in Illinois. For advertising revenue from broadcasting, the customer is the advertiser and the service is received in Illinois if the commercial domicile of the advertiser is in Illinois. For situations where film or radio programming is broadcast for a fee received from the recipient of the broadcast, the portion of the service that is received in Illinois is measured by the portion of the recipients of the broadcast located in Illinois. As such, the fee or other remuneration for such service that is included in the Illinois numerator of the sales factor is the total of those fees or other remuneration received from recipients in Illinois. A taxpayer may determine the location of the recipients of its broadcast using the address of the recipient shown in its contracts with the recipient or using the billing address of the recipient in the taxpayer's records. (35 ILCS 5/304(a)(3)(B-7))

The "throwout rule" (35 ILCS 5/304(a)(3)(C-5)(iv)), excluding the gross receipts of any sale sourced to a state in which the taxpayer is not subject to tax from the numerator and denominator of the sales factor, does not apply to receipts from the sale of broadcasting services; see *General Information Letter IT10-0004-GIL*, Illinois Department of Revenue, February 16, 2010, CHH Illinois Tax Reports, ¶402-094.

"Film" or "film programming" is the broadcast on television of any and all performances, events, or productions, including but not limited to news, sporting events, plays, stories, or other literary, commercial, educational, or artistic works, either live or through the use of video tape, disc, or any other type of format or medium. Each episode of a series of films produced for television constitutes a separate film notwithstanding that the series relates to the same principal subject and is produced during one or more tax periods. A similar definition applies to "radio" or "radio programming."(35 ILCS 5/304(a)(3)(B-7))

When film or radio programming is broadcast for a fee from the person providing the programming, the portion of the broadcast service that is received by the station, network, or cable system in Illinois is measured by the part of recipients of the broadcast located in Illinois. Accordingly, the amount of revenue related to this type of arrangement that is included in the Illinois numerator of the sales factor is the total fee or other total remuneration from the person providing the programming related to that broadcast multiplied by the Illinois audience factor for that broadcast.

When film or radio programming is provided by a taxpayer that is a network or station to a customer for broadcast in exchange for a fee from that customer, the broadcasting service is received at the location of the office of the customer from which the services were ordered in the regular course of the customer's trade or business. Accordingly, in such a case, the revenue derived by the taxpayer that is included in the taxpayer's Illinois numerator of the sales factor is the revenue from such customers who receive the broadcasting service in Illinois.

When film or radio programming is provided by a taxpayer that is not a network or station to another person for broadcasting in exchange for a fee from that person, the broadcasting service is received at the location of the office of the customer from which the services were ordered in the regular course of the customer's trade or business. As such, the revenue derived by the taxpayer that is included in the taxpayer's Illinois numerator of the sales factor is the revenue from customers who receive the broadcasting service in Illinois. (35 ILCS 5/304(a)(3)(B-7))

• *Construction contractors*

Illinois has not adopted MTC regulation IV.18(d), which provides special apportionment factors for construction contractors. Construction contractors in Illinois are subject to the same allocation and apportionment provisions as other corporations.

• *Financial organizations*

A single-factor formula is used to apportion the business income of financial organizations.

The apportionment rules for financial organizations were amended effective for tax years ending on or after December 31, 2008. The post-2008 formula is determined by multiplying the business income of a financial organization by a fraction, the numerator of which is its gross receipts from sources in Illinois or otherwise attributable to Illinois' marketplace and the denominator of which is its gross receipts everywhere during the taxable year. Previously, interest income was only included in the numerator if it was received in Illinois from Illinois customers. (35 ILCS 5/304(c)(3); 86 Ill. Adm. Code Sec. 100.3405)

A financial organization's receipts from investment assets and activities and trading assets and activities are included in the receipts factor as follows (35 ILCS 5/304(c)(3)(viii)):

    (1) Interest, dividends, net gains, and other income from investment assets and activities and from trading assets and activities shall be included in the receipts factor.

    (2) The numerator of the receipts factor includes interest, dividends, net gains, and other income from investment assets and activities and from trading assets and activities described in paragraph (1) that are attributable to Illinois.

Income from assets and activities that are properly assigned to a fixed place of business of the taxpayer within Illinois are attributed to the state and included in the numerator. The denominator is the gross income from all assets and activities (35 ILCS 5/304(c)).

The presumption that an investment or trading asset or activity has been properly assigned by the taxpayer may be rebutted by the Department. If the fixed place of business cannot be determined, the asset or activity will be assigned to the state in which the taxpayer's commercial domicile is located (35 ILCS 5/304(c)).

Special provisions apply with respect to interest from federal funds sold and securities purchased under resale agreements and to the amount by which income from trading assets and activities exceeds amounts paid in lieu of interest, amounts paid in lieu of dividends, and losses from such assets and activities.

Practitioner Comment: Marketplace Rule

Beginning with the 2008 tax year, a financial organization apportions its business income by a fraction, "the numerator of which is its gross receipts from sources in this State or otherwise attributable to this State's marketplace and the denominator of which is its gross receipts everywhere during the taxable year." P.A. 95-233 (S.B. 1544), Laws 2007, further explains how this rule is to be applied. For example, interest income and other receipts from credit card receivables are sourced to Illinois if the card charges are regularly billed to a customer in Illinois (35 ILCS 5/305(c)(3)).

Horwood Marcus & Berk Chartered

An Illinois provision adds to the MTC definition of "financial organization" the following organizations: bank holding companies, building and loan associations, small loan companies, sales finance companies, or any person that is owned by a bank or bank holding company (35 ILCS 5/1501(a)(8)). Definitions and examples are discussed in a regulation (86 Ill. Adm. Code Sec. 100.9710).

CCH Advisory: Investment Companies

Subsidiaries that were created to manage the parent corporation's investments were not financial organizations entitled to single-factor apportionment. Instead, they were part of a unitary business with the parent because the group was engaged in the same business activity, shared corporate officers and directors, and the parent maintained substantial control over activities of the subsidiaries. The subsidiaries were more like the taxpayer's treasury department than investment companies that provide investment services to the public (*Automated Data Processing, Inc.*, Illinois Appellate Court, First District, No. 1-99-0324, May 16, 2000, 313 Ill. App. 3d 433, 729 N.E.2d 897, CCH ILLINOIS TAX REPORTS, ¶401-145).

International banking facility: An "international banking facility" is a set of asset and liability accounts segregated on the books of a depository institution, United States branch or agency of a foreign bank, or an Edge or Agreement Corporation that includes only international banking facility time deposits and extensions of credit (35 ILCS 5/1501(a)(25)).

The adjusted income of an international banking facility is its income reduced by the amount of the floor amount. The "floor amount" is the amount, if any, determined by multiplying the income of the facility by a fraction that is determined as follows (35 ILCS 5/304(c)(2)(B)):

(1) The numerator is the average aggregate of the financial organization's loans to foreign banks, foreign-domiciled borrowers (except when secured primarily by real estate), and foreign governments and other foreign official institutions, as reported for its branches, agencies, and offices within Illinois on its "Consolidated Report of Condition," filed with the Federal Deposit Insurance Corporation and other regulatory authorities for 1980, minus the average aggregate of such loans (other than loans of an international banking facility), as reported by the financial institution for its branches, agencies, and offices within Illinois, on the corresponding Schedule and lines of the Consolidated Report of Condition for the current taxable year. The average aggregate in both cases is determined on a quarterly basis. The amount determined by the computation for the current year may not exceed that determined by the computation for 1980.

(2) The denominator is the average aggregate of the international banking facility's loans to banks in foreign countries, foreign-domiciled borrowers (except when secured primarily by real estate), and foreign governments and other foreign official institutions that were recorded in its financial accounts for the current taxable year.

Federally regulated exchanges: For taxable years ending on or after December 31, 2012, business income of a federally regulated exchange may, at the option of the federally regulated exchange, be apportioned to Illinois by multiplying the income by a fraction, the numerator of which is its business income from sources within this State, and the denominator of which is its business income from all sources (35 ILCS 5/304(c-1)). The business income within Illinois of a federally regulated exchange is the sum of the following:

(1) Receipts attributable to transactions executed on a physical trading floor if that physical trading floor is located in Illinois.

(2) Receipts attributable to all other matching, execution, or clearing transactions, including without limitation receipts from the provision of matching, execution, or clearing services to another entity, multiplied by (i) for taxable years ending on or after December 31, 2012, but before December 31, 2013, 63.77%; and (ii) for taxable years ending on or after December 31, 2013, 27.54%.

(3) All other receipts not governed by subparagraphs (1) or (2) to the extent the receipts are characterized for sales factor purposes as Illinois sales.

Practitioner Comment: Illinois Reduces Tax Liability for CME Group and Sears Holding Corp.

Public Act 97-0636 (SB 397), Laws 2012, significantly reduces the tax burdens of CME Group and Sears Holdings Corp. by reducing receipts attributable to Illinois for federally regulated exchanges to 27.54% after December 31, 2013, and by extending the Sears Economic Development Area an additional 15 years. Despite Illinois' budgetary issues, the Governor and legislature still recognize the need for maintaining a solid corporate tax base in Illinois. Therefore, both CME Group and Sears Holding Corp. were able to negotiate certain benefits to maintain a significant presence in Illinois. While not available to all entities, it is never out of the realm of possibility to negotiate additional benefits to remain in or move to Illinois. As reflected in this legislation, the benefits can be obtained by either a statutory change or through negotiation with the Illinois Department of Economic Opportunity and Commerce.

Jordan M. Goodman, Horwood Marcus & Berk, Chartered

• *Public utilities*

Illinois has not adopted the UDITPA provision that precludes apportionment of income from the business activity of a public utility. Public utilities are subject to the allocation and apportionment provisions in the same manner as other corporations. See below for special rules applicable to pipeline companies.

• *Insurance companies*

The business income of an insurance company, other than a company whose principal business consists of writing premiums for reinsurance (see following), is apportioned to Illinois by multiplying the income by a fraction the numerator of which is the sum of the direct premiums written for insurance upon property or risk in Illinois and the denominator of which is direct premiums written everywhere.

The term "direct premiums written" means the total amount of direct premiums written, assessments, and annuity considerations as reported for the taxable year on the annual statement filed by the company with the Illinois Director of Insurance (35 ILCS 5/304(b)(1)).

Out-of-state insurance companies: The apportionment provisions apply the same whether an insurance company is domiciled in Illinois or outside Illinois. However, an insurance company formed under the laws of a state that imposes a retaliatory tax on Illinois insurance companies may reduce the otherwise-applicable income and replacement tax rates imposed on that company by Illinois so that the total amount of Illinois income and replacement tax imposed on the foreign insurance company is equal to the amount of income tax that its home state would have imposed on its Illinois income. (35 ILCS 5/201(d-1); *General Information Letter IT 11-0019-GIL*, Department of Revenue, September 30, 2011, CCH Illinois Tax Reports, ¶ 402-420)

Reinsurance: If the principal source of premiums written by an insurance company consists of premiums for reinsurance accepted by the company, business income is apportioned to Illinois by multiplying the income by a fraction the numerator of which is the sum of the direct premiums written for insurance upon property or risk in Illinois plus premiums for reinsurance accepted in respect of property or risk in Illinois. The denominator of the fraction is the sum of direct and reinsurance premiums written everywhere by the company.

¶1108

Premiums written for reinsurance accepted in respect of property or risk in Illinois may, at the election of the reinsurance company, be determined either (1) on the basis of the proportion that premiums written for reinsurance accepted from companies commercially domiciled in Illinois bear to premiums written for reinsurance accepted from all sources or (2) in the proportion that the sum of the direct premiums written for insurance upon property or risk in Illinois by each ceding company from which reinsurance is accepted bears to the sum of the total direct premiums written by each ceding company for the taxable year (35 ILCS 5/304(b)(2)). This election made by a company for its first taxable year ending on or after December 31, 2011, is binding for that company for that taxable year and for all subsequent taxable years, and may be altered only with the written permission of the Department of Revenue, which shall not be unreasonably withheld.

• *Railroads, pipeline companies, airlines, and other transportation services*

The formula used to apportion income for transportation businesses includes a numerator that is (1) all receipts from any movement or shipment of people, goods, mail, oil, gas, or any other substance (other than by airline) that both originates and terminates in Illinois, plus (2) that portion of the person's gross receipts from movements or shipments of people, goods, mail, oil, gas, or any other substance (other than by airline) passing through, into, or out of Illinois, that is determined by the ratio that the miles traveled in Illinois bears to total miles from point of origin to point of destination. The denominator is all revenue derived from the movement or shipment of people, goods, mail, oil, gas, or any other substance (other than by airline).

Airlines: Business income derived from furnishing airline transportation services is apportioned to Illinois by multiplying that income by a fraction, the numerator of which is the revenue miles of the person in Illinois, and the denominator of which is the revenue miles of the person everywhere. (35 ILCS 5/304(d)(3); 86 Ill. Adm. Code Sec. 100.3450).

Practitioner Comment: Rule for Transportation Companies

The regulation implements statutory amendments to the apportionment formula for business income derived from providing transportation services. The regulation is retroactive to December 31, 2008. The regulation includes definitions of "revenue mile" and "in this state."

The apportionment fraction for non-airlines (trucking companies) is based on actual receipts and mileage.

The fraction for airline transportation companies is based on the amount of revenue miles within the state and miles everywhere.

For tax years ending prior to December 31, 2008, business income for transportation companies was apportioned to the state by multiplying the income by a fraction, the numerator was revenue miles in Illinois and the denominator was the revenue miles everywhere.

Horwood Marcus & Berk, Chartered

Practitioner Comment: Apportionment of Pipeline Revenue

Under prior law, the Illinois Appellate Court held that taxpayers, who operated natural gas pipelines in Illinois, were required to include all miles of natural gas pipelines that traveled through Illinois in the numerator of their apportionment factor. For tax years 1998 through 2000, the taxpayers amended their corporate income tax returns to exclude the pipeline miles that traveled through Illinois. The taxpayers argued that their revenue from "pass-through revenue miles" should be excluded from the computation of the numerator because the natural gas transportation services neither originated nor terminated in Illinois. The Circuit Court agreed with this argument, and noted that an amendment to Section 304(d)(2) of the Income Tax Act, which provides that business income from pipeline transportation must be apportioned by multiplying income by the fraction of a company's pipeline miles in Illinois over pipeline miles everywhere, was enacted subsequent to the tax years at issue. Reversing the Circuit Court, the Appellate Court noted that the taxpayers were sufficiently present in Illinois to be subject to tax and that the inclusion of the flow-through miles in the numerator did not violate the United States Constitution.

The Appellate Court ruled in favor of the Department of Revenue even though the pipeline apportionment statute in effect during the years in issue did not expressly include "pass-through" miles in the numerator and statutory but a statutory amendment, which went into effect after the years in question, expressly included pass-through miles in the numerator. Despite this seemingly substantive change in the statute, the Appellate Court concluded that the taxpayer's position would create a tax "gap" in violation of the Illinois Supreme Court's decision in *GTE Automatic Electric, Inc. v. Allphin*, 68 Ill. 2d 326 (1977). This case should also be contrasted with the Appellate Court's decision in Northwest Airlines, Inc. v. Department of Revenue, 295 Ill. App. 3d 889, 892 (1998) where the Court concluded that an airline's "fly over" miles could not be included in the numerator of the apportionment formula. (*Panhandle Eastern Pipeline Co. v. Hamer*, Illinois Supreme Court, No. 09 L 051281, December 7, 2012; CCH ILLINOIS TAX REPORTS, ¶402-593)

David A. Hughes, Esq., Horwood Marcus & Berk Chartered

Motor carriers (prior law): The Illinois Appellate Court concluded that an interstate motor carrier must include its pass-through miles driven in the numerator of its Illinois apportionment factor because it had both a physical and economic presence in Illinois. The Department contended that the taxpayer's "pass-through miles" in Illinois should be included in the taxpayer's Illinois numerator for purposes of income tax because the revenue miles were in Illinois. The Court agreed. The court found that physical presence "in this State" is more broadly defined to include, not only being within Illinois borders, but also having a presence or existence in Illinois. This broad definition encompassed plaintiff whose trucks and employees were physically present in the state as they pass-through the boundaries of Illinois. Plaintiff's trucks traveled through Illinois on its roadways.

By utilizing the state's infrastructure and roadways, plaintiff's property and employees were physically present in Illinois. Plaintiff was also conducting the economic activity of providing shipping services involving travel through Illinois. Moreover, the record demonstrated plaintiff alleged it paid Illinois fuel tax, which indicated that plaintiff engaged in additional economic activities with Illinois suppliers. The court therefore concluded that pass-through miles were In Illinois, as the taxpayer's trucks and employees maintained a physical and economic presence while driving through Illinois. (*Witte Bros. Exch., Inc. v. Dep't of Revenue*, 2013 IL App (1st) 120850, 997 N.E.2d 903, reh'g denied (Nov. 1, 2013); CCH ILLINOIS TAX REPORTS, ¶402-712)

¶1109 Allocation of Nonbusiness Income

Law: Income Tax Act, Sec. 301 [35 ILCS 5/301]; Income Tax Act, Sec. 303 [35 ILCS 5/303]; Income Tax Act, Sec. 305 [35 ILCS 5/305]; Income Tax Act, Sec. 1501(a)(1), (2) [35 ILCS 5/1501]; 86 Ill. Adm. Code Sec. 100.3010; 86 Ill. Adm. Code Sec. 100.3210 (CCH ILLINOIS TAX REPORTS, ¶11-515).

Under UDITPA, adopted by Illinois, "business income" is apportioned, and "nonbusiness income" is allocated (¶1105). Nonbusiness income is all income other than "business income," which is defined as income arising from transactions and activities in the regular course of the taxpayer's trade or business (35 ILCS 5/1501(a)(1)). UDITPA provides rules for allocating rents and royalties from real or tangible personal property, capital gains, interest, dividends, and patent or copyright royalties to the extent that they constitute nonbusiness income. Illinois provisions for allocating nonbusiness income are substantially the same as those of UDITPA and MTC with these exceptions: (1) Illinois has not adopted the MTC rule that permits allocation of nonbusiness income regardless of whether a corporation is "taxable in another state," and (2) items of income and deduction not explicitly allocated or apportioned under the law and regulations are allocated to the state in which the corporation had its commercial domicile at the time the item was paid, incurred, or accrued. Expenses attributable to both business and nonbusiness income may be prorated to distribute the deduction fairly (86 Ill. Adm. Code Sec. 100.3010(e)).

Although, Illinois has adopted the UDITPA definitions, effective for tax years beginning on or after January 1, 2003, a taxpayer may annually elect to classify income (other than compensation) as either business or nonbusiness income (see ¶ 1106).

Under UDITPA, once income has been determined to be allocable nonbusiness income, it is assigned on the basis of the following allocation rules. The regulations issued by the Multistate Tax Commission do not deal with rules of allocation for nonbusiness income.

Payments received from the assignment of an Illinois lottery prize are allocable to Illinois for purposes of computing income tax liability to the extent that such payments constitute nonbusiness income (35 ILCS 5/303(e)).

• *Rents and royalties from real and tangible personal property*

Nonbusiness net rents and royalties from real property located in the taxing state are assigned to the taxing state (35 ILCS 5/303(c)). Nonbusiness net rents and royalties from tangible personal property are assigned to the taxing state on the basis of the extent to which the property was "utilized" in the taxing state. There is also a throwback rule: if the property was utilized in a state in which the taxpayer is not taxable and the taxing state is the commercial domicile of the taxpayer, the rents and royalties from the personal property are thrown back to the taxing state in their entirety. "Commercial domicile" is defined as the principal place from which the trade or business of the taxpayer is directed or managed (35 ILCS 5/1501(a)(2)). A regulation adds that the principal place of direction is generally the offices of the principal executives. When executive authority is scattered, the place of daily operational decision making is controlling.

The extent of utilization in the taxing state is determined by a fraction the numerator of which is the number of days the property was in the taxing state during the rental or royalty period and the denominator of which is the total number of days of the rental or royalty period. This fraction is multiplied by the income being allocated. If the physical location of the property cannot be ascertained, it will be deemed utilized in the state in which it was located at the time the rental or royalty payor obtained possession (86 Ill. Adm. Code Sec. 100.3210).

• *Capital gains and losses*

Like other nonbusiness income derived from real property, nonbusiness capital gains and losses from sales of real property located in the taxing state are assigned to the taxing state (35 ILCS 5/303(b)).

Nonbusiness gains from sales of tangible personal property are assigned to the taxing state if the property had a situs in the state at the time of sale. Again, there is a throwback rule: If the taxpayer is not taxable in the state in which the property had its situs at the time of sale and if the taxpayer's commercial domicile is the taxing state, the gains are assigned to the taxing state (35 ILCS 5/303(b)).

Nonbusiness gains from sales of intangible personal property are assigned to the taxing state if the taxpayer's commercial domicile is the taxing state.

• *Interest and dividends*

Interest and dividends, to the extent they constitute nonbusiness income, are assigned to the taxing state if the taxpayer's commercial domicile is the taxing state (35 ILCS 5/301(c)(2)(B)).

• *Patent and copyright royalties*

Royalties derived from patents and copyrights are assigned to the taxing state to the extent that they are utilized by the payor in the state. There is a throwback rule: If the patent or copyright is utilized by the payor in a state in which the taxpayer is not taxable and the taxpayer's commercial domicile is the taxing state, the royalties are thrown back to the taxing state (35 ILCS 5/303(d)(1)).

Patents are utilized in the taxing state to the extent that they are employed in production in the state or to the extent a patented product is produced in the state. If the basis of receipts from patent royalties does not permit allocation to states or if the accounting procedures do not reflect in which states actual utilization took place, the patent is deemed utilized in the state of the taxpayer's commercial domicile (35 ILCS 5/303(d)(2)).

Copyrights are utilized in a state to the extent that printing or other publication originates in the state. As in the case of patents, if the basis of receipts does not permit allocation to states or if the accounting procedures do not reflect in which states actual utilization took place, the copyright is deemed utilized in the state of the taxpayer's commercial domicile. (35 ILCS 5/303(d)(2)(B))

• *Taxable income of an investment partnership*

Taxable income of an investment partnership that is distributable to a nonresident partner is treated as nonbusiness income and allocated to the partner's state of residence, unless the partner has made an election to treat all such income as business income or the income is from investment activity (35 ILCS 5/305(e)(5)):

— that is directly related to any other business activity conducted in Illinois by the nonresident partner;

— that serves an operational function to any other business activity of the nonresident partner; or

— where assets of the investment partnership were acquired with working capital from a trade or business in Illinois in which the nonresident partner owns an interest.

CORPORATE INCOME TAX

CHAPTER 12

RETURNS AND PAYMENTS; CREDITS AGAINST TAX

¶1201 Returns and Payment of Tax

Law: Income Tax Act, Sec. 502(a), (f) [35 ILCS 5/502]; Income Tax Act, Sec. 503(b) [35 ILCS 5/503]; Income Tax Act, Sec. 504 [35 ILCS 5/504]; Income Tax Act, Sec. 505(a), (b) [35 ILCS 5/505]; Income Tax Act, Sec. 506(b) [35 ILCS 5/506]; Income Tax Act, Sec. 601(a) [35 ILCS 5/601]; Income Tax Act, Sec. 601.1 [35 ILCS 5/601.1]; Income Tax Act, Sec. 602(a) [35 ILCS 5/602]; Income Tax Act, Sec. 803 [35 ILCS 5/803]; Income Tax Act, Sec. 804 [35 ILCS 5/804; 86 Ill. Adm. Code 100.5020](CCH Illinois Tax Reports, ¶ 89-102, ¶ 89-104).

Forms: IL-1120; IL-1120-ES; IDR 916, Signature Declaration; IL-505-B, Automatic Extension Payment.

Income and replacement taxes are reported together by for-profit corporations filing Form IL-1120 and by exempt corporations reporting unrelated business income on Form 990T. S corporations, which are not subject to income tax, report only the replacement tax on Form 1120-ST.

Due dates: Effective for taxable years beginning after 2015, a C corporation must file a federal income tax return and the corresponding Illinois return by April 15 or the 15th day of the fourth month following the close of the corporation's fiscal year (86 Ill. Adm. Code 100.5020). Previously, returns had to be filed on or before the 15th day of the third month following the close of the corporation's taxable year (35 ILCS

5/505). Returns for exempt corporations reporting unrelated business income are due by the 15th day of the fifth month following the close of the taxable year; employee trusts described by IRC Sec. 401(a) report by the 15th day of the fourth month following the taxable year.

Signature: The signing of the return, required of an authorized officer or fiduciary, constitutes a declaration that the statements within are made under penalty of perjury (35 ILCS 5/504).

EFT: A taxpayer with an annual corporate income tax liability of $20,000 or more must make all payments to the Department of Revenue by electronic funds transfer (EFT) (35 ILCS 5/601.1). See ¶2402. See also ¶609 in the "Personal Income" division of this *Guidebook* for payment of withheld taxes by electronic funds transfer.

Practitioner Comment: Tax Shelter Disclosure Requirements

Following California's lead in enacting tax shelter legislation in October 2003, the Illinois General Assembly in July 2004 also enacted tax shelter legislation. Illinois taxpayers are now required to file with the Department a copy of their federal disclosure statement with respect to reportable transactions.

See ¶2503 for penalties that are imposed for failure to disclose a reportable transaction.

Horwood Marcus & Berk Chartered

• *Extensions*

Effective for taxable years beginning after 2015, taxpayers that are unable to file an Illinois corporate income tax return by the original due date will be granted an automatic extension of six months (previously seven months) or one month beyond an approved federal extension if the taxpayer is granted a longer extension to file its federal return. A corporation must attach a copy of any approved federal extension to its Illinois return when it is filed. There is no paper or electronic filing requirement for Illinois extensions, but 100% of any outstanding tax liability must be paid by the original due date of a corporation's return to avoid penalties. Subscribers can view the amended regulation. (86 Ill. Adm. Code 100.5020)

A filing extension does not extend the time for payment of the tax (35 ILCS 5/602(a)). See the discussion of interest and penalties at ¶802.

If the IRS has granted an extension in excess of six months, the Illinois Director of Revenue may also grant such an extension (35 ILCS 5/505). Corporations that have applied for a federal extension of time to file are automatically granted an equivalent Illinois extension plus an additional month. A copy of the federal extension must be filed.

The Department of Revenue (DOR) may extend the due date for payment to a date that is no later than the due date for the payment of the Illinois income taxpayer's federal tax liability.

• *Federal return changes*

If a corporation's federal taxable income is recomputed by the IRS so as to affect the corporation's base income (this specifically includes net income, net loss, or any income tax credit), for the Illinois income tax, the taxpayer must notify the Department of Revenue within 120 days after (1) the recomputation of federal taxable income was agreed to or finally determined, (2) a federal tax deficiency was paid, or (3) a tentative federal carryback adjustment, abatement, or credit was assessed or paid (35 ILCS 5/506(b)).

¶1201

• *Composite returns*

Composite returns may be filed on behalf of nonresident and resident individuals, trusts, and estates who derive income from Illinois and who are partners or S corporation shareholders or who transact insurance business under a Lloyd's plan of operation. See ¶501.

Effective for taxable years beginning after 2014, nonresident S corporation shareholders, members of pass-through entities classified as partnerships for federal purposes, trust beneficiaries, and certain insurance underwriters are no longer permitted to file composite income and replacement tax returns. See ¶858.

• *Estimated tax payments*

A corporation that expects to have an Illinois income tax liability in excess of $400 must make payments of estimated tax; S corporations are not included in the requirement (35 ILCS 5/803). The estimates are made on Form IL-1120-ES and filed with the Illinois Department of Revenue, P.O. Box 19045, Springfield, IL 62794-9045.

The first payment of estimated tax for a calendar year taxpayer is due on or before April 15th of the taxable year; the second, on or before June 15th; the third, on or before September 15th; and the fourth, on or before December 15th. If the payments are made on a fiscal year basis, the months of the fiscal year are substituted for the corresponding calendar year months. Short-year filers use the same due dates, except that the final payment is due on the 15th day of the last month of the short year.

An underpayment of estimated tax occurs if (1) the estimate is not paid as required, (2) the estimate paid is less than 90% of the tax liability shown on the return for the taxable year, or (3) the estimate paid is less than 90% of the tax liability for the taxable year in cases in which no return was filed. In addition, penalty for underpayment may be avoided if any of the following exceptions are met: estimated tax paid equals (1) the amount shown on the return for the previous year, provided that it is not a short year; (2) the amount that would be due if the current year's income were placed on an annualized basis (35 ILCS 5/804).

Required annual payment: The required annual payment is the lesser of ((35 ILCS 5/804(c)):

— 90% of the tax shown on the return (or if no return is filed, 90% of the tax for that year), or

— 100% of the tax shown on the return of the previous year if the taxpayer filed a return for a taxable year of 12 months.

Period of underpayment: The period of underpayment runs from the date the installment was due until the earlier of the date on which paid or the date the return is due, without extensions. Payments of estimated tax are credited against unpaid installments in the order in which installments are due. Penalties for underpaid estimated taxes are discussed at ¶802.

Electronic transfer: Taxpayers with annual corporate income tax liability of $20,000 or more must make estimated payment by electronic funds transfer (EFT) (35 ILCS 5/601.1). See ¶2402.

Abatement of penalty: Penalties may be abated for reasonable cause. See ¶2503.

Practitioner Comment: Penalty Relief Limited

Section 804 of the Illinois Income Tax Act [35 ILCS 5/804] prescribes the amount of estimated tax that a taxpayer must pay to avoid penalties for the underpayment of estimated tax. A corporate taxpayer must be aware of not only the amounts that must be paid to avoid penalties, but also that penalties may be waived if the taxpayer can

¶1201

demonstrate reasonable cause. Both Illinois case law and the Department's regulations require that a taxpayer exercise ordinary care and prudence in estimating and paying its tax installments to satisfy the reasonable cause requirement. In evaluating whether a taxpayer has established reasonable cause for abatement of penalties, the Department will generally look at the taxpayer's level of sophistication, filing history, and good faith in timely paying and properly maintaining its estimated taxes to determine if reasonable cause exists.

Indeed, this very issue was addressed by the Illinois Appellate Court in *Hollinger International v. Bower*, 363 Ill. App. 3d 313 (2005), CCH ILLINOIS TAX REPORTS, ¶401-617. The Appellate Court reversed the circuit court's decision and refused to abate estimated tax penalties even though the taxpayer relied on its long-time CPA firm – which had never previously erred in estimating the company's taxes – to prepare the installment payments because the corporation itself had "sophisticated and experienced" employees working on its behalf. In this case, the taxpayer measured its first and second quarter estimated tax payments for 1998 based on its estimated tax liability for 1997 (the return was on extension). As it turned out, the taxpayer was not eligible to use the safe harbor of basing its installment payments on its 1997 liability because, due to unforeseen midyear adjustments, there was no tax liability in 1997. This opinion appears out of step with an entire body of federal case law standing for the proposition that a taxpayer can avoid penalties upon showing of reasonable cause when the taxpayer relies on the advice of a trusted attorney or accountant in preparing taxes; however, the Hollinger court does focus on the ability of the taxpayer's own employees to determine the taxpayer's own estimated tax payments rather than the taxpayer's reliance on the outside CPA firm to make such determinations.

Jennifer A Zimmerman, Esq., Horwood Marcus & Berk Chartered

• *Tax Preparers*

Effective for taxable years beginning on or after January 1, 2017, preparers of Illinois corporate income tax returns must include their preparer tax identification number (PTIN) on any return or claim for a tax refund prepared by the preparer. (35 ILCS 35/10; 86 Ill. Adm. Code 9910).

The term "income tax return preparer" means any person who prepares for compensation, or who employs one or more persons to prepare for compensation, any Illinois income tax return or refund claim. The preparation of a substantial portion of a return or claim for refund will be treated as the preparation of that return or claim for refund. (35 ILCS 5/1501(a)(26); 86 Ill. Adm. Code 9910) The PTIN requirement applies only to a preparer who would be considered the "signing tax return preparer" under federal regulations and only to an income tax return preparer who holds an active PTIN at the time of filing the Illinois return or claim for refund. If there is an employment relationship or association between the individual required to sign a return and another person, the name, Employer Identification Number (EIN), and signature of that other person must be included on the filed return or claim for refund when required by department forms (86 Ill. Adm. Code 9910).

The PTIN information allows the department to identify preparers who prepare fraudulent or otherwise erroneous returns, and returns reflecting unsubstantiated tax positions. The department will share and exchange PTIN information with the Internal Revenue Service (IRS) on income tax return preparers who are suspected of fraud, disciplined, or barred from filing tax returns with the department or the IRS. The department will share similar enforcement or discipline information with other states (86 Ill. Adm. Code 9910).

The department may investigate the actions of any income tax return preparer doing business in Illinois and may bar or suspend an income tax return preparer from filing returns for good cause. A penalty of $50 for each offense, up to $25,000, may be imposed against any preparer for failing to provide his or her PTIN, unless it is shown that the failure is due to reasonable cause and not due to willful neglect. (35 ILCS 35/15, Laws 2016; 86 Ill. Adm. Code 9910)

Practitioner Comment: Tax Preparer Oversight Act

The DOR's objective in instituting the Tax Preparer Oversight Act (35 ILCS 35/1) is to recognize and document questionable return practices by income tax return preparers. The DOR is also required to establish communications protocols with the Commissioner of the Internal Revenue Service to exchange PTIN information of income tax preparers suspected of fraud or barred from filing returns. As a result, tax preparers should be aware that the Department and IRS will be dually monitoring the tax positions of income tax preparers in search of potential patterns of errors.

Samantha K. Breslow, Esq., Horwood Marcus & Berk, Chartered

¶1202 Credits Against Tax—In General

Law: Corporate Accountability for Tax Expenditures Act, Sec. 25 [20 ILCS 715/25]; Civil Administrative Code, Sec. 605 [20 ILCS 605/605-320]; Income Tax Act, Sec. 201(l) [35 ILCS 5/201(l)]; Income Tax Act, Sec. 206(a) [35 ILCS 5/206(a)]; Income Tax Act, Sec. 206(b) [35 ILCS 5/206(b)]; Income Tax Act, Sec. 215 [35 ILCS 5/215]; Income Tax Act, Sec. 250 [35 ILCS 5/250]; Income Tax Act, Sec. 405 [35 ILCS 5/405] (CCH Illinois Tax Reports, ¶12-001).

Credits available to corporate taxpayers include those for investments in qualified property, for the hiring of employees to work in enterprise zones, for amounts spent on vocational training, for dependent care assistance programs, for amounts paid for environmental remediation costs, for coal research donations, for increasing qualified research activities, and for investment in affordable housing. In addition, an income tax credit is provided for a percentage of amounts paid for the personal property replacement income tax.

Sunset date for credits: Any credit that is enacted after September 16, 1994, must be limited by a sunset date. If a "reasonable and appropriate" sunset date is not specified, then the credit will expire five years after the effective date of the enacting law (35 ILCS 5/250).

The sunset date is extended five years for all tax exemptions, credits, or deductions that would have expired in 2011-2013 (35 ILCS 5/250).

• *Requirements for development assistance*

The Corporate Accountability for Tax Expenditures Act imposes minimum recapture, or "claw back," requirements for credits against Illinois corporate income taxes (20 ILCS 715/25).

The Act also establishes a new definition of "development assistance" that encompasses all the aforementioned incentives, provides for developmental assistance agreements between state bodies granting incentives and incentive recipients, establishes standardized application requirements for developmental assistance, and requires annual reporting to the Legislature.

Details of the Act are discussed at ¶401.

• *Reporting requirements for recipients of tax incentives*

An annual reporting requirement is imposed on Illinois taxpayers that receive corporate income tax credits, personal income tax credits, sales tax exemptions, or the abatement of property tax under the Economic Development for a Growing Economy Tax Credit Act, the River Edge Redevelopment Zone Act, or the Enterprise Zone Act, including the High Impact Business program (20 ILCS 605/605-320). Recipients of such incentives must provide the Department of Commerce and Economic Opportunity the following:

— a detailed list of the occupation or job classifications and number of new employees or retained employees to be hired in full-time, permanent jobs;

— a schedule of anticipated starting dates of the new hires and the actual average wage by occupation or job classification; and

— total payroll to be created as a result of the incentives.

See also *Informational Bulletin FY 2014-11,* Illinois Department of Revenue, March 2014.

• *Enterprise zones and river edge redevelopment zones defined*

Enterprise zone: A contiguous area within a municipality and/or an unincorporated area in which pervasive poverty, unemployment, and economic distress exits. Enterprise zones range from a half square mile to 15 square miles (20 ILCS 655/4). An enterprise zone will exist for 30 years or for a lesser number of years as specified in the zone designation (20 ILCS 655/5.3).

River edge redevelopment zone: A contiguous area adjacent to or surrounding a river that (65 ILCS 115/10-4):

(1) comprises a minimum of one half square mile and not more than 12 square miles, exclusive of lakes and waterways;

(2) satisfies any additional criteria established by the Department of Commerce and Economic Opportunity;

(3) is entirely within a single home rule municipality; and

(4) has at least 100 acres of environmentally challenged land within 1500 yards of the riverfront.

Designation: A home-rule municipality may designate a river edge redevelopment zone (65 ILCS 115/10-5).

Extension: Enterprise zone credits may be extended by municipal or county ordinance for an additional 10 years. In addition, any credit that is scheduled to expire before July 1, 2016, may be extended by municipal or county ordinance until July 1, 2016. Applications for an extension to July 1, 2016, had to be submitted by December 31, 2014. (20 ILCS 655/5.3(c))

• *Mergers and acquisitions*

Applicable to all acquisitions described in IRC Sec. 381(a) regarding carryovers in certain corporate acquisitions, all of an acquired corporation's corporate income tax credits and NOLs (¶ 1013) may be claimed by the acquiring corporation (35 ILCS 5/405). The adoption of these federal provisions concerning successor organizations by Illinois in 1999 is applicable retroactively to all acquisitions occurring in tax years ending after 1986. However, transitional rules apply concerning a taxpayer's eligibility for refunds and assessment reductions for pre-1999 tax liabilities.

¶1203 Investment Credits—Qualified Investments

Law: Income Tax Act, Sec. 201(e) [35 ILCS 5/201(e)] (CCH Illinois Tax Reports, ¶ 12-055b).

There are three credits related to qualified property placed into service in a taxable year (35 ILCS 5/201(e), (f), (h); 35 ILCS 5/206). The replacement tax investment credit for qualified investments is discussed below. The investment credit for enterprise zone investments is discussed at ¶ 1204 and the investment credit for high impact businesses is discussed at ¶ 1205.

Investment Credits

Credit Sec.	Tax Applies	Placed in Service	Nature of Property	Relation to Other Credits	Rate	Recapture	Carryover
201(e)	PPRIT	Post July 1, 1984	Manufacturing Retailing, Mining	Excludes 201(f)	0.5% basis	Yes 48 mo.	Conditional
201(f)	Income	Post June 30, 1983	Placed in Enterprise Zone	Excludes 201(e)	0.5% basis	Yes 48 mo.	5-year
201(h)	Income	Post 1985	Tangible, depreciable, IRC Sec.179(d) purchase	Excludes 201(f)	0.5% basis	Yes 48 mo.	5-year

• *Replacement tax investment credit*

Differing from the other credits in that it is applied against the personal property tax replacement income tax liability, this credit is granted for investments in qualified property placed in service after July 1, 1984, but prior to January 1, 2014. The amount of the credit is 0.5% of the basis of the qualified property. In common with the other credits, "qualified property" is tangible property, new or used, including buildings and structural components of buildings and signs that are real property, but not including land or improvements to real property that are not a structural component of a building, such as landscaping, sewer lines, local access roads, fencing, parking lots, and other appurtenances, depreciable for federal purposes, and acquired by purchase as defined by IRC Sec. 179(d). In addition, the property must be used by a taxpayer that is primarily engaged in manufacturing operations, mining coal or fluorite, or in retailing, or was placed in service on or after July 1, 2006, in a River Edge redevelopment zone; and must not have previously been used in Illinois in such a manner and by such a person as would have qualified for this credit or the enterprise zone credit (see below). A regulation defines qualified operations in detail (86 Ill. Adm. Code Sec. 100.2100). Three-year ACRS property does not qualify for the replacement tax credit or the enterprise zone credit.

Applicable to taxable years beginning with 2009, the term "tangible personal property" has the same meaning as it does for retailers' occupation tax purposes and does not include the generation, transmission, or distribution of electricity (35 ILCS 5/201(e)(3)). This amendment effectively overturns the decision by the Illinois Supreme Court in *Exelon Corp. v Illinois Department of Revenue*, discussed below.

Practitioner Comment: Retailing Electricity

In *Exelon Corp. v. Illinois Department of Revenue*, Illinois Supreme Court, No.105582, Modified Upon Denial of Rehearing July 15, 2009, CCH ILLINOIS TAX REPORTS, ¶ 401-994, the Illinois Supreme Court reversed the Appellate Court's decision and held that for purposes of the Corporate Income and Replacement Tax, electricity constitutes tangible personal property. Unicom, a predecessor of Exelon, filed amended tax returns for 1995 and 1996, claiming investment credits for its purchases on the basis that it was a retailer of tangible personal property, namely, electricity. The Department denied the claim for the investment credits and Exelon protested the denial. Exelon included with its Motion for Summary Judgment an un-rebutted affidavit and expert report that concluded that as a matter of scientific fact, "electricity is physical and material." However, relying on *Farrand Coal Co. v. Alphin*, 10 Ill. 2d 507 (1957), an Illinois sales tax case concerning the taxation of electricity, the Administrative Law Judge (ALJ) found that the General Assembly did not intend to include electricity within the meaning of tangible personal property.

On appeal, the Illinois Supreme Court found that any reference to the characterization of electricity in *Farrand Coal* was dicta and was not to be relied upon. The Court clarified that the focus of *Farrand Coal* was on the consumption of coal and not on the characterization of electricity. The Court noted that it could not ignore the laws of physics and that several other state courts had held that electricity constituted tangible property. Relying on the expert's report, the Court concluded that electricity was tangible personal property. The parties had agreed that if electricity was found to be tangible personal property, then Exelon would be engaged in retailing as defined by Section 201(e) and the statutory requirements for the investment credit would be met.

The Court's holding that electricity was tangible personal property applied prospectively; thus, although Exelon met the statutory requirements for the credit, its refund was denied. The Court determined that a prospective application was appropriate because it was an issue of first impression and it would allow the General Assembly to provide direction. The Court's invitation was accepted by the General Assembly and Public Act 96-115, Laws 2010, which clarifies that electricity cannot be classified as tangible personal property for purposes of the investment tax credit, was signed into law.

The classification of electricity as tangible personal property is likely to give rise to some interesting issues. Revenues from the sale of electricity, because it had been characterized as an intangible, had historically been sourced for apportionment purposes using Cost of Performance. The more interesting issues resulting from the reversal of 52 years of policy may arise with respect to non-income taxes. Does the characterization of electricity as tangible personal property subject the commodity to a sales tax? Is the Electricity Excise Tax imposed in lieu of a sales tax? Would the manufacturing machinery and equipment exemption now apply to the generation of electricity?

Marilyn A. Wethekam, Esq., Horwood Marcus & Berk Chartered

CCH Advisory: Offsite Property

Case law has upheld the taxpayer's right to include property supporting retail operations that is not directly used at the retail site. Warehouse equipment, as well as a fleet of trucks, was eligible for the credit (*American Stores*, Illinois Appellate Court, First Dist., No. 1-96-4444, May 1, 1998; CCH ILLINOIS TAX REPORTS, ¶ 400-927).

"Placed in service" is assigned the meaning of IRC Sec. 46, the investment credit provision. The basis of qualified property for all the investment credits is the basis used to compute the depreciation deduction for federal income tax purposes. If the federal basis of the property is increased after it is placed in service in Illinois, the amount of the increase is deemed to be property placed in service on the date of the increase.

Bonus credit: An additional credit of 0.5% is allowed for qualified property placed in service if the taxpayer's base employment in Illinois has increased by 1% or more over the preceding year. A taxpayer who is new to Illinois is presumed to meet the 1% increase in base employment for the first year. If the increase in Illinois base employment is less than 1% in any year, the additional credit is limited to the percentange of increase times a fraction the numerator of which is 0.5% and the denominator of which is 1%. The additional credit may not, however, exceed 0.5%.

Carryovers: The credit may be carried over for five taxable years. The credit must be applied to the earliest year for which there is a tax liability.

Recapture of credit: If, within 48 months after being placed in service, the property ceases to qualify for the credit or is moved outside the state, the taxpayer's income tax will be increased by the amount of credit already allowed with respect to the property.

CCH Advisory: Sale and Leaseback Triggers Recapture

Property that at one time qualified for Illinois corporate income tax investment and enterprise zone credits ceased to be qualified for such credits following the sale/

leaseback of the property within 48 months after its acquisition. After the sale and leaseback, the property was no longer depreciable by the taxpayer, nor was it "acquired by purchase," both of which are qualifications for claiming the credit (*The May Department Stores Co. v. Department of Revenue*, Ill CirCt, Cook County, No. 98 L 50450, February 5, 1999; CCH ILLINOIS TAX REPORTS, ¶ 401-002).

¶ 1204 Investment Credits—Enterprise Zone or River Edge Redevelopment Zone Investments

Law: Income Tax Act, Sec. 201(f) [35 ILCS 5/201(f)]; 86 Ill. Adm. Code Sec. 100.2100 (CCH ILLINOIS TAX REPORTS, ¶ 12-060).

Corporations are allowed a nonrefundable credit against the income tax for investments in qualified property that is placed in service during the taxable year in an enterprise zone or, for property placed in service on or after July 1, 2006, a River Edge redevelopment zone. "Qualified property" and "placed in service" are defined as for the replacement tax credit (see ¶ 1203). In contrast to the replacement credit, the property does not require a specific use (86 Ill. Adm. Code Sec. 100.2100). For a chart that lists the differences and similarities between the three investment credits, see ¶ 1203.

Credit amount: The amount of the credit is 0.5% of the basis of the property, defined, as for the replacement credit, as that used to compute depreciation for federal purposes. Unused credit may be carried over five years. Amounts carried over are applied to the earliest tax year possible. The credit extends to partnerships, S corporations, and to LLCs treated as partnerships. The credit is passed through to partners, S corporation shareholders, or LLC members.

Bonus credit: An additional credit of 0.5% is allowed for qualified property placed in service during the taxable year in a River Edge redevelopment zone, provided the property is placed in service on or after July 1, 2006, and the taxpayer's base employment in Illinois has increased by 1% or more over the preceding year. A taxpayer who is new to Illinois is presumed to meet the 1% increase in base employment for the first year. If the increase in Illinois base employment is less than 1% in any year, the additional credit is limited to the percentange of increase times a fraction the numerator of which is 0.5% and the denominator of which is 1%. The additional credit may not, however, exceed 0.5%.

Jobs credit: The $500 corporation and personal income tax credit for each job created in a river edge redevelopment zone and foreign trade zone or subzone was eliminated for high-impact and other enterprise zone businesses by P.A. 97-905 (S.B. 3616), Laws 2012, effective August 7, 2012. The credit was repealed, effective July 25, 2013 (P.A. 98-0109 (S.B. 20), Laws 2013).

Practitioner Comment: Enterprise Zone Program Extended

On August 7, 2012, the Governor approved SB 3616 and created Public Act 97-0905 which extended and amended the Illinois Enterprise Zone Act. Per the original legislation, the 97 existing enterprise zones would have expired in 2013. Preventing this expiration, the amendment extends the enterprise zone program for 25 years and allows the Department of Commerce and Economic Opportunity to grant extensions until 2016 after which current zones would have to reapply. Additionally, the amendment provides for the creation of five new enterprise zones over the next 20 years.

Aside from extending the existing act, the amendment makes a handful of other substantive changes to the Enterprise Zone Act. Most significantly, the amendment adds section 3(f) which creates new standards for evaluating what areas qualify as enterprise zones and section 5.2.1 which mandates the creation of an Enterprise Zone Board. While previously an area had to be "depressed" and satisfy additional department criteria, the amendment creates a list of ten specific factors of which an area must meet at least three to be considered to be an enterprise zone. Further streamlining evaluation, the amendment assigns a point value to each criterion. To evaluate communities, the amendment created the Enterprise Zone Board composed of the Director of Commerce and Economic Opportunity, the Director of Revenue, and 3 appointees of the governor. While the impact of the amendments remain to be seen, they do indicate that enterprise zones will be present in Illinois for the foreseeable future and new designations will be evaluated by an independent committee based on more discrete factors.

Breen M. Schiller, Esq., Horwood Marcus & Berk, Chartered

¶1205 Investment Credits—Investment in High Impact Businesses

Law: Income Tax Act, Sec. 201(h) [35 ILCS 5/201(h)] (CCH ILLINOIS TAX REPORTS, ¶12-055).

A credit against the income tax is available for investing in qualified property placed in service during the tax year in a business designated as a high impact business. The property of the business cannot be located in an enterprise zone. For a chart that lists the differences and similarities between the three investment credits, see ¶1203.

To qualify as a high impact business, a business (other than an energy-related business) must intend to invest at least $12 million that will be placed in service in qualified property and create 500 full-time-equivalent jobs in Illinois, or must intend to invest at least $30 million that will be placed in service in qualified property and to retain 1,500 full-time jobs in Illinois. "Qualified property" is property that is tangible, depreciable under IRC Sec. 167, and acquired by purchase as defined at IRC Sec. 179(d). All businesses must certify to the Department of Commerce and Economic Opportunity that the creation or expansion of facilities would not be possible without the credits or exemptions.

Energy-related businesses: The credit is also available to businesses that encourage the establishment of new or expanded coal-fired electricity generation facilities, associated coal production facilities, or electricity transmission facilities. In the case of a coal-fired generation facility or a coal production facility, the facility must create at least 150 new jobs.

New gasification facilities have been added to the type of business that can qualify as high impact businesses. With certain pilot projects excepted, a "new gasification facility" is a newly constructed coal gasification facility that generates chemical feedstocks or transportation fuels derived from coal, that supports the creation or retention of Illinois coal-mining jobs, and that qualifies for financial assistance from the Illinois Department of Commerce and Economic Opportunity before December 31, 2006.

Credit amount: The credit is equal to 0.5% of the basis of such property and is not available until the minimum investments in qualified property, as required by Sec. 5.5 of the Enterprise Zone Act, have been satisfied. The credit applicable to such minimum investments must be taken in the taxable year in which the investments were completed. The credit for additional investments beyond the minimum investment by a high impact business is available only in the taxable year in which the property is placed in service and cannot reduce a taxpayer's tax liability below zero. For purposes of computing the credit amount, the basis of the qualified property is the basis used in computing the federal depreciation deduction.

With respect to an energy-related business, the credit is not available until the facility is operational.

For related sales and use tax exemptions available to high-impact businesses, see ¶1702.

¶1205

Recapture of credit: A taxpayer that has received the credit and that later relocates its entire facility in violation of its contract with a local taxing authority, will have its income tax increased for the taxable year in which the facility was relocated by an amount equal to the credit received.

Carryovers: The credit may be carried forward and applied to the tax liability of the five taxable years following the excess credit year. The credit must be applied to the earliest year for which there is liability.

See ¶1017 for a deduction for dividends paid by a corporation designated as a high impact business and ¶1003 for a deduction by financial organizations of interest income received on loans secured by property eligible for the high-impact business investment credit.

¶1206 New Jobs Tax Credit (expired)

Law: Income Tax Act, Sec. 201(g) [35 ILCS 5/201(g)] (CCH ILLINOIS TAX REPORTS, ¶12-060a).

This credit was eliminated for enterprise zones, effective August 7, 2012, and for foreign trade zones or subzones and River Edge redevelopment zones, effective July 25, 2013 (35 ILCS 5/201(g)). However, eligibility for high impact business credits was extended to a business that invests a minimum of $500 million and creates 125 jobs at a newly constructed or upgraded fertilizer plant. Applications for the credit had to be submitted to the Department of Revenue within 60 days after July 25, 2013 (P.A. 98-0109 (S.B. 20), Laws 2013).

Prior to repeal, corporations were allowed a $500 income tax credit for each eligible employee hired to work in a foreign trade zone or subzone, an enterprise zone, or a River Edge redevelopment zone during the tax year (former 35 ILCS 5/201(g)).

Excess credit may be carried forward five years.

See also the Small Business Jobs Creation Credit, discussed at ¶1221.

¶1207 EDGE Job Creation Credit

Law: Income Tax Act, Sec. 211 [35 ILCS 5/211]; Economic Development for a Growing Economy Tax Credit Act, Sec. 5-5 [35 ILCS 10/5-5]; Economic Development for a Growing Economy Tax Credit Act, Sec. 5-20 [35 ILCS 10/5-20]; 14 Ill. Adm. Code 527.30; 86 Ill. Adm. Code 100.129 (CCH ILLINOIS TAX REPORTS, ¶12-085).

Eligible businesses that enter into an agreement before June 30, 2022, with the Illinois Department of Commerce and Economic Opportunity (DCEO) to expand operations or relocate in Illinois resulting in job creation or retention may be awarded a credit against Illinois corporate income tax liability under the Economic Development for a Growing Economy Credit Act (EDGE credit) (35 ILCS 5/211). Eligible entities include individuals, corporations, partnerships, or other entities with Illinois income tax liability, including shareholders or partners of a pass-through entity (35 ILCS 5/211; 35 ILCS 10/5-5).

Qualifications: Effective beginning September 18, 2017, credit applicants with more than 100 employees must invest at least $2.5 million in capital improvements that are placed in service in the state. There is no capital investment requirement for businesses with 100 or fewer employees. (35 ILCS 10/5-20). New jobs created in the state on the date a credit application is filed with the Department of Commerce and Economic Opportunity (DCEO) must be equal to the lesser of 50 new employees or:

— 10% of the full-time employees employed world-wide by businesses with more than 100 employees; or

— 5% of the full-time employees employed world-wide by businesses with 100 or fewer employees. (35 ILCS 10/5-20)

A "full-time employee" is an individual who is employed for consideration for at least 35 hours each week or who renders any other standard of service generally accepted by industry custom or practice as full-time employment (35 ILCS 10/5-5). An employee of a professional employer organization is a full-time employee if employed in the service of the applicant for at least 35 hours each week or who renders any other standard of service generally accepted by industry custom or practice as full-time employment to applicant.

Amount of credit: The credit is equal to the lesser of:

— 50% of the income tax withheld from new employees, plus 10% of their training costs; or

— 100% of the income tax withheld from new employees (35 ILCS 10/5-5).

If the business is located in an underserved area that meets certain poverty, unemployement, and federal assistance rates, then the amount of the credit may not exceed the lesser of:

— 75% of the income tax withheld from new employees, plus 10% of their training costs; or

— 100% of the income tax withheld from new employees (35 ILCS 10/5-5).

Businesses that agree to hire the required number of new employees may claim an additional credit of 25% of the income tax withheld for employees that are retained at the same location as the new employees (35 ILCS 10/5-5).

Carryover: Unused credits may be carried forward and applied to the tax liability of the five tax years following the excess credit year.

A taxpayer may not generally claim the credit for jobs relocated from one site in Illinois to another, although there are exceptions.

Eligible costs: The aggregate amount of costs include the following: (1) capital investment including, but not limited to, equipment, buildings, and land; (2) infrastructure development; (3) debt service, except refinancing of current debt; (4) research and development; (5) job training and education; (6) lease costs; or (7) relocation costs.

Loss of credit: The agreement that taxpayers must enter into with the DCEO must provide that if the taxpayer does not meet either the investment requirement or the job creation and retention requirement specified in the agreement during the five-year period beginning on the first day of the first taxable year in which the agreement is executed and ending on the last day of the fifth taxable year after the agreement is executed, then (1) the agreement is automatically terminated on the last day of the fifth taxable year after the agreement is executed and (2) the taxpayer is not entitled to the award of any credits for any of that five-year period. Effective beginning September 18, 2017, the agreement must also include a provision specifying that, if the taxpayer ceases principal operations with the intent to shut down the project in the state permanently during the term of the agreement, then the entire credit amount awarded to the taxpayer before the date the taxpayer ceases principal operations must be returned to the DCEO and reallocated to the local workforce investment area in which the project was located. (35 ILCS 10/5-50)

Pass-through entities: Pass-through entities that are awarded a credit may treat the credit as a tax payment. The term "tax payment" is also defined as a composite payment made by a pass-through entity on behalf of any of its shareholders or partners to satisfy such shareholders' or partners' taxes. (35 ILCS 10/5-15(g))

¶1207

¶1208 TECH-PREP Youth Vocational Program Credit

Law: Income Tax Act, Sec. 209 [35 ILCS 5/209] (CCH ILLINOIS TAX REPORTS, ¶ 12-120).

A taxpayer that is primarily engaged in manufacturing is allowed a credit against the income tax and the personal property tax replacement income tax for expenditures for cooperative secondary school youth vocational programs in Illinois that are certified as qualifying TECH-PREP programs by the State Board of Education and the Department of Revenue (35 ILCS 5/209).

Credit amount: The credit is equal to 20% of the taxpayer's direct payroll expenditures in the tax year for which the vocational program credit is claimed. If the amount of the credit exceeds the tax liability for the year, the excess may be carried forward for two taxable years following the excess credit year.

Planning considerations: The vocational programs must prepare students to be technically skilled workers and meet the performance standards of business and industry and the admission standards of higher education.

The credit may also be claimed for personal services rendered to the manufacturer by a TECH-PREP student or instructor when those services would be subject to withholding tax if the student or instructor was an employee of the taxpayer and a TECH-PREP credit is not claimed for the services by another taxpayer.

¶1209 Dependent Care Assistance Program Credit

Law: Income Tax Act, Sec. 210 [35 ILCS 5/210] (CCH ILLINOIS TAX REPORTS, ¶ 12-110).

A taxpayer that is primarily engaged in manufacturing is entitled to a credit against the income tax and the personal property tax replacement income tax for expenditures in providing on the Illinois premises of the taxpayer's workplace an on-site facility dependent care assistance program under IRC Sec. 129 (35 ILCS 5/210). The amount of the credit equals 5% of the amount of expenditures by the taxpayer in the tax year for which the credit is claimed. If the amount of the credit exceeds the tax liability for the year, the excess may be carried forward for two years following the excess credit year.

¶1210 Employee Child Care Facilities Credit

Law: Income Tax Act, Sec. 210.5 [35 ILCS 5/210.5]; 86 Ill. Adm. Code 100.2196 (CCH ILLINOIS TAX REPORTS, ¶ 12-110a).

A credit is allowed for 30% of the start-up costs incurred by corporations to provide child care facilities for children of employees and 5% of the annual expenses of the child care facilities (35 ILCS 5/210.5; 86 Ill. Adm. Code Sec. 100.2196). Start-up costs include planning, site-preparation, construction, renovation, or acquisition of a child care facility.

The credit cannot reduce the corporation's liability below zero. A corporation may provide and operate such a facility independently or in partnership with other corporations. Any excess credit may be carried forward for five tax years. The regulations clarify that the credit is not available to S corporations or shareholders of S corporations (86 Ill. Adm. Code 100.2196).

¶1211 Research Expenditures Credit

Law: Income Tax Act, Sec.201(k) [35 ILCS 5/201(k)]; 86 Ill. Admin. Code 100.2160(c); 86 Ill. Admin. Code 100.5270(d)(5) (CCH ILLINOIS TAX REPORTS, ¶ 12-085).

For tax years beginning after December 31, 2004 and before January 1, 2022, corporations are allowed to take a credit against corporate income taxes for qualifying expenditures that are used to increase research activities in Illinois (35 ILCS 5/201(k)). The definition of "Qualifying research expenditures" is the same as that in IRC Sec. 41, which provides that "qualified research expenses" is the sum of the in-house research expenses and contract research expenses paid or incurred by the taxpayer pursuant to carrying on trade or business, including wages paid to employees, amounts paid for supplies, or payments to third parties that conduct research on behalf of the taxpayer (86 Admin. Code 100.2160(c)).

Credit amount: The credit equals 6.5 % of qualifying expenditures (35 ILCS 5/201(k); 86 Ill. Admin. Code 100.2160(c)).

Planning considerations: The taxpayer may elect to have the unused credit carried over as a credit against tax liability for the following five taxable years or until it has been fully used, whichever occurs first. (35 ILCS 5/201(k); 86 Ill. Admin. Code 100.2160(c)).

The credit may be passed through by partnerships, S corporations, and limited liability companies (LLCs) to corporations that are partners, shareholders of the S corporation, or owners of the LLC (35 ILCS 5/201(k)).

In the case of taxpayers filing combined returns, for purposes of determining entitlement to the credit during a combined-return year, the increase in research activities shall be determined with respect to research activities conducted by all members of the combined group in Illinois and not an individual member's research activities. The regulations provide a series of examples that illustrate the application of the research and development credit in combined return situations (86 Ill. Admin. Code 100.5270(d)(5)).

¶1212 River Edge Redevelopment Zone Site Remediation Credit

Law: Income Tax Act, Sec. 201(n) [35 ILCS 5/201(n)] (CCH ILLINOIS TAX REPORTS, ¶12-080).

A taxpayer is allowed a credit for certain amounts paid for unreimbursed eligible remediation costs at a site in a River Edge redevelopment zone (35 ILCS 5/201(n)).

"Unreimbursed eligible remediation costs" means costs approved by the Illinois Environmental Protection Agency that were paid in performing environmental remediation at a site within a River Edge redevelopment zone for which a no further remediation letter was issued and recorded by the Agency. "Related party" includes the persons disallowed a deduction under IRC Sec. 267(b), (c), and (f)(1) by virtue of being a related taxpayer, as well as any of its partners. "Taxpayer" includes a person whose tax attributes the taxpayer has succeeded to under IRC Sec. 381 (35 ILCS 5/201(n)).

Credit amount: The credit equals 25% of the unreimbursed eligible remediation costs in excess of $100,000 per site (35 ILCS 5/201(n)).

Planning considerations: The credit must be claimed for the taxable year in which Agency approval of the eligible remediation costs is granted. The credit is not available if the taxpayer or any related party caused or contributed to a release of regulated substances on, in, or under the site that was identified and addressed by the remedial action pursuant to the Site Remediation Program of the Environmental Protection Act. This credit is not subject to the automatic sunset provision that applies to most other income tax credits.

Carryover: Unused credit amounts may be carried forward for five tax years.

Credit transfers: A credit may be sold to a buyer as part of a sale of all or part of the remediation site for which the credit was granted. To perfect the transfer, the assignor must record the transfer in the chain of title for the site and provide written notice to the Director of the Illinois Department of Revenue of the assignor's intent to sell the remediation site and the amount of the tax credit to be transferred as a portion of the sale.

¶1212

¶1213 Affordable Housing Credit

Law: Housing Development Act, Sec. 7.28 [20 ILCS 3805/7.28]; Income Tax Act, Sec. 214 [35 ILCS 5/214]; 47 Ill. Adm. Code 355.103 et seq. (CCH ILLINOIS TAX REPORTS, ¶12-105).

An income tax credit is available to a taxpayer who makes a donation between January 1, 2002, and December 31, 2021, in connection with the acquisition, construction, rehabilitation, and financing of an affordable housing project (20 ILCS 3805/7.28).

An affordable housing project is either (1) a rental project in which at least 25% of the units have rents not exceeding 30% of the gross monthly income of a household earning the maximum income for a low income household or (2) a unit for sale to low income households who will pay no more than 30% of their gross household income for mortgage principal, interest, property taxes, and property insurance upon the purchase of the unit.

A donation includes money, securities, or real or personal property that is donated to a not-for-profit sponsor and that is used solely for costs associated with either the purchasing, constructing, or rehabilitating an affordable housing project, an employer-assisted housing project, general operating support, or technical assistance.

A low income household is a household whose adjusted income is less than or equal to 60% of the median income of the geographical area of the household's affordable housing project, adjusted for family size.

Credit amount: The amount of the credit is 50% of the value of the donation (20 ILCS 3805/7.28). The minimum amount of a donation is $10,000.

Planning considerations: A taxpayer must complete and remit an application to the Illinois Housing Development Authority indicating the taxpayer's ability to meet the requirements imposed by the Act, the financial feasibility of the project, the chance of successful construction, evidence of site control, the amount of the proposed donation, and the location of the project. The agency will issue of certificate of approval to qualifying taxpayers (47 Ill. Adm. Code 355.301).

Funds used by a donor to acquire an ownership interest in an affordable housing project will not qualify as a donation.

If the amount of the credit exceeds the tax liability for the year, the excess may be carried forward for five taxable years following the excess credit year (35 ILCS 5/214).

Transfer provisions: A donor may transfer the tax credit to another individual or entity if the transfer is made to an individual or entity that has purchased land for the affordable housing project or another donor that has made a donation to the affordable housing project for which a certificate was issued (35 ILCS 5/214). The certificate must indicate the name of the original donor and the name of the entity to which the certificate is transferred.

¶1214 Film and Live Theater Production Services Credits

Law: Income Tax Act, Sec. 213 [35 ILCS 5/213]; Film Production Services Tax Credit Act of 2008 [35 ILCS 16/1] *et seq.*; Live Theater Production Tax Credit Act, Secs. 30 and 45 [35 ILCS 17/30; 35 ILCS 17/45]; Income Tax Act, Secs. 213 and 222 [35 ILCS 5/213; 35 ILCS 5/222]; 86 Ill. Admin. Code Sec. 100-2185; 14 Ill. Adm. Code 528.10 *et seq.*; 14 Ill. Adm. Code 532.10 *et seq.* (CCH ILLINOIS TAX REPORTS, ¶12-085a).

Film producers are allowed a nonrefundable credit against Illinois corporate income tax and personal income tax for a portion of the salary or wages paid to employees for services on an accredited production in Illinois (35 ILCS 5/213).

"Accredited production" means a film, video, or television production in which the Illinois production spending (for productions beginning before May 1, 2006, aggregate Illinois labor expenditures) exceed $100,000 for productions of 30 minutes or longer, or $50,000 for productions of less than 30 minutes (35 ILCS 15/10). An accredited production must be certified by the Department of Commerce and Economic Opportunity (DCEO) and excludes certain types of programming, such as news or current events, talk shows, game and awards shows, sports events, and productions produced primarily for industrial, corporate, or institutional purposes. An applicant proposing a film or television production in Illinois may apply to the DCEO for an accredited production certificate, which would certify that the production meets credit guidelines.

The credit includes an "accredited animated production," which is defined as an accredited production in which movement and characters' performances are created using a frame-by-frame technique and a significant number of major characters are animated. Motion capture by itself is not an animation technique. (35 ILCS 16/10)

"Illinois production spending" means the expenses incurred by the applicant for an accredited production, including, without limitation, all of the following: (1) expenses to purchase, from vendors within Illinois, tangible personal property that is used in the accredited production; (2) expenses to acquire services, from vendors in Illinois, for film production, editing, or processing; and (3) the compensation, not to exceed $100,000 for any one employee, for contractual or salaried employees who are Illinois residents performing services with respect to the accredited production.

Credit amount: For an accredited production beginning on or after January 1, 2009, the credit equals (1) 30% (formerly, 20%) of the Illinois production spending for the taxable year plus (2) 15% of the Illinois labor expenditures generated by the employment of residents of geographic areas of high poverty or high unemployment (as determined by the DCEO). A taxpayer's Illinois labor expenditures are limited to the first $100,000 of wages paid or incurred to each employee of a production beginning on or after May 1, 2006. (35 ILCS 16/10)

Planning considerations: A film producer must file an application with the DCEO for the credit. If the application is approved, the DCEO will issue a certificate stating the amount of the tax credit to which the applicant is entitled. The credit may be passed through partnerships to partners and through subchapter S corporations to shareholders.

Applicants requesting credits for an accredited animated production commencing on or after July 1, 2010, may make an application to the DCEO in each taxable year beginning with the taxable year in which the production commences and ending with the taxable year in which production is complete (35 ILCS 16/44).

The film production services credit may not be claimed for tax years beginning on or after May 6, 2021 (35 ILCS 16/42). The General Assembly may extend the sunset date by five-year intervals.

Carryover: If the amount of the credit exceeds the film producer's tax liability for the year, the excess may be carried forward for up to five taxable years (35 ILCS 5/213). The credit may not be carried back. The credit must be applied to the earliest year for which there is a tax liability. If there are credits from more than one taxable year that are available to offset a tax liability, the earliest credit must be applied first.

Credit transfers: A film producer earning the credit is specifically allowed to transfer the credit within one year after the credit is awarded, in accordance with rules adopted by the Department of Commerce and Economic Opportunity (35 ILCS 5/213; 14 Ill. Adm. Code 528.85).

Live theater production credit: Certain taxpayers who are theater producers, owners, licensees, or operators, or who otherwise present live stage presentations, may claim a nonrefundable credit against their income tax liability, effective for tax years beginning on or after January 1, 2012 and before January 1, 2022, equal to 20% of the

Illinois labor expenditures for each tax year, plus 20% of the Illinois production spending for each tax year, plus 15% of the Illinois labor expenditures generated by the employment of Illinois residents in geographic areas of high poverty or high unemployment in each tax year. (35 ILCS 5/222; 35 ILCS 17/10-45; 14 Ill. Adm. Code 532.10–532.120)

Eligibility for the credit is determined by the Department of Commerce and Economic Opportunity (35 ILCS 17/10-30). A total of $2 million in credits are to be awarded each year on a first come, first served basis. The tax credit award may not be carried back and can be carried forward five years (35 ILCS 5/222(e)).

¶1215 Credit for Wages Paid to Ex-Offenders

Law: Income Tax Act, Sec. 216 [35 ILCS 5/216] (CCH ILLINOIS TAX REPORTS, ¶ 12-126).

A credit may be taken for wages paid to qualified ex-offenders. (35 ILCS 5/216) "Qualified ex-offender" means any person who:

(1) is an eligible offender, as defined under Sec. 5-5.5-5 of the Unified Code of Corrections;

(2) was sentenced to a period of incarceration in an Illinois adult correctional center; and

(3) was hired by the taxpayer within three years after being released from an Illinois correctional center.

An offender required to register under the Sex Offenders Registration Act is not qualified. (35 ILCS 5/216(c))

Qualified wages:

(1) include only wages that are subject to federal unemployment tax under IRC Sec. 3306, without regard to any dollar limitation contained in the section;

(2) do not include any amounts paid or incurred by an employer for any period to any qualified ex-offender for whom the employer receives federally funded payments for on-the-job training of that qualified ex-offender for that period; and

(3) include only wages attributable to service rendered during the one-year period beginning with the day the qualified ex-offender begins work for the employer.

Credit amount: The credit equals 5% of the qualified wages paid by the taxpayer during the taxable year to one or more Illinois residents who are qualified ex-offenders. The total credit allowed to each taxpayer with respect to each qualified ex-offender may not exceed $1500 for all taxable years.

Planning considerations: If the taxpayer has received any payment from a program established under Sec. 482(e)(1) of the federal Social Security Act with respect to a qualified ex-offender, the amount of the qualified wages must be reduced by the payment amount.

Carryover: If the amount of the credit exceeds the tax liability for the tax year, the excess may be carried forward and applied to the tax liability of the five taxable years following the excess credit year. If there are credits for more than one year that are available to offset a liability, the earlier credit must be applied first.

¶1216 Credit for Hiring Post-9/11 Veterans

Law: Income Tax Act, Sec. 217.1 [35 ILCS 5/217.1] (CCH ILLINOIS TAX REPORTS, ¶ 12-127).

An income tax credit is available for employing qualified veterans initially hired by the taxpayer on or after June 1, 2012. A "qualified veteran" is a person who was an honorably-discharged member of the Armed Forces of the United States, the Illinois

National Guard, or any reserve component of the Armed Forces of the United States who served on active duty on or after September 11, 2001. Additionally, the veteran must have been unemployed for an aggregate period of four weeks or more during the six-week period ending on the Saturday immediately preceding the date he or she was hired by the taxpayer. (35 ILCS 5/217.1)

Credit amount: The credit is equal to 20% of the gross wages paid to the qualified veteran, but may not exceed $5,000 (35 ILCS 5/217.1).

Planning considerations: The sunset date for claiming a veterans jobs credit for qualified veterans was tax years beginning on or after January 1, 2015 (35 ILCS 5/217(a); 35 ILCS 5/250(a)). However, the Illinois jobs credit for qualified unemployed veterans is scheduled to sunset for tax years after 2016 (35 ILCS 5/217.1(a)).

Unused credit may be carried forward for five years, and taxpayers claiming this credit may not claim a different credit for the same veteran for that taxable year. (35 ILCS 5/217.1)

¶1217 New Markets Credit

Law: New Markets Development Program Act, Sec. 663 [20 ILCS 663/1 *et seq.*](CCH ILLINOIS TAX REPORTS, ¶12-085b).

The New Markets Development Program Act includes a credit against the corporate and personal income, franchise, and the insurance and gross premiums taxes for taxpayers who make qualified cash equity investments in a qualified community development entity. This credit is set to expire after fiscal year 2021. (20 ILCS 663/1, 20 ILCS 663/50)

A "qualified equity investment" is any equity investment in, or long-term debt security issued by, a qualified community development entity that (1) is acquired after the effective date of this legislation at its original issuance solely in exchange for cash; (2) has at least 100% (85% for investments made before January 1, 2017) of its cash purchase price used by the issuer to make qualified low-income community investments in the state; and (3) is designated by the issuer as a qualified equity investment and is certified by the Department of Commerce and Economic Opportunity as not exceeding the annual cap. This term includes any qualified equity investment that does not meet the provisions of item (1) of this definition if the investment was a qualified equity investment in the hands of a prior holder. (20 ILCS 663/5)

Credit amount: Upon certification, taxpayers who make qualified equity investments earn a vested right to tax credits, as follows (20 ILCS 663/10):

— on each credit allowance date of the investment, the purchaser of the investment, or subsequent holder of the investment, is entitled to a tax credit during the taxable year including that credit allowance date;

— the tax credit amount is equal to the applicable percentage (0% for each of the first two credit allowance dates, 7% for the third, and 8% for the next four credit allowance dates) for such credit allowance date multiplied by the purchase price paid to the issuer of the qualified equity investment; and

— the amount of the tax credit claimed can not exceed the amount of the state tax liability of the holder, or the person or entity to whom the credit is allocated for use, for the tax year for which the tax credit is claimed.

The total amount of credits allowed under this program is capped at $20 million per year (20 ILCS 663/20). Unused credits may be carried forward up to 5 years. (20 ILCS 663/15)

Credits received under the program are not refundable or saleable on the open market. Credits earned by a pass-through entity are to be allocated to the partners, members, or shareholders of that entity according to their agreement. (20 ILCS 663/15)

Recapture: The Department of Revenue will recapture the credit, in whole or in part, if any amount of the federal tax credit available with respect to a qualified equity investment that is eligible for a tax credit under this program is recaptured under IRC Sec. 45D, the issuer redeems or makes principal repayment with respect to a qualified equity investment prior to the seventh anniversary of the issuance of the qualified equity investment, or the issuer fails to invest at least 100% (85% for investments made before January 1, 2017) of the cash purchase price of the qualified equity investment in qualified low-income community investments in the state within 12 months of the issuance of the qualified equity investment and maintain such level of investment in qualified low-income community investments in Illinois until the last credit allowance date for such qualified equity investment. (20 ILCS 663/40)

¶1218 Credit for Employers Who Match Employees' College Savings Contributions

*Law:*Income Tax Act, Sec. 218 [35 ILCS 5/218.] (CCH ILLINOIS TAX REPORTS, ¶12-055c).

Applicable to tax years 2009 through 2020, a credit is available for employers who make matching contributions to a College Savings Pool Account (pool) or to the Illinois Prepaid Tuition Trust Fund (trust) in the same year as a contribution made by an employee (35 ILCS 5/218(a)).

Credit amount: The credit is in the amount of 25% of the employer's contribution up to $500 per employee (35 ILCS 5/218(a)).

Planning considerations: The credit may not be carried back and may be carried forward up to five years (35 ILCS 5/218(c)).

An addition modification to the taxpayer's base income is required for the amount of the credit (¶2010).

¶1219 Credits for Historic Structure Rehabilitation

Law: Income Tax Act, Sec. 219 [35 ILCS 5/219], Income Tax Act, Sec. 221 [35 ILCS 5/221](CCH ILLINOIS TAX REPORTS, ¶12-090).

Instead of a general credit for rehabilitation or restoration of historic structures, Illinois has enacted credits for specific rehabilitation projects, as follows:

• *River Edge Redevelopment Zone projects*

For tax years beginning after 2011 and ending before 2022, an historic preservation income tax credit is allowed for a portion of the qualified expenditures incurred pursuant to a qualified rehabilitation plan by a qualified taxpayer during the taxable year in the restoration and preservation of a qualified historic structure located in a River Edge Redevelopment Zone (35 ILCS 5/221). The total amount of expenditures must equal at least $5,000 and must exceed 50% of the purchase price of the property.

A "qualified historic structure" means a certified historic structure as defined under IRC Sec. 47(c)(3). A "qualified rehabilitation plan" means a project that is approved by the Historic Preservation Agency as being consistent with the standards in effect on July 28, 2011, for rehabilitation as adopted by the U.S. Secretary of the Interior. (35 ILCS 5/221(d))

A "qualified taxpayer" means the owner of the qualified historic structure or any other person who qualifies for the federal rehabilitation credit that is allowed by IRC Sec. 47 with respect to the qualified historic structure. A "qualified expenditure" means all the costs and expenses that are defined as qualified rehabilitation expenditures under IRC Sec. 47 that were incurred in connection with a qualified historic structure. (35 ILCS 5/221(d))

Credit amount: The credit is allowed in an amount equal to 25% of the qualified expenditures incurred (35 ILCS 5/221(a)), but may not reduce a taxpayer's liability to less than zero (35 ILCS 5/221(c)).

Planning considerations: In order to obtain the credit, a taxpayer must apply with the Department of Commerce and Economic Opportunity, and the department, in consultation with the Historic Preservation Agency, must determine the amount of eligible rehabilitation costs and expenses. The Historic Preservation Agency must also determine whether the rehabilitation is consistent with the standards of the U.S. Secretary of the Interior for rehabilitation. (35 ILCS 5/221(b))

Jobs credit: The zone jobs credit is no longer available in river edge redevelopment zones; see ¶ 404.

River Edge Redevelopment Zones are authorized in Aurora, East St. Louis, Elgin, Rockford, and Peoria (65 ILCS 115/10-5.3).

• *Peoria project*

An income tax credit is available for the renovation of qualified historic structures in the city of Peoria (namely, the Hotel Pere Marquette). A "qualified taxpayer" is the owner of the qualified historic structure or any other person who may qualify for the federal rehabilitation credit allowed by IRC Sec. 47. "Qualified expenditures" means all the costs and expenses defined as qualified rehabilitation expenditures under IRC Sec. 47 that were incurred in connection with a qualified historic structure. (35 ILCS 5/219)

Credit amount: The credit is allowed in an amount equal to 25% of the qualified expenditures incurred by a qualified taxpayer during the taxable year in the restoration and preservation of the structure pursuant to a qualified rehabilitation plan, provided that the total amount of such expenditures is at least $5,000 and it exceeds 50% of the purchase price of the property.

Planning considerations: The credit may be claimed for taxable years beginning on or after January 1, 2010, and ending on or before December 31, 2015. The project must be approved by the Historic Preservation Agency as being consistent with the standards in effect for rehabilitation as adopted by the federal Secretary of the Interior. Unused credit can be carried forward for up to 10 years and may be transferred. The total amount of credits that can be awarded to one qualified rehabilitation plan is $10 million.

If the taxpayer is a corporation having a federal Subchapter S election, a partnership, or a limited liability company, the credit may be claimed by the shareholders of the corporation, the partners of the partnership, or the members of the limited liability company in the same manner as those shareholders, partners, or members account for their proportionate shares of the income or losses of the corporation, partnership, or limited liability company, or as provided in the bylaws or other executed agreement of the corporation, partnership, or limited liability company. Credits granted to a partnership, a limited liability company taxed as a partnership, or other multiple owners of property will be passed through to the partners, members, or owners respectively on a pro rata basis or pursuant to an executed agreement among the partners, members, or owners documenting any alternate distribution method. (P.A. 96-0933 (S.B. 2534), Laws 2010)

¶1220 Angel Investor Credit

Law: Income Tax Act, Sec. 220 [35 ILCS 5/220.]; 14 Ill. Adm. Code 531.10 through 531.90 (CCH ILLINOIS TAX REPORTS, ¶ 12-055d).

Effective for taxable years 2011 through 2021, a nonrefundable and nontransferable tax credit may be claimed for a portion of a taxpayer's equity investment of at least $10,000 made directly in a qualified new business venture. Taxpayers eligible to apply for the credit include a corporation, partnership, limited liability company, or a natural person that makes an investment in a qualified new business venture. The term "applicant" does not include a corporation, partnership, limited liability company, or a natural person who has a direct or indirect ownership interest of at least 51% in the profits, capital, or value of the investment or a related member. (35 ILCS 5/220)

Credit amount: The credit may be claimed in an amount equal to 25% of the taxpayer's investment made directly in a qualified new business venture. (35 ILCS 5/220(b)) The maximum amount of a taxpayer's investment that may be used as the basis for a credit is $2 million for each investment. (35 ILCS 5/220(c)) The annual cap on credits is $10 million of which:

— $500,000 is reserved for businesses owned by minorities, women, and individuals with a disability; and

— $500,000 is reserved for businesses that are located in counties with a population of 250,000 or less.

Planning considerations: A business venture must satisfy the following conditions before it can be registered as a qualified business (35 ILCS 5/220(e)):

— it has its headquarters in Illinois;

— at least 51% of its employees are employed in Illinois;

— it has the potential for increasing jobs or capital investments, or both, in Illinois and either, (1) it is principally engaged in innovation in manufacturing, biotechnology, nanotechnology, communications, agricultural sciences, clean energy creation or storage technology, processing or assembling products (including medical devices, pharmaceuticals, computer software or hardware, semiconductors, other innovative technology products, or other products that are produced using manufacturing methods that are enabled by applying proprietary technology), or providing services that are enabled by applying proprietary technology, or (2) it is undertaking pre-commercialization activity related to proprietary technology that includes conducting research, developing a new product or business process, or developing a service that is principally reliant on applying proprietary technology;

— it is not principally engaged in real estate development, insurance, banking, lending, lobbying, political consulting, professional services provided by attorneys, accountants, business consultants, physicians, or health care consultants, wholesale or retail trade, leisure, hospitality, transportation, or construction, except construction of power production plants that derive energy from a renewable energy resource, as defined in the Illinois Power Agency Act;

— it has fewer than 100 employees;

— it has been in operation in Illinois for not more than 10 consecutive years prior to the year of certification; and

— it has received not more than $10 million in aggregate private equity investment in cash and not more than $4 million in investments that qualified for tax credits under this section.

The businesses must have applied for and received certification for the taxable year in which the investment was made prior to the date on which the investment was made (35 ILCS 5/220(b)).

Unused credit may be carried forward for five years.

¶1221 Small Business Job Creation Credit

Law: Income Tax Act, Sec. 25 [35 ILCS 25/10—26/30]; 14 Ill. Adm. Code 529.10 through 529.110; 86 Ill. Adm. Code Sec. 100-7380 (CCH ILLINOIS TAX REPORTS, ¶ 12-070).

A credit against withholding tax is available to businesses with 50 or fewer employees that hire new, full-time Illinois employees during an incentive period beginning on July 1 and ending on June 30 of the following year. The first incentive period began on July 1, 2010 and the last incentive period will end on June 30, 2016. The required net increase in the number of employees is based on the employer's number of Illinois employees as of June 30 of the incentive period. To qualify for the credit, a new job must pay at least $25,000 annually and must be sustained for at least one year. (P.A. 96-0888 (ILCS 25/25(a), (e), & (f)); 14 Ill. Adm. Code 150.529 through 529.110; 86 Ill. Adm. Code Sec. 100-7380(b))

Credit amount: The credit is equal to $2,500 for each new employee (35 ILCS 25/25(d)). Businesses that hire employees who participated as worker-trainees in the Put Illinois to Work Program (Program) during 2010 are also eligible for the credit. In the first calendar year ending on or after July 1, 2011, or the date of hire, whichever is later, an applicant is entitled to one-half of the allowable credit for each new employee who previously worked in the Program and who is employed for at least six months after the date of hire. In the first calendar year ending on or after December 31, 2011, or the date of hire, whichever is later, an applicant is entitled to one-half of the allowable credit for each new employee who previously worked in the Program who is employed for at least 12 months after the date of hire. (35 ILCS 25/25(a)(1); 35 ILCS 25/35; 86 Ill. Adm. Code Sec. 100-7380(b))

The credit will be allowed as a credit to an applicant for each full-time employee hired during the incentive period that results in a net increase in full-time Illinois employees, where the net increase in the employer's full-time Illinois employees is maintained for at least 12 months (35 ILCS 25/25(a)(2)).

Planning considerations: The determination of whether an employer has 50 or fewer employees includes all employees in every location, including Illinois and out-of-state employment totals. Related businesses are treated as one business for this determination.

An individual for whom a W-2 is issued by a professional employer organization (PEO) is a full-time employee if he or she is employed in the service of the taxpayer for a basic wage for at least 35 hours each week or renders any other standard of service generally accepted by industry custom or practice as full-time employment. A PEO does not include a regulated day and temporary labor service agency. (35 ILCS 25/10)

The credit is administered by the Department of Commerce and Economic Development. Eligible companies can apply for the credit online. Applications for the credit may be submitted as soon as an eligible employee is hired and begins providing services. The total amount of credits issued is capped at $50 million.

The state has created a website that allows taxpayers to register, keep abreast of any announcements, as well as obtain general information concerning the credit: **http://jobstaxcredit.illinois.gov/.**

¶1222 Credit for Hospital Owners

Law: Income Tax Act, Sec. 223 [35 ILCS 5/223] (CCH ILLINOIS TAX REPORTS, ¶ 12-128).

For tax years ending on or after December 31, 2012, a credit against personal and corporate income taxes is available for qualified hospital owners (35 ILCS 5/223). The credit applies to owners of hospitals licensed under the Hospital Licensing Act, but not to organizations that are exempt from federal income taxes.

Credit amount: The credit is equal to the lesser of (35 ILCS 5/223):

— the amount of real property taxes paid during the tax year on real property used for hospital purposes during the prior tax year; or

— the cost of free or discounted services provided during the tax year pursuant to the hospital's charitable financial assistance policy, measured at cost.

Planning considerations: The credit may be passed through to partners of partnerships and shareholders of S corporations (35 ILCS 5/223(b)).

Unused credit may be carried forward for five years. The credit will be applied to the earliest year for which there is a tax liability. If there are credits from more than one tax year that are available to offset a liability, the earlier credit will be applied first. (35 ILCS 5/223(b))

¶1223 Invest in Kids Credit

Law: Income Tax Act, Sec. 224 [35 ILCS 5/224] (CCH ILLINOIS TAX REPORTS, ¶12-030a).

Effective for taxable years beginning on or after January 1, 2018 and ending before January 1, 2023, taxpayers who have been awarded a tax credit certificate by the Illinois Department of Revenue (DOR) for making a qualified contribution to nonprofit organizations that use at least 95% of the contribution received during a taxable year for scholarships to low-income elementary or high school students may claim a credit against Illinois corporate income tax liability. (35 ILCS 5/224)

Credit amount: The credit is equal to 75% of the total amount of qualified contributions made by the taxpayer during a taxable year up to a maximum of $1 million. The total amount of all credits the DOR may award in any calendar year may not exceed $75 million. If the annual cap is not reached by June 1 of a given year, remaining credits will be awarded on a first-come, first-served basis. (Uncodified § 10, (S.B. 1947) Laws 2017)

Planning considerations: The credit may be passed through to partners of partnerships and shareholders of S corporations (35 ILCS 5/224).

Unused credits may be carried forward and applied to a taxpayer's tax liability for up to 5 taxable years following the excess credit year. (35 ILCS 5/224)

CORPORATE INCOME TAX
CHAPTER 13
ADMINISTRATION, ASSESSMENT, COLLECTION

¶1301 Tax Administered by Department of Revenue

Law: Income Tax Act, Sec. 901(a) [35 ILCS 5/901]; Income Tax Act, Sec. 1401 [35 ILCS 5/1401] (CCH ILLINOIS TAX REPORTS, ¶89-060).

Comparable Federal: Secs. 7801—7805.

The Illinois income tax is administered and collected by the Department of Revenue (DOR) (35 ILCS 5/901(a)). The Department is authorized to make and enforce reasonable rules and regulations and to prescribe forms relating to the administration and enforcement of the income tax law.

For additional information on the authority of the DOR, see ¶2401.

For Department of Revenue contact information, see Chapter 27.

¶1302 Assessment

Law: Income Tax Act, Sec. 503(e) [35 ILCS 5/503]; Income Tax Act, Sec. 903 [35 ILCS 5/903]; Income Tax Act, Sec. 904 [35 ILCS 5/904]; Income Tax Act, Sec. 914 [35 ILCS 5/914] (CCH ILLINOIS TAX REPORTS, ¶89-162, 89-164).

Comparable Federal: Secs. 6201—6204, 6211, 6212, 6501, 6502 (U.S. MASTER TAX GUIDE, ¶2711—2740).

The Illinois income tax, like other income taxes, is normally self-assessed. However, if a taxpayer fails to satisfy its tax liability or fails to file a return, the tax will be assessed by the Department, and a notice sent to the taxpayer to pay the amount assessed (35 ILCS 5/903(a)).

The Department is authorized to inspect the books and records of taxpayers (35 ILCS 5/914). If a taxpayer fails to sign an income tax return within 30 days after proper notice and demand for signature by the Department of Revenue, the return will be considered valid and any amount shown due on the return will be deemed assessed (35 ILCS 5/503(e)).

Practitioner Comment: Bypass Administrative Hearing, "Pay-to-Play"

A taxpayer wishing to challenge a proposed income tax assessment is not limited to the Department of Revenue's administrative law judge system. As an alternative, a taxpayer may pay the proposed deficiency under protest and raise the dispute directly in the circuit court. Under the State Officers and Employees Money Disposition Act (30 ILCS 230/1 *et seq.*), a taxpayer may deposit a disputed tax payment into a special escrow fund and then obtain a court order enjoining the State Treasurer from transferring the payment until the case is ultimately resolved. Although this involves actually paying a proposed assessment, many taxpayers pursue this alternative because they perceive that the circuit court is a more impartial forum than the Department's internal hearing officer system.

Horwood Marcus & Berk Chartered

For information on penalties and interest, see ¶ 2503. For information on dispute resolution and appeals, see ¶ 2601.

¶ 1303 Notice and Hearing on Assessment

Law: Income Tax Act, Secs. 901—908 [35 ILCS 5/901—5/908]; Income Tax Act, Sec. 914 [35 ILCS 5/914]; Income Tax Act, Sec. 918 [35 ILCS 5/918]; Income Tax Act, Sec. 1201 [35 ILCS 5/1201]; Income Tax Act, Sec. 1202 [35 ILCS 5/1202] (CCH ILLINOIS TAX REPORTS, ¶ 89-228, 89-234).

Comparable Federal: Sec. 6201 (U.S. MASTER TAX GUIDE, ¶ 2711).

After determining the amount of tax due from a taxpayer, the Department must give notice to the taxpayer of its intent to assess the tax. A taxpayer may protest a proposed assessment of tax by filing a written protest with the Department within 60 days after the issuance of a notice of deficiency (150 days if the taxpayer is outside the United States). If a protest is filed, the Department must reconsider the proposed assessment and, if the taxpayer has requested it, grant the taxpayer a hearing (35 ILCS 5/908).

After a hearing, the Department will mail to the taxpayer a notice of its decision. The taxpayer may file a written request for a rehearing within 30 days after the mailing of the notice of the Department's decision. The Department's action on the taxpayer's protest becomes final 30 days after issuance of notice of a decision or, if a timely request for a rehearing is made, upon the issuance of a denial of the request or the issuance of a notice of final decision (35 ILCS 5/908).

The provisions of the Administrative Review Act apply to and govern all proceedings for the judicial review of final actions of the Department (35 ILCS 5/1201). The circuit court of the county in which the taxpayer has his residence or commercial domicile has power to review all final administrative decisions of the Department (35 ILCS 5/1202). If the taxpayer has no residence or commercial domicile in Illinois, the circuit court of Cook County will review the administrative decisions.

For information on audit procedures, see ¶ 2501. For additional information on appeals, see ¶ 1305 and ¶ 2601.

CCH Advisory: Independent Tax Tribunal

On and after July 1, 2013, the Department of Revenue no longer hears protests of notices of tax liability or deficiencies for any taxes administered by the department or revocations of licenses issued by the department. Instead, an Independent Tax Tribunal Board exercises and administers all rights, powers, duties, and responsibilities pertaining to protests of notices of tax liability or deficiencies for all taxes administered by the department or revocations of licenses issued by the department. See ¶ 1305.

¶ 1304 Statute of Limitations

Law: Income Tax Act, Sec. 905 [35 ILCS 5/905]; Income Tax Act, Sec. 911 [35 ILCS 5/911]; Income Tax Act, Sec. 1101 [35 ILCS 5/1101] (CCH ILLINOIS TAX REPORTS, ¶ 89-164, 89-190).

Comparable Federal: Sec. 6501 (U.S. MASTER TAX GUIDE, ¶ 2726, 2738).

Generally, a notice of deficiency must be issued not later than three years after the date the return was filed (35 ILCS 5/905(a)(1)). However, if the taxpayer omitted from base income an amount properly includible therein that is in excess of 25% of the base income stated in the return, a notice of deficiency may be issued not later than six years after the date the return was filed (35 ILCS 5/905(b)(1)). If a taxpayer fails to file a return or files a false and fraudulent return with intent to evade the tax, or if a taxpayer fails to notify the Department of a change in the federal return (¶1202) or fails to report a change or correction that is treated in the same manner as if it were a deficiency for federal income tax purposes, a notice of deficiency may be issued at any time (35 ILCS 5/905(b)). If notice is given to the Department of a change in the federal return, a notice of deficiency may be issued at any time within two years after the date notification is given; however, the amount of any proposed assessment is limited to the amount of any deficiency resulting from recomputation of base income to give effect to the items reflected in the reported alteration (35 ILCS 5/905(e)(2)).

The period of limitations may be extended by written agreement between the taxpayer and the Department (35 ILCS 5/905(f)). In addition, a taxpayer at any time may waive the restrictions on assessment and collection of the whole or any part of an assessment by a signed written notice filed with the Department.

Notice of lien: The three-year limitations period on the right of the Illinois Department of Revenue to file a notice of lien against taxpayers that refuse or neglect to pay corporate income tax, personal income tax, or sales tax does not run during the term of a repayment plan into which the taxpayer has entered with the department, so long as the taxpayer remains in compliance with the terms of the repayment plan. (35 ILCS 5/1101(d))

• *Erroneous refund*

If an erroneous refund has been made, a notice of deficiency may be issued at any time within two years from the making of the refund, or within five years from the making of the refund if it appears that any part of the refund was induced by fraud or the misrepresentation of a material fact (35 ILCS 5/905(g)). The amount of any proposed assessment is limited to the amount of the erroneous refund.

When there has been an income tax refund that was attributable to a net loss carryback and the refund is subsequently determined to have been erroneous because of a reduction in the amount of the net loss that was originally carried back, a notice of deficiency for the erroneous refund may be issued at any time during the same time period in which a notice of deficiency can be issued on the loss year creating the carryback amount and subsequent erroneous refund (35 ILCS 5/905(g)). No claim for refund is allowed to the extent that the refund is the result of an amount of net loss incurred in any taxable year for which no return was filed within three years of the due date (including extensions) of the return for the loss year (35 ILCS 5/911(h)).

• *Date of filing*

For purposes of the statute of limitations, a return filed before the last day prescribed by law (including any extension) is considered to have been filed on the last day (35 ILCS 5/905(h)).

Practitioner Comment: Statute of Limitations

A notice of deficiency is not barred by the statute of limitations if the Department issues the notice not later than three years after the date the return was filed. Individual taxpayers may presume, as a general rule, that if they filed their 2005 Illinois Form 1040 on April 15, 2006, the Department has until April 15, 2009 to issue a notice of deficiency. However, the Department maintains that it may issue a timely notice on or before October 15, 2009, even though the taxpayer never requested an extension to file the return.

The Department's rationale is based on the fact that Illinois law deems a tax return that was filed before the last day prescribed by law (including extensions thereof) to have been filed on such last day. Further, the Department has adopted a regulation that states that the Department will grant individual taxpayers an automatic extension of six months to file their IL 1040, without the taxpayer needing to file any application form.

Thus, even though an individual taxpayer may have filed its federal and Illinois tax returns on or before April 15th and not requested any extension of time to file, the Department deems the last day for filing to be October 15th. As such, the Department maintains that it has three years from October 15th to issue a timely notice. It is questionable whether the Department's position is a valid interpretation of Illinois law.

Horwood Marcus & Berk Chartered

• *Withholding tax deficiency*

A notice of deficiency for withholding tax liability must be issued no later than three years following the 15th day of the fourth month following the close of the calendar year in which the withholding was required (35 ILCS 5/905(j)).

¶1305 Appeals

Law: Income Tax Act, Sec. 1201 [35 ILCS 5/1201]; Income Tax Act, Sec. 1202 [35 ILCS 5/1202]; Administrative Review Act, Sec. 3-104 [735 ILCS 5/3-104](CCH ILLINOIS TAX REPORTS, ¶89-236).

Comparable Federal: Secs. 6512, 7422.

Taxpayers may seek review of a final decision of the Department in the circuit court of the county of residence or commercial domicile, or in Cook County if the residence or commercial domicile is outside Illinois (35 ILCS 5/1202).

Tax Tribunal: Illinois has created a tax tribunal independent of the state Department of Revenue (DOR) to resolve some tax disputes between the DOR and taxpayers prior to requiring the taxpayer to pay the amounts in issue. Beginning on January 1, 2014, the tribunal provides administrative hearings in all tax matters except those matters reserved to the DOR or another entity by statute. The tribunal does not have jurisdiction over property tax issues.

With certain limitations, the tribunal has original jurisdiction over all determinations of the DOR reflected on a notice of deficiency, notice of tax liability, notice of claim denial, or notice of penalty liability issued under specified taxes administered by the DOR. However, the jurisdiction is limited to notices where either the amount at issue in a notice or the aggregate amount in multiple notices issued for the same year or audit period exceeds $15,000. Generally, no person can contest any matter within the jurisdiction of the tribunal in any action, suit, or proceeding in court in the state. Taxpayers may be required to post a bond, and there is a $500 filing fee for petitions.

The tribunal may decide questions regarding the constitutionality of statutes and rules as applied to the taxpayer, but it may not determine that a statute or rule is unconstitutional on its face. Proceedings before the tribunal are tried *de novo*. Hearings are open to the public, and rules of evidence and privilege as applied in civil cases in circuit courts are be followed. Taxpayers have the burden of proof on issues of fact. (P.A. 97-1129 (H.B. 5192), Laws 2012)

For additional information, see ¶2601.

¶1306 Jeopardy Assessments

Law: Income Tax Act, Sec. 1102 [35 ILCS 5/1102] (CCH ILLINOIS TAX REPORTS, ¶89-168).

Comparable Federal: Secs. 6861, 6863 (U.S. MASTER TAX GUIDE, ¶2713, 2778).

If the Department finds that a taxpayer is planning to depart from the state or to conceal himself or his property, or that collection will be jeopardized by delay, the Department may give the taxpayer notice of such findings and make demand for immediate return and payment of any amounts due (35 ILCS 5/1102(a)(1)). Upon such demand, the amount due is considered assessed and is immediately due and payable.

If the taxpayer does not comply within five days with the notice or show to the Department that such findings are erroneous, the Department may file a notice of jeopardy assessment lien in the office of the county recorder of deeds in any county in which property of the taxpayer is located and notify the taxpayer (35 ILCS 5/1102(a)(2)).

If the taxpayer believes that some or all of the amount for which a jeopardy assessment has been filed is not owed or that no jeopardy to the revenue in fact exists, the taxpayer may protest within 20 days after being notified of the filing of a jeopardy assessment lien and request a hearing (35 ILCS 5/1102(c)). After the hearing, the Department will notify the taxpayer of its decision as to whether or not the jeopardy assessment lien will be released.

Practitioner Comment: Bulk Sales Notice

As a general rule, a buyer of assets is not liable for the seller's historical tax liabilities. However, pursuant to Section 902 of the Illinois Income Tax Act, the buyer of the assets of an Illinois business is potentially liable for any unpaid taxes, including corporate income taxes that the seller may owe, except if the buyer or seller timely discloses the sale to the Department of Revenue and requests that the Department determine the seller's taxes due. These rules are designed to protect both the buyer and the Department of Revenue. If there are outstanding income tax liabilities and the parties do not timely notify the Department of the sale, the Department of Revenue has no obligation to collect the liability from the seller (rather than the buyer) and is not bound by any representation or agreement between the parties. Indeed, the Department of Revenue is not bound by an indemnification agreement between the parties. It is advisable for the buyer to enter into an agreement with the seller whereby the seller indemnifies the buyer for historical tax liabilities. In practice, some parties choose not to alert the Department of the sale because it will cause an audit, but instead will rely solely on the indemnification agreement.

Practitioners must be aware that while Act Section 902 applies only to income tax, other Illinois tax acts have similar bulk sale rules for those taxes. In addition, local taxing jurisdictions, such as the City of Chicago, may have their own bulk sale rules.

Jennifer A Zimmerman, Esq., Horwood Marcus & Berk Chartered

¶1307 Collection of Unpaid Tax

Law: Income Tax Act, Secs. 901—902 [35 ILCS 5/901—5/902]; Income Tax Act, Sec. 1101 [35 ILCS 5/1101]; Income Tax Act, Secs. 1103—1110 [35 ILCS 5/1103—5/1110] (CCH ILLINOIS TAX REPORTS, ¶89-162—89-176).

Comparable Federal: Secs. 6321—6344 (U.S. MASTER TAX GUIDE, ¶2726, 2735).

If the income tax due is not paid at the time required, the Department will make a demand for payment on the delinquent taxpayer. If the tax remains unpaid for 10 days after demand and no proceedings have been taken to review the tax, the Department may issue a warrant, directed to any sheriff or other person authorized to serve process, commanding the officer to levy upon and sell the real and personal property of the taxpayer, without exemption, found within his jurisdiction, for the payment of the tax, including penalties, interest and the cost of executing the warrant. Following a demand, any officer or employee of the Department is authorized to (1) serve process to levy on accounts and other intangibles of a taxpayer held by a financial institution and (2) levy on the salaries, wages, commissions, and bonuses of any employee, except employees of other states, by serving notice of the levy on the employer (35 ILCS 5/1109).

For additional information on collection, see ¶2502.

- *Transferee liability*

Illinois law contains provisions holding a purchaser or transferee of a major portion of taxpayer's stock of goods or business personally liable for any unpaid income tax, interest, and penalties of the seller, to the extent of the value of the property sold or transferred. The law provides for collection of the tax due from the buyer or the transferee if the purchaser has (1) failed to report the transaction to the Chicago office of the Department 10 days following sale, or (2) failed to withhold a sufficient amount from the purchase price to cover the unpaid liability. The obligation on the buyer to withhold arises following the Department's determination as to whether there is any unpaid tax debt due from the seller after being notified of the pending transaction by either the seller or buyer (35 ILCS 5/902(d)).

- *Lien for income taxes*

The income tax, together with interest and penalties, is a lien in favor of the state against all real and personal property of the taxpayer. If the lien arises from an assessment pursuant to a notice of deficiency, the lien does not attach until all proceedings in court for review of the assessment have terminated or the time for the taking thereof has expired without proceedings being instituted. The lien terminates unless a notice of lien is filed within three years from the date all review proceedings in court have terminated to the time for the taking thereof has expired without proceedings being instituted. If the lien results from the filing of a return without payment of the tax or penalty shown due, the lien terminates unless a notice of lien is filed within three years from the date the return was filed; for purposes of this provision, a tax return filed before the regular due date, including extensions, is deemed to have been filed on the last day. Liens continue for 20 years from the date of filing the notice of lien unless sooner released or otherwise discharged (35 ILCS 5/1101).

An income tax lien does not have preference over the rights of any bona fide purchaser, mortgagee, judgment creditor or other lien holder arising prior to the filing of a regular notice of lien or a notice of jeopardy assessment lien in the office of the recorder of deeds of the county in which the property subject to the lien is located (35 ILCS 5/1103(a)).

The limitations period on the right of the Illinois Department of Revenue to file a notice of lien against taxpayers that refuse or neglect to pay corporate income tax, personal income tax, or sales tax does not run during the term of a repayment plan into which the taxpayer has entered with the department, so long as the taxpayer remains in compliance with the terms of the repayment plan. (35 ILCS 5/1101(d))

¶1308 Refunds, Penalties, Records

Illinois statutory provisions relating to refunds, penalties, and records are equally applicable to individual and corporate taxpayers and are covered in detail in the "Personal Income Tax" division at Chapter 8. Also, see "Taxpayer Rights and Remedies," at ¶2601.

PART IV
FRANCHISE TAX
CHAPTER 14
CORPORATIONS SUBJECT TO TAX

¶1401 Illinois Franchise Tax/Income Tax Compared

The Illinois franchise tax is a tax based on the paid-in capital of a corporation. It is initially imposed at the beginning of the corporation's first year of doing business in the state. The tax paid at that time represents the corporation's franchise tax liability for the following 12 months. The corporate income tax, on the other hand, is imposed on income earned in the preceding taxable year. In the last year of corporate existence in Illinois, a corporation has already paid in advance its franchise tax liability. However, the same corporation is required to file a short return to fulfill its responsibility for income tax for the part of the year it did business in the state.

¶1402 Nature of Tax and Taxpayers

Law: Business Corporation Act of 1983, Sec. 13.05 [805 ILCS 5/13.05]; Business Corporation Act of 1983, Sec. 13.75 [805 ILCS 5/13.75]; Business Corporation Act of 1983, Sec. 14.05 [805 ILCS 5/14.05]; Business Corporation Act of 1983, Sec. 15.35 [805 ILCS 5/15.35]; Business Corporation Act of 1983, Sec. 15.65 [805 ILCS 5/15.65] (CCH ILLINOIS TAX REPORTS, ¶ 5-015).

The Illinois franchise tax is imposed on domestic corporations (*i.e.,* organized in Illinois) and foreign corporations that transact business in Illinois. Domestic corporations are subject to the taxes for the privilege of exercising their franchises in Illinois. Foreign corporations are subject to tax for the privilege of exercising their authority to do business in the state (805 ILCS 5/15.35; 805 ILCS 5/15.65; 805 ILCS 5/13.05).

• *Corporations not subject to tax*

Foreign and domestic homestead associations, building and loan associations, banks, and insurance companies are not subject to the franchise tax (805 ILCS 5/13.05; 805 ILCS 5/14.05).

The following activities do not constitute transacting business by a foreign corporation in Illinois (805 ILCS 5/13.75):

— maintaining, defending, or settling any proceeding;

— holding meetings of the board of directors or shareholders or other activities regarding internal corporate affairs;

— maintaining bank accounts, maintaining offices or agencies for the transfer, exchange, and registration of corporate securities or maintaining trustees or depositaries for the securities;

— selling through independent contractors;

— soliciting or obtaining orders through mail, employees, agents, or otherwise, provided the orders require acceptance outside Illinois before becoming contracts;

— creating or acquiring indebtedness, mortgages, and security interests in property;

— securing or collecting debts or enforcing mortgages and security interest in property securing the debts;

— owning property;

— conducting an isolated transaction that is completed within 120 days and is not part of a repeated transaction; or

— having a corporate officer or director who is an Illinois resident.

Practitioner Comment: Limited Liability Companies

A limited liability company is not subject to a franchise tax at the entity level, regardless how it is treated for federal tax purposes. However, a corporate member of a limited liability company may be subject to a franchise tax. Prior to May 2003, the Secretary of State required a foreign corporation to be qualified in Illinois if it was a member of a member-managed LLC or the manager of a manager-managed LLC. In May 2003, the Secretary of State amended the regulations to delete that requirement. Now, a foreign corporation serving as a member or manager of an LLC must provide evidence of its existence upon request of the Secretary of State.

Horwood Marcus & Berk Chartered

¶1403 Description and Basis of Franchise Taxes

Law: Business Corporation Act of 1983, Sec. 1.80 [805 ILCS 5/1.80]; Business Corporation Act of 1983, Sec. 9.20 [805 ILCS 5/9.20]; Business Corporation Act of 1983, Sec. 15.35 [805 ILCS 5/15.35]; Business Corporation Act of 1983, Sec. 15.40 [805 ILCS 5/15.40]; Business Corporation Act of 1983, Sec. 15.65 [805 ILCS 5/15.65]; Business Corporation Act of 1983, Sec. 15.70 [805 ILCS 5/15.70] (CCH ILLINOIS TAX REPORTS, ¶5-020).

Domestic and foreign corporations are subject to the franchise tax on total "paid-in capital" represented in Illinois at the time the corporation is first authorized to do business in the state. Thereafter, corporations pay the tax annually (on the same "paid-in capital" basis) and after events (*e.g.*, issuance of shares, statutory mergers or consolidations) causing increases in the entity's "paid-in capital" (see below for a definition of "paid-in capital").

• *Initial franchise tax*

The initial franchise tax on domestic corporations is based on the corporation's "paid-in capital" disclosed in its first report of issuance of shares (805 ILCS 5/15.35; 805 ILCS 5/15.40). The tax is paid at the same time the report is filed (¶1405).

The initial franchise tax on a foreign corporation is based on the corporation's "paid-in capital" disclosed in its application for authority to do business in Illinois (805 ILCS 5/15.65; 805 ILCS 5/15.40). The tax is paid at the same time the application is filed (¶1405).

• *Additional taxes*

The incidence of the additional franchise tax is triggered by events that increase a domestic or foreign corporation's paid-in capital. The tax is imposed at the time any of the following events are reported to the Department: (1) the issuance of additional shares; (2) an increase in the paid-in capital without the issuance of additional shares; or (3) the filing of a report of cumulative changes in paid-in capital, an interim annual report, or a final transition annual report that results in an increase in paid-in capital.

¶1403

The tax is based on the increased amount of paid-in capital disclosed in the report or amendment over the amount last reported in a required document other than the corporation's annual report (805 ILCS 5/15.35(b); 805 ILCS 5/15.65(b)).

An additional franchise tax is also imposed if a statutory merger or consolidation results in an increase in the paid-in capital of the new or surviving entity when compared to the aggregate paid-in capital of the entities that entered into the merger or consolidation. The tax is paid by the new or surviving corporation at the time a report is filed (other than the annual report) disclosing the increase (805 ILCS 5/15.35(c); 805 ILCS 5/15.65(c)).

CCH Advisory: Sale of Assets Triggered Franchise Tax Increase

When the sole shareholder of an Illinois corporation sold all its stock to another entity, which then made an IRC Sec. 338(h)(10) election to treat the transaction as a purchase of assets, the corporation became liable for additional Illinois franchise tax.

Although no monetary value was actually added to the corporation, the push-down accounting adjustments made for federal income tax purposes increased the corporation's paid-in capital account, triggering the additional franchise tax liability (*E & E Hauling, Inc.*, Ill AppCt, First Dist., Fourth Div., No. 1-97-3174, June 17, 1999; CCH ILLINOIS TAX REPORTS, ¶401-041).

• *Franchise tax obligations of merged or consolidated corporations*

Following a statutory merger or consolidation, the surviving or new corporation is also required to pay the last franchise tax obligations of the corporations merged or consolidated into the new entity. For example, such an obligation would arise in cases in which a merged corporation issued shares prior to the merger, but had not reported the increase in paid-in capital by the time of the merger. This tax is generally computed by multiplying the paid-in capital of each of the corporations as last reported by them in any document other than the annual report for the period from the end of their taxable year to the next succeeding anniversary month of the surviving or new corporation. However, if the merged or consolidated corporation's last taxable year ends within the two-month period immediately preceding the anniversary month of the surviving or new corporation, the tax is computed for the period from the end of that year to the anniversary month of the surviving or new corporation in the succeeding calendar year. See below for the definitions of "taxable period" and "anniversary month" (805 ILCS 5/15.35(c); 805 ILCS 5/15.65(c)).

The surviving corporation in a vertical merger between a parent corporation and its subsidiary may report a reduction in paid-in capital based on the economic realities of the merger and generally accepted accounting principles.

Practitioner Comment: Horizontal and Vertical Mergers

The Secretary of State follows a so-called "rule of aggregation" for computing the paid-in-capital of the survivor of a horizontal merger. See Ill. Attorney General Opinion No. 92-017 (Sep. 24, 1992), CCH ILLINOIS TAX REPORTS, ¶400-603. Under this rule, the paid-in-capital of the corporation surviving a horizontal merger, i.e., a combination where neither of the merging corporations owns shares of the other, is the sum of the paid-in-capital of each of the merging corporations. In view of this rule, corporations may wish to avoid using highly capitalized corporations as acquisition vehicles.

The Secretary of State has historically also applied this "rule of aggregation" in the case of certain vertical mergers, i.e., when a parent and a subsidiary corporation combine. But, since 1993, the Secretary of State has developed a policy for vertical mergers based on the 1992 Attorney General Opinion. Under this policy, a subsidiary corporation's paid-in capital may be eliminated, up to the amount of the parent's investment in the subsidiary. This occurs whether or not the merger is upstream (subsidiary into parent) or downstream (parent into subsidiary). The Secretary of State's treatment of vertical mergers is the subject of litigation. (See *American Cyanamid Co. v. White*, Doc. No. 03 MR 310 (filed Aug. 1, 2003) (administrative review)).

Horwood Marcus & Berk Chartered

Practitioner Comment: Reverse Triangular Mergers

The Illinois franchise tax consequences of a reverse triangular merger and a horizontal merger differ even though both types of mergers may be treated the same for all substantive purposes including accounting, financial reporting, federal and state income tax. The result of a horizontal merger is that one surviving corporation remains, while in a reverse triangular merger, two corporations survive, a parent corporation and a subsidiary.

With a horizontal merger, that is, a combination where neither of the merging corporations owns shares of the other, the surviving corporation's paid-in capital is the sum of the paid-in capital of each of the merging corporations (*i.e.*, the "rule of aggregation" applies).

In a reverse triangular merger, the following events commonly occur: a parent company acquires the target company by creating a wholly-owned, limited purpose subsidiary, which is merged into the acquired company. The stock in the subsidiary held by the parent is exchanged for newly issued shares in the acquired company, and the shares of the acquired company held by its shareholders are exchanged for stock of the parent. Thus, immediately after the merger, the acquired company becomes a wholly-owned subsidiary of the parent. The limited-purpose subsidiary disappears after merging into the acquired company.

As a result of a reverse triangular merger, the parent measures its paid-in capital by taking into account its consideration received for issuing its stock to purchase the acquired company, and its consideration is valued at the acquired company's fair market. The parent company's consideration is not the book value of the acquired company's paid-in capital (that is, the rule of aggregation does not apply). The aggregation rule does not apply because the parent is not a party to, nor the survivor of, a statutory merger. An Illinois court held that the disparate treatment between horizontal and reverse triangular mergers does not violate the Uniformity Clause of the Illinois Constitution (*USX Corp. v. White*, 2004 Ill. App. Lexis 183 (March 1, 2004), CCH Illinois Tax Reports, ¶401-458).

Horwood Marcus & Berk Chartered

Real estate entities: If a taxpayer is liable for Illinois corporate franchise taxes as a result of a transfer of a controlling interest in a real estate entity, the taxpayer is entitled to a real estate transfer tax exemption to the extent of the corporate franchise tax paid as a result of the transfer (¶2208).

• *Annual franchise tax*

Domestic corporations and foreign corporations transacting business in the state are subject to an annual franchise tax payable each year at the time of the filing of the annual report. The annual franchise tax is based on the amount of the corporation's paid-in capital represented in Illinois on the third month preceding the corporation's anniversary month. The annual report must include a statement, expressed in dollars, of the value of all property owned by a corporation, wherever located, and the value of property located within Illinois, and the gross amount of business, defined as "gross receipts, from whatever source derived," transacted by the corporation in Illinois. If these data are not completed in the annual report, the franchise tax will be computed on the basis of the entire paid-in capital (805 ILCS 5/15.70; 805 ILCS 5/15.35(c); 805 ILCS 5/15.65(c)).

¶1403

• *"Paid-in capital" defined*

The franchise taxes are based on amounts of "paid-in capital" represented in Illinois. Generally, the amount of paid-in capital for Illinois purposes is determined by multiplying the paid-in capital by a fraction composed of the following: the sum of the value of the corporation's property located in Illinois plus the gross amount of receipts from business in the state over the sum of property and receipts everywhere. However, a corporation may elect in its annual report to have its franchise tax based on its entire paid-in capital rather than on the amount allocated to Illinois.

The amount of paid-in capital represented in the state for corporations involved in a statutory merger or consolidation is determined separately for each of the merged or consolidated corporations (805 ILCS 5/15.40; 805 ILCS 5/15.70).

"Paid-in capital" is all of the following: (1) the sum of cash and other consideration received, less expenses in connection with the issuance of shares; (2) cash and other consideration contributed to the corporation by shareholders; and (3) amounts added or transferred to "paid-in capital" by action of the Board of Directors or shareholders related to a stock dividend or stock split. If the latter addition to paid-in capital was accomplished through a redemption of corporate stock, the cost of redeeming the stock is subtracted from the amount of the addition (805 ILCS 5/1.80(j)).

A corporation can reduce its paid-in-capital by a resolution of its board of directors charging against its paid-in-capital the following: paid-in capital represented by the shares acquired and canceled by the corporation to the extent of the cost from the paid-in capital of the reacquired and canceled shares or a lesser amount as elected by the corporation; dividends paid on preferred shares; or distributions as liquidating dividends. Another allowable method would be pursuant to an approved reorganization in bankruptcy that provides for the reduction. The paid-in capital should not be reduced to an amount less than the aggregate par value of all issued shares having a par value. The annual basis of the franchise tax will not be reduced until the required report is filed in the office of the Secretary of State (¶1405).

• *"Taxable period" and "anniversary month" defined*

"Taxable period" is the 12-month period commencing with the first day of the second month preceding the corporation's anniversary month in the preceding year and prior to the first day of the second month immediately preceding its anniversary month in the current year. However, if a corporation has established an extended filing month, "taxable period" is the 12-month period ending with the last day of its fiscal year immediately preceding the extended filing month (805 ILCS 5/1.80(w)).

"Anniversary month" means the month in which the anniversary of the issuance of incorporation or authority of a corporation occurs (805 ILCS 5/1.80(o)).

¶1404 Rate of Tax

Law: Business Corporation Act of 1983, Sec. 15.45 [805 ILCS 5/15.45]; Business Corporation Act of 1983, Sec. 15.75 [805 ILCS 5/15.75] (CCH Illinois Tax Reports, ¶5-200).

The initial franchise tax is payable at a rate of $1/15$ of 1% ($1.50 per $1,000) of paid-in capital for the 12-month period starting on the first day of the month in which the Certificate of Incorporation is issued to the corporation. The tax may not be less than $25 or more than $2 million plus either

(1) $1/10$ of 1% of the basis for domestic corporations (805 ILCS 5/15.45); or

(2) $1/20$ of 1% of the basis for foreign corporations (805 ILCS 5/15.75).

Practitioner Comment: No "Max Tax" on Capital Increases

There is no maximum for the additional franchise tax on the issuance of additional shares or the increase in paid-in-capital without the issuance of shares.

Fred O. Marcus, Esq., Horwood Marcus & Berk Chartered

The annual franchise tax is payable at a rate of $1/10$ of 1% for the 12-month period from the first day of the anniversary month of the corporation or, in cases in which a corporation has established an extended filing month, the extended filing month. The minimum tax is $25, and the maximum is $2 million (805 ILCS 5/15.45; 805 ILCS 5/15.75).

Generally, the additional franchise taxes are payable at a rate of $1/15$ of 1% for each calendar month, or fraction of the month between the date of each increase in paid-in capital and the next anniversary month of the corporation. However, if the increase occurs within the two-month period immediately preceding the anniversary month, the tax is computed from the period from the date of the increase until the anniversary month of the succeeding calendar year (805 ILCS 5/15.45).

In addition to the tax, the Secretary of State charges a fee of $75 for filing an annual report, interim report, or final transition annual report.

¶1405 Reports and Payments

Law: Business Corporation Act of 1983, Sec. 9.20 [805 ILCS 5/9.20]; Business Corporation Act of 1983, Sec. 14.05 [805 ILCS 5/14.05]; Business Corporation Act of 1983, Sec. 14.15 [805 ILCS 5/14.15]; Business Corporation Act of 1983, Sec. 14.20 [805 ILCS 5/14.20]; Business Corporation Act of 1983, Sec. 14.25 [805 ILCS 5/14.25]; Business Corporation Act of 1983, Sec. 15.10 [805 ILCS 5/15.10]; Business Corporation Act of 1983, Sec. 15.35 [805 ILCS 5/15.35]; 14 Ill. Adm. Code Sec. 150.620 (CCH ILLINOIS TAX REPORTS, ¶5-105).

Forms: Domestic Corporation Annual Report; Foreign Corporation Annual Report.

Domestic corporations, with the exception of certain financial businesses that are not subject to franchise tax (¶1402), and foreign corporations authorized to do business in the state are required to file the annual report and pay the franchise tax to the Secretary of State within 60 days immediately preceding the first day of the corporation's anniversary month (805 ILCS 5/14.05; 805 ILCS 5/15.35(d); 805 ILCS 5/15.10; 14 Ill. Adm. Code 150.620).

Amended reports: A corporation can amend its most recently filed annual report to denote any subsequent changes in the (1) names and addresses of its officers and directors, (2) principal place of business, or (3) corporation's status as a minority or female owned business (14 Ill. Adm. Code 150.631).

• *Reports of issuance of shares and increase in paid-in capital*

The articles of incorporation of each domestic corporation are deemed the entity's first reporting of its issuance of shares. The amount received as consideration for the shares is the paid-in capital amount used to compute the initial franchise tax basis, and the initial franchise tax is paid along with the filing of the articles of incorporation or the filing of application for authority (in the case of a foreign corporation). (805 ILCS 5/14.15; 805 ILCS 5/15.35(a)).

Domestic and foreign corporations authorized to do business in Illinois are required to report an issuance of shares or an increase in paid-in capital and pay the tax after the issuance or increase. Specifically, any domestic or foreign corporation that has effected a change in the number of shares issued or the amount of paid-in-capital and has not otherwise reported the changes must file a report detailing the changes. The report must be filed no later than the time the corporation's annual

¶1405

report is due and no later than the time of filing the articles of merger, consolidation or amendment to the articles of incorporation that addressed the changes (805 ILCS 5/15.35(b); 805 ILCS 5/14.20; 805 ILCS 5/14.30).

Practitioner Comment: Increase in Paid-in Capital

Illinois imposes additional franchise taxes and license fees whenever there is an increase in "paid-in capital," such as the issuance of additional shares (for example, the exercise of stock options), or an increase in paid-in capital without the issuance of additional shares (for example, by a merger or consolidation). These additional franchise taxes and license fees are reported to the Illinois Secretary of State on a special filing, not the annual report form.

Illinois has a seven year statute of limitations for assessing annual franchise taxes. However, there is no statute of limitations for additional franchise taxes and license fees if the special filing required to report that change was not filed. Illinois law imposes penalties at 10%, and the legislature recently increased the interest rate from 12% to 24% annually (apparently retroactively).

Horwood Marcus & Berk Chartered

• *Reports following statutory mergers or consolidations*

The surviving or new corporation following a statutory merger or consolidation is required to file a report of changes in paid-in capital effected by the merger or consolidation and pay the tax within 60 days after the date of such event (805 ILCS 5/15.35; 805 ILCS 5/14.25).

• *Reports of reductions in paid-in capital*

A corporation effecting a reduction in paid-in capital in connection with the acquisition and cancellation of its shares is required to file a report within 60 days after the acquisition and cancellation (805 ILCS 5/14.25; 805 ILCS 5/14.30).

Until the cumulative report of changes in paid-in capital has been filed showing the reduction in paid-in capital, the basis of the annual franchise tax will not be reduced (¶1403). The annual franchise tax for any taxable year will not be reduced if the report is not filed prior the first day of the anniversary month. If a corporation has established an extended filing month, the report must be filed during the extended period and before payment of the annual franchise tax. A corporation that reduced its paid-in capital after December 31, 1986, by one or more of the methods described at ¶1403, may report the reduction subject to the stated restrictions. A reduction in paid-in capital that has been reported will have no effect on a taxable year ending before the report is filed.

• *New markets credit*

The New Markets Development Program Act includes a credit against the corporate and personal income, franchise, and the insurance and gross premiums taxes for taxpayers who make qualified cash equity investments in a qualified community development entity. This credit is set to expire after 2017. (20 ILCS 663/1, 20 ILCS 663/50)

For details about this credit, see ¶1217.

¶1406 Assessment and Collection

Law: Business Corporation Act of 1983, Sec. 12.40 [805 ILCS 5/12.40]; Business Corporation Act of 1983, Sec. 13.55 [805 ILCS 5/13.55]; Business Corporation Act of 1983, Sec. 15.80 [805 ILCS 5/15.80]; Income Tax Act, Sec. 14 Ill. Adm. Code Sec. 150.600 (CCH ILLINOIS TAX REPORTS, ¶5-150).

The Secretary of State mails a notice of delinquency to each corporation that fails to file its annual report and pay the annual franchise tax within the prescribed time.

See ¶1405 for the return due dates. The notice informs the corporation of its franchise tax assessment and the amount of penalties assessed against the corporation for its failures to file and pay. See ¶1408 for the franchise tax penalty provisions. The failure of the corporation to receive the notice does not relieve it of its obligation to pay the assessed tax or penalties (805 ILCS 5/15.80; 14 Ill. Adm. Code Sec. 150.600).

• *Proceeding for dissolution*

If the delinquent annual franchise tax and related penalties are not paid within 90 days of the notice of delinquency, the Illinois Secretary of State will (1) issue a certificate of dissolution dissolving a domestic corporation; or (2) issue a certificate of revocation revoking the authority of a foreign corporation (805 ILCS 5/15.80; 805 ILCS 5/12.40; 805 ILCS 5/13.55).

• *Assessment as lien*

The tax and penalties assessed in the notice of delinquency as well as interest and collection costs are deemed a prior lien on the real and personal property of the corporation from the due date of the delinquent franchise tax until the date the tax, interest, penalties, and costs have been paid (805 ILCS 5/15.80).

• *Statute of limitations*

The Secretary of State has seven years in which to institute proceedings for failure to pay the tax due (805 ILCS 5/15.90).

¶1407 Remedies

Law: Business Corporation Act of 1983, Sec. 1.17 [805 ILCS 5/1.17]; Business Corporation Act of 1983, Sec. 15.80 [805 ILCS 5/15.80]; Business Corporation Act of 1983, Sec. 15.90 [805 ILCS 5/15.90] (CCH Illinois Tax Reports, ¶5-180).

A corporation may petition the Secretary of State for a refund or adjustment of the franchise tax, license fee, penalty, or interest claimed to have been erroneously paid or claimed to be payable. The Secretary of State has the authority to hear and determine objections to any assessment of the franchise tax and, after a hearing, to change or modify any such assessment prior to payment (805 ILCS 5/1.17; 805 ILCS 5/15.80).

Practitioner Comment: Judicial Review

A corporation wishing to challenge a proposed franchise tax assessment is not limited to the Secretary of State's internal hearing officer system. As an alternative, a corporation may pay the proposed deficiency under protest and raise the dispute directly in the circuit court. Under the State Officers and Employees Money Disposition Act (30 ILCS 230/1 *et seq.*), a corporation may deposit a disputed tax payment into a special escrow fund and then obtain a court order enjoining the State Treasurer from transferring the payment until the case is ultimately resolved. Although this involves actually paying a proposed assessment, many litigants pursue this alternative because they perceive the circuit court as a more independent forum than the hearing officer system.

Fred O. Marcus, Esq., Horwood Marcus & Berk Chartered

Statute of limitations: Taxpayers must apply for refunds within three years of payment of the tax (805 ILCS 5/1.17).

¶1408 Penalties

Law: Business Corporation Act of 1983, Sec. 16.05 [805 ILCS 5/16.05]; Business Corporation Act of 1983, Sec. 16.10 [805 ILCS 5/16.10] (CCH Illinois Tax Reports, ¶5-210).

Domestic and foreign corporations are subject to penalties of 10% of the amount of annual franchise tax for a failure to file the annual report or report of cumulative changes in paid-in capital and pay the tax by the due date. In addition, there is added a penalty and interest of 2% of the amount of the franchise tax delinquency for each month or fraction of the month that the failure to pay the delinquency continues. Corporations that fail to file a report of cumulative changes in paid-in capital are subject to interest at the rate of 2% of the tax due per each month of delinquency (805 ILCS 5/16.05).

CCH Advisory: Suit Not Barred by Failure to Pay

A California corporation with an Illinois office engaged in leasing advertising equipment was entitled to maintain civil actions in Illinois, even though it failed to pay its Illinois franchise tax, because the failure to pay Illinois franchise tax served only as a temporary impediment to the completion of the actions and not as a complete bar from proceeding in the actions (*Lease Partners Corp. v. R&J Pharmacies, Inc., et al.*, Illinois Appellate Court, First District, Nos. 1-00-2664, 1-00-2667, and 1-00-2668 (consolidated), March 26, 2002, CCH ILLINOIS TAX REPORTS, ¶401-336).

• *Failure to file issuance of shares or increased capital reports*

Each domestic or foreign corporation that fails to file a report of issuance of shares or a report of an increase in paid-in capital (without such an issuance of shares) and pay the tax is subject to a penalty of 2% per month or fraction of the month that such failure to pay continues (805 ILCS 5/16.05).

• *Penalties imposed on corporate officers and directors*

Officers and directors of domestic or foreign corporations who (1) fail to answer truthfully or fully interrogatories propounded to them by the Department, or (2) sign any report or statement filed with the Secretary of State that they know to be false in any material statement are guilty of a Class C misdemeanor (805 ILCS 5/16.10).

PART V
SALES AND USE TAXES
CHAPTER 15
PERSONS AND SALES SUBJECT TO TAX

(For purposes of convenience, throughout the sales and use tax division, the retailers' occupation (sales) tax, use tax, service occupation tax, and service use tax are frequently referred to as the ROT, UT, SOT, and SUT, respectively.)

¶1501 History of the Taxes

The Illinois retailers' occupation (sales) tax was enacted by Act of June 28, 1933, the use tax by Act of July 14, 1955, the service occupation tax by Act of July 10, 1961, and the service use tax by Act of July 10, 1961. (For convenience, throughout the discussion of these taxes, they will be referred to respectively as the ROT, the UT, the SOT, and the SUT).

The Illinois Sales Tax Reform Act (P.A. 85-1135, Laws 1988) restructured Illinois sales tax law, granting home rule counties the power to enact retailers' occupation (sales) tax, service occupation (sales) tax, and use tax. The Government Tax Reform Validation Act enacted in 1999 (P.A. 91-0051 (S.B. 144), Laws 1999, effective June 30, 1999) addressed those provisions that had been declared unconstitutional as violative of the single-subject clause of the Illinois Constitution in *Oak Park Arms Associates v. Whitley*, Ill CirCt, Cook County, No. 92 L 51045, August 26, 1998; CCH ILLINOIS TAX

REPORTS, ¶ 400-951. The order invalidating the act was later vacated on December 7, 1998. See CCH ILLINOIS TAX REPORTS, ¶ 61-710.

The Illinois Uniform Sales and Use Tax Administration Act (P.A. 92-221, Laws 2001) is discussed at ¶ 1811.

¶1502 Overview of Illinois Sales and Use Tax

Although the Illinois sales and use tax operates like the sales and use taxes of other states, it *appears* to be far more complicated because of the manner in which it has been enacted.

It is called an occupation tax, for example, rather than a sales tax. The label is not significant, however, because the tax is measured by sales transactions, as are all sales taxes.

Sales tax is a combination of "occupation" taxes that are imposed on sellers' receipts and "use" taxes that are imposed on amounts paid by purchasers. Sales tax is the combination of all state, local, mass transit, water commission, home rule occupation and use, non-home rule occupation and use, and county public safety/transportation taxes.

"Sales tax" is imposed on a seller's receipts from sales of tangible personal property for use or consumption, though tangible personal property does not include real estate, stocks, bonds, or other "paper" assets representing an interest. The term "sales tax" actually refers to several tax acts.

The law is contained in four separate acts: the Retailers' Occupation Tax Act, the Use Tax Act, the Service Occupation Tax Act, and the Service Use Tax Act. Some of the provisions in the four acts are parallel, others differ in wording but are the same in substance; some adopt by reference provisions in one of the other acts (usually the Retailers' Occupation Tax Act), and still others differ slightly because of the nature of the tax. This elaborate statutory scheme makes a simple presentation of the tax more difficult than it otherwise would be.

The fundamental rate for:

— qualifying food, drugs, and medical appliances is 1%;

— items required to be titled or registered is 6.25%;

— other general merchandise is 6.25%.

Depending upon the location of the sale, the actual sales tax rate may be highter than the fundamental rate because of home rule, non-home rule, water commission, mass transit, and county public safety/transportation sales taxes.

Finally, the Service Occupation Tax Act (and its complementary Service Use Tax Act) may be initially confusing because the tax is *not* upon services, as the name would indicate, but merely upon the transfer of property incident to a service.

Privilege tax on marijuana sales: Effective January 1, 2014, through June 30, 2020, Illinois imposes a 7% tax on the sales price per ounce on the privilege of cultivating medical cannabis. The privilege tax is paid by a cultivation center, not a dispensing organization or a qualifying patient, and is imposed in addition to all other Illinois state and local occupation and privilege taxes. (Uncodified Secs. 190—215, Compassionate Use of Medical Cannabis Pilot Program Act). For details, see ¶ 1520.

• *Local taxes*

Certain local taxes are permitted in addition to the state taxes. For detailed explanation, see ¶ 1518. For local rates, see ¶ 1601.

Home rule units of local government are authorized to impose a home rule sales tax (in 0.25% increments). The tax is imposed on the same general merchandise base as the state sales tax, excluding titled or registered tangible personal property (such as vehicles, watercraft, aircraft, trailers, and mobile homes), and qualifying food, drugs, and medical appliances.

Non-home rule municipalities also may impose a municipal retailers' occupation (sales) tax, municipal service occupation (sales) tax, and municipal use tax in 0.25% increments (but not to exceed 1%). A municipality may not impose a retailers' occupation tax without imposing a service occupation tax at the same rate, and vice versa. The taxes are collected by the Department of Revenue.

Special non-home rule units of local government are authorized to impose a non-home rule sales tax (in 0.25% increments). The tax is imposed on the same general merchandise base as the state sales tax, excluding titled or registered tangible personal property (such as vehicles, watercraft, aircraft, trailers, and mobile homes) and qualifying food, drugs, and medical appliances. In addition, a 1.25% Chicago home rule use tax is imposed on automobiles and other titled or registered items sold by dealers located in the counties of Cook, Kane, Lake, McHenry, DuPage, and Will selling items that will be registered to an address within the corporate limits of Chicago.

¶1503 Great Lakes States Information Exchange Agreement

(CCH ILLINOIS TAX REPORTS, ¶ 61-480.)

Illinois has joined four other Great Lakes region states as a signatory to a tax information and cooperative enforcement agreement. The other participants in the agreement are Indiana, Minnesota, Michigan, and Ohio. Wisconsin, an original signatory, has withdrawn from the agreement. Under the agreement, the member states will cooperate to obtain the registration of out-of-state companies and exchange information on interstate shipments to individuals and companies to facilitate the collection of taxes and the enforcement of tax laws of the agreement participants.

Practitioner Comment: Obligation to Respond to Questionnaire

Members of the Great Lakes Information Sharing Agreement gather multistate information about a business by issuing a Great Lakes Questionnaire. It is unclear whether a business is obligated to respond to the questionnaire. Generally, a state is limited in the type of information it can request from a business. A state is usually limited to requesting information about the type of tax at issue and only for the years in issue. The Great Lakes Questionnaire usually requests information for the state issuing the questionnaire, and the other member states as well. It can be argued that the business's activities in the other states is irrelevant to the state issuing the questionnaire and therefore a business cannot be forced to respond.

Jordan M. Goodman, Esq., Horwood Marcus & Berk Chartered

¶1504 ROT—Persons Engaged in Selling at Retail

Law: Retailers' Occupation Tax Act, Sec. 1 [35 ILCS 120/1]; Retailers' Occupation Tax Act, Sec. 2 [35 ILCS 120/2]; 86 Ill. Adm. Code Sec. 130.2145 (CCH ILLINOIS TAX REPORTS, ¶ 60-020, 60-570).

The ROT is imposed on "persons engaged in the business of selling tangible personal property at retail" (35 ILCS 120/2). Although this may sound like a simple statement, there has been much litigation over the meanings of "persons," "selling at retail," and "tangible personal property." The Illinois Supreme Court has held that wholesalers selling goods only for resale are not required to obtain resale numbers from their purchasers because the statutory requirement that "no sale shall be made tax-free on the ground of being a sale for resale unless the purchaser has an active registration number or resale number from the Department of Revenue and furnishes the number to the seller in connection with certifying to the seller that any sale to such purchaser is nontaxable because of being a sale for resale" applies only to retailers. The court held wholesalers exempt from the requirement since it is the effect of the statute to impose the retailers' occupation (sales) tax on wholesalers despite uncontroverted evidence that wholesalers are not engaged in the business of selling property at retail (*Dearborn Wholesale Grocers, Inc. v. Robert Whitler* (1980, SCt), 82 Ill2d 471, 413 NE2d 370; CCH Illinois Tax Reports, ¶ 61-650.18).

The ROT is imposed on a seller's receipts from sales of tangible personal property for use or consumption. If the seller (typically an out-of-state business, such as a catalog company or a retailer making sales on the Internet) does not charge Illinois sales tax, the purchaser must pay the use tax directly to the state of Illinois (¶ 1511). There is no requirement that the tax be passed on to the consumer—this is a matter strictly between the seller and the buyer. However, it should be noted that in actual practice the retailer collects the *use* tax from the purchaser (the Illinois use tax is imposed on the use of tangible personal property within the state) and remits the retailers' occupation (sales) tax to the state. The retailer is not required to remit the use tax collected when the ROT applies to the gross receipts from the same transaction.

See ¶ 1512 for a discussion concerning use tax and Internet/electronic commerce transactions.

"Person" defined: "Person" means any natural individual, firm, partnership, association, joint stock company, joint adventure, public or private corporation, or a receiver, executor, trustee, conservator, or other representative appointed by order of any court (35 ILCS 120/2).

"Sale at retail" defined: "Sale at retail" means any transfer, for a valuable consideration, of the ownership of, or title to, tangible personal property to a purchaser, for the purpose of use or consumption and not for the purpose of resale in any form as tangible personal property. Property is considered to be purchased for the purpose of resale, despite first being used, to the extent to which it is resold as an ingredient of any intentionally produced product or byproduct of manufacturing (for this purpose, slag produced as an incident to manufacturing pig iron or steel and sold is considered to be an intentionally produced byproduct of manufacturing) (35 ILCS 120/2).

Sales of tangible personal property, which property, to the extent not first subjected to a use for which it was purchased, as an ingredient or constituent, goes into and forms a part of tangible personal property subsequently the subject of a sale at retail are not sales at retail.

Airlines: Airlines are subject to the retailers' occupation tax and the use tax on food and beverages purchased in Illinois and given to passengers without a separate charge (86 Ill. Adm. Code Sec. 130.2145). Airlines are also liable for tax on purchases of meals served to crew members.

Sales of airline tickets are not considered a sale of tangible personal property and are not subject to sales or use tax (*General Information Letter ST 12-0058-GIL*, Illinois Department of Revenue, November 2, 2012, CCH Illinois Tax Reports, ¶ 402-613).

Meeting facilities: When meeting rooms are rented or leased with food provided, the taxability of the food depends on the outcome of the true-object test—if only snacks or nonalcoholic beverages are transferred incidental to the renting of a room, the true object of the transaction will be deemed to be the rental of the room, and the charges for the room rental will not be subject to tax. However, if any food other than snacks is provided or alcohol is served, the true object of the transaction will be deemed to be the sale of food or beverages, and the charges for the room rental will be considered part of the seller's taxable gross receipts. (86 Ill. Adm. Code Sec. 130.2145)

¶1504

Maintenance agreements: Tangible personal property purchased by a serviceperson (¶1508) is subject to the retailers' occupation tax when it is purchased for transfer by the service provider pursuant to a completion of a maintenance agreement.

Tire retailers—Fee for recycling used tires: Retailers of tires must collect a fee on each tire sold and delivered in Illinois for the purpose of recycling and disposing of used tires (¶2212). The fee is to be added to the sales price of the tire and is not includible in taxable gross receipts. For guidance on the tire user fee, see *PIO-55, Tire User Fee,* Illinois Department of Revenue, March 2011, CCH ILLINOIS TAX REPORTS,¶402-299.

¶1505 ROT—Seller Must Determine Whether or Not a Sale Is for Resale

Law: Retailers' Occupation Tax Act, Sec. 2c [35 ILCS 120/2c] (CCH ILLINOIS TAX REPORTS, ¶60-650).

A seller of tangible personal property must determine, at the time the seller makes sales to a purchaser who may use or consume the property or who may resell the property, whether the purchaser is, in fact, buying for purposes of resale or for purposes of use (35 ILCS 120/2c). Except for sales to totally exempt purchasers, sellers should obtain a certificate of resale from purchasers making purchases for resale. The Illinois Supreme Court has held that wholesalers are not required to obtain resale certificates because the resale certificate requirement applies only to retailers (¶1504). A sale is tax-free as a sale for resale if the purchaser has an active registration number or resale number from the Department of Revenue and furnishes that number to the seller. Further, the statutes create a rebuttable presumption that a sale is not for resale when the purchaser fails to present an active registration number or resale number and certification to the seller.

This determination is not necessary as to sales made to a totally exempt body, such as a governmental body or a corporation, society, association, foundation, or institution organized and operated exclusively for charitable, religious, or educational purposes (¶1702).

A purchaser who is not registered with the Department and who makes purchases for resale must apply to the Department for a resale number, unless the purchaser is an out-of-state purchaser who will always resell and deliver the property to customers outside Illinois (35 ILCS 120/2c). See also *General Information Letter ST 13-0018-GIL,* Illinois Department of Revenue, April 23, 2013, CCH ILLINOIS TAX REPORTS,¶402-657.

Blanket and percentage exemption certificates: If all the sales made by a seller to a particular purchaser are for resale, the seller may accept a blanket resale certificate covering all sales to the purchaser. Or, if all sales of certain types of goods to a particular purchaser are for resale, the seller may accept a blanket resale certificate covering purchases of that item.

If a purchaser knows that a certain percentage of all purchases from a seller will be made for resale, the seller may accept a percentage certificate of resale specifying that a certain portion of the sales made by the seller to the purchaser will be made for resale. (*General Information Letter ST 11-0063-GIL,* Illinois Department of Revenue, August 12, 2011, CCH ILLINOIS TAX REPORTS,¶402-406)

Practitioner Comment: Resale Certificates

All sales in Illinois are presumed to be at retail. It is the seller's obligation to establish that the sale is not subject to tax because it is a sale for resale. Illinois does not have a particular form that must be used as a resale certificate; however, either the Department's Form CRT-61, or the Multistate Tax Commission's Uniform Sales & Use Tax

Certificate may be used. To be valid and create a presumption that the sale is for resale, the form or statement must include: (1) the seller's name and address; (2) the purchaser's name and address; (3) a description of the property being purchased; (4) a statement that the property is being purchased for resale; (5) the purchaser's signature and date of signing; and (6) either an Illinois registration number, an Illinois resale number, or a certification of resale to an out-of-state purchaser.

Jordan M. Goodman, Esq., Horwood Marcus & Berk Chartered

Electronic resale certificates: An electronic resale certificate should contain all of the information required by the state, and that it does not find that simply requiring a customer to check a box on an online application to acknowledge the customer's eligibility for resale or exemption adequate to meet the signature requirement required by law. If a signature is not obtained in accordance with the Department's rules, a sale will be presumed to be a sale at retail. (*General Information Letter ST 10-0009*, Illinois Department of Revenue, February 25, 2010, CCH ILLINOIS TAX REPORTS, ¶ 402-086)

Alternative documentation of sale for resale: The Illinois Department of Revenue issued a general information letter discussing whether a taxpayer's acceptance of documents from a purchaser in lieu of a resale certificate would suffice for the resale sales tax exemption. The department clarified that the documents provided by the taxpayer's purchaser did not contain required information to prove that the sale was for resale. The department stated that if a purchaser failed to provide a valid certificate of resale and an active registration or resale number, then the sale would be presumed to be a sale not for resale. However, this presumption could be rebutted by providing other evidence, such as a purchaser's invoice showing that the item was actually resold, along with an explanation of why the purchaser could not obtain a resale number and certifying that the purchase was for resale. If the taxpayer chose to accept the purchaser's documents as proof of resale, the Illinois auditor may ask for additional information to rebut the presumption that the sale was not for resale. (*General Information Letter ST 15-0010-GIL,* Illinois Department of Revenue, January 12, 2015, CCH ILLINOIS TAX REPORTS, ¶ 402-939)

Motor fuel resales: Motor fuel retailers may not make sales for resale at the pump or accept certificates of resale for these transactions because the transactions are in conflict with reporting and payment procedures governing prepayment of Illinois sales tax on motor fuel. Motor fuel retailers may make exempt sales provided the sales are documented and information from the exempt entity is maintained in the retailers' books and records. (*Informational Bulletin FY 2008-09,* Illinois Department of Revenue, April 2008, CCH ILLINOIS TAX REPORTS, ¶ 401-879; see also *General Information Letter ST 13-0056-GIL,* Illinois Department of Revenue, October 8, 2013, CCH ILLINOIS TAX REPORTS, ¶ 402-740)

¶1506 ROT—Persons Engaged in Renting or Leasing Tangible Personal Property

Law: Retailers' Occupation Tax Act, Sec. 1c [35 ILCS 120/1c]; Use Tax Act, Sec. 2 [35 ILCS 105/2]; 86 Ill. Adm. Code Sec. 130.2010 (CCH ILLINOIS TAX REPORTS, ¶ 60-460, 60-570).

Persons who lease or rent tangible personal property to others for use by the lessees are not subject to the ROT as resellers if the rental or lease agreement is a *bona fide* agreement. However, such lessors are users of the property they rent or lease and are subject to the use tax when purchasing the property which they subsequently rent or lease to others. (35 ILCS 120/1c)

Persons who purport to rent or lease tangible personal property to other persons, but in fact sell such property to the nominal bailee or lessee for use or consumption, are liable for the ROT. Such a transaction is considered to be a conditional sale (86 Ill.

¶1506

Adm. Code Sec. 130.2010). Conditional sales are usually characterized by a nominal or one dollar purchase option at the end of the lease term. The lessors/retailers generally owe sales tax on any installment payments they receive under the contract. Buyers who purchase items for resale under conditional sales contracts can provide certificates of resale to suppliers and avoid paying tax on the purchases. A true lease generally has no buy-out provision at the end of the lease. Any buy-out provision must be a fair market value buy-out option to maintain the character of a true lease. Lessors are deemed the end users of the property leased and owe use tax on their cost price of the property. No tax is imposed on the rental receipts. (*General Information Letter ST 13-0026-GIL*, Illinois Department of Revenue, May 28, 2013, CCH ILLINOIS TAX REPORTS, ¶ 402-673)

A person engaged in the business of leasing or renting motor vehicles, aircraft, or watercraft who sells a used motor vehicle or aircraft or watercraft to a purchaser for his use and not for the purpose of resale, is a retailer engaged in the business of selling tangible personal property at retail under this Act to the extent of the value of the vehicle, aircraft, or watercraft sold. For reporting requirements, see ¶ 1802.

Persons engaged in the business of renting or leasing automobiles are subject to the Automobile Renting Occupation and Use Tax Act (¶ 1517).

- *Vehicles to be leased for more than one year*

Illinois has added sales and use tax provisions pertaining to the purchase of vehicles to be leased for over one year (35 ILCS 105/2; 35 ILCS 105/2; *Information Bulletin FY 15-03*, Illinois Department of Revenue, December 2014).

Selling price of leased vehicles: For motor vehicles described at ¶ 1517 sold on or after January 1, 2015, for the purpose of leasing the vehicle for a defined period that is longer than one year, "selling price" or "amount of sale" means the consideration received by a lessor under a lease contract, including amounts due at lease signing and all monthly or other regular payments charged over the term of the lease. (35 ILCS 105/2; see also *General Information Letter ST 15-0060-GIL*, Illinois Department of Revenue, October 20, 2015, CCH ILLINOIS TAX REPORTS, ¶ 403-044)

Also included in the "selling price" is any amount received by the lessor from the lessee for the leased vehicle that is not calculated at the time the lease is executed, including, but not limited to, excess mileage charges and charges for excess wear and tear.

Practitioner Comment: Vehicles Sold for Leasing

Any motor vehicle sold on or after January 1, 2015 for the purpose of leasing the vehicle for a defined period longer than one year, and is a motor vehicle of the second division that is a self-contained motor vehicle, a van, or has a gross weight rating of 8,000 lbs. or less, or is a motor vehicle of the first division, then the "selling price" or "amount of sale" means the consideration received by the lessor pursuant to the lease contract, including amounts due at lease signing and all regular payments over the lease term. The selling price also includes amounts received by the lessor that are not calculated at the time the lease is executed, including excess mileage charges and charges for wear and tear. (35 ILCS 105/2)

Practitioner Comment: In what was likely an attempt to establish competitiveness with others states' leasing laws, Illinois changed the way it defines "selling price" in the context of leasing certain motor vehicles. Illinois now defines the selling price of leased motor vehicles as the actual selling price, or the amount due at lease signing, plus the total amount of payments over the term of the lease. At the termination of the lease, the lessor must report any additional tax on costs such as excess wear and tear, retaining the motor vehicle beyond the term of the lease, or others, which were not anticipated at the outset of the lease. Prior to January 1, 2015, the selling price was based on the lessor's cost of the vehicle. The change also eliminated the trade-in credit for vehicles subject to the new selling price. Notably, this change does not affect the way selling price is computed for semi-trucks and other over the road trucks designed for pulling or carrying freight or cargo. Selling price for these types of vehicles will remain the lessor's cost of the vehicle and a trade in credit will be available. However, practitioners and industry members should be aware of a rolling stock exemption that may apply to many of these types of vehicles. In spite of the changes, who the use tax is imposed on does not change. In Illinois, the lessor is deemed to be the user of the property in a lease and subject to use tax. Thus, use tax will remain imposed on the lessor. However, practically speaking, lessors will generally build this cost into the price of the lease and recoup its cost of use tax.

David W. Machemer, Esq., Horwood Marcus & Berk, Chartered

Reporting and paying tax: For sales that occur in Illinois, with respect to any amount received by the lessor from the lessee for the leased vehicle that is not calculated at the time the lease is executed, the lessor does not incur use tax on those amounts, and the retailer that makes the retail sale of the motor vehicle to the lessor is not required to collect the use tax or pay the sales tax on those amounts. However, the lessor must report and pay to the Department of Revenue sales and use taxes on those amounts received in the same form in which the retailer would have reported and paid such amounts if the retailer had accounted for the tax to the department. For amounts received by the lessor that are not calculated at the time the lease is executed, the lessor must file the return and pay tax by the due date otherwise required for returns other than transaction returns. If the retailer is entitled to a collection allowance for reporting and paying the tax, then the lessor will also be entitled to a collection allowance with respect to the tax paid by the lessor for any amount received by the lessor from the lessee for the leased vehicle that is not calculated at the time the lease is executed. (35 ILCS 105/2; 35 ILCS 105/2)

Traded-in property: The "selling price" of a motor vehicle that is sold on or after January 1, 2015, for the purpose of leasing for a defined period of longer than one year will not be reduced by the value of or credit given for traded-in tangible personal property owned by the lessor. The "selling price" also will not be reduced by the value of or credit given for traded-in tangible personal property owned by the lessee, regardless of whether the trade-in value thereof is assigned by the lessee to the lessor. (35 ILCS 105/2; 35 ILCS 105/2)

Vehicle sales after lease contract ends: In the case of a motor vehicle that is sold for the purpose of leasing for a defined period of longer than one year, the sale occurs at the time of the delivery of the vehicle, regardless of the lease payment due dates. A lessor who incurs a sales tax liability on the sale of a motor vehicle coming off-lease may not take a credit against that liability for use tax paid on the lessor's purchase of the motor vehicle if the "selling price" was calculated using the definition of "selling price" as described above. A credit also is not available for any tax the lessor paid with respect to any amount received by the lessor that was not calculated at the time the lease was executed. (35 ILCS 105/2; 35 ILCS 105/2)

Electronic filing required: All lessors must electronically file and pay the tax due under these provisions. This rule does not apply to leases of motor vehicles for which, at the time the lease is entered into, the term of the lease is not a defined period, including leases with a defined initial period with the option to continue the lease on a month-to-month or other basis beyond the initial defined period. (35 ILCS 105/2; 35 ILCS 105/2)

CCH Advisory: Defined Lease Periods

Lease payments made on cars leased for a period of 12 months plus one day with an option to continue leasing on a monthly basis were not subject to Illinois sales and use tax because the cars were not being leased for a defined period. The taxable selling price for cars does not include leases where the lease term is not a defined period, such as a defined initial period with the option to continue the lease on a month-to-month or other basis beyond the initial defined period. However, tax is due on the leasing company's purchases of the leased cars. (*Private Letter Ruling, ST 14-0006-PLR,* Illinois Department of Revenue, October 20, 2014, CCH Illinois Tax Reports,¶402-888)

¶1507 ROT—Sales by or to Banks and Savings and Loan Associations

86 Ill. Adm. Code Sec. 130.2085 (CCH Illinois Tax Reports, ¶60-370).

Sales to financial institutions: Retail sales to national banks, state chartered banks, federal or state savings and loan associations, and other privately owned financial institutions are subject to tax (86 Ill. Adm. Code Sec. 130.2085). Sales of building materials and fixtures to construction contractors for incorporation into real estate owned by banks and savings and loan associations are also taxable, even though the real estate is used for bank or savings and loan association purposes.

However, sales to federal reserve banks, federal land banks, and federal home loan banks are exempt under the exemption for sales to governmental bodies (¶1702).

Sales by financial institutions: State chartered banks and both federally and state chartered savings and loan associations, which engage in selling tangible personal property at retail, are liable for the tax on their receipts from such sales. National banks that engage in selling tangible personal property at retail also are liable for the tax on their receipts from such sales.

¶1508 SOT—Persons Engaged in the Business of Making Sales of Service

Law: Service Occupation Tax Act, Sec. 2 [35 ILCS 115/2]; Service Occupation Tax Act, Sec. 3 [35 ILCS 115/3]; 86 Ill. Adm. Code Sec. 130.2165 (CCH Illinois Tax Reports, ¶60-020, 61-210).

The SOT is imposed on persons engaged in the business of making sales of service and is generally based on the retail price of tangible personal property transferred either in the form of tangible personal property or in the form of real estate as an incident to a "sale of service" (35 ILCS 115/2). Although this tax is imposed on the service provider, suppliers may elect to collect the tax when the cost to the service person is less than 35% of the total service cost. When the selling price of property being transferred is more than 35% of the total bill, sales tax is paid directly to the Department (¶1606).

"Sale of service" defined: A "sale of service" means any transaction *except* the following (35 ILCS 115/2):

— a retail sale of tangible personal property taxable under the ROT or under the UT;

— a sale of tangible personal property for the purpose of resale made in compliance with the ROT;

— a sale or transfer of tangible personal property as an incident to the rendering of service for or by any governmental body or exempt charitable, religious or educational organization;

— a sale or transfer of tangible personal property as an incident to the rendering of service for interstate carriers for hire for use as rolling stock moving in interstate commerce or leases of tangible personal property for one year or longer, executed or in effect at the time of purchase, to interstate carriers for hire for use as rolling stock moving in interstate commerce;

— a sale or transfer of tangible personal property as an incident to the rendering of service for owners, lessors, or shippers of property that is utilized by interstate carriers for hire for use as rolling stock moving in interstate commerce;

— the repairing, reconditioning, or remodeling for a common carrier by rail of tangible personal property received by the carrier in Illinois and transported by the carrier out of the state;

— a sale or transfer of tangible personal property that is produced by the seller on a special order for an interstate carrier by rail in such a way as to be subject to the SOT or the SUT rather than the ROT or the UT and that is received by the carrier in Illinois for transportation out of the state;

— a sale or transfer of machinery and equipment used primarily in the process of the manufacturing or assembling of tangible personal property for wholesale or retail sale or lease, whether such sale or lease is made directly by the manufacturer or by some other person, whether the materials used in the process are owned by the manufacturer or some other person, or whether such sale or lease is made apart from or as an incident to the seller's engaging in a service occupation and the applicable tax is the SOT or SUT, rather than the ROT or UT;

— the sale or transfer of distillation machinery and equipment for the production of ethyl alcohol for use as motor fuel, sold as a unit or kit for assembly or installation and for the personal use of the buyer; and

— sales of service in which the aggregate annual cost price of tangible personal property transferred as an incident to the sales of service is less than 35% (75% in the case of servicemen transferring prescription drugs or servicemen engaged in graphic arts production) of the aggregate annual total gross receipts from all sales of service.

Sales in interstate commerce: If tangible personal property is transferred incident to the sale of services, the service provider will be liable to pay either SOT or use tax depending upon the provider's activities. The interstate commerce exemption is available for a service provider who resells tangible personal property incident to a sale of service agreement and makes delivery of the property from a point in Illinois to a point outside Illinois, provided delivery is made and the goods are not returned. Unregistered *de minimis* service providers may also claim this exemption. However, tax is due if the property is delivered or mailed to locations in Illinois. Proper documentation is required for each transaction in interstate commerce or else the exemption may be denied. (*General Information Letter ST 15-0084-GIL*, Illinois Department of Revenue, October 19, 2015, CCH ILLINOIS TAX REPORTS, ¶ 403-037)

Taxation of nursing homes is discussed in *Information Bulletin FY 91-53*, Department of Revenue; CCH ILLINOIS TAX REPORTS, ¶ 400-512, and taxation of dentists, optometrists, and dental and eyewear laboratories is discussed in *Information Bulletins FY 91-54* and *91-55*, Department of Revenue; CCH ILLINOIS TAX REPORTS, ¶ 400-516 and 400-517.

"Transfer" defined: "Transfer" means any transfer of the title to property or of the ownership of property, whether or not the transferor retains title as security for the payment of amounts due him from the transferee (35 ILCS 115/2).

"Person" defined: "Person" means any natural individual, firm, partnership, association, joint stock company, joint venture, public or private corporation, and any receiver, executor, trustee, conservator, or other representative by order of any court (35 ILCS 115/2).

"Serviceman" defined: "Serviceman" means any person who is engaged in the occupation of making sales of service (35 ILCS 115/2; 35 ILCS 115/3).

¶1508

Practitioner Comment: Veterinarians Are Subject to SOT and ROT

Illinois veterinarians are engaged in a service occupation, and accordingly many veterinarians calculate their sales tax liability as a serviceperson when they sell prescription products such as certain types of pet foods and flea powders. However, the Department maintains that veterinarians are subject to ROT when they sell tangible personal property that is available at retail stores, even though the veterinarian prescribed the product. See General Info. Ltr. 03-ST-0025. See also 86 Ill. Adm. Code Sec. 130.2165.

Horwood Marcus & Berk Chartered

"*Supplier*" *defined:* "Supplier" means any person who makes sales of tangible personal property to servicemen for purposes of resale as an incident to a sale of service.

¶1509 SOT—Sales by Supplier to Serviceperson Presumed Exempt

Law: Service Occupation Tax Act, Sec. 4 [35 ILCS 115/4] (CCH ILLINOIS TAX REPORTS, ¶60-650).

In the absence of an exemption certificate, the fact that tangible personal property was sold by a supplier for delivery to a person residing in or engaged in business in Illinois is prima facie evidence that the property was sold for the purpose of resale as an incident to a taxable sale of service (35 ILCS 115/4). "Supplier" and "sale of service" are defined at ¶1508.

¶1510 SOT—Tax in Addition to Other Taxes

Law: Service Occupation Tax Act, Sec. 16 [35 ILCS 115/16] (CCH ILLINOIS TAX REPORTS, ¶60-020).

The SOT is imposed in addition to all other occupation or privilege taxes imposed by the state or its municipal corporations or political subdivisions (35 ILCS 115/16).

¶1511 UT—Use of Property Purchased at Retail

Law: Use Tax Act, Sec. 2 [35 ILCS 105/2]; Use Tax Act, Sec. 3 [35 ILCS 105/3]; Use Tax Act, Sec. 3-45 [35 ILCS 105/3-45]; Use Tax Act, Sec. 4 [35 ILCS 105/4]; Watercraft Use Tax Law [35 ILCS 158-5 *et seq.*](CCH ILLINOIS TAX REPORTS, ¶60-020, 60-510, 60-645, 60-740).

The use tax is imposed on the privilege of using, in Illinois, tangible personal property purchased at retail from a retailer (35 ILCS 105/3). The use tax is an additional privilege tax and does not replace the sales tax. However, retailers are not required to remit both taxes to the state. They must collect the use tax from the purchaser, but need not pay it over to the state if the ROT covers the same sale (35 ILCS 105/3-45).

Evidence that tangible personal property was sold by any person for delivery to a person residing or engaged in business in Illinois is prima facie evidence that the property was sold for use in Illinois.

Lease-purchase agreements: The lessee/purchaser under a conditional sale lease with an out-of-state lessor is obligated to self-assess and remit use tax when the lessor does not have nexus with Illinois and is not registered with the DOR. The lessee/purchaser is required to register with the department since it is liable for use tax on installment payments under the lease. A conditional sale is one where the lessor is guaranteed at the time of the lease that the leased property will be sold. (*General Information Letter ST 12-0035-GIL*, Illinois Department of Revenue, July 20, 2012, CCH ILLINOIS TAX REPORTS,¶402-550)

Individual taxpayers: The Illinois Department of Revenue has issued guidance on the Illinois use tax for individual taxpayers. The guidance generally discusses what use tax is, why taxpayers should voluntarily pay the tax, and the use tax rates imposed by Illinois. It also explains how use tax liability arises, the availability of credits for sales taxes paid to another state, and the filing requirements for reporting various transactions, including acquisitions of motor vehicles, watercraft, aircraft, trailers and mobile homes. The guidance also indicates where to get forms and assistance for reporting and paying use tax. (*PIO-36 --Illinois Use Tax for Individual Taxpayers,* Illinois Department of Revenue, September 2010, CCH ILLINOIS TAX REPORTS,¶402-221; also available at **http://tax.illinois.gov/Publications/PIOs/PIO-36.pdf**)

CCH Advisory: Consignee of Boat on Customs Declaration

A customs declaration designating an individual as the consignee of a boat that entered the United States from a foreign country was, by itself, insufficient to establish that the individual was the owner of the boat or exercised ownership rights for purposes of assessing Illinois use tax. Under Illinois case law and the Uniform Commercial Code, the type of consignment transaction at issue did not confer transferable ownership rights. The designation of the individual as a consignee only indicated that the individual was transferred possession of the boat. The taxpayer claimed that he obtained temporary custody of the boat to use it before deciding whether to buy it and that he later returned the boat to the owner (*Administrative Hearing Decision No. UT 06-1*, Illinois Department of Revenue, January 4, 2006, CCH ILLINOIS TAX REPORTS, ¶401-702).

"Sale at retail" defined: "Sale at retail" means any transfer, for a valuable consideration, of the ownership of, or title to, tangible personal property to a purchaser, for the purpose of use, and not for the purpose of resale in any form as tangible personal property. Property is deemed to be purchased for the purpose of resale, despite first being used, to the extent to which it is resold as an ingredient of an intentionally produced product or byproduct of manufacturing (this includes, for example, slag produced as an incident to manufacturing pig iron or steel and sold) (35 ILCS 105/2).

Practitioner Comment: Internet Cigarette Purchases

In 2005, the Department of Revenue increased its enforcement of unpaid cigarette use taxes by sending tax bills to thousands of Illinois residents. The Department is able to enforce unpaid taxes on Internet cigarette purchases because the federal Jenkins Act requires out-of-state cigarette vendors to provide the names and addresses of purchasers to the Department. Illinois tax liabilities for periods prior to July 1, 2002 are subject to double interest and penalties because those taxes were eligible for tax amnesty. The Board of Appeals can abate penalties and interest due to reasonable cause (see ¶2503).

Horwood Marcus & Berk Chartered

"Sale at retail" includes any transfer made for resale, unless made in compliance with the provisions of the ROT regarding use of resale numbers. A transaction in which possession of the property is transferred, but the seller retains title as security, is also a sale (35 ILCS 105/2).

Tangible personal property that is purchased by a serviceperson (¶1508) is subject to the use tax when it is purchased for transfer by the serviceperson pursuant to completion of a maintenance agreement.

"Retailer" defined: "Retailer" means and includes every person engaged in the business of making sales at retail. A person engaged in a business that is not taxable because it involves the sale of realty or contracts to improve real estate, who, in the course of business, transfers tangible personal property, which does not become real estate, to users or consumers in the finished form in which it was purchased, which

property does not become real estate, is a retailer to the extent of the value of the tangible personal property transferred (35 ILCS 105/2).

"Use" defined: "Use" means the exercise of any right or power over tangible personal property incident to the ownership of the property, except that it does not include the sale of such property in any form as tangible personal property in the regular course of business to the extent that such property is not first subjected to a use for which it was purchased, and does not include the use of such property by its owner for demonstration purposes. Property is considered to be purchased for the purpose of resale, despite first being used, to the extent to which it is resold as an ingredient of an intentionally produced product or byproduct of manufacturing (35 ILCS 105/2). A restaurant was liable for Illinois use tax on the cost price of meals and drinks given to customers as "comps" because the meals and drinks were gifts. When retailers take an item from inventory and "use" the item by gifting it to someone, a use tax liability is incurred. (*General Information Letter ST 10-0093-GIL,* Illinois Department of Revenue, October 11, 2010; CCH ILLINOIS TAX REPORTS, ¶ 402-236)

Also, "use" does not mean the interim use of property by a retailer before sale or the physical incorporation of property, to the extent not first subjected to a use for which it was purchased, as an ingredient or constituent, into other tangible personal property that (a) is sold in the regular course of business or (b) the person incorporating the ingredient or constituent therein has undertaken at the time of purchase to cause to be transported in interstate commerce to destinations outside Illinois.

Practitioner Comment: Shared Imaging, LLC v. Hamer, 2017 IL App (1st) 152817, P1 (Ill. App. Ct. 1st Dist. June 28, 2017)

On June 28, 2017, the Illinois Appellate Court reversed the Circuit Court's decision and held that Shared Imaging, LLC (the "Taxpayer") is entitled to a depreciation deduction on the selling price of units of equipment that occurred prior to their return to Illinois, a credit for taxes paid to other states for the periods before the units were returned to Illinois, and abatement of penalties on those units of equipment that were acquired outside of Illinois but returned to Illinois after the initial storage.

The case addressed whether 11 medical equipment units, which were acquired both within Illinois and outside the state, stored within Illinois, and then leased outside the state were subject to Illinois use tax. The Appellate Court broke from the Circuit Court with respect to the applicability of the depreciation deduction, holding that although storage may constitute use within the meaning of the Act, the initial temporary storage of property prior to out-of-state use is not counted as the "first use" of the property for determining whether the depreciation deduction applies. Additionally, the Appellate Court awarded Shared Imaging credit for taxes paid to other jurisdictions, holding that to the extent Shared Imaging paid taxes to other states on the sale or use of the property prior to their return to Illinois, it is entitled to a credit for taxes paid to the other states. However, the Appellate Court affirmed the Circuit Court's decision that although the temporary storage exemption initially applies to items bought outside of Illinois and stored in Illinois for less than two months before being leased exclusively outside of Illinois, their return to Illinois for further storage is taxable use, defeating the exemption's requirement of use solely outside of Illinois.

The Appellate Court's decision is significant because it provides clarity to the temporary storage exemption, where the Court acknowledges there is an "absence of guiding case law." For example, the Court establishes that a period of less than two months is "temporary" within the meaning of the Act, whereas Illinois law was previously silent as to the definition of the term. Further, the Court codifies a "one-time" rule for purposes of the temporary storage exemption, meaning that if items return to the state subsequent to their initial storage, even if just for purposes of additional storage, the items are not eligible for either the temporary or expanded temporary storage exemption. This is significant for lessors who have a storage facility located in the state, because if an item of property returns to the facility beyond the initial period of storage, the temporary and expanded temporary storage exemption no longer apply.

Samantha K. Breslow, Esq., Horwood Marcus & Berk Chartered

Donations: A manufacturer's charitable donations of tangible personal property withdrawn from its inventory are subject to Illinois use tax because donating property from inventory is considered the end use of the property. Donations to charities are taxable regardless of whether the donee is a tax exempt organization. Use tax is based on the cost price of the donated property. (*General Information Letter ST 10-0027-GIL*, Illinois Department of Revenue, March 31, 2010, CCH ILLINOIS TAX REPORTS, ¶ 402-110)

CCH Advisory: Use Tax Charged on Free Flu Shots

A company that plans to administer free flu vaccines to individuals without insurance would be liable for Illinois use tax on the cost of the vaccines. The flu vaccines do not require prescriptions and the free program would not be a coupon program that will be reimbursed by any manufacturer. When property is purchased and then given away, the donor has made a taxable use of the property by making a gift. The donor is deemed the end user of the property who is subject to use tax, rather than the donee. (*General Information Letter ST09-0118-GIL*, Illinois Department of Revenue, September 3, 2009)

Aircraft use tax: An aircraft use tax is imposed on the use in Illinois of any aircraft acquired, transferred, or purchased after June 30, 2003 (35 ILCS 158/15-5; 35 ILCS 158/15-25). For basis of the tax, see ¶ 1607. For the tax rate, see ¶ 1601.

The aircraft use tax will not apply if (1) the use of the aircraft is subject to Illinois use tax, (2) the aircraft is bought and used by a governmental agency or by a charitable, religious, or educational entity, (3) the use of the aircraft is exempt from use tax to prevent actual or likely multistate taxation, or (4) the aircraft is transferred as gift to a surviving spouse in the administration of an estate.

Practitioner Comment: Use of Airplane in Illinois Created Nexus; Tax Not Apportioned

In *Irwin Industrial Tool Co. v. Dep't of Revenue*, 394 Ill. App. 3d 1002 (1st Dist. 2009), CCH ILLINOIS TAX REPORTS, ¶ 402-013, the Illinois Appellate Court held that the Department properly imposed a use tax on the entire purchase price of an airplane that came into Illinois, used Illinois airports but was purchased and hangared outside the state.

The Taxpayer argued that it did not have substantial nexus because it spent less than 4% of its total ground time in Illinois. The Appellate Court disagreed, finding that the airplane's physical presence in Illinois was not merely coincidental, but rather the Taxpayer had availed itself of the privilege of doing business in Illinois. The court concluded that there was a sufficient connection between Illinois and both the Taxpayer and the taxable property.

Taxpayer also argued that Illinois could not constitutionally tax 100 percent of the purchase price on the basis that the tax violated the "external consistency" requirement of fair apportionment. However, the court found overwhelming precedent establishing that a use tax need not be apportioned as long as there is a credit provision in place. The court noted that to apportion the use tax based on actual usage would be both burdensome and impractical. Therefore, the taxpayer was liable for use tax on the full value of the airplane.

Although Irwin is not a sales tax case, the underlying rationale for the apportionment of sales taxes is seen in the Court's reasoning. Sales taxes are not normally apportioned because a sale by definition occurs in only one place. A traditional sales tax is imposed on a unique event (transfer of title or delivery of goods) that occurs in a single jurisdiction. Therefore, there is no risk of multiple states taxing the same transaction. Here, the Taxpayer argued that the rationale underlying the hesitation to require apportionment or division of a sales tax base should not apply to use taxes; and that unlike a sale, a use of property can occur in a number of states.

On September 23, 2010, the Supreme Court of Illinois upheld the decision of the Appellate Court in *Irwin*. The Supreme Court of Illinois found that the owner of an airplane which was delivered in Arkansas and hangared in Nebraska, but which made frequent trips to Illinois, was subject to Illinois Use Tax for the entire value of the airplane. The Supreme Court reasoned that the Illinois use tax based on the full purchase price of the airplane is externally consistent (*i.e.* the State is taxing only the portion of revenues that result from the in-state component of the activity being taxed) and thus fairly apportioned because no tax had been paid on the airplane in another state, and even if it had been, the Use Tax Act provides an exemption for sales and use taxes paid to other states.

The Illinois Supreme Court paid lip service to the taxpayer's external consistency argument but ultimately concluded that the state could impose a use tax even though the airplane in issue spent less than 4% of its time in Illinois. Several courts around the country have concluded that a credit provision saves an otherwise invalid tax from an internal consistency challenge. But the external consistency test is separate and by relying on a credit provision to uphold the use tax on *Irwin*, the Illinois Supreme—arguably impermissibly—blends the two tests.

Breen M. Schiller, Esq., Horwood Marcus & Berk Chartered

Watercraft use tax: Use tax is owed when a watercraft acquired by gift, donation, transfer, or non-retail purchase is used in Illinois. Individuals, businesses, and other entities that use a watercraft in the state will pay the watercraft use tax on the watercraft's purchase price, including the value of any motor sold with, or as a part of, the transaction (35 ILCS 158/15-15).

For basis of the tax, see ¶1607. For the tax rate, see ¶1601.

CCH Caution: Adding Name to Registration May Trigger Watercraft Use Tax

An owner of a watercraft registered in Illinois in the owner's name would incur Illinois watercraft use tax liability if he or she were to add on the Illinois registration the name of a limited liability company (LLC) of which he or she is the sole owner. The addition of a second party to an Illinois title and registration is a transfer subject to watercraft use tax because the tax applies to any nonretail transfer of watercraft, with very limited exceptions (*General Information Letter ST 05-0091-GIL*, Illinois Department of Revenue, October 3, 2005, CCH ILLINOIS TAX REPORTS, ¶401-610).

Private vehicle use tax: see ¶2204.

¶1512 UT and SUT—Taxable Nexus

Law: Use Tax Act, Sec. 2 [35 ILCS 105/2]; Service Use Tax Act, Sec. 2 [35 ILCS 110/2](CCH ILLINOIS TAX REPORTS, ¶60-025).

For purposes of imposing use tax on interstate sales of tangible personal property, certain solicitations are considered as being made by a "retailer maintaining a place of business in Illinois," and therefore sales resulting from such solicitations are subject to Illinois use or service use taxes. "Maintaining a place of business in the state" includes the following activities (35 ILCS 105/2; 35 ILCS 110/2):

— having an office, distribution house, sales house, warehouse, or other place of business (the ownership of property located at the premises of a printer with which a retailer has contracted for printing and that consists of the final printed product, property that becomes a part of the final printed product, or copy from which the printed product is produced will not result in the retailer being deemed to have or maintain an office, distribution house, sales house, warehouse, or other place of business in Illinois);

— having an agent operating within Illinois under the authority of the retailer; and

— engaging in activities in Illinois that would constitute maintaining a place of business in the taxpayer's state of domicile.

In addition, the following activities will render a business subject to the tax:

— telecommunications or television shopping systems;

— contracts with broadcasters or publishers in Illinois advertising primarily to consumers located in Illinois;

— mail, if the solicitations are substantial and recurring and if the retailer benefits from any banking, financing, debt collection, telecommunications, or marketing activities occurring in Illinois, or receives benefit from locating authorized installation, servicing, or repair facilities in Illinois;

— businesses owned or controlled by the same interests that own or control a retailer engaged in the same or similar business in Illinois;

— franchises; and

— advertising over cable television in Illinois.

See also *General Information Letter ST 07-0033-GIL,* Illinois Department of Revenue, May 17, 2007, CCH ILLINOIS TAX REPORTS, ¶401-826.

Two additional types of retailers are included under the definition of a "retailer maintaining a place of business in Illinois," as follows:

(1) the retailer that has a contract with a local person in the state through whom the retailer sells the products, which are same or similar to those of a local person and

(2) the retailer that provides a commission or other consideration to a local person for the sales of tangible personal property (TPP) of the retailer.

Effective September 12, 2016, the statutory nexus provisions applying to retailers that receive commissions from persons using the same trademarks or from persons with whom the retailers have referral contracts are included in the rules. Amendments also include nexus presumption rebuttal documentation requirements for these retailers and examples of successful and unsuccessful rebuttal of the presumption of nexus. (86 Ill. Adm. Code Sec. 150.201)

Sales of services with delivery of personal property in interstate commerce: The interstate commerce exemption is available for a service provider who resells tangible personal property incident to a sale of service agreement and makes delivery of the property from a point in Illinois to a point outside Illinois, provided delivery is made and the goods are not returned. Unregistered *de minimis* service providers may also claim this exemption. However, tax is due if the property is delivered or mailed to locations in Illinois. Proper documentation is required for each transaction in interstate commerce or else the exemption may be denied. *(General Information Letter ST 15-0084-GIL,* Illinois Department of Revenue, October 19, 2015, CCH ILLINOIS TAX REPORTS, ¶403-037)

Although Illinois has expanded its nexus provisions, the U.S. Supreme Court in the 1967 *National Bellas Hess* case (386 US 753) ruled that an out-of-state vendor cannot be compelled to collect the state's use tax on sales made to the state's residents unless the vendor has retail outlets, solicitors, or property within the state. In *Quill Corp. v. North Dakota* (1992, US SCt) 112 SCt 1904, the U.S. Supreme Court held that physical presence in the state is required for creating nexus under the Commerce Clause, but not under the Due Process Clause.

The Illinois Supreme Court held that a Missouri retail furniture store was liable for the collection of Illinois use tax on merchandise it delivered to customers in Illinois *(Brown's Furniture, Inc.* (1996, SCt) 171 Ill2d 410, 422, *cert. denied,* US SCt, October 7, 1996; CCH ILLINOIS TAX REPORTS, ¶ 400-764). The court determined that the

Missouri retailer had sufficient nexus with Illinois because it made 942 deliveries in the state during the 10-month audit period at issue and it advertised extensively in the state.

Government contractors: No person may enter into a contract with a state agency or enter into a subcontract subject to the Procurement Code unless the person and all of its affiliates collect and remit Illinois use tax on all sales of tangible personal property into Illinois, regardless of whether the person or affiliate is a retailer maintaining a place of business within Illinois. Every bid and contract must contain a certification that the bidder or contractor is in compliance with this use tax collection and remittance requirement and that the bidder or contractor acknowledges that the contracting state agency may void the contract if the certification is false. (Ill. Procurement Code, Sec. 50-12.) Local governments may also adopt these requirements.

- *"Click-through" nexus*

The Illinois Supreme Court struck down the state's "click-through" nexus law (35 ILCS 105/2(1.1); 35 ILCS 110/2(1.1)), holding that the law impermissibly discriminated against electronic commerce, violating the federal Internet Tax Freedom Act (ITFA).

A trade group that represented businesses engaged in performance marketing brought action against Director of the Illinois Department of Revenue alleging that portions of the "click-through" nexus law, which required out-of-state internet retailers and servicemen to collect state use tax if they had a contract with a person in Illinois who displayed a link on his or her website that connected an Internet user to that remote retailer or serviceman's website, were preempted by federal law and violated the commerce clause of the United States Constitution. The Illinois Supreme Court found that, under the "click-through" nexus law, performance marketing over the Internet provided the basis for imposing a use tax collection obligation on an out-of-state retailer when a threshold of $10,000 in sales through the clickable link was reached. However, national, or international, performance marketing by an out-of-state retailer that appears in print or on over-the-air broadcasting in Illinois, and that reaches the same dollar threshold, did not trigger an Illinois use tax collection obligation. The relevant provisions of the Act therefore imposed a discriminatory tax on electronic commerce within the meaning of the ITFA. Accordingly, the court concluded that the definition provisions contained in the Act were expressly preempted by the ITFA and are therefore void and unenforceable. (*Performance Marketing Ass'n, Inc. v. Hamer,* 2013 IL 114496, 998 N.E.2d 54, CCH ILLINOIS TAX REPORTS, ¶ 402-719).

Practitioner Comment: Statutory Basis of the **Performance Marketing** *Decision*

The Performance Marketing decision sidestepped the constitutional questions at issue, and instead concluded that because the law singled out electronic commerce, it violated the ITFA. This is one of the very first state supreme court decisions striking down a state tax as violating the ITFA's prohibition on discriminating against electronic commerce. As a result of this opinion, the Illinois General Assembly has already passed, and the Governor has approved P.A. 98-1089, a new version of the law that applies to transactions beyond the Internet.

Christopher T. Lutz, Esq., Horwood Marcus & Berk, Chartered

Public Act 98-1089 provides that a retailer having a contract with a person within Illinois in which the Illinois person, for a commission or other consideration based upon the sale of the tangible personal property by the retailer, directly or indirectly refers potential customers to the retailer will have sales tax nexus with the state (35 ILCS 105/2(1.1); 35 ILCS 110/2(1.1)). A retailer meeting these criteria may rebut the presumption that nexus exists by submitting proof that the referrals or other activities pursued within Illinois were not sufficient to meet the nexus standards of the United States Constitution during the preceding four quarterly periods. P.A. 98-1089 was a legislative fix to the Illinois Supreme Court's decision in *Performance Marketing Association, Inc. v. Hamer*, above, in which the Illinois Supreme Court struck down the first iteration of Illinois' "Amazon law" because the law violated the Internet Tax Freedom Act. Unlike the original Act, Public Act 98-1089 does not appear to specifically discriminate against electronic commerce. Requirements and examples pertaining to the P.A. 98-1089 are set forth in *Informational Bulletin FY 2015-07*, Illinois Department of Revenue, December 2014, CCH Illinois Tax Reports, ¶ 402-896; see also *General Information Letter ST 15-0019-GIL*, Illinois Department of Revenue, March 18, 2015, CCH Illinois Tax Reports, ¶ 402-944.

Practitioner Comment: "Amazon" Nexus

An Illinois Cook County Circuit Court held that the State's "Amazon" law violated the Commerce Clause of the U.S. Constitution. The law, passed in March 2011, required remote sellers to collect sales taxes if they sold through in-state affiliates receiving a commission. In its order for summary judgment, the Court found that the law failed the substantial nexus requirement for state use tax collection and reporting obligations under the Commerce Clause. In addition, the Court found that the law was preempted by the Internet Tax Freedom Act, which serves as a federal moratorium against discriminatory state taxes on electronic commerce. The decision has been appealed to the Illinois Supreme Court. (*Performance Marketing Association v. Hamer*, Dkt. No. 2011-CH-26333 (Cook County Cir. Ct., May 7, 2012, CCH Illinois Tax Reports, ¶ 402-482)) Many online retailers have responded to the laws in Illinois and other states by terminating their affiliate programs. With the Illinois court providing the first judicial response to the click-through nexus laws since a 2010 New York appellate court ruling, this decision is just the first step in a long battle over the constitutionality of these laws. Although the PMA welcomed the decision, Judge Cepero's ruling is unlikely to be the final word on the Illinois Amazon tax.

Breen M. Schiller, Esq., Horwood Marcus & Berk Chartered

Nexus issues determined on audit: The issue of how nexus is determined for sales and use tax purposes is not addressed in general terms by statute or regulations in Illinois. Determinations of nexus are made only within the context of individual audits where all relevant facts and circumstances of a taxpayer's activities in Illinois can be weighed (*General Information Letter IT 99-0057-GIL*, Department of Revenue, May 24, 1999; CCH Illinois Tax Reports, ¶ 401-092).

• *Electronic commerce transactions*

The Illinois retailers' occupation (sales) and use tax treatment of computer software sales, licenses, and maintenance agreements is outlined in a general information letter issued by the Illinois Department of Revenue. A license of software is not taxable if the license is evidenced by a written agreement signed by the licensor and customer and if the license restricts the customer's duplication, use, and transfer of the software and meets other specific requirements. (*General Information Letter ST 10-0003-GIL*, Illinois Department of Revenue, January 29, 2010, CCH Illinois Tax Reports, ¶ 402-080; see also ¶ 1701)

Cloud computing: The IDOR has stated that it is evaluating the taxability of SaaS, cloud computing, computer software Application Service Providers (ASPs) and similar transactions and will make a determination regarding taxability that will operate prospectively (*General Information Letter ST 15-0015-GIL*, Illinois Department of Revenue, March 16, 2015, CCH Illinois Tax Reports, ¶ 402-942).

Whistleblower lawsuits against online retailers: A law firm (relator) that brought "qui tam" complaints against several online retailers alleging that the retailers failed to collect Illinois use taxes on sales by their dot.com subsidiaries to Illinois residents was dismissed as a party plaintiff in the lawsuits because it was not the original source of the information found in the complaints. Rather, the allegations in the relator's complaints were supported by or substantially similar to information in previous public disclosures that were readily available in the news media or in transcripts from congressional hearings. The motion to dismiss was filed by the State of Illinois, which intervened in the lawsuits (*State ex rel Beeler v. Target Corporation*, Illinois Appellate Court, First District, Nos. 1-04-2001 and 1-04-3159, August 25, 2006, CCH Illinois Tax Reports, ¶ 401-714).

Practitioner Comment: "Whistelblower" Lawsuits

Shipping and handling charges: The Cook County Circuit Court determined that under the Illinois False Claims Act ("IFCA"), the relator failed to demonstrate that the taxpayer had actual knowledge it was required to pay tax on shipping and handling charges, acted in deliberate ignorance of Illinois tax law, or acted with reckless disregard when it did not collect or remit tax on Internet or catalog sales. The relator plaintiff brought suit claiming that the taxpayer had failed to collect tax on shipping and handling charges, thus violating the IFCA. The Court determined that rather than showing the taxpayer merely remitted tax incorrectly, the relator was required to show that the taxpayer had actual knowledge it was required to pay, acted in deliberate ignorance, or acted with reckless disregard when it did not collect tax. Prior to the relator's suit, the Department of Revenue had conducted an audit of the taxpayer, concluding that the taxpayer was not required to collect or remit tax on its shipping charges. Therefore, the Court concluded, the relator failed to meet his burden in showing that the taxpayer had actual knowledge it should have collected, or that the taxpayer acted with reckless disregard or deliberate ignorance of the applicable tax laws. (*Illinois ex rel. Schad Diamond and Shedden v. National Business Furniture LLC*, No. 12 L 84; No. 11 L 828)

After a victory for the taxpayer at trial in the Circuit Court, the Appellate Court affirmed and concluded the relator "needed to prove the defendant ignored obvious warning signs, buried its head in the sand, and refused to learn information from which its duty to pay money to the State would have been obvious," and the relator failed to meet this burden. The Appellate Court determined that the Circuit Court's finding that the defendant did not act with reckless disregard was not contrary to the manifest weight of the evidence. There was no knowing violation of the Act by the defendant taxpayer because the "pertinent area of the law is unclear and specific factual analysis must be completed to determine" a retailer's use tax liability. (*Illinois ex. rel. Schad Diamond and Shedden v. National Business Furniture LLC*, 2016 IL App (1st) 150526; CCH Illinois Tax Reports, ¶ 403-115)

Practitioner Comment: Taxpayers have been the subject of hundreds of these whistleblower/*qui tam* cases over the years, mostly by the same serial relator. The good news from this case is that both the circuit and appellate courts in Illinois should ultimately get to the correct result in support of the taxpayer defendants, as they did here, when all of the facts are laid out. Unfortunately, the State of Illinois, which can take control of these *qui tam* cases if it chooses to intervene, has historically chosen not to support the defendants throughout these cases. The State has refrained from intervening and has thus allowed this relator to prosecute these cases without check, even after being presented with a taxpayer's good facts early on in the case. Unless the legislature unexpectedly decides to revise the Illinois False Claims Act to exempt sales tax, these *qui tam* claims will continue to be filed. If you own a business that sells into Illinois, there are steps you can take to help protect yourself for the future. Since these cases are premised on an allegation that a taxpayer defrauded the State of Illinois, it is less about getting it right and more important to conduct the necessary due diligence and stay informed about the Illinois sales tax laws. The numerous rules about sales and use tax collection and remittance can be confusing. Failing to follow the Illinois tax laws may result in a future assessment, but if you don't ignore "obvious warning signs" and haven't "buried [your] head in the sand," this case is precedent for being able to avoid the additional fraud liability.

Nexus: In another of the *qui tam* cases filed under the Illinois False Claims Act, the circuit court ruled in favor of the defendant taxpayer after a bench trial. This case was based on another sales tax issue, a nexus question. The majority of the court's analysis was whether a Lush Internet, Inc. affiliate, Lush Cosmetics, Inc., a separate entity that owned and operated retail stores in Illinois, was sufficient to establish the requisite physical presence in, or nexus to, Illinois and obligate Lush Internet to collect and remit use tax on its internet sales to Illinois customers. The relator brought the suit against Lush Internet, a Nevada corporation that owned and operated a website that sold products to Illinois customers, claiming it had nexus with Illinois through its agency relationship with Lush Cosmetics, a New York corporation that owned and operated retail stores in Illinois. The trial court focused its analysis on whether Lush Internet had sufficient nexus under the Commerce Clause despite not having a physical presence in Illinois. For its determination of whether Lush had substantial nexus with Illinois, the court relied heavily on the precedent of *Quill Corp. v. N.D.*, 504 U.S. 298 (1992) and *Brown's Furniture, Inc. v. Wagner*, 171 Ill. 2d 410 (1996). Based on the evidence at trial, the court found relator did not sufficiently prove that "Lush Cosmetics' employees or personnel performed more than the slightest activities on behalf of Lush Internet and failed to prove that Lush Internet had a substantial nexus to Illinois." Order, p. 9. The court further determined the facts did not establish that there was nexus through an agency relationship between the two affiliates. Despite the fact that Lush Internet benefited from in-state marketing performed by Lush Cosmetics on behalf of Lush Internet, the trial court still held that relator did not prove by a preponderance of the evidence that Lush Internet had sufficient nexus with Illinois through its agency relationship with Lush Cosmetics. *(State of Illinois, ex rel. Stephen B. Diamond, P.C. v. Lush Internet, Inc.*, No. 13 L 009147 and 12 L 6782)

Practitioner Comment: While the outcome from this circuit court decision is definitely a positive result, it raises some important questions as these qui tam cases relate to state sales and use tax. First, should a Circuit Court judge need to fully determine whether or not substantial nexus exists in a case filed under the Illinois False Claims Act? Based on other cases, including the National Business Furniture decision discussed above, it seems the sole analysis should be whether the defendant acted knowingly to defraud the State, regardless of the ultimate nexus determination. Next, if a Circuit Court judge does make a nexus determination in a *qui tam* case, is the Illinois Department of Revenue bound by that finding? I suspect the Department may think not. Finally, can businesses that are diligent with their internal procedures do anything more to protect themselves from having to incur significant time and money defending these cases all the way through a trial for the necessary relief? While the answer is unfortunately no, carefully organizing your corporate structure and obtaining advice from outside experts should help to avoid liability under a similar sales tax fraud allegation. The relator did file a Notice of Appeal on this ruling, so keep an eye on this important review by the Illinois Appellate Court.

David S. Ruskin, Esq., Horwood Marcus & Berk, Chartered

• *Streamlined Sales Tax Agreement*

Illinois is not a member of the Streamlined Sales and Use Tax (SST) Agreement because, although it has enacted legislation authorizing it to enter into the Agreement, it has not yet enacted the changes to its laws necessary to comply with the Agreement's requirements. See ¶1811 for details.

¶1513 UT—In Addition to Other Taxes

Law: Use Tax Act, Sec. 15 [35 ILCS 105/15] (CCH ILLINOIS TAX REPORTS, ¶60-020).

The use tax is imposed in addition to all other occupation or privilege taxes imposed by the state or by any municipal corporation or political subdivision. Although state use taxes are usually complementary to sales taxes, the Illinois use tax, as stated above, is specifically made an additional tax. However, from the standpoint of the retailer, it is complementary because the retailer is relieved from remitting use taxes collected on sales also covered by the ROT (35 ILCS 105/15).

¶1514 SUT—Property Acquired as an Incident to Purchase of a Service

Law: Service Use Tax Act, Sec. 2 [35 ILCS 110/2]; Service Use Tax Act, Sec. 3 [35 ILCS 110/3]; Service Use Tax Act, Sec. 3-10 [35 ILCS 110/3-10]; 86 Ill. Adm. Code Sec. 130.2085 (CCH Illinois Tax Reports, ¶60-020, 61-210).

The service use tax is imposed on the privilege of using in Illinois real or tangible personal property acquired as an incident to the purchase of a service from a serviceperson, and is based on the cost price to the serviceperson of property transferred as an incident to the sale of service (35 ILCS 110/2; 35 ILCS 110/3). The service use tax and the service occupation tax are related in the same manner as the use tax and the retailers' occupation tax—although the SUT is an additional tax rather than a complementary tax to the SOT, the relationship is complementary because the serviceperson is relieved from remitting to the Department of Revenue SUT collected on transactions to which the SOT applies.

While the SOT involves only the serviceperson and the supplier, the SUT involves a third person—the serviceperson's customer.

The substance and provisions of the SOT rules and regulations are incorporated by reference as the rules and regulations relating to the SUT, to the extent to which they are compatible with the SUT (86 Ill. Adm. Code Sec. 160.145; see also *General Information Letter ST 10-0046-GIL*, Illinois Department of Revenue, May 27, 2010, CCH Illinois Tax Reports, ¶402-137 and *General Information Letter ST 12-0059-GIL*, Illinois Department of Revenue, November 29, 2012, CH Illinois Tax Reports, ¶402-614).

"Sale of service" is defined at ¶1508.

¶1515 SUT—Sales to Persons Residing or Engaged in Business in Illinois Presumed Taxable

Law: Service Use Tax Act, Sec. 4 [35 ILCS 110/4] (CCH Illinois Tax Reports, ¶60-020).

Evidence that property was sold by any person for delivery to a person residing or engaged in business in Illinois is prima facie evidence that such property was sold for use in Illinois and the use is, therefore, presumed taxable (35 ILCS 110/4).

¶1516 SUT—Tax in Addition to Other Taxes

Law: Service Use Tax Act, Sec. 16 [35 ILCS 110/16] (CCH Illinois Tax Reports, ¶60-020).

The SUT is imposed in addition to all other occupation or privilege taxes imposed by the state or by any municipal corporation or political subdivision (35 ILCS 110/16).

¶1517 Automobile Renting Occupation and Use Tax Act

Law: Automobile Renting Occupation and Use Tax Act, Sec. 2 [35 ILCS 155/2]; Automobile Renting Occupation and Use Tax Act, Sec. 3 [35 ILCS 155/3](CCH Illinois Tax Reports, ¶60-570, 61-710).

An automobile renting occupation and use tax is imposed on persons engaged in the business of renting or leasing automobiles in lieu of the ROT and UT taxes (35 ILCS 155/3). Home rule units (¶1518) may impose and collect a *use* tax on vehicles, but no local sales tax on vehicles is permitted.

An "automobile" is defined as (35 ILCS 155/2):

(1) any motor vehicle of the first division, or

(2) a motor vehicle of the second division that:

(A) is a self-contained motor vehicle designed or permanently converted to provide living quarters for recreational, camping or travel use, with direct walk through access to the living quarters from the driver's seat;

(B) is of the van configuration designed for the transportation of not less than 7 nor more than 16 passengers; or

(C) has a Gross Vehicle Weight Rating of 8,000 pounds or less.

For sales and use tax treatment when such vehicles are purchased to be leased for more than one year, see ¶1506.

For additional information, see *Publication 114, Automobile Renting Occupation and Use Tax*, Illinois Department of Revenue, March 2014, CCH ILLINOIS TAX REPORTS, ¶402-789.

¶1518 Municipal, County, and Regional Taxation

Law: Retailers Occupation Tax Act, Sec. 2-12 [35 ILCS 120/2-12]; Illinois Municipal Code, Sec. 8-11-1 [65 ILCS 5/8-11-1]; Illinois Municipal Code, Secs. 8-11-1.1—8-11-1.4 [65 ILCS 5/8-11-1.1—5/8-11-1.4]; Illinois Municipal Code, Secs. 8-11-1.6—8-11-1.8 [65 ILCS 5/8-11-1.6—5/8-11-1.8]; Illinois Municipal Code, Sec. 8-11-5 [65 ILCS 5/8-11-5]; Illinois Municipal Code, Sec. 8-11-6 [65 ILCS 5/8-11-6]; Illinois Municipal Code, Sec. 8-11-6a [65 ILCS 5/8-11-6a]; Counties Code, Secs. 5-1006—5-1009 [55 ILCS 5/5-1006—5/5-1009]; Counties Code, Sec. 5-1032 [55 ILCS 5/5-1032]; Counties Code, Sec. 5-1033 [55 ILCS 5/5-1033]; Regional Transportation Authority Act, Sec. 4.03 [70 ILCS 3615/4.03]; Regional Transportation Authority Act, Sec. 4.03.1 [70 ILCS 3615/4.03.1]; Local Mass Transit District Act, Sec. 5.02(a) [70 ILCS 3610/5.02]; 86 Ill. Adm. Code 220.115, 86 Ill Adm. Code 270.115, 86 Ill. Adm. Code 320.115, 86 Ill. Adm. Code 370.115, 86 Ill Adm. Code 395.115, 86 Ill. Adm. Code 630.120, 86 Ill. Adm. Code 670.115, Ill Adm. Code 690.115, 86 Ill. Adm. Code 693.115, and 86 Ill. Adm. Code 695.115 (CCH ILLINOIS TAX REPORTS, ¶61-710).

The taxes levied by municipalities and counties are levied on the same transactions that are subject to the state taxes, and are collected by the state along with the state taxes (¶1802). The tax base is basically the same as that of the state tax.

Jurisdiction to tax: Imposition of local sales and use taxes takes effect when "selling" occurs in a jurisdiction. The most important element of selling is the seller's acceptance of a purchase order. If a purchase order is accepted in a jurisdiction that imposes a local tax, that local tax will be incurred and the fact that the item is shipped from outside the state or from another Illinois location would be immaterial. If a purchase order is accepted outside Illinois, but the property being sold is located in an inventory in an Illinois jurisdiction that imposes a local tax, the location of the property at the time of sale will determine where the seller is engaged in business for the purpose of imposing local sales tax. If the retailer has nexus, but both the purchase order acceptance and the location of the property are outside Illinois at the time of sale, such sales will only be subject to use tax at the state rate (*General Information Letter ST 07-0043-GIL*, Illinois Department of Revenue, May 22, 2007, CCH ILLINOIS TAX REPORTS, ¶401-827).

• *Home rule taxes*

Home rule municipalities may impose a home rule municipal retailers' occupation (HRMROT), home rule municipal service occupation (HRMSOT), and home rule municipal vehicle use (HRMVUT) taxes in increments of $1/4$ of 1%. Home rule counties may impose a home rule county retailers' occupation (HRCROT), home rule county service occupation (HRCSOT), and home rule county vehicle use (HRCVUT) taxes in increments of $1/4$% of 1%. These home rule taxes are in addition to the $6^1/4$% state sales (ROT), service (SOT), and use (UT) taxes, as well as to the transit and water commission taxes. Home rule municipalities and counties cannot impose a retailers' occupation tax without also imposing a service occupation tax. For information on home rule cities and counties imposing local taxes, see ¶1601.

¶1518

Home rule cities are those with populations of over 25,000 that have been granted self-governing authority either by referendum or by the state constitution. A county that has a chief executive officer elected by the electors of the county is a home rule county.

Home rule municipalities and home rule counties may not impose the HRMROT and HRMSOT on tangible personal property (such as automobiles) that are titled or registered with an agency of Illinois state government. Home rule municipalities are authorized to impose a use tax (HRMUT) and home rule counties are authorized to impose a use tax (HRCUT) on the privilege of using, in such jurisdiction, any item purchased at retail that is titled or registered to the resident purchaser with an agency of the Illinois state government. Home rule units can also impose and collect their own taxes on utilities, hotels/motels, parking, real estate transfers, restaurants, alcohol, and cigarettes. However, a home rule city that did not impose a sales, use, or other tax before July 1, 1993, that was based on the number of units of cigarettes or tobacco products sold or used may not impose such a tax after that date.

In addition, home rule units cannot impose caps or ceilings on purchase prices for tax purposes.

Practitioner Comment: Planning Opportunity

Local home rule taxes are imposed where the sales orders are accepted. Many local home rule jurisdictions have entered into agreements with businesses to relocate their operations, particularly their sales offices, to their home rule jurisdiction. These agreements are generally mutually beneficial to the local jurisdictions and the businesses. The local jurisdictions benefit because additional local sales revenue is generated within their jurisdiction and allocated to that particular jurisdiction. The businesses benefit from this type of agreement because they generally get a percentage of the increased tax revenue generated for the local jurisdiction.

However, in 2004, the Illinois General Assembly amended the Counties Code and the Municipal Code to effectively close this planning opportunity with respect to new agreements. Local government units may file suit against a county or municipality (but not the taxpayer) that enters into an agreement to share or rebate any portion of sales tax and violates the law. If the local governmental unit prevails, it is entitled to damages in the amount of the tax revenue it was denied as a result of the agreement, statutory interest, costs, reasonable attorney's fees, and an amount equal to 50% of the tax (55 ILCS 5/5-1014.3; 65 ILCS 5/8-11-21).

Jordan M. Goodman, Esq., Horwood Marcus & Berk Chartered

Additional tax: Home rule cities with a population of two million or more are authorized to impose an additional use tax at a rate that is an increment of 0.25% up to 1%. The tax is on the privilege of using any item of tangible personal property, other than titled or registered tangible personal property, that is purchased at retail from a retailer located outside the corporate limits of the municipality. To avoid double taxation, purchases outside the corporate limits of the municipality for which a home rule municipal tax has been paid are exempt from the additional use tax.

Soft drinks tax: Home rule municipalities with populations in excess of 1 million are authorized to impose soft drink retailers' occupation taxes and fountain soft drink taxes. Soft drink tax rates must be in increments of $1/4$ of 1%, with a maximum rate of 3%. Fountain soft drink taxes may not exceed 9% of the cost price of the drinks. "Soft drinks" are complete, ready-to-use, nonalcoholic drinks, both carbonated and non-carbonated, including soda water, cola, fruit juice, vegetable juice, carbonated water, and other preparations that are contained in a closed or sealed can, carton, or container, regardless of size. "Fountain soft drinks" are soft drinks prepared by a retail seller by mixing syrup or concentrate with water by hand or through a soft drink dispensing machine. The Chicago soft drink tax is discussed at ¶ 2308.

¶1518

• *Non-home rule taxes*

Non-home rule municipalities may impose a municipal retailers' occupation (sales) tax, municipal service occupation (sales) tax, and a municipal use tax. The rate of tax must be imposed in increments of 0.25% and may not exceed 1%. A municipality may not impose a retailers' occupation (sales) tax without imposing a service occupation (sales) tax at the same rate, and vice versa.

Exemptions: Municipal retailers' occupation (sales) tax and municipal service occupation (sales) tax may not be imposed on sales of food to be consumed off the premises where sold (except for alcoholic beverages, soft drinks, and food that has been prepared for immediate consumption) and sales of medicines, drugs, medical appliances, insulin, urine testing materials, syringes, and needles used by diabetic persons.

• *Adoption of ordinance or resolution*

Beginning January 1, 2014, for county sales tax, county school facility occupation tax, and non-home rule municipality tax purposes, the results of any election authorizing the imposition or increase of any of these taxes and the ordinance adopted to impose the tax or increase the rate must be certified by the county clerk and filed with the Department of Revenue on or before May 1 or October 1. The same rule applies to any ordinance adopted to lower a tax rate or discontinue a tax. For ordinances filed on or before May 1, the department will administer and enforce the tax as of the following July 1. For ordinances filed on or before October 1, the department will administer and enforce the tax as of the following January 1. (55 ILCS 5/5-1006.5; 55 ILCS 5/5-1006.7)

• *Automobile renting occupation and use taxes*

Municipalities are authorized to impose an automobile renting occupation tax of up to 1% of the gross receipts of persons engaged in the business of renting automobiles (¶1517 for the state tax). Counties are authorized to impose a tax of up to 1% of the gross receipts of all persons engaged in the business of renting automobiles in the county but outside of any municipality.

Regional Transportation Authority: The Board of the Regional Transportation Authority (RTA) is authorized to impose an automobile renting occupation tax of up to 1% of the gross receipts of persons engaged in the business of renting an automobile within Cook County and up to $1/4$ of 1% of the gross receipts of such business located in DuPage, Kane, Lake, McHenry, and Will Counties. The Board may also impose a tax of up to 1% of the rental price in Cook County and up to $1/4$ of 1% in DuPage, Kane, Lake, McHenry, and Will Counties for the privilege of using in the metropolitan region an automobile that is rented outside Illinois but titled or registered in Illinois.

Metro East Mass Transit District: The Board of the Metro East Mass Transit District (MED) may impose an automobile renting occupation tax of up to 1% of the gross receipts of persons engaged in the business of renting automobiles in the district. The board is also authorized to impose a tax of up to 1% of the rental price for the privilege of using in the district an automobile that is rented outside Illinois but titled or registered in Illinois.

• *County tax for public safety, public facilities, or transportation*

All counties are authorized to impose a sales tax (ROT and SOT), subject to voter approval, to provide revenue to be used exclusively for public safety, public facilities, or transportation purposes. The tax must be imposed in increments of $1/4$ of 1%. (55 ILCS 5/5-1006.5)

¶1518

• *County tax for school facilities*

All counties, except Cook County, are authorized to impose a sales tax (ROT and SOT) up to 1%, subject to voter approval, to provide revenue to be used exclusively for school facility purposes. The tax must be imposed in increments of $1/4$ of 1%. (55 ILCS 5/5-1006.7)

• *Regional taxes*

RTA taxes: The Regional Transportation Authority (RTA) ROT, SOT, and UT are imposed in Cook, DuPage, Kane, Lake, McHenry, and Will Counties at different rates. (70 ILCS 3615/4.03(e), (f), (g); *Informational Bulletin FY 2008-13*, Illinois Department of Revenue, February 2008, CCH ILLINOIS TAX REPORTS, ¶ 401-862) For rates, see ¶ 1601.

MED-MT taxes: The Metro East Mass Transit District (MED-MT) may impose ROT, SOT, and UT. (70 ILCS 3610/5.01(b), (c), (d)) Some taxing districts, but not all, within Madison County and St. Clair County have imposed the MED-MT retailers' occupation tax.

MPEA: The Metropolitan Pier and Exposition Authority (MPEA) imposes a food and beverage tax, an occupation tax on the gross receipts of hotel operators in Chicago, and an occupation tax on airport transit operators, as well as an automobile renting occupation tax and the automobile renting use tax. (70 ILCS 210/13)

• *Tax rate shopping*

In *Hartney Fuel Oil Co. v. Illinois Dept. of Revenue,* the Illinois courts upheld a taxpayer's plan to source sales to a low rate city instead of a higher rate city. The taxpayer, Hartney, is a family-owned oil distribution business founded in 1916. Hartney's headquarters are located in Forest View, Illinois, a suburb of Chicago. Hartney relocated its sales office a number of times over the years, seeking the lowest marginal sales tax rate on its sales. It moved its sales office from Forest View in 1985 to Elmhurst, then to Burr Ridge, then to Peru and most recently to Mark, Illinois, where sales tax is limited to the 6.5% statewide tax. Hartney entered into an agreement with Mark in which Hartney shared a portion of local sales tax revenues, generated from Hartney's sales, as an incentive for Hartney choosing to locate its sales office in Mark. In its decision, a Putnam County Circuit Court addressed the issue of where sales are sourced for local sales tax purposes.

On audit, the Illinois Department of Revenue sourced Hartney's sales to Forest View, Illinois and issued a multi-million dollar assessment against Hartney for local sales taxes imposed on these sales in Forest View. Hartney filed suit in Circuit Court protesting the Department's assessment. The Circuit Court struck down the Department's assessment, ruling that Hartney had proved by a preponderance of the evidence that fuel sales were completed at its dedicated sales office in Mark, Illinois, and that these sales must be sourced to Mark and not to Forest View, Illinois. The court found that customers, having been provided bid pricing information and the option of purchasing fuel from Hartney or elsewhere, could choose to purchase from Hartney. The court ruled that the determinative fact in sourcing Hartney's sales to Mark was that each sale was completed upon the sales representative's acceptance of customer purchase order at Hartney's Mark, Illinois sales office. The court ruled that because purchase order acceptance created a contractually binding agreement by Hartney to sell fuel oil to customers, under Illinois law the sales must be sourced to Mark, Illinois.

The appellate court rejected the defendants' argument that not enough selling activities occurred in Mark to justify the finding that Mark is the taxing jurisdiction. The defendants argued that additional factors, such as where credit decisions were made, must be considered. The court stressed the plain language of the statute requiring the acceptance of purchase orders as fixing the situs of sales tax liability and further refused to create a "legal fiction" by applying a test or factors that do not exist in the statute. (*Hartney Fuel Oil Co. v. Illinois Dept. of Revenue*, Nos. 08-MR-11, 08-MR-13, 08-MR-15 (Jan. 26, 2011), CCH ILLINOIS TAX REPORTS,¶402-324, affirmed, *Hartney Fuel Oil Co. v. Hamer*, Appellate Court of Illinois, Third District, Nos. 3-11-0144 and 3-11-0151, September 17, 2012, CCH ILLINOIS TAX REPORTS,¶402-545)

The Illinois Circuit Court of Cook County later held that a company's use of an order acceptance office in Sycamore, IL would not violate the ruling in *Hartney* that taxpayers were entitled for prior periods to utilize order acceptance offices as a means of situsing sales. Nonetheless, the court did not reach a final judgment, as the taxpayer had not shown that orders were actually accepted in Sycamore. (*The Regional Transportation Authority v. United Aviation Fuels Corp. et al.*; 13 CH 1023)

Practitioner Comment: Hartney v. Illinois DOR

The assessments issued by the Department of Revenue in this case and many similar ones represent an apparent change in policy by the Department of what comprised a sales office. Hartney, like many other retailers obtained a private letter ruling from the Department prior to setting up the new sales office. While technically not binding for the years at issue, the Department should put the taxpayers on notice prior to issuing assessments.

Jordan Goodman, Esq., Horwood Marcus & Berk Chartered

• *Sourcing rules for specific transactions*

Sourcing rules provide for the location where a retailer is deemed to be engaged in the business of selling tangible personal property for sales tax, use tax, service occupation tax, service use tax and local sales tax purposes. The rules do not apply to retailers with respect to any activity not described in the rules. (35 ILCS 120/2-12)

Over-the-counter transactions will be deemed to occur at the retailer's same place of business where the buyer is present and pays for the property if the retailer regularly stocks the property or similar property for sale at the retailer's place of business, the buyer had no prior commitment to the retailer, and either (35 ILCS 120/2-12(1))

    (1) the buyer takes possession of the property at the same place of business, or

    (2) the retailer delivers or arranges for the property to be delivered to the buyer.

Sales of property where the purchase is made and paid for over the phone, in writing or via the Internet are deemed to occur at the retailer's same place of business if the retailer regularly stocks the property or similar property for sale at the retailer's place of business, the buyer had no prior commitment to the retailer, and the buyer takes possession of the property at the retailer's place of business. (35 ILCS 120/2-12(2))

Leases for a nominal amount: Effective July 23, 2015, a retailer selling tangible personal property to a nominal lessee or bailee pursuant to a lease with a dollar or other nominal option to purchase is engaged in the business of selling at the location where the property is first delivered to the lessee or bailee for its intended use. (35 ILCS 120/2-12(5))

Vending machine sales: A retailer's vending machine sales are deemed to occur at the location of the vending machine when the sale is made, if (35 ILCS 120/2-12(3)):

    (1) the vending machine is operated by coin, currency, credit card, token, coupon or similar device;

    (2) the food, beverage or other property is contained in, and dispensed from, the vending machine; and

    (3) the buyer takes possession of the item immediately.

¶1518

Minerals: A producer of coal or other mineral mined in Illinois is deemed to be engaged in the business of selling at the place where the coal or other mineral mined is extracted from the earth. "Extracted from the earth" means the location at which the coal or other mineral is extracted from the mouth of the mine. A "mineral" includes not only coal, but also oil, sand, stone taken from a quarry, gravel and any other thing commonly regarded as a mineral and extracted from the earth. (35 ILCS 120/2-12(4))

Sourcing local taxes: In response to the *Hartney* decision above, the Illinois Department of Revenue issued emergency regulations, effective January 22, 2014, and finalized effective June 25, 2014, for sourcing local retailers' occupation tax liabilities. The rules cover the following local taxes: home rule county retailers' occupation tax (86 Ill. Adm. Code 220.115), home rule municipal retailers' occupation tax (86 Ill Adm. Code 270.115), Regional Transportation Authority retailers' occupation tax (86 Ill. Adm. Code 320.115), Metro East Mass Transit District retailers' occupation tax (86 Ill. Adm. Code 370.115), Metro East Park and Recreation District retailers' occupation tax (86 Ill Adm. Code 395.115), County Water Commission retailers' occupation tax (86 Ill. Adm. Code 630.120), special county retailers' occupation tax for public safety (86 Ill. Adm. Code 670.115), Salem Civic Center retailers' occupation tax (86 Ill Adm. Code 690.115), non-home rule retailers' occupation tax (86 Ill. Adm. Code 693.115) and county motor fuel tax (86 Ill. Adm. Code 695.115). The rules for each tax contain similar provisions.

Under *Hartney,* local retailers' occupation tax is imposed on the retail business of selling and is not based on the jurisdiction in which a sale takes place. A retailer is engaged in the business of selling in only one location. The regulations now require a fact-specific inquiry into the composite of selling activities that comprise a retailer's business to determine which jurisdiction has taxing authority. "Selling activities" refers to those activities that comprise an occupation, the business of which is to make retail sales of tangible personal property, and includes the composite of many activities extending from preparing for and obtaining orders for goods to the final consummation of a sale by the passing of title and payment of the purchase price. Further, the taxing statutes intend that a seller incurs tax in a jurisdiction if the seller enjoyed the greater part of governmental services and protection in that jurisdiction.

A seller incurs tax in a local jurisdiction if the seller's predominant and most important selling activities take place in that jurisdiction. This standard applies to both intrastate and interstate retailers. Isolated or limited business activities do not constitute engaging in the business of selling in a jurisdiction when other more significant selling activities occur outside the jurisdiction, and the seller predominantly takes advantage of government services provided by other jurisdictions. The Department of Revenue may also apply the substance-over-form rule when reviewing multijurisdictional sales transactions.

Presumptions are made that over the counter sales, sales through vending machines, and sales from vehicles carrying an uncommitted stock of goods, as described in the rules, occur in a single location. The rules also provide presumptions for determining location with regard to in-state inventory/out of state selling activity, sales over the Internet, leases with an option to purchase, and sales of coals or other minerals.

The regulations provide primary selling activities factors for retailers operating in multiple jurisdictions to determine the location of a sale. Factors include the location of sales personnel, the location where the seller takes action that binds it to the sale, the location where payment is tendered and received or from which invoices are issued, the location of inventory, and the location of the retailer's headquarters. If a seller engages in three or more primary selling activities in one location for a sale, the seller remits the local tax for the jurisdiction of that location. Where no jurisdiction has more than two primary selling activities, the rules provide secondary selling activities factors to consider, including the location of marketing and solicitation and the location of title passage. When both primary and secondary factors are considered, the sale takes place where its inventory is located or its headquarters, wherever more selling activities occur. A seller whose place of business cannot be determined applying the sales activities factors is presumed to be engaged in the business of selling at the location of its headquarters.

Practitioner Comment: Factors in Determining Origin of a Sale

Most states determine local sales tax based on location of delivery of the product. Illinois, however, has always determined local sales tax based on origin of the sale (order acceptance) rather than destination (delivery point). The *Hartney* decision did not invalidate the origin rule *per se*, but instead said that an origin rule based on order acceptance only was improper. Although some taxpayers and practitioners lobbied the Department of Revenue to adopt a destination rule for local sales tax sourcing, the Department ultimately chose to amend its origin-based sourcing regulation to include other factors in addition to mere order acceptance. These other factors include, among other things, the location of sales personnel; the location where payment is tendered and received; the location of inventory; and the location of the retailer's headquarters.

David A. Hughes, Esq., Horwood Marcus & Berk, Chartered

Practitioner Comment: New Regulations Challenged

The new regulations attempt to provide a "totality of the circumstances" test, as required by the *Hartney* decision. However, the Regional Transportation Authority has already brought suit, alleging that the regulations do not sufficiently adhere to the ruling in *Hartney*. From the taxpayer's perspective, the provision in the regulations which provide that an out-of-state seller who satisfies the primary five factors in a jurisdiction other than Illinois nonetheless will have its sales sourced to the location where its Illinois inventory sits is cause for concern. This rule essentially evaporates the 11-part test for out-of-state sellers with inventory in the state, converting the test into a one-part test.

Christopher T. Lutz, Esq., Horwood Marcus & Berk, Chartered

Sourcing—prior law: Before the *Hartney* decision, local taxes administered by the Illinois Department of Revenue were imposed on a sale when the sale location was within a local taxing jurisdiction. If a sale occurred outside Illinois, but the property sold was located in an inventory of the business located in Illinois, the applicable local tax was the tax of the local jurisdiction in which the property was located at the time of sale. When both the sale and the location of the property sold were outside Illinois, no local tax is incurred. (*General Information Letter ST 11-0035-GIL*, Illinois Department of Revenue, May 13, 2011, CCH Illinois Tax Reports, ¶ 402-357)

¶1519 Hotel Operators' Occupation Tax Act

Law: Hotel Operators' Occupation Tax Act, Sec. 1 [35 ILCS 145/1]; Hotel Operators' Occupation Tax Act, Sec. 2 [35 ILCS 145/2]; Hotel Operators' Occupation Tax Act, Sec. 3 [35 ILCS 145/3] (CCH Illinois Tax Reports, ¶ 60-480).

A statewide hotel operators' occupation tax is imposed on individuals or companies engaged in the business of renting, leasing, or letting rooms in a hotel, motel, inn, tourist home (or court), lodging house, rooming house or apartment house (35 ILCS 145/2; 35 ILCS 145/3; 35 ILCS 145/1). In general, the tax is in addition to all other state or local occupation or privilege taxes.

Operators subject to the occupation tax can pass the tax along to their customers in the form of a separately stated, additional charge. For additional information, see

General Information Letter ST 05-0133-GIL, Illinois Department of Revenue, December 22, 2005, CCH ILLINOIS TAX REPORTS, ¶401-648 and *General Information Letter ST 13-0028-GIL,* Illinois Department of Revenue, May 28, 2013, CCH ILLINOIS TAX REPORTS, ¶402-675.

¶1520 Tax on Cultivation of Medical Marijuana

Law: Compassionate Use of Medical Cannabis Pilot Program Act, Secs. 190—220; Use Tax Act, Sec. 3-10 (35 ILCS 105/3-10); 86 Ill. Adm. Code Sec. 429.105 *et seq.* (CCH ILLINOIS TAX REPORTS, ¶60-250).

Effective January 1, 2014, through June 30, 2020, Illinois imposes a tax on the sales price per ounce on the privilege of cultivating medical cannabis. The privilege tax is paid by a cultivation center, not a dispensing organization or a qualifying patient, and is imposed in addition to all other Illinois state and local occupation and privilege taxes. A "cultivation center" is a facility operated by an organization or business that is registered by the Department of Agriculture to perform necessary activities to provide only registered medical cannabis dispensing organizations with usable medical cannabis. (Uncodified Secs. 190—215, Compassionate Use of Medical Cannabis Pilot Program Act)

Beginning January 1, 2014, "prescription and nonprescription drugs" includes medical cannabis purchased from a registered dispensing organization under the Compassionate Use of Medical Cannabis Pilot Program Act for purposes of the sales, use, retailers' occupation and service occupation taxes (35 ILCS 105/3-10).

A surcharge is also imposed on income arising from the sale or exchange of capital assets, depreciable business property, real property used in the trade or business, and Section 197 intangibles of any registrant organization., as discussed at ¶102, ¶903.

Rate of tax: The tax is imposed at the rate of 7% of the sales price per ounce. For purposes of computing the tax on medical cannabis infused products, the sales price is the cultivation center's average sales price per gram of high grade cannabis flowers as determined on a monthly basis. The tax on medical cannabis concentrate or extract is calculated based on the sales price of the quantity of concentrate or extract sold. (Uncodified Sec. 200, Compassionate Use of Medical Cannabis Pilot Program Act; 86 Ill. Adm. Code Sec.429.110).

Planning considerations: Persons subject to the privilege tax must apply to the Department of Revenue for a certificate of registration. The department will prescribe and furnish application forms. A retailer that holds a certificate of registration for the collection of retailers' occupation (sales) taxes does not need to register separately to do business to sell medical cannabis.

The department has the power to administer and enforce the medical cannabis privilege tax law. The department and persons subject to the law will have the same rights, remedies, privileges, immunities, powers and duties, be subject to the same conditions, restrictions, limitations penalties and definitions of terms, and employ the same modes of procedures prescribed by certain provisions of the Retailers' Occupation Tax Act and the Uniform Penalties Act. (Uncodified Sec. 205, Compassionate Use of Medical Cannabis Pilot Program Act)

On or before the 20th day of each calendar month, persons subject to the privilege tax must file a return with the department. The amount of tax due must be submitted at the time a return is filed. The department may adopt rules related to enforcing the medical cannabis privilege tax law. (Uncodified Sec. 205, Compassionate Use of Medical Cannabis Pilot Program Act)

Beginning January 1, 2014, "prescription and nonprescription drugs" includes medical cannabis purchased from a registered dispensing organization under the

Compassionate Use of Medical Cannabis Pilot Program Act for purposes of the sales, use, retailers' occupation and service occupation taxes (35 ILCS 105/3-10).

¶1521 Rental Purchase Agreement Occupation and Use Tax Act

> *Law:* Rental Purchase Agreement Occupation and Use Tax Act, P.A. 100-437 (S.B. 1434), Laws 2017, (CCH ILLINOIS TAX REPORTS, ¶60-460).

Illinois has enacted two 6.25% taxes on transactions involving merchandise rented or used by consumers. The rental purchase agreement occupation tax (rental sales tax) is imposed on transactions where a consumer rents merchandise. And the rental purchase agreement use tax (rental use tax) is imposed on a consumer's use of rented merchandise. Both taxes go into effect on January 1, 2018. Transactions subject to these taxes will not also be subject to Illinois sales and use tax. In addition, the legislation includes a one-time use tax credit for taxpayers that will be liable for the new taxes.

SALES AND USE TAXES

CHAPTER 16

BASIS AND RATE OF TAX

(For purposes of convenience, throughout the sales and use tax division, the retailers' occupation (sales) tax, use tax, service occupation tax, and service use tax are frequently referred to as the ROT, UT, SOT, and SUT, respectively.)

¶1601 Rate of Tax—State, Transportation Authority, and Local ROT, SOT, UT, and SUT

Law: Retailers' Occupation Tax Act, Sec. 2 [35 ILCS 120/2]; Retailers' Occupation Tax Act, Sec. 2-10 [35 ILCS 120/2-10]; Service Occupation Tax Act, Sec. 3 [35 ILCS 115/3]; Service Occupation Tax Act, Sec. 3-10 [35 ILCS 115/3-10]; Use Tax Act, Sec. 3 [35 ILCS 105/3]; Use Tax Act, Sec. 3-10 [35 ILCS 105/3-10]; Service Use Tax Act, Sec. 3 [35 ILCS 110/3]; Service Use Tax Act, Sec. 3-10 [35 ILCS 110/3-10]; Hotel Operators' Occupation Tax Act, Sec. 3 [35 ILCS 145/3]; Illinois Municipal Code, Sec. 8-11-1 [65 ILCS 5/8-11-1]; Illinois Municipal Code, Secs. 8-11-5—8-11-8 [65 ILCS 5/8-11-5—5/8-11-8]; Counties Code, Secs. 5-1006—5-1008 [55 ILCS 5/5-1006—5/5-1008]; Counties Code, Sec. 5-1032 [55 ILCS 5/5-1032]; Counties Code, Sec. 5-1033 [55 ILCS 5/5-1033]; Prepaid Wireless 9-1-1 Surcharge Act, Sec. 15 [50 ILCS 753/15]; Regional Transportation Authority Act, Sec. 4.03 [70 ILCS 3615/4.03]; Local Mass Transit District Act, Sec. 5.01 [70 ILCS 3610/5.01]; Water Commission Act of 1985, Sec. 4(b) [70 ILCS 3720/4]; 86 Ill. Adm. Code Sec. 130.311 (CCH ILLINOIS TAX REPORTS, ¶ 60-110, 61-735, 60-020, 61-210, 61-710, 61-720).

In Illinois, sales tax is a combination of "occupation" taxes that are imposed on sellers' receipts (the ROT and SOT), and "use" taxes that are imposed on amounts paid by purchasers (UT and SUT). Sellers owe the occupation tax to the Illinois Department of Revenue, and they reimburse themselves for this liability by collecting use tax from the buyers. Sales tax is, therefore, the combination of all state, local, mass transit, water commission, home-rule occupation and use, non-home rule occupation and use, and county public-safety taxes.

The statewide sales tax rate for general merchandise is 6.25%.

The statewide rate for food (that is, food not prepared by the retailer for immediate consumption, such as grocery store food items), drugs, and medical appliances (including prescribed FDA Class III medical devices (generally, high risk devices that are subject to premarket approval) used for cancer treatment and related accessories and components) is 1% (*Informational Bulletin FY 2017-04*, Illinois Department of Revenue, August 2016, CCH ILLINOIS TAX REPORTS, ¶ 403-121). Modifications made to a motor vehicle for the purpose of rendering it usable by a disabled personalso qualify for the reduced rate of tax.

Food: A general information letter provides a summary of the sales tax rates for food. The letter discusses how the proper rate is determined and notes that the administrative rules contain a Food Flow Chart as a quick rate reference for most retailers. (*General Information Letter ST 11-0109-GIL,* Department of Revenue, December 29, 2011, CCH ILLINOIS TAX REPORTS,¶ 402-441; see also *General Information Letter ST 13-0061-GIL,* Illinois Department of Revenue, October 22, 2013, CCH ILLINOIS TAX REPORTS,¶ 402-741).

Medical cannabis: Beginning January 1, 2014, medical cannabis and medical cannabis-infused products sold by a registered dispensing organization are considered prescription and nonprescription medicines and drugs subject to the low 1% tax rate. Cannabis paraphernalia is subject to the general merchandise rate of 6.25%. Medical cannabis is also subject to the Metro East Mass Transit District Retailers' Occupation Tax and the Regional Transportation Authority Retailers' Occupation Tax. (86 Ill. Adm. Code Sec. 130.311)

Automobile, aircraft, and watercraft rental and use taxes: A 5% tax is imposed upon persons in the business of renting automobiles, and a 5% tax is imposed on the rental price paid upon the privilege of using an automobile, pursuant to the Illinois automobile renting and occupation and use tax. The aircraft use tax and the watercraft use tax are imposed at the rate of 6.25%.

Hotel operators' occupation tax: The hotel operators' occupation tax is imposed at a rate of 5% of 94% of the gross rental receipts, plus an additional tax of 1% of 94% of gross rental receipts.

As a result of the combination of the statewide rate, together with mass transit district taxes (metro-east mass transit district (MED) and regional transportation authority (RTA)), the Metropolitan Pier and Exposition Authority (MPEA) food and beverage tax, county home-rule tax, county public-safety tax, water commission taxes, municipal home-rule occupation and use taxes, and non-home rule occupation and use taxes, the actual sales tax rate may be higher. In addition, all counties, municipalities, the MED, and the RTA have the authority to impose automobile rental occupation and use taxes up to 1%. The Illinois Department of Revenue is authorized to collect for, and to share collected revenues with, state and local governments.

Sourcing: Sourcing of local taxes is discussed at ¶ 1518.

Prepayment of tax on motor fuels: See ¶ 18022.

• *Wireless 911 surcharge*

The prepaid wireless 911 surcharge on retail transactions was increased to 3% from 1.5%, effective October 1, 2015. A local wireless surcharge imposed by a governmental unit or emergency telephone system board must not exceed $2.50 per commercial mobile radio service connection or in-service telephone number billed on a monthly basis, effective January 1, 2016. Entities exempt from Illinois sales tax are exempt from the 911 surcharge. (Prepaid Wireless 9-1-1 Surcharge Act, Sec. 15 [50 ILCS 753/15]; *Informational Bulletin FY 2012-01,* Department of Revenue, September 2011, CCH ILLINOIS TAX REPORTS,¶ 402-416; see also *Publication 113, Retailer's Overview of Sales and Use Tax and Prepaid Wireless E911 Surcharge,* Department of Revenue, October 2014, CCH ILLINOIS TAX REPORTS,¶ 402-908)

The 911 surcharges are administered and enforced under existing sales tax provisions to the extent practicable. Procedures for registration and payment of the 911 surcharges are substantially the same as those that apply for sales tax purposes. (50 ILCS 753/20)

¶1601

State and local 911 surcharges are imposed on customers, but sellers are liable for remitting all 911 surcharges they collect (Sec. 15(c), P.A. 97-463 (S.B. 2063), Laws 2011). A seller may deduct and retain 3% of the 911 surcharges it collects and timely remits to the Illinois Department of Revenue with a timely filed return (50 ILCS 753/20(b)).

Additional information is provided at ¶2207.

• *Regional tax rates*

RTA taxes: The Regional Transportation Authority (RTA) ROT is imposed in Cook County at the following rates: (1) 1.25% on sales of food for off-premises consumption (except alcohol, soft drinks, and food prepared for immediate consumption), prescription and nonprescription medicines, drugs, medical appliances and insulin, urine testing materials, and syringes and needles used by diabetics; and (2) 1% on other taxable sales. In DuPage, Kane, Lake, McHenry, and Will Counties, the RTA tax is imposed at the rate of 0.75% on all taxable sales. (70 ILCS 3615/4.03(e); *Informational Bulletin FY 2008-13*, Illinois Department of Revenue, February 2008, CCH ILLINOIS TAX REPORTS, ¶401-862)

The RTA's SOT is imposed at the same rates as listed above for the ROT, except that in Cook County it is also imposed on food prepared for immediate consumption and transferred incident to a sale of service by an entity licensed under the Hospital Licensing Act, the Specialized Mental Health Rehabilitation, or the Nursing Home Care Act. (70 ILCS 3615/4.03(f))

The RTA's use tax is imposed at the rate of 1% in Cook County and 0.75% in DuPage, Kane, Lake, McHenry, and Will Counties (collar counties). (70 ILCS 3615/4.03(g); *Informational Bulletin FY 2008-13*, Illinois Department of Revenue, February 2008, CCH ILLINOIS TAX REPORTS, ¶401-862)

MED-MT taxes: A Metro East Mass Transit District (MED-MT) may impose retailers' occupation tax, service occupation tax, and use tax at the rate of 0.25%. (70 ILCS 3610/5.01(b), (c), (d)) Some taxing districts, but not all, within Madison County and St. Clair County have imposed the MED-MT retailers' occupation tax.

MPEA: The Metropolitan Pier and Exposition Authority (MPEA) imposes several local taxes. The rate of the food and beverage tax imposed by the MPEA is 1% on the gross receipts from sales of food, alcoholic beverages, and soft drinks. (70 ILCS 210/13)

The MPEA imposes an occupation tax of 2.5% on the gross receipts of hotel operators in Chicago. An automobile renting occupation tax and the automobile renting use tax are imposed by the MPEA at the rate of 6%. (70 ILCS 210/13)

The MPEA also imposes an occupation tax on airport transit operators at the following rates (70 ILCS 210/13):

— $4 per taxi or livery vehicle departure with passengers for hire from commercial service airports (those receiving scheduled passenger service and enplaning more than 100,000 passengers a year) in the metropolitan area;

— For each departure with passengers for hire from a commercial service airport in the metropolitan area in a bus or van operated by a person other than a person described below: $18 per vehicle with a capacity of 1-12 passengers; $36 per vehicle with a capacity of 13-24 passengers; and $54 per vehicle with a capacity of over 24 passengers;

— For each departure with passengers for hire from a commercial service airport in the metropolitan area in a bus or van operated by a person regulated under federal or state law, operating scheduled service from the airport, and charging fares on a per passenger basis: $2 per passenger for hire in each vehicle.

• *STAR bond districts*

Municipalities and counties may issue sales tax and revenue (STAR) bonds to promote new development of land that has been determined to be a blighted area. Blighted areas may be designated STAR bond districts. Local governments may pass ordinances imposing new retailers' occupation and service occupation taxes in the districts to pay off the STAR bonds. (Sec. 10, P.A. 96-939 (S.B. 2093), Laws 2010, effective June 24, 2010)

If additional sales taxes are imposed in a STAR bond district, both a STAR bond ROT and a STAR bond SOT must be imposed. A municipality may impose the two taxes only within the portion of the STAR bond district that is located within the municipality's boundaries. The STAR bond ROT and the STAR bond SOT may not exceed 1%, respectively, and may be imposed only in 0.25% increments on an annual basis. The STAR bond ROT is imposed on all persons engaged in the business of selling tangible personal property, other than an item of property registered or titled with a state agency. The STAR bond SOT is imposed on all persons engaged in the business of making sales of service, who, as an incident to making those sales of service, transfer tangible personal property within the STAR bond district, either in the form of tangible personal property or in the form of real estate as an incident to a sale of service. Neither tax may be imposed on food for human consumption that is to be consumed off the premises where it is sold (other than alcoholic beverages, soft drinks, and food that has been prepared for immediate consumption), prescription and nonprescription medicines, drugs, medical appliances, modifications to a motor vehicle for the purpose of rendering it usable by a disabled person, and insulin, urine testing materials, syringes, and needles used by diabetics, for human use.

STAR bond sales taxes and penalties are assessed, collected and enforced by the Department of Revenue. Retailers in a STAR bond district are responsible for charging sales taxes, but will be held harmless if they were incorrectly included or excluded from the list of those required to collect tax.

Sellers subject to STAR bond district sales taxes may reimburse themselves for their seller's tax liability by separately stating the tax as an additional charge, which charge may be stated in combination, in a single amount, with state taxes that sellers are required to collect under the Use Tax Act, in accordance with such bracket schedules as the department may prescribe.

• *Local tax rates*

Sales Tax Rate Reference Manual, ST-25, which formerly contained charts of various local sales taxes, is no longer published by the Illinois Department of Revenue. In its place, an online Tax Rate Finder is provided for obtaining local tax rates. A link to the Tax Rate Finder can be found at **https://mytax.illinois.gov/_/**

¶1602 Discount—State ROT, SOT, UT, and SUT

> *Law:* Retailers' Occupation Tax Act, Sec. 3 [35 ILCS 120/3]; Service Occupation Tax Act, Sec. 9 [35 ILCS 115/9]; Use Tax Act, Sec. 9 [35 ILCS 105/9]; Service Use Tax Act, Sec. 9 [35 ILCS 110/9](CCH ILLINOIS TAX REPORTS, ¶ 60-570, 61-220).

Retailers remitting the ROT, SOT, UT, or SUT to the state are allowed a discount of 1.75% or $5 per calendar year, whichever is greater, of the state, local, mass transit, and water commission tax liability to reimburse the retailer for expenses incurred in collecting the tax, keeping records, preparing and filing returns, remitting the tax, and supplying data to the Department on request. No discount is allowed when use tax is remitted directly to the Department by a user (35 ILCS 105/9; 35 ILCS 110/9; 35 ILCS 115/9; 35 ILCS 120/3).

Tire recycling fee: Retailers of tires, who are required to collect the fee for recycling used tires (¶1504, 2212), are given a collection allowance of 10¢ per tire. However, when a retailer of tires remits the tire user fee to a supplier of tires, rather than the Department of Revenue (¶ 1802), and the supplier agrees to remit the fee to the Department, the tire supplier is entitled to the collection allowance of 10¢ per tire. The collection allowance is available only if the retailer's tire user fee return is timely filed and only for the amount that is timely paid. For additional information on the tire user fee, see *PIO-55, Tire User Fee*, Illinois Department of Revenue, March 2011, CCH ILLINOIS TAX REPORTS, ¶ 402-299.

¶ 1603 Credit for Tax Paid Another State—UT and SUT

Law: Use Tax Act, Sec. 3-55 [35 ILCS 105/3-55]; Service Use Tax Act, Sec. 3 [35 ILCS 110/3]; Service Use Tax Act, Sec. 3-45 [35 ILCS 110/3-45](CCH ILLINOIS TAX REPORTS, ¶ 60-020, 60-450, 61-270).

The use tax or service use tax does not apply to the use in Illinois of tangible personal property acquired outside Illinois and brought into Illinois by a person who has already paid a tax in another state in respect to the sale, purchase, or use of the property, to the extent of the amount of tax paid and properly due to the other state. Thus, in effect, a credit is allowed against the Illinois tax due for any tax paid to another state on the sale, purchase, or use of property acquired outside Illinois and later brought into Illinois for use (35 ILCS 105/3-55; 35 ILCS 110/3; 35 ILCS 110/3-45).

Practitioner Comment: Credits Properly Paid

In order to qualify for a credit for taxes paid to another state, Illinois insists that the taxes were properly paid. If the tax was erroneously paid to another state, Illinois will not allow a credit. Furthermore, if the tax was properly paid to another state, Illinois will allow only a credit for the amount of tax that would have been due had the property been used first in Illinois. In other words, Illinois will not allow a business to benefit from another state's higher tax rates.

Furthermore, to qualify for a credit for taxes paid to other states, the property must be acquired outside Illinois. The Illinois circuit court has held that the term "acquire" means "to become the owner of the property." As such, the court held that a taxpayer who leased equipment in Pennsylvania and paid Pennsylvania use taxes on the lease payments, then moved the equipment to Illinois and later bought out the lease, was not eligible for a credit against its Illinois use tax, for Pennsylvania use taxes paid, when buying the equipment in Illinois, because the taxpayer "acquired" the equipment in Illinois (*SunGard Planning Solutions v. Bower*, Doc. No. 99 L 50577, Circuit Court of Cook County, May 6, 2003, CCH ILLINOIS TAX REPORTS, ¶ 401-408 (no appeal filed)).

Jordan M. Goodman, Esq., Horwood Marcus & Berk Chartered

¶ 1604 Manufacturer's Purchase Credit (expired)

Law: Use Tax Tax Act, Sec. 3-85 [35 ILCS 105/3-85]; Service Use Tax Act, Sec. 2 [35 ILCS 110/3-70]; 86 Ill. Adm. Code 130.331 (CCH ILLINOIS TAX REPORTS, ¶ 60-510).

Through August 30, 2014, a manufacturer's purchase credit (MPC) against the use tax or service use tax was earned when tax-exempt purchases were made of machinery and equipment or graphic arts machinery and equipment (¶ 1702). Purchases of fuel that is used or consumed in a manufacturing facility could qualify for the credit; see *General Information Letter ST 10-0119-GIL*, Illinois Department of Revenue, December 22, 2010, CCH ILLINOIS TAX REPORTS, ¶ 402-266.

Calculation of MPC: Taxpayers could earn MPC at the rate of 50% of the state (but not local) sales and use taxes paid on tax-exempt purchases of machinery and equipment. (35 ILCS 105/3-85; 35 ILCS 110/3-70; 86 Ill. Adm. Code 130.331).

Application of MPC: To use the MPC, the manufacturer had to provide the seller of production-related tangible personal property with a Manufacturer's Purchase

Credit Certificate (Form ST-16-C). The certificate could be used by the retailer or service provider to satisfy liability under the ROT or SOT (sales tax), but the amount could not exceed 6.25% of the receipts subject to tax from a qualifying purchase.

¶1605 Basis of Tax—ROT

Law: Retailers' Occupation Tax Act, Sec. 1 [35 ILCS 120/1]; Retailers' Occupation Tax Act, Sec. 2 [35 ILCS 120/2]; 86 Ill. Adm. Code Secs. 130.1995, 130.2125, 130.401, 130.410, 130-415, 130.425, 130.435, 130.445, 130.450, 130.455 (CCH ILLINOIS TAX REPORTS, ¶ 60-020, 61-110, 61-130, 61-150, 61-160, 61-170, 61-210).

The ROT is imposed on persons engaged in the business of selling tangible personal property at retail and is based on the gross receipts from sales (35 ILCS 120/2). Since the ROT is imposed as a privilege tax on the retailer, rather than on the sales, it is the retailer who is responsible for the amount due based on gross receipts. The price charged and the manner in which the tax is passed on to the purchaser is immaterial to the state.

• *Definitions*

"Gross receipts" defined: "Gross receipts" from the sale of tangible personal property at retail means the total selling price or the amount of such sales. Receipts from charge and time sales generally are included in gross receipts only as and when payments are received by the seller. Receipts or other consideration derived by a seller from the sale, transfer, or assignment of accounts receivable to a wholly owned subsidiary are not payments prior to the time the purchaser makes payment on the accounts (35 ILCS 120/1).

Practitioner Comment: Meaning of "Gross Receipts"

Even though Illinois' sales tax is calculated on the taxpayer's gross receipts, the tax is on the business of selling and not on the sale itself. The term "gross receipts" means "the total selling price or amount of such sales," which the Department has interpreted to mean "all the consideration actually received by the seller, except traded-in tangible personal property." Illinois law does not limit gross receipts or consideration to that which the retailer receives from the purchaser.

An Illinois court held that a car dealer may not reduce its sales tax liability by reducing its gross receipts by a rebate paid by the car manufacturer to the car buyer because the rebate did not impact the dealer's gross receipts (*Keystone Chevrolet Co. v. Kirk*, 69 Ill.2d 483 (1978), CCH ILLINOIS TAX REPORTS, ¶ 200-964). Likewise, an Illinois court held a car dealer must include within its taxable gross receipts the amount that the dealer receives from the car manufacturer pursuant to an "Employee/Retiree New Vehicle Purchase/ Lease Program," even though the car buyer was unaware of the payment and even though the rebate amount was accounted for by the car manufacturer and dealer as an inventory purchase price adjustment (*Ogden Chrysler Plymouth, Inc. v. Bower*, 348 Ill. App. 3d 944 (2004), CCH ILLINOIS TAX REPORTS, ¶ 401-467).

David A. Hughes, Esq., Horwood Marcus & Berk Chartered

Practitioner Comment: Sales Commissions

The Illinois Circuit Court in Cook County held in *Clearchoice Mobility, Inc. v. Hamer*, Illinois Circuit Court, 1st Judicial Circuit, No. 2010 L 051694, Mar. 7, 2013; CCH ILLINOIS TAX REPORTS, No ¶ 402-633, that the commissions paid by a telecommunications provider to a cellular phone company for the sale of postpaid cellphone plans are not subject to sales tax. Clearchoice Mobility sells cellular phones on behalf of AT&T and derives revenue from those sales and separately from commissions paid by AT&T for each sale. Following an audit, the Department of Revenue assessed sales tax on these commissions.

Clearchoice argued that there is no statutory language under the Retailers' Occupation Tax ("ROT") permitting the taxation of these commissions as they constitute compensation for other services and are not part of "gross receipts." The Department of Revenue argued the commissions constitute gross receipts and are taxable under the ROT. However, the court found that the legislature intended the ROT to apply only to the sale of tangible personal property and prepaid cellular phone arrangements. The court noted that the post-paid cellular service plans are not tangible personal property and that the commissions were paid not for the sale of the phone itself but for the activation of the plan. The Department of Revenue also suggested that the commissions were taxable under the longstanding policy of the Department. The court quickly rejected this argument, noting that for such a policy to control, it must be correct under the law.

The court accordingly found the commissions paid to Clearchoice for post-paid cell phone plan activations are not within the taxable scope of the ROT. As the plans are not tangible personal property, the commissions are not subject to sales tax. However, the court did find that the commissions for pre-paid plans were within the scope and taxable under ROT as a specific taxable transaction.

There are a number of these cases pending at both the administrative level before the Department's administrative hearings and in Circuit Court. Even after this taxpayer victory, the Department is unwilling to concede or settle any of the pending matters. Instead, the Department has taken the position that each matter must be evaluated individually. However, the Department did float around global settlement terms that were almost universally rejected by the taxpayer community. For the time being, both sides seem to be waiting for legislative guidance out of Springfield.

Breen M. Schiller, Esq., Horwood Marcus & Berk, Chartered

"Selling price" or the "amount of sale" means the consideration for a sale valued in money, whether received in money or otherwise (35 ILCS 120/1). This includes cash, credits, and property other than tangible personal property and services, but does not include the value of, or credit given for, trade-in tangible personal property, interest or finance charges extended on account of credit, or charges added to prices by a seller on account of ROT or local tax liability or on account of the seller's liability to collect the use tax. The trade-in deduction is limited to items of like kind and character as the item being sold.

"Selling price" or "amount of sale" does not include amounts added to prices by sellers because of their duty to collect any tax imposed by the Chicago Regional Transportation Authority. "Like kind and character" is given a liberal construction and includes any type of motor vehicle traded in for any other type of motor vehicle and any type of farm or agricultural implement traded in for any other type of farm or agricultural implement. However, a trade-in does not qualify for the deduction if its sale by the retailer would be exempt as an occasional or isolated sale. No deduction from the selling price is allowed for the cost of the property sold, the cost of material used, labor or service cost, or any other expenses. A deduction is allowed for refunds made to purchasers for returned property, if the receipts from the sale of the property were previously included in gross receipts and the tax was paid (86 Ill. Adm. Code Secs. 130.401, 130.410, 130.425, 130.455).

"Deal of the Day" vouchers: So-called Deal-of the-Day vouchers, such as those sold on websites like **Groupon.com**, are subject to sales tax on redemption by the voucher purchaser, not at the time of sale by the voucher retailer. The purchaser is buying the right to redeem the voucher, which is a nontaxable sale of an intangible. For examples of taxability when such a voucher is presented for payment, see *General Information Letter ST 12-0009-GIL*, Department of Revenue, February 28, 2012, CCH ILLINOIS TAX REPORTS, ¶ 402-456.

Layaways: Layaway fees are taxable on receipt. Nonrefundable layaway fees are taxable as they are similar to handling charges, which are a taxable cost of doing business. Sales tax is refundable on the return of a product purchased on layaway, except for sales tax paid on any nonrefundable fees. Any cancellation fee is not taxable because it is not imposed on a sale. (*General Information Letter ST 12-0007-GIL*, Department of Revenue, January 31, 2012, CCH ILLINOIS TAX REPORTS, ¶ 402-448)

Trading stamps: A retail grocer that transferred tangible personal property for trading stamps was liable for Illinois sales and use tax based on the retail value of the property. The item's retail value is its advertised or stated price or value. (*General Information Letter ST 11-0093-GIL*, Department of Revenue, November 10, 2011, CCH ILLINOIS TAX REPORTS, ¶ 402-437)

Gift cards: Sales of gift cards and coupons that give buyers the right to redeem those cards for tangible personal property are not subject to Illinois retailers' occupation (sales) tax because the cards and coupons are not tangible personal property. Rather, the gift cards and coupons are intangibles. However, when the customer redeems the gift cards or coupons for tangible personal property, the retailers are liable for charging tax based on the gross receipts from those redemption sales. On the subject of nexus, the Department of Revenue notes that even if an out-of-state retailer does not have sufficient nexus to be subject to the sales tax laws, Illinois customers will incur use tax on their purchases of goods from the retailer and have a duty to self-assess. (*General Information Letter ST 10-0052-GIL*, Illinois Department of Revenue, June 4, 2010, CCH ILLINOIS TAX REPORTS, ¶ 402-154)

Sales of repossessed assets: A bank that sold assets on which it foreclosed after a borrower's loan default would not be liable for Illinois sales tax on the asset sales provided the bank disclosed the owner of the repossessed property and did not take title to the property. Sales of repossessed items of tangible personal property by lending agencies and finance companies are taxable, with some exceptions. In addition, the occasional sale exemption may apply to the asset sales if the bank were determined to not hold itself out to the public as a retailer engaged in the business of selling tangible personal property. (*General Information Letter ST 14-0035-GIL*, Illinois Department of Revenue, July 29, 2014, CCH ILLINOIS TAX REPORTS, ¶ 402-836)

- *Discounts and rebates*

The value of discount coupons is not includible in gross receipts because it is never actually received by the retailer. For guidelines representing the Department of Revenue's position regarding the treatment of discount coupons, see *General Information Letter ST 16-0030 GIL*, Illinois Department of Revenue, July 21, 2016, CCH ILLINOIS TAX REPORTS, ¶ 403-130.

Practitioner Comment: Coupons

The Illinois Appellate Court affirmed the Circuit Court's finding that Sears Roebuck & Co. ("Sears") violated the Illinois Consumer Fraud and Deceptive Business Act by overcharging Aliano ("Plaintiff") sales tax on his purchase of a digital television converter box *Aliano v. Sears Roebuck & Co.*, 2015 IL App (1st) 143367).

At the time of purchase, Plaintiff presented a $40 coupon that was valid towards the purchase of the converter box. The coupon allowed Sears to seek reimbursement from the federal government for the lesser of the $40 coupon or the purchase price of the converter box. Sears applied sales tax to the original purchase cost, rather than reducing the selling price by the coupon amount. One year prior to the Plaintiff's purchase, the Illinois Department of Revenue issued guidance on the definition of "purchase price" which is to be reduced by the coupon amount.

Practitioner Comment: Coupons used to decrease the amount a consumer pays for a product may or may not be subject to the Illinois Retailers Occupation Tax ("ROT").

Generally, store coupons which reduce the price of the object sold will not be considered part of the purchase price as the store is not made whole for the value of the coupon. Contrastingly, the value of a manufacturer's coupon is most often subject to the ROT. The explanation for the difference is explained by looking at the total consideration received by the seller. With a store coupon, the seller is not reimbursed by any source. Thus only the amount paid by the customer is subject is subject to the ROT.

¶1605

Manufacturers' coupons generally allow for the seller to submit the coupon back to the manufacturer for full reimbursement of the value of the coupon. Here the seller receives consideration from both customer and the manufacturer. And it is the total consideration received that is subject to the ROT. In *Sears,* the Illinois Department of Revenue had issued a ruling that the reimbursement by the Government Agency would not count towards consideration to the seller and thus not included in the base subject to the ROT. The circuit court judge found that Sears had knowledge of the Department's position and still chose to impose tax on the full selling price of the converters and was found in violation of the Illinois Consumer Fraud and Deceptive Business Act.

Jordan M. Goodman, Esq., Horwood Marcus & Berk, Chartered

When a retailer receives no discount coupon reimbursement, the amount of the discount given to a purchaser is not subject to tax. When a retailer receives full or partial coupon reimbursement from a manufacturer, distributor, or other source, the amount of the coupon reimbursement is subject to tax; see *General Information Letter ST 15-0029-GIL,* Illinois Department of Revenue, May 18, 2015, ¶ 402-968. However, payment received by the retailer for handling charges or administrative expenses in processing coupons is not subject to tax. When a gift coupon entitles a person to obtain an item free of any charge and not conditioned on the purchase of other property, no tax liability is incurred on the retailer's part. However, the donor of the coupon incurs use tax liability on the cost price of all tangible personal property actually transferred as a result of the coupon (86 Ill. Adm. Code Sec. 130.2125).

Discount cards: Discount cards sold through retail locations which allow cardholders to receive discounted prices for prescription drugs at selected pharmacies are not subject to sales and use tax because a discount card is not considered tangible personal property. Rather, a sale of a discount card represents the sale of an intangible (*General Information Letter ST 05-0050-GIL,* Illinois Department of Revenue, June 23, 2005, CCH ILLINOIS TAX REPORTS, ¶ 401-571).

Manufacturers' rebates: Manufacturers' rebates cannot be subtracted from the selling price or added to the trade-in value in determining the sales tax due. The tax applies to gross receipts from retail transactions, including any amounts received through a manufacturer's rebate program. A rebate differs from a discount (see above) in that the manufacturer encourages sales by reimbursing the dealer or consumer after the sale rather than before the sale (*Informational Bulletin FY 91-44,* Department of Revenue; CCH ILLINOIS TAX REPORTS, ¶ 400-518).

Automobile dealer commissions, rebates, and incentives: The dealer commission provided under various "employee discount" incentive programs sometimes offered by the automotive industry is required to be included in the dealer's taxable gross receipts because it is a form of rebate or reimbursement received by the dealer from the manufacturer for a discount provided to the purchaser on the purchase price of a vehicle (*General Information Letter ST 05-0121-GIL,* Illinois Department of Revenue, November 29, 2005, CCH ILLINOIS TAX REPORTS, ¶ 401-632).

If an automobile dealer accepts a manufacturer's rebate provided by a customer as part of the payment for the purchase of an automobile or other type of vehicle, the amount of the reimbursement or payment paid by the manufacturer to the dealer is part of the taxable gross receipts received by the dealer. (86 Ill. Adm. Code 130.2125)

The tax treatment of automobile dealer incentives depends upon whether the dealer receives a payment from a source other than the purchaser that is conditioned upon the retail sale of an automobile. If the dealer receives a payment as an incentive for the retail sale of an automobile, the amount of that reimbursement or payment is part of the taxable gross receipts received by the dealer. If a dealer receives payment in exchange for the purchase of an automobile from a supplier or manufacturer, and that payment is not conditioned upon the sale of that automobile to a retail consumer, the amount of that payment is not part of the dealer's taxable gross receipts. A payment is not part of the dealer's taxable gross receipts if, at the time of the retail sale, the payment is contingent on the dealer making or having made any additional retail sales. In addition, a dealer incentive or bonus that is contingent on the dealer meeting certain manufacturer-required marketing standards, facility standards, or sales and service department satisfaction goals is not part of the dealer's taxable gross receipts, even if the incentive or bonus is calculated using the gross receipts, Manufacturer's Suggested Retail Price (MSRP), or a flat amount per vehicle. (86 Ill. Adm. Code 130.2125; see also *Mattoon Kawasaki Yamaha Inc. v. The Department of Revenue*, Appellate Court of Illinois, Fourth District, No. 4-12-1116, October 23, 2013, CCH ILLINOIS TAX REPORTS, ¶ 402-720)

• *Transportation and delivery charges*

If transportation or delivery charges for delivering property to customers are included in the selling price of the property sold, the charge is an element of cost to the seller and may not be deducted in determining gross receipts. However, if the seller and buyer agree on the transportation or delivery charge separately from the selling price of the property, then the charge is a separate service charge, and need not be included in the gross receipts that are the base for computation of the ROT liability. Mere separate billing of the delivery charges is not sufficient to exclude them from gross receipts; the buyer and seller must contract separately for the transportation costs. However, a business, such as a home catering service, may not even deduct contracted-for delivery expenses when the delivery is inseparably linked to the taxpayer's business (*Gapers, Inc. v. Department of Revenue* (1973, App Ct), 13 IllApp3d 199; CCH ILLINOIS TAX REPORTS, ¶ 200-671; see also *Kean v. Wal-Mart Stores, Inc.*, 235 Ill. 2d 351, 919 N.E.2d 926 (November 20, 2009), CCH ILLINOIS TAX REPORTS, ¶ 402-040, *General Information Letter ST 10-0092-GIL*, Illinois Department of Revenue, October 7, 2010, CCH ILLINOIS TAX REPORTS, ¶ 402-235, *General Information Letter ST 12-0029-GIL*, Illinois Department of Revenue, June 15, 2012, CCH ILLINOIS TAX REPORTS, ¶ 402-548, and *General Information Letter ST 15-0068-GIL*, Illinois Department of Revenue, October 26, 2015, CCH ILLINOIS TAX REPORTS, ¶ 403-058). Transportation or delivery costs paid by a seller in acquiring property for sale are merely costs of doing business and are not deductible from gross receipts (86 Ill. Adm. Code Sec. 130.415).

Practitioner Comment: Shipping Charges May Be Taxable

In *Kean v. Wal-Mart Stores, Inc.*, (cited above), the Illinois Supreme Court affirmed the appellate court's decision dismissing a class action lawsuit that alleged that Wal-Mart had erroneously charged sales tax on shipping charges included on an Internet purchase made by a Wal-Mart customer. The Illinois Supreme Court determined that the primary inquiry was whether shipping was separately contracted for by the parties. If there was no separate agreement for shipping, as the Court found in this case, then the charges must be included in the retailer's gross receipts and are subject to tax. The plaintiffs were required to have the product delivered, so the selling price included the shipping cost.

The Court was not persuaded by the plaintiffs' argument that Wal-Mart's policy of not refunding shipping charges was an indication that the parties were separately agreeing to shipping. Plaintiffs' argument that the conclusion was inconsistent with the Department's letter rulings was also rejected, because the court found that the information had no precedential effect. Furthermore, the court rejected plaintiffs' argument that because taxing statutes must be strictly construed and because the ROTA and Use Tax Act only apply to retailers and users of tangible personal property, the delivery services were not taxable. The Court held that there was an inseparable link between the sale and delivery, because the delivery was not an option. The delivery was part of what was being sold and therefore was part of the selling price.

The *Kean* case is an example of how taxpayers' tax collection and remittance procedures are being challenged by third parties. Typically, lawsuits are between taxpayers and Departments of Revenue, not third party consumers. However, third parties are using unique methods, such as class action lawsuits or *qui tam* actions, to present arguments challenging taxpayers' tax collection and remittance procedures. Taxpayers must now be ready to defend their tax practices, not only to Departments of Revenue, but against their customers as well.

Breen Schiller, Horwood Marcus & Berk, Chartered

The Department of Revenue has revised its regulations (86 Ill. Adm. Code Sec.130.410; 86 Ill. Adm. Code 130.415) regarding transportation and delivery charges in light of the decision in *Kean v. Wal-Mart Stores, Inc.,* 235 Ill. 2d 351, 919 N.E.2d 926 (2009), CCH ILLINOIS TAX REPORTS, ¶402-040), which held that transportation and delivery charges are taxable when an "inseparable link" exists between the sale and delivery of merchandise. See also (*General Information Letter ST 15-0069-GIL,* Illinois Department of Revenue, October 26, 2015, CCH ILLINOIS TAX REPORTS, ¶403-059.

Practitioner Comment: Shipping and Handling

Effective April 1, 2016, the Illinois Department of Revenue amended its shipping and handling regulations (see above) to confirm to the Illinois Supreme Court's decision in *Kean v. Wal-Mart Stores, Inc.,* 235 Ill. 2d 351 (2009). The Department implemented safe harbor provisions for tax periods falling between November 19, 2009 and April 1, 2016 for those taxpayers who computed their sales tax liability based on the prior regulation or the newly amended regulation.

Outgoing transportation and delivery charges are part of the gross receipts and subject to Retailers' Occupation Tax when there is an inseparable link between the sale of the tangible personal property and the outgoing transportation and delivery of the property. An inseparable link exists when the transportation charges are not separately stated on the invoice or when the transportation charges are separately identified, but the seller does not offer the purchaser the option to receive the tangible personal property in any manner except by the payment of such charges (*i.e.,* in store pickup is not an option).

Practitioner Comment: Two questions that remain open after this amendment is whether the pickup option must be for no charge, and if a pick up option is available, whether the delivery option(s) and pickup option are all considered services separate from the sale of the tangible personal property excluded from gross receipts subject to the Retailer's Occupation Tax.

Based on a private letter ruling that has yet to be published, as long as a pickup option is available, if the delivery option is chosen, the delivery charge is excluded from gross receipts regardless of whether the pickup option is for a charge or no charge. However, if there is a charge for pickup, the Department views such charge as an incoming transportation and delivery charge of the retailer which is a business expense to the retailer which may not be deducted from the gross receipts, though the retailer may pass those costs on to its customers by quoting and billing those costs separately from the price of the tangible personal property sold.

Jennifer A. Zimmerman, Esq., Horwood Marcus & Berk, Chartered

---

Quit tam *actions:* See also ¶1512.

• *State and federal taxes*

In calculating taxable receipts, the Illinois motor fuel tax may be deducted, since this tax is on the consumer and is not considered part of the selling price of the fuel. Illinois cigarette taxes may similarly be deducted in calculating taxable receipts and no deduction is allowed from gross receipts for Illinois alcoholic liquor taxes (86 Ill. Adm. Code Sec. 130.435).

Taxes paid to the federal government by a retailer who is required to collect such taxes from customers and remit them are deductible, as are federal excise taxes imposed on property sold at retail (as distinguished from wholesale or manufacturers' taxes). Federal excise taxes imposed on the manufacture or production of tangible personal property, processing taxes, compensating taxes, importation taxes, and taxes on floor stocks are not deductible, including taxes on manufacturers of tobacco products and alcoholic liquors. Gross receipts include amounts collected representing the Illinois liquor gallonage taxes, but not amounts representing Cook County gallonage taxes. Also, federal taxes on tangible personal property sold by a wholesaler, importer, manufacturer or other producer (such as the taxes on gasoline, tires, *etc.*) are not deductible (86 Ill. Adm. Code Sec. 130.445).

• *Installation, alteration, and special service charges*

Charges for installation, alteration, or other special services on tangible personal property sold by a retailer are taxable if the charges are included in the selling price of the property sold, regardless of whether billing is stated separately. However, if the buyer and seller contract separately for the installation or alteration charges, the charges are not a part of the selling price and may be deducted in computing taxable receipts (86 Ill. Adm. Code Sec. 130.450).

Personalized greeting cards: Sales of personalized greeting cards are not subject to the ROT because the sellers of such cards are primarily engaged in a service occupation in producing or procuring the personalized greeting cards, which have no commercial value for the seller's customers (86 Ill. Adm. Code Sec. 130.1995).

¶1606 Basis of Tax—SOT

Law: Service Occupation Tax Act, Sec. 2 [35 ILCS 115/2]; Service Occupation Tax Act, Sec. 3 [35 ILCS 115/3]; Service Occupation Tax Act, Sec. 3-10 [35 ILCS 115/3-10]; Service Occupation Tax Act, Sec. 9 [35 ILCS 115/9]; 86 Ill. Adm. Code Sec. 140.305 (CCH Illinois Tax Reports, ¶60-020, 60-635, 61-110, 61-210).

The service occupation tax is measured by the "selling price" of tangible personal property transferred by a service provider as an incident to a sale of service (35 ILCS 115/3). "Selling price" means all the consideration actually received by the service provider, whether paid in money or otherwise, including cash, credits, or services. Selling price is determined without a deduction for the service provider's cost of the property sold or any other expense incurred by the seller. (35 ILCS 115/2)

At the annual election that any registered service provider makes for each fiscal year, sales of service in which the aggregate annual cost price of tangible personal property transferred as an incident to the sale of service is less than 35% (75% in the case of service providers transferring prescription drugs or service providers engaged in graphic arts production) of the aggregate annual total gross receipts from all sales of service, the service occupation tax will be based on the service provider's cost price of the tangible personal property transferred as an incident to the sale of those services.

Provisions regarding deductibility of transportation or delivery charges and treatment of refunds are similar to those provided under the ROT (¶1605) (86 Ill. Adm. Code Sec. 140.305).

¶1607 Basis of Tax—UT

Law: Use Tax Act, Sec. 2 [35 ILCS 105/2]; Use Tax Act, Sec. 3 [35 ILCS 105/3]; Use Tax Act, Sec. 3-10 [35 ILCS 105/3-10]; Use Tax Act, Sec. 9 [35 ILCS 105/9]; Aircraft Use Tax Law, Sec. 10-15 [35 ILCS 157/10-15]; Watercraft Use Tax Law, Sec. 15-15 [35 ILCS 158/15-15]; 86 Ill. Adm. Code Sec. 150.1101 (CCH Illinois Tax Reports, ¶60-020, 60-740, 61-110, 61-140, 61-180).

The use tax is generally imposed on the "selling price" of tangible personal property purchased at retail and used in Illinois. However, in cases where property used or consumed is a by-product or waste product refined, manufactured, or produced from property purchased at retail, the tax is imposed on the lower of the selling price of the property purchased or the fair market value of the property used or consumed. "Selling price" means the consideration for a sale valued in money, whether received in money or otherwise, and includes cash, credits, and property other than tangible personal property and service, but does not include the value of traded-in tangible personal property. (35 ILCS 105/2)

Practitioner Comment: Avoiding Use Tax on Promotional Items

Retailers owe Illinois use tax on inventory withdrawn and used as promotional give-away items. However, retailers can avoid self-assessing use tax if they choose to sell the inventory for any price, even a penny. Changing the nature of the transaction to a taxable sale from a taxable use may significantly reduce taxes sales/use taxes owed. For example, the Department has stated that cell phone retailers owe use tax on the cost price of phones that they give away to customers, but if they charge a $1, sales tax is due on $1 gross receipt. *General Info. Letter 94-ST-0245* (July 1, 1994).

Horwood Marcus & Berk Chartered

Aircraft use tax: An aircraft use tax must be paid by persons who use an aircraft in Illinois that was acquired by gift, donation, transfer, or nonretail purchase (35 ILCS 157/10-15). The purchaser, transferee, or donee must submit a return and payment to the Department of Revenue within 30 days after the date of purchase, donation, or other transfer or the date the aircraft is brought into the state, whichever is later. Payment of the tax is required in order to secure state registration of the aircraft. For the tax rate, see ¶1601.

A transfer is taxable even if the beneficial ownership of the aircraft will not change after the transfer; see *General Information Letter ST 12-0062-GIL*, Illinois Department of Revenue, December 20, 2012, CCH ILLINOIS TAX REPORTS,¶402-616.

The aircraft use tax will not apply if: (1) the use of the aircraft is otherwise subject to Illinois use tax, (2) the aircraft is bought and used by a governmental agency or by a charitable, religious, or educational entity, (3) the use of the aircraft is exempt from use tax to prevent actual or likely multistate taxation, or (4) the aircraft is transferred as gift to a surviving spouse in the administration of an estate.

Watercraft use tax: Use tax is imposed on any watercraft acquired by gift, transfer, or purchase (35 ILCS 158/15-15). The tax applies to the watercraft and the value of any motor that is a part of the transaction. Taxpayers must file a Form RUT-75, Aircraft/Watercraft Use Tax Return, no later than 30 days from the acquisition date or date the watercraft is brought into Illinois, whichever is later. For the tax rate, see ¶1601.

• *Trade-ins*

The trade-in deduction is limited to items of like kind and character as the item being sold. "Selling price" does not include any amounts added to prices by sellers because of their duty to collect any tax imposed by the Chicago Regional Transportation Authority (35 ILCS 105/2). "Like kind and character" is given a liberal construction and includes any type of motor vehicle traded in for any other type of motor vehicle and any type of farm or agricultural implement traded in for any other type of farm or agricultural implement. However, a trade-in does not qualify for the deduction if its sale by the retailer would be exempt as an occasional or isolated sale (86 Ill. Adm. Code Sec. 150.1101). No deduction is allowed for the cost of the property sold, materials used, labor or service cost, or any other expenses. However, finance or interest charges appearing as separate items on the bill of sale or contract and amounts on account of ROT, UT, or local ROT taxes are not included. Installment payments may be included in taxable receipts as received during such tax return period, except in the case of motor vehicles and aircraft.

• *Property used outside the state*

If property was acquired outside Illinois and used outside the state before being brought to Illinois for use, but is nevertheless taxable by Illinois, the "selling price" on which the use tax is based is reduced by an amount representing a reasonable allowance for depreciation for the period of use outside the state (35 ILCS 105/2).

Practitioner Comment: Part-Time Use of Property in Illinois

The Illinois Appellate Court upheld the Department's assessment of use taxes on the entire purchase price of an airplane, even though the airplane was purchased outside of Illinois, the airplane was never hangered in Illinois, and the airplane spent only 4% of its time on the ground in Illinois. See *Irwin Industrial Tool Co. v. Ill. Dep't of Revenue*, Doc. No. 1-07-3331 & 08-0750 (Ill. App. Ct. 1st Dist. Sept. 11, 2009).

The taxpayer purchased the airplane from a seller in Kansas, delivery was accepted in Arkansas, and the airplane was subsequently hangered in Nebraska, and all maintenance was done in Nebraska. The airplane was used by the company for various purposes, including visiting customers, employee travel among offices, and matters related to acquisitions and lawsuits. For the 24-months ending April 2002, the airplane flew 290 days, including 734 flight segments, of which 269 originated or ended in Illinois. No use tax was paid in Nebraska because an exemption applied. No use tax was paid to Illinois either.

The Department assessed use tax on the entire purchase price of the airplane, and the company argued that the assessment was unconstitutional because, among other reasons, the tax was not fairly apportioned to its use in Illinois. The circuit court agreed with the company, but the appellate court reversed. The appellate court reasoned that Illinois' use tax was fairly apportioned because the tax was both internally consistent (which the company did not dispute) and externally consistent. External consistency is concerned about the relationship between the taxing state and entity and, specifically, whether the "State's tax reaches beyond that portion of value that is fairly attributable to economic activity within the taxing State." Even though the airplane was used only part-time in Illinois, the court held that Illinois' allowance of a credit for taxes paid to other states satisfies the requirement of external consistency and, therefore, the tax was "fairly apportioned" and constitutional.

Horwood Marcus & Berk, Chartered

Practitioner Comment: Trade-In Planning

As discussed above, Illinois allows a deduction from the selling price for the credit given for traded-in tangible personal property (including motor vehicles) that is of like kind and character as that which is being sold. The Department interprets the phrase "like kind and character" broadly. A regulation states that "the real test [for whether property is of like kind and character] is whether the retail sale of the traded-in tangible personal property by the person who accepts it in a trade would be subject to Retailers' Occupation Tax, or whether such sale would be exempt as an isolated or occasional sale." Thus, a trade-in of a used tennis racquet to the tennis pro-shop for a new tennis racquet would qualify for a trade-in credit. Likewise, a trade-in of the used tennis racquet to a sporting goods store for downhill skis would qualify for a trade-in credit. However, the trade-in of the tennis racquet to a ski store for new skis may not qualify for a trade-in credit.

Jordan M. Goodman, Esq., Horwood Marcus & Berk Chartered

¶1608 Basis of Tax—SUT

Law: Service Use Tax Act, Sec. 2 [35 ILCS 110/2]; Service Use Tax Act, Sec. 3 [35 ILCS 110/3]; Service Use Tax Act, Sec. 3-10 [35 ILCS 110/3-10](CCH ILLINOIS TAX REPORTS, ¶ 60-020, 61-110, 61-210).

¶1608

The service use tax is based on the selling price to the service provider of tangible personal property transferred as an incident to the sale of service (35 ILCS 110/3). "Selling price" means the consideration received by the service provider for the purchase valued in money, whether paid in money or otherwise, including cash, credits and services, and is determined without deduction for the service provider's cost of the property sold or any other expenses of the service provider (35 ILCS 110/2).

At the election that any registered service provider makes for each fiscal year, sales of service in which the aggregate annual cost price of tangible personal property transferred as an incident to the sale of service is less than 35% (75% in the case of servicepersons transferring prescription drugs or servicepersons engaged in graphic arts production) of the aggregate annual total gross receipts from all sales of service, the service use tax will be based on the serviceperson's cost price of the tangible personal property transferred as an incident to the sale of those services (35 ILCS 110/3-10).

• *Subcontracted services*

If the service provider contracts out part or all of the services required, it is presumed that the selling price to the service provider of the property transferred by the subcontractor is equal to 50% of the subcontractor's charges to the service provider in the absence of proof of the consideration paid by the subcontractor for the property or in the absence of proof that the SUT was paid by the subcontractor (35 ILCS 110/2).

• *Property used outside the state*

If property acquired by a service provider as an incident to a sale of service was acquired outside Illinois and used outside the state before being brought to Illinois and is nevertheless taxable by Illinois, the "selling price" on which the tax is based may be reduced by an amount representing a reasonable allowance for depreciation for the period of use outside the state. (35 ILCS 110/3-10)

¶1609 Basis of Tax—Automobile Renting Occupation and Use Tax Act

Law: Automobile Renting Occupation and Use Tax Act, Secs. 2—4 [35 ILCS 155/2—155/4]; 86 Ill. Adm. Code Sec. 180 (CCH ILLINOIS TAX REPORTS, ¶ 61-735, 60-570, 61-710).

The automobile renting occupation and use tax is based on gross receipts received from renting or leasing automobiles in Illinois. "Renting" means any transfer of the possession or right to possession of an automobile to a user for valuable consideration for a period of one year or less (35 ILCS 155/2; 35 ILCS 155/3).

An "automobile" is defined as (35 ILCS 155/2):

(1) any motor vehicle of the first division, or

(2) a motor vehicle of the second division that:

(A) is a self-contained motor vehicle designed or permanently converted to provide living quarters for recreational, camping or travel use, with direct walk through access to the living quarters from the driver's seat;

(B) is of the van configuration designed for the transportation of not less than 7 nor more than 16 passengers; or

(C) has a Gross Vehicle Weight Rating of 8,000 pounds or less.

Basis of tax: For purposes of the automobile renting occupation tax, "rental price" includes all consideration received from renting or leasing automobiles and is determined without any deduction for the cost of the property rented, the cost of materials used, the cost of labor or service, or any other expense. When the rental price is paid to the rentor in installments, the amount of installment payments must only be included by the rentor in the gross receipts when the installments are received by the rentor. "Rental price" does not include compensation paid to a rentor by a rentee in consideration of a waiver by the rentor of any right of action or claim against the rentee for loss or damage to the rented automobile. It also does not include separately stated charges for insurance, recovery of refueling costs, or other separately stated charges that are not for the use of tangible personal property. Receipts from these sources must be included in gross receipts and then deducted prior to computing the amount of tax due (35 ILCS 155/2).

• *Exclusions*

"Gross receipts" does not include making a charge for the use of an automobile when the renter furnishes a service of operating an automobile in such a way that the renter remains in possession of the automobile; the term also does not include a dealer's charge for the use of an automobile as a demonstrator in connection with the dealer's business of selling. An exclusion applies to receipts received by an automobile dealer from a manufacturer or service contract provider as reimbursement for the use of an automobile by a person while that person's automobile is being repaired by the automobile dealer, provided that the repair is made pursuant to a manufacturer's warranty or service contract and the reimbursement is made merely for the dealer to recover the costs of operating the automobile as a loaner vehicle (35 ILCS 155/2).

¶1610 Basis of Tax—Hotel Operators' Occupation Tax Act

Law: Hotel Operators' Occupation Tax Act, Secs. 2—4 [35 ILCS 145/1—145/9](CCH ILLINOIS TAX REPORTS, ¶ 60-480).

The hotel operators' occupation tax(HOOT) is imposed on individuals or companies engaged in the business of renting, leasing, or letting rooms in a hotel, motel, inn, tourist home (or court), lodging house, rooming house or apartment house (35 ILCS 145/2; 35 ILCS 145/3). In general, the tax is in addition to all other state or local occupation or privilege taxes.

Homeowners and other taxpayers who rent rooms to the general public may be liable for the HOOT.

A hotel operator is not exempt from tax when a room is rented to an exempt entity. Hotel operators may collect an amount from their customers that reimburses the operators for the tax liability, and the holding of an "E" number does not exempt a customer from paying a reimbursement charge (*General Information Letter ST 11-0036-GIL*, Illinois Department of Revenue, May 23, 2011, CCH ILLINOIS TAX REPORTS, ¶ 402-358).

Basis of tax: The hotel operators' occupation tax is based on gross rental receipts, which is the consideration received for occupancy, valued in money, and includes all receipts, cash, credits and property or services of any kind.

Permanent residents: Excluded from gross rental receipts are all proceeds that come from renting to permanent residents, that is, persons who have occupied or have the right to occupy one or more rooms in an accommodation for a period of at least 30 days. Returns may be reported on either a gross receipts or gross billing basis (35 ILCS 145/2; 35 ILCS 145/3).

Receipts from hotel rooms rented by an airline for periods longer than 30 days were not subject to the hotel operators' occupation tax, because rooms rented to permanent residents are not taxable. The airline, which rented the rooms under a binding rental contract for its crew members' use, was considered a "permanent resident." If the rental contract did not unconditionally obligate the airline to pay for a specific number of rooms for at least 30 consecutive days, the hotel would be required to charge and collect the tax. (*General Information Letter ST 10-0081-GIL*, Illinois Department of Revenue, September 8, 2010, CCH ILLINOIS TAX REPORTS, ¶ 402-205)

¶1610

CCH Advisory: Redemption of Hotel's Reward Points for Free Lodging

A hotel chain operating a rewards program for frequent guests does not incur Illinois hotel operators' occupation tax liability on a customer's redemption of reward points for complimentary lodging. Guests earn points each time they pay for a stay at one of the taxpayer's hotels. Hotel tax is remitted by guests on their initial stay. The hotel pays about 4% of room revenues from these guests into the taxpayer's central reward point program fund, and when a guest redeems points, the hotel's fund account is credited an amount to cover the guest's complimentary stay. Reimbursement of hotel fees comes from an account held and owned entirely by the taxpayer and not from a third party. The tax consequences would change if a third party pays any reimbursement of the lodging fees to the hotels. (*Private Letter Ruling, ST 05-0015-PLR,* Illinois Department of Revenue, October 6, 2005, CCH ILLINOIS TAX REPORTS, ¶401-606).

SALES AND USE TAXES
CHAPTER 17
EXEMPTIONS

(For purposes of convenience, throughout the sales and use tax division, the retailers' occupation (sales) tax, use tax, service occupation tax, and service use tax are frequently referred to as the ROT, UT, SOT, and SUT, respectively.)

¶1701 In General

The application of every exemption that is enacted after September 16, 1994, must be limited by a sunset date. If a "reasonable and appropriate" sunset date is not specified, the exemption will expire five years after the effective date of the enacting law.

Guidance: Additional information on exemptions may be found in *Publication 104, Common Sales Tax Exemptions and E911 Surcharge Exemptions,* Illinois Department of Revenue, November 2015, CCH ILLINOIS TAX REPORTS, ¶ 403-031.

• *Requirements for development assistance*

The Corporate Accountability for Tax Expenditures Act (P.A. 93-552 (H.B. 235), Laws 2003) imposes minimum recapture requirements for credits against Illinois High Impact Business Zone Illinois retailers' occupation (sales) tax, service occupation (sales) tax, service use tax, and use tax.

The Act also establishes a new definition of "development assistance" that encompasses all the aforementioned incentives, provides for developmental assistance agreements between state bodies granting incentives and incentive recipients, establishes standardized application requirements for developmental assistance, and requires annual reporting to the Legislature.

Details of the Act are discussed at ¶ 401.

¶1702 ROT/UT/SOT/SUT—Exemptions

Law: Retailers' Occupation Tax Act, Sec. 1 [35 ILCS 120/1]; Retailers' Occupation Tax Act, Sec. 1a-1 [35 ILCS 120/1a-1]; Retailers' Occupation Tax Act, Sec. 1d [35 ILCS 120/1d]; Retailers' Occupation Tax Act, Secs. 1j.1, 1j.2 [35 ILCS 120/1j.1, 120/1j.2]; Retailers' Occupation Tax Act, Sec. 1k [35 ILCS 120/1k]; Retailers' Occupation Tax Act, Sec. 1m [35 ILCS 120/1m]; Retailers' Occupation Tax Act, Sec. 1n [35 ILCS 120/1n]; Retailers' Occupation Tax Act, Sec. 2 [35 ILCS 120/2]; Retailers' Occupation Tax Act, Sec. 2-5 [35 ILCS 120/2-5]; Retailers' Occupation Tax Act, Sec. 2-6 [35 ILCS 120/2-6]; Retailers' Occupation Tax Act, Sec. 2-7 [35 ILCS 120/2-7]; Retailers' Occupation Tax Act, Sec. 2-9 [35 ILCS 120/2-9]; Retailers' Occupation Tax Act, Sec. 2-10 [35 ILCS 120/2-10]; Retailers' Occupation Tax Act, Sec. 2-20 [35 ILCS 120/2-20]; Retailers' Occupation Tax Act, Sec. 2-25 [35 ILCS 120/2-25]; Retailers' Occupation Tax Act, Sec. 2-54 [35 ILCS 120/2-54]; Retailers' Occupation Tax Act, Sec. 2-60 [35 ILCS 120/2-60]; Service Occupation Tax Act, Sec. 2 [35 ILCS 115/2]; Service Occupation Tax Act, Sec. 2b [35 ILCS

115/2b]; Service Occupation Tax Act, Sec. 3 [35 ILCS 115/3]; Service Occupation Tax Act, Sec. 3-5 [35 ILCS 115/3-5]; Service Occupation Tax Act, Sec. 3-8 [35 ILCS 115/3-8]; Service Occupation Tax Act, Sec. 3-10 [35 ILCS 115/3-10]; Service Occupation Tax Act, Sec. 3-15 [35 ILCS 115/3-15]; Service Occupation Tax Act, Sec. 3-20 [35 ILCS 115/3-20]; Service Occupation Tax Act, Sec. 3-25 [35 ILCS 115/3-25]; Service Occupation Tax Act, Sec. 3-30 [35 ILCS 115/3-30]; Service Occupation Tax Act, Sec. 3-45 [35 ILCS 115/3-45]; Use Tax Act, Sec. 2 [35 ILCS 105/2]; Use Tax Act, Sec. 2a-1 [35 ILCS 105/2a-1]; Use Tax Act, Sec. 2c [35 ILCS 105/2c]; Use Tax Act, Sec. 3 [35 ILCS 105/3]; Use Tax Act, Sec. 3-5 [35 ILCS 105/3-5]; Use Tax Act, Sec. 3-8 [35 ILCS 105/3-8]; Use Tax Act, Sec. 3-10 [35 ILCS 105/3-10]; Use Tax Act, Sec. 3-15 [35 ILCS 105/3-15]; Use Tax Act, Sec. 3-20 [35 ILCS 105/3-20]; Use Tax Act, Sec. 3-25 [35 ILCS 105/3-25]; Use Tax Act, Sec. 3-30 [35 ILCS 105/3-30]; Use Tax Act, Sec. 3-35 [35 ILCS 105/3-35]; Use Tax Act, Sec. 3-40 [35 ILCS 105/3-40]; Use Tax Act, Sec. 3-50 [35 ILCS 105/3-50]; Use Tax Act, Sec. 3-55 [35 ILCS 105/3-55]; Use Tax Act, Sec. 3-60 [35 ILCS 105/3-60]; Use Tax Act, Sec. 3-70 [35 ILCS 105/3-70]; Service Use Tax Act, Sec. 2 [35 ILCS 110/2]; Service Use Tax Act, Sec. 2b [35 ILCS 110/2b]; Service Use Tax Act, Sec. 3 [35 ILCS 110/3]; Service Use Tax Act, Sec. 3-5 [35 ILCS 110/3-5]; Service Use Tax Act, Sec. 3-8 [35 ILCS 110/3-8]; Service Use Tax Act, Sec. 3-10 [35 ILCS 110/3-10]; Service Use Tax Act, Sec. 3-15 [35 ILCS 110/3-15]; Service Use Tax Act, Sec. 3-20 [35 ILCS 110/3-20]; Service Use Tax Act, Sec. 3-25 [35 ILCS 110/3-25]; Service Use Tax Act, Sec. 3-30 [35 ILCS 110/3-30]; Service Use Tax Act, Sec. 3-35 [35 ILCS 110/3-35]; Service Use Tax Act, Sec. 3-45 [35 ILCS 110/3-45]; Service Use Tax Act, Sec. 3-50 [35 ILCS 110/3-50]; Service Use Tax Act, Sec. 3-60 [35 ILCS 110/3-60]; Municipal Code, Sec. 11-65-10 [65 ILCS 11-65-10]; Municipal Code, Sec. 11-65-10 [65 ILCS 11-65-10]; 86 Ill. Adm. Code 130.315; 86 Ill. Adm. Code 130.321; 86 Ill. Adm. Code 130.330; 86 Ill. Adm. Code 130.345; 86 Ill. Adm. Code 130.350; 86 Ill. Adm. Code 130.351; 86 Ill. Adm. Code 130.2080 (CCH ILLINOIS TAX REPORTS, ¶ 60-230, 60-250, 60-300, 60-310, 60-360, 60-390, 60-420, 60-450, 60-510, 60-520, 60-530, 60-560, 60-580, 60-610, 60-620, 60-630, 60-640, 60-650, 60-645, 60-740, 61-010).

The exemptions discussed below are provided under the ROT/UT/SOT/SUT.

• *Agriculture*

Illinois provides various exemptions relating to agriculture.

Seeds and fertilizer: Sales of seeds to farmers and other persons who use the seeds to raise vegetables, crops, or plants for sale are deemed sales for resale not subject to the ROT and UT. Sales of fertilizer to purchasers engaged in the business of producing agricultural products for sale are exempt (86 Ill. Adm. Code 130.2110).

Farm chemicals: Proceeds from the sale of farm chemicals are exempt from the ROT and UT (35 ILCS 105/3-5; 35 ILCS 120/2-5). "Farm chemicals" are chemical products used in production agriculture, the products of which are to be sold, or in the production or care of animals or their by-products that are to be sold, such as stock sprays, disinfectants, stock tonics, serums, vaccines, poultry remedies and other medicinal preparations and conditioners, water-purifying products, insecticides, and weed killers. The exemption includes sales of chemicals used to raise dairy cows for the production of milk that is to be sold for human consumption (*General Information Letter ST 11-0066-GIL*, Department of Revenue, August 19, 2011, CCH ILLINOIS TAX REPORTS, ¶ 402-407). However, the exemption does not include weed control chemicals used to spray native prairie grasses, because the chemicals were used as food plots for wildlife and not used in raising crops for resale (*General Information Letter ST 11-0061-GIL*, Department of Revenue, August 11, 2011, CCH ILLINOIS TAX REPORTS, ¶ 402-405).

See also "Farm machinery," below.

Breeding; racing: Sales of bulls, stallions, and other breeding livestock for breeding purposes are not subject to tax. Sales and use of semen for artificial insemination of livestock for direct agricultural production are also exempt (86 Ill. Adm. Code 130.2100).

¶1702

Horses, or interests in horses, registered with and meeting requirements of the Arabian Horse Club Registry of America, Appaloosa Horse Club, American Quarter Horse Association, United States Trotting Association, or Jockey Club, and used for breeding or racing for prizes, are exempt from ROT, SOT, UT, and SUT (35 ILCS 105/3-5; 35 ILCS 110/3-50; 35 ILCS 115/3-5; 35 ILCS 120/2-5).

For additional information, see *General Information Letter ST 13-0001-GIL,* Illinois Department of Revenue, January 9, 2013, CCH ILLINOIS TAX REPORTS, ¶ 402-634.

Feed: Feed sold to prepare livestock or poultry for market or to produce eggs or dairy products for sale is not subject to the ROT and UT (86 Ill. Adm. Code 130.2100). "Feed" is salt, grains, tankage, oyster shells, mineral supplements, vitamins, limestone, and other generally recognized animal feeds.

• *Aircraft and related exemptions*

An exemption is allowed for (1) an aircraft that is sold in Illinois and leaves the state within 15 days after the sale and the aircraft is not based or registered in Illinois after the sale, (2) an aircraft temporarily located in Illinois for a prepurchase evaluation, and (3) an aircraft that is temporarily located in Illinois for post-sale customization and leaves the state within 15 days (35 ILCS 105/3-55(h-2); 86 Ill. Adm. Code 150.310; 86 Ill. Adm. Code Sec. 130.605). For additional details, see ¶ 1703.

Aircraft maintenance facility machinery: Machinery and equipment purchased by qualified interstate carriers for hire and used in the operation of aircraft maintenance facilities located in enterprise zones are exempt. The machinery and equipment must be used primarily for the maintenance, rebuilding, or repair of aircraft, aircraft parts, and auxiliary equipment that is owned or leased by a carrier and used as rolling stock moving in interstate commerce. To qualify for the exemption, the interstate carrier for hire must make an investment of $400 million or more in an enterprise zone, create at least 5,000 full-time jobs in the zone, locate in a county with between 150,000 to 200,000 inhabitants that contains three enterprise zones as of December 31, 1990, and enter into a legally binding agreement with the Department of Commerce and Community Affairs to comply with these requirements. The exemption also applies to purchases of tangible personal property that is used or consumed in the qualified aircraft maintenance facility, including repair and replacement parts (35 ILCS 105/12; 35 ILCS 110/12; 35 ILCS 115/12; 35 ILCS 120/1m; 35 ILCS 120/1n).

Aircraft support center purchases: An aircraft support center that is certified by, and enters into, an agreement with the Illinois Department of Commerce and Community Affairs to invest at least $30 million into a federal Air Force base located in Illinois and that generates at least 750 full-time jobs at an airport located on the base that is used by military and civilian personnel, is exempt from ROT, SOT, SUT, and UT on purchases of jet fuel and petroleum products that are used or consumed by the aircraft support center directly in the process of maintaining, rebuilding, or repairing aircraft. The aircraft support center must apply for a certificate of eligibility for exemption and the certificate must be presented to the center's supplier when making an initial purchase, along with a certification that the items are exempt. Subsequent purchases may be made by indicating the exempt status on the face of the purchase orders (35 ILCS 120/1o; 35 ILCS 115/12; 35 ILCS 105/12; 35 ILCS 110/12).

Aircraft repair parts and materials: Materials, parts, equipment, components, and furnishings that are incorporated into or upon an aircraft as part of the modification, refurbishment, completion, replacement, repair, or maintenance of the aircraft are exempt from Illinois retailers' occupation (sales) tax, service occupation tax, use tax, and service use tax. The exemption includes consumable supplies, such as adhesive, tape, sandpaper, general purpose lubricants, cleaning solution, latex gloves, and protective films. The exemption does not include items used in modifying, replacing, repairing, and maintaining aircraft engines or power plants. The exemption does not cover aircraft operated by a commercial air carrier providing scheduled passenger air service pursuant to authority issued under Part 121 or Part 129 of the Federal Aviation Regulations. (35 ILCS 105/3-5; 35 ILCS 110/3-5; 35 ILCS 115/3-5; 35 ILCS 120/2-5)

Practitioner Comment: Use Tax Exemption for Aircraft Parts

On August 23, 2013, the General Assembly amended 35 ILCS 110/3-4 to provide that the exemption only to the use of qualifying tangible personal property be persons who modify, refurbish, complete, repair, replace, or maintain aircraft, and who also meet the pre-existing requirements under the Act. P.A. 98-0534.

Marilyn A. Wethekam, Esq., Horwood Marcus & Berk, Chartered

The exemption is available only to persons who modify, refurbish, complete, repair, replace, or maintain aircraft and who (1) hold an Air Agency Certificate and are empowered to operate an approved repair station by the Federal Aviation Administration, (2) have a Class IV Rating, and (3) conduct operations in accordance with Part 145 of the Federal Aviation Regulations.

Aircraft fuel: See "Fuels and petroleum products" below.

• *Arts and cultural programs*

Sales of personal property to, and the use of personal property by, nonprofit arts or cultural organizations that are exempt under IRC Sec. 501(c)(3) and that are organized and operated primarily for the presentation or support of arts or cultural programming, activities, or services (including symphony orchestras, theatrical groups, arts and cultural services organizations, local arts councils, visual arts organizations, and media arts organizations) are exempt from Illinois sales and use tax (35 ILCS 105/3-5; 35 ILCS 110/3-5; 35 ILCS 115/3-5; 35 ILCS 120/2-5).

Such organizations may not make tax-free purchases unless they have an identification number issued by the Department of Revenue.

• *Charitable, religious, or educational institutions*

The following sales by exclusively charitable, religious, and educational organizations are exempt (35 ILCS 105/2; 35 ILCS 120/1; 86 Ill. Adm. Code 130.2005):

— sales made to the organizations' members, students, or patients primarily for the purposes of the selling organization (such as Bible sales by a church to its members);

— infrequent sales that are noncompetitive with business establishments (such as sales of Girl Scout cookies); and

— sales at social activities (such as dinners, carnivals, and rummage sales) held occasionally (not more than twice yearly).

The use tax does not apply to nonprofit organizations operated primarily for the recreation of persons 55 years of age or older (86 Ill. Adm. Code Secs. 130.2005, 150.325; CCH ILLINOIS TAX REPORTS, ¶ 67-255, 68-736). See ¶1703 for the ROT/UT exemption for sales to such organizations. See also "Schools," below.

Sales of religious materials: The U.S. Supreme Court has upheld the imposition of the sales tax on religious materials sold at evangelistic crusades and the imposition of the use tax on mail-order sales of these materials (*Jimmy Swaggart Ministries v. Board of Equalization of California* (1990, US SCt), 493 US 378, 110 SCt 688; CCH ILLINOIS TAX REPORTS, ¶ 400-422).

Limited liability companies: Sales to limited liability companies (LLCs) organized and operated exclusively for educational purposes are exempt. However, LLCs that are engaged in offering professional, trade, or business seminars; courses in self-improvement; and correspondence courses are not operated exclusively for educational purposes.

¶1702

Sales to university students: University food facilities must maintain an auditable and verifiable record system for tacking tax-free sales to students in food facilities open to the public. On-campus, non-university restaurant sales are all taxable. Sales of nonfood items on campus, including by the school, are taxable to students as ongoing competitive sales. (*General Information Letter ST 11-0108-GIL,* Department of Revenue, December 28, 2011, CCH ILLINOIS TAX REPORTS,¶402-440)

• *Coal-burning devices*

The purchase, use, and transfer of property defined as "low sulfur dioxide emission coal fueled devices" are exempt. "Low sulfur dioxide emission coal fueled devices" are devices sold, used, or intended for the purpose of burning, combusting, or converting locally available coal in a manner that eliminates or significantly reduces the need for additional sulfur dioxide abatement otherwise required under state or federal air emission standards. Such devices include all machinery, equipment, and structures and all related apparatus of a coal gasification facility, including coal-feeding equipment, designed to convert locally available coal into a low-sulfur gaseous fuel and to manage all waste and byproduct streams (35 ILCS 105/2a-1; 35 ILCS 110/2b; 35 ILCS 115/2b; 35 ILCS 120/1a-1).

• *Common carriers*

Sales of personal property to a common carrier by rail or motor are exempt if the carrier receives possession of the property in Illinois and transports the property outside the state (86 Ill. Adm. Code 130.2090). See also "Rolling stock," below.

• *Computer software*

Computer software is specifically subject to tax as tangible personal property. However, custom-made software (adapted to specific individualized requirements) or software used to operate exempt machinery used in manufacturing or assembling is exempt (35 ILCS 105/37; 35 ILCS 105/3-25; 35 ILCS 110/30; 35 ILCS 110/3-25; 35 ILCS 115/; 35 ILCS 115/3-25; 35 ILCS 120/20; 35 ILCS 120/2-25; 86 Ill. Adm. Code 130.1935; see also *General Information Letter ST 12-0022-GIL,* Department of Revenue, April 27, 2012, CCH ILLINOIS TAX REPORTS,¶402-490).

The Illinois retailers' occupation (sales) and use tax treatment of computer software sales, licenses, and maintenance agreements is outlined in a general information letter issued by the Illinois Department of Revenue. A license of software is not taxable if the license is evidenced by a written agreement signed by the licensor and customer and if the license restricts the customer's duplication, use, and transfer of the software and meets other specific requirements. (*General Information Letter ST 10-0003-GIL,* Illinois Department of Revenue, January 29, 2010, CCH ILLINOIS TAX REPORTS,¶402-080)

The term "computer software" includes software used to operate machinery and equipment used in (1) the generation of electricity for wholesale or retail sale; (2) the generation or treatment of natural or artificial gas for wholesale or retail sale that is delivered to customers through pipes, pipelines, or mains; or (3) the treatment of water for wholesale or retail sale that is delivered to customers through pipes, pipelines, or mains (35 ILCS 105/3-25; 35 ILCS 110/3-25; 35 ILCS 115/3; 35 ILCS 120/2-25).

Software maintenance: Maintenance agreements that cover computer software are treated the same as maintenance agreements for other types of tangible personal property. If the charges for the agreements are included in the selling price of the property, those charges are subject to tax. However, no tax is incurred on the maintenance services or parts when the repair or servicing is performed. On the other hand, if the repair or maintenance agreements are sold separately from the property, those agreements are not taxable. However, when maintenance or repair services or parts are provided under those agreements, the service providers incur use tax based on their cost price of the items transferred to customers. (*General Information Letter ST 10-0003-GIL*, Illinois Department of Revenue, January 29, 2010, CCH ILLINOIS TAX REPORTS, ¶ 402-080; see also *General Information Letter ST 13-0027-GIL*, Illinois Department of Revenue, May 28, 2013, CCH ILLINOIS TAX REPORTS, ¶ 402-674)

Licensed canned software: The licensing of canned computer software by a software developer to its customer met the requirements for exemption from Illinois sales tax. The software license (1) was evidenced by a written agreement signed by the licensor and the customer, (2) restricted the customer's duplication and use of the software, and (3) prohibited the customer from licensing, sublicensing, or transferring the software to a third party (except to a related party) without the permission and continued control of the licensor. In addition, the licensor had a policy of providing another copy at minimal or no charge if the customer lost or damaged the software, or permitting the licensee to make and keep an archival copy. Finally, the customer was required to destroy or return all copies of the software to the licensor at the end of the license period. Neither the transfer of the software at issue nor any subsequent software update was subject to sales tax (*Private Letter Ruling, ST 05-0009-PLR*, Illinois Department of Revenue, August 25, 2005, CCH ILLINOIS TAX REPORTS, ¶ 401-582; see also *Private Letter Ruling, ST 16-0003-PLR*, Illinois Department of Revenue, March 23, 2016, CCH ILLINOIS TAX REPORTS, ¶ 403-117).

Software license agreements that authorize the transfer of the software without permission of the licensor are subject to sales and use tax. A software license must meet numerous requirements to constitute a nontaxable retail sale, including that the license agreement be in writing and restrictions on the duplication and transferring of the software. (*General Information Letter ST 14-0034-GIL*, Illinois Department of Revenue, July 29, 2014, CCH ILLINOIS TAX REPORTS, ¶ 402-835; see also *Private Letter Ruling, ST 14-0004-PLR*, Illinois Department of Revenue, July 24, 2014, CCH ILLINOIS TAX REPORTS, ¶ 402-833)

A reseller of software will not be liable for sales tax, where a license agreement exists between the original seller of the software and the customer, provided that the reseller maintains a copy of the signed license agreement in its records and other criteria concerning the license transaction are met (*General Information Letter ST 13-0032-GIL*, Illinois Department of Revenue, June 19, 2013, CCH ILLINOIS TAX REPORTS, ¶ 402-689).

CCH Caution: Online Acceptance of Software License Terms

Software license agreements in which a customer electronically accepts the terms by clicking "I accept" while online do not meet the exemption requirement of a written agreement signed by the licensor and customer (*Private Letter Ruling, ST 06-0010-PLR*, Illinois Department of Revenue, June 29, 2006, CCH ILLINOIS TAX REPORTS, ¶ 401-712).

Providing an electronic signature whereby a customer electronically accepts the terms of a software license agreement by clicking "I agree" on the Web page being viewed does not satisfy the exemption requirement of a written "signed" agreement by the licensor and customer. Therefore, the transfer of the software and any subsequent software updates are taxable (*Private Letter Ruling, ST 06-0005-PLR*, Illinois Department of Revenue, May 16, 2006, CCH ILLINOIS TAX REPORTS, ¶ 401-707).

An electronic resale certificate should contain all of the information required by the state, and that it does not find that simply requiring a customer to check a box on an online application to acknowledge the customer's eligibility for resale or exemption adequate to meet the signature requirement required by law. The department further emphasizes that if a signature is not obtained in accordance with its rules, a sale will be presumed to be a sale at retail. (*General Information Letter ST 10-0009*, Illinois Department of Revenue, February 25, 2010, CCH ILLINOIS TAX REPORTS, ¶ 402-086)

¶ 1702

Software upgrades and technical support: The provision of software upgrades and technical support to Illinois customers by out-of-state computer software developers may be exempt from retailers' occupation (sales) tax if the software was a custom software program and the developer sold the maintenance agreement in conjunction with the sale of the custom computer software. With regard to technical support and maintenance, the computer software developer provided its customers with access to a technical support center via e-mail or telephone. No physical property was delivered to the customer. Therefore, the software would be exempt from retailers' occupation (sales) tax if it was custom software. However, if maintenance or parts were provided for particular pieces of equipment for stated periods of time at predetermined fees, the service provider would incur a use tax for the property transferred to the customer incident to completion of the maintenance service. (*General Information Letter ST 01-0206-GIL*, Illinois Department of Revenue, September 28, 2001, CCH ILLINOIS TAX REPORTS, ¶ 401-306.)

Sales of customer lists: Sales of Internet names and digital signatures acquired by an online service were not subject to retailers' occupation (sales) or service occupation (sales) taxes because the names did not constitute tangible personal property subject to tax. Further, the names were deemed custom computer software because each name was a unique identifier customized for individual customers. However, any software used to create, encrypt, decrypt, or read digital signatures may be subject to tax. (*General Information Letter ST 01-0148-GIL*, Illinois Department of Revenue, August 6, 2001, CCH ILLINOIS TAX REPORTS, ¶ 401-316.)

Digitized products: Information or data that is downloaded electronically, such as downloaded books, musical recordings, newspapers or magazines, does not constitute the transfer of tangible personal property. These types of transactions represent the transfer of intangibles and are thus not subject to retailers' occupation and use taxes (86 Ill. Adm. Code 130.2105(a)(3)).

A company in the business of providing business financial information online is not liable for Illinois sales and use tax on fees charged customers for accessing an online database when the company does not transfer any software or other tangible personal property to those customers. Information or data that is electronically transferred or downloaded is not considered the transfer of tangible personal property. (*General Information Letter ST 10-0121-GIL*, Illinois Department of Revenue, December 22, 2010, CCH ILLINOIS TAX REPORTS, ¶ 402-268)

Practitioner Comment: Licensed Software

Canned, modified or custom software that is transferred subject to a license agreement (arguably, even a perpetual license) is not subject to Illinois sales tax if: (1) there is a written agreement signed by the licensor and customer; (2) the agreement restricts the customer's duplication and use of the software; (3) the agreement prohibits the customer from licensing, sublicensing, or transferring the software to a third party; (4) the licensor provides another copy of the software at minimal or no charge if the customer loses or damages the software; and (5) the customer destroys or returns all copies of the software to the licensor at the end of the license period. But, if the software license is exempt from Illinois sales/use taxes, it might be subject to Chicago personal property lease transaction taxes (see ¶ 2304).

Jordan M. Goodman, Esq., Horwood Marcus & Berk Chartered

- *Convention halls*

A municipality may incorporate a public facilities corporation for the purposes of acquiring a site for a municipal convention hall; constructing, building, and equipping a hall on that site; and collecting revenues from the hall without profit to the hall, its officers, or its directors (65 ILCS 5/11-65-10). The use or sale of tangible personal property sold to a public facilities corporation for purposes of constructing or furnishing the hall is exempt from the state use and occupation taxes (65 ILCS 5/11-65-15). In addition, all real property and a hall owned by the corporation armotore exempt from property tax. These exemptions also apply to any existing corporations and halls that otherwise comply with the law.

- *County fair associations*

Sales to a nonprofit Illinois county fair association for use in conducting, operating, or promoting a county fair are exempt (35 ILCS 105/3-5; 35 ILCS 110/3-5; 35 ILCS 115/3-5; 35 ILCS 120/2-5).

- *Drugs*

Sales of prescription and nonprescription drugs are taxed at the special rate of 1%. See below under "Medicines and medical appliances" for further details. Drugs purchased for use by a person receiving medical assistance under the Illinois Public Aid Code and residing in a licensed long-term care facility are exempt from the service occupation tax. Nonprofit organizations that sell food in a food distribution program at a price below the retail cost of the food are exempt from the retailers' occupation, service occupation, use, and service use taxes on their purchases of drugs (35 ILCS 105/3-10; 35 ILCS 110/3-10; 35 ILCS 115/3-100; 35 ILCS 120/2-10).

Beginning January 1, 2014, the definition of "prescription and nonprescription drugs" for purposes of the sales, use, retailers' occupation and service occupation taxes includes medical cannabis purchased from a registered dispensing organization under the Compassionate Use of Medical Cannabis Pilot Program Act (discussed at ¶1520).

- *Enterprise zones, River Edge redevelopment zones, and high impact businesses*

Purchases of manufacturing machinery and equipment used by a qualified business located in an enterprise zone are exempt. Included in the exemption are repair and replacement parts, fuels, raw materials, and supplies (35 ILCS 105/120; 35 ILCS 110/12; 35 ILCS 115/12; 35 ILCS 120/1d; 86 Ill. Adm. Code 130.1951).

To qualify for the exemption, businesses are required to meet one of the following conditions: (1) creation of 200 full-time jobs in Illinois; (2) retention of 2,000 full-time jobs in Illinois; or (3) investment of $40 million. In addition, the businesses must be located in the enterprise zone and must retain 90% of the jobs in place when the exemption is granted. A construction contractor or other entity must not make tax-free purchases unless it has an active exemption certificate or high impact business location certificate at the time of purchase (35 ILCS 120/5k; 35 ILCS 120/5l).

Building materials: An exemption from ROT, SOT, UT, and SUT is provided for building materials that are to be physically incorporated into real estate in an enterprise zone established by a county or municipality or River Edge redevelopment zone. The exemption may be limited by specific enterprise zone ordinance requirements (20 ILCS 655/5.5; 35 ILCS 120/5k; 35 ILCS 110/12; *General Information Letter ST 13-0007-GIL*, Illinois Department of Revenue, February 5, 2013, CCH ILLINOIS TAX REPORTS, ¶402-637).

Beginning July 1, 2013, the building materials exemption will be available only to those contractors or other entities with a certificate issued by the Illinois Department of Revenue. When purchasing tax exempt building materials, the purchaser must submit a signed statement to the retailer that contains the certificate number, the zone, the project, and the materials being purchased. Form EZ-1, *Building Materials Exemption Certification,* contains all necessary information and will be provided to certificate holders when they receive their certificates. (*Informational Bulletin FY 2013-16,* Illinois Department of Revenue, June 2013, CCH ILLINOIS TAX REPORTS, ¶ 402-664)

A retailer must obtain the purchaser's building materials exemption certificate to document the exemption (20 ILCS 655/8.1(a); 35 ILCS 120/2-54(d)). A construction contractor or other entity must not make tax-free purchases unless it has an active exemption certificate at the time of purchase. On request from the corporate authorities of a municipality in which a building project is located, the Department of Revenue will issue a River Edge building materials exemption certificate for each construction contractor or other entity identified by the corporate authorities.

High impact business: A "high impact business" is an energy-related business that intends to invest at least $12 million in placing qualified property in service and to create 500 full-time equivalent jobs or one that intends to invest at least $30 million in placing qualified property in service and to retain 1,500 full-time jobs. (20 ILCS 655/5.5) A high impact business may qualify for the above building materials exemption even if it is not located within an enterprise zone. See "High impact businesses" below for additional information:

— a business that intends to establish new electric generating facilities through newly constructed generation plants or expand an existing generation plant;

— a business that intends to establish new coal mines, re-establish coal production at a closed coal mine, or expand production at an existing coal mine;

— a business that intends to establish a new gasification facility;

— a business that intends to establish new transmission facilities or upgrade existing transmission facilities that transfer electricity from supply points to delivery points;

— a business that intends to establish a new wind power facility or expand an existing electric generation facility using wind energy devices with a nameplate capacity of at least 0.5 megawatts.

Reporting requirements: High impact businesses and businesses receiving tax incentives in enterprise zones and river edge redevelopment zones must file certain reports, depending on the tax benefits claimed; see *Informational Bulletin FY 2014-11,* Illinois Department of Revenue, March 2014, CCH ILLINOIS TAX REPORTS, ¶ 402-780.

• *Farm machinery*

Sales of new or used farm machinery or equipment certified by the purchaser to be used primarily for production agriculture or Illinois or federal agricultural programs and sales of replacement parts for such machinery and equipment are exempt. Aquaculture is included within "production agriculture." Equipment purchased for lease is included in the exemption (86 Ill. Adm. Code Sec. 130.305). Horticultural polyhouses or hoop houses used for propagating, growing, or overwintering plants are considered farm machinery and equipment and are exempt. The farm machinery exemption also includes husbandry tools and instruments, registered nurse wagons, agricultural chemical and fertilizer spreaders, and agricultural chemical tender tanks and dry boxes. Also exempt are computers, sensors, software, and related equipment used primarily in the computer-assisted operation of production agriculture facilities, equipment, and activities such as the collection, monitoring, and correlation of animal crop data for purposes of formulating animal diets and agricultural chemicals, and precision farming equipment that is installed or purchased for installation on farm machinery and equipment.

¶1702

For examples of exempt machinery and equipment, see *General Information Letter ST 10-0026-GIL,* Illinois Department of Revenue, March 31, 2010, CCH ILLINOIS TAX REPORTS, ¶ 402-108.

Trailers used to transport crops, animal food products or animals do not qualify for the farm machinery and equipment exemption (*Compliance Alert: CA-2016-16,* Illinois Department of Revenue, June 2016, CCH ILLINOIS TAX REPORTS, ¶ 403-111).

• *Federal, state, and local governments*

Sales to and by a federal, state, or local governmental body, agency, or instrumentality are exempt (35 ILCS 105/3-5; 35 ILCS 120/2-5).

Documentation of exemption: Sales to a governmental body are subject to the Illinois retailers' occupation tax, the service occupation tax and the use tax, unless the governmental body has an active exemption identification "E-number." Sales to individual employees of the governmental body holding the E-number are not exempt. Sales to a governmental body holding an E-number may be documented by retaining a copy of the exemption letter or by recording the E-number in the seller's books and records. (*General Information Letter ST 10-0044-GIL,* Illinois Department of Revenue, May 18, 2010, CCH ILLINOIS TAX REPORTS, ¶ 402-135).

Retailers may not accept U.S. Government Bank cards beginning January 1, 2015, without an E-number. Sales made to individual government employees who will be reimbursed by the government are taxable even if the employee provides an E-number (86 Ill. Adm. Code Sec. 130.2080; 86 Ill. Adm. Code Sec. 130. ILLUSTRATION A, Illinois Department of Revenue, effective January 15, 2015).

Government contractors: Tangible personal property purchased by a government contractor is exempt where the contract with the government unit explicitly requires the contractor to sell the items purchased to the government unit. The contract must state that the government unit requires the contractor to provide the tangible personal property to the government unit but does not have to be item specific. For example, within the contract a statement that title to all tangible personal property must be transferred to the government unit is sufficient to allow for the exemption.

The supplier of the tangible personal property must keep a certificate of resale in its records (86 Ill. Adm. Code 130.2076).

Telecommunications: The Telecommunications Excise Tax Act does not authorize an exemption for a purchase of telecommunications by local governmental units. The exemptions available for sales tax purposes are not available for the telecommunications excise tax (*General Information Letter ST 12-0026-GIL,* Illinois Department of Revenue, June 15, 2012, issued September 2012, CCH ILLINOIS TAX REPORTS, ¶ 402-546).

• *Food*

Food sales for consumption off the premises are taxed at a special reduced rate (¶ 1601). Nonprofit organizations that sell food in a food distribution program at a price below the retail cost of the food are exempt from the retailers' occupation, service occupation, use, and service use taxes on their purchases of food for consumption off the premises. Until July 1, 2016, food for consumption off the premises purchased for use by a person receiving medical assistance under the Illinois Public Aid Code and residing in a licensed long-term care facility or an entity licensed under the MR/DD Community Care Act was exempt from the service occupation tax and use taxes. (35 ILCS 115/3-5; 35 ILCS 110/3-5; 35 ILCS 115/3-5; 35 ILCS 120/2-5)

In Cook County, a Regional Transportation Authority service occupation tax rate of 1.25% is imposed on a serviceman's cost price of food prepared for immediate consumption and transferred incident to a sale of service by an entity that is licensed under the MR/DD Community Care Act and is located in the metropolitan region. (70 ILCS 3615/4.03(f))

¶1702

The reduced rate does not apply to alcoholic beverages, candy, soft drinks, and food prepared for immediate consumption.

Food products are subject to the regular tax rate when they are served for immediate consumption and when facilities are provided for consumption on the seller's premises (86 Ill. Adm. Code Sec. 130.310). However, food prepared for immediate consumption and transferred incidental to a sale of service by an entity licensed under the Hospital Licensing Act, the Nursing Home Care Act, the Specialized Mental Health Rehabilitation Act, or the Child Care Act is subject to the reduced rate of SOT or SUT.

All food products sold through a vending machine, except soft drinks, hot food products, and candy are taxed at the reduced rate (35 ILCS 115/3-10; 35 ILCS 110/3-10; 35 ILCS 115/3-10; 35 ILCS 120/2-10).

The use of items such as nonreusable paper plates and cups, napkins, straws, and other packaging materials by persons engaged in the business of operating an eating establishment is considered a sale for resale and is exempt from tax.

Candy: "Food for human consumption that is to be consumed off the premises where it is sold," which qualifies for the reduced rate, does not include candy. "Candy" is defined as a preparation of sugar, honey, or other natural or artificial sweeteners in combination with chocolate, fruits, nuts, or other ingredients or flavorings in the form of bars, drops, or pieces. However, candy does not include any preparation that contains flour or requires refrigeration. (35 ILCS 115/3-10; 35 ILCS 110/3-10; 35 ILCS 115/3-10; 35 ILCS 120/2-10; *Informational Bulletin FY 2010-01,* Illinois Department of Revenue, July 2009, CCH ILLINOIS TAX REPORTS, ¶ 401-995)

Soft drinks: "Soft drinks," which are ineligible for the reduced rate, are defined as "non-alcoholic beverages that contain natural or artificial sweeteners". However, "soft drinks" do not include beverages that contain milk or milk products, soy, rice or similar milk substitutes, or greater than 50% of vegetable or fruit juice by volume. (35 ILCS 115/3-10; 35 ILCS 110/3-10; 35 ILCS 115/3-10; 35 ILCS 120/2-10; *Informational Bulletin FY 2010-01,* Illinois Department of Revenue, July 2009, CCH ILLINOIS TAX REPORTS, ¶ 401-995)

• *Fuels and petroleum products*

Fuels to operate vessels on rivers bordering Illinois are not taxable when delivered to the vessel while afloat (35 ILCS 120/2-5; 86 Ill. Adm. Code 130.315).

Gasohol: In 2017, the Illinois legislature passed Senate Bill 9 and its first budget in over two years. Public Act 100-0022, effective July 6, 2017, implements the following change. Effective July 1, 2017, tax incentives related to gasohol were eliminated. Prior to the passage of Senate Bill 9 (Budget Bill), 80% of the proceeds from the sale of gasohol were subject to tax. With the passage of the bill, 100% of the proceeds from the sale of gasohol are taxable effective July 1, 2017. (35 ILCS 115/3-10; 35 ILCS 110/3-10; 35 ILCS 115/3-10; 35 ILCS 120/2-10)

Biodiesel and blended fuels: In 2017, the Illinois legislature passed Senate Bill 9 and its first budget in over two years. Public Act 100-0022, effective July 6, 2017, implements the following change. Sales of blended ethanol and 100% biodiesel fuels are not subject to Illinois Service Use Tax on or before on or before December 31, 2023. Prior to the passage of Senate Bill 9 (Budget Bill), these fuels would have been subject to tax effective December 31, 2018. (35 ILCS 115/3-10; 35 ILCS 110/3-10; 35 ILCS 115/3-10; 35 ILCS 120/2-10)

"Majority blended ethanol fuel" means motor fuel that contains not less than 70% and no more than 90% denatured ethanol and no less than 10% and no more than 30% gasoline (35 ILCS 105/3-44).

Jet fuel and petroleum products: Until August 16, 2018, jet fuel and petroleum products sold for a flight engaged in foreign trade or engaged in trade between the United States and any of its possessions is exempt (35 ILCS 105/3-5(12); 35 ILCS 110/3-5(8); 35 ILCS 115/3-5(8); 35 ILCS 120/2-5(22); 86 Ill. Adm. Code Sec. 130.321). Also, jet fuel and petroleum products sold to and used by a high-impact service facility located in an enterprise zone are exempt from sales and use tax. However, the business enterprise must have waived its right to exemption for charges imposed under the Public Utilities Act. (35 ILCS 115/3-12; 35 ILCS 110/3-12; 35 ILCS 115/3-12; 35 ILCS 120/2-1j)

• *Game or game birds*

Purchases of game or game birds at a game breeding and hunting preserve area are exempt (35 ILCS 115/3-5; 35 ILCS 110/3-5; 35 ILCS 115/3-5; 35 ILCS 120/2-5).

• *Graphic arts machinery and equipment*

In 2017, the Illinois legislature passed Senate Bill 9 and its first budget in over two years. Public Act 100-0022, effective July 6, 2017, implements the following change. The exemption from Illinois Retailers' Occupation Tax and Use Tax for machinery and equipment used for graphic arts was reinstated effective July 1, 2017. The exemption is included in the manufacturing and assembling machinery and equipment exemption. This exemption had previously sunset on August 30, 2014. Graphic arts equipment is defined as "graphic arts machinery and equipment, including repair and replacement parts, both new and used, and including that manufactured on special order, certified by the purchaser to be used primarily for graphic arts production, and including machinery and equipment purchased for lease. Equipment includes chemicals or chemicals acting as catalysts but only if the chemicals or chemicals acting as a catalyst effect a direct and immediate change upon a graphic arts product." (35 ILCS 115/3-5; 35 ILCS 110/3-5; 35 ILCS 115/3-5; 35 ILCS 120/2-5).

Practitioner Comment: Past versions of the Illinois graphic arts exemption have always contained automatic sunset provisions. The latest bill, however, makes the credit permanent and exempt from any sunset laws. The exemption becomes part of the manufacturing machinery and equipment exemption. *David W. Machemer, Esq., Horwood Marcus & Berk Chartered*

• *High-impact business*

A "high impact business" is one that intends to invest at least $12 million in placing qualified property in service and to create 500 full-time equivalent jobs or one that intends to invest at least $30 million in placing qualified property in service and to retain 1,500 full-time jobs (20 ILCS 655/5.5). Eligible businesses include the following (20 ILCS 655/5.5):

— a business that intends to establish new electric generating facilities through newly constructed generation plants or expand an existing generation plant;

— a business that intends to establish new coal mines, re-establish coal production at a closed coal mine, or expand production at an existing coal mine;

— a business that intends to establish a new gasification facility;

— a business that intends to establish new transmission facilities or upgrade existing transmission facilities that transfer electricity from supply points to delivery points;

— a business that intends to establish a new wind power facility or expand an existing electric generation facility using wind energy devices with a name-plate capacity of at least 0.5 megawatts.

¶1702

Tangible personal property to be used or consumed by a qualified high-impact business in the manufacture or assembly of tangible personal property for wholesale or retail sale or lease is exempt. Included in the exemption are repair and replacement parts, equipment, manufacturing fuels, and material and supplies. (35 ILCS 115/3-12; 35 ILCS 110/3-12; 35 ILCS 115/3-12; 35 ILCS 120/1d) A high impact business may qualify for the building materials exemption available to enterprise zone businesses even if it is not located within an enterprise zone.

Other tax benefits: For information on income tax benefits available to high-impact businesses, see ¶ 1205.

- *High-impact service facility machinery*

Machinery or equipment used in the operation of a high-impact service facility located in an enterprise zone is exempt. Exempt machinery and equipment include (1) motor-driven heavy equipment, other than rolling stock, that is used to transport parcels, machinery, or equipment, (2) trailers used to ship parcels, (3) equipment used to maintain and provide in-house services within the confines of the facility, and (4) automated machinery and equipment used to transport parcels and all component parts and computer software contained in the electronic control systems. (35 ILCS 115/3-12; 35 ILCS 110/3-12; 35 ILCS 115/3-12; 35 ILCS 120/2-1j)

- *Hospitals*

Tangible personal property sold to, or used by, owners of one or more hospitals licensed under the Hospital Licensing Act or operated under the University of Illinois Hospital Act, or a hospital affiliate that is not already exempt for sales and use tax purposes and meets the exemption requirements, is exempt from sales tax, use tax, service occupation tax (SOT) and service use tax (SUT) (35 ILCS 105/3-8; 35 ILCS 110/3-8; 35 ILCS 115/3-8; 35 ILCS 120/2-9).

A qualifying hospital satisfies the requirements for an exemption if the value of qualified services or activities performed by the hospital for the hospital year equals or exceeds the relevant hospital entity's estimated property tax liability for the calendar year in which the exemption or renewal of exemption is sought. The property tax liability is the amount of liability before any property tax exemption is deducted. (35 ILCS 105/3-8(b); 35 ILCS 110/3-8(b); 35 ILCS 115/3-8(b); 35 ILCS 120/2-9(b))

The following services and activities will be considered for purposes of qualifying for the exemption: charity care, health services to low-income and underserved individuals, subsidy of state or local governments, support for state health care programs for low-income individuals, dual-eligible subsidy, relief of the burden of government related to health care, or any other activity by the entity that the department determines relieves the burden of government or addresses the health of low-income or underserved individuals. (35 ILCS 105/3-8(c); 35 ILCS 110/3-8(c); 35 ILCS 115/3-8(c); 35 ILCS 120/2-9(c))

The services or activities must relate to the hospital that includes the property subject to the property tax liability. In a multi-state hospital system, the services must occur in Illinois and the property tax liability must be an Illinois liability. A hospital may elect to use either the value of the services or activities for the hospital year or the average value of those services or activities for the three fiscal years ending with the hospital year. (35 ILCS 105/3-8(d); 35 ILCS 110/3-8(d); 35 ILCS 115/3-8(d); 35 ILCS 120/2-9(d))

- *Intermodal terminal facility areas*

An exemption is allowed for qualified sales of building materials to be incorporated into real estate in a redevelopment project area within an intermodal terminal facility area by remodeling, rehabilitating, or new construction as part of an industrial or commercial project for which a Certificate of Eligibility for Sales Tax Exemption has been issued to the taxpayer. (35 ILCS 115/3-12; 35 ILCS 110/3-12; 35 ILCS 115/3-12; 35 ILCS 120/2-6; 86 Ill. Adm. Code 130.1953)

• *Internet access charges*

Charges for Internet access that do not include charges for the telephone line or other transmission charges or charges for canned computer software or other tangible personal property are generally not subject to ROT, UT, or telecommunications tax. Digital subscriber line (DSL) services purchased, used, or sold by providers of Internet access are exempt, effective July 1, 2008. DSL services purchased, used, or sold by nonproviders of Internet access remain subject to telecommunications tax (*Informational Bulletin FY 2008-18,* Illinois Department of Revenue, March 2006, CCH ILLINOIS TAX REPORTS, ¶401-670).

Federal Internet Tax Freedom Act: The federal Internet Tax Freedom Act (P.L. 105-277, 112 Stat 2681), as amended by P.L. 107-75, P.L. 108-435, and P.L. 110-108, bars state and local governments from imposing multiple and discriminatory taxes on electronic commerce, including taxes on Internet access, except those that were imposed and enforced prior to October 1, 1998. This moratorium expires on November 1, 2014.

• *Internet sales*

Charges for an online training course and live data feeds over the Internet are not subject to Illinois sales tax, use tax, service occupation tax, or service use tax because the viewing and downloading of text and other data over the Internet is not considered to be a transfer of tangible personal property. However, the transfer of any canned software or update of canned software is considered the transfer of tangible personal property and is subject to sales and use tax, regardless of the means of delivery (*General Information Letter ST 05-0057-GIL,* Illinois Department of Revenue, July 15, 2005, ILLINOIS TAX REPORTS, ¶401-573).

Shipping charges: Shipping charges on purchases of merchandise from a retailer's Internet store were properly included in the selling price of the merchandise and thus were subject to Illinois retailers' occupation (sales) and use tax. Customers could not submit their Internet orders unless and until they selected a shipping option. Because customers were required to buy the delivery service, the cost of shipping was part of the taxable selling price. (*Kean v. Wal-Mart Stores, Inc.,* Illinois Supreme Court, No. 107771, November 19, 2009, CCH ILLINOIS TAX REPORTS, ¶402-040)

• *Interstate commerce*

Sales by businesses engaged in interstate commerce are exempt if Illinois taxation is prohibited under the United States Constitution or under federal statute (¶1512; see also ¶1508).

Temporary storage (expired): Tangible personal property was exempt (through June 30, 2016) if purchased from an Illinois retailer by a taxpayer engaged in centralized purchasing activities in Illinois who, upon receipt of the property, temporarily stored the property in Illinois for the purpose of (1) transporting it outside the state for use or consumption solely outside Illinois, or (2) being processed, fabricated, or manufactured into, attached to, or incorporated into other tangible personal property outside Illinois and consumed solely outside Illinois. (35 ILCS 105/3-55; 35 ILCS 110/3-45; 35 ILCS 115/3-5; 35 ILCS 120/2-5)

On or after July 1, 2016, holders of expanded temporary storage permits issued by the Illinois Department of Revenue no longer can make tax-free purchases of tangible personal property using their expanded temporary storage permits, and retailers should no longer allow a sales tax exemption for purchases made by

¶1702

expanded temporary storage permit holders. *(Informational Bulletin FY 2016-12,* Illinois Department of Revenue, June 2016, CCH ILLINOIS TAX REPORTS, ¶ 403-110)

Practitioner Comment: Leveling the Playing Field

For many years now, Illinois has had a temporary storage exemption from use tax that allowed a buyer to purchase goods from a seller located outside of Illinois and not pay Illinois use tax if the goods were going to be incorporated into another product and shipped outside of Illinois for use outside of Illinois. (55 ILCS 105/3-55(e)). This exemption did not apply to sales made by Illinois retailers. Thus, if the buyer was going to incorporate its purchase into another product and ship it outside Illinois, it was more effective from a tax prospective for a buyer to make its purchase from an out-of-state seller so that the use tax exemption would apply.

In order to level the playing field between Illinois and out-of-state retailers, the Illinois General Assembly added a sales/use tax exemption, effective January 1, 2002, that allows Illinois retailers to sell property tax-free to a taxpayer engaged in centralized purchasing activities in Illinois who will temporarily store the property in Illinois for the purpose of (1) subsequently transporting it outside Illinois for use or consumption thereafter solely outside Illinois, or (2) being processed, fabricated, or manufactured into, attached to, or incorporated into other tangible personal property to be transported outside Illinois and consumed solely outside Illinois (35 ILCS 120/2-5(38)).

Jordan M. Goodman, Esq., Horwood Marcus & Berk Chartered

• *Legal tender, currency or gold or silver coinage*

Proceeds from the sale of bullion, legal tender, currency medallions, or gold or silver coinage issued by the United States, Illinois, or any foreign country are exempt (35 ILCS 115/3-5; 35 ILCS 110/3-5; 35 ILCS 115/3-5; 35 ILCS 120/2-5). "Bullion" means gold, silver, or platinum in a bulk state with a purity of 980 or more parts per 1,000.

• *Maintenance agreements*

Transfers of tangible personal property pursuant to a maintenance agreement are exempt from the service occupation and service use taxes. However, purchases of such tangible personal property by service providers are subject to the retailers' occupation and use taxes (¶ 1504, ¶ 1511).

• *Mandatory service charges*

A mandatory service charge that is stated on a customer's bill separately from the charge for food and beverages is exempt (35 ILCS 115/3-5; 35 ILCS 110/3-5; 35 ILCS 115/3-5; 35 ILCS 120/2-5).

This exemption applies to the extent that the charges are turned over as tips or as a substitute for tips to the employees who participated directly in preparing, serving, hosting, or cleaning up the food or beverages for which the service charge is imposed.

• *Manufacturing*

Sales of machinery and equipment, including chemical catalysts effecting a direct and immediate change, used primarily in the manufacturing or assembling of tangible personal property for wholesale or retail sale or lease are exempt (35 ILCS 105/3-50).

The manufacturer's exemption from the ROT, the UT, the SOT, and the SUT applies to purchases of machinery, equipment, and material that are primarily (more than 50%) used in a manufacturing process or an assembling process that results in the production of tangible personal property for sale or lease. Machinery and equipment used to repair or maintain other exempt machinery or equipment, or to manufacture exempt machinery and equipment for in-house use are exempt. Lessors of qualified machinery and equipment qualify for the exemption. (35 ILCS 105/3-50, 120/2-45, 110/2, 115/2, 105/3-85, and 110/3-70)

The exemption includes replacement machinery and parts and equipment used in the maintenance or repair of such machinery. Ready-mix concrete trucks have been held exempt under these provisions by the Illinois Supreme Court (*Van's Material Co., Inc. v. Department of Revenue* (1989, SCt), 131 Ill2d 196, 545 NE2d 695; CCH ILLINOIS TAX REPORTS, ¶ 400-412). Sales of computers are exempt when used to operate machinery and equipment in a computer-assisted design or a computer-assisted manufacturing (CAD/CAM) system. However, computer equipment used to assist in design work in connection with the taxpayer's business of manufacturing special order machinery and equipment was not exempt, because the computer equipment, though essential to the taxpayer's business, was not directly used to manufacture the special order machinery and equipment. (*Administrative Hearing Decision No. ST 01-16*, Illinois Department of Revenue, Office of Administrative Hearings, August 20, 2001, CCH ILLINOIS TAX REPORTS, ¶ 401-298)

Also exempt is machinery or equipment used in the operation of a high-impact parcel service facility located in an enterprise zone.

Catalysts: The Illinois Circuit Court held that if chemicals cause a direct and immediate physical change to a product in the manufacturing process, the chemicals qualify for a use tax exemption for manufacturing. A glass manufacturer was entitled to a refund because the nitrogen and hydrogen used in its manufacturing process qualify for the exemption for machine and equipment used primarily in the manufacturing or assembling of tangible personal property for wholesale or retail sale or lease under 35 ILCS 105/3-5(18). The exemption includes chemicals that "effect a direct and immediate change upon a product being manufactured." (35 ILCS 105/3-50(4))

The Court determined that the chemicals need not react with the final product to effect a direct and immediate change to the glass. The chemicals used had the effect of changing the glass' temperature, physical composition and texture; therefore, the glass being manufactured underwent a recognizable immediate physical change. Further, the effects were direct, because no further steps in the manufacturing process were required to cause a range of vital changes on the glass. As a result, the Court determined the chemicals were catalysts and qualified for the exemption. (*PPG Industries, Inc. v. The Department of Revenue*, Circuit Court, Cook County Judicial Circuit, No. 13 L 050140, September 9, 2014, CCH ILLINOIS TAX REPORTS, ¶ 402-886)

Practitioner Comment: Exemption for Catalytic Chemicals

The Circuit Court reversed the administrative hearings decision (No. UT 13-07) which had held that the chemicals in this case were not exempt because they did not directly contact the glass, *i.e.* the product being manufactured. The administrative hearings decision's interpretation of the exemption was narrower than provided by the statute, which opened the door it to be challenged and overruled by the Circuit Court.

Jennifer A. Zimmerman, Esq., Horwood Marcus & Berk, Chartered

---

Exclusions from exemption: The machinery and equipment exemption does not apply to machinery and equipment, repair and replacement parts, or in-house manufactured machinery and equipment used in (35 ILCS 105/3-50; 35 ILCS 120/2-45; 86 Ill. Adm. Code 130.330):

— the generation of electricity for wholesale or retail sale;

— the generation or treatment of natural or artificial gas for wholesale or retail sale that is delivered to customers through pipes, pipelines, or mains; or

— the treatment of water for wholesale or retail sale that is delivered to customers through pipes, pipelines, or mains.

Special ordered equipment: Sales of special machinery, tools, dies, jigs, patterns, gauges, or other similar equipment are exempt from ROT if the purchaser employs the seller primarily for the seller's skill to design and produce the property on special order, if the property has use or value only for the specific purpose for which it is produced, and if the property has commercial value only to the purchaser. The seller is considered to be engaged in a service occupation and is liable for SOT. (86 Ill. Adm. Code 130.2115)

Scrap: A manufacturer was not qualified for a manufacturing exemption on the 1% to 2% of its purchased materials that were spoiled or damaged in the manufacturing process and discarded. Property used or consumed in the manufacturing process is taxable to the extent it is not physically incorporated into the item that is manufactured and subsequently sold. Raw materials that become scrap are subject to tax on their cost price. Materials that are subject to some production process and then are spoiled are subject to tax on the lower of their fair market value or cost price (*General Information Letter ST 05-0097-GIL,* Illinois Department of Revenue, October 13, 2005, CCH ILLINOIS TAX REPORTS, ¶401-611).

• *Medicines and medical appliances*

Prescription and nonprescription medicines, drugs, medical appliances, hearing aids, eyeglasses, contact lenses, insulin, urine-testing utensils, syringes, and needles used by diabetics are subject to a 1% tax (86 Ill. Adm. Code Sec. 130.310). Through June 30, 2016, these items were exempt from the service occupation tax and use tax when purchased for use by a person receiving medical assistance under the Illinois Public Aid Code and residing in a licensed long-term care facility, nursing home, an intermediate care facility for the developmentally disabled, or a long-term care for under age 22 facility (35 ILCS 105/3-5(30)).

In order for a medicine or drug to qualify for the 1% rate of tax, the medicine or drug must purport to have a medicinal quality on its label. A medicinal claim is a written claim on the label that the product is intended to cure or treat disease, illness, injury, or pain or that the product is intended to mitigate the symptoms of such disease, illness, injury, or pain. The low rate of tax applies only to medicines and medical appliances for human use (86 Ill. Adm. Code Sec. 130.310).

Modifications to a motor vehicle for the purpose of rendering it usable by a disabled person are taxable at the 1% sales and use tax rate (¶1601). For information on what equipment and modifications qualify for the reduced rate, see *General Information Letter ST 10-0041-GIL,* Illinois Department of Revenue, May 14, 2010, CCH ILLINOIS TAX REPORTS, ¶402-132.

Medical appliances: In order for an item to qualify as a medical appliance the item must be intended by its manufacturer for use in directly substituting for a malfunctioning part of the body. (86 Ill. Adm. Code 130.310(c))

Grooming and hygiene products: "Nonprescription medicines and drugs" (which qualify for the reduced rate) do not include grooming and hygiene products, which are defined as soaps and cleaning solutions, shampoo, toothpaste, mouthwash, antiperspirants, and sun tan lotions and screens, unless those products are available by prescription only, regardless of whether the products are over-the-counter-drugs. An "over-the-counter-drug" is a drug for human use that contains a label that identifies the product as a drug as required by federal regulation (21 C.F.R. §201.66). The over-the-counter-drug label includes (1) a "Drug Facts" panel or (2) a statement of active ingredients contained in the compound, substance, or preparation. (35 ILCS 115/3-10; 35 ILCS 110/3-10; 35 ILCS 115/3-10; 35 ILCS 120/2-10; *Informational Bulletin FY 2010-01,* Illinois Department of Revenue, July 2009, CCH ILLINOIS TAX REPORTS, ¶401-995)

Feminine hygiene products: Beginning January 1, 2017, menstrual pads, tampons, and menstrual cups are exempt from Illinois sales and use taxes (35 ILCS 105/3-5(37); (35 ILCS 110/3-5(29); (35 ILCS 155/3-5(30); (35 ILCS 120/3-5(42); *Informational Bulletin FY 2017-03*, Illinois Department of Revenue, August 2016, CCH ILLINOIS TAX REPORTS,¶ 403-120).

Veterinarians: A regulation addresses the difficulties experienced by veterinarians in determining their tax obligations. In particular, the determination of tax liability for service transactions has been complicated by changes in the way that many veterinary products, such as flea and tick medications, are marketed. The regulation sets out the requirements that must be met in order to establish a service (or retail) transaction. (86 Ill. Adm. Code Sec. 130.2165)

• *Mining*

Exemptions from sales tax, use tax, service occupation tax, and service use tax are available for the purchase of equipment used for coal and aggregate exploration, mining, off-highway hauling, processing, maintenance, and reclamation, including replacement parts and equipment purchased for lease (35 ILCS 105/3-5(16); 35 ILCS 110/3-5(12); 35 ILCS 115/3-5(12); 35 ILCS 120/2-5(21)). The exemptions are scheduled to sunset effective August 16, 2018.

Regulations provide examples of exempt equipment and activities that do and that do not constitute coal exploration, mining, off-highway hauling, processing, or maintenance (86 Ill. Adm. Code 130.350; 86 Ill. Adm. Code 130.351; 86 Ill. Adm. Code 130.345).

• *Motor vehicles*

A motor vehicle purchased by a nonresident who has a driveaway vehicle permit or out-of-state registration plates that the buyer will attach to the vehicle upon returning to his or her home state is exempt (35 ILCS 105/3-55). However, the exemption does not apply if the other state does not allow a reciprocal exemption for the use of a motor vehicle sold and delivered in that state to an Illinois resident to be titled in Illinois (*Informational Bulletin FY 2005-13*, Illinois Department of Revenue, January 2005, CCH ILLINOIS TAX REPORTS, ¶ 401-523). See also ¶ 1703.

The Department of Revenue publishes a chart that lists the states that do not provide a reciprocal exemption to Illinois residents and specifies the tax rate to be used to compute tax due on vehicles/trailers purchased in Illinois by residents of such states. These states and tax rates are: Arizona (5.6%), California (6.25%), Florida (6.0%), Hawaii (4.0%), Indiana (6.25%), Massachusetts (6.25%), Michigan (6.0%), and South Carolina (5.0% up to a maximum of $300) (*Reciprocal—Non-Reciprocal Vehicle Tax Rate Chart*, Illinois Department of Revenue, January 2016, CCH ILLINOIS TAX REPORTS,¶ 403-084).

If the motor vehicle is then used in Illinois for 30 or more days in a calendar year, the purchaser is liable for use tax on the purchase price of that vehicle (see ¶ 1703).

Documentation of nonresidency: A retailer claiming the exemption must keep evidence that the purchaser is not a resident of Illinois, along with the records related to the sale. If the purchaser is a natural person, the retailer's retention of a copy of the purchaser's permanent non-Illinois driver's license is prima facie evidence that the purchaser is a nonresident eligible for the exemption. The retailer must also obtain and keep a certification of nonresidency from the purchaser. A corporation, partnership, limited liability company, trust, or other purchaser that is not a natural person will be deemed a resident of the state or foreign country under whose laws the purchaser was incorporated, created, or organized, as well as the state or foreign country of the purchaser's commercial domicile, if different. The retailer must obtain from the purchaser and retain a certificate of this information. (86 Ill. Adm. Code 130.605)

¶1702

CCH Advisory: Sales of RVs and Trailers Registered in Indiana Exempt

Recreational vehicles or cargo trailers sold by Illinois dealers, with delivery in Illinois, but titling and registration in Indiana, are exempt from Illinois sales and use tax if (1) a drive-away permit is issued or (2) the Indiana purchaser has vehicle registration plates to transfer to the vehicle upon returning to Indiana. Watercraft trailers may qualify for the exemption if they meet the definition of a "cargo trailer" (*Informational Bulletin FY 2006-11*, Illinois Department of Revenue, June 2006, CCH ILLINOIS TAX REPORTS, ¶401-676).

The exemption for purchases of motor vehicles by nonresidents does not apply to (1) a watercraft, personal watercraft, or boat equipped with an inboard motor, (2) all-terrain vehicles, (3) motorcycles or motor driven cycles not properly manufactured or equipped for general highway use, (4) off-highway motorcycles, or (5) snowmobiles. If a watercraft, personal watercraft, or boat is included with the sale of a trailer, the trailer may qualify for exemption. If the two items are sold together for one non-itemized price, only the gross receipts representing the selling price of the trailer are exempt. (86 Ill. Adm. Code Sec. 130.605)

Practitioner Comment: Motor Vehicle Exemption for Out-of-State Buyers

Dealers are required to collect Illinois sales tax from certain Illinois nonresidents on motor vehicles and trailer sales. Specifically, the Illinois' "out-of-state buyer" exemption is no longer available to nonresidents when the vehicle will be titled in a state that does not give Illinois residents an "out-of-state buyer" exemption on vehicles to be titled in Illinois.

When the law changed, Illinois dealers were required to charge sales tax on vehicles purchased by Indiana and Michigan residents, but the "out-of-state buyer" exemption applied to Iowa and Missouri residents. When the exemption does not apply, the applicable tax rate is the lesser of the nonresident's state sales tax rate or 6.25%.

Horwood Marcus & Berk Chartered

A motor vehicle is exempt if it is donated to a public school or a qualified private or vocational school that is determined by the Illinois Department of Revenue to be organized and operated exclusively for educational purposes.

Rental vehicles: Tax does not apply to motor vehicles used for automobile renting as defined in the Automobile Renting Occupation and Use Tax Act (¶1509, ¶1517)(35 ILCS 105/3-5(10); 35 ILCS 110/2(4a-5); 35 ILCS 115/2(d-1.1); 35 ILCS 120/2-5(5); 86 Ill. Adm. Code Sec. 130.120; *Informational Bulletin FY 2008-12*, Illinois Department of Revenue, February 2008, CCH ILLINOIS TAX REPORTS, ¶401-860). The exemption was repealed from September 1, 2007, through January 10, 2008.

Interim use exemption: A leased motor vehicle is eligible for the interim use exemption if the leased vehicle remains in the vehicle dealer's inventory and is available for sale during the lease period. For example, if a dealer enters into a lease of a vehicle with a lessee and simultaneously sells the vehicle to a third party, then the lease of the vehicle does not subject the dealer to use tax liability. However, the dealer's sale of the vehicle, with or without the lease, to a third party is taxable and the third party incurs use tax liability.

This exemption also applies to vehicles leased by a vehicle manufacturer to its employees. (86 Ill. Adm. Code 150.306.)

Motor vehicles subject to the replacement tax: The proceeds from the selling price of a passenger car that was subject to the former vehicle replacement tax (¶2209) are exempt.

- *Newsprint and ink*

The purchase and transfer of newsprint and ink for the primary purpose of conveying news is exempt. An Illinois Supreme Court decision held that sales of publications furnishing business and financial information to investors were exempt under the newsprint exemption (*Moody's Investors Service, Inc. v. Department of Revenue* (1984, SCt), 101 Ill2d 291, 461 NE2d 972; CCH ILLINOIS TAX REPORTS, ¶ 60-175.15; see also *General Information Letter ST 12-0010-GIL*, Department of Revenue, February 29, 2012, CCH ILLINOIS TAX REPORTS, ¶ 402-457). However, the newsprint and ink exemption does not extend to the transfer of news by CD-Rom discs (*General Information Letter ST 05-0112-GIL*, Illinois Department of Revenue, November 7, 2005, CCH ILLINOIS TAX REPORTS, ¶ 401-628).

- *Nonprofit organizations for the elderly*

Proceeds from sales to a nonprofit corporation, society, association, foundation, institution, or organization that is operated primarily for the recreation of persons 55 years of age or older are exempt. Also exempt are sales by a nonprofit organization organized and operated as a service enterprise for the benefit of persons 65 years of age or older, provided that the property was not purchased by the enterprise for the purpose of reselling it; however, sales by limited liability companies are excluded from this exemption. (35 ILCS 115/3-5; 35 ILCS 120/2-5)

- *Photo-processing equipment*

Photo-processing equipment, including repair and replacement parts and equipment purchased for lease, certified by the purchaser to be used primarily for photo processing, is not subject to state use tax, service use tax, and retailers' occupation (sales) tax (35 ILCS 115/3-5; 35 ILCS 110/3-5; 35 ILCS 115/3-5; 35 ILCS 120/2-5). For purposes of the exemption, photo processing is deemed to be a manufacturing process of tangible personal property for resale. However, the use of photographs, including negatives and positives, that are the product of photo processing is subject to the state use tax and retailers' occupation (sales) tax with the exception of photographs produced to advertise motion pictures.

- *River Edge redevelopment project*

An exemption is allowed for qualified sales of building materials to be incorporated into real estate within a River Edge redevelopment zone by remodeling, rehabilitating, or new construction as part of an industrial or commercial project for which a Certificate of Eligibility for Sales Tax Exemption has been issued to the taxpayer (35 ILCS 120/2-54; 86 Ill. Adm. Code 130.1954). The building materials qualify for the exemption if they are incorporated into the commercial portion of a multi-use development project that also includes residential units; see *General Information Letter ST 15-0071-GIL*, Illinois Department of Revenue, October 15, 2015, CCH ILLINOIS TAX REPORTS, ¶ 403-060.

- *Rolling stock*

The following sales of rolling stock moving in interstate commerce are exempt: (1) sales to interstate carriers; or (2) sales to lessors for which a lease of one year or longer to interstate carriers is executed or in effect at the time of sale (35 ILCS 105/3-55; 35 ILCS 110/2; 35 ILCS 115/2; 35 ILCS 120/2-5; 86 Ill. Adm. Code 130.340). The sale of property that is utilized by interstate carriers or attached to rolling stock moving in interstate commerce is also exempt.

"Rolling stock" includes the transportation vehicles of any kind of interstate transportation company for hire (railroad, bus line, airline, trucking company, etc. (86 Ill. Adm. Code 130.340(b)). The exemption for the use of rolling stock moving in interstate commerce is limited to transportation vehicles that, during a 12-month period, have carried persons or property for hire in interstate commerce for greater than 50% of either their total trips or total miles (35 ILCS 105/3-61(e); 35 ILCS 110/3-51(e); 35 ILCS 115/2d(e); 35 ILCS 120/2-51(e)). The taxpayer must make an irrevocable election at the time of purchase whether to use the trips or mileage method. The election to use either trips method or the mileage method will remain in effect for the duration of the purchaser's ownership of the item. For purposes of determining qualifying trips or miles, motor vehicles that carry persons or property for hire, even just between points in Illinois, will be considered used for hire in interstate commerce if the motor vehicle transports persons whose journeys or property whose shipments originate or terminate outside Illinois).

For motor vehicles, the exemption is available only for limousines and motor vehicles whose gross vehicle weight rating exceeds 16,000 pounds (35 ILCS 105/3-51(c); *Informational Bulletin FY 2008-03,* Illinois Department of Revenue, October 2007, CCH ILLINOIS TAX REPORTS, ¶401-818).

Documentation: A trucking company may use intrastate trips to qualify its trucks for the Illinois rolling stock exemption from retailers' occupation (sales) tax if the company can document that the shipment of products either originated or terminated outside Illinois. If the initial documentation for a shipment of products from outside Illinois indicates that the Illinois destination is a specific warehouse, any subsequent shipment of the products from that warehouse to another Illinois destination will not qualify as part of an interstate trip for purposes of the rolling stock exemption. However, if the initial documentation indicates that the ultimate destination is an Illinois location via the Illinois warehouse, then the travel of products from the warehouse to the destination can count as part of the interstate trip. (*General Information Letter ST 10-0019-GIL,* Illinois Department of Revenue, March 19, 2010, CCH ILLINOIS TAX REPORTS, ¶402-105)

The rolling stock exemption from Illinois sales tax applies to product shipments when (1) the carrier for hire has documented that the products originated or terminated outside Illinois, and (2) the products were shipped to an Illinois location by the carrier. (*General Information Letter ST 14-0046-GIL,* Illinois Department of Revenue, September 4, 2014, CCH ILLINOIS TAX REPORTS, ¶402-885)

• *Sales for resale*

A sale of tangible personal property for the purpose of resale is exempt (35 ILCS 105/2; 35 ILCS 120/1). See ¶1505.

• *Schools*

Sales by teacher-sponsored student organizations affiliated with Illinois elementary or secondary schools are exempt.

Personal property, including food, purchased through fundraising events for the benefit of a public or private elementary or secondary school, a group of those schools, or one or more school districts is exempt from sales and use taxes if the events are sponsored by an entity recognized by the school district that consists primarily of volunteers and includes parents and teachers of the school children. These exemptions do not apply to personal property purchased through fundraising events (1) for the benefit of private home instruction or (2) for which the fundraising entity purchases the personal property sold at the events from another individual or entity that sold the property for the purpose of resale by the fundraising entity and that profits from the sale to the fundraising entity. These exemptions are not subject to any sunset date provisions and, thus, are available indefinitely.

• *Telecommunications*

Telecommunications generally are subject to the telecommunications excise tax and the telecommunications infrastructure maintenance fee, discussed at ¶2207.

Equipment installed in aircraft: Proceeds from sales and use of equipment that is operated by a telecommunications provider licensed as a common carrier by the FCC and that is permanently installed in or affixed to aircraft moving in interstate commerce are exempt.

Prepaid calling arrangements: Prepaid telephone calling arrangements are subject to retailers' occupation (sales), service occupation (sales), use, and service use tax as tangible personal property, regardless of the form the arrangements may be embodied or transmitted. Prepaid telephone calling arrangements are not considered "telecommunications" subject to the telecommunications infrastructure maintenance fee (35 ILCS 635/10(b)).

The term "prepaid telephone calling arrangements" means the right to exclusively purchase prepaid telephone or telecommunications services in order to originate intrastate, interstate, or international telecommunications using an access number or authorization code and includes the recharge of such services. However, purchases that are reflected by the service provider as a credit on a customer account under an existing subscription plan are not included (35 ILCS 120/2-27). For additional information, see *General Information Letter ST 13-0009-GIL,* Illinois Department of Revenue, February 5, 2013, CCH ILLINOIS TAX REPORTS,¶ 402-639 and *General Information Letter ST 13-0053-GIL,* Illinois Department of Revenue, September 11, 2013, CCH ILLINOIS TAX REPORTS,¶ 402-738.

• *Transportation*

Sales tax exemptions were created in conjunction with enactment of the Illinois Public-Private Partnerships for Transportation Act. One of the express intentions of the Act is to authorize transportation agencies to enter into public-private agreements related to the development, operation, and financing of transportation facilities (Sec. 5, P.A. 97-502 (H.B. 1091), Laws 2011).

"Qualified sales" of building materials to be incorporated into a project authorized under the Act are exempt from sales tax (35 ILCS 120/1r). Incorporation into a project includes remodeling, rehabilitating, or new construction. A "qualified sale" is a sale of building materials that will be incorporated into a project for which a Certificate of Eligibility for Sales Tax Exemption was issued by the agency that authorized the project.

A retailer must obtain a copy of the Certificate of Eligibility for Sales Tax Exemption from the buyer in order to document the sale. The legislation specifies the contents of the Certificate.

South Suburban Airport building materials: A sales tax exemption is available for retailers that make a qualified sale of building materials to be incorporated into the South Suburban Airport by remodeling, rehabilitating, or new construction (35 ILCS 120/1s). To document the exemption, the retailer must obtain from the purchaser a copy of a certificate of eligibility for sales tax exemption issued by the Department of Transportation (DOT). In addition, the retailer must obtain a certificate from the purchaser that contains the following (35 ILCS 120/1s(c)):

— a statement that the building materials are being purchased for incorporation in the South Suburban Airport in accordance with the Public-Private Agreements for the South Suburban Airport Act;

— the location or address of the project into which the building materials will be incorporated;

— the name of the project;

— a description of the building materials being purchased; and

— the purchaser's signature and date of purchase.

¶1702

A "qualified sale" is a sale of building materials that will be incorporated into the South Suburban Airport for which a certificate of eligibility for sales tax exemption has been issued by the DOT (35 ILCS 120/1s(b)).

• *Utilities*

Transactions involving the following are exempt from retailers' occupation (sales) tax, use tax, service occupation tax (SOT), and service use tax (SUT) (35 ILCS 105/3; 35 ILCS 110/3; 35 ILCS 115/3; 35 ILCS 120/2):

— electricity delivered to customers by wire;

— natural or artificial gas that is delivered to customers through pipes, pipelines, or mains; and

— water that is delivered to customers through pipes, pipelines, or mains.

¶1703 ROT/UT—Exemptions

Law: Retailers' Occupation Tax Act, Sec. 1 [35 ILCS 120/1]; Retailers' Occupation Tax Act, Sec. 2-5 [35 ILCS 120/2-5]; Use Tax Act, Sec. 2 [35 ILCS 105/2]; Use Tax Act, Sec. 3-5 [35 ILCS 105/3-5]; 86 Ill. Adm. Code 130.110; 86 Ill. Adm. Code Sec. 130.2075, 86 Ill. Adm. Code 150.310; 86 Ill. Adm. Code Sec. 150.1201 (CCH Illinois Tax Reports, ¶60-250, 60-330, 60-380, 60-390, 60-450, 60-560, 60-570, 60-590, 60-760, 61-010).

The exemptions discussed below are provided under the ROT/UT.

• *Aircraft*

An exemption is allowed for (1) an aircraft that is sold in Illinois and leaves the state within 15 days after the sale, (2) an aircraft temporarily located in Illinois for a prepurchase evaluation, and (3) an aircraft that is temporarily located in Illinois for post-sale customization and leaves the state within 15 days (35 ILCS 105/3-55(h-2); 86 Ill. Adm. Code 150.310). See also *Informational Bulletin FY 2008-02*, Illinois Department of Revenue, September 2007, CCH Illinois Tax Reports, ¶401-811.

• *Construction contractors*

Sales by construction contractors of materials and fixtures integrally incorporated into a structure are exempt when installed incident to the construction contract because sales tax has been paid by the contractor. Sales of personal property by contractors are taxable when sold without installation because the property is purchased tax-free by the contractor as items bought for resale (86 Ill. Adm. Code Secs. 130.1940, 150.1201).

Practitioner Comment: Retailer, Service Provider, or Construction Contractor

The Illinois Independent Tax Tribunal granted the Illinois Department of Revenue's summary judgment motion, denying Nokia Siemens Networks US, LLC's cross-motion for summary judgment and protest of a use tax assessment on equipment sold to T-Mobile USA. Nokia based its cross-motion for summary judgment on the claim that if classified as a "construction contractor," it was exempt from paying use tax because the equipment was not affixed to real estate and the contract for the equipment did not state a fixed price for the equipment. The Tribunal concluded first that Nokia was acting as a construction contractor because it was responsible for installing equipment and providing other services to T-Mobile's telecommunications structures. Further, the Tribunal determined that whether or not the Power Modules were removable from the cabinets on the cell towers, the Power Modules were not exempt from use tax because use tax is imposed on all items of tangible personal property in a telecommunications construction contract. Lastly, the Tribunal decided that Nokia was not permitted to use resale exemption certificates to offset its use tax liability on the Power Modules sold to T-Mobile because Nokia was assessed use tax, and not Retailer's Occupation Tax. (*Nokia Siemens Networks US LLC v. Dep't of Revenue*, Illinois Independent Tax Tribunal, 14 TT 10, Dec. 22, 2015, CCH Illinois Tax Reports, ¶403-070)

Practitioner Comment: For Illinois sales/use tax purposes, taxpayers fall into one of three buckets: retailer, service provider, or construction contractor. A retailer collects tax from its customer while a construction contractor pays use tax on the materials it purchases to perform construction contracts. The distinction between a retailer and a construction contractor is often difficult to discern and some taxpayers who consider themselves retailers—such as Nokia Siemens in the case described above—get burned when the DOR classifies them as a construction contractor. This trap for the unwary is even deeper for taxpayers like Nokia that sell telecommunication systems because of an obscure DOR rule that says a seller of a telecommunication system sold at one contract price is per se subject to use tax (and not retailer's occupation tax or "sales tax") even though the system is not permanently affixed and could be removed from the real estate. To make matters worse, the Tribunal concluded in this case that Nokia was still subject to use tax even though it accepted a resale certificate from its customer, thereby underscoring that resale certificates in certain circumstances are not necessarily "get out of jail free" cards.

David A. Hughes, Esq., Horwood Marcus & Berk, Chartered

Sales of materials to construction contractors for incorporation into real estate owned by nonprofit organizations, governmental bodies, or public improvements are exempt (86 Ill. Adm. Code Sec. 130.2075, 86 Ill. Adm. Code Sec. 150.1201). The exemption applied to purchases of building materials by a lessee for incorporation into property owned by a city and leased to the lessee under a 99-year lease (*Private Letter Ruling, ST 05-0025-PLR*, Illinois Department of Revenue, December 22, 2005, CCH ILLINOIS TAX REPORTS, ¶ 401-640).

Use tax: When a construction contractor permanently affixes tangible personal property to real property, the contractor is deemed the end user of that property and incurs use tax liability based on the cost price of the property. Because the contractor's customers incur no use tax liability, the contractor has no legal authority to collect the use tax from them. However, many construction contractors pass on the amount of their use tax liabilities to customers in the form of higher prices or by including provisions in their contracts that require customers to reimburse them for their tax liability. This reimbursement cannot be billed as "sales tax," but can be listed on the bill as a reimbursement of tax. (*General Information Letter ST 10-0001-GIL*, Illinois Department of Revenue, January 12, 2010, CCH ILLINOIS TAX REPORTS, ¶ 402-081)

CCH Advisory: Carpet

The Department of Revenue has clarified that installation of carpet by means of tacks, staples, tacking strips, or gluing is considered permanent installation. Retailers must pay tax on their purchases of carpet that is sold installed by such methods, but tax is not collected from the customer when the sale includes permanent installation (*Informational Bulletin FY 2000-18*, Department of Revenue, May 2000; CCH ILLINOIS TAX REPORTS, ¶ 401-195).

Carpet purchased tax-free from an out-of-state supplier is subject to use tax; use tax on the cost price must be included (Line 12a of Form ST-1).

A retail sale made to a construction contractor that qualifies for the enterprise zone exemption, though not subject to tax, must be reported as a deduction (Item 12 of Form ST Worksheet).

Construction contracts for the improvement of real estate that include engineering, installation, and maintenance of voice, data, video, security, and telecommunication systems do not constitute engaging in the business of selling tangible personal property at retail if the systems are sold at one specified contract price and the contractor has paid sales tax on the purchases. However, a person engaged in a construction contract to engineer, install, and maintain an integrated system of products and who transfers tangible personal property to users or consumers in the finished form in which it was purchased but that was not engineered or installed under the terms of the contract is engaged in the business of selling tangible personal property at retail to the extent of the value of the tangible personal property that was transferred.

Taxable property purchased out of state: If tangible personal property is purchased outside Illinois, then a contractor must self-assess and remit use tax to the department. However, the contractor may take a tax credit for sales tax paid in another state on the purchase. (*General Information Letter ST 15-0032-GIL*, Illinois Department of Revenue, June 18, 2015, CCH ILLINOIS TAX REPORTS, ¶ 402-970)

• *Farm chemicals*

Proceeds from the sale of farm chemicals are exempt. "Farm chemicals" are any chemical products used in the production of crops. Examples of exempted items are stock sprays, disinfectants, stock tonics, serums, vaccines, poultry remedies, and other medicinal preparations and conditioners; water-purifying products; insecticides; and weed killers. The farm chemicals exemption applies only if the product's label indicates that it is used exclusively on farm animals (*Allemed, Inc. v. Department of Revenue* (1981, Ill AppCt), 101 IllApp3d 746, 428 NE2d 714; CCH ILLINOIS TAX REPORTS, ¶ 60-250.50).

• *Fuel for river vessels*

Sales of fuel consumed or used on the operation of barges, ships, or vessels that transport property or convey passengers for hire on rivers bordering Illinois are exempt if the fuel is delivered to the barge, ship or vessel while afloat (86 Ill. Adm. Code Sec. 130.315).

• *Isolated or occasional sales*

An isolated or occasional sale of tangible personal property by a retailer who is not engaged in the business of selling such property is exempt (35 ILCS 105/2; 35 ILCS 120/1; 86 Ill. Adm. Code 130.110). The sale by a manufacturer of machinery that has been used in its business and that the taxpayer no longer needs is an example of an exempt occasional sale.

Purchase for resale: When an item is purchased by an occasional seller with the intent to resell the item, the occasional seller purchasing the item is deemed a retailer. Accordingly, the initial purchase is a purchase for resale and the subsequent sale at retail is subject to retailers' occupation (sales) tax when the item is sold (86 Ill. Adm. Code Sec. 130.110).

• *Manufacturing*

Chemicals used: The Illinois Circuit Court held that if chemicals cause a direct and immediate physical change to a product in the manufacturing process, the chemicals qualify for a use tax exemption for manufacturing. A glass manufacturer was entitled to a refund because the nitrogen and hydrogen used in its manufacturing process qualify for the exemption for machine and equipment used primarily in the manufacturing or assembling of tangible personal property for wholesale or retail sale or lease under 35 ILCS 105/3-5(18). The exemption includes chemicals that "effect a direct and immediate change upon a product being manufactured." (35 ILCS 105/3-50(4))

The Court determined that the chemicals need not react with the final product to effect a direct and immediate change to the glass. The chemicals used had the effect of changing the glass' temperature, physical composition and texture; therefore, the glass being manufactured underwent a recognizable immediate physical change. Further, the effects were direct, because no further steps in the manufacturing process were required to cause a range of vital changes on the glass. As a result, the Court determined the chemicals were catalysts and qualified for the exemption. (*PPG Industries, Inc. v. The Department of Revenue*, Circuit Court, Cook County Judicial Circuit, No. 13 L 050140, September 9, 2014, CCH ILLINOIS TAX REPORTS, ¶402-886)

Practitioner Comment: Exemption for Catalytic Chemicals

The Circuit Court reversed the administrative hearings decision, which had held that the chemicals in this case were not exempt because they did not directly contact the glass, *i.e.* the product being manufactured. The administrative hearings decision's interpretation of the exemption was narrower than provided by the statute, which opened the door for it to be challenged and overruled by the Circuit Court.

Jennifer A. Zimmerman, Esq., Horwood Marcus & Berk, Chartered

---

• *Meals served under a federal nutrition program*

Meals served pursuant to grants or contracts under Title VII of the Older American Act of 1965 to participants in the federal Nutrition Program for the Elderly are exempt if served in return for contributions by the participants that correspond to federal guidelines.

• *Motor vehicles*

Motor vehicles sold to nonresidents: Sales of motor vehicles delivered in Illinois to nonresidents are exempt, if (1) the vehicle is not required to be titled in Illinois and (2) a driveway decal permit is issued (35 ILCS 105/3-55). The exemption does not apply if the other state does not allow a reciprocal exemption for the use of a motor vehicle sold and delivered in that state to an Illinois resident to be titled in Illinois (*Informational Bulletin FY 2005-13*, Illinois Department of Revenue, January 2005, CCH ILLINOIS TAX REPORTS, ¶401-523). The Department of Revenue publishes a chart that lists the states that do not provide a reciprocal exemption to Illinois residents and specifies the tax rate to be used to compute tax due on vehicles/trailers purchased in Illinois by residents of such states; see ¶1702.

If a purchaser of a motor vehicle claims an exemption on a vehicle for which a drive-away decal has been issued, then uses the vehicle in Illinois for more than 30 days in a calendar year, the purchaser is liable for use tax on the motor vehicle (86 Ill. Adm. Code 150.310). A credit will be given for any tax that was properly due and paid in another state.

For additional information on this exemption, see *Motor vehicles* at ¶1702.

• *Out-of-state florists*

A transaction in which a purchase order is received by an out-of-state florist who then arranges for an Illinois florist to deliver the property in Illinois to the purchaser or the purchaser's donee is exempt. However, a purchase order received by an Illinois florist who arranges for a florist in another state to deliver the property to the purchaser or the purchaser's donee constitutes a taxable sale.

• *Printed matter*

Sales of newspapers and magazines are exempt. However, sales of books and sheet music are subject to tax (86 Ill. Adm. Code Sec. 130.2105).

¶1704 UT/SUT—Exemptions

Law: Use Tax Act, Sec. 3-55 [35 ILCS 105/3-55]; Use Tax Act, Sec. 3-70 [35 ILCS 105/3-70]; Service Use Tax Act, Sec. 3-45 [35 ILCS 110/3-45]; Service Use Tax Act, Sec. 3-60 [35 ILCS 110/3-60] (CCH ILLINOIS TAX REPORTS, ¶60-450, 61-010).

The exemptions discussed below are provided under the UT/SUT.

- *Locomotive fuel*

Fuel purchased outside Illinois and brought into the state in the fuel supply tanks of locomotives engaged in freight hauling and passenger service is exempt from use tax and service use tax. (35 ILCS 105/3-55; 35 ILCS 110/3-45)

- *Property acquired outside of Illinois by nonresident*

Property acquired outside the state and brought into the state by a nonresident individual is exempt if (1) used by the nonresident for at least three months before bringing the property into the state or (2) brought into Illinois for his or her own use while temporarily in or passing through the state. However, when a business operating outside Illinois moves its office, plant, or other business facility to Illinois, the business will be subject to the use tax on items of tangible personal property that are titled or registered in Illinois or whose registration with the United States government must be filed with the state of Illinois. (35 ILCS 105/3-55; 35 ILCS 110/3-45)

The exemption was not allowed to be claimed by a single-member LLC organized in another state (*JB4 Air LLC v. Department of Revenue*, Illinois Appellate Court, Second District, No. 2-07-1254, March 10, 2009, CCH ILLINOIS TAX REPORTS,¶ 401-950; see also *Administrative Hearing Decision No. UT 11-08*, Department of Revenue, August 26, 2011, CCH ILLINOIS TAX REPORTS,¶ 402-399). Likewise, a corporation with a sole shareholder was not allowed to claim the exemption (*Administrative Hearing Decision No. UT 11-11*, Department of Revenue, February 25, 2011, CCH ILLINOIS TAX REPORTS,¶ 402-413)

Practitioner Comment: Property Relocated to Illinois

The Illinois Appellate Court held that a nonresident, single-member limited liability company owed use taxes on assets owned by the LLC when the Illinois nonresident member relocated to Illinois. See *JB4 Air LLC v. Ill. Dep't of Rev.*, supra. Illinois law does grant a use tax exemption for tangible personal property that is acquired outside this State by a nonresident individual who then brings the property to this State for use here and who has used the property outside this State for at least three months before bringing the property to this State. The court held that this exemption applies only to property owned by an individual, and not to property owned by an LLC or other entities.

Although Illinois grants a similar exemption for property owned by a business that relocates to Illinois, that exemption does not apply to titled or registered property. Yet, if the member had liquidated the LLC at least three months prior to moving to Illinois, it would appear as though Illinois use taxes may have been avoided on the property owned by the LLC that was relocated to Illinois.

Horwood Marcus & Berk, Chartered

- *Relocated businesses*

A business that moves to Illinois or opens an office, plant, or other business facility in the state is exempt from the Illinois use tax on property that was used outside Illinois for at least three months before being moved into the state. (35 ILCS 105/3-70; 35 ILCS 110/3-60)

- *Temporary storage in state*

The temporary storage in Illinois of property acquired outside the state is exempt if (1) after its storage it is used solely outside the state, (2) it is incorporated into other property that is used solely outside the state, or (3) it is altered by any of the following processes before use outside the state: converting, fabricating, manufacturing, printing, processing, or shaping. (35 ILCS 115/3-5; 35 ILCS 110/3-5; 35 ILCS 115/3-5; 35 ILCS 120/2-5)

The temporary storage in Illinois of building materials and fixtures that are acquired by an Illinois registered combination retailer/construction contractor and that are then incorporated into real property located outside Illinois is exempt.

A private letter ruling held that computer equipment acquired outside of Illinois on behalf of a customer and then temporarily stored in a taxpayer's warehouse in Illinois (where title is transferred to the customer) for final shipment outside of the state qualified for the temporary storage exemption from use tax. In addition, the exemption is available when the equipment is acquired outside of Illinois and temporarily stored in the warehouse, where the taxpayer performs services on the equipment before it is shipped outside of Illinois.

The exemption is not available when the equipment is stored in the taxpayer's warehouse (where title is transferred only after 180 days) until further shipping instructions from the customer to a location outside of Illinois. However, the transaction may qualify for the interstate commerce exemption (see ¶1702). *(Private Letter Ruling, ST 15-0016-PLR, Illinois Department of Revenue, November 13, 2015, CCH ILLINOIS TAX REPORTS, ¶ 403-085)*

¶1705 Automobile Renting Occupation and Use Tax Act—Exemptions

Law: Automobile Renting Occupation and Use Tax Act, Secs. 3 and 4 [35 ILCS 155/3, 155/4]; 86 Ill. Adm. Code Sec. 180.130 (CCH ILLINOIS TAX REPORTS, ¶ 60-570).

The following are excluded from the automobile renting occupation and use tax: governmental bodies; charitable, religious, or educational institutions; and nonprofit organizations that are organized primarily for the recreation of persons 55 years of age or older.

The following transactions are exempt (35 ILCS 155/3, 155/4):

— isolated or occasional rentals;

— those protected by the Commerce Clause of the U.S. Constitution;

— those in which the rentor operates the vehicle, so that the rentor or rentor's agent remains in possession;

— transactions in which the rental charge covers only the costs of operating the vehicle as a demonstrator; and

— the renting of automobiles for one year or less to persons who will rerent the automobiles for a period of one year or less.

(86 Ill. Adm. Code Sec. 180.130)

¶1706 Local ROT, UT, and SOT—Exemptions

Law: Illinois Municipal Code, Sec. 8-11-1 [65 ILCS 5/8-11-1]; Illinois Municipal Code, Sec. 8-11-5 [65 ILCS 5/8-11-5]; Illinois Municipal Code, Sec. 8-11-6 [65 ILCS 5/8-11-6]; Counties Code, Secs. 5-1006—5-1009 [55 ILCS 5/5-1006—5/5-1009] (CCH ILLINOIS TAX REPORTS, ¶ 61-730).

The exemptions under the municipal and county taxes are the same as those under the state taxes.

¶1707 Hotel Operators' Occupation Tax Act—Exemptions

Law: Hotel Operators' Occupation Tax Act, Secs. 3 and 9 [35 ILCS 145/3, 145/9](CCH ILLINOIS TAX REPORTS, ¶ 60-480).

Exempted from the hotel operators' occupation tax are persons who rent, lease or let rooms only to permanent residents (35 ILCS 145/9). Also, the tax is not imposed on the privilege of engaging in any business involved in interstate commerce or anything else when that business may not, under the Constitution and federal statutes, be made subject to taxation by the State of Illinois (35 ILCS 145/3). In addition, the tax does not apply to gross rental receipts for which the hotel operator is prohibited from obtaining reimbursement of the tax from the customer because of a federal treaty.

Room rentals to religious, charitable, or educational organizations are not exempt from Illinois hotel operators' occupation tax, even if the organizations possess a tax exemption identification number ("E" number) that exempts their purchases from sales tax, use tax, service occupation tax, service use tax, and local occupation and use taxes. (*General Information Letter ST 05-0127-GIL*, Illinois Department of Revenue, December 16, 2005, CCH ILLINOIS TAX REPORTS, ¶ 401-645)

SALES AND USE TAXES
CHAPTER 18
RETURNS, PAYMENT, AND ADMINISTRATION

(For purposes of convenience, throughout the sales and use tax division, the retailers' occupation (sales) tax, use tax, service occupation tax, and service use tax are frequently referred to as the ROT, UT, SOT, and SUT, respectively.)

¶1801 Licensing and Registration

Law: Retailers' Occupation Tax Act, Sec. 2a [35 ILCS 120/2a]; Retailers' Occupation Tax Act, Sec. 2b [35 ILCS 120/2b]; Retailers' Occupation Tax Act, Sec. 2i [35 ILCS 120/2i]; Retailers' Occupation Tax Act, Sec. 13 [35 ILCS 120/13]; Service Occupation Tax Act, Sec. 6 [35 ILCS 115/6]; Service Occupation Tax Act, Sec. 10a [35 ILCS 115/10a]; Use Tax Act, Sec. 2 [35 ILCS 105/2]; Use Tax Act, Sec. 6 [35 ILCS 105/6]; Use Tax Act, Sec. 10a [35 ILCS 105/10a]; Use Tax Act, Sec. 13 [35 ILCS 105/13]; Service Use Tax Act, Sec. 2 [35 ILCS 110/2]; Service Use Tax Act, Sec 6 [35 ILCS 110/6]; Service Use Tax Act, Sec. 7 [35 ILCS 110/7]; Service Use Tax Act, Sec. 10a [35 ILCS 110/10a]; Service Use Tax Act, Sec. 14 [35 ILCS 110/14]; Service Use Tax Act, Sec. 15 [35 ILCS 110/15]; Hotel Operators' Occupation Tax Act, Sec. 5 [35 ILCS 145/5]; 86 Ill. Adm. Code 130.701; 86 Ill. Adm. Code Secs. 130.1301, 130.1305, 130.1310; 86 Ill. Adm. Code Secs. 140.1201, 140.1205, 140.1210; 86 Ill. Adm. Code Sec. 150.805; 86 Ill. Adm. Code Sec. 160.130; (CCH ILLINOIS TAX REPORTS, ¶ 60-480, 60-570, 61-220, 61-240, 61-530).

Forms: ST-1, Sales and Use Tax Return; PST-1, Prepaid Sales Tax Return; ST-2, Multiple Site Form; STS-80, Request for Vending Machine Decals.

Licensing and registration provisions relating to the ROT, UT, SOT, and SUT are discussed below.

• *Retailers' occupation tax*

Every person engaging in the business of selling tangible personal property at retail in Illinois must obtain a certificate of registration (35 ILCS 120/2a; 86 Ill. Adm. Code Sec. 130.701). "Engaging in business" includes persons who hold themselves out as being engaged, or who habitually engage, in selling tangible personal property at retail, including special order producers whose products, when sold to users, serve substantially the same function as stock or standard items, or persons who engage in the business of transferring tangible personal property upon the redemption of trading stamps. Application for a permit must be made to the Department of Revenue and a bond or other security must be provided.

The Illinois Department of Revenue has issued a general information letter discussing sales and use tax nexus rules. The letter notes which types of retailers are or are not required to register with Illinois to collect sales and use tax. Retailers without nexus that are not required to register sometimes do register in order to collect the use tax that would otherwise be payable by Illinois customers. (*General Information Letter ST 13-0069-GIL*, Illinois Department of Revenue, November 26, 2013, CCH ILLINOIS TAX REPORTS, ¶ 402-760)

If a registered retailer states that the retailer operates other places of business from which the retailer engages in the business of selling tangible personal property at retail in Illinois, the Department must give the retailer a subcertificate of registration for each place of business. When the same person engages in two or more businesses of selling tangible personal property at retail in Illinois, and the businesses are substantially different in character or operate under different trade names or under substantially dissimilar circumstances, the Department may require or permit such person to apply for and obtain a separate certificate of registration (35 ILCS 120/2a; 86 Ill. Adm. Code Sec. 130.701).

Effective June 1, 2014, an application for a certificate of registration to engage in the business of selling tangible personal property at retail must include, in the case of a publicly traded corporation, the name and title of the chief financial officer, chief operating officer, and any other officer or employee with responsibility for preparing sales and use tax returns, along with the last four digits of their Social Security numbers (35 ILCS 120/2a).

Bond requirement: Vendors making retail sales of property or maintaining a place of business in Illinois must furnish a bond or irrevocable bank letter of credit not to exceed the lesser of three times the vendor's average monthly tax liability or $50,000 (35 ILCS 120/2a; 86 Ill. Adm. Code Sec. 130.701).

Notice: If a taxpayer holding a certificate of registration is in default for delinquent returns or payments, the Department, not less than 60 days (120 days prior to June 1, 2015) before the expiration date of the certificate, must give notice to the taxpayer of the account period for the delinquent returns and the amount of tax, penalty, and interest due. The Department must also notify the taxpayer that the certificate will not be renewed unless the taxpayer has filed the delinquent return and paid the delinquent taxes, penalties, and interest. The Department may approve a renewal if the returns are filed and a percentage of the delinquent payment is made and the taxpayer waives all limitations on the Department to collect the balance of the delinquent amounts (35 ILCS 120/2a; 86 Ill. Adm. Code Sec. 130.701).

Vending machines: An applicant for a certificate of registration who will sell tangible personal property at retail through vending machines must indicate the number of vending machines that will be operated and then notify the Department of Revenue, upon request, of the number of machines in use (35 ILCS 120/2a; 86 Ill. Adm. Code Sec. 130.701).

CCH Advisory: Out-of-State Sellers of Alcoholic Beverages

A general information letter discusses the sales and use tax responsibilities of out-of-state retailers selling and shipping alcoholic beverages to Illinois residents. Sales or use tax is due on sales of liquor by the out-of-state retailers, provided they have sufficient nexus with Illinois. However, the retailers who do not have sufficient nexus with Illinois are not required to collect and remit sales or use tax. In such a case, the Illinois customers incur use tax liability and are required to self-assess and remit use tax to the department.

Out-of-state wineries that intend to sell wine directly to Illinois residents must complete an Application For State Of Illinois Winery Shipper's License and must register to collect and remit Illinois use tax for all gallons of wine sold by the licensee and shipped to persons in Illinois. Sales tax is not due on shipping charges, if a seller and the buyer agree on transportation or delivery charges separately from the selling price of tangible personal property that is sold. (*General Information Letter ST 15-0030-GIL,* Illinois Department of Revenue, June 5, 2015, CCH Illinois Tax Reports,¶ 402-969)

• *Service occupation tax*

A service provider who is registered under the ROT, SUT, or UT need not obtain a separate registration certificate under the SUT (35 ILCS 115/6). However, a service provider who is not registered under one of the above taxes and who is maintaining a place of business in Illinois must register under the SOT. Security requirements and provisions for registration of more than one place of business are the same as under the ROT.

• *Use tax*

A retailer who is registered under the ROT need not obtain a separate certificate of registration under the use tax (35 ILCS 105/6). However, a retailer maintaining a place of business in Illinois, who is not registered under the ROT, must apply to the Department for a certificate of registration. Security requirements and provisions for registration of more than one place of business are the same as under the ROT.

The U.S. Supreme Court, in *National Bellas Hess, Inc. v. Department of Revenue* (1967, US SCt), 87 SCt 1389, 386 US 753; CCH Illinois Tax Reports, ¶ 200-434, held that Illinois could not require a foreign mail order company to collect and remit use tax on sales made to Illinois residents when the company's only activity in the state was solicitation of sales by catalogs and flyers followed by delivery of the goods by mail or common carrier.

Effective January 1, 2015, out-of state retailers are required to register in Illinois and collect use tax when an Illinois person refers customers to them in exchange for a commission, and the Illinois person provides the customers with a promotional code; see *Informational Bulletin FY 2015-07,* Illinois Department of Revenue, December 2014, CCH Illinois Tax Reports,¶ 402-896. See also ¶ 1502.

• *Service use tax*

A service provider who is registered under the ROT, SOT, or UT need not obtain a separate registration certificate under the SUT (35 ILCS 110/6). However, a service provider who is not registered under one of the above taxes and who is maintaining a place of business in Illinois must register under the SUT. Security requirements and provisions for registration of more than one place of business are the same as under the ROT.

• *Leased departments*

When a person engaging in the business of selling tangible personal property at retail leases to other persons certain parts of the premises in which the lessor conducts his business, the lessee may file his or her own tax return if the lessee operates under a separate trade name and a separate identity from the lessor is made known to the general public. If the lessee operates under the identity of the lessor, then the lessor should account to the state for the lessee's tax (86 Ill. Adm. Code Sec. 130.1301; 86 Ill. Adm. Code Sec. 130.1305; 86 Ill. Adm. Code Sec. 130.1310). The same rule applies with respect to a service provider or supplier who leases to other persons certain parts of the lessor's business premises (86 Ill. Adm. Code Sec.; 86 Ill. Adm. Code Sec. 140.1201; 86 Ill. Adm. Code Sec. 140.1205; 86 Ill. Adm. Code Sec.140.1210).

• *Person not maintaining a place of business in Illinois*

A person not maintaining a place of business in Illinois may be licensed to collect the SOT, UT or SUT, if satisfactory security is provided to insure collection and payment of the tax (35 ILCS 105/6; 35 ILCS 115/6; 35 ILCS 110/7; 35 ILCS 105/13; 35 ILCS 110/14; 86 Ill. Adm. Code Sec. 160.130; 86 Ill. Adm. Code Sec. 150.805).

• *Hotel operators' occupation tax*

A person or company engaged in the business of renting, leasing, or letting rooms in an accommodation in Illinois must first obtain a certificate of registration from the Department of Revenue (35 ILCS 145/5).

• *Automobile renting occupation and use tax*

Persons engaged in the business of renting automobiles who are already registered under the ROT Act need not obtain a separate registration for their automobile rental business (*Informational Bulletin No. FY82-14*, Department of Revenue, November 1981).

CCH Caution: Collected Tax Is Held in Trust

Any person who collects, withholds, or receives an Illinois tax, or any amount represented to be a tax, from another person is deemed to hold the amount so collected or withheld in trust for the benefit of the Illinois Department of Revenue and is liable to the Department for the amount so collected or withheld plus any accrued interest and penalty on that amount. For information on penalties and interest, see ¶ 2503.

• *Denial or revocation of registration*

The Department of Revenue has the authority to refuse to issue a certificate of registration, permit, or license to a taxpayer that is in default for any tax or fee administered by the department. The DOR may refuse to issue a certificate of registration to any person who is or has been named as a corporate officer, a partner, a manager or member of a limited liability company, or the owner of the applicant that is in default only for amounts that are established as a final liability within the 20 years before the date of the DOR's notice of refusal. If the DOR's decision to revoke a certificate of registration has become final, it also has the authority to disallow the sales and use tax discount that is available to retailers and service providers for the purpose of offsetting tax collection and reporting costs. (35 ILCS 120/2a)

Practitioner Comment: Refusal to Issue Certificate of Registration for Unpaid Tax Debt

On August 16, 2013, the General Assembly permitted the Department of Revenue to deny a certificate of registration, permit, or license if a person who is either an owner, partner, officer, manager, or member of the company is in default for moneys due under the tax or fee Act upon which the certificate of registration, permit, or license is required or any other tax or fee Act administered by the Department. (P.A. 98-0496).

Breen M. Schiller, Esq., Horwood Marcus & Berk, Chartered

¶1802 Returns and Payment of Tax

Law: Retailers' Occupation Tax Act, Sec. 2d [35 ILCS 120/2d]; Retailers' Occupation Tax Act, Sec. 3 [35 ILCS 120/3]; Service Occupation Tax Act, Sec. 9 [35 ILCS 115/9]; Service Occupation Tax Act, Sec. 15 [35 ILCS 115/15]; Use Tax Act, Sec. 9 [35 ILCS 105/9]; Use Tax Act, Sec. 10 [35 ILCS 105/10]; Service Use Tax Act, Sec. 9 [35 ILCS 110/9]; Service Use Tax Act, Sec. 10 [35 ILCS 110/10]; Service Use Tax Act, Sec. 15 [35 ILCS 110/15]; Hotel Operators' Occupation Tax Act, Sec. 6 [35 ILCS 145/6]; Uniform Penalty and Interest Act, Secs. 3-1—3-6 [35 ILCS 735/3-1—735/3-6]; Tax Delinquency Amnesty Act [35 ILCS 745/10]; Aircraft Use Tax Law, Sec. 157 (35 ILCS 157/10-15); Income Tax Act, Sec. 5 (35 ILCS 5/502.1); 86 Ill. Adm. Code Sec. 130.501; 86 Ill. Adm. Code Sec. 130.502; 86 Ill. Adm. Code Sec. 130.510; 86 Ill. Adm. Code Sec. 130.535; 86 Ill. Adm. Code Sec. 130.540; 86 Ill Adm. Code Sec. 130.552; 86 Ill. Adm. Code Sec. 140.126(c); 86 Ill. Adm. Code Sec. 140.401; 86 Ill. Adm. Code Sec. 150.130; 86 Ill. Adm. Code Sec. 150.701; 86 Ill. Adm. Code Sec. 150.901a; 86 Ill. Adm. Code Sec. 160.135; 86 Ill. Adm. Code Sec. 180.140; 86 Ill. Adm. Code Sec. 750.300 (CCH ILLINOIS TAX REPORTS, ¶ 60-480, 61-220, 61-230, 61-520, 61-710).

Forms: ST-1, Sales and Use Tax Return; PST-1, Prepaid Sales Tax Return; ST-2, Multiple Site Form; ST-556, Sales Tax Transaction Form; CDF-7, Commercial Distribution Fee (CDF) Sales Tax Exemption; MC-1, Medical Cannabis Cultivation Privilege Tax Return; RUT-7, Rolling Stock Certification; ST-587, Equipment Exemption Certificate.

Monthly returns and payment of tax, due on or before the 20th day of each month, are required under all the state and local occupation and use taxes. However, the Department may permit quarterly returns or annual returns for taxpayers with low average monthly liabilities (35 ILCS 105/9; 35 ILCS 110/9; 35 ILCS 115/9; 35 ILCS 120/3; 86 Ill. Adm. Code Sec. 130.501; 86 Ill. Adm. Code Sec. 140.401; 86 Ill. Adm. Code Sec. 150.901a; 86 Ill. Adm. Code Sec. 160.135).

Retailers, suppliers, and service providers who sell out or discontinue their business must file a final return with the Department of Revenue not more than one month after discontinuing business.

CCH Advisory: Use Tax Reporting

In lieu of filing monthly use tax returns, individuals may elect to report their use tax liability on their standard individual income tax return if their annual individual use tax liability does not exceed $600. If an individual chooses to report use tax owed on the income tax return, the use tax may be:

— treated as being due at the same time as the income tax obligation,

— assessed, collected, and deposited in the same manner as income taxes, and

— treated as an income tax liability for all purposes.

The income tax return instructions must explain the imposition of the use tax and how to pay and report use tax when filing the income tax return. (35 ILCS 5/502.1)

• *Annual returns*

Taxpayers with an average monthly tax liability of $50 or less may file annual returns, due on January 20 (35 ILCS 105/9; 35 ILCS 110/9; 35 ILCS 120/3).

The decision to permit annual filing will be based on information obtained by the department, including registration and audit information regarding the retailer's average monthly liability. The department will periodically review taxpayer information, including returns filed by the taxpayer, to determine if any changes have occurred that require the taxpayer to file returns on other than an annual basis. The department will notify the taxpayer if a change in filing frequency is required. (86 Ill. Adm. Code Sec. 130.510)

• *Quarterly returns*

Taxpayers with an average monthly tax liability of $200 or less may file quarterly returns (35 ILCS 105/9; 35 ILCS 110/9; 35 ILCS 120/3).

The decision to permit quarterly filing will be based on information obtained by the department, including registration and audit information regarding the retailer's average monthly liability. The department will periodically review taxpayer information, including returns filed by the taxpayer, to determine if any changes have occurred that require the taxpayer to file returns on other than a quarterly basis. The department will notify the taxpayer if a change in filing frequency is required. (86 Ill. Adm. Code 130.502). Quarterly returns for the preceding quarter are due by April 20, July 20, October 20, and January 20.

¶1802

• *Quarter-monthly payments by large liability taxpayers*

A taxpayer whose average monthly liability under the ROT, UT, SOT, SUT, and under the municipal and county ROT and SOT is equal to or more than $20,000 during the preceding four calendar quarters is required to make payments four times during each month (known as the "quarter-monthly basis"). Quarter-monthly payments are due on the 7th, 15th, 22nd, and the last day of the month (payment cards are entitled "RR-3 Quarter Monthly Payment"). The quarter-monthly payment amount is equal to 22.5% of the taxpayer's actual liability for the month, 25% of the taxpayer's liability for the same calendar month of the preceding year (35 ILCS 105/9; 35 ILCS 120/3; 86 Ill. Adm. Code Sec. 130.535).

• *Electronic funds transfer payments*

A taxpayer whose tax liability for all occupation and use taxes is $20,000 or more must make all tax payments by electronic funds transfer (EFT). (35 ILCS 105/9; 35 ILCS 110/9; 35 ILCS 115/9; 35 ILCS 120/3; 86 Ill. Adm. Code Sec. 750.300).

The Illinois Department of Revenue has no statutory authority to waive the mandatory electronic funds transfer (EFT) payment requirements for a carpet installation company with an average monthly Illinois ROT, SOT, UT, or SUT liability of $20,000 or more. Although a statutory amendment regarding carpet installation changed the company's status from a retailer that collected sales tax from its customers to a construction contractor that had to pay sales tax to its carpet suppliers, resulting in a change in the taxability of the company's business, the company was required to make quarter monthly payments by EFT since its tax liability during the preceding four complete calendar quarters was $20,000 or more. However, a petition for a change in reporting status on the basis that a substantial change occurred causing the company to anticipate that its average monthly tax liability would fall below the $20,000 threshold could be filed (*General Information Letter ST 00-0224-GIL*, Department of Revenue, October 19, 2000; CCH ILLINOIS TAX REPORTS, ¶ 401-185).

• *MyTax Illinois program*

Registration information and a current list of forms that may be filed through MyTax Illinois is located on the DOR's website at **https://mytax.illinois.gov/_/#1**.

• *Transaction reporting for motor vehicles, aircraft, watercraft, and trailers*

ROT and UT returns on sales of motor vehicles, aircraft, watercraft, and trailers must be filed on a transaction reporting basis; that is, a separate return for each item sold or for multiple items of the same kind sold to a single purchaser. Transaction reporting returns (Form ST-556) must be filed not later than 20 days after the date of delivery of the property. The return and remittance (or proof of exemption from use tax) may be transmitted to the Department by way of the state agency with which the property must be titled or registered, if the Department and agency determine that this will expedite the processing of applications for title or registration. An annual information return is also required. Details of reporting are discussed in a regulation (86 Ill. Adm. Code Sec. 130.540).

Aircraft and watercraft use taxes: The purchaser, transferee, or donee of an aircraft or watercraft must submit a return and payment to the Department of Revenue within 30 days after the date of purchase, donation, or other transfer or the date the aircraft or watercraft is brought into the state, whichever is later. Payment of the tax is required in order to secure state registration of the aircraft or watercraft (35 ILCS 105/10; 35 ILCS 157/10-15).

Practitioner Comment: Penalty for Failure to File Transaction Report

Public Act 99-0335 amends the Uniform Penalty and Interest Act by clarifying that the $100 penalty for failure to file a transaction reporting return only applies when a properly prepared and filed return would not result in the imposition of a tax. Prior to

¶1802

the amendment, 35 ILCS 735/3-3(a-15) applied the $100 penalty regardless of whether a tax is imposed. Additionally, the 2% penalty imposed under 35 ILCS 735/3-3(a-10) does not apply to transaction reporting returns that would not result in the imposition of a tax when properly prepared and filed.

Horwood Marcus & Berk, Chartered

• *Direct payment by purchaser*

Under the UT, if a purchaser purchases property from a retailer for use in Illinois and does not pay the tax to the retailer, the purchaser must file a return and pay the tax directly to the Department. If the purchaser only occasionally incurs liability for direct payment, he need not register with the Department. However, if the purchaser has a frequently recurring direct tax liability, he or she must register (35 ILCS 105/3-45; 35 ILCS 105/10; 86 Ill. Adm. Code Sec. 150.130; 86 Ill. Adm. Code Sec. 140.126(c); 86 Ill. Adm. Code Sec. 150.701).

Similar provisions apply under the SOT and SUT relating to service providers who purchase property for resale as an incident to a sale of service and do not pay the tax to the supplier and to purchasers of service who do not pay the tax to the service provider when they acquire property as an incident to a sale of service.

Direct pay permits: A retailer of tangible personal property is not required to collect tax from a purchaser if the purchaser provides the retailer with a copy of a valid direct pay permit issued by the Department of Revenue and the purchaser assumes the retailer's obligation to pay all taxes related to the retail sale directly to the Department (35 ILCS 120/2-10.5; 35 ILCS 105/3-10.5).

Electronic resale certificates: An electronic resale certificate should contain all of the information required by the state, and that it does not find that simply requiring a customer to check a box on an online application to acknowledge the customer's eligibility for resale or exemption adequate to meet the signature requirement required by law. The department further emphasizes that if a signature is not obtained in accordance with its rules, a sale will be presumed to be a sale at retail. (*General Information Letter ST 10-0009*, Illinois Department of Revenue, February 25, 2010, CCH ILLINOIS TAX REPORTS, ¶ 402-086)

• *Annual ROT and SOT information returns required*

The Department of Revenue is authorized, by separate written notice, to require a taxpayer to file an annual information return for the tax year specified in the notice. Returns are due within 60 days after receipt of the notice and must contain a statement of gross receipts as shown by the taxpayer's last state income tax return and a schedule reconciling that amount with the amount reported to the Department for purposes of the ROT and SOT Taxpayers who are not required to file federal income tax returns are exempted from the requirement of filing the information returns (35 ILCS 115/9; 35 ILCS 120/3).

• *Alcoholic liquor retailers and manufacturers*

A retailer of alcoholic liquor who is not a distributor or manufacturer must file a statement with the Department of Revenue, at a time prescribed by the Department, showing the total amount paid for alcoholic liquor purchased during the preceding month. Also, every distributor, importing distributor, and manufacturer of alcoholic liquor must file a statement, by electronic means, no later than the 10th day of the month for the preceding month, showing the total gross receipts from alcoholic liquor sold or distributed during the preceding month to purchasers. The statement must identify the purchaser, the purchaser's tax registration number, and other information reasonably required by the Department (35 ILCS 120/3; 86 Ill Adm. Code 130.552).

A copy of the monthly statement must be sent to the retailer no later than the 10th day of the month for the preceding month.

- *Fair, art show, and flea market reports*

A person, including any transit merchant, who promotes, organizes, or provides retail selling space for concessionaires or other types of sellers at fairs, art shows, flea markets, and similar exhibitions, must file a report with the Department of Revenue providing information about the merchant's business not later than the 20th day of the month next following the month during which the sale event was held. The Department, however, may require daily reports and payments if there is a risk of revenue loss (35 ILCS 120/3).

- *Payment of tax by manufacturers and wholesalers*

Manufacturers, importers, and wholesalers whose products are sold at retail in Illinois by numerous retailers may, if they wish, assume the responsibility for accounting and paying to the Department all taxes accruing under the ROT, SOT, or UT, if the retailers (or service providers) do not make written objections to the Department (35 ILCS 105/9; 35 ILCS 115/9; 35 ILCS 120/3).

- *Separate returns*

When the same person has more than one business registered with the Department under separate registrations under any of the four taxes, the person must file separate returns for each such registered business (35 ILCS 105/9; 35 ILCS 110/9; 35 ILCS 115/9; 35 ILCS 120/3).

- *Home rule sales taxes*

All home rule city sales taxes (¶1518) are collected by the Department of Revenue. Payment of state and local sales taxes can be made using one combined rate of tax that is printed on the Sales and Use Tax Return Form ST-1 (*Information Bulletin FY 91-2*, Department of Revenue, July 1, 1990; CCH ILLINOIS TAX REPORTS, ¶400-452).

- *Penalties and interest*

Civil penalties and interest and criminal penalties are discussed at ¶2503.

For abatement of penalties and interest resulting from certified audits, see ¶2402.

- *Prepaid sales tax on motor fuel*

Motor fuel retailers are required to prepay a portion of the tax to the distributor, supplier, or other reseller of motor fuel; liquid propane gas is excluded from the prepayment requirement (35 ILCS 120/2d; 86 Ill. Adm. Code Sec. 130.701). Retailers are entitled to take credit on the sales tax return for the amount of the prepaid sales tax. Motor fuel resellers are not required to collect and remit prepaid sales tax on motor fuel delivered to their company-owned retail outlets. Registered distributors, suppliers and other resellers of motor fuel must remit to the Department the prepaid sales tax and provide each prepaying motor fuel retailer with a statement confirming the amount of sales tax prepaid. The vendor's discount (¶1602) does not apply to prepaid sales tax.

The DOR generally will determine the per-gallon retailers' occupation (sales) tax rate on January 1 and July 1. The DOR will establish the rate by multiplying the average selling price of motor fuel in the state during the previous six months by 6.25%. For qualifying biodiesel blends and gasohol, the semiannual rates will be 80% of the general rate set for motor fuels. The DOR will provide notice of the rates at least 20 days prior to each January 1 and July 1 by publishing the rates on the department's Website at **http://tax.illinois.gov/TaxRates/PrepaidSalesTax.htm**. Publication of the rates on the DOR Website constitutes sufficient notice of the rates. (35 ILCS 120/2d(d))

¶1802

• *Automobile renting use tax*

Persons engaged in the automobile rental business in Illinois must file a return on or before the last day of each month covering transactions for the preceding month (86 Ill. Adm. Code Sec. 180.140).

• *Hotel operators' occupation tax*

Every operator engaged in renting, leasing, or letting rooms must file a return and send a payment to the Department of Revenue no later than the last day of each month covering transactions for the preceding month (35 ILCS 145/6).

The Department may authorize quarterly or annual reports if the operator's average monthly tax liability does not exceed a specified amount. If the operator goes out of business or ceases to have a tax liability, the operator must file a final return not more than one month after discontinuance. If an individual or company has more than one business registered with the Department of Revenue, that individual or company cannot file a consolidated return but must file separate returns for each of the registered businesses.

Collection discount: The operator filing the return may deduct a discount of 2.1% or $25 per calendar year, whichever is greater, to reimburse the operator for the expenses incurred in keeping records, preparing and filing returns, remitting the tax, and supplying data to the Department.

• *Tire user fee*

Instead of tire retailers filing returns, they may remit the tire user fee (¶1504) to the tire suppliers who then file a return (Form ST-8) and remit the fee to the Department of Revenue. Suppliers who enter into agreements with tire retailers to collect and remit the tire user fee are liable for the tax on all tires sold to the tire retailers.

• *Tax on cultivation of medical marijuana*

On or before the 20th day of each calendar month, persons subject to the privilege tax on the cultivation of medical marijuana (¶1520) must file a return with the department. The amount of tax due must be submitted at the time a return is filed. The department may adopt rules related to enforcing the medical cannabis privilege tax law. (Uncodified Sec. 205, Compassionate Use of Medical Cannabis Pilot Program Act)

Cannabis cultivation centers must file Form MC-1, Medical Cannabis Cultivation Privilege Tax Return, to report the privilege tax due on cultivated medical cannabis and Form ST-1, Sales and Use Tax and E911 Surcharge Return, to report sales tax due on sales of medical cannabis and medical cannabis infused products through July 1, 2020. Free samples of medical cannabis given away by medical cannabis cultivation centers and medical cannabis dispensaries are subject to 1% use tax. (*Informational Bulletin FY 2017-02,* Illinois Department of Revenue, August 2016, CCH ILLINOIS TAX REPORTS, ¶403-119)

¶1803 Records

Law: Retailers' Occupation Tax Act, Sec. 7 [35 ILCS 120/7]; Service Occupation Tax Act, Sec. 11 [35 ILCS 115/11]; Use Tax Act, Sec. 11 [35 ILCS 105/11]; Service Use Tax Act, Sec. 11 [35 ILCS 110/11]; 86 Ill. Adm. Code Sec. 140.701; 86 Ill. Adm. Code Sec. 150.1301 (CCH ILLINOIS TAX REPORTS, ¶61-260).

Persons subject to the ROT, SOT, UT, or SUT must keep books and records of all sales of tangible personal property, together with invoices, bills of lading, sales records, copies of bills of sale, inventories prepared as of December 31 of each year (or otherwise annually as has been the custom in the specific trade) and other pertinent papers and documents. A seller claiming deductions on the tax return must keep records showing the names and addresses of customers, the character of the transactions, the date of every transaction, receipts realized, and such other information as is necessary to establish the nontaxable character of each transaction (35 ILCS 105/11; 35 ILCS 110/11; 35 ILCS 115/11; 35 ILCS 120/7).

Books and records must be preserved until the expiration of the periods during which the Department i; 86 Ill. Adm. Code Sec. 150.1301;.

See also ¶2403, concerning recordkeeping and confidentiality.

¶1804 ROT—Sales of Stock of Goods, Furniture or Fixtures, or Machinery and Equipment

Law: Retailers' Occupation Tax Act, Sec. 5j [35 ILCS 120/5j]; Service Occupation Tax Act, Sec. 12 [35 ILCS 115/12]; Use Tax Act, Sec. 12 [35 ILCS 105/12]; Service Use Tax Act; Sec. 12 [35 ILCS 110/12]; 86 Ill. Adm. Code Sec. 130.1701; 86 Ill. Adm. Code Sec. 140.1601 (CCH ILLINOIS TAX REPORTS, ¶60-590).

If a taxpayer whose business is subject to tax sells or transfers, outside the usual course of business, the major part of the following: (1) the stock of goods that the taxpayer is engaged in the business of selling; (2) furniture or fixtures; (3) machinery and equipment; or (4) real property, the taxpayer must pay the Department any tax due up to the time of the sale or transfer. The seller or purchaser *may* notify the Department, at least 10 business days before the date of the intended sale or transfer, and request an audit to determine the tax due. In any event, the purchaser *must*, no later than 10 business days after the sale or transfer, notify the Department of the sale and withhold from the sales price an amount sufficient to pay any tax (including any penalty or interest) due and unpaid by the seller, until the purchaser or transferee receives a certificate from the Department indicating that no tax is due from the seller. A purchaser or transferee of a taxpayer's business or stock of goods becomes personally liable for the unpaid tax debts of the seller on failure to file a report of sale with the Department (35 ILCS 120/5j; 86 Ill. Adm. Code Sec. 130.1701; 86 Ill. Adm. Code Sec. 140.1601).

Practitioner Comment: Bulk Sale Notices

Often, instead of notifying the Department of Revenue that an extraordinary sale is going to occur, sellers represent to the buyer that all state and local taxes are paid and warranty that if state and local taxes are owed that the seller will reimburse the buyer for any liabilities. This representation and warranty can be a dangerous undertaking for a buyer. If the Department determines that a liability is owed, the Department can collect the liability directly from the buyer under the theory of successor liability. The Department has no obligation to collect the liability from the seller and is not bound or restricted in anyway by the representation and warranty. Buyers can only protect themselves by filing a "bulk sale notice" with the Department.

It should also be noted that bulk sales notices must be filed with the Chicago Department of Revenue if any of the assets sold reside within the city limits. In addition, any person or firm purchasing or otherwise acquiring another business should request the seller to produce a certificate from the Director of Employment Security stating that it owes no contributions, interest, or penalties (see ¶2102).

Jordan M. Goodman, Esq., Horwood Marcus & Berk Chartered

¶1805 Administration

Law: Retailers' Occupation Tax Act, Sec. 1 [35 ILCS 120/1]; Retailers' Occupation Tax Act, Sec. 11a [35 ILCS 120/11a]; Retailers' Occupation Tax Act, Sec. 12 [35 ILCS 120/12]; Service Occupation Tax Act, Sec. 2 [35 ILCS 115/2]; Service Occupation Tax Act, Sec. 20a [35 ILCS 115/20a]; Use Tax Act, Sec. 1a [35 ILCS 105/1a]; Use Tax Act, Sec. 12b [35 ILCS

105/12b]; Service Use Tax Act, Sec. 2 [35 ILCS 110/2]; Service Use Tax Act, Sec. 20a [35 ILCS 110/20a] (CCH ILLINOIS TAX REPORTS, ¶ 60-030).

Taxes administratively collected by the Illinois Department of Revenue on behalf of local governments are as follows:

— Chicago home rule municipal soft drink retailers' occupation tax;

— county motor fuel tax;

— countywide share of state taxes;

— county share of state taxes;

— DuPage water commission taxes;

— home rule and non-home rule sales taxes;

— hotel taxes (metropolitan pier and exposition authority (MPEA) hotel operators' occupation tax, municipal hotel operators' occupation tax (Chicago), sports facilities authority hotel operators' occupation tax);

— local automobile renting occupation and use taxes;

— mass transit district taxes (metro-east mass transit district (MED) taxes and regional transportation authority (RTA) taxes);

— Metropolitan Pier and Exposition Authority (MPEA) taxes (automobile renting occupation and use taxes, hotel operators' occupation tax, and food and beverage tax);

— municipal share of state taxes; and

— special county retailers' occupation tax for public safety/transportation.

The Department is authorized to make, promulgate, and enforce necessary and reasonable rules and regulations relating to the administration and enforcement of the law (35 ILCS 105/12; 35 ILCS 110/12; 35 ILCS 115/125; 35 ILCS 120/12).

For a discussion of the Taxpayers' Bill of Rights, see ¶ 2601.

¶1806 Assessment

Law: Retailers' Occupation Tax Act, Sec. 4 [35 ILCS 120/4]; Retailers' Occupation Tax Act, Sec. 5a [35 ILCS 120/5a]; Retailers' Occupation Tax Act, Sec. 12 [35 ILCS 120/12]; Service Occupation Tax Act, Sec. 12 [35 ILCS 115/12]; Use Tax Act, Sec. 12 [35 ILCS 105/12]; Service Use Tax Act, Sec. 12 [35 ILCS 110/12] (CCH ILLINOIS TAX REPORTS, ¶ 61-410, 61-430, 61-520).

The Illinois occupation and use taxes are generally self-assessed in that they are based on gross receipts or selling price of tangible personal property. However, if a return filed shows an incorrect amount of tax due, the Department may correct the return and assess any additional tax due by means of a deficiency notice. A notice of deficiency becomes a final assessment unless a protest and request for a hearing are filed within 60 days after the notice is issued.

Except in the case of a fraudulent return, or with the consent of the taxpayer, no notice of tax liability can be issued on and after each January 1 and July 1 covering gross receipts received during any period more than three years prior to such January 1 and July 1 (in the case of the SOT, UT, and SUT, the date the tax was due rather than the date the gross receipts were received governs) (35 ILCS 120/5).

If a taxpayer fails to sign a sales or use tax return within 30 days after proper notice and demand for signature by the Department of Revenue, the return will be considered valid and any amount shown due on the return will be deemed assessed.

If the Department of Revenue's correction of a sales tax return is the result of an understatement of tax by the taxpayer due to a mathematical error, the Department must notify the taxpayer that the excess amount is due and has been assessed (35 ILCS 120/4). This notice is not considered a notice of tax liability and the taxpayer does not have any right of protest.

Practitioner Comment: Informal Conference Board

In 2001, the Illinois Department of Revenue created a forum called the Informal Conference Board for resolving tax disputes before the issuance of a notice of tax liability or claim denial. A taxpayer may submit a settlement proposal or request a penalty waiver either with the initial request to the Board or at any time during the process before the Board. The Board's decision may not be appealed. However, if the Board does not grant the relief that the taxpayer has requested, the taxpayer may still seek relief via the regular administrative process or circuit court. For additional information on dispute resolution and appeals, see ¶ 2701.

Jordan M. Goodman, Esq., Horwood Marcus & Berk Chartered

• *Jeopardy assessments*

If the Department finds that a taxpayer is about to leave the state, conceal himself or his property, or do any other act tending to prejudice or render wholly or partly ineffectual proceedings to collect tax unless proceedings are brought without delay, or if the Department finds that collection of the amount due will be jeopardized by delay, the Department will give the taxpayer notice of its findings and demand immediate return and payment of the tax, upon which the tax will become immediately due and payable. If the taxpayer does not comply with the notice or show that the findings are erroneous, within five days after notice, the Department may file a notice of jeopardy assessment lien (35 ILCS 120/5a; 35 ILCS 120/5c).

A taxpayer who believes that no tax is owed or that there is no jeopardy may protest within 20 days after notice of the jeopardy assessment lien and may request a hearing. After the hearing, the Department will notify the taxpayer whether or not the lien will be released (35 ILCS 120/5a).

Practioner Comment: Voluntary Payment Doctrine

The Illinois Appellate Court upheld the circuit court's dismissal of plaintiff Edward Karpowicz's complaint alleging that Papa Murphy's International, LLC ("PMI") and P-Cubed Enterprises LLC ("P-Cubed") violated the Illinois Consumer Fraud and Deceptive Business Practices Act (*Karpowicz v. Papa Murphy's International LLC*, No. 5-15-0320, July 5, 2016, CCH Illinois Tax Reports, ¶ 403-112).

The Plaintiff alleged that the 9% sales tax charged by PMI, a franchisor of pizza stores that sold "take-and-bake" pizzas was an unfair and deceptive act in violation of the Consumer Fraud Act because a 1% sales tax rate should apply to food sold by a retailer without facilities for on-premises consumption of food. The Tribunal held for PMI and P-Cubed, finding that Plaintiff's suit was barred by the voluntary payment doctrine because the payment was not made under duress as pizza did not constitute a "necessity."

Practitioner Comment: Taxpayers who challenge the collection of use or sales taxes need to be aware of the voluntary payment doctrine. It has been a long standing principle that taxes that are paid voluntarily even if erroneous may not be recovered without statutory authority. (See: *Getto v. City of Chicago*, 86 ILL. 2d 39, 1981). To recover taxes that were voluntarily paid it is necessary not only to show that the taxing jurisdiction's claim to the tax was unlawful but also the payment of that tax was not voluntary. To establish the payment was not voluntary the taxpayer has to establish that there was some necessity that amounted to a compulsion and the payment was made under the influence of that compulsion. (*Illinois Glass Co. v. Chicago Telephone Co.* 234 Ill. 535, 1908). In other words, the payment had to be made under duress. Taxpayers may avoid the application of the voluntary payment doctrine by following the procedures set forth in the Protest Fund Act. This Act provides that a consumer who intends to contest the a collection of a use tax may do so by paying the tax under protest and then suing the retailer, the Director of Revenue and the Illinois Treasurer to request that the funds be segregated into a protest fund. (30 ILCS 230/2).

Marilyn A. Wethekam, Esq., Horwood Marcus & Berk, Chartered

¶1807 Refunds and Credits; Bad Debts

Law: Retailers' Occupation Tax Act, Sec. 2-40 [35 ILCS 120/2-40]; Retailers' Occupation Tax Act, Secs. 6—6c [35 ILCS 120/6—120/6c]; Service Occupation Tax Act, Secs. 17—20 [35 ILCS 115/17—115/20]; Use Tax Act, Secs. 19—22 [35 ILCS 105/19—105/22]; Service Use Tax Act, Secs. 17—20 [35 ILCS 110/17—110/20]; Counties Code, Secs. 5-1006— 5-1007 [55 ILCS 5/5-1006—5/5-1007]; Illinois Municipal Code, Sec. 8-11-1 [65 ILCS 5/8-11-1]; Illinois Municipal Code, Sec. 8-11-5 [65 ILCS 5/8-11-5]; 86 Ill. Adm. Code Sec. 130.1501 (CCH Illinois Tax Reports, ¶60-570, 61-270, 61-610).

Forms: ST-6, Claim for Verified Overpayment; ST-557, Claim for Credit for Repossession of Motor Vehicles.

Cash refunds or credit memoranda are authorized for return of overpayments of state occupation and use taxes (35 ILCS 120/6; 35 ILCS 110/17; 35 ILCS 115/17; 35 ILCS 105/19; 86 Ill. Adm. Code Sec. 130.1501). The Department does not automatically issue credit memoranda for overpayments of quarter-monthly payments (¶1802) unless requested by the taxpayer.

A credit memorandum may be applied against liability under any of the state taxes. It may be assigned by the taxpayer to another taxpayer who is subject to tax.

A seller that refunds tax to a customer that paid sales tax on a purchase, but later provided an exemption certificate, may not make an adjustment on its sales tax return to reflect the customer refund. The seller must file a claim for credit or refund with the department. Further, the seller's customers may not file a credit or claim for refund with the department for taxes that were paid to the seller. (*General Information Letter ST 13-0029-GIL,* Illinois Department of Revenue, June 10, 2013, CCH Illinois Tax Reports, ¶402-686)

Claims filed on and after each January 1 and July 1 are not allowed as to taxes, penalties or interest erroneously paid more than three years prior to such January 1 or July 1.

Practitioner Comment: Statute of Limitations

In *American Airlines, Inc. v. Illinois Department of Revenue,* Docket. No. 1-08-2985, Illinois Appellate Court (December 18, 2009), CCH Illinois Tax Reports, ¶402-055, the Illinois Appellate Court reversed the Illinois Circuit Court's decision and held that sales tax refund claims filed by a taxpayer, after the statute of limitations had run, did not relate back to and amend the taxpayer's timely-filed refund claims. After filing timely sales/ use tax returns, American Airlines informed the Department that it had identified additional flights that were not originally included in its initial claims and filed amended sales/use tax returns. The Department then issued a notice to American Airlines that the original claims had been approved but that the amended claims were time barred. The Court rejected American Airline's argument that the relation-back doctrine, which is recognized for federal income tax purpose, was applicable to Illinois' sales/use tax laws. Rather, the court found that each claim was independent and therefore independently subject to the statute of limitations. The Court stated that "each time an amount is claimed, it is subject to the operative statute of limitations, so that even a so-called amended claim that seeks an additional amount, albeit for the same type of exemption, would have to independently satisfy the statute of limitations."

Marilyn A. Wethekam, Esq., Horwood Marcus & Berk Chartered

If a seller, supplier, or service provider collects amounts from a purchaser in excess of the amount of tax due on a transaction, the purchaser is given the legal right to claim a refund from the seller. However, if the excess amounts collected are not refunded to the purchaser, they must be remitted to the state.

When there is an erroneous refund of tax, a notice of tax liability may be issued by the Department of Revenue anytime within three years of the refund or within five years if the refund was induced by fraud or misrepresentation.

• *Returned motor vehicles*

A retailer of a motor vehicle is entitled to a sales tax (ROT) refund or credit memorandum when the manufacturer of a motor vehicle sold by the retailer accepts the return of that automobile and refunds to the purchaser the selling price as provided in the New Vehicle Buyer Protection Act. The amount of the refund or credit is equal to the amount of tax paid by the retailer on the initial sale of the vehicle (35 ILCS 120/6).

• *Other credits*

Credit for tax paid to another state: See ¶ 1603.

Manufacturer's purchase credit (expired): See ¶ 1604.

• *Sunset dates for credits*

Application of any credit enacted after September 16, 1994, must be limited by a sunset date. If a "reasonable and appropriate" sunset date is not specified, then the credit will expire five years after the effective date of the enacting law (35 ILCS 105/3-90; 35 ILCS 110/3-70; 35 ILCS 115/3-55).

For a discussion of the Taxpayers' Bill of Rights, see ¶ 806.

• *Bad debts*

Effective July 1, 2015, a retailer may claim a deduction for Illinois sales tax due and payable if the tax has become a bad debt and the following three conditions are met (35 ILCS 120/6d(a)):

> (1) the tax is represented by amounts that are found to be worthless or uncollectible;

> (2) the tax has been charged off as bad debt on the retailer's books and records; and

> (3) the tax has been claimed on the retailer's federal income tax return as a bad debt deduction.

Separate rules apply for credit card purchases. When taxes were paid with a credit card purchase, for example, a deduction is available only for debts written off on or after January 1, 2016. If a retailer deducts a bad debt but later collects the tax due, the retailer must include the tax in the retailer's next return and remit the tax. (35 ILCS 120/6d(b))

The Department of Revenue will issue rules for taking a bad sales tax debt deduction.

Practitioner Comment: Bad Debt Refunds and Third-party Financing

The Illinois Appellate Court upheld the denial of Home Depot's claim for a refund of sales tax (*Home Depot v. Hamer*, Illinois Appellate Court (1st Dist.) Docket No. 4-09-0611 (May 5, 2010) (Petition for Leave to Appeal Pending). Home Depot claimed that the refund was based on sales taxes it paid on transactions that were financed through its private label credit card (PLCC) but that were never completed because the purchasers defaulted on the payments. The Department denied the refund because it found that the unrelated third parties, which served as the financing company for the PLCC program, bore the burden of the bad debt rather than Home Depot).

On appeal, Home Depot argued that the Department misconstrued the financing agreements, and that Home Depot both directly and indirectly compensated the third party for the bad-debt losses. Applying the clear error standard of review, the court rejected the argument and held that Home Depot did not overcome the prima facie case established by the Department. The court found that three of the four revenue streams, which Home Depot maintained were the ways it compensated the third party for the bad-debt losses, could not reasonably be claimed as reimbursements. The Court did not address the argument that the Department added a requirement to the regulation "that the party seeking the refund must be the party who wrote off the receivable on the federal income-tax return," because it affirmed the Department's decision based on the determination that Home Depot did not bear the burden of the bad-debt losses.

The decision makes it clear that under the Illinois statue when a retailer sells its accounts receivable to an unrelated third party the retailer may not take the deduction for bad debts because it is the third party that actually incurred the bad debt.

Marilyn A. Wethekam, Esq., Horwood Marcus & Berk Chartered

Practitioner Comment: Intrastate Tax Collection Reciprocity Act

On February 9, 2011, Senate Bill 1395 was introduced creating the Intrastate Tax Collection Reciprocity Act (ITCRA). The ITCRA provides that if a taxpayer is due a refund, and if the taxpayer has also incurred a tax liability under one or more of these Acts, then the taxpayer may apply with the Department of Revenue to offset the amount of the refund from the amount of his or her tax liability. The ITCRA would be applicable to any taxpayer who is due a refund, and who has incurred a tax liability under the Illinois Income Tax Act, the Use Tax Act, the Service Use Tax Act, the Service Occupation Tax Act, the Retailers' Occupation Tax Act, the Cigarette Tax Act, the Cigarette Use Tax Act, the Tobacco Products Tax Act of 1995, the Motor Fuel Tax Law, the Hotel Operators' Occupation Tax Act, the Electricity Excise Tax Law, the Gas Revenue Tax Act, or the Gas Use Tax Law.

If passed, S.B. 1395 would have provided some needed relief for taxpayers who have outstanding tax refunds that the Department has not been able to pay. However, even with today's economic climate, this bill did not make it beyond the Senate committees.

Breen M. Schiller, Esq., Horwood Marcus & Berk Chartered

Practitioner Comment: Citi Bank, N.A. v. Illinois Department of Revenue, 2016 IL App (1st) 133650

The Illinois Appellate Court determined that a bank was entitled to a refund of Retailer's Occupation Tax on uncollectible debt from installment contracts financed by Citibank. While the customer made the purchase from an Illinois retailer, Citibank later acquired the consumer charge accounts from the Illinois retailers. The Illinois retailers were the entities responsible for remitting the applicable ROT to the Illinois Department of Revenue. When Citibank acquired the accounts from the Illinois retailers, it acquired all rights related to the accounts, including the right to later claim a sales tax refund for defaulted accounts. Some of the consumers ultimately defaulted leaving unpaid balances for which Citibank sought a refund for related to amounts attributable to financed sales taxes. The Illinois Circuit Court ruled in favor of Citibank and the Department of Revenue appealed.

On appeal, the Department alleged that Citibank lacked standing because it was not the retailer that remitted tax to the state and under the applicable statute, only the person who remitted such tax to the state had standing to file a refund claim. However, the appellate court did not agree and found that the refund rights were assigned from the retailer to Citibank and that in essence, Citibank stepped into the shoes of the retailer. The Court relied on the longstanding principle that common law and statutory rights are assignable, unless a statute or public policy clearly indicates otherwise. Following the assignment, "the assignee stands in the shoes of the assignor with respect to the rights, title, and interest in the thing assigned." ¶ 32 citing *Collins Co. v. Carboline Co.*, 125 Ill. 2d 498, 512 (1988). The Department of Revenue has appealed the Appellate Court's decision to

This decision should be contrasted with the unpublished decision of the Illinois Appellate Court in *Home Depot USA v. Hamer*, No. 4-09-0611 (May 5, 2010). In the *Home Depot* case, the Appellate Court ruled that a retailer was not entitled to a sales tax bad debt deduction on receivables that it sold to an unrelated bank because Home Depot did not bear the economic burden of the bad debt. Instead, at least according to the *Home Depot* court, the economic burden of the bad debt is borne by the bank that purchased the ultimately worthless receivable. Without actually relying on the *Home Depot* decision, the *Citi Bank* court implicitly recognized this fact by permitting Citi Bank to claim a sales tax refund on the bad debts in issue. If the Appellate Court had denied Citi Bank its refund claim, then the net result of the *Home Depot* and *Citi Bank* decisions would have been that neither the retailer nor the financing party could claim a sales tax refund on a bad debt.

David A. Hughes, Esq., Horwood Marcus & Berk Chartered

¶1808 Refund or Credit for Building Material Sales to High-Impact Businesses

Law: Retailers' Occupation Tax Act, Sec. 5*l* [35 ILCS 120/5*l*](CCH ILLINOIS TAX REPORTS, ¶60-360).

Retailers making sales of building materials to "high-impact" businesses (¶1017) are entitled to credit or refund of sales or use taxes paid (35 ILCS 120/5). Sales that are also exempt under enterprise zone provisions (¶1702) are not eligible for additional credit.

¶1809 Credit for Erroneous Payment by Retailer to Vendor

Law: Retailers' Occupation Tax Act, Sec. 6 [35 ILCS 120/6]; Use Tax Act, Sec. 19 [35 ILCS 105/19](CCH ILLINOIS TAX REPORTS, ¶61-610).

If a retailer fails to pay the retailers' occupation tax or use tax on the gross proceeds from the sale of an item and is later required to make that payment, the retailer may take a credit for an erroneous tax payment made to the vendor on the purchase of the item. (The erroneous payment to the vendor arises if the retailer does not first use the item before reselling it.) If the credit is taken, the retailer's vendor may neither refund the tax to the retailer nor file a claim for a refund or credit with the Department (35 ILCS 120/6; 35 ILCS 105/19).

¶1810 Absorption of Tax Prohibited—SOT and UT

Law: Use Tax Act, Sec. 7 [35 ILCS 105/7]; Service Occupation Tax Act, Sec. 7 [35 ILCS 115/7] (CCH ILLINOIS TAX REPORTS, ¶61-210, 61-530).

Both the SOT and UT laws contain provisions prohibiting a retailer or supplier from advertising or holding out to the public or to any purchaser or service provider that the tax will be assumed or absorbed or that it will not be added to the selling price of the property sold, or, if added, that it will be refunded (other than a refund of tax when the selling price is refunded upon return of the merchandise, or when the seller refunds the tax to the purchaser to support a tax claim filed with the Department). (35 ILCS 105/7; 35 ILCS 115/7)

Unlawful advertisement: A flyer advertising that an Illinois retailer would be responsible for retailers' occupation (sales) tax on customer purchasers made in the store on a specific date was illegal. The flyer contained a one-inch headline indicating "TAX-FREE DAY!!" and included the following language: "You pay . . . No State Sales Tax! No County Sales Tax! No City Sales Tax!"

Illinois requires retailers to collect a use tax from purchasers by adding the tax to the selling price of the tangible personal property sold when sold for use. Therefore, it was unlawful for the retailer to advertise that the tax would be assumed or absorbed by the retailer. The retailer was guilty of a Class A misdemeanor for the advertisement (*General Information Letter ST 01-0173-GIL*, Illinois Department of Revenue, September 25, 2001, CCH ILLINOIS TAX REPORTS, ¶401-297; see also *General Information Letter ST 15-0042-GIL*, Illinois Department of Revenue, June 25, 2015, CCH ILLINOIS TAX REPORTS,¶402-977).

¶1811 Streamlined Sales and Use Tax Agreement

Law: Simplified Sales and Use Tax Administration Act, Sec.1, *et seq.* [35 ILCS 171/1] (CCH ILLINOIS TAX REPORTS, ¶60-098).

The purpose of the Streamlined Sales and Use Tax (SST) Agreement is to simplify and modernize sales and use tax administration in the member states in order to substantially reduce the burden of tax compliance.

Illinois is not a member of the Agreement because, although it has enacted legislation authorizing it to enter into the Agreement, it has not yet enacted the changes to its laws necessary to comply with the Agreement's requirements. However, as an Advisor State to the Governing Board it will serve in an *ex officio* capacity on the Board, with nonvoting status, and may speak to any matter presented to the Board for its consideration. It will also have input through its representation on the State and Local Advisory Council, which advises the Board on matters pertaining to the administration of the Agreement.

The text of the Agreement and a list of current members can be found at **www.streamlinedsalestax.org**.

• *Outline of the Agreement*

A state that wishes to become a member of the Agreement must certify that its laws, rules, regulations, and policies are substantially compliant with each of the requirements of the Agreement. The requirements of the Agreement include the following:

— a central online registration system for all member states;

— an amnesty for uncollected or unpaid tax for sellers that register to collect tax, so long as they were not previously registered in the state;

— the use of new technology models for tax collection, including certified service providers (CSPs);

— a monetary allowance for CSPs;

— relief from liability for collecting the incorrect amount of tax as a result of relying on data that each member state must provide in the form of a taxability matrix;

— state level administration of local sales and use taxes;

— a single state and local tax base in each state;

— adequate notice to sellers of changes in tax rates, the tax base, and jurisdictional boundaries;

— a single tax rate per taxing jurisdiction, with the exception that a state (but not a locality) may have a second rate on food and drugs;

— uniform, destination-based sourcing rules;

— direct pay authority for holders of permits;

— limitations on exemptions to make them simpler to administer;

— uniform returns and remittances;

— uniform rules for bad debt deductions;

— limitations on sales tax holidays;

— elimination of most caps and thresholds;

— a uniform rounding rule;

— customer refund procedures that limit a purchaser's ability to sue for a return of over-collected tax from the seller;

— uniform definitions, including uniform product definitions; and

— a "books-and-records" standard for certain bundled transactions.

Uniform exemption certificate: The SST Governing Board has approved a uniform exemption certificate. Although full member states may continue to use their pre-existing exemption certificates, they must also accept the uniform certificate. Associate member and nonmember states may, but are not required to, accept the certificate.

PART VI
ESTATE TAXES
CHAPTER 19
ESTATE AND GENERATION-SKIPPING TRANSFER TAXES

¶1901 The Law

Illinois estate tax is covered in 35 ILCS 405 Illinois Estate and Generation-Skipping Transfer Tax Act. Comprehensive coverage of estate and inheritance taxes is provided in Wolters Kluwer, CCH Multistate Inheritance Tax Reporter. For more information go to CCHGroup.com or contact an account representative at 888-CCH-REPS (888-224-377).

PART VII
PROPERTY TAXES
CHAPTER 20
PROPERTY TAXES

¶2001 Scope of Chapter

The property taxes in Illinois apply to all real property, except for specified exemptions. While there is provision for a state property tax, none is currently imposed, and so the taxes are essentially local. No tax is levied on personal property.

The property tax cycle extends over a two-year period: property is assessed during the first year (¶2005) and property tax bills are paid during the second year (*e.g.*, tax for the 2016 assessment year is paid in 2017).

This chapter is intended to be a general survey of the property taxes and is not intended to provide detailed coverage. It outlines primarily the property subject to taxation, the assessment procedure, the basis and rate of the tax, and the requirements for filing returns and making payments. For additional information, see PTAX-1004, *The Illinois Property Tax System*, Illinois Department of Revenue, October 2014, CCH ILLINOIS TAX REPORTS, ¶402-905.

• *Tax rate information*

The Illinois Department of Revenue (DOR) maintains on its Website a database of local rates of corporate and personal income, property, sales and use (use and occupation), and excise tax rates for taxing districts in the state. The database, called Tax Rate Finder, is located at **https://www.revenue.state.il.us/app/trii/**.

Rate information for property taxes includes:

— the name of each taxing district;

— a list of all funds for which taxes were extended;

— the corresponding rate for each fund; and

— the district's total rate.

Rate information for property taxes is updated annually on January 1 with the most recent rate information available.

¶2002 Imposition of Tax

Law: Property Tax Code, Sec. 1-50 [35 ILCS 200/1-50]; Property Tax Code, Sec. 9-145 [35 ILCS 200/9-145]; Property Tax Code, Sec. 9-175 [35 ILCS 200/9-175]; Property Tax Code, Sec. 18-125 [35 ILCS 200/18-125]; Property Tax Code, Sec. 18-185 *et seq.* [35 ILCS 200/18-185 *et seq.*] (CCH ILLINOIS TAX REPORTS, ¶ 20-010, 20-405, 20-605).

The tax is imposed by various local taxing units at the county level and lower, such as city, school district, sanitary district, park district, and the like. Property is subject to the combined tax rates of the various districts in which it is located.

Real property in Illinois is generally valued on the basis of its fair cash value. (35 ILCS 200/9-145) Special assessment rules apply to farmland, pollution control facilities, open-space land, coal, and airports.

The date for assessed valuation of real property is January 1. (35 ILCS 200/9-175)

Hospital provider assessment: See ¶2213.

Hydraulic fracturing tax: "New property" includes any increase in assessed value due to oil or gas production from an oil or gas well required to be permitted under the Hydraulic Fracturing Regulatory Act (see ¶2214) that was not produced in or accounted for during the previous levy year (35 ILCS 200/18-185).

• *Property Tax Extension Limitation Law*

Illinois has a law designed to limit the increases in property tax extensions for non-home rule districts when property values and assessments are increasing faster than the rate of inflation. However, the Property Tax Extension Limitation Law (PTELL) (35 ILCS 200/18-185 *et seq.*) is not a "tax cap" and does not cap either individual property tax bills or individual property assessments (see *PIO-62, An Overview of the Property Tax Extension Limitation Law by Referendum,* Illinois Department of Revenue, February 2012, CCH ILLINOIS TAX REPORTS,¶402-455; see also *Property Tax Extension Limitation Law Technical Manual,* PTAX-1080, December 2013).

The extension limitation generally is equal to (35 ILCS 200/18-185):

— the lesser of 5% or

— the percentage increase in the Consumer Price Index during the 12-month calendar year preceding the levy year or

— the rate of increase approved by voters.

Property tax maximum rate referenda ballots must provide specific information, and all referendum questions proposed must conform to language requirements. (35 ILCS 200/18-125; 35 ILCS 200/18-190; 35 ILCS 200/18-205)

CCH Advisory: New Rate Required a Voter Referendum

For purposes of the Illinois property tax extension limitation law (PTELL), a county's 1997 first-time levy and collection of a tax for operation of a detention home constituted a "new rate," which should have been submitted to direct referendum of the county voters prior to extending the levy, according to the Illinois Supreme Court. A contrary appellate court ruling in the case was reversed, and a 1997 opinion on which the appellate court relied was reversed in part.

Although the statute authorizing the detention home tax was enacted prior to the effective date of PTELL, the unambiguous language in PTELL that required that a "new rate" be submitted for referendum did not apply only to rates authorized by statutes enacted after PTELL's effective date. In addition, the county's levies for the same purpose over the four years after the initial levy also were invalid because they had not been submitted to referendum. The purpose of PTELL was to provide greater citizen control over the levy of taxes they are required to pay, and the protections contemplated by the statute were ignored in this case. Where the requirements of a statute are designed for the protection of taxpayers, those provisions are mandatory and a disregard of them will render the tax illegal. Without a valid preexisting levy, each successive levy was an attempt to impose the levy for the first time. (*Acme Markets, Inc. v. Callanan,* Illinois Supreme Court, Docket No. 106198, October 29, 2009, CCH ILLINOIS TAX REPORTS,¶402-037)

District boundaries: PTELL applied to all portions of a school district after territory in a county that had not considered a PTELL referendum was annexed into the district.

Although PTELL had no provisions addressing this situation, it also had no provisions for reexamination of a PTELL district's status because of a subsequent change in its boundaries. In addition, the district had not met referendum requirements of districts in more than one county to make PTELL inapplicable to the district. Finally, there was no basis for holding that PTELL applied to the part of the district that fell within the county that prior to the annexation had voted for PTELL but not in the very small part of the district that fell within the other county. (*Board of Education of Auburn Community Unit School District No. 10 v. Department of Revenue,* Illinois Supreme Court, Docket Nos. 110395, 110422, May 19, 2011, CCH ILLINOIS TAX REPORTS, ¶ 402-336)

For additional information on PTELL, see *PIO-62, An Overview of the Property Tax Extension Limitation Law by Referendum,* Illinois Department of Revenue, February 2012, CCH ILLINOIS TAX REPORTS, ¶ 402-455; see also *Property Tax Extension Limitation Law Technical Manual,* PTAX-1080, December 2013.

¶2003 Property Subject to Tax

Law: Illinois Const., Art. IX, Sec. 5, Illinois Development Finance Authority Act, Sec. 7.80 [20 ILCS 3505/7.80]; County Historic Preservation Act, Sec. 4(14) [55 ILCS 5/5-30004]; Property Tax Code, Sec. 1-30 [35 ILCS 200/1-30]; Property Tax Code, Sec. 1-130 [35 ILCS 200/1-130]; Property Tax Code, Secs. 18-165—18-178 [35 ILCS 200/18-165—18-178]; Property Tax Code, Sec. 18-184.10 [35 ILCS 200/18-184.10]; Property Tax Code, Sec. 21-95 [35 ILCS 200/21-95]; Property Tax Code, Sec. 24-5 [35 ILCS 200/24-5]; Longtime Owner-Occupant Property Tax Relief Act, Sec. 10—20 [35 ILCS 250/10—250/20]; 35 ILCS 515/1, et seq.; 86 Ill. Adm. Code 110.116 (CCH ILLINOIS TAX REPORTS, ¶ 20-010, 20-315).

In general, all real property in the state is taxable but personal property is not. Real estate is taxable where it is located.

Practitioner Comment: Farm Crops

The Illinois Supreme Court determined that crops growing on a farm are personal property not subject to property tax while stock growing at a nursery is taxable as real estate because of the importance of food crops and because nursery stock has the characteristics of growing trees permanently located on real estate (*Knupper et al. v. Property Tax Appeal Board,* 61 Ill. App.3d 884, 378 N.E.2d 340 (2nd Dist. 1978), CCH ILLINOIS TAX REPORTS, ¶ 200-996).

David A. Hughes, Esq., Horwood Marcus & Berk Chartered

To comply with the Illinois constitutional mandate abolishing personal property taxes, the corporate personal property tax was declared unconstitutional by the Illinois Supreme Court (*Client Follow-Up Co. v. Hynes* (1979, SCt), 75 Ill2d 208, 390 NE2d 847, CCH ILLINOIS TAX REPORTS, ¶ 201-022). Thereafter, the legislature enacted the personal property tax replacement income tax (replacement tax). See the discussion of the replacement tax at ¶ 902.

Mobile homes and manufactured homes: Homes located in mobile home parks are taxed according to the mobile home local services tax (35 ILCS 515/1). Mobile homes and manufactured homes that are sold and transferred from a mobile home park to private property, or that are already located on private property, are subject to property tax, whether or not the mobile home or manufactured home is affixed to, or installed on, a permanent foundation or is considered real property under other Illinois law (35 ILCS 200/1-130).

The owner of an inhabited mobile home or manufactured home outside of a mobile home park must record a mobile home registration form in the county where the home is located (35 ILCS 515/4).

Mobile homes and manufactured homes located on a dealer's lot for resale purposes or as a temporary office are not subject to the mobile home local services tax (35 ILCS 515/1).

In light of a "grandfather clause" in a new law generally requiring mobile and manufactured homes installed outside a mobile home park to be taxed as real property, the requirement did not apply to a manufactured home whose owner failed to register the home and pay a privilege tax after its installment outside a mobile home park just months before the effective date of the new law. The property owners had installed a manufactured home on their property in 2010 but did not register the home with the local tax assessor within 30 days as required by the Mobile Home Local Services Act then in effect. The local county assessor did not conduct a new assessment of the property in 2010 and it was, therefore, assessed and taxed as a vacant lot under the old law. After the law was amended, the manufactured home was assessed as real property in 2011. However, under the old law, failure to record or surrender the title or certificate of origin did not prevent the home from being assessed and taxed as real property, and assessing officials had to assess and tax property according to its proper classification regardless of whether homeowners complied with the registration requirement. (*Jones v. State of Illinois Property Tax Appeal Board*, Appellate Court of Illinois, Fifth District, No. 5-16-0199, August 1, 2017, CCH ILLINOIS TAX REPORTS, ¶ 403-258)

Leaseholds: Although some land in the state may be exempt from taxation, leases of such land are taxable to the lessee (35 ILCS 200/9-195). The lessee of tax-exempt property is liable for tax on the property, and no tax lien attaches to the exempt interest in the property. A concession permit agreement between a private company and a city park district that allowed the company to use certain areas within a park to operate a restaurant and store was held to be a nontaxable license rather than a taxable lease for Illinois property tax assessment purposes (*Millennium Park Joint Venture, LLC*, Illinois Appellate Court, First District, No. 1-07-3141, June 29, 2009).

• *Abatement of tax*

Some property, while not exempt, is given preferred treatment either through special methods of valuation or in the form of property tax abatements. Enterprise zone property and property of a commercial or, under certain circumstances, industrial firm are examples of the latter category. The purpose of such programs is to encourage businesses to locate or rehabilitate property within a taxing district by offering financial incentives in the form of property tax abatements. As a practical matter, the effect of an abatement is to reduce or eliminate property taxes on a specific parcel of property.

Reporting requirement for certain abatements: An annual reporting requirement is imposed on Illinois taxpayers that receive abatement of property taxes under the Economic Development for a Growing Economy Tax Credit Act, the River Edge Redevelopment Zone Act, or the Enterprise Zone Act, including the High Impact Business program.

Recipients of such incentives must provide the Department of Commerce and Economic Opportunity with the following (20 ILCS 605/605-320):

— a detailed list of the occupation or job classifications and number of new employees or retained employees to be hired in full-time, permanent jobs;

— a schedule of anticipated starting dates of the new hires and the actual average wage by occupation or job classification; and

— total payroll to be created as a result of the incentives.

Abatement of taxes for property in a business corridor: Property that is not otherwise exempt from property tax and is situated in a qualifying business corridor created by an intergovernmental agreement is entitled to a property tax abatement. A qualifying "business corridor" is property that encompasses territory along the common border of two disadvantaged municipalities and is (1) undeveloped or underdeveloped and (2) not likely to be developed without the creation of the business corridor. A "disadvantaged municipality" is one with (1) a per capita equalized assessed valuation less than 60% of the state average and (2) more than 15% of its population below the national poverty level. A corridor agreement can only be adopted after each of the municipalities holds a public hearing on the issue. The abatement under any such agreement cannot exceed 10 years in duration. [35 ILCS 200/184.10]

Abatement of taxes for property leased to housing authorities: Noncommercial properties containing multifamily dwellings or certain multi-building developments in Cook County or Chicago that are leased for a minimum of 20 years to a state housing authority for use as low-rent housing are eligible for abatement from Illinois property taxes in the form of a reduction in payments due under the lease (35 ILCS 200/18-177).

Abatement of taxes for new or expanding industry: Local taxing districts may voluntarily abate taxes of a commercial or industrial firm that:

(1) uses its property for collecting, separating, storing, or processing recyclable materials;

(2) moves into the taxing district from another state or country during the preceding calendar year;

(3) expands its current facility within the taxing district; or

(4) is newly created within the state during the preceding calendar year.

The abatement is for a 10 year period. The total abated taxes cannot exceed $4 million (35 ILCS 200/18-165).

Buildings, structures, or other improvements developed for leasehold interests under U.S. military public/private residential developments (PPV leases) have been added to the list of properties for which taxing districts can abate all or part of property taxes due (35 ILCS 200/18-165).

Abatement of taxes on donations to job-training and counseling programs: Municipalities are authorized to abate municipal taxes in an amount not to exceed 50% of a taxpayer's donations of not less than $10,000 to a qualified program in an area designated as a target area for the creation or expansion of job-training and counseling programs, youth day-care centers, housing projects for senior adults, youth recreation programs, alcohol and drug abuse prevention programs, mental health counseling programs, domestic violence shelters, and other approved program. (65 ILCS 5/8-3-18)

Abatement of taxes on enterprise zone property: Local property tax abatement is authorized for real property located within an enterprise zone or a River Edge redevelopment zone. The amount of tax that may be abated cannot exceed the amount attributable to new construction, renovation, or rehabilitation (35 ILCS 200/18-170; *Information Bulletin FY 2014-11*, Illinois Department of Revenue, March 2014).

Practitioner Comment: Treatment in Cook County

Cook County offers special property tax treatment for enterprise zones. Improvements to enterprise zone property are assessed at 16% of market value for eight years. The tax rate itself remains the same but a taxpayer's liability is reduced because of the reduced property value. These special incentives also apply to the purchase of existing buildings in enterprise zones provided that the buildings have been vacated for 24 continuous months.

David A. Hughes, Esq., Horwood Marcus & Berk Chartered

Abatement of taxes on commercial or industrial development: A taxing district may abate its property taxes on a commercial or industrial development of at least 500 acres located within the district. The abatement must not exceed a period of 20 years and the aggregate amount of abated taxes for all taxing districts combined must not exceed $12 million (35 ILCS 200/18-165).

A commercial or industrial firm that expands a facility or its number of employees also may be abated by the taxing district. The abatement may not exceed a period of 10 years and the aggregate amount of the abated taxes may not exceed $4 million (35 ILCS 200/18-165).

Abatement of taxes under the Corporate Headquarters Relocation Act: The Corporate Headquarters Relocation Act authorizes taxing districts, other than school districts, to abate eligible corporations' property taxes or to enter into an agreement with an eligible corporation to make payments to that corporation for up to 20 years and authorizes school districts to abate taxes or enter into an agreement with an eligible corporation to make payments if the municipality agrees to provide equal funding to the school district (35 ILCS 200/18-165).

Abatement of taxes for high-impact businesses: Illinois businesses that encourage the establishment of new coal-powered electric generation facilities and certain related industries that would also encourage the creation of new jobs are eligible for property tax abatements. Qualifying businesses are also eligible for retailers' occupation (sales) tax exemptions on purchases of building materials and equipment (35 ILCS 200/18-165).

Abatement of taxes for academic or research institutes: A taxing district may abate property taxes on the property of an academic or research institute if the following requirements are satisfied:

(1) it is an exempt organization under IRC Sec. 501(c)(3);

(2) it operates for the benefit of the public by performing scientific research and making the results of the research available to the interested public on a nondiscriminatory basis; and

(3) it employs more than 100 employees.

The abatement will be for 15 years, at a minimum, and the aggregate amount of the abated taxes for all districts combined will be $5 million (35 ILCS 200/18-165).

Abatement of taxes on senior housing facilities: A taxing district may voluntarily abate property taxes on property that is devoted to affordable housing for seniors. These properties must have people living in housing provided by the state or a federal program designed by the Department of Human Rights to assist the elderly. Qualified occupants must be 55 years or older and have an annual income that does not exceed 80% of the gross median income as determined by the U.S. Department of Housing and Urban Development. The abatement may not exceed 15 years (35 ILCS 200/18-165).

Abatement of taxes in housing opportunity areas: For tax years 2004 through 2024, an owner of property located within a housing opportunity area who has a housing choice voucher contract with a housing authority may apply to the housing authority for an annual abatement of property tax. "Housing opportunity area" means a census tract where less than 10% of the residents live below the poverty level and that is located within a qualified township (35 ILCS 200/18-173).

The property's value may be reduced by a percentage calculated as follows: 19% of the equalized assessed value of the property multiplied by a fraction, the numerator of which is the number of qualified units and the denominator of which is the total number of dwelling units located within the property. A qualified unit must meet certain housing quality standards and must be rented to and occupied by a tenant who is participating in a housing choice voucher program. No more than 2 units or 20% of the total units contained within the property, whichever is greater, may be considered qualified units. No property may receive an abatement for more than 10 tax years (35 ILCS 200/18-173).

Abatement of taxes on residence of the spouse of a fallen police officer, soldier, or rescue worker: The governing body of any county or municipality may abate any percentage of the taxes levied by the county or municipality on each parcel of qualified property in the county or municipality that is owned and used as the principal residence by an unremarried surviving spouse of a fallen police officer, soldier, or rescue worker (35 ILCS 200/18-178). The governing body may provide for the percentage amount and duration of an abatement.

A "fallen police officer or rescue worker" is an individual who dies as a result of or in the course of employment as a police officer or while in the active service of a fire, rescue, or emergency medical service. A "fallen soldier" is an individual who dies while on active duty as a member of the United States Armed Services, including the National Guard, serving in Iraq or Afghanistan. (35 ILCS 200/18-178)

Abatement of taxes on foreclosed property acquired by governmental units: Due and unpaid Illinois property taxes and existing liens for unpaid property taxes are abated for property that is acquired by a county, municipality, school district, park district, or forest preserve district through foreclosure of a lien; a judicial deed; foreclosure of receivership certificate lien; acceptance of a deed of conveyance in lieu of foreclosing any lien against the property; or when acquiring property under certain federal programs. In addition, unpaid taxes and tax liens are abated on property acquired by any county, municipality, school district, park district, or forest preserve district under the terms of an annexation agreement, development agreement, donation agreement, plat of subdivision or zoning ordinance and that was transferred to the government unit by an entity that has been or is being dissolved or has been or is in bankruptcy proceedings. (35 ILCS 200/21-95)

Abatement of taxes on historical society property: For assessment years through 2018, property of qualifying historical societies may have all or a portion of their taxes abated. The abatement must be approved by a majority vote of a governing taxing district, and the society must qualify as an exempt organization under IRC Sec. 501(c)(3). (35 ILCS 200/18-165)

• *Longtime Owner-Occupant Property Tax Relief Act*

Longtime owner-occupants may be granted an exemption or deferral (or a combination of the two) by counties for that portion of an increase in real property taxes that is due to an increase in the market value of the real property as a consequence of the refurbishing or renovating of other residences or the construction of new residences in long-established residential areas or areas of deteriorated, vacant, or abandoned homes and properties. The exemption or deferral may be effective until the longtime owner-occupant transfers title to the property. Municipalities and school districts with populations in excess of 500,000 are required to participate in this program if they lie within a county that has a population of three million or more that has enacted ordinances or resolutions that permit its school districts and municipalities to decide whether they will participate in the program (35 ILCS 250/15).

A "longtime owner-occupant" is a person who, for at least 10 continuous years, has owned and occupied the same dwelling place as a principal residence and domicile (five continuous years for persons receiving assistance in the acquisition of the property as part of a government or nonprofit housing program).

See also ¶2004 for additional information on the longtime occupant homestead exemption.

• *Senior citizens tax deferral*

Persons 65 years of age or older, who have a total household income of less than $55,000 and meet certain other qualifications, may defer all or part of the real estate taxes and special assessments on their principal residences. The deferral is similar to a loan against the property's market value. A lien is filed on the property in order to ensure repayment of the deferral. The state pays the property taxes and then recovers the money, plus 6% annual interest, when the property is sold or transferred. The deferral must be repaid within one year of the taxpayer's death or 90 days after the property ceases to qualify for deferral. The maximum amount that can be deferred, including interest and lien fees, is 80% of the taxpayer's equity interest in the property, but not more than $5,000 per taxpayer (320 ILCS 30/1; 320 ILCS 30/3; 320 ILCS 30/2).

When a homestead exemption has been granted and an applicant then becomes a resident of a facility licensed under the Assisted Living and Shared Housing Act, the Nursing Home Care Act, the Specialized Mental Health Rehabilitation Act, or the MR/DD Community Care Act, the exemption shall be granted in subsequent years so long as the residence continues to be occupied by the qualified applicant's spouse or if remaining unoccupied, is still owned by the qualified applicant for the homestead exemption (35 ILCS 15/172).

To apply for real estate tax deferrals, Form PTAX-1017-TD, Application for Deferral of Real Estate Taxes, and Form PTAX-1018-TD, Real Estate Tax Deferral and Recovery Agreement, must be completed. To apply for special assessment deferrals, Form PTAX-1017-SA, Application for Deferral of Special Assessment, and Form PTAX-1018-SA, Special Assessments Deferral and Recovery Agreement, must be completed.

• *Repeal of rebate*

An Illinois city's repeal of a property tax rebate ordinance did not result in either an unlawful taking of property or a denial of due process in violation of the federal Constitution. In this case the ordinance constituted a special remedial statute, and the unconditional repeal of a special remedial statute without a saving clause stops all pending actions where the repeal finds them. A right derived from a remedial statute is not a vested right, and the Legislature has ongoing authority to repeal or amend the statute. (*Bell v. City of Country Club Hills*, U.S. Court of Appeals, Seventh Circuit, Nos. 16-1245, 16-1448, November 8, 2016, CCH ILLINOIS TAX REPORTS ¶ 403-151)

¶2004 Property Exempt

Law: Ill. Const. Art. IX, Sec. 6; County Economic Development Project Area Property Tax Allocation Act, Sec. 7.80 [20 ILCS 3505/7.80]; County Historic Preservation Act, Sec. 4(14) [55 ILCS 5/5-30004]; Property Tax Code, Sec. 1-30 [35 ILCS 200/1-30]; Property Tax Code, Sec. 10-23 [35 ILCS 200/10-23]; Property Tax Code, Sec. 10-300 [35 ILCS 200/10-300]; Property Tax Code, Sec. 15-50 [35 ILCS 200/15-50]; Property Tax Code, Secs. 15-35—15-180 [35 ILCS 200/15-35—15-180]; Property Tax Code, Secs. 18-165—18-177 [35 ILCS 200/18-165—18-177]; Property Tax Code, Sec. 24-5 [35 ILCS 200/24-5] (CCH ILLINOIS TAX REPORTS, ¶ 20-190, 20-510).

The following are the main exemptions and partial exemptions from the property tax:

• *Government or public property*

Property owned and used by the United States government (in *United States of America v. Hynes et al.*, a U.S. district court held that assessment of property taxes on federal buildings being acquired in Illinois on an installment basis and used exclusively for federal government purposes violated the Supremacy Clause of the U.S. Constitution and that the Illinois statute allowing such property to be taxed discriminated against the federal government or those with whom it dealt; see CCH ILLINOIS TAX REPORTS, ¶ 400-526). Also exempt is the following:

— property owned by the state;

— property owned by local governments and used for public purposes, including the Illinois Sports Facility Authority and Illinois Research Park Authority, and including leased property, applicable to leases entered into on or after January 1, 1994;

— property owned by an airport authority, including property leased to private individuals, as long as the primary use of the property is consistent with the maintenance of a public airport (35 ILCS 200/15-160; *Harrisburg-Raleigh Airport Authority v. Department of Revenue* (1989, SCt), 126 IllApp2d 326, 533 NE2d 1072; CCH ILLINOIS TAX REPORTS, ¶ 400-360; but see *Moline School District No. 40 v. Quinn,* Appellate Court of Illinois, Third District, No. 3-14-1505, July 15, 2015, CCH ILLINOIS TAX REPORTS,¶ 402-974; affirmed, *Moline School District No. 40 Board of Education v. Quinn,* Supreme Court of Illinois, No. 119704, June 16, 2016, CCH ILLINOIS TAX REPORTS,¶ 403-108);

— property owned by a municipal transportation system; property owned by the following parties is exempt: a municipal corporation of 500,000 or more used for public transportation purposes and operated by the Chicago Transit Authority; the Regional Transportation Authority; any service or board of the Regional Transportation Authority; the Northeast Illinois Regional Commuter Railroad Corporation; the Chicago Transit Authority; or property owned by the Metropolitan Water Reclamation District in Cook County;

— property owned by a municipality of 500,000 or more that is used for tollroad or tollbridge purposes and is leased to a person whose property does not qualify for exemption;

— property owned by a municipality with a population of over 500,000 inhabitants that is leased, sold, or transferred to another entity and immediately thereafter is the subject of a leaseback agreement that gives the municipality: (1) a right to use, control, and possess the property, or (2) a right to require the other entity to use the property in the performance of services for the municipality;

— property owned by a municipality with a population of over 500,000 inhabitants, or a unit of local government whose jurisdiction includes territory located in whole or in part within a municipality with a population of over 500,000 inhabitants, shall remain exempt from taxation and any leasehold interest in that property is not subject to taxation under Section 9-195 if the property, including dedicated public property, is used by a municipality or other unit of local government for the purpose of an airport or parking or for waste disposal or processing and is leased for continued use for the same purpose to another entity whose property is not exempt (35 ILCS 200/15-185); and

— all property owned by the state or the Illinois State Toll Highway Authority that is defined as a "transportation project" under the Illinois Public-Private Partnerships for Transportation Act, used for transportation purposes, and leased for those purposes to another entity whose property is not exempt will remain exempt (35 ILCS 200/15-55(g)).

Practitioner Comment: Special Legislation

The Illinois Supreme Court struck down a property tax exemption finding that it violated the special legislation clause of the Illinois Constitution. A business located in the Moline School District operated in the aviation industry as a Fixed Base Operator ("FBO"). FBOs operate at airports and provide support services such as hangaring, maintenance and repair, and fueling. Illinois levies property taxes on the leasehold interests of FBOs. The FBO had threatened expansion in other states where FBOs were exempt from property tax. In response, Illinois enacted special legislation that exempted FBOs located in Moline School District from property taxes. Plaintiff, a local school district, stood to lose $150,000 per year in tax revenue. The District filed suit challenging the statute as a violation on a number of constitutional grounds. The FBO located in the Moline School District intervened. The Court found the legislation violated the special legislation clause of the Illinois Constitution because the exemption was not rationally related to a legitimate state interest. The Court took issue with the fact that there was no requirement in the legislation that the FBO actually use the money saved by the tax exemption for expansion in Illinois. (*Moline School District No. 40 Board of Education v. Quinn*, Supreme Court of Illinois, No. 119704, June 16, 2016, CCH ILLINOIS TAX REPORTS, ¶ 403-108)

Marilyn A. Wethekam, Esq., Horwood Marcus & Berk, Chartered

Library systems and public library districts: All property used exclusively for public purposes belonging to a library system established under the Illinois Library System Act or belonging to a public library district established under the Public Library District Act of 1991 (P.A. 91-0897 (S.B. 1296), Laws 2000).

• *Cemeteries*

Lands used exclusively as graveyards are constitutionally and statutorily exempt from property taxes (Ill. Const., Art. IX, Sec. 6; Property Tax Code, Sec. 15-45 [35 ILCS 200/15-45]).

• *Developer's exemption*

See ¶ 2005.

• *Educational property*

Property owned by nonprofit schools and military schools, and property on or adjacent to school grounds that is used by research, academic, or professional organizations to advance the field of study taught by the school (the exemption for property adjacent to school grounds was upheld by the Illinois Supreme Court in *The Chicago Bar Association v. Department of Revenue* (1993, SCt), 163 Ill2d 300, 644 NE2d 117; CCH ILLINOIS TAX REPORTS, ¶ 400-693).

Practitioner Comment: Satisfying the "Educational Purposes" Test

The Illinois Appellate Court held that a not-for-profit corporation that owned a fraternity house near the main campus of the University of Chicago did not qualify for a real estate exemption for property "used for college, university or other educational purposes." See *Illinois Beta House Fund Corp. v. Ill. Dep't of Rev.*, 382 Ill. App. 3d 426 (1st Dist. 2008), CCH ILLINOIS TAX REPORTS, ¶ 401-880. The court reasoned that an applicant for an "educational purposes" real estate exemption must show the primary use of the property is by an association of learning institutions or some other legal entity that is closely affiliated with and functions on behalf of a learning association. The court noted that the applicant's purpose and efforts were on behalf of a fraternal organization, and not on behalf of a learning organization. Moreover, the school exercises no authority over the fraternity and its articles of incorporation and its by-laws indicate that it is not closely affiliated with the university.

Horwood Marcus & Berk, Chartered

• *Nonprofit charitable organizations*

Property of the following entities when it is used exclusively for charitable or beneficent purposes, and not leased or used with a view to profit (35 ILCS 200/15-65):

      (1) institutions of public charity;

      (2) beneficent and charitable organizations;

      (3) old people's homes;

¶ 2004

(4) facilities for developmentally disabled;

(5) facilities for educational, social, and physical development;

(6) health maintenance organizations;

(7) facilities used to distribute, sell, or resell donated goods;

(8) free public libraries; and

(9) certain historical societies.

Low-income housing projects: A property tax regulation clarifies charitable exemption requirements for some low-income housing projects. Specifically, the exemption deals with low-income housing projects that are owned and managed by an Illinois charity or an entity controlled by an Illinois charity that utilizes federal tax credits as a financing mechanism. (86 Ill. Adm. Code 110.116)

All property of housing authorities created under the Housing Authorities Act is exempt, if the property and improvements are used for low rent housing and related uses. The exemption is not lost to a housing authority when title is held by an entity that is organized as a partnership or a limited liability company (LLC) in which the housing authority or one of its affiliates is a general partner or managing member. The exemption also is not lost if the entity is holding title for the purpose of owning and operating a residential rental property that has received an allocation of federal low-income housing tax credits for 100% of the dwelling units involved. (35 ILCS 200/15-95)

Practitioner Comment: Exclusive Use

Property of charitable organizations qualifies for a property tax exemption if: (1) the property is used exclusively for charitable purposes; and (2) the property is owned by a charitable organization. The Illinois Supreme Court outlined the criteria used in evaluating whether property is exempt from taxation based on a charitable use. (*Methodist Old Peoples Home v. Corzen,* 233 N.E.2d 537, 39, Ill.2d 149 (1968), CCH ILLINOIS TAX REPORTS, ¶ 200-452.) Later cases have stated that the factors outlined by the Methodist Old Peoples Home court are merely guidelines and not definite requirements. (*Lutheran General Healthcare System and Healthcare Medical Foundation v. Illinois Department of Revenue,* 231 Ill. App.3d 652, 595 N.E.2d 1214 (2nd Dist. 1992), CCH ILLINOIS TAX REPORTS, ¶ 400-590.)

David A. Hughes, Esq., Horwood Marcus & Berk Chartered

Practitioner Comment: Satisfying the Exclusive Charitable Use Test

On March 18, 2010, the Illinois Supreme Court affirmed the Appellate Court's judgment that upheld the Illinois Department of Revenue's decision to deny Provena Hospitals' claim to a charitable exemption from real property taxes for 2002. The Illinois Appellate Court held that Provena, a nonprofit hospital, was not eligible for a real estate exemption for property owned by a public charity institution and actually and exclusively used for charitable or beneficial purposes. See *Provena Covenant Medical Center v. Ill. Dep't of Rev.,* 384 Ill. App. 3d 734 (4th Dist. 2008), CCH ILLINOIS TAX REPORTS, ¶ 401-901, affirmed, Illinois Supreme Court, Docket No. 107328, 236 Ill.2d 368, 925 N.E.2d 1131 (March 18, 2010), CCH ILLINOIS TAX REPORTS, ¶ 402-092. Provena Hospitals, is a not-for-profit corporation under Illinois law, and is exempt from both federal income tax under IRC Sec. 501(c)(3) and from Illinois incomes taxes and sales/use taxes. Provena claimed that it was also exempt from real property taxes because the real estate was owned by a public charity and it was "actually and exclusively used for charitable or beneficent purposes."

In its plurality decision, the Supreme Court applied a significantly deferential standard of review, holding that it must affirm the Director's decision, unless it was "clearly erroneous." In affirming the Director's decision, the Court noted that "if there is any doubt as to applicability of an exemption, it must be resolved in favor of requiring that tax to be paid." The Court found that the decision was not clearly erroneous because

Provena's funds were not mainly derived from charity, Provena had failed to establish by clear and convincing evidence that it dispensed "charity" (free/discounted services) to everyone who needed it, and Provena did not establish that its charitable activities helped to alleviate the financial burden of the local taxing bodies in performing their governmental functions.

The Illinois Supreme Court affirmed the Appellate Court's judgment that upheld the Illinois Department of Revenue's decision to deny Provena Hospitals' claim to a charitable exemption from real property taxes for 2002. Under Federal law, new charity hospital provisions were created by the Patient Protection and Affordable Care Act that require tax-exempt hospitals to regularly assess the health needs of the community, develop financial assistance policies, limit some of the charges associated with charity care, and reform the collection processes. The enactment of the new Federal provisions creates a new question for Illinois hospitals: if the hospital satisfies the federal criteria, will it be enough to meet Illinois' requirements? The answer to this question may determine whether or not we will see this issue litigated again.

Breen M. Schiller, Esq., Horwood Marcus & Berk, Chartered

Citing the "considerable uncertainty surrounding the test for charitable property tax exemption" following the Illinois Supreme Court decision in *Provena*, the Illinois legislature established criteria to be applied on a case-by-case basis for exemption applicants. Any hospital property parcel or portion thereof that is owned, leased, licensed, or operated by a for-profit entity cannot qualify for an exemption (35 ILCS 200/15-86).

Generally, a hospital applicant will be issued a charitable exemption if the value of services or activities listed in the new exemption criteria for the year at issue (hospital year) equals or exceeds the relevant hospital entity's estimated property tax liability for the year for which the exemption is sought. Services or activities that will be considered in determining that value are (Property Tax Code Sec. 15/86(e) [35 ILCS 200/15-86(e)]):

— charity care;

— health services to low-income or underserved individuals;

— subsidy of state or local governments;

— support for state health care programs for low-income individuals;

— subsidy of dual-eligible Medicare/Medicaid patients;

— relief of the burden of government related to health care of low-income individuals; and

— any other activity by the hospital entity that the Department of Revenue determines relieves the burden of government or addresses the health of low-income or underserved individuals.

The Illinois Supreme Court vacated a ruling that a statutory exemption for certain hospital property was facially unconstitutional because the order containing the underlying issue that was appealed to the intermediate appellate court was not an appealable order. The trial court had granted summary judgment on the issue of what law applied to the statutory exemption at issue, and taxing districts appealed. In its ruling, the intermediate appellate court addressed several issues, including whether it had appellate jurisdiction, whether the exemption could be sought as it was in the proceedings below, and whether the legislature intended for the statute at issue to apply retroactively.

The supreme court determined that the intermediate appellate court lacked appellate jurisdiction because the appealed order did not resolve the exemption claim, but resolved only an issue that was part of or ancillary to the claim. What law governs a claim is not itself a "claim," as it resolves nothing other than the standard by which the underlying claim will be adjudicated.

In addition, the appealed order did not qualify as a declaratory judgment because a declaration of what section of law applied to the exemption claim would do nothing to aid in the termination of the controversy or some part thereof. Finally, the supreme court declined to exercise its supervisory authority and address the merits of the appeal because (1) neither the supreme court rules nor the declaratory judgment statute was intended to facilitate piecemeal litigation and (2) courts should avoid reaching constitutional issues where, as in this case, those issues might become moot on remand. (*Carle Foundation v. Cunningham Township,* Supreme Court of Illinois, Nos. 120427, 120433, March 23, 2017, CCH ILLINOIS TAX REPORTS, ¶ 403-206; vacating ruling in *Carle Foundation v. Cunningham Township,* Appellate Court of Illinois, Fourth District, Nos. 4-14-0795, 4-14-0845, January 5, 2016, CCH ILLINOIS TAX REPORTS, ¶ 403-075)

Practitioner Comment: What is "Charitable" Use?

An Administrative Law Judge for the Department ruled that a housing corporation, despite its nonprofit status, did not qualify for real estate tax exemptions, because the corporation did not obtain its funds from charity. Noting that "[t]here is nothing particularly kind or benevolent about selling somebody something [,]" the ALJ opined that if such a nonprofit corporation were to be considered "charitable," so too would all landlords renting at a rate below what they thought they could charge on the open market. Reasoning that statutes exempting property from taxation must be strictly construed against exemption, the ALJ held that a nonprofit corporation renting property below "fair market rent" could not qualify for the charitable exemption. (*Lake County Residential Development Corp v. Dep't of Revenue,* Dkt No. 10-PT-0047 (2/9/12); CCH ILLINOIS TAX REPORTS, ¶ 20120810013)

The question of whether an organization is truly "charitable" for tax purposes has become a controversial one in Illinois. Under case law that dates back to the 1960s, Illinois courts have historically applied a 6-part test to determine whether an organization provides sufficient charitable care to qualify as a tax exempt organization. In 2010, the Illinois Supreme Court applied the 6-part test in *Provena Covenant Medical Center v. Dept. of Revenue.* Focusing on the fifth and sixth factors—dispensing charity to all who need and apply for it and placing no obstacles in their way—the Illinois Supreme Court concluded that Provena was not sufficiently charitable to qualify for a property tax exemption. Provena was only one of many hospitals and other organizations whose tax exempt status was challenged by the Department of Revenue.

Due both to political pressure and the difficulty in applying the 6-part charitable organization test set forth in the case law, the Governor's office and the General Assembly intervened in an effort to bring some clarity to this issue. In 2012, the General Assembly passed and the Governor signed new legislation, which provides a bright line, objective, quantifiable test for determining whether an organization provides enough charitable care to earn tax exempt status. Pursuant to P.A. 97-688, Laws 2012, a charitable exemption is now allowed for hospital property if the value of certain specified services or activities equals or exceeds the hospital's estimated property tax liability for the year for which the exemption is sought. See 35 ILCS 200/15-86. A comparable exemption also applies for sales and use tax. See 35 ILCS 120/2-9(a); 35 ILCS 105/3-8(a).

David A. Hughes. Esq., Horwood Marcus & Berk, Chartered

Religious property: Property used for religious purposes, including property that is (35 ILCS 200/15-40):

    (1) owned by a church or religious institution;

    (2) used by a church and school,

    (3) used as housing facilities for ministers of such churches or institutions; or

    (4) used as orphanages.

¶2004

Practitioner Comment: Profit Motive

An Administrative Law Judge held that real property owned by a nonprofit religious corporation was subject to tax because the parcels of land were not used exclusively for religious purposes. The taxpayers owned two parcels of land that were rented to the federal government. The Department initially denied an application for a property tax exemption for the property. The taxpayers pointed to Section 15-65 of the Property Tax Code for the proposition that "property shall not lose its exemption if a charitable organization leases property to an entity that would otherwise be exempt under the code." The religious organization contended that because the lessee, the federal government, was exempt under the code, it should not have been required to pay property tax. The Department, on the other hand, noted that Section 15-65 excludes from exemption property that is rented in order to make a profit. The ALJ concluded that the religious organization rented the property in order to make a profit, and as a result, the Department's denial of the taxpayer's exemption application was affirmed. (*Application of Catholic Charities Housing Development Corporation*, Dkts. 10-PT-0048 and 07-16-876 (3/29/12); CCH ILLINOIS TAX REPORTS, ¶ 20120810019)

Breen M. Schiller, Esq., Horwood Marcus & Berk, Chartered

Fraternal or veterans' organizations: Real property owned and used by certain fraternal or veterans' organizations qualifies for an assessment freeze. For fraternal organization property, the valuation is generally 15% of its final assessed value (35 ILCS 200/10-355; 86 Ill. Adm. Code 110.113):

    (1) for the year 2001;

    (2) for each year the property qualifies; or

    (3) for property qualifying after 2002, the year in which the property first becomes qualified.

For veterans' organization property, the valuation is generally 15% of its final assessed value (35 ILCS 200/10-300):

    (1) for the year 1999;

    (2) for each year the property qualifies; or

    (3) for property qualifying after 2002, the year in which the property first becomes qualified.

The assessed value of real property owned by such organization and used by its members and guests for parking at the principal building for the post, camp, or chapter is eligible for an assessment freeze. Improvements that increase the assessed value of the property are assessed at 15% of the final assessed value of the improvements for the year in which the improvements were completed (35 ILCS 200/10-300).

Fraternal organizations qualifying for the assessment freeze are organizations that prohibit gambling and the use of alcohol on the property, are exempt under IRC Sec. 501(c)(10), and whose members directly or indirectly provide financial support for charitable works; and organizations whose members provide, directly or indirectly, financial support for charitable works, including medical care, drug rehabilitation, or education (35 ILCS 200/10-360).

Housing: A specially adapted home for a disabled veteran or a disabled veteran's spouse (up to $70,000 of assessed value) (35 ILCS 200/15-165) and township housing for senior citizens.

• *Homesteads*

Illinois provides multiple homestead exemptions, as discussed below. Although the Illinois Supreme Court has held that the annual homestead exemption may be granted only when the owner lives on the premises (*McKenzie* (IL SCt 1983), 98 IL2d 87; CCH ILLINOIS TAX REPORTS, ¶ 201-328), the Illinois Attorney General determined that a lessee of a single-family residence who occupied the residence had a leasehold interest in the property, was liable for the property tax, and qualified for the homestead exemption (*Opinion of the Attorney General*, No. 96-031, November 27, 1996; CCH ILLINOIS TAX REPORTS, ¶ 400-826).

In all Illinois counties except for Cook County, if a property owner fails to file an application for any homestead exemption provided under Article 15 of the property tax code during the previous assessment year and qualifies for the exemption, the chief county assessment officer or the board of review shall issue a certificate of error setting forth the correct taxable valuation of the property. (35 ILCS 200/14-20)

For information on tax liens that may be imposed for erroneous property tax exemptions in Cook County, see ¶ 2009.

Institutionalized patients: Individuals who are granted either a disabled persons' homestead exemption, a senior citizen homestead exemption, or a senior citizen assessment freeze homestead exemption for their residences will continue to be eligible for those exemptions under certain circumstances if they subsequently become residents of a facility licensed under the Nursing home Act, the Assisted Living and Shared Housing Act, the Specialized Mental Health Rehabilitation Act, or the MR/DD Community Care Act. An exemption will continue so long as the residence (1) continues to be occupied by the qualifying individual's spouse or (2) if unoccupied, is still owned by the qualified individual. (35 ILCS 200/15-168; 35 ILCS 200/15-170; 35 ILCS 200/15-172)

CCH Advisory: Pro Rata Homestead Exemption

Property that is first occupied as a residence after January 1 of any assessment year by a person who is eligible for the senior citizens homestead exemption must be granted a *pro rata* exemption for the assessment year. The amount of the *pro rata* exemption is the exemption allowed in the county, divided by 365 and multiplied by the number of days during the assessment year the property is occupied as a residence by a person eligible for the exemption (35 ILCS 200/15-170).

General homestead exemption: This annual exemption is available for residential property that is occupied as the principal dwelling place by the owner or a lessee with an equitable interest in the property and an obligation to pay the property taxes on the leased property. The amount of exemption is the increase in the current year's equalized assessed value (EAV), above the 1977 EAV, up to a maximum of $6,000 for 2009 through 2011. For taxable years 2012 through 2016, the maximum reduction is $7,000 in Cook County and $6,000 in all other counties. For taxable year 2017 and thereafter, the maximum reduction is $10,000 in Cook County and $6,000 in all other counties. Owners who, for the taxable year, have not been granted a senior citizens assessment freeze homestead exemption under Section 15-172 or a long-time occupant homestead exemption under Sec. 200/15-177, an additional exemption of $5,000 is available for owners with a household income of $30,000 or less (35 ILCS 200/15-175).

Leaseholds: When considering whether to grant a homestead exemption from property tax for a leasehold, a county assessor may require the following information (35 ILCS 200/15-175):

— a notarized and signed application for the exemption;

— a copy of the lease at the time the application is filed;

— that the lease expressly states that the lessee is liable for property tax payments;

— that the lease include certain specific language; and

— that the owner of the property notify the assessor if there is a change in the lease.

Nursing home residents: If a person awarded the exemption subsequently becomes a resident of a licensed nursing home or assisted care facility or a facility licensed under the MR/DD Community Care Act, the exemption will continue (i) so long as the residence continues to be occupied by the qualifying person's spouse who is age 65 or older or (ii) if the residence remains unoccupied but is still owned by the person qualified for the homestead exemption. (35 ILCS 200/15-170)

*Alternative general homestead exemption (obsolete):*In lieu of the general homestead exemption, a county could adopt ordinances to establish an annual homestead exemption equal to a reduction in the property's equalized assessed value (35 ILCS 200/15-176(a)). A county wanting to subject itself to the alternative general homestead exemption had to enact an ordinance within six months of August 1, 2010 (35 ILCS 200/15-176(k)). The amount of the exemption was the equalized assessed value of the homestead property for the current tax year, minus the adjusted homestead value, with the certain exceptions (35 ILCS 200/15-176(e))

Longtime occupant homestead exemption: If a county elected to be subject to the alternative general homestead exemption, then, for taxable years 2007 and thereafter, qualified homestead property is entitled to an annual homestead exemption equal to a reduction in the property's equalized assessed value (35 ILCS 200/15-177). The amount of the exemption is the greater of (35 ILCS 200/15-177(d)):

(1) the equalized assessed value of the homestead property for the current tax year minus the adjusted homestead value; or

(2) the general homestead deduction.

Senior citizens assessment freeze homestead exemption: This exemption allows qualifying senior citizens to elect to maintain the EAV of their homes at the base year EAV and prevent any increase in that value due to inflation. The exemption applies to real property occupied as a residence by senior citizens who are, among other things, at least 65 years old and who have a total household income of at most $55,000 for taxable years 2008 through 2016. For taxable year 2017, the income limit if $65,000 in Cook County and $55,000 in all other counties. For taxable years 2018 and thereafter, the limit is $65,000 in all counties. Qualified individuals must complete and file Form PTAX-340, Senior Citizens Assessment Freeze Homestead Exemption Application and Affidavit, each year with the CCAO ([35 ILCS 200/15-172], ¶109-667).

If a person awarded the exemption subsequently becomes a resident of a licensed nursing home or assisted care facility or a facility licensed under the MR/DD Community Care Act, the exemption will continue (i) so long as the residence continues to be occupied by the qualifying person's spouse or (ii) if the residence remains unoccupied but is still owned by the person qualified for the homestead exemption. (35 ILCS 200/15-172)

Senior citizens homestead exemption: This exemption allows a reduction in the EAV of the property that a person 65 years of age or older is obligated to pay taxes on, and owns and occupies, or leases and occupies, as a residence. Generally, the initial application, Form PTAX-324, Application for Senior Citizens Homestead Exemption, is required and is filed with the CCAO (35 ILCS 200/15-170).

For taxable years 2013 through 2016, the maximum reduction is $5,000 in all counties. For taxable years 2017 and thereafter, the maximum reduction is $8,000 in Cook County is $5,000 in all other counties. (35 ILCS 200/15-170)

Senior citizens property tax deferral: See ¶ 2003.

CCH Advisory: Decreased Property Value May be Reflected

If the equalized assessed value of a senior citizen's homestead declines below the base year value, the lower equalized assessed value may become the new base year value upon which property tax is imposed. However, decrease in equalized assessed value may not become the base year value if the decrease is due to a temporary irregularity that reduces equalized assessed value for one or more years (Property Tax Code Sec. 15-172 [35 ILCS 200/15-172]).

Disabled persons' homestead exemption: A $2,000 annual homestead exemption is granted to disabled persons. The disabled person will receive the homestead exemption upon meeting the following requirements (35 ILCS 200/15-168):

— The property must be occupied as the primary residence by the disabled person;

— The disabled person must be liable for paying the real estate taxes on the property; and

— The disabled person must be an owner of record of the property or have a legal or equitable interest in the property as evidenced by a written instrument.

In the case of a leasehold interest in property, the lease must be for a single family residence.

A person who is disabled during the taxable year is eligible to apply for the exemption during that taxable year. Application must be made during the application period in effect for the county of residence. If a person awarded the exemption subsequently becomes a resident of a licensed nursing home facility or a facility licensed under the MR/DD Community Care Act, the exemption will continue (i) so long as the residence continues to be occupied by the qualifying person's spouse or (ii) if the residence remains unoccupied but is still owned by the person qualified for the homestead exemption (35 ILCS 200/15-168(a)).

A "disabled person" means a person unable to engage in any substantial gainful activity by reason of a medically determinable physical or mental impairment which can be expected to result in death or has lasted or can be expected to last for a continuous period of not less than 12 months. Claimants must submit proof of disability, which may include certification of Social Security disability, an Illinois "Person with a Disability Identification Ccard," or the results of a physical examination by an approved physician (35 ILCS 200/15-168(b)).

Accessibility Improvements: for elderly or disabled persons' access that are made to residential property will not increase the assessed valuation of the property for a period of seven years after the improvements are completed (35 ILCS 200/10-23). "Accessibility improvement" refers to a home modification listed with the federal Department of Human Services including, but not limited to, the installation of ramps and grab-bars, widening of doorways, and other changes to enhance the independence of a disabled or elderly individual.

Disabled veterans' homestead exemption: An annual homestead exemption is granted for property that is used as a qualified residence by a disabled veteran with a service-connected disability certified by the U.S. Department of Veterans' Affairs (35 ILCS 200/15-169).

For taxable years 2015 and thereafter, the annual homestead amounts for veterans with certified service-connected disabilities is:

— $2,500 for disabilities of 30% or more, but less than 50%;

— $5,000 for disabilities of 50% or more, but less than 70%; and

— total exemption for disabilities of 70% or more.

Before 2015, the exemption amounts were as follows:

— for veterans with a service-connected disability of at least 70%, the annual exemption was $5,000; and

— for veterans with a service-connected disability of at least 50%, the annual exemption was $2,500.

Surviving spouse: The exemption carries over to the benefit of the veteran's surviving spouse as long as the spouse holds the legal or beneficial title to the homestead, permanently resides thereon, and does not remarry. If the surviving spouse sells the property, an exemption not to exceed the amount granted from the most recent ad valorem tax roll may be transferred to his or her new residence as long as it is used as his or her primary residence and he or she does not remarry. Tthe exemption can apply to veterans who become residents of qualifying nursing home facilities or a facility of the U.S. Department of Veterans Affairs (35 ILCS 200/15-169(b-5)). The exemption will continue so long as the residence either is occupied by the veteran's spouse or remains unoccupied but is still owned by the veteran.

A taxpayer who claims an exemption under 35 ILCS 200/15-165 or 15-168 may not claim this exemption.

Application must be made during the application period in effect for the county of his or her residence. "Veteran" means an Illinois resident who has served as a member of the United States Armed Forces on active duty or State active duty, a member of the Illinois National Guard, or a member of the United States Reserve Forces and who has received an honorable discharge.

Disabled veterans' exemption for adapted housing: This exemption may be up to $100,000 ($70,000, prior to 2015) of the assessed value for certain types of housing that is adapted for the disabled veteran's use and that is owned and used by a disabled veteran or his or her unmarried surviving spouse. Beginning in 2015, the exemption is available when a veteran has been killed in the line of duty, even if the exemption was not taken before the veteran's death. The Illinois Department of Veterans' Affairs determines the eligibility for this exemption, which must be reestablished annually (35 ILCS 200/15-165).

Returning veterans' homestead exemption: A $5,000 homestead exemption is granted for property that is owned and occupied as the principal residence of a veteran returning from an armed conflict involving the U.S. Armed Forces. A "veteran" means an Illinois resident who has served as a member of the U.S. Armed Forces, a member of the Illinois National Guard, or a member of the United States Reserve Forces. The exemption is applicable to the year following the year in which the veteran returns from active duty (35 ILCS 200/15-167(b)).

Homestead improvement exemption: A homeowner may exempt the following:

— up to $75,000 of actual value of improvements made to a homestead owned and used exclusively for residential purposes, if the increase in value is due solely to the new improvement of an existing structure, the exemption being applicable for four years from the date on which the improvement is completed and occupied or until the next following quadrennial assessment of the property, whichever is later (the exemption is not available to property that has increased in value because of a general increase in the value of property in the area

(*Opinion of the Attorney General,* October 25, 1994; CCH ILLINOIS TAX REPORTS, ¶400-682)); in counties of fewer than three million inhabitants, a taxpayer whose assessment has been changed due to an assessable improvement must either be notified that the taxpayer may be eligible for the exemption or the exemption must be automatically granted; structures that are rebuilt following a cata-strophic event also qualify for the exemption; however, a structure that was damaged by flooding is not eligible unless it is located within a local jurisdiction that participates in the National Flood Insurance Program; in order to qualify for the exemption, structures must be rebuilt within two years of the catastrophic event; for residential structures in counties with three million or more inhabi-tants that are rebuilt following a catastrophic event, applications must be sub-mitted to the chief county assessment officer with a valuation complaint and a copy of the building permit; and

— maintenance and repair work to residential real estate owned and used exclusively for residential purposes.

The homestead improvement exemption may be granted automatically or Form PTAX-323, Application for Homestead Improvement Exemption, may be required by the chief county assessment officer (35 ILCS 200/15-180).

Natural disaster homestead exemption: A homestead exemption against Illinois property tax will be granted for homestead properties containing a residential struc-ture that has been rebuilt following a natural disaster occurring in taxable year 2012 or any taxable year thereafter. A "natural disaster" means an occurrence of wide-spread or severe damage or loss of property, resulting from any catastrophic cause including, but not limited to, fire, flood (subject to certain restrictions), earthquake, wind, storm, or extended period of severe inclement weather. No proclamation of disaster by either the President of the United States or the Governor of Illinois is required for classification of an occurrence as a "natural disaster" for purposes of this exemption. (35 ILCS 200/15-173(b))

The amount of the exemption is the equalized assessed value (EAV) of the residence in the first taxable year for which the taxpayer applies for the exemption minus the base amount, which is the EAV of the residence in the taxable year prior to the taxable year in which the disaster occurred. (35 ILCS 200/15-173(c))

In order to be eligible for the exemption, the residential structure must be rebuilt within two years of the date of the natural disaster and may not have more than 110% of the square footage of the original residential structure. The initial application for the exemption must be made no later than the first taxable year after the structure is rebuilt, and the exemption will continue until the taxable year in which the property is sold or transferred. (35 ILCS 200/15-173(c))

An application for the exemption must be submitted to the chief county assess-ment officer by July 1 of each taxable year, although counties are permitted to establish a different date. This exemption is exclusive of an existing "catastrophic event" exemption for the same natural disaster or catastrophic event. The natural disaster exemption carries over to the benefit of a surviving spouse so long as the spouse holds the legal or beneficial title to the homestead and permanently resides there. (35 ILCS 200/15-173(d))

• *Miscellaneous exemptions*

Other property eligible for exemptions includes:

— community college district property not leased for profit (35 ILCS 200/15-135);

— property belonging to nonprofit health maintenance organizations (35 ILCS 200/15-65);

— property belonging to a forest preserve district in counties with a population of less than three million (35 ILCS 200/15-150);

— municipal property used for the maintenance of the poor (35 ILCS 200/15-60);

— property located outside municipal corporate limits when used as a tuberculosis sanitarium, a penal farm colony, or farm, garden, or nursery to grow trees and plants to be used to beautify and maintain parks, buildings, and other public grounds (35 ILCS 200/15-60);

— city property outside its boundaries used exclusively for public or municipal purposes (35 ILCS 200/15-60); and

— graveyards (35 ILCS 200/15-45).

Taxes on exempt property that is leased to another whose property is not exempt will be collected in the same manner as on property that is not exempt and the lessee is liable for those taxes (35 ILCS 200/15-10).

The U.S. Supreme Court has held that a Maine tax exemption for property owned by charitable institutions that was limited to property of organizations serving primarily Maine residents violated the Commerce Clause of the U.S. Constitution. Thus, a Maine town was prohibited from denying an exemption to a religious summer camp operated by a nonprofit organization serving primarily out-of-state residents (*Camps Newfound/Owatonna, Inc. v. Town of Harrison* (1997, US SCt), 117 SCt 1590; CCH ILLINOIS TAX REPORTS, ¶ 400-853).

Parking areas: A parking area owned by an exempt religious institution that is leased or rented to a mass transportation entity for the limited free parking of the commuters of the mass transportation entity is exempt from Illinois property tax. In addition, a parking area owned by an exempt religious institution will remain exempt if it is leased to a municipality for nominal consideration (i.e., insurance and maintenance) if the municipality uses the parking area for free public parking. Parking areas used and owned by exempt school districts, nonprofit hospitals, schools, and charitable institutions generally are exempt if not leased or used for profit. (35 ILCS 200/15-125)

¶2005 Appraisal and Assessment

Law: Ill. Const., Art. IX, Sec. 4; County Economic Development Project Area Property Tax Allocation Act, Sec. 7.80 [20 ILCS 3505/7.80]; County Historic Preservation Act, Sec. 4(14) [55 ILCS 5/5-30004]; Property Tax Code, Sec. 1-30 [35 ILCS 200/1-30]; Property Tax Code, Sec. 1-50 [35 ILCS 200/1-50]; Property Tax Code, Sec. 9-145 [35 ILCS 200/9-145]; Property Tax Code, Sec. 9-175 [35 ILCS 200/9-175]; Property Tax Code, Sec. 9-260 [35 ILCS 200/9-260]; Property Tax Code, Sec. 9-265 [35 ILCS 200/9-265]; Property Tax Code, Sec. 10-20 [35 ILCS 200/10-20]; Property Tax Code, Sec. 10-160 [35 ILCS 200/10-160]; Property Tax Code, Sec. 10-370(b) [35 ILCS 200/10-370(b)]; Property Tax Code, Sec. 10-375(c) [35 ILCS 200/10-375(c)]; Property Tax Code, Sec. 15-50 [35 ILCS 200/15-50]; Property Tax Code, Sec. 16-50 [35 ILCS 200/16-50]; Property Tax Code, Secs. 16-55, 16-65, 16-183 [35 ILCS 200/16-55; 35 ILCS 200/16-65; 35 ILCS 200/16-183]; Property Tax Code, Secs. 18-165—18-177 [35 ILCS 200/18-165—18-177]; Property Tax Code, Sec. 21-15 [35 ILCS 200/21-15]; Property Tax Code, Sec. 24-5 [35 ILCS 200/24-5]; Property Tax Code, Sec. 27-75 [35 ILCS 200/27-75]; Illinois Real Property Appraisal Manual, Department of Revenue, revised July 1995 (CCH ILLINOIS TAX REPORTS, ¶ 20-190, 20-605, *et seq.*).

Illinois property is assessed by county assessors at its "fair cash value." The legal assessment level on any parcel of property (except in Cook County) is 33^1/3% of fair cash value, with the exception of farmland and farm-related buildings, and coal (35 ILCS 200/9-145). Cook County classifies property and assesses classes at different percentages of market value. (Cook County Real Property Assessment Classification Ordinance, Sec. 2)

Land used for agricultural purposes is eligible for assessment under the farmland assessment law (discussed below), which allows such land to be assessed on the basis of its economic productivity value rather than at one-third of its market value. (35 ILCS 200/10-115) Minerals and mineral rights, except coal, are assessed separately from the other part of the land at $33^1/3\%$ of fair cash value; coal is assessed on the basis of its "reserve economic value" (35 ILCS 200/9-145). Subsurface mineral rights in land may be separately assessed only when their ownership has been severed from the surface rights (*Opinion of the Attorney General,* February 4, 1992; CCH ILLINOIS TAX REPORTS, ¶ 400-564).

Practitioner Comment: Income Approach Was Insufficient

There are three fundamental ways to measure an asset: (1) the asset reproduction cost approach; (2) the sales comparison / market approach; and (3) the income approach, which is based on the economic principal of expectation. Omni Chicago, a property on North Michigan Avenue in Chicago, sought to have its assessment reduced. It alleged that the sales comparison method was not appropriate because the property possessed a "unique character" and there were no sales of similar properties, and that the cost method was inappropriate because the adjustments would be too subjective. Thus, it valued its property based on the income approach. *Cook County Bd. of Review v. Ill. Property Tax Appeal Bd.*, 384 Ill. App. 3d 472 (1st Dist. 2008), CCH ILLINOIS TAX REPORTS, ¶ 401-906.

The Illinois Appellate Court held that, absent a contemporaneous arm's length sale, the sales comparison approach is the preferred method. Further, the sales comparison method approach may be omitted only "if the subject property is so unique as to not be salable, for which no market exists." The court found that the Property Tax Appeal Board had a list of 34 sales in the Cook County Board of Review's report offered as comparables. As such, the court held that Omni's failure to consider the sales comparison approach in determining market value meant that Omni failed to meet its burden of demonstrating that the assessment was incorrect by clear and convincing evidence.

Horwood Marcus & Berk, Chartered

Practitioner Comment: Component-In-Place Method

Industrial property is generally valued pursuant to the "component-in-place method" whereby each component part of a building is analyzed and priced separately. An extensive set of component-in-place schedules used for pricing industrial buildings is available from the Illinois Department of Revenue.

David A. Hughes, Esq., Horwood Marcus & Berk Chartered

Assessment lowered by PTAB: If the Property Tax Appeal Board (PTAB) lowers the assessment on a parcel on which an owner-occupied residence is located, the reduced assessment, subject to equalization, remains in effect for the rest of the general assessment period unless the parcel is subsequently sold in an arm's-length transaction establishing a fair cash value on which the Board's assessment is based or the decision of the board is overruled (35 ILCS 200/16-185).

Practitioner Comment: Notice of Tax Increase

Under the Truth In Taxation Law, taxing districts are required to publish notices if the district's proposed levies are at least 5% greater than the amount billed to taxpayers for the prior year. Districts must hold public hearings regarding any proposed tax increases and they may not increase levies by more than 5% unless the taxing district certifies that it has complied with all publication and hearing requirements (35 ILCS 200/18-55 *et seq.*). For additional information on assessment notices, see ¶ 2007.

David A. Hughes, Esq., Horwood Marcus & Berk Chartered

¶ 2005

Tax rates: Tax rates, determined on the local level, are subject to legal maximums and are based on the dollars requested by the taxing bodies and the total equalized assessed value within that taxing district. The county clerk takes the amount requested by a taxing district and divides that by the total equalized assessed value for the district to determine the rate (up to the legal maximum rate) each taxpayer will be expected to pay per $100 of equalized assessed value of the individual property (35 ILCS 200/18-45).

The rate of tax is the sum of the individual levies of the various taxing districts in which the property is located. While there is no specified rate a district must levy, a maximum amount is usually provided by statute. Illinois property tax maximum rate referenda ballots must provide more specific information, and all referendum questions proposed must conform to specific wording requirements (35 ILCS 200/18-125).

Equalization of assessments among counties is accomplished by a state-determined "equalization factor," more commonly known as a multiplier, which is applied to the local nonfarm assessments to bring the median level of real estate assessments in a county to the state-mandated level of $33^1/_3$% (35 ILCS 200/17-25).

Assessment caps: Counties may adopt ordinances to cap property tax assessment increases at 7% per year. However, the exemption from higher increases may not exceed $20,000.

• *Farmland*

The Illinois Department of Revenue has published guidelines for the valuation of farmland to achieve equitable assessment within and among counties in the state. Generally, the guidelines define land use, describe the assessment process, and discuss adjustment factors and alternative land uses. The publication also provides a chart of certified values and assessments ($ per acre) for use with Bulletin 810 productivity indexes, as well as a Bulletin 810 slope and erosion adjustment table (*Publication 122, Instructions for Farmland Assessments,* Illinois Department of Revenue, September 2015, CCH ILLINOIS TAX REPORTS, ¶ 403-013).

Wooded acreage: Wooded acreage that was classified as farmland during the 2006 assessment year is assessed by multiplying the current fair cash value of the property by a transition percentage. That percentage is determined by dividing the property's 2006 equalized assessed value as farmland by the 2006 fair cash value of the property (35 ILCS 200/10-510). "Wooded acreage" is defined as any parcel of unimproved real property that (35 ILCS 200/10-505):

— can be defined as "woodlands" by the U.S. Department of Interior Bureau of Land Management;

— is at least five contiguous acres;

— does not qualify as cropland, permanent pasture, other farmland, or wasteland;

— is not managed under a forestry management plan and is not considered other farmland;

— does not qualify for another preferential assessment under the Illinois property tax code; and

— was owned by the taxpayer on October 1, 2007.

A Department of Revenue publication covers the options for preferential assessment of wooded acreage for property tax purposes. Specific topics include assessment for purposes of forestry management, conservation stewardship, and transition percentage (*Publication 135, Preferential Assessments for Wooded Acreage,* Illinois Department of Revenue, July 2009, CCH ILLINOIS TAX REPORTS, ¶ 401-998).

¶2005

• *Unimproved land*

The Conservation Stewardship Law (35 ILCS 200/10-400) allows for the conservation, management, and assessment of unimproved land generally suitable for the perpetual growth and preservation of that land in Illinois. "Unimproved land" means woodlands, prairie, wetlands, or other vacant and undeveloped land that is not used for any residential or commercial purposes that materially disturbs the land. "Managed land" refers to unimproved land of at least five contiguous acres that is subject to a conservation management plan (35 ILCS 200/10-405; 17 Ill. Adm. Code 2580.10, et seq.).

Qualifying managed land is valued at 5% of its fair cash value (35 ILCS 200/10-420(a)). This special valuation does not apply to land that has been (35 ILCS 200/10-420(b)):

— assessed as farmland;

— valued as either vegetative filter strips, non-clear cut land, or open-space land;

— certified as providing a defined public benefit; or

— dedicated as a nature preserve or a nature preserve buffer.

Taxpayers requesting special valuation must submit a conservation management plan to the state Department of Natural Resources. If that agency approves the plan, it will certify its approval to the state Department of Revenue. Plan approval is required every 10 years, and plans will be revised when necessary or appropriate. If a taxpayer receiving the special valuation does not comply with the plan during a taxable year, the taxpayer must pay to the county the difference between the taxes paid and the taxes that would have been paid without the special valuation (35 ILCS 200/10-425).

Unimproved land assessment does not apply in Cook County (35 ILCS 200/10-420(a)).

Vacant platted land: From August 14, 2009, through calendar year 2011 in all counties except for Cook County, the assessed valuation for qualifying vacant property that has been platted and subdivided was determined based on the assessed value assigned to the property when last assessed prior to its last transfer or conveyance. An initial sale of any qualifying platted lot or a transfer to a holder of a mortgage pursuant to a mortgage foreclosure proceeding or pursuant to a transfer in lieu of foreclosure does not disqualify the lot from the assessed valuation provision. In addition, the replatting of a subdivision or portion of a subdivision does not disqualify the lot from the assessed valuation provision. (35 ILCS 200/10-31)

In 2012, the law reverted to its terms in effect prior to August 14, 2009. Under that version of the law, the assessed valuation of qualifying platted and subdivided property is determined annually based on the estimated price the property would bring at a fair voluntary sale for use by the buyer for the same purposes for which the property was used when last assessed prior to its platting (35 ILCS 200/10-30(d)). This provision does not apply to property in a special service area for which the *ad valorem* taxes are extended solely upon the equalized assessed value of the land without regard to improvements (35 ILCS 200/27-75).

Developer's relief: Except in Cook County, the improvement of platted and subdivided property into separate lots with streets, sidewalks, curbs, gutters, sewer, water, and utility lines does not increase its valuation until a habitable structure is completed on the lot, the property is used for any business, commercial, or residential purpose, or the lot is sold. The land must be:

— platted and subdivided in accordance with the Plat Act (765 ILCS 205/0.01, et seq.);

— platted after January 1, 1978;

— in excess of ten acres at the time of platting; and

— vacant land or be used as a farm at the time of platting.

Generally, until a subdivided lot has a completed habitable structure, the property is assessed yearly based on the estimated price it would bring at a fair voluntary sale for use by the buyer for the same purpose for which it was used before platting (35 ILCS 200/10-30; *Publication 134, Developer's Exemption, Property Tax Code, Section 10-30*, Illinois Department of Revenue, October 2007, CCH ILLINOIS TAX REPORTS, ¶401-832)

• *Historic buildings and historical societies*

Tax incentives are provided to owner-occupiers of historic buildings who rehabilitate their property. The assessed valuation of qualifying structures may not be increased during an eight-year period; thereafter, the valuation may be increased at a graduated rate for the next four years. Historic buildings include owner-occupied multifamily residences (35 ILCS 200/10-45).

Illinois taxing districts, with voter approval, may abate any portion of taxes due on property of qualifying historical societies through assessment year 2013. Qualifying societies are those that qualify as exempt organizations under IRC Sec. 501(c)(3). (35 ILCS 200/18-165)

• *Land used for open space*

An open space assessment based on the value of the land for open space purposes is available in every county that classifies property for taxation (Cook County). Valuation is made on the basis of the land's fair cash value, estimated at the price it would bring at a fair, voluntary sale for use by the buyer for open space purposes (35 ILCS 200/10-155). Property leased to a park or conservation district for $1 or less per year and used exclusively as open space is exempt (35 ILCS 200/15-105).

Golf courses: Improvements underlying portions of a golf course's property could qualify for open-space status if they conserved landscaped areas by facilitating the existence of the golf course. Under Illinois law, the property of golf courses that conserved landscaped areas qualified as open-space, which during the tax year at issue was assessed at a rate of $1,000 per acre in the county. A golf course typically requires certain appurtenances in order to function, such as parking areas, a building in which to conduct the course business (i.e., a clubhouse), and perhaps a building to support the physical maintenance of the course. Without such improvements, many golf courses would not exist. Since those improvements facilitate the existence of the golf course, and the course conserves landscaped areas, such improvements also can be said to conserve landscaped areas. On remand, the improvements at issue (a swimming pool, a clubhouse, a horse riding area, a stable, a parking lot, a driveway, and tennis courts) should be evaluated to determine whether they conserve landscaped areas by facilitating the existence of the golf course. (*Onwentsia Club v. Illinois Property Tax Appeal Board*, Appellate Court of Illinois, Second District, No. 2-10-0388, June 16, 2011, CCH ILLINOIS TAX REPORTS, ¶402-353)

Another case held that the term "conserve" must be construed narrowly. Therefore, there must be some substantial nexus between the land considered as open space and the landscaped area it is claimed to conserve—the improvement in question must directly relate to and facilitate the existence of the golf course. The court found that nexus did not exist between the golf course and a swimming pool, tennis facilities, the riding arena and the stable. The court remanded to the Property Tax Appeal Board the question of whether maintenance buildings, parking lots, driveways and the clubhouse have nexus with the golf course. (*The Lake Co. Board of*

Review v. Illinois Property Tax Appeal Board, Appellate Court of Illinois, Second District, No. 02-12-0429, March 26, 2013, CCH ILLINOIS TAX REPORTS, ¶ 402-632)

Application: In all Illinois counties except for Cook County, a person liable for property tax on land used for open-space purposes must file a verified application for additional open-space valuation with the chief county assessment officer by June 30 of each year that the valuation is desired. The file date in Cook County is January 31. If an application is not filed by January 31 or June 30, as applicable, the right to claim the valuation for that year is waived. (35 ILCS 200/10-160)

• *Vegetative filter strips*

Effective through December 31, 2026, land located between a farm field and an area to be protected, including surface water, streams, rivers, or sinkholes, will be assessed as vegetative filter strips and will receive a special valuation. The land must be at least 66 feet wide and contain vegetation that has a dense top growth, forms a uniform ground cover, has a heavy fibrous root system, and tolerates pesticides used in the farm field. (35 ILCS 200/10-152)

• *Nature preserves*

Value of property dedicated as a nature preserve under the Illinois Natural Areas Preservation Act that is encumbered by a public easement is reduced for assessment purposes to a level at which its valuation is $1 per acre (35 ILCS 200/9-145).

• *Solar energy heating or cooling system*

A taxpayer who installs a solar energy heating or cooling system may apply to have the improvements valued at the lesser of their value as equipped with the solar energy system or their value as if equipped with a conventional heating or cooling system (35 ILCS 200/10-10).

• *Railroads*

The Department of Revenue, rather than local assessors, assesses the operating property of railroads in Illinois (35 ILCS 200/9-70). Nonoperating or noncarrier real estate of railroads is assessed by local officials (35 ILCS 200/9-75). Railroads are taxed on the percentage of their operating property in Illinois. This is determined by adding the percentages of the track mileage in Illinois as opposed to total track mileage, revenues attributable to Illinois as opposed to total revenues, and the reproduction cost of operating property within Illinois as opposed to total operating property. The percentage thus obtained is applied to the total value of operating property to obtain the value of taxable property in Illinois (35 ILCS 200/9-70).

Applicable to calendar years 2010-2019, any increase in railroad operating property's overall valuation that is directly attributable to qualifying development of higher-speed passenger rail transportation is excluded from the valuation of the real property improvements. Railroad companies must continue to include information pertaining to any of those potential increases in the property's overall valuation in their property and information schedules. (P.A. 97-481 (H.B. 1518), Laws 2011)

• *Model homes*

A single-family dwelling or condominium unit that is not occupied as a dwelling but is used as a display or demonstration model home is assessed in the same manner that the tract or lot was assessed prior to construction of the dwelling. The valuation of the property is not affected if the display or model home contains home furnishings, appliances, offices, and office equipment used to further sales activities. The special valuation is available for a 10-year period (35 ILCS 200/10-25).

• *Property in state of disrepair*

Maintenance and repairs of property that improve the overall exterior and interior appearance and quality of a residence by restoring it from a state of disrepair to a standard state of repair do not constitute material alterations to the existing character and condition of the residence that would trigger an increase in the assessed valuation of the property (35 ILCS 200/10-20).

• *Military public/private residential development leasehold*

Valuation and abatement provisions have been adopted for PPV leases, which are leasehold interests in U.S. military public/private residential developments at military training facilities, military bases, and related military support facilities. All interests enjoyed pursuant to Chapter 159 (Real Property; Related Personal Property; and Lease of Non-Excess Property) and Chapter 169 (Military Construction and Military Family Housing) of Title 10 of the U.S. Code are considered leaseholds for purposes of these provisions. The provisions apply beginning January 1, 2006, and ending December 31, 2055 (formerly, 2017). A PPV lease must be valued at its fair cash value using certain PPV-related provisions that must be determined by using an income capitalization approach. (35 ILCS 200/10-370(b); 35 ILCS 200/10-375(c)).

For naval training facilities, naval bases, and naval support facilities, "net operating income" means all revenues received minus the actual expenses before interest, taxes, depreciation, and amortization (prior to tax year 2017, minus the lesser of 62% of all revenues or actual expenses before interest, taxes, depreciation, and amortization). For all other military training facilities, military bases, and related military support facilities, the definition, including the 42%-of-revenue figure, remains the same. (35 ILCS 200/10-370(b))

• *Wind energy devices*

The fair cash value of wind energy devices is determined by subtracting the allowance for physical depreciation from the trended real property cost basis (35 ILCS 200/10-605). Functional obsolescence and external obsolescence may further reduce the fair cash value of the wind energy device, to the extent they are proved by the taxpayer by clear and convincing evidence. A "wind energy device" is any device, with a nameplate capacity of at least 0.5 megawatts, that is used in the process of converting kinetic energy from the wind to generate electric power for commercial sale (35 ILCS 200/10-600). These valuation provisions are applicable through 2021.

• *Revaluation of tornado-affected small business property*

Certain commercial and industrial property owned by a small business that was involved in a tornado disaster will be valued for property tax purposes under modified criteria for a specified period. The property must be rebuilt within two years after the date of the tornado disaster, and the square footage of the rebuilt structure may not be more than 110% of the square footage of the original structure. (35 ILCS 200/10-700)

A "qualified parcel of property" means property owned and used exclusively for commercial or industrial business that has been rebuilt following a tornado disaster occurring in taxable year 2013 or any taxable year thereafter. "Modified equalized assessed value" means, in the first taxable year after a tornado disaster occurs, the equalized assessed value of the property in the base year (the taxable year prior to the taxable year in which the tornado occurred), and in the second taxable year after the tornado disaster, the modified equalized assessed value for the previous taxable year, increased by 4%.

A qualified parcel of property will be valued at the lesser of:

    (1) its modified equalized assessed value,

    (2) 33 1/3% of its fair cash value, or

    (3) if applicable, the fair cash value as required by county ordinance.

The applicable method of valuation will continue until the earlier of a change in use or ownership of the property or the 15th taxable year after the tornado disaster. (35 ILCS 200/10-700)

• *Assessment freeze program for targeted areas*

Between January 1, 2015, and June 30, 2029, the chief county property tax assessor of any Illinois county may reduce the assessed value of improvements to residential real property in qualifying targeted areas (*i.e.,* a distressed community that meets geographic, poverty, and unemployment criteria set forth under federal law). for 10 taxable years, subject to a number of conditions. Applications for the benefit under the community stabilization assessment freeze pilot program must be submitted between January 1, 2015, and December 31, 2019. (35 ILCS 200/15-174)

The preferred assessments will apply only if all of the following factors are met:

— the improvements are residential;

— the parcel was purchased or otherwise conveyed to the taxpayer after January 1 of the taxable year, but not as a result of a tax sale;

— the parcel is located in a targeted area;

— the taxpayer either:

(a) occupies single family home improvements as a primary residence or,

(b) for residences of one to six units that will not be owner-occupied, replaces two primary building systems (electricity; heating; plumbing; roofing; exterior doors and windows; floors, walls, and ceilings; elevators; health and safety; and energy conservation improvements);

— the transfer from the holder of the prior mortgage to the taxpayer was an arm's length transaction;

— an existing residential dwelling structure of not more than six units was either unoccupied at the time of conveyance for at least six months or was ordered by a court to be deconverted in accordance with provisions governing distressed condominiums;

— the parcel is clear of unreleased liens and has no outstanding tax liabilities attached against it; and

— the purchase price did not exceed the Federal Housing Administration's loan limits then in place for the area in which the improvement is located.

For the first seven years after the improvements are placed in service, the assessed value of the improvements must be reduced by an amount equal to 90% of the difference between the base year assessed value of the improvements and the assessed value of the improvements in the current taxable year. In the eighth year, the percentage will decrease to 65%, and in the ninth year it will decrease to 35%. The benefit will cease in the tenth taxable year.

Among other restrictions, if there is a transfer of ownership during the period of the assessment freeze, the benefits of the program will apply after the transfer only if the property conveyance is from an owner who does not occupy the improvements as a primary residence to an owner who will do so, and all other requirements of the program continue to be met. (35 ILCS 200/15-174)

• *Omitted property*

Property that has not been assessed in any given year is assessed as "omitted property" on discovery of this fact by the board of review or the Cook County assessor (35 ILCS 200/9-260; 35 ILCS 200/16-50; 35 ILCS 200/9-265). Assessments of omitted property are also made when there has been a defect in the description or assessment (35 ILCS 200/9-265). A defective description or assessment includes a description or assessment of real property omitting improvements with the result that part of the taxes on the total value of the property as improved remain unpaid.

Effective June 1, 2014, except in Cook County, a chief county assessment officer who discovers that a property improperly was granted a homestead exemption may consider that property as omitted property for that taxable year only (35 ILCS 200/9-265).

County assessors are authorized to assess omitted property for the current assessment year and three prior years. After providing notice and an opportunity to be heard, the assessor is required to render a decision on the omitted assessment, whether or not the omitted assessment was contested, and must mail a notice of the decision to the taxpayer of record or to the party that contested the omitted assessment. The notice of decision must contain a statement that the decision may be appealed to the board of review. (35 ILCS 200/9-260)

In Cook County, omitted property assessments are made by the county assessor either on the assessor's own initiative or on the order of the board of appeals when the assessor fails to act. In all other counties, the board of review has the exclusive authority to list and assess all omitted property. (ILCS 200/9-260; 35 ILCS 200/9-265)

Interest: Omitted property assessments are subject to interest at the annual rate of 10% beginning two years after the date the correct tax bill should have been received. Interest may be waived under certain circumstances (35 ILCS 200/9-265) When the interest has been waived, the owner is not charged with any penalty for nonpayment of taxes until the owner receives actual notice of, and is billed for, the principal amount of back taxes (35 ILCS 200/21-15).

¶2006 Equalization

Law: Ill. Const., Art. IX, Sec. 4; Property Tax Code, Sec. 1-55 [35 ILCS 200/1-55]; Property Tax Code, Sec. 8-5(6) [35 ILCS 200/8-5]; Property Tax Code, Sec. 9-205 [35 ILCS 200/9-205]; Property Tax Code, Sec. 9-210 [35 ILCS 200/9-210]; Property Tax Code, Sec. 9-250 [35 ILCS 200/9-250]; Property Tax Code, Sec. 10-135 [35 ILCS 200/10-135]; Property Tax Code, Sec. 10-200 [35 ILCS 200/10-200]; Property Tax Code, Sec. 10-1535 [35 ILCS 200/10-155]; Property Tax Code, Sec. 10-156 [35 ILCS 200/10-156]; Property Tax Code, Sec. 16-60 [35 ILCS 200/16-60]; Property Tax Code, Sec. 16-65 [35 ILCS 200/16-65]; Property Tax Code, Sec. 16-205 [35 ILCS 200/16-205]; Property Tax Code, Sec. 17-5 [35 ILCS 200/17-5]; Property Tax Code, Sec. 17-25 [35 ILCS 200/17-25]; Property Tax Code, Sec. 18-155 [35 ILCS 200/18-155] (CCH ILLINOIS TAX REPORTS, ¶20-720).

The Illinois Constitution provides that taxes on real property must be levied uniformly by valuation (Ill. Const., Art. IX, Sec. 4(a)). To achieve this objective, a method exists for equalizing the valuation of property within a taxing jurisdiction (township, county, assessment district) and throughout the state. Equalization of assessment levels within counties occurs prior to equalization among counties by the state.

The Department of Revenue acts as an equalizing authority for Cook County as a whole and among counties statewide. The equalized assessed value of all the property in Cook County is the equalized assessed value of the property for the year immediately preceding the levy year.

In Illinois, the equalization factor, whether determined on a local level or county level, is commonly referred to as a "multiplier." This factor or multiplier is the percentage applied to bring assessments up or down to the statutorily mandated level of $33^1/_3$%. State multipliers are not applied to farm acreage and farm buildings or to coal assessments (35 ILCS 200/10-135; 35 ILCS 200/10-200).

If, after calculating an apportioned property tax levy among counties, the Illinois Department of Revenue determines that an over-apportionment has taken place, the department will notify the county clerk and county treasurer of each county affected by the incorrect apportionment and provide those county clerks and county treasurers with correct apportionment data, applicable for taxable year 2015 and thereafter. (35 ILCS 200/10-155; 35 ILCS 200/10-156)

The Illinois Department of Revenue has issued a publication to explain generally the sales ratio and equalization procedures authorized by the state property tax law. Along with discussions of sales ratio studies, assessment levels, and equalization, the publication covers applicable statutes. (*Publication-136, Property Assessment and Equalization,* Illinois Department of Revenue, April 2016, available at **http://www.revenue.state.il.us/Publications/Pubs/PUB-136.pdf**)

¶2007 Payment of Taxes

Law: Property Tax Code, Sec. 9-260 (35 ILCS 200/9-260); Property Tax Code, Sec.12-50 (35 ILCS 200/12-50); Property Tax Code, Sec.16-115 (35 ILCS 200/16-115); Property Tax Code Secs. 20-5—20-85 [35 ILCS 200/20-5—20-85]; Property Tax Code, Secs. 21-15—21-40 [35 ILCS 200/21-15—21-40](CCH Illinois Tax Reports, ¶20-756).

Generally, real property taxes are paid each year in two equal installments, due 30 days after a real estate tax bill is mailed (35 ILCS 200/21-15). Cook County and certain other counties use an accelerated or estimated tax billing system (35 ILCS 200/21-20; 35 ILCS 200/21-25; 35 ILCS 200/21-30). Partial payments are permitted. Penalties are added if the tax is paid after the due date.

The county treasurer is the *ex officio* county collector in all Illinois counties. County collectors are authorized to collect taxes on real property located in their counties.

Payment of the tax must be made to the county collector in legal tender, cashier's check, certified check, postal or money orders, personal or corporate check, or in some counties by credit card. Cook County generally is required to accept payment by credit card for each installment of property taxes, although the taxpayers must also pay any credit card service charges or fees (35 ILCS 200/20-25(b)). However, the county need not accept payment by credit card for delinquent payments or for purposes of any tax sale or scavenger sale.

There is no extension of time for payment and discounts are not given for early payment.

Payment under specification: A tax collector may, but is not required to, receive taxes on part of a property when a particular specification of the part is furnished. If the tax on the remainder of the property remains unpaid, the collector must enter that specification in his or her return so that the part on which the tax remains unpaid may be clearly known (35 ILCS 200/20-210; see *Bigelow Group, Inc. v. Rickert,* Illinois Appellate Court, Second District, No. 2-06-0879, October 24, 2007, CCH Illinois Tax Reports, ¶401-828).

Military personnel: A person in the military service is afforded protection under federal law from the loss of real or personal property through enforcement of the collection of taxes when the property is occupied by his or her dependents as a dwelling or by employees for professional, business, or agricultural purposes (50 USC §560). Property may be sold to enforce tax collection only by court permission upon application by the tax collector.

Unpaid Illinois property tax due on property owned by a National Guard member or reservist in the Armed Forces of the United States called to active duty outside the United States is not deemed delinquent and no interest or penalty will accrue until 180 days after the reservist returns from active duty (35 ILCS 200/21-15).

• *Tax bills—Notice*

Tax bills are mailed by the county or town collector the year following the year the assessments are made. Tax bills are prepared in triplicate for each installment and mailed at least 30 days before the due date. Where tax bills are mailed to a mortgage lender, a copy of the bill must be sent by the lender to the borrower within 15 days of the receipt of the bill. If the county uses the accelerated billing method, the copy is mailed to the borrower with the final installment. Failure to mail a bill or to receive one, however, does not affect the validity of the tax or relieve the taxpayer of tax liability.

As an alternative to mailing the bill and at the request of the taxpayer, the bill can be sent by e-mail (35 ILCS 200/20-20). Beginning in 2015, the taxpayer's request must be in writing. A taxpayer who makes such a request must notify the collector of any subsequent change in the e-mail address.

The county tax bill or a separate statement accompanying the bill must show:

(1) the assessed value of the property;

(2) the county and state equalization factors;

(3) the equalized assessment resulting from the application of the equalization factors;

(4) the dollar amount of tax levied allocable to a school district for payment of community college district tuition;

(5) itemization of the tax rates extended by each of the taxing districts; and

(6) information that certain taxpayers may be eligible for tax exemptions, abatements, and other assistance programs.

Tax bills issued by counties that utilize electronic data processing equipment will also include the dollar amount of tax that is allocated to each taxing district, the total tax rate, the total amount due, and the amount by which the total tax and the tax allocable to each taxing body differs from the previous tax bill. Payment postmarked on or before the due date are considered timely.

Assessment notices: For all Illinois counties except Cook County, the chief county assessment officer must publish a list of property for which assessments have been added or changed since the preceding assessment, together with the amounts of the assessments (except those changed by equalization) (35 ILCS 200/12-10). Publication of assessments in each year of general assessments must include:

— a statement that property generally is required to be assessed at 331/3 % of fair market value;

— contact information, including any website, of the local assessor;

— advice to taxpayers of steps to follow if they believe the full fair market value of the house is incorrect or the assessment is not uniform;

— a statement of the deadline date for filing an appeal;

— a brief explanation of the relationship between the assessment and the tax bill; and

— a notice of possible eligibility for some homestead exemptions.

Notice of an increase or decrease in property tax assessment by a board of review may, under certain circumstances, be given to the taxpayer's attorney or, in Cook County, by e-mail. A board of review in Cook County may send electronic notices of assessment changes to taxpayers whose e-mail address appears in either the assessment records or a complaint filed with the board. If the taxpayer has been represented by an attorney, the notice will be sent to the attorney, whether by mail or by e-mail. In all other counties, the notice will be mailed to the taxpayer's attorney if the taxpayer was represented by an attorney. (35 ILCS 200/12-50)

A complaint that property in Cook County was overassessed, underassessed, or exempt may be filed electronically and signed with the electronic signature of either the complaining party or the complaining party's attorney (35 ILCS 200/16-115). The legislation provides definitions for "electronic," "electronic record," and "electronic signature."

• *Time for payment*

With certain exceptions discussed below, all real estate taxes are payable in two equal installments. The first installment is due on the later of June 1 or the day after the date specified on the real estate tax bill as the first installment due date, and the second installment is due on the later of September 1 or the day after the date specified on the real estate tax bill as the second installment due date. These dates may be modified by ordinance. If either due date falls on a Sunday or legal holiday, the due date is extended to the succeeding business day. Payments postmarked on or before the due date are considered timely (35 ILCS 200/21-15).

Cook County: Cook County accelerates its tax payment procedure. Under this system, the first installment, billed January 31, is equal to 50% of the preceding year's tax bill and is due by March 1 (or no later than June 1, by ordinance). The second installment is to be mailed June 30 and covers the balance of taxes due, computed by subtracting the first billing from the total taxes for the present year.

Omitted property: County assessors may assess properties that may have been omitted from local Illinois property tax assessments for up to three years prior to the current assessment year. County property taxes based on an omitted assessment must be prepared and mailed at the same time as the estimated first installment property tax bill for the preceding year. The omitted assessment tax bill will be due on the date on which the second installment property tax bill for the preceding year becomes due. Any taxes for omitted assessments will be deemed delinquent after the due date of the second installment tax bill and will bear interest at the rate of 1.5% per month until paid or forfeited (35 ILCS 200/9-260).

Late payments: In all cases, if the tax payment is late, the tax becomes delinquent 30 days after the due date, at which time interest is charged. A tax bill payment received by mail, and postmarked on or before the required due date, is not delinquent.

The legislature has also authorized a third billing method in counties with populations of less than two million. The county board may defer the delinquency date for half of each installment of real estate taxes for 60 days.

¶2008 Administration

Law: Civil Administrative Code, Sec. 2505/2505-560 [20 ILCS 2505/2505-560] (CCH ILLINOIS TAX REPORTS, ¶91-870a).

The Illinois property tax is administered at several governmental levels under the supervision of the Department of Revenue. Counties (the particular official depending on the size of the county) administer the taxes imposed on land within their geographic jurisdiction. The Department of Revenue equalizes property statewide as an adjunct to its supervisory authority over the local assessing officials.

Administrative review tribunals hear appeals on assessments of individual parcels of property. The Property Tax Appeal Board reviews decision by local boards of review on alleged overassessments.

The State's Attorney represents the state in collection proceedings.

Taxpayer Action Boards: A Taxpayer Action Board is created in each of the following counties: Cook, DuPage, Kane, Kendall, Lake, McHenry, and Will. The seven members of each board will serve two-year terms, and each board will oversee various assessment procedures and propose appropriate changes. (20 ILCS 2505/2505-560)

Practitioner Comment: Local Rules

The Illinois Appellate Court determined that a county board of review may reject tax appeals sent by any delivery carrier other than U.S. mail as untimely. The Court held that the Kane County Board of Review had the authority to make reasonable rules that did not necessarily mimic the Illinois Supreme Court rules, including modifying the "mailbox rule." Petitioners argued that because the powers, duties, role, and function of the Board were "quasi-judicial," the Illinois Supreme Court Rules applied to the Board. Consequently, Petitioners contended that since the Illinois Supreme Court Rules allowed for third-party commercial carriers as acceptable deliverers of documents, their appeals were timely filed. Instead, the Appellate Court held the Board was not limited in its authority to make rules that follow the Illinois Supreme Court. Accordingly, the Board had the authority to determine that only delivery via U.S. mail was acceptable. (*BLTREJV3 Chicago LLC v. Kane County. Board. of Review*, 2014 IL App (2d) 140164, Sept. 3, 2014, CCH ILLINOIS TAX REPORTS, ¶ 402-844)

Horwood Marcus & Berk, Chartered

¶2009 Delinquencies

Law: Property Tax Code, Sec. 9-275 [35 ILCS 200/9-275]; Secs. 21-75—21-410 [35 ILCS 200/21-75—21-410] (CCH ILLINOIS TAX REPORTS, ¶ 20-758 *et seq.*).

In Illinois, real estate taxes become a prior lien against the land on January 1 of each year (35 ILCS 200/21-75).

The assessee receives notice by mail of the tax liability on an annual basis. Individuals who do not pay their annual real estate taxes and lienholders of record are notified of the impending tax sale by certified mail before the tax collector's annual application for judgment and order for sale of delinquent real estate is filed with the circuit court. If the taxes and costs are not paid by the owner or any lienholder, and if the circuit court grants the collector's application, the delinquent property is offered for sale at a public auction.

Payments: County tax collectors must accept payment of delinquent taxes from the property owners on or before the business day preceding the day the taxes are sold (35 ILCS 200/21-165). In addition, the county treasurer must keep the treasurer's office open from 8:00 am to 4:00 pm on the business day before the commencement of a tax sale and during the same hours each day the tax sale is pending (55 ILCS 5/3-10008). Home rule units are not permitted to impose restrictions inconsistent with either of those changes.

Tax sales; redemption: The annual sale is the initial device for collecting unpaid tax debts and is a sale for the full amount of taxes owed on the property. A certificate of sale for each delinquent parcel of real estate is awarded to each successful bidder. The owner of the property or other interested party may redeem the property within the specified time period by paying the delinquent tax plus a penalty, interest, and costs. For most property, the minimum length of the redemption period under the Illinois Constitution is two years from the date of the tax sale. However, a six-month period is applicable to vacant nonfarm real estate, commercial property, industrial property, and improvements having seven or more residential units on which taxes have been delinquent for more than two years, and a period of two and one-half years is applicable to improvements having no more than six dwelling units. The constitutional periods have been lengthened or shortened by statute, and the statutory deadlines for redemption are discussed in CCH ILLINOIS TAX REPORTS at ¶ 20-760.

Tracts offered for sale but not sold are forfeited to the state. The purchaser's interest is perfected against *bona fide* purchasers when the purchaser records a tax deed to the property (*Smith v. SIPI, LLC*, U.S. Court of Appeals for the Seventh Circuit, No. 08-2880, July 27, 2010, CCH ILLINOIS TAX REPORTS, ¶ 402-156).

Notices: When it is certified that assessments and taxes of delinquent property previously forfeited to the state equal or exceed the value of the property, that property can be sold to the highest bidder with 10 days' notice in counties with less than 10,000 inhabitants and 30 days' notice in all other counties (35 ILCS 200/21-225).

The county collector, at least 10 days before an authorized tax sale, may post on the collector's website a list of all properties eligible to be sold that will include the street address on file with the collector and the PIN number of each property, but the posting may not include the name of the property owner (35 ILCS 200/21-118).

Bidding process: Either (35 ILCS 200/21-205)

— the collector will employ an automated bidding system that is programmed to accept the lowest redemption qualifying price bid, or

— all tax sales shall be digitally recorded with video and audio.

All hardware and software used with respect to required automated means must be certified by the Department of Revenue and recertified every five years. If tax sales are digitally recorded and no automated bid system is used, the recordings must be maintained for at least three years from the date of the tax sale. (35 ILCS 200/21-205)

A qualifying owner of property sold to recover delinquent taxes who is injured by the sale must bring an action for indemnity within 10 years after the date the tax deed was issued. Previously, there was no deadline.

CCH Advisory: Lien Registry—2018

Effective January 1, 2018, for taxes administered by the Department of Revenue (DOR), a state tax lien registration program has been established to provide a uniform state-wide system for filing notices of tax liens that are in favor of or enforced by the DOR. The scope of the program is real property and personal property, tangible and intangible, of taxpayers or other persons against whom the DOR has liens pursuant to law for unpaid final tax liabilities.

If any person neglects or refuses to pay any final tax liability, the DOR may file in the registry a notice of tax lien within three years from the date of the final liability. The lien is perfected at the time of the filing and attaches to all after-acquired property of the debtor. The notice of lien is a lien for 20 years from the date of the filing unless the DOR files an earlier release of lien in the registry (35 ILCS 750/1-15).

The tax buyer must file a petition for tax deed in the circuit court before the redemption period expires. At the same time, the tax buyer must serve notice upon all owners, occupants, and parties interested in the real estate. Petitions must contain the address, room number, and time at which the petition for tax deed is set for hearing. If the redemption period expires without a response from parties interested in the real estate, the tax buyer may apply for a deed to the property after proving compliance with statutory service requirements.

Seizure of personal property: In addition to the annual tax sale of delinquent properties, the personal property of a taxpayer who is delinquent in payment of real estate taxes may be seized. The county may at any time bring a civil action in the name of the state against the property owner personally for taxes on property that has been forfeited. Also, should the property remain tax delinquent for two years or more, the law provides for a tax "scavenger" sale. There is a right to redemption under these enforcement proceedings, but the period of redemption varies on some property. Taxes delinquent for 20 years are presumed uncollectible (35 ILCS 200/21-260).

Liability of mortgage lender: Liability for any unpaid property taxes, including interest, that become delinquent through the fault of a mortgage lender extends to the mortgage lender responsible for servicing the mortgage and is not the responsibility of the mortgagor if the lender (1) holds funds in escrow to pay the taxes, and (2) the funds are sufficient to pay the taxes after deducting all reasonably anticipated hazard insurance premiums, mortgage insurance premiums, and any other assessments to be paid from the escrow under the terms of the mortgage. If unpaid property taxes become delinquent through the fault of the mortgage lender (*i.e.,* the mortgage lender received from the owner all payments due under the terms of the mortgage), the interest assessed for the delinquent taxes will be charged against the mortgage lender. In addition, the mortgage lender must pay the taxes due, redeem the property, and take all the necessary steps to remove any liens accruing against the property. The mortgage lender will not be deemed to be at fault if the mortgagor directed the lender in writing not to pay the property taxes or if the failure to pay was the result of inadequate or inaccurate parcel information (35 ILCS 200/21-15).

Indemnity: Any owner of property sold who sustains loss or damage by reason of the issuance of a tax deed and who is barred or is in any way precluded from bringing an action for the recovery of the property has the right to indemnity for the loss or damage sustained. An action for indemnity must be brought within 10 years after the date the tax deed was issued. (35 ILCS 200/21-305)

• *Erroneous homestead exemptions*

Property tax provisions concerning homestead exemptions granted erroneously are subject to penalties and interest on the "erroneous exemption principal amount," instead of on back taxes due and owing. The "erroneous exemption principal amount" means the total amount of property tax principal that would have been billed to a property index number but for the erroneous homestead exemption or exemptions a taxpayer received (35 ILCS 200/9-275(a)).

The chief county assessment officer must notify taxpayers if the officer discovers that their homestead exemptions from property tax are erroneous. The notice of discovery must identify the property, state the tax, interest and other fees due, inform the taxpayer that a lien will be placed on the property within three years, and inform the taxpayer that the amount due plus interest and fees may be paid up to 30 days after a lien is put on the property for the taxes. (35 ILCS 200/9-275(c))

A taxpayer was liable for a homestead exemption erroneously granted over a three-year period on a property she inherited because the taxpayer had improperly taken simultaneous homestead exemptions on two different properties. The General Assembly clearly and unequivocally had expressed its intention that the newly enacted section of the statute applied to exemptions erroneously taken in "any of the three collection years immediately prior to the current collection year." (*Mulry v. Berrios,* Appellate Court of Illinois, First District, No. 2017 IL App (1st) 152563, March 16, 2017, CCH Illinois Tax Reports, ¶ 403-204) In another case, no constitutional defect was found in a county's recovery of delinquent taxes from a taxpayer who had claimed homestead exemptions on 11 different properties, only one of which was his principal residence. (*Cuevas v. Berrios,* Appellate Court of Illinois, First District, No. 1-15-1218, 1-16-0602, March 31, 2017, CCH Illinois Tax Reports, ¶ 403-218)

• *Erroneous homestead exemptions in Cook County; Amnesty*

In Cook County, when the chief county assessment officer determines that one or more erroneous homestead exemptions was applied to the property, the erroneous exemption principal amount, together with all applicable interest and penalties, will constitute a lien on the property receiving the erroneous homestead exemption (35 ILCS 200/9-275(c)). A lien will not be filed if the property owner pays the erroneous exemption principal amount, plus penalties and interest, within 30 days of service of the notice of intent to record a lien.

¶2009

The chief assessment officer of Cook County, Illinois, can record liens against certain property in the county that has received one or more erroneous homestead exemptions from property tax. In addition, an amnesty period is established in which some property owners can pay any taxes due as a result of this law without having to pay interest or penalties. The law applies to the following homestead exemptions: (1) disabled veterans, (2) returning veterans, (3) disabled persons, (4) disabled veterans standard homestead, (5) senior citizens, (6) senior citizens assessment freeze, (7) general homestead, (8) alternative general homestead, and (9) long-time occupant.

An "erroneous homestead exemption" is a homestead exemption that was granted for real property in a taxable year if the property was not eligible for that exemption in that taxable year. If the taxpayer receives an erroneous homestead exemption under a single Code section for the same property in multiple years, that exemption is considered a single erroneous homestead exemption. However, if the taxpayer receives erroneous homestead exemptions under multiple Code sections for the same property, or if the taxpayer receives erroneous homestead exemptions under the same Code section for multiple properties, then each of those exemptions is considered a separate erroneous homestead exemption. (35 ILCS 200/9-275(a))

The chief county assessment officer is required to include in each assessment notice during any general assessment year information on homestead exemptions, including penalties and interest that may be incurred for erroneous exemptions received in earlier years. The notice also must inform owners of a 60-day grace period in which to pay the tax and avoid penalties. (35 ILCS 200/9-275(b))

Liens: Penalties and limitations periods, as well as access to amnesty provisions, depend, in part, on the number of erroneous exemptions. A lien can be recorded against property in the county if the property owner received (35 ILCS 200/9-275(c)):

— one or two erroneous homestead exemptions for real property, including at least one erroneous exemption granted for the property against which the lien is sought, during any of the three assessment years immediately prior to the assessment year in which the notice of intent to record a lien is served; or

— three or more erroneous exemptions for real property, including at least one erroneous exemption granted for the property against which the lien is sought, during any of the six assessment years immediately prior to the assessment year in which the notice of intent to record a lien is served.

Along with identifying the property, the specific erroneous homestead exemption granted, and the arrearage of taxes, a notice of intent to record a tax lien must inform the owner of the right to request a hearing and appeal a hearing officer's ruling, as well as inform the owner that the amount due, plus interest and penalties, must be paid within 30 days. A lien may not be filed sooner than 60 days after:

(1) notice is delivered to the owner if no hearing is requested or

(2) the conclusion of the hearing and appeals, if requested.

Penalties and interest: For owners of property that received one or two erroneous exemptions in the immediately preceding three assessment years, the applicable tax arrearage and 10% annual interest will be charged against the property. For owners of property that receive three or more erroneous exemptions in the immediately preceding six assessment years, the arrearage, a penalty of 50% of the total amount of arrearage for each year, and 10% annual interest will be charged against the property. (35 ILCS 200/9-275(f))

• *Court invalidates Cook County tax on nontitled personal property*

A Cook County trial court has granted summary judgment to two law firms, ruling that Cook County's nontitled personal property use tax ordinance is invalid. The Cook County Department of Revenue argued that the tax was not prohibited by the state law, because it was imposed on the value of the property, rather than on the

¶2009

sales price. The court held that the tax violated state law prohibiting a home rule county from imposing, under its home rule authority, a use tax, sales tax or other tax on the use, sale or purchase of tangible property based on the gross receipts from such sales or the selling price of the property. In addition, the court held the tax is an *ad valorem* tax on personal property in violation of the Illinois Constitution. Finally, the court held that the tax is *per se* discriminatory against interstate commerce in violation of the U.S. Constitution. (*Reed Smith, LLP et al. v. Ali, Director of the Cook County Department of Revenue, et al.*, Nos. 13 L 050454 and 13 L 050470, Circuit Court of Cook County, October 11, 2013)

Decision on appeal: The trial court's grant of injunctive relief in favor of two taxpayers and against enforcement of the tax ordinance was affirmed. The court considered the intent of the county ordinance to determine the meaning of "value" because, as the term was used in the ordinance, its meaning could be vague. The court noted the following three items:

— the preamble to the county ordinance enacting the tax acknowledged an increasing loophole by which county citizens could avoid sales tax on non-titled personal property used in the county;

— "use" was defined as the exercise of any right to or power over personal property incident to the ownership of it; and

— if the property was delivered to a location in the county or the purchaser merely resided in the county, then the property was *prima facie* "first subject to use" in the county on the delivery date.

So viewed, the court concluded that the use tax was, in reality, a prohibited sales tax upon the purchase of the property, so therefore there was no need to determine whether it violated either the U.S. Constitution or the Illinois Constitution. (*Reed Smith LLP v. Ali*, Appellate Court of Illinois, First District, Nos. 1-13-2646, 1-13-2654, 1-13-3350, 1-13-3352, August 4, 2014, CCH ILLINOIS TAX REPORTS, ¶ 402-831) (¶ 2305)

¶2010 Remedies

Law: Property Tax Code, Sec. 9-10 [35 ILCS 200/9-10]; Property Tax Code, Sec. 9-85 [35 ILCS 200/9-85]; Property Tax Code, Secs. 14-15—14-25 [35 ILCS 200/14-15—14-25]; Property Tax Code, Secs. 16-75—16-195 [35 ILCS 200/16-95—16-195] (CCH ILLINOIS TAX REPORTS, ¶ 20-902 *et seq.*).

A comprehensive set of administrative and legal remedies is afforded under the Property Tax Code for taxpayers aggrieved by the assessment placed on their property. In all but a limited number of circumstances, it is necessary for the taxpayer to seek review of a property tax assessment at the appropriate administrative tribunal prior to appealing to the courts. Generally, a complaint must be filed within 30 calendar days after the date of publication of the assessment list (35 ILCS 200/16-55).

The appeal mechanism differs between Cook County and the rest of the Illinois counties. In counties other than Cook, the taxpayer must first present a complaint to the county board of review. If dissatisfied with the board's decision, the taxpayer may then select one of two mutually exclusive routes of challenging the board's decision. First, the taxpayer may appeal to the Illinois Property Tax Appeal Board, whose decision is subject to court review under the Administrative Review Law. Such an appeal does not delay the extension of taxes on the assessment, but if the taxpayer prevails he or she is entitled to an abatement or refund. Alternatively, the taxpayer may pay the taxes under protest and file objections to the collector's application for judgment in the circuit court (35 ILCS 200/12-50).

Practitioner Comment: Presenting New Evidence to the PTAB

In August 2002, an Illinois court held that the Illinois Property Tax Appeal Board (PTAB), as an appeal board, may not review issues that were not raised by the parties before the Cook County Board of Review (Board). Further, the Illinois court held that PTAB may only consider facts, data, and testimony that the parties introduced before the Board (*Cook County Bd. of Review v. Property Tax Appeal Bd.*, 339 Ill. App. 3d 529 (2002); see also *Cook County Bd. of Review v. Property Tax Appeal Bd. and The Lurie Company*, 345 Ill. App. 3d 539 (2003), CCH ILLINOIS TAX REPORTS, ¶ 401-449).

In July 2003, the Illinois General Assembly amended the Property Tax Code to provide that PTAB "shall not be limited to the evidence presented to the board of review of the county." The amended law further states that "a party participating in the hearing before the PTAB is entitled to introduce evidence that is otherwise proper and admissible without regard to whether that evidence has previously been introduced as a hearing before the board of review of the county" (35 ILCS 200/16-180).

The General Assembly stated that its amendment shall be construed as declaratory of existing law and not as a new enactment. However, the amendment does not appear to completely reverse the Appellate Court's decisions in the above cited cases, because the amendment was silent about whether parties could raise new issues before the PTAB.

Horwood Marcus & Berk Chartered

Judicial review: When a change in assessed valuation is $300,000 or more, review is directly in the Illinois Appellate Court for the district in which the property is located. An action to review a final board decision, when a change in assessed valuation is less than $300,000, begins with the filing of a complaint and summons in circuit court within 35 days from the date that a copy of the decision sought to be reviewed is served upon the party affected by the decision. (35 ILCS 200/16-195)

A Cook County taxpayer may begin the appeal process by filing a complaint with the Cook County assessor. Taxpayers may take the case to the Cook County Board of Review initially, without filing with the assessor. If dissatisfied with the results, taxpayers have the option of filing a tax objection complaint in the circuit court of Cook County or filing for review with the state Property Tax Appeal Board.

Other remedies, such as mandamus, injunction, or certiorari, are available but severely restricted.

Equitable relief: Illinois circuit courts have general equitable jurisdiction to determine whether an intended abatement of taxes within an enterprise zone has been properly applied to extend and collect property taxes, even though that determination may result in detriment to a taxpayer who could only protest the issue under the exclusive jurisdiction of the state property tax code. Seven counties and a community college district (objectors) brought suit for equitable and declaratory relief against one county treasurer's abatement of property tax in an enterprise zone for construction of an ethanol plant. Where a tax objection procedure provides a taxpayer with an adequate remedy at law, the taxpayer may not seek equitable relief. However, in this case, the objectors were seeking to have another property owner's taxes increased, and the property code did not provide such a remedy. Therefore, the objectors were not barred from seeking equitable relief, and the trial court had equitable jurisdiction over their complaint. (*Board of Trustees of Illinois Valley Community College District No. 513 v. Putnam County*, Appellate Court of Illinois, Third District, No. 3-13-0344, July 9, 2014, CCH ILLINOIS TAX REPORTS, ¶ 402-824)

Refunds: Duplicate payments of Illinois real estate taxes could not be characterized as something other than tax payments or as unclaimed property, and claims for return of the payments were subject to the property tax code's five-year statute of limitations for refund claims, according to the Illinois Supreme Court. A class action brought in 2005 to recover duplicate payments in 1990 was untimely and properly was dismissed (*Santos Alvarez v. Maria Pappas, Treasurer and ex-officio Collector of Cook County, Illinois,* Illinois Supreme Court, Docket No. 104922, April 17, 2008, CCH ILLINOIS TAX REPORTS, ¶ 401-878).

• *Errors and mistakes*

Certificates of error are issued to correct mistakes or errors that are discovered before judgment or order for sale (¶ 2009). In counties other than Cook County, the chief county assessment officer and the board of review may draw up and issue a certificate for mistakes, other than errors of judgment as to valuation. (35 ILCS 200/14-20; 35 ILCS 200/16-75)

Certificates of error may be issued on court or Department of Revenue exemption approvals if (35 ILCS 200/14-25):

(1) the property became tax exempt at an earlier time, limited to certificates for the three preceding assessment years;

(2) the owner failed to file an application for exemption; or

(3) the property was erroneously assessed after the exemption claim is approved.

In counties with a population of less than three million, if an owner fails to file an application for the Senior Citizens Assessment Freeze Homestead Exemption during the previous year and qualifies for it, the chief county assessor may issue a certificate of error providing the correct taxable value of the property (35 ILCS 200/14-20).

Sales to counties or municipalities: Property sold at a tax sale for delinquent Illinois property taxes is a sale in error if a lien becomes null and void because the property has been acquired by a county or municipality or the property is owned by the state, a municipality, or a taxing district (55 ILCS 5/5-1080).

Homestead exemptions: If a certificate of error results in the allowance of a homestead exemption not previously allowed, the county collector must pay the taxpayer 6% interest on the amount of the exemption (35 ILCS 200/20-175).

Time limitation: The certificate of error must be executed no more than three years after the date on which the annual judgment and order of sale for that tax year was first entered (35 ILCS 200/14-15).

Cook County: In Cook County, certificates of error originate with the county assessor upon discovery of assessment errors or mistakes. There is no language prohibiting issuance on the basis of errors of judgment, a restriction that applies to the rest of the Illinois counties. The certificate needs to be endorsed only by the county assessor unless the assessment has been appealed to the Cook County Board of Review, in which case both must endorse the certificate. The certificate may be received in evidence in any court of competent jurisdiction. A certificate of error proceeding is separate and distinct from the procedures available to a taxpayer under complaint provisions (35 ILCS 200/14-15).

Interest on refunds of protested payments: The interest rate on refunds on protested Illinois property tax payments is the lesser of either 5% or the percentage increase in the Consumer Price Index for All Urban Consumers during the 12-month calendar year preceding the levy year for which the refund was made (35 ILCS 200/23-20).

PART VIII
MISCELLANEOUS TAXES
CHAPTER 21
UNEMPLOYMENT COMPENSATION

¶2101 Unemployment Compensation

Illinois unemployment insurance tax is covered in the Unemployment Insurance Act (820 ILCS 405/100—405/3200). Comprehensive coverage of unemployment insurance is provided in Wolters Kluwer, CCH Unemployment/Social Security Reporter. For more information go to CCHGroup.com or contact an account representative at 888-CCH-REPS (888-224-7377).

MISCELLANEOUS TAXES
CHAPTER 22
OTHER STATE TAXES

¶2201 Scope of Chapter

This chapter deals with the Illinois taxes that have not been previously discussed. The discussion here will indicate in general terms the persons subject to the tax, the basis and rate of the tax, and payments and reports due.

For a discussion of the Taxpayers' Bill of Rights, see ¶ 806.

¶2202 Alcoholic Beverage Taxes

Law: Liquor Control Act of 1934 [235 ILCS 5/8-1]

The Illinois alcoholic beverage tax is covered in Liquor Control Act of 1934 Sec. 8-1 [235 ILCS 5/8-1]). Current tax rates per gallon are:

— beer and cider containing not less than 0.5% nor more than 7% alcohol by volume . . . . $0.231.

— alcoholic liquor other than beer with an alcohol content of up to 14%; alcoholic liquor with an alcohol content of more than 14% and less than 20% . . . . $1.39.

— alcoholic liquor with an alcohol content of 20% or more . . . . $8.55.

(http://www.revenue.state.il.us/TaxRates/Excise.htm)

Comprehensive coverage of taxation of alcohol, as well as licensing and distribution information is provided in Wolters Kluwer, CCH Liquor Control Law Reporter. For more information go to CCHGroup.com or contact an account representative at 888-CCH-REPS (888-224-7377).

¶2203 Motor Fuel Taxes

Law: Motor Fuel Tax Law, Secs. 1—20 [35 ILCS 505/1—20]; Environmental Impact Fee Law, Sec. 310 [415 ILCS 125/310]; 86 Ill. Adm. Code 500 (CCH ILLINOIS TAX REPORTS, ¶ 40-001, 40-005).

Forms: RMFT-2, Application for Licensing and/or Permit; RMFT-5, Motor Fuel Distributor/Supplier Tax Return; RMFT-5-US, Underground Storage Tank Tax and Environmental Impact Fee Receiver Return; RMFT-11, Motor Fuel Tax Refund Claim; RMFT-71,

Liquefied Petroleum Gas Tax Return; MFUT-12, Application for Motor Fuel Use Tax License and Decals; MFUT-15, IFTA Quarterly Return.

All motor fuels used in motor vehicles on public highways and waterways in the state are subject to the tax, which is collected and paid by distributors [35 ILCS 505/6].

Practitioner Comment: No Refunds for Diesel Consumed While Idling on Private Property

The Appellate Court upheld the denial of the motor fuel tax refund claims filed by US Xpress Leasing for diesel fuel when its vehicles exited the public highways for refueling, cargo loading, and cab climate control. See *US Xpress Leasing Inc. v. Ill. Dep't of Rev.*, 385 Ill. App. 3d (1st Dist. 2008), CCH ILLINOIS TAX REPORTS, ¶ 401-903. The basis for its refund claims was that Illinois' motor fuel tax is imposed upon "the use of motor fuel upon highways of this State by commercial motor vehicles," and it was not using the motor fuel on public highways.

The court held that the statutory bar on refunds for idle time "clearly and unambiguously prohibits receiving a tax refund for fuel consumed in Illinois by commercial vehicles while idling whether that idling takes place on a public highway or on private property". Although the Motor Fuel Law states that a person who "uses [tax-paid] motor fuel for any purpose other than operating a motor vehicle upon the public highways or waters, shall be reimbursed and repaid the amount so paid," the next paragraph includes a sentence that states: "No claim based upon idle time shall be allowed."

In denying the refund claims, the court reasoned that "[w]hen read as a whole, the Law imposes a tax on motor fuel consumed by commercial motor vehicles while operating in Illinois." As such, the court read out of the imposition clause the fact that such fuel must be used "upon highways" in Illinois. Upon finding that the imposition clause reached and authorized taxation of fuel used off public highways, the court then found no exemption based solely on the "specific locations of consumption." Instead, the court found that the enumerated exemptions from the tax were all based upon the "specific purposes of fuel consumption," and no exemption is allowed for idle time.

Horwood Marcus & Berk, Chartered

Dyed diesel fuel transactions must be reported separately from other transactions. See *PIO-71, Dyed Diesel Fuel Enforcement Program*, Illinois Department of Revenue, August 2014, CCH ILLINOIS TAX REPORTS, ¶ 402-851.

Exemptions: The following tax-free sales by a distributor are exempt from the motor fuel tax [35 ILCS 505/6; 35 ILCS 505/2]:

    (1) sales to a valid licensed distributor or supplier;

    (2) sales in which delivery is made to a purchaser outside the state;

    (3) sales made to the federal government or its instrumentalities;

    (4) sales made to a municipal corporation that owns a local transportation system;

    (5) sales to privately-owned public utilities that own and operate vehicles used for transporting seven or more passengers;

    (6) sales of special fuel to a qualified user (other than a licensed distributor or supplier) for use other than in motor vehicles; and

    (7) sales of gasoline to be used by aircraft.

Also, Illinois motor fuel taxes or fees may not be imposed on the importation or receipt of diesel fuel sold to, or used by, a registered rail carrier or one otherwise recognized by the Illinois Commerce Commission as a rail carrier used directly in railroad operations [35 ILCS 505/2a].

¶2203

The collection of tax on 1-K kerosene is prohibited except when the 1-K kerosene is delivered directly into a storage tank that is located at a facility that has withdrawal facilities that are readily accessible to and capable of dispensing 1-K kerosene into the fuel supply tanks of motor vehicles [35 ILCS 505/2].

Sunset date for exemptions enacted after September 16, 1994: The application of an exemption enacted after September 16, 1994, must be limited by a sunset date [35 ILCS 505/2c]. If a "reasonable and appropriate" sunset date is not specified, then the exemption will expire five years after the effective date of the enacting law.

Refunds on exempt purchases: Claims for refund of motor fuel tax paid on exempt purchases must be filed within two years after the date the tax was paid [35 ILCS 505/13]. No claim for refund based upon the use of undyed diesel fuel is allowed except for fuel used in a manufacturing process where the undyed fuel becomes part of a product or by-product other than motor fuel and the process results in a product or by-product that is unsuitable for the intended use of fuel. Further, a claim for refund is also allowed for undyed diesel fuel used in testing machinery and equipment in a manufacturing process:

(a) by a manufacturer for research and development;

(b) by a commercial motor vehicle for any purpose other than operating the commercial motor vehicle on public highways;

(c) by a unit of local government when operating an airport;

(d) by refrigeration units that are permanently mounted to a semitrailer when the refrigeration unit has a fuel supply system dedicated solely for the operation of the refrigeration units; and

(e) by power take-off equipment.

A refund of tax paid on undyed diesel fuel unintentionally mixed with dyed diesel fuel may be claimed under certain circumstances.

Practitioner Comment: Constitutionality of Motor Fuel Tax

The Illinois Motor Fuel Tax Act was originally enacted in 1929 and since then, it has survived multiple constitutional challenges. Early attempts to invalidate the Motor Fuel Tax Act pursuant to the Equal Protection and Due Process Clauses of the United States Constitution were unsuccessful. For instance, a court found that the Motor Fuel Tax Act does not discriminate against the use of gasoline versus the use of kerosene oil and electricity, which were not subject to tax. *People v. Deep Rock Oil Corp.,* 343 Ill. 388, 175 N.E. 572 (1931). The matter of classification was within legislative discretion since it bore a reasonable relation to the purposes of the Act. *Id.* Furthermore, since the tax is classified as an excise or privilege tax, and not a property tax, more than one tax on the same conduct is allowed. *Id.* However, the tax imposed cannot exceed a reasonable rate of taxation for the privilege enjoyed. *Id.*

Under the Motor Fuel Tax Law, the user of the motor fuel is ultimately responsible for payment of the tax. However, the burden of collecting the tax falls upon the vendor of the fuel. Even if the vendor fails to collect the tax at the time of sale, the vendor is still liable; thus, the vendor must pay the tax from his own funds or seek collection of the tax from his customers. *Midland Oil Co. v. State,* 10 Ill. Ct. Cl. 635 (1939) as cited by *Beck v. Dept. of Revenue,* 121 Ill. App. 3d 666, 671, 460 N.E.2d 24, 26 (1984), CCH ILLINOIS TAX REPORTS, ¶ 201-379.

Jennifer A. Zimmerman, Esq., Horwood Marcus & Berk Chartered

• *Basis and rate of tax*

The motor fuel tax rate is 19¢ per gallon, and the diesel fuel rate is 21.5¢ per gallon. Beginning July 1, 2017, the rate for compressed natural gas (CNG) is 19¢ per gasoline gallon equivalent, and the rate for liquefied natural gas (LNG) and liquefied petroleum gas (LPG) is 21.5¢ per diesel gallon equivalent. [35 ILCS 505/2]

Fuel use tax: An additional tax ("Part B"), set annually by the Department of Revenue, is imposed on "commercial motor vehicles," which are defined as motor vehicles used, designed, or maintained for the transportation of persons or property and either having two axles and a gross weight or registered gross weight exceeding 26,000 lbs. (11,793 kg.), or having three or more axles, regardless of weight, or a vehicle that is used in combination, when the weight of the combination exceeds 26,000 lbs. gross vehicle weight. Commercial motor vehicles operated solely within Illinois using only motor fuel purchased in Illinois are excluded from the definition, as are school buses, recreational vehicles, and vehicles operated by the state or by the United States. (35 ILCS 505/13a; 35 ILCS 505/1.16)

For the second half of 2017, Part B per-gallon rates are diesel, 11.9¢; gasoline and gasohol, 11.7¢; liquefied petroleum gas (LPG), 13.8¢; liquefied natural gas (LNG), 12¢; and compressed natural gas (CNG), 10.1¢. Therefore, the total motor fuel taxes imposed in the second half of 2017 on commercial motor vehicles (Part A plus Part B) are as follows: diesel, 33.4¢; gasoline and gasohol, 30.7¢; and LPG, 35.3¢; LNG, 35.5¢; and CNG, 29.1¢. (*Informational Bulletin FY 2017-10-A*, Department of Revenue, June 2017)

Receivers' tax: Between January 1, 1990, and January 1, 2025, a tax of 0.3¢ per gallon of motor fuel is imposed on the privilege of being a receiver of fuel for sale or use. Proceeds are designated for the Underground Storage Tank Fund. Certain fuels used by airlines and railroads are exempt, as are fuels delivered outside the state or to another receiver. (35 ILCS 505/2a)

Environmental impact fee: Effective through January 1, 2025, an environmental impact fee of $60 per 7,500 gallons is imposed on all receivers of fuel that sell or use the fuel in Illinois. A receiver is subject to the fee whether or not the fuel is intended to be used for operation of motor vehicles on the public highways or waterways (415 ILCS 125/390; 86 Ill. Adm. Code Sec. 501.200).

The following sales are exempt from the fee:

(1) sales to other licensed receivers;

(2) sales of diesel fuel used by registered or recognized rail carriers for direct railroad operations;

(3) sales of aviation fuel and kerosene imported or received at O'Hare or Midway Airports and sold to or used by air carriers that hold certificates of public convenience and necessity or foreign air carrier permits issued by the U.S. Department of Transportation;

(4) sales made and delivered to customers outside Illinois; and

(5) sales of diesel fuel consumed in ships, barges, or vessels primarily used in interstate commerce for hire on rivers bordering Illinois are exempt if the fuel is delivered by a licensed receiver to the purchaser's barge, ship, or vessel while it is floating on a bordering river.

Local taxes: Information on county motor fuel taxes is available in *Publication-115, County Motor Fuel Tax*, Illinois Department of Revenue, October 2015, CCH ILLINOIS TAX REPORTS, ¶ 403-030.

CNG as "motor fuel": The Illinois Independent Tax Tribunal denied petitioner's claim for refund of Illinois Motor Fuel Tax on its purchases of compressed natural gas (CNG) on the basis that CNG falls within the taxable definition of "motor fuel" under the Illinois Motor Fuel Tax Law Act (MFTL Act), 35 ILCS 505/1.1. In this case, the basis of petitioner's argument was that CNG is a gas and the term "motor fuel" was defined to only to include liquids. CNG is often touted as a clean, affordable and abundant fuel source. At all times during the petitioner's use of CNG, including in its natural state, CNG remained a gas. It was never in liquid form.

The Court, in finding that CNG was subject to the tax, relied on the MFTL Act's definition of motor fuel, which included "among other things" before defining specific kinds of motor fuel subject to tax. While CNG was not included in the list of defined fuels, the act's definition was flexible enough to include liquid and non-liquid fuels. Moreover, the MFTL Act's definition of "gallon" specifically allowed for the measure of gaseous substances such as CNG. Lastly, CNG was referenced by description in the MFTL Act and the Illinois Retailers' Occupation Act, thus evidencing the legislative intent to include CNG as a taxable motor fuel. (*Waste Management of Illinois, Inc. v. Illinois Department of Revenue*, Illinois Independent Tax Tribunal, 15 TT 130, October 3, 2016, CCH ILLINOIS TAX REPORTS, ¶ 403-135)

• *Reports and payment*

Motor fuel distributors must secure a license and file a bond with the Department to guarantee payment of the tax.

Distributors and suppliers of motor fuel and suppliers of special fuel must file reports on or before the twentieth day of each month on the amount of fuel sold by them during the preceding month. Licensed motor fuel distributors and special fuel suppliers, receivers, and blenders, must separately report their gasoline and special fuel blending activities. Beginning July 1, 2017, this reporting requirement does not extend to liquefied natural gas (LNG) unless it is (1) dispensed into the fuel supply tank of any motor vehicle or (2) it is delivered into a storage tank located at a facility that has withdrawal facilities that are readily accessible to and are capable of dispensing LNG into the fuel supply tanks of motor vehicles. [35 ILCS 505/5]

A seller, distributor, or supplier that timely reports and remits Illinois motor fuel tax, special fuel tax, and the environmental impact fee is entitled to a discount of 1.75% for reimbursement of expenses incurred in keeping records, preparing and filing returns, collecting and remitting the tax, and supplying data to the Department on request [35 ILCS 505/5].

All Illinois motor fuel distributors, motor fuel suppliers, and motor fuel receivers must file their motor fuel tax returns and pay the tax using an electronic filing and payment method. For all reporting periods beginning with December 2015, the following forms must be electronically filed:

— RMFT-5, Motor Fuel Distributor/Supplier Tax Return;

— RMFT-5-X, Amended Motor Fuel Distributor/Supplier Tax Return;

— RMFT-5-US, Underground Storage Tank Tax and Environmental Impact Fee Receiver Return; and

— RMFT-5-US-X, Amended Underground Storage Tank Tax and Environmental Impact Fee Receiver Return.

The forms must be filed using MyTaxIllinois, which is available on the Department of Revenue (DOR) website at **http://tax.illinois.gov/**. Payments also can be made through MyTaxIllinois, or they can be made using the ACH method.

Returns not filed electronically will be treated as nonfiled and collection discounts will be disallowed. Motor fuel returns and schedules still must be filed by the 20th day of each month. (*Informational Bulletin FY 2016-06*, Illinois Department of Revenue, November 2015, CCH ILLINOIS TAX REPORTS, ¶ 403-054)

A refund or credit is allowed for erroneously paid taxes.

Losses of fuel as a result of evaporation or shrinkage due to temperature variation must be reported. For the six-month period from January to June or the six-month period from July to December, the net losses of fuel as the result of evaporation or shrinkage due to temperature variations may not exceed 1% of the total gallons in storage at the beginning of each period plus the receipts of gallonage for the period minus the gallonage remaining in storage at the end of each period. Any loss in excess of 1% is subject to tax.

The Department of Revenue will cancel a license due to the lack of activity over a two month period. Lack of activity is defined as having no taxable transactions within a two month period.

Self-use biodiesel: Private producers of biodiesel fuel or biodiesel blends for self use must file reports and pay the tax. Those who produce fewer than 5,000 gallons of biodiesel per year must report and pay the tax annually. Both the return and the payment are due by January 20 of the following year.

If a biodiesel producer's total production of those fuels is 5,000 gallons or more per year, the producer must file a return and pay the tax monthly. For each month, the return and payment are due between the first and 20th days of the following month. [35 ILCS 505/2d]

Recordkeeping: Records may be kept on microfilm, microfiche, or other computerized or condensed record storage system. Electronic imaging of original records is generally acceptable provided that the records are complete and contain the information put on quarterly reports and are accessible. During an audit, a taxpayer may be expected to produce a hard copy of an imaged document. If a taxpayer destroys the original document, it must be able to produce a legible image of that original. (*General Information Letter ST 13-0013-GIL,* Illinois Department of Revenue, March 29, 2013, CCH ILLINOIS TAX REPORTS,¶ 402-654)

Administration: The tax is administered by the Department of Revenue. For contact information, see Chapter 27.

International Fuel Tax Agreement (IFTA): A motor carrier may operate in Illinois by securing motor fuel use tax license and decals issued by any member jurisdiction of the International Fuel Tax Agreement. For additional information, see *Illinois Motor Fuel Use Tax Carrier Compliance Manual,* available from the Illinois Department of Revenue at **http://tax.illinois.gov/Publications/MotorFuel/MFUT-53.pdf**.

Interstate motor carriers must file quarterly returns on or before the last day of the month next succeeding each quarter. Illinois return filings, decal applications, and payments made pursuant to IFTA must be made electronically through MyTax Illinois (*Informational Bulletin FY 2013-03,* Illinois Department of Revenue, August 31, 2012, CCH ILLINOIS TAX REPORTS,¶ 402-542).

¶2204 Motor Vehicle Registration

Law: Illinois Vehicle Code Sec. 2-101 [625 ILCS 5/2-101]; Illinois Vehicle Code Sec. 3-414 [625 ILCS 5/3-414]; Illinois Vehicle Code Secs. 3-805—3-818 [625 ILCS 5/3-805—3-818]; Illinois Vehicle Cde Sec. 3-1001 [625 ILCS 5/3-1001]; 86 Ill. Adm. Code 151.101 (CCH ILLINOIS TAX REPORTS, ¶ 37-101).

The tax is imposed on commercial and non-commercial vehicles operated within the state. This includes automobiles, motorcycles, road tractors, buses, semitrailers, trailers, trucks, and truck tractors.

Exemptions: Among the vehicles exempt are those owned by nonresidents, farm vehicles not ordinarily used on the road, vehicles owned by the state, and vehicles owned by disabled veterans.

• *Basis and rate*

There is a wide variety of fees, based upon classification. The annual fee for registration of motor vehicles of the first division (automobiles) other than motorcycles, motor driven cycles, and pedalcycles is $98. The fee for motorcycles, motor driven cycles, and pedalcycles is $38. There are no reduced fees for partial year registration of motor vehicles.

The registration fees for both the two-year registration period for ceremonial plates and the fiscal year fee for vehicles of the second division with a maximum gross weight of 8,000 pounds are $98. The fees for certificates of title (except for all-terrain vehicles or off-highway motorcycles), duplicate certificates of title, and corrected certificates of title are each $95.

The Secretary of State may provide for the staggering of registrations of vehicles carrying not more than ten passengers. The Secretary may require that any vehicle of the second division also be registered on a staggered basis.

Second division motor vehicles (motor trucks, trailers, and buses designed for carrying more than ten persons) have a $10 registration fee, plus either (1) a flat weight tax, or (2) a mileage weight tax. Other second division vehicles include recreational vehicles, trailers, farm trucks, and farm trailers.

Commercial distribution fee: Owners of vehicles of the second division with a gross vehicle weight that exceeds 8,000 pounds must pay an annual commercial distribution fee to the Secretary of State for the use of the public highways, state infrastructure, and state services. The fee is equal to 36% of the Illinois motor vehicle registration taxes and fees incurred by the vehicle. Owners of vehicles of the second division with a gross vehicle weight of 8,000 pounds or less must pay the commercial distribution fee if they claimed a rolling stock sales tax exemption for the vehicles.

Reduced fees: Qualified senior citizens (in general, those with incomes below $16,000) and disabled persons or one who is the spouse of such a person pay a $24 annual fee for basic automobile registration (excluding vanity plates).

Vehicle use tax: A vehicle use tax is imposed for the privilege of using a motor vehicle in Illinois. The use tax is based on the selling price of the motor vehicle and, for vehicles selling for less than $15,000, ranges from $25 to $390 (depending on the age of the motor vehicle). If the selling price is $15,000 or more, the tax ranges from $750 to $1,500. Transfers to a surviving spouse are exempt from the vehicle use tax.

Private vehicle use tax: A tax is imposed on the privilege of using a motor vehicle in Illinois that is acquired by gift, transfer, or purchase (625 ILCS 5/3-1001; 86 Ill. Adm. Code 151.101). With certain exceptions, the amount of tax assessed is based on the model year of the car unless the purchase price is $15,000 or greater. A tax rate of $15 applies under the following circumstances:

(1) the transferee or purchaser of the motor vehicle is the spouse, mother, father, brother, sister or child of the transferor;

(2) the transfer is a gift to a beneficiary in the administration of an estate and the beneficiary is not a surviving spouse, or

(3) when the motor vehicle has once been subjected to the Illinois Retailers' Occupation Tax or Use Tax and is transferred in connection with the organization, reorganization, dissolution or partial liquidation of an incorporated or unincorporated business wherein the beneficial ownership is not changed.

A taxpayer was liable for the standard Illinois private vehicle use tax on the transfer of a car to his stepson because the lower tax rate applicable to transfers to a child does not extend to stepchildren (General Information Letter ST 12-0061-GIL, Illinois Department of Revenue, December 7, 2012, CCH ILLINOIS TAX REPORTS, ¶ 402-615).

Gross receipts tax: A gross receipts tax is imposed on motor carriers of passengers, rail carriers, and common carriers by pipeline. The tax rate is determined annually by the Illinois Commerce Commission and may not exceed 0.1% of gross receipts for each calendar year. The rate applicable to rail carriers is set by statute at 0.15%.

Two additional annual fees are imposed on rail carriers: a route fee of $45 per route mile of railroad owned in Illinois as of January 1 of the year the fee is due; and a railroad-highway grade crossing fee of $28 per crossing location as of January 1 of the year the fee is due. Both fees are due by February 1 of each calendar year.

Driver's licenses: The fee for an original or renewal driver's license is $30, except for applicants ages 18-20 and above 68, who pay $10.

Administration: The tax is administered by the Secretary of State. For contact information, see Chapter 27.

¶2205 Cigarette and Tobacco Taxes

Law: Cigarette Tax Act Secs. 1, 3*et seq.* [35 ILCS 130/1; 35 ILCS 130/3-10; 35 ILCS 130/3-15; 35 ILCS 130/4g]; Cigarette Use Tax Act Sec. 1 *et seq.* [35 ILCS 135/1] (CCH ILLINOIS TAX REPORTS, ¶ 55-002 *et seq.*).

Forms: RC-1-A, Cigarette Tax Stamp Order-Invoice; RC-6, Cigarette Revenue Return; RC-6-A, Out-of-State Cigarette Revenue Return; RC-16, Cigarette Tax Claim for Credit; RC-44, Cigarette Use Tax Return; TP-1, Tobacco Products Tax Return.

The Cigarette Tax Act imposes a tax on the occupation of selling cigarettes at retail. Payment of the tax or responsibility to pay the tax is evidenced by stamps or imprints on cigarette packages. The state also imposes a complementary cigarette use tax. When the cigarette tax is paid, the cigarette use tax, which is a privilege tax imposed on the user, is not applicable. The Cigarette Use Tax Act largely duplicates the Cigarette Tax Act, and its purpose is to prevent tax evasion by means of interstate purchases of cigarettes for personal use. Effective August 1, 2012, the Cigarette Machine Operators' Occupation Tax is imposed on operators of machines that make or fabricate cigarettes.

Beginning January 1, 2016, a license from the Illinois Department of Revenue will be required by anyone who engages in business as a retailer of cigarettes or tobacco products (35 ILCS 130/4g). Each applicant for a license will be required to file an application electronically and to pay a fee of $75 for each place of business at which the applicant proposes to sell cigarettes or tobacco products at retail. (35 ILCS 130/4g; *Informational Bulletin FY 2016-03,* Illinois Department of Revenue, October 2015, CCH ILLINOIS TAX REPORTS, ¶ 403-029)

The cigarette tax is imposed on retailers and users of cigarettes, although distributors of cigarettes are responsible for collecting the tax and prepaying it to the state. All distributors must be licensed. Distributors of cigarettes are required to pay an annual license fee of $250 to defray the cost to the Department of coding and/or serializing cigarette tax stamps. A person is not a "retailer" or a "distributor" if the person transfers cigarettes to a not-for-profit research institution that (1) conducts tests concerning the health effects of tobacco products and (2) does not offer the cigarettes for resale (P.A. 95-462 (S.B. 1433), Laws 2007).

Effective July 1, 2013, a "cigarette" is defined as any roll for smoking made wholly or in part of tobacco (1) irrespective of size or shape, whether or not such tobacco is flavored, adulterated, or mixed with any other ingredient, and the wrapper is made of paper or any other substance or material except tobacco (35 ILCS 130/1; 35 ILCS 135/3).

Effective July 1, 2013, "little cigars" are defined under the tobacco products tax act as "any roll, made wholly or in part of tobacco, where such roll has an integrated cellulose acetate filter and weighs less than four pounds per thousand and the wrapper or cover of which is made in whole or in part of tobacco". (35 ILCS 143/10-5; see also *Informational Bulletin FY 2014-01,* Illinois Department of Revenue, July 31, 2013, CCH ILLINOIS TAX REPORTS, ¶ 402-709)

Practitioner Comment: Cigar Association of America v. Hamer, No. 12 L 50133

On June 14, 2012 the Illinois legislature amended the Cigarette Tax Act and Cigarette Use Tax Act to expand the definition of the term "cigarette." The Department of Revenue issued an information bulletin based on the amendments, specifically including little cigars within the definition of "cigarettes". A collection of tobacco distributors and trade associations including the Cigar Association of America ("CAA") challenged the constitutionality of the amendments and sought injunctive relief. In its request for an injunction, CAA argued that the amendments and bulletin were unconstitutionally vague, violated the Uniformity Clause of the Illinois Constitution, and conflicted with the Federal Cigarette Labeling and Advertising Act. The Circuit Court issued a preliminary injunction, rejecting the Department's argument that losses were speculative and finding that the amendments definition of cigarette placed plaintiffs at risk for civil and criminal penalties. The court agreed with the plaintiff's contention that they had a likelihood of success on the merits given the vagueness of the statute. The court held the vague criteria allowed for inconsistent and overly broad enforcement of the statute. The court also agreed with the plaintiff's other substantive claims, including: (1) the court found that the different language in the amendments and in federal labeling laws for cigarettes impermissibly created a conflict which would force plaintiffs to comply with one statute while violating the other; and (2) the court noted the amendments' classification of cigars and cigarettes as the same product violated the uniformity clause.

Breen M. Schiller, Esq., Horwood Marcus & Berk, Chartered

Distributors of tobacco products are required to be licensed by the Department of Revenue and file a bond when applying for a license. Distributors include manufacturers or wholesalers located outside Illinois engaged in the business of selling tobacco products from outside Illinois to retailers or consumers located in Illinois. "Tobacco products" are cigars; little cigars; cheroots; stogies; periques; granulated, plug cut, crimp cut, ready rubbed, and other smoking tobacco; snuff or snuff flour; cavendish; plug and twist tobacco; fine-cut and other chewing tobacco; shorts, refuse scraps, clippings, cuttings, and sweepings of tobacco; and other kinds and forms of tobacco prepared to be suitable for chewing or smoking in a pipe or for both chewing and smoking. Tobacco purchased for manufacture of cigarettes is not a "tobacco product."

Practitioner Comment: Internet Cigarette Purchases

In 2005, the Department of Revenue increased its enforcement of unpaid cigarette use taxes by sending tax bills to thousands of Illinois residents. The Department is able to enforce unpaid taxes on Internet cigarette purchases because the federal Jenkins Act requires out-of-state cigarette vendors to provide the names and addresses of purchasers to the Department. Illinois tax liabilities for periods prior to July 1, 2002 are subject to double interest and penalties because those taxes were eligible for tax amnesty. The Board of Appeals can abate penalties and interest due to reasonable cause (see ¶2503).

Horwood Marcus & Berk Chartered

CCH Advisory: Internet Seller of Cigarettes Subject to Illinois Law

A New Mexico-based cigarette seller was subject to personal jurisdiction in an Illinois federal district court for alleged violations of, among other statutes, Illinois cigarette tax law and the federal Jenkins Act based on the seller's failure to report to Illinois its Internet sales to Illinois residents. The seller's contacts with Illinois were sufficient to satisfy due process minimum contact requirements. The seller's statement on its Web site that it would ship to any state in the country except for New York was important to this issue for two reasons. First the statement made the seller's argument that it did not purposefully avail itself of doing business in Illinois ring "particularly hollow" because the statement showed that the seller was expressly electing to do business with the residents of 49 states, was ready and willing to do business with Illinois residents, and knowingly did business with Illinois residents. Second, the fact that the seller excluded New York residents from its customer pool showed that the seller knew that conducting business with residents of a particular state could subject it to jurisdiction there and how to protect itself from being haled into court in any particular state. (*Illinois v. Hemi Group LLC*, U.S. Court of Appeals, Seventh Circuit, No. 09-1407, September 14, 2010, CCH ILLINOIS TAX REPORTS, ¶ 402-196).

Exemptions: The following are exempt from the cigarette tax:

(1) sales free from taxation under the laws and Constitution of the United States;

(2) sales of cigarettes for use aboard ships engaged in foreign commerce; and

(3) sales directly to military hospitals and installations.

Cigarettes on which the occupation tax has been paid are not subject to the use tax.

Persons who make, manufacture, or fabricate cigarettes as a part of a correctional industries program for sale to residents of penal institutions or to resident patients of state-operated mental health facilities are excluded from the definition of "distributor." Persons who transfer to residents of penal institutions or resident patients of state-operated mental health facilities ownership of cigarettes made, manufactured, or fabricated as a part of a correctional industries program are excluded from the definition of "retailer."

Anyone who transfers cigarettes to a not-for-profit research institution that conducts tests concerning the health effects of tobacco products and who does not offer cigarettes for resale is excluded from the definitions of (1)"retailer" in Illinois cigarette tax regulations and (2) "distributor" in cigarette use tax regulations. In addition, anyone who transfers cigarettes to a not-for-profit research institution for qualifying research is excluded from the definitions of "retailer" and "distributor" in cigarette tax regulations. (86 Ill. Adm. Code Secs. 440.30 and 450.10)

The tobacco products tax is not imposed on any activity in interstate commerce that may not be taxed under the laws and Constitution of the United States.

Sunset date for exemptions enacted after September 16, 1994: The application of every exemption enacted after September 16, 1994, must be limited by a sunset date. If a "reasonable and appropriate" sunset date is not specified, then the exemption will expire five years after the effective date of the enacting law.

• *Basis and rate of tax*

Cigarette taxes: The rate of cigarette tax and cigarette use tax is 99 mills per cigarette. That translates to a rate of $1.98 per pack of 20 cigarettes. An additional tax of $3 per pack of 20 cigarettes is imposed in Cook County, and an additional tax of 68¢ is imposed in Chicago.

Payment is shown by affixing a stamp to each package. The distributors' collection discount is 1.75% of the first $3 million of cigarette taxes paid during the year and 1.5% for amounts above $3 million.

Tobacco products tax: Tobacco products are taxed at a rate of 36% (formerly, 18%) of the wholesale price of tobacco products sold. Beginning July 1, 2013, little cigars are taxed at the same rate as cigarettes and are required to be stamped in the same manner as cigarettes.

Practitioner Comment: Tax on "Little Cigars"

On August 9, 2013, the General Assembly imposed a tax on "little cigars," as they are defined in the Tobacco Products Act of 1995. The Act requires that distributors of little cigars must remit a tax of 36% of the wholesale price, which is to be remitted by purchasing tax stamps from the Department and affixing them to packages of the little cigars in the same manner as cigarettes under the Cigarette Tax Act. The Act further specifies that packages that do not bear the tax stamp under the Act will be considered contraband. (P.A. 98-0273).

Breen M. Schiller, Esq., Horwood Marcus & Berk, Chartered

Moist snuff is taxed at a rate of 30¢ per ounce. The tax rate imposed per ounce of moist snuff may not exceed 15% of the tax imposed upon a package of 20 cigarettes; see *General Information Letter ST 13-0017-GIL*, Illinois Department of Revenue, March 31, 2013, CCH ILLINOIS TAX REPORTS, ¶ 402-653.

• *Returns and payments*

Distributors and manufacturers must file monthly reports on the amount of cigarettes received and sold. Distributors' reports are due on the 15th and manufacturers' on the 5th day of the month. Payment is made at the time of the report.

Practitioner Comment: Secondary Distributors

The Cigarette Tax Act and the Cigarette Use Tax Act were amended on July 12, 2010 to require secondary distributors to be licensed, maintain specific records, and submit reports to the Department. A "secondary distributor" is defined as any person engaged in the business of selling cigarettes who purchases stamped original packages of cigarettes from a licensed distributor, sells 75% or more of those cigarettes to retailers for resale, and maintains an established business where a substantial stock of cigarettes is available to retailers for resale (P.A. 96-1027 (HB 5833), Laws 2010).

Marilyn A. Wethekam, Esq., Horwood Marcus & Berk Chartered

Tobacco distributors must file returns on or before the 15th day of each month covering the preceding calendar month.

Payment for cigarette tax stamps and cigarette use tax stamps must be made by means of electronic funds transfer.

Penalties: Any person other than a licensed distributor possessing not fewer than 10 but not more than 100 packages of cigarettes not stamped will be fined $10 for each package. Further, any person other than a licensed distributor who sells, offers for sale, or has in his possession for sale up to 100 nonstamped or tax imprinted packages will be charged with a Class A misdemeanor for the first offense and a Class 4 felony for each subsequent offense.

Contraband: It is unlawful to knowingly possess or possess for sale contraband cigarettes (35 ILCS 130/3-10(a)(4)). "Contraband cigarettes" are cigarettes (35 ILCS 130/1):

— that do not have required tax stamps or are improperly stamped;

— for which federal taxes have not been paid;

— that bear counterfeit stamps;

— manufactured, fabricated, assembled, processed, packaged, or labeled by any person other than the owner of the trademark rights in the cigarette brand, or a person directly authorized by that owner;

— imported into the U.S. in violation of federal law;

— that have false manufacturing labels, or

— that are discussed in a broad enforcement provision.

In addition, the definition of "contraband cigarettes" includes cigarettes made or fabricated by a person holding a cigarette machine operator license under the terms of the Cigarette Machine Operators' Occupation Tax Act in the possession of manufacturers, distributors, secondary distributors, manufacturer representatives, or other retailers for the purpose of resale. Such cigarettes fall within the definition regardless of whether the tax has been paid on them.

The knowing possession for sale of contraband cigarettes will result in the forfeiture of the product and related machinery and equipment used to produce or falsely mark contraband cigarettes. (35 ILCS 130/3-15)

Licensing: Beginning January 1, 2016, a license from the Illinois Department of Revenue will be required by anyone who engages in business as a retailer of cigarettes or tobacco products, pursuant to amendments of the cigarette tax act, the cigarette use tax act, and the tobacco products tax act (35 ILCS 130/4g; 35 ILCS 143/10-21). Each applicant for a license will be required to file an application electronically and to pay a fee of $75 for each place of business at which the applicant proposes to sell cigarettes or tobacco products at retail. Anyone seeking a retailer's license under the cigarette tax act and the tobacco products tax act also must be registered under the terms of the state retailers' occupation tax act. Licensed retailers may purchase.

(1) cigarettes for sale only from a licensed distributor, secondary distributor, or manufacturer representative (35 ILCS 130/4h); and

(2) tobacco products for sale only from a licensed distributor or secondary distributor (35 ILCS 143/10-22).

Certain original invoices must be preserved on the licensed premises for a period of 90 days after a purchase. Criminal penalties also are specified for certain violations.

Administration: The cigarette and tobacco products taxes are administered by the Department of Revenue. For contact information, see Chapter 27.

• *Cigarette Machine Operators' Occupation Tax Act*

A tax is imposed on all persons engaged in the business of operating a cigarette machine. Persons engaged in the business of renting, leasing or selling cigarette machines are exempt from the Act, but they must provide notice of the Act's requirements to any potential buyer, lessee or lessor of a cigarette machine. (Sec. 1-10, Cigarette Machine Operators' Occupation Tax Act, P.A. 97-688 (S.B. 2194), Laws 2012; *Informational Bulletin FY 2013-01,* Illinois Department of Revenue, July 2012, CCH ILLINOIS TAX REPORTS, ¶ 402-522)

A "cigarette machine" is a machine, equipment or device used to make or fabricate cigarettes, but does not include a handheld, manually operated device used by consumers to make roll-your-own cigarettes. A "cigarette machine operator" (operator) is any person who is engaged in the business of operating a cigarette machine in Illinois and is licensed by the Department of Revenue as an operator.

Basis and rate of tax: The basis of the cigarette machine operator tax is every cigarette made or fabricated in a cigarette machine owned by a licensed operator (Sec. 1-10, Cigarette Machine Operators' Occupation Tax Act, P.A. 97-688 (S.B. 2194), Laws 2012; *Informational Bulletin FY 2013-01,* Illinois Department of Revenue, July 2012, CCH ILLINOIS TAX REPORTS, ¶ 402-522).

Rate of tax: The tax rate is the same as the state's cigarette tax.

Reports and payments: Returns must be filed and tax must be remitted by the 15th day of each month covering the preceding calendar month. Operators may take a credit against tax due for taxes imposed and paid under the state's tobacco products tax law on qualifying tobacco products sold to a customer and used in a rolling machine located at the operator's place of business. (Sec. 1-40, Cigarette Machine Operators' Occupation Tax Act, P.A. 97-688 (S.B. 2194), Laws 2012)

Administrative provisions: Operators must be licensed before engaging in the business of operating a cigarette machine. Each place of business at which a person wants to procure a cigarette machine operator license requires a license application, payment of a $250 annual license fee, and filing of a joint and several surety bond in an amount of $2,500. Applicants also must meet several eligibility requirements. Taxpayers licensed and bonded for five years and who have not been delinquent or deficient in payment of the tax will not be required to furnish a bond to renew their license.

Operators may reimburse themselves for their tax liability by separately stating the tax as an additional charge to users of the cigarette machines. The reimbursement charge must not include any credits against the tax for which the operator qualifies. A customer can claim a refund from the operator if the customer was charged a reimbursement fee on cigarettes not subject to the tax or paid a fee greater than the actual tax. If the customer does not ask for a refund, the operator must remit the amounts to the department.

The Act places restrictions on the type of tobacco used in cigarette machines and the tubes to be used in such machines. Cigarettes made or fabricated by a cigarette machine operator may not be sold or distributed to, or possessed by, manufacturers, distributors, secondary distributors, manufacturer representatives, or retailers, except for operators. An operator may not purchase unstamped cigarettes from a manufacturer or distributor. The Act places requirements on operators and the sale of cigarettes, including a requirement that a cigarette machine have a secure meter that counts the number of cigarettes made.

The Act also covers audits of returns, failure to file returns, taxpayer protests, claims for credit or refunds, the maintenance of records, penalties, and civil and criminal legal proceedings for violations of the Act. The department and (for specifications relating to cigarette tubes) the Attorney General are authorized to issue regulations under the Act.

¶2206 Insurance Taxes

Law: Insurance Code, Secs. 407—446 [215 ILCS 5/407—446] (CCH ILLINOIS TAX REPORTS, ¶88-001 *et seq.*).

A privilege tax on net receipts is imposed on all insurance companies doing business in the state. A gross premiums tax is imposed on surplus line agents licensed to do business in the state. There is also a fire marshal's tax on fire risk premiums of all companies and on individuals writing special insurance.

The Illinois Appellate Court held that an insurance company (Scioto) formed by Wendy's International Inc. to provide insurance policies to Wendy's and its affiliates was an insurance company for Illinois income tax purposes. The court found that the facts indicated Scioto was a *bona fide* insurance company for purposes of federal income tax law as it met the requirements during the applicable years and engaged in the necessary risk shifting and risk distribution. No evidence suggested Scioto Insurance Company was formed as a sham business or lacked a valid business purpose. Given this, along with the treatment of Scioto by the IRS and the advantages of conformity with federal law, Scioto constituted an insurance company for federal income tax purposes and should have been treated in a similar fashion for purposes of the Illinois Income Tax Act. (*Wendy's Int'l, Inc. v. Hamer*, 2013 IL App (4th) 110678, 996 N.E.2d 1250, reh'g denied (Nov. 6, 2013))

Exemptions: Fraternal benefit societies are exempt from the taxes. Also exempt are premiums on annuities.

Retaliatory taxes: The retaliatory tax is applied when an out-of-state company's state of incorporation imposes higher taxes on Illinois insurance companies that are doing business in that other state. Definitions relating to the retaliatory tax imposed on certain out-of-state insurance companies doing business in Illinois have been amended, effective January 9, 2015. The terms "penalties," "fees," "charges," and "taxes" now include the penalties, fees, charges, and taxes collected on a cash basis. Further, the term "taxes" means the aggregate Illinois corporate income taxes paid during the calendar year for which the retaliatory tax calculation is being made, less the recapture of any Illinois corporate income tax cash refunds to the extent that the amount of tax refunded was reported as part of the Illinois basis in the calculation of the retaliatory tax for a prior tax year. However, the recaptured refund is limited to the amount necessary to make the Illinois basis equal to the out-of-state insurance company's basis in its state of incorporation for such tax year. (215 ILCS 5/444(c))

• *Basis and rate of tax*

The privilege tax is 0.5% of the net taxable premium written. However, the tax on premium derived from any accident and health insurance or on any insurance business written by any company operating as a health maintenance organization, voluntary health service plan, dental service plan, or limited health service organization is 0.4% of the net taxable premium written.

Net taxable premium written is, generally, gross premiums reduced by returned premiums and dividends paid on insurance policies.

The tax due is reduced by (1) Illinois income taxes paid for the preceding year to the extent they exceed 1.5% of the net taxable premium written for that year, and (2) any fire department taxes paid during the preceding year.

The tax on surplus line agents is 3.5% of gross premiums. The fire marshal's tax is a maximum of 1% of the gross premiums attributable to fire, sprinkler leakage, riot, civil commotion, explosion, and motor vehicle fire risk insurance.

Foreign companies are subject to retaliatory taxes (but see *U.S. Liability Insurance Co. v. Illinois Department of Insurance,* Appellate Court of Illinois, Fourth District, No. 4-12-1125, March 3, 2014, CCH ILLINOIS TAX REPORTS,¶402-776 and *United States Liability Insurance Co. v. Department of Insurance,* Appellate Court of Illinois, Fourth District, No. 4-12-1125, May 9, 2014, CCH ILLINOIS TAX REPORTS, ¶402-801).

Industrial insureds: The Insurance Code applies to transactions in Illinois involving contracts of insurance independently procured directly from an unauthorized insurer by industrial insureds. Consequently, insureds are subject to tax on premiums paid to captive insurers even when the payments are paid out-of-state on an out-of-state insurance policy.

A 90-day reporting requirement is imposed for contracts of insurance effective January 1, 2015 or later. Further, within 30 days after filing the report to the Surplus Line Association of Illinois, the insured must pay the Director for the use and benefit of the State a sum equal to the gross premium of the contract of insurance multiplied by the surplus line tax rate. A surplus line producer must maintain separate records of business transacted for 7 years from the policy effective date. (215 ILCS 5/121-2.08)

Practitioner Comment: Tax Imposed on Insured

Public Act 98-0978 is an attempt to work around the rule established in *State Board of Insurance v. Todd Shipyards Corp.,* 370 U.S. 451 (1962), which held that states may not tax insurance premiums paid out-of-state on an out-of-state insurance policy where the only connection between the state and the insurance transaction is the property located in the state. Doing so, the Supreme Court held, violates the Due Process Clause of the United States Constitution.

This law effects a work-around of that limitation because the tax is imposed on the insured rather than the insurer. On April 21, 2015, the Illinois Senate unanimously passed SB 1573, which would exempt captive insurance companies from this treatment. The general consensus is that this tax, indirectly imposed on captive insurers, was slipped into the bill, and was neither debated nor intended to be the outcome of the original bill. SB 1573 was referred to the House Rules Committee on April 21, 2015, where it has remained. Even if passed, the exemption of premiums paid to captive insurers would only become effective January 1, 2016.

Christopher T. Lutz, Esq., Horwood Marcus & Berk, Chartered

Financial regulation fee: The fee, which ranges from $150 to $37,500, is based on premium income and is collected by the Director of Insurance from every domestic and foreign insurance company to fund the internal costs and expenses of examining and analyzing the company's financial condition.

• *Credit against tax*

The New Markets Development Program includes a credit against the insurance and gross premiums taxes for taxpayers who make qualified cash equity investments in a qualified community development entity. Corporate taxpayers doing insurance business in Illinois who claim a credit against the net receipts tax as part of the insurance premiums tax scheme are not required to pay any retaliatory tax related to that claim for the tax credit. This credit is set to expire for years after 2012. (20 ILCS 663/1; 20 ILCS 663/50; 215 ILCS 5/444)

For additional details of this credit, see ¶1217.

• *Reports and payments*

Insurers whose annual tax was more than $5,000 make payments on a quarterly basis on April 15, June 15, September 15, and December 15. Insurers whose annual tax was less than $5,000 for the preceding taxable year make their payments with the annual return due March 1. Returns, accompanied by payment, of surplus line agents are due semiannually on February 1 and August 1 covering the preceding half-calendar year. An annual report, due in March, of the applicable premiums is required of all companies for the purposes of the fire marshal's tax; payment is also due in March.

When a qualifying contract of insurance is independently procured directly from an unauthorized insurer by an industrial insured, the insured must file a report with the Illinois Director of Insurance within 90 days of the effective date of the contract and, within 30 days after filing the report, pay the surplus lines tax on the gross premium of the contract. In addition, the insured must withhold the amount of the taxes and countersignature fee from the amount of premium charged by and otherwise payable to the insurer for the insurance. If the insured fails to withhold those amounts, then the insured will be liable for them. (215 ILCS 5/445)

Administration: The taxes are administered by the Director, Department of Insurance. For contact information, see Chapter 27.

CCH Advisory: Payment of unclaimed benefits

Under the terms of the Unclaimed Life Insurance Benefits Act (ULIBA; P.A. 99-893 (H.B. 4633), Laws 2016), authorized insurers regulated by the Illinois Department of Insurance must make good faith efforts to locate and pay beneficiaries' proceeds under unclaimed life insurance policies. If benefits are due and the insurer cannot locate the beneficiaries or owners, the benefits from the policy, annuity contract, or retained asset account must be reported and delivered to the state treasurer pursuant to the terms of the Uniform Disposition of Unclaimed Property Act (UPA). The ULIBA does not amend, modify, or supersede the UPA. It is applicable to policies, annuity contracts, and retained asset accounts in force on or after January 1, 2017.

Each insurer must perform an initial comparison of its insureds', annuitants', and retained asset account holders' in-force policies, annuity contracts, and retained asset accounts by using the full U.S. Social Security Administration's Death Master File or similar database to determine whether a person has died. The initial comparison must be completed by December 31, 2017. Following the initial comparison, each insurer must conduct a similar comparison at least semiannually. For potential matches identified in a search, the insurer will have 120 days from the date the insured's name was matched (date of death notice) to determine whether benefits are due. (P.A. 99-893 (H.B. 4633), Laws 2016)

¶2207 Public Utilities Taxes

Law: Gas Use Tax Law Sec. 5-10 [35 ILCS 173/5-10]; Electricity Excise Tax Law [35 ILCS 640/2-1 *et seq.*]; Gas Revenue Tax Act [35 ILCS 615/1 *et seq.*]; Public Utilities Act [220 ILCS 5/1-101 *et seq.*]; Public Utilities [Electricity]Revenue Act [35 ILCS 620/1 *et seq.*]; Telecommunications Excise Tax Act [35 ILCS 630/1 *et seq.*]; Telecommunications Municipal Infrastructure Maintenance Fee Act [35 ILCS 635/1 *et seq.*]; Water Company Invested Capital Tax Act [35 ILCS 625/1 *et seq.*] (CCH Illinois Tax Reports, ¶80-031, *et seq.*).

Forms: IVT-4, Electricity Distribution and Invested Capital Tax Return; RG-1, Gas Revenue Tax Return; RG-12, Gas Revenue and Gas Use Tax Affidavit; IDR 909, Qualified Solid Waste Energy Facility Payment Form; RPU-13, Electricity Excise Tax Return; RT-2, Telecommunications Excise Tax Return; RT-10, Telecommunications Infrastructure Maintenance Fees Return.

Taxes are imposed on suppliers of electricity, light, and gas and on the origination or reception of telecommunications within the state. Persons who resell telecommunications, such as hotels and universities, must collect and pay the telecommunications excise tax (*Information Bulletin FY 91-3*, Department of Revenue; CCH Illinois Tax Reports, ¶400-470). Taxes imposed include a gross receipts tax, electricity distribution and excise taxes, and a privilege tax on gross receipts. The telecommunications excise tax, enacted in 1985 and upheld by the U.S. Supreme Court in *Goldberg v. Sweet; GTE Sprint Communications Corp. v. Sweet* (1989, US SCt), 488 US 252, 109 SCt 582; CCH Illinois Tax Reports, ¶400-355, replaces a former message tax. There is also a fee for the issuance of securities by a public utility and municipal infrastructure maintenance fees imposed on telecommunications retailers. Local taxes are authorized; see below.

• *Gas and electricity*

Public utilities subject to regulation by the Illinois Commerce Commission must also pay a privilege tax on gross revenue for each fiscal year to cover maintenance expenses of the Commission. The rate cannot exceed 0.1%. The Commission has set the rate at 0.1% of gross revenues since July 1, 1988.

Practitioner Comment: Tax on Consumer

The Public Utilities Revenue Act authorizes the imposition of a tax upon electric cooperatives, electric utilities and alternative retail electric suppliers. Generally, a tax is imposed on persons engaged in the business of selling electricity for further use. Even though electric utilities and electric cooperatives are subject to these taxes, they have been given the authority by the Illinois legislature to pass that burden onto their customers as an additional charge on their bills. As a result, the true taxpayer under the Public Utilities Revenue Act is the consumer who purchases the electricity, and not the entity that supplies it. Therefore, it is likely that any taxpayer who overpays a tax to a utility must attempt to recover the overpayment from the utility, not the Department of Revenue.

Jennifer A. Zimmerman, Esq., Horwood Marcus & Berk Chartered

Facilities and persons engaged in the business of selling compressed natural gas at retail to the public for use only as a motor fuel are included within the Public Utilities Act.

The invested capital tax is the lesser of (1) the current tax calculation or (2) an amount equal to 0.8% times the utility's gas plant service for the taxable period ending December 3, 1996, as modified by an adjustment factor.

Electricity distribution and excise taxes: The electricity distribution tax is determined on the basis of the number of kilowatt hours distributed to a purchaser in Illinois. Accompanying the tax is an electricity assistance charge that must be collected by a distributor of electricity and natural gas. A municipal electric utility or an electric cooperative may elect to collect this charge from its customers and remit it to the Department of Revenue. This charge is used to assist low-income residential customers in obtaining energy services.

Practitioner Comment: Power Distributor

An out-of-state electricity supplier that sells electricity to end users in Illinois is not subject to Illinois' Electricity Distribution Tax if the supplier does not deliver the electric energy to the end users over facilities owned, leased, or controlled by the supplier. If the supplier pays transportation charges to an Illinois Public Utility to deliver the electricity, the utility would be subject to the electricity distribution tax and be required to collect the Electricity Excise Tax from end users (other than self-assessing purchasers). (Ill. ST 02-0030-GIL, February 4, 2002)

Marilyn A. Wethekam, Esq., Horwood Marcus & Berk Chartered

An electricity excise tax is imposed on the privilege of electric use measured by the number of kilowatt hours delivered to a purchaser. The excise tax is collected from the purchaser unless the delivering supplier is notified by the Department of Revenue that the purchaser is registered as a self-assessing purchaser.

Practitioner Comment: Gas Revenue Tax Act—Limited Tax Base

The Gas Revenue Tax Act is imposed on all persons who sell, distribute, supply or furnish natural gas for use or consumption to end users in Illinois. The Gas Revenue Tax Act does not apply to customers who are subject to the Gas Use Tax. The Gas Revenue Tax Act also does not apply to any transaction in interstate commerce, or to the extent a transaction may not, under the U.S. Constitution and statutes, be subject to tax in Illinois, so practitioners should be aware that given these limitations, many entities are not subject to this Act.

However, it is important to the note that under current federal law, a tax such as this could constitutionally be applied to some transactions in interstate commerce. See *Complete Auto Transit v. Brady*, 430 U.S. 274 (1977), CCH ILLINOIS TAX REPORTS, ¶ 200-884.

However, it is the Department's position, as provided in Attorney General Opinion 95-101, that it is up to the Legislature to amend the Gas Revenue Tax Act to provide for an expanded tax base.

Jennifer A. Zimmerman, Esq., Horwood Marcus & Berk Chartered

Exemptions: The following are exempt from the electricity excise tax and gas revenue taxes:

— sales to the federal government;

— sales to other departments of the utility; and

— sales to enterprise zone or high-impact businesses (see ¶ 1205) for state taxes and municipal taxes as authorized by municipal authorities.

The utility gross receipts tax does not apply to transactions taxed under the gas use tax law. The tax on suppliers of electricity does not apply to sales of electricity to municipal transportation companies.

For tax years before 2018, a certified business located in an enterprise zone or high-impact foreign trade zone or subzone may be exempt from additional charges added to its utility bills as a pass-on of municipal and state utility taxes on electricity, gas, and telecommunications. Such businesses will be exempt from the additional charges, provided that they (1) create at least 200 full-time equivalent (FTE) jobs; (2) make investments of at least $175 million that create at least 150 new FTE jobs; or (3) make investments that cause the retention of a minimum of 750 FTE jobs per year in 2013 through 2017 in the manufacturing sector, as defined by the North American Industry Classification System, in an area in Illinois in which the unemployment rate is above 9% (220 ILCS 5/9-222.1). The business must be certified by the Department of Commerce and Community Affairs (DCCA).

The exemption period cannot exceed 30 years. The exemption of a percentage of gross receipts requires adoption by municipal ordinance for municipal taxes. The percentage of exemption from state taxes is specified by the DCCA.

Payment: A taxpayer with an annual electricity excise tax liability of $200,000 or more must make all payments to the Department of Revenue by electronic funds transfer (EFT).

Sunset date for exemptions enacted after September 16, 1994: The application of an exemption enacted after September 16, 1994, must be limited by a sunset date. If a "reasonable and appropriate" sunset date is not specified, then the exemption will expire five years after the effective date of the enabling law.

Credit: Public utilities that are required by federal law to purchase electricity from qualified solid waste energy facilities are entitled to credits against the electricity excise tax. The credits are equal to the amount, if any, by which payments for such electricity exceed (1) the then current rate at which the utility must purchase the output of qualified facilities pursuant to the federal Public Utility Regulatory Policies Act of 1978, less (2) any costs, expenses, losses, damages or other amounts incurred by the utility, or for which it becomes liable, arising out of its failure to obtain such electricity from such other sources. A delivering supplier that is required or authorized to collect the electricity excise tax must make a return on or before the 15th day of each month stating the preceding month's amount of credits to which the taxpayer is entitled on account of purchases of electricity from a qualified solid waste energy facility (Electricity Excise Tax Law Sec. 2-9 [35 ILCS 640/2-9]).

A "qualified solid waste energy facility" means a facility that qualifies under the Local Solid Waste Disposal Act to use methane gas generated from landfills as its primary fuel and that possesses characteristics that would enable it to qualify as a cogeneration or small power production facility under federal law (Public Utilities Act Sec. 8-403.1 [220 ILCS 5/8-403.1]). Through January 2013, each qualified solid waste energy facility that sells electricity to an electric utility pursuant to a long-term contract at a purchase rate equal to the average amount per kilowatt hour paid by the unit of local government in which the electricity generating facilities are located must file a form with and pay to the state treasurer by the 15th of each month an amount equal to $^6/_{10}$ of a mill ($0.0006) per kilowatt hour of electricity for which payment was received at that purchase rate during the immediately preceding month.

Rate and basis: Gross receipts taxes are levied at the rate of 5% of the gross receipts of the utility, or, alternatively 0.32¢ per kilowatt-hour of electricity and 2.4¢ per therm of gas sold to customers, whichever rate is lower. Any charge for gas or gas services to a customer who acquired contractual rights for the direct purchase of gas or gas services originating from an out-of-state supplier or source on or before March 1, 1995, except for those charges solely related to the local distribution of gas by a public utility, is not included in gross receipts for purposes of the Gas Revenue Tax Act.

Practitioner Comment: Self-Assessing Purchaser

The rate of tax and tax base turn on whether the tax is collected from the consumer or a self-assessing purchaser. If the tax is collected by the delivering supplier, the rate is a tiered-rate determined by the amount of kilowatt hours purchased. If the purchaser is a "self-assessing purchaser," e.g., one who is not purchasing for residential use, the tax is imposed at the rate of 5.1% of the purchase price.

Marilyn A. Wethekam, Esq., Horwood Marcus & Berk Chartered

• *Gas use tax*

A gas use tax is imposed on the use in Illinois of gas obtained in a purchase of out-of-state gas. "Gas" is defined as any gaseous fuel distributed through a pipeline system.

Exemptions: The gas use tax does not apply to gas that is:

(1) used by business enterprises located in an enterprise zone;

(2) used by governmental bodies or qualified charitable, religious, or educational entities;

(3) used in the production of electric energy;

(4) used in a petroleum refinery operation;

(5) purchased by persons for use in liquefaction and fractionation processes that produce value added natural gas byproducts for resale; or

(6) used in the production of anhydrous ammonia and downstream nitrogen fertilizer products for resale.

In addition, a purchaser may claim a credit against the gas use tax to the extent of any taxes paid to another state on the gas.

Rate of tax: Self-assessing purchasers must pay gas use tax at the rate of 2.4¢ per therm or 5% of the purchase price for the billing period, whichever is the lower rate.

Returns and payment: Self-assessing purchasers must register with the Department of Revenue by completing Form REG-10, Gas Use Tax Self-Assessing Purchaser Application. They must file a return and pay the tax directly to the Department on or before the 15th day of each month for the preceding calendar month.

Purchasers may elect to pay tax at the rate of 2.4¢ per therm to a delivering supplier that maintains a place of business in Illinois. The tax must be separately stated from the selling price of the gas. The delivering supplier must make a return to the Department on or before the 15th day of each month for the preceding calendar month.

The Department may permit annual or quarterly returns for purchasers or suppliers with low average monthly tax liabilities. Purchasers or suppliers with an average monthly liability of $10,000 or more during the preceding calendar year (excluding the month of highest liability and the month of lowest liability) must make quarter-monthly estimated tax payments.

• *Telecommunications*

Telecommunications are taxed at the rate of 7% of the gross receipts of the utility (see below for discussion of the telecommunications infrastructure maintenance fee). Prepaid telephone calling arrangements are not subject to Illinois telecommunications excise tax or telecommunications municipal infrastructure maintenance fees.

Internet access and DSL: Charges for Internet access that do not include charges for the telephone line are generally not subject to telecommunications tax. Digital subscriber line (DSL) services purchased, used, or sold by providers of Internet access, as well as by nonproviders of Internet access, are subject to telecommunications tax (*Informational Bulletin FY 2006-09*, Illinois Department of Revenue, March 2006, CCH Illinois Tax Reports, ¶ 401-670).

The Illinois Department of Revenue has issued a general information letter to Internet service providers regarding the application of the federal moratorium on taxing Internet access on the Illinois telecommunication excise tax. Purchases of Internet bandwidth by an Internet service provider for the purpose of distribution would be subject to the moratorium, if the bandwidth sold enables the customers to access content, information or other services over the Internet. (*General Information Letter ST 15-0034-GIL*, Illinois Department of Revenue, June 18, 2015, CCH Illinois Tax Reports, ¶ 402-971)

Cloud computing: Certain cloud computing services used through a customer's existing telecommunications, Internet or network connections were not telecommunications services subject to the Illinois telecommunications excise tax. The cloud-based applications and services provided by the company are services that support a customer's telecommunication equipment, including its voice, video, messaging, presence, audio, web conferencing and mobile capabilities. (*General Information Letter ST 13-0074-GIL*, Illinois Department of Revenue, November 26, 2013, CCH Illinois Tax Reports, ¶ 402-764)

Practitioner Comment: Telecom Excise Taxes on VoIP

Providers of "voice over Internet protocol" (VoIP) allow users to make calls over the Internet, and the in-state or nationwide data service charges may be a flat monthly fee, regardless of distance or time. The Department maintains that charges for VoIP constitute charges for the act or privilege of originating or receiving telecommunications in Illinois, and as such, are subject to Illinois' telecommunications excise tax, as well as Illinois' telecommunications infrastructure maintenance fee and the simplified municipal telecommunications tax act. Illinois sources VoIP telecommunications made or received on a mobile device based on the customer's place of primary use as defined in the Mobile Telecommunications Sourcing Conformity Act. See *General Info. Letter 05-ST-0008*(Jan. 12, 2005).

The federal moratorium on Internet access taxes is now permanent. However, the federal law states that it does not affect the imposition of taxes on a charge for voice or similar services utilizing the Internet. Thus, Illinois' taxation of VoIP charges does not violate that Act.

Horwood Marcus & Berk Chartered

Telecommunication surcharges: As part of amending emergency telephone safety statutes to create a single statewide 911 system, Illinois legislation also amends and enacts public utilities and related telecommunications surcharges and taxes, as follows (P.A. 99-06 (S.B. 96), Laws 2015; see also *Publication 113, Retailer's Overview of Sales and Use Tax and Prepaid Wireless E911 Surcharge*, Department of Revenue, October 2014, CCH Illinois Tax Reports, ¶ 402-908):

Statewide surcharge: Beginning January 1, 2016, Illinois imposes a statewide surcharge on, with certain exceptions, customers of telecommunications carriers and wireless carriers. Each carrier generally imposes a monthly surcharge of $0.87 for each network connection and for each qualifying commercial mobile radio service (CMRS) connection. The surcharge does not apply to network connections provided for use with pay telephone services, and multiple surcharges are required for certain multiple voice grade communications channels.

State and local taxes do not apply to the surcharges, and the surcharges must be stated as separate items on subscriber bills. The carrier collecting the surcharge may deduct 3% of the gross amount of the surcharge to reimburse the carrier for expenses of accounting and collecting the surcharge. The surcharges must be remitted, either by check or by electronic transfer, to the Department of Revenue within 30 days of being collected.

Local wireless surcharge: A local wireless surcharge imposed by a governmental unit or emergency telephone system board must not exceed $2.50 per commercial mobile radio service connection or in-service telephone number billed on a monthly basis. The surcharge will be imposed based on the municipality or county encompassing the customer's place of primary use as defined in the Mobile Telecommunications Sourcing Conformity Act.

Prepaid wireless 911 surcharge: The prepaid wireless 911 surcharge on retail transactions will increase to 3% from 1.5%, effective October 1, 2015. The reduction of the surcharge for municipalities having a population over 500,000 from 9% to 7% will not apply until December 31, 2020. Under previous legislation, the reduction would have occurred July 1, 2017. The surcharge is not imposed on the provider or consumer of the federally funded Lifeline service where the consumer does not pay the provider for the service.

Local tax rates: For a complete listing of statewide telecommunications tax rates, see the Tax Rate Finder on the Department of Revenue's website at **tax.illinois.gov**. See also ¶2309 for information on the Chicago telecommunications tax.

Returns and payments: Returns and payments for the gross receipts tax are filed with the Department of Revenue on or before the 15th day of each month for taxpayers whose average monthly tax liability exceeds $1,000 but is less than $25,000. If the taxpayer's average monthly tax liability does not exceed $1,000, quarterly returns are authorized, due on or before the last day of April, July, October, and January for the preceding calendar quarter. If the average monthly tax liability does not exceed $400, an annual return is authorized, due on or before January 31 for the preceding year. Taxpayers whose average monthly tax liability is $25,000 or more must file quarter-monthly.

Telecommunication service providers who have an average monthly tax liability of more than $1,000 must make their tax payments by EFT and file their returns (Form RT-2) and schedules electronically.

Taxpayers whose average monthly liability under the telecommunications tax, gas revenue tax, or electricity tax was $10,000 or more during the preceding calendar year (excluding the month of highest liability and the month of lowest liability), and who are not operated by a unit of local government, must make estimated payments on or before the 7th, 15th, 22nd, and last day of the month.

Utilities that owe less than $10,000 in tax for the maintenance of the Illinois Commerce Commission must, on or before March 31 next following the end of the calendar year, file an annual gross revenue return and pay the amount of tax due.

Administration: The tax is administered by the Department of Revenue. For contact information, see Chapter 27.

- *Invested capital tax on water and gas companies*

An additional tax is imposed on retailers of water companies, and persons engaged in the business of distributing, supplying, furnishing, or selling gas, in an amount equal to 0.8% per year of their invested capital. Invested capital is the amount equal to the average of the balances at the beginning and end of the taxable period of a utility's total stockholders' equity and total long-term debt, less investments in and advances to all corporations (35 ILCS 620/2a.1(b)). Persons who are not regulated by the Illinois Commerce Commission or who are not required, in the case of telephone cooperatives, to file reports with the Rural Electrification Administration, or who are subject, in the case of water companies, to the invested capital tax only with respect to transactions between the seller and tenants of buildings owned or operated by the seller, are exempt from the invested capital tax. Payment is made in four installments, the first three based on the estimated tax due for the year.

The tax was upheld by the Illinois Supreme Court in *Continental Illinois National Bank & Trust Co. of Chicago v. Zagel* (1979, SCt), 78 Ill2d 387, 410 NE2d 491; CCH ILLINOIS TAX REPORTS, ¶ 201-059.

- *Telecommunications infrastructure maintenance fee*

A state infrastructure maintenance fee is imposed on telecommunications retailers, except cellular and wireless providers, at the rate of 0.5% of the gross charges made from Illinois service addresses (35 ILCS 635/15).

Local power to tax: Municipalities are authorized to levy a telecommunications tax, discussed above.

CCH Advisory: Local Telecommunications Fee

The Illinois telecommunications municipal infrastructure maintenance fee, imposed to compensate municipalities for telecommunications retailers' use of public rights-of-way, violated the Uniformity Clause of the Illinois Constitution because, as applied to wireless telecommunications retailers, the fee was intended to compensate municipal governments for the physical occupation of public rights-of-way but wireless telecommunications providers do not physically occupy any public rights-of-way. Thus, it was unreasonable to include wireless providers within the classification of entities subject to the fee (*PrimeCo Personal Communications, L.P., et al.*, Illinois Supreme Court, Nos. 89075 and 89084, March 29, 2001; CCH ILLINOIS TAX REPORTS, ¶ 401-234).

Jurisdiction to tax: The federal Mobile Telecommunications Sourcing Act (P.L. 106-252, 4 USC §§ 116—126) provides that mobile telecommunications services are taxable only in the state and locality where the customer resides or maintains its primary business address, and any other state or locality is prohibited from taxing the services, regardless of where the services originate, terminate, or pass through. The Act does not apply to prepaid telephone calling services or air-ground service.

A state or a company designated by the political subdivisions of a state may provide an electronic database identifying the proper taxing jurisdiction for each street address in that state. If the provider of mobile telecommunications services uses such a database, it will be held harmless from any tax otherwise due solely as a result of an error in the database. If no such database exists, then a provider employing an enhanced zip code and exercising due diligence in assigning a street address to a taxing jurisdiction will be held harmless for any incorrect assignment.

Illinois has adopted the provisions of the federal act (P.A. 92-0474 (H.B. 843), Laws 2001).

¶2207

¶2208 Real Estate Transfer Tax

Law: Property Tax Code, Sec. 31-5 [35 ILCS 200/31-5]; 86 Ill. Adm. Code, Sec. 120.5 (CCH ILLINOIS TAX REPORTS, ¶37-051).

Forms: Form PTAX-203, Illinois Real Estate Transfer Declaration.

The tax is imposed on the transfer of real estate as represented by a deed or a beneficial interest in a land trust in Illinois.

• *Real estate entities*

A transfer of a controlling interest in a real estate entity owning property in Illinois is subject to real estate transfer tax, regardless of whether a transfer is made by one or more related transactions or involves one or more persons or entities and regardless of whether a document is recorded. A "real estate entity" is defined as any person or entity that exists for the purpose of holding title to or beneficial interest in real property. An entity is presumed to be a real estate entity if it owns, directly or indirectly, real property having a fair market value greater than 75% of the total fair market value of all of the entity's assets, determined without deduction for any mortgage, lien, or encumbrance. A "beneficial interest" includes the beneficial interest in an Illinois land trust, the lessee interest in a ground lease (including any interest in related improvements) that provides for a term of 30 or more years when all options to renew or extend are included, and the indirect interest in real property as reflected by a controlling interest in a real estate entity. A "controlling interest" means more than 50% of the fair market value of all ownership interests or beneficial interests in a real estate entity.

An interest in a cooperative is considered a beneficial interest in real property that is subject to the tax (*Informational Bulletin,* Vol. 2009 No. 3, Chicago Department of Revenue, April 2009).

• *Exemptions*

Certain transactions are exempt from the transfer tax and its filing requirements. For exempt transactions under Sec. 31-45 of the Property Tax Code, no declaration is required, but a notation of exempt status must appear on the face of the deed or trust document. See 35 ILCS 200/31-45(a), (c)—(j), and (*l*). For exempt transactions under Sec. 31-45, subsections (b), (k), and (m), of the Property Tax Code, a completed transfer declaration must be filed with the recorder of deeds or registrar of titles. See ILCS 200/31-45(b), (k), and (m). In addition, the following transactions are exempt:

— a transfer qualifying for exempt status under subsection (b) is exempt from the filing requirements only if the Administrator of Veterans' Affairs of the United States is the grantee pursuant to a foreclosure proceeding; and

— a transfer qualifying for exempt status under subsection (k) must involve a simultaneous exchange and not a delayed exchange pursuant to IRC Sec. 1031 (commonly known as a "Starker" exchange). However, revenue stamps must be affixed to the deed or trust document for any difference in money paid.

Real estate entities: If a taxpayer is liable for Illinois corporate franchise taxes as a result of a transfer of a controlling interest in a real estate entity, the taxpayer is entitled to a real estate transfer tax exemption to the extent of the corporate franchise tax paid as a result of the transfer.

Mortgage assignments: Mortgage assignments were not subject to Chicago real estate transfer tax because mortgages do not convey equitable ownership in real property. The transfer tax is imposed on transfer of beneficial interests in real property. A beneficial interest in property is controlling or equitable ownership of the property, not merely owning title to the property. (*City of Chicago v. Elm State Property LLC,* Appellate Court of Illinois, First District, No. 1-15-2552, 1-15-2553, December 22, 2016, CCH ILLINOIS TAX REPORTS, ¶403-202)

• *Rate and basis*

The tax is levied at the rate of 50¢ per $500 of value or fraction thereof. "Value" is the full consideration for the property as stated in a declaration filed by the parties at the time the deed is recorded. If the property transferred remains subject to an existing mortgage, only the owner's equity (not the outstanding mortgage amount) is included in the base for computing the tax. Counties may impose a tax at 25¢ per $500 of value. Home rule municipalities may also impose an additional tax. Chicago imposes the tax at the rate of $3.75 per $500 of the transfer price.

The transfer tax is not based on full actual consideration but rather on net consideration. In computing the amount of tax due, errors occur by erroneously claiming or inflating various exclusions. For example, the mortgage exclusion should be taken only if the deed or trust document states that the transferred property remains subject to a mortgage at the time of the transfer.

The full actual consideration (sale price) must be stated in the transfer declaration. This value is the amount actually paid, excluding any amount credited against the purchase price or refunded to the buyer for improvements or repairs to the property. Included in the consideration are the following values:

— the amount of outstanding mortgages to which the property remains subject at the time of the transfer;

— the amount for other real estate transferred in a simultaneous exchange between buyer and seller;

— the amount for items of personal property transferred from buyer to seller; and

— the amount representing noncash consideration, such as assuming or forgiving debt or other liability of seller by buyer.

• *Returns and payment*

A single website, MyDec (**http://tax.illinois.gov/LocalGovernment/PropertyTax/ MyDec/**) has replaced the EZDec system for filing Illinois, Cook County, and Chicago real property transfer tax declarations.

Payment: The tax, evidenced by stamps affixed to the deed, is payable at the time the deed is recorded or within three business days after the transfer is effected, whichever is earlier. Transactions subject to the state transfer tax must be reported on Form PTAX-203, Illinois Real Estate Transfer Declaration. Also, additional supplemental information must be reported at that time for transactions involving certain categories of commercial or industrial property for which the full actual consideration is over $1 million. The form for this purpose is Form PTAX-203-A, Illinois Real Estate Transfer Tax Declaration Supplemental Form A. If these reporting requirements have not been satisfied, then the recorder or registrar cannot accept and record or register the deed or trust document.

Individuals: Form PTAX-203, Illinois Real Estate Transfer Declaration, is completed by the buyer and seller and filed at the county in which the property is located. The form must be filed with the county recorder of deeds or registrar of titles. The county transfer tax is also paid at the time of recordation or registration.

Administration: The tax is collected by the various county recorders of deeds or registrars of titles through the sale of revenue stamps. However, the Department of Revenue is authorized to prescribe reasonable rules and regulations for the administration of the tax and to prescribe the form of the tax stamps to ensure the same stamp evidences payment of both the state and the county real estate transfer tax.

¶2208

¶2209 Video Gaming Tax

Law: Video Gaming Act, Sec. 1 *et. seq.* [625 ILCS 5/3-2001](CCH ILLINOIS TAX REPORTS, ¶35-001).

For purposes of the Video Gaming Act, a tax of 30% is imposed on "net terminal income," which means money put into a video gaming terminal minus credits paid out to players (Video Gaming Act, Sec. 30). Non-home rule units of government may not impose any annual fee for the operation of a video gaming terminal in excess of $25.

Nonrefundable applications for video gaming licenses are set at $5,000 for manufacturers, distributors, and terminal operators; $2,500 for suppliers; $100 for technicians; and $50 for terminal handlers. Maximum annual fees for each licenses are $10,000 for each manufacturer and distributor; $5,000 for each terminal operator; $2,000 for each supplier; $100 for each technician, licensed establishment, and video gaming terminal; and $50 for each terminal handler. (Video Gaming Act, Sec. 45)

The state's percentage of net terminal income must be reported and remitted within 15 days after the 15th day of each month. However, video terminal operators must remit and pay the tax within 15 days after the end of each month. A video terminal operator's failure to report or false report of the amount due constitutes a Class 4 felony and could result in termination of the operator's license. Payments not remitted when due are subject to a monthly penalty assessment of 1.5%. In addition, the video gaming act is subject to rules promulgated for the state riverboat gambling tax where there is no conflict between the laws. (Video Gaming Act, Sec. 60)

¶2210 Timber Purchase Tax

Law: Professions and Occupation, Sec. 735/8 [225 ILCS 735/8]; Professions and Occupation, Sec. 735/9a [225 ILCS 735/9a] (CCH ILLINOIS TAX REPORTS, ¶31-001).

A tax is imposed on purchasers of timber. A tax is also imposed on growers, on the gross value of timber utilized, processed, or held for resale by the grower. Excluded from the tax is timber occasionally used or processed by the grower for his own use and not for resale.

Rate of tax: The tax is 4% of the purchase price or gross value of the timber. The 4% tax is deducted from the purchase payment and forwarded by the buyer to the Department of Natural Resources. Every timber grower pays an amount equal to 4% of the gross value to the Department of Natural Resources. The fees are deposited in a special fund.

¶2211 Gambling and Live Adult Entertainment Taxes

Law: Bingo License and Tax Act, Sec. 1 [230 ILCS 25/1, *et seq.*]; Charitable Games Tax Act, Sec. 2 [230 ILCS 30/1, *et seq.*;] Pull Tabs and Jar Games Act [230 ILCS 20/1 *et seq.*]; Riverboat Gambling Act [230 ILCS 10/1 *et seq.*]; Live Adult Entertainment Facility Surcharge Act, Sec. 1 [35 ILCS 175-5 *et seq.*]; 86 Ill. Adm. Code 3000 (CCH ILLINOIS TAX REPORTS, ¶35-001).

Taxes on selected gambling activities are briefly discussed below.

• *Bingo games*

The Bingo License and Tax Act restricts the conducting of bingo games to licensees that are determined by the Department of Revenue to be a bona fide religious, charitable, labor, fraternal, youth athletic, senior citizen, educational, or veterans' organization organized in Illinois, operating without profit to its members, and in existence in Illinois for a period of five continuous years immediately preceding application for a license. A license authorizes the licensee to conduct the game of "bingo," in which prizes are awarded on the basis of designated numbers or symbols on a card conforming to numbers or symbols selected at random. (Bingo License and Tax Act, Sec. 1 [230 ILCS 25/1])

Rate and basis of tax: The bingo tax is imposed at the rate of 5% of the gross proceeds of any game of bingo conducted by the licensee. (Bingo License and Tax Act, Sec. 3 [230 ILCS 25/3])

The Charitable Games Tax Act restricts the conducting of charitable games to licensees that are determined by the Department of Revenue to be qualified charitable, religious, fraternal, veterans, labor, or educational organizations, operating without profit, and exempt from federal income taxation under Secs. 501(c)(3), 501(c)(4), 501(c)(5), 501(c)(8), 501(c)(10), or 501(c)(19) of the Internal Revenue Code. (Charitable Games Tax Act, Sec. 2 [230 ILCS 30/2]) Qualified organizations must have been in existence in Illinois for a period of five years immediately before making application for a license. (Charitable Games Tax Act, Sec. 3 [230 ILCS 30/3])

Rate and basis of tax: The charitable games tax is imposed at the rate of 3% of the gross proceeds of any charitable game conducted by the licensee. (Charitable Games Tax Act, Sec. 9 [230 ILCS 30/9])

• *Pull tabs and jar games*

The Illinois Pull Tabs and Jar Games Act imposes a gross receipts tax on nonprofit charitable, religious, and educational organizations that conduct pull tabs and jar games. "Pull tabs" and "jar games" are defined as games using single-folded or banded tickets or a card, the face of which is initially covered or otherwise hidden from view in order to conceal numbers or symbols, some of which are winners. Players with winning tickets receive a prize stated on a promotional display. "Pull tabs" also means a game in which prizes are won by pulling a tab from a board, thereby revealing a number that corresponds to the number for a given prize.

Rate and basis of tax: The tax is imposed at a rate of 5% of gross receipts from pull tabs and jar games (Pull Tabs and Jar Games Act, Sec. 5 [230 ILCS 20/5]).

Returns and payment: The tax must be paid quarterly together with a report describing the games conducted. Payment must be received within the first 20 days of April, July, October, and January.

Administration: The pull tabs and jar games tax is administered by the Department of Revenue.

• *Riverboat gambling*

An admission tax and a gross receipts privilege tax are imposed upon the licensed owner conducting riverboat gambling.

Rate and basis of tax: The admission tax rate is based on the number of admissions in 2004. For licensees that admitted at most one million persons in 2004, the rate is $2 per person admitted. For all other licensees, the rate is $3 per person admitted.

The privilege tax is based on the adjusted gross receipts received by a licensed owner from authorized gambling games. Rates range from 15% of annual adjusted gross receipts up to and including $25 million to 50% of annual adjusted gross receipts in excess of $200 million.

Returns and payment: The privilege taxes must be paid by the licensed owner to the State Gaming Board by 3:00 p.m. on the day after the wagers were made. Licensed owners are required to keep books and records and file an audit of all financial transactions with the Gaming Board within 90 days after the end of each quarter of each fiscal year.

Administration: The riverboat gambling tax is administered by the Illinois Gaming Board.

¶2211

Practitioner Comment: Riverboat Surcharges Are Lawful

The Illinois Supreme Court upheld, over constitutional challenges, the surcharge on riverboat casinos with adjusted gross receipts over $200 million. See *Empress Casino Joliet Corp v. Giannoulias,* 231 Ill.2d 62 (2008), CCH ILLINOIS TAX REPORTS, ¶ 401-885.

There were nine riverboat casinos in Illinois, and four of them had adjusted gross receipts of over $200 million and, therefore, were subject to the tax. The proceeds from the surcharge were to be distributed to five horse racing tracks located in Illinois.

The Plaintiffs alleged that the tax was unconstitutional by violating the Illinois Uniformity Clause and other constitutional provisions. Under Illinois law, legislation regarding a non-property tax classification survives scrutiny under the uniformity clause if it is: (1) based on a real and substantial difference between the people taxed and those not taxed, and (2) bears some reasonable relationship to the object of the legislation or to public policy. The court found that the legislative intent behind the surcharge was to offset the adverse impact that the casinos had on the race horsing industry. The court upheld the surcharge on the basis that the tax bears a reasonable relationship with that objective. Further, the court found that there was no "real and substantial difference" between casinos based on whether or not their adjusted gross receipts were in excess of $200 million because "the uniformity clause allows sub-classifications and exclusions as long as they are reasonable."

Horwood Marcus & Berk, Chartered

• *Live entertainment surcharge*

An annual surcharge is imposed on each operator of a live adult entertainment facility in Illinois (35 ILCS 175/10; *Informational Bulletin FY 2013-11,* Illinois Department of Revenue, February 2013, CCH ILLINOIS TAX REPORTS, ¶ 402-627). A "live adult entertainment facility" is a striptease club or other business that serves or permits the consumption of alcohol on its premises and, during at least 30 consecutive or nonconsecutive days in a calendar year, offers or provides activities by employees, agents, or contractors of the business that involve nude or partially denuded individuals that, when considered as a whole, appeal primarily to an interest in nudity or sex (35 ILCS 175/5). An "operator" is any person who owns or operates a live adult entertainment facility in Illinois.

Rate of surcharge: An operator may elect to pay the surcharge in one of two ways. The operator may choose to pay $3 per person admitted to the facility or a flat amount based on the gross receipts of the facility. If an operator has not filed its sales and use tax returns for the prior year by January 20, then the operator must pay the surcharge using the per-person method. (35 ILCS 175/10(a))

The operator is not required to impose a $3 fee on each customer, but has the discretion to determine how it will derive the money to pay the surcharge. The amount of the flat surcharge is based on the gross receipts of the facility during the preceding calendar year as determined for sales and use tax purposes. If the receipts are equal to or greater than $2 million, the surcharge is $25,000. If the receipts are equal to or greater than $500,000, but less than $2 million, the surcharge is $15,000. If the receipts are less than $500,000, the surcharge is $5,000. (35 ILCS 175/10(a))

Returns: The returns for the annual surcharge are due on January 20 each year and must be filed electronically (35 ILCS 175/10(c), (d)). If an operator stops operating a live adult entertainment facility, the operator must file a final return not more than one calendar month after discontinuing the business.

¶2212 Environmental Taxes and Fees

Law: Environmental Protection Act, Secs. 55.8—55.10 [415 ILCS 5/55.8—55.10], Environmental Protection Act, Sec. 1009.6 [415 ILCS 5/9]; Environmental Protection Act, Sec. 1022.2 [415 ILCS 5/22.2]; Environmental Protection Act, Sec. 1022.8 [415 ILCS 5/22.8]; Environmental Protection Act, Sec. 1039.5(18) [415 ILCS 5/39.5]; Environmental Protection Act, Sec. 55.8 [415 ILCS 5/55.8]; Environmental Protection Act, Sec. 55.10 [415 ILCS 5/55.10]; Low-Level Radioactive Waste Management Compact, Sec. 241-13 [420 ILCS 20/13]; Drycleaner Environmental Response Trust Fund Act, Sec. 5 [415 ILCS 135/5]; Drycleaner Environmental Response Trust Fund Act, Sec. 65 [415 ILCS 135/65]; Drycleaner Environmental Response Trust Fund Act, Sec. 77 [415 ILCS 135/77](CCH ILLINOIS TAX REPORTS, ¶ 37-151, 60-570).

Forms: DS-1, Dry Cleaning Solvent Tax Return; ST-8, Tire User Fee Return.

Illinois imposes taxes and fees related to environmental pollution and protection, as discussed below.

• *Hazardous waste disposal fees*

The Environmental Protection Agency collects from the owner or operator of each hazardous waste disposal site the following fees (415 ILCS 5/22.2):

— 9¢ per gallon or $18.18 per cubic yard of hazardous waste disposed at a hazardous waste disposal site if the disposal site is located off the site where the waste was produced, up to a maximum amount of $30,000 with respect to waste generated by a single generator and deposited in monofills;

— 9¢ per gallon or $18.18 per cubic yard of hazardous waste disposed if the disposal site is located on the site where the waste was produced, up to a maximum fee of $30,000 per year for each such disposal site;

— if the hazardous waste disposal site is an underground injection well, $6,000 per year if not more than 10 million gallons per year are injected, $15,000 per year if more than 10 million gallons but not more than 50 million gallons per year are injected, and $27,000 per year if more than 50 million gallons per year are injected; and

— 3¢ per gallon or $6.06 per cubic yard of hazardous waste received for treatment at a hazardous waste treatment site if the treatment site is located off the site where the waste was produced and if the treatment site is owned, controlled, and operated by a person other than the generator of the waste.

Waste disposal site fees: The owner or operator of a hazardous waste disposal site or management facility must pay annual fees as follows (415 ILCS 5/22.8):

— hazardous waste disposal site receiving waste produced offsite, $70,000;

— hazardous waste disposal site receiving waste produced onsite, $18,000;

— hazardous waste disposal site that is an underground injection well, $14,000;

— hazardous waste management facility treating hazardous waste by incineration, $4,000;

— hazardous waste management facility treating hazardous waste by process other than incineration, $2,000;

— hazardous waste management facility storing hazardous waste in a surface impoundment or pile, $2,000;

— hazardous waste management facility storing hazardous waste other than in a surface impoundment or pile, $500; and

— for a large quantity hazardous waste generator required to submit an annual or biennial report for hazardous waste generation, $500.

• *Low-level radioactive waste disposal fees*

The Department of Nuclear Safety collects from each generator of low-level radioactive wastes a fee of $3 per cubic foot of waste stored in Illinois for shipment, storage, treatment, or disposal.

The minimum fee is $50. Nuclear power reactors generally are not subject to the fee.

¶2212

• *Air pollution fees*

Sites that are permitted under an air pollution operating permit to emit regulated pollutants must pay to the Illinois Environmental Protection Agency an annual fee generally based on the tonnage of pollutants emitted annually, as follows:

— less than 25 tons, $200;

— at least 25 tons, but less than 100 tons, $1,800; and

— at least 100 tons, $3,500.

Fees under Clean Air Act permit program: For each 12-month period after the date on which the U.S. Environmental Protection Agency approves or conditionally approves Illinois' Clean Air Act Permit Program (CAAPP), a stationary source of air pollutants must pay an air pollution fee as follows (415 ILCS 5/39.5):

— A source allowed to emit less than 100 tons of all regulated air pollutants, or less than 100 tons of a regulated air pollutant that is subject to any standard under Sec. 112 of the Clean Air Act (42 USC §7412), must pay a fee of $1,800 per year; and

— A source allowed to emit 100 tons or more per year of all regulated air pollutants will be assessed by the Illinois Environmental Protection Agency an annual fee of $18 per ton for the allowable emissions of all regulated air pollutants at that source during the term of the permit. The applicant or permittee may pay the fee annually or semiannually for fees greater than $5,000. If the fee is greater than $100,000, the full amount must be paid by July 1 for the subsequent year, or 50% of the fee may be paid on July 1 on and January 1 of the following year.

• *Dry-cleaning solvent tax*

A tax is imposed on the purchase of dry-cleaning solvents by persons who operate dry-cleaning facilities in Illinois. Dry-cleaning solvents include chlorine-based or hydrocarbon-based products that are used as a primary cleaning agents in dry-cleaning operations. The tax is scheduled for repeal on January 1, 2020. (415 ILCS 135/65; *Informational Bulletin FY 2010-07*, Illinois Department of Revenue, January 2010, CCH ILLINOIS TAX REPORTS, ¶402-062)

Exemptions: The following facilities are not considered dry-cleaning facilities for purposes of this tax: a facility located on a United State military base; an industrial laundry, commercial laundry, or linen supply facility; a penal institution that is engaged in dry-cleaning only as part of a correctional industries program; a not-for-profit health care facility; or a facility located or previously located on state or federal property.

Rate of tax: The tax on chlorine-based solvents is $3.50 per gallon and the tax on petroleum-based solvents is $0.35 per gallon. For green solvents, the tax rate is $1.75 per gallon unless the green solvent is used at a virgin facility, in which case the rate is $0.35 per gallon. A "virgin facility" is a drycleaning facility that has never had chlorine-based or petroleum-based solvents stored or used at the property prior to becoming a green solvent drycleaning facility. The tax rate is determined annually by the Drycleaner Environmental Response Trust Fund Council.

Payment: The tax is paid to the Department of Revenue on or before the 25th day of the month following the quarter for which the return is filed. Beginning in 2010, a seller of drycleaning solvents may, at the time of filing an Illinois drycleaning solvent tax return, deduct from the amount of tax due 1.75% of that amount or $5 per calendar year, whichever is greater. Failure to timely file returns and to provide data requested by the Department of Revenue will result in disallowance of the reimbursement discount. (415 ILCS 135/65)

The Illinois Department of Revenue reminds taxpayers of changes to the law imposing a dry-cleaning solvent tax that are effective as of January 1, 2010. Among other items, the tax is imposed on the purchase (formerly, the use) of solvents. (*Informational Bulletin FY 2010-07*, Illinois Department of Revenue, January 2010, CCH ILLINOIS TAX REPORTS, ¶ 402-062)

• *Tire user fee*

Any person offering or selling tires at retail in Illinois must collect a tire user fee of $2.50 for every new or used tire sold and delivered in the state (415 ILCS 5/55.8). The fee is collected from the purchaser and is added to the selling price of the tire and must be listed separately on the bill of sale. The fee is not included in the state or local retailers' occupation tax or the state use tax. Chicago also imposes a tire fee (¶ 2314).

The fee applies to tires for highway vehicles, special mobile equipment, and farm equipment and to aircraft tires.

Exemptions: Tires excluded from the fee are, generally, those tires that are placed on a vehicle that is not transported or drawn upon a highway, i.e., race cars, fork lifts, all-terrain vehicles, and lawn and garden tractors. The fee does not apply to mail-order sales of tires nor to tires that are included in the retail sale of a motor vehicle. Also, the fee does not apply to the sale of reprocessed tires. A "reprocessed tire" is a used tire that has been recapped, retreaded, or regrooved and that has not been placed on a vehicle wheel rim. However, used tires sold at retail that have not been "reprocessed" are not exempt.

Reports and payments: The fee is reported and paid to the Department of Revenue by the retail seller on a quarterly basis by the 20th of the month following the end of a calendar quarter (415 ILCS 5/55.10). Instead of filing returns, a retailer of tires may pay the fee to its supplier of tires at the time of purchase, if the supplier is a registered retailer and arranges to collect and remit the fee to the Department.

A credit of 10¢ per tire is allowed either the retail seller or the tire supplier for incurred expenses, provided that the retailer's tire user fee return is timely filed and timely paid (415 ILCS 5/55.8). Retail sellers choosing to pay the fee to their suppliers are not entitled to the credit.

The Illinois Department of Revenue has issued guidance discussing the tire user fee. The notice discusses what tires are subject to the fee, what tires are excluded from the fee, and what retail sales are exempt. Some retail sales of tires exempt from Illinois sales tax may be subject to the fee. The notice also provides contact information for persons required to register to collect and pay the fee, notifies retailers that the fee is not included in sales price for sales tax purposes, and discusses when to pay the fee and file the tire user fee return. (*PIO-55, Tire User Fee*, Illinois Department of Revenue, March 2011, CCH ILLINOIS TAX REPORTS, ¶ 402-299)

• *Motor fuels environmental impact fee*

An environmental impact fee is imposed until January 1, 2025, on receivers of fuel intended to be used on the public highways or waterways of Illinois. Details are discussed at ¶ 2203.

¶2213 Hospital Provider Assessment

Law: Public Aid Code, Sec. 5A-1 *et seq.* [305 ILCS 5/5A-1 *et seq.*](CCH ILLINOIS TAX REPORTS, ¶ 35-051).

Illinois imposes an annual assessment on hospital providers' inpatient and outpatient services. The assessments are scheduled for repeal at the end of calendar year 2018 (305 ILCS 5/5A-2).

Rates: The hospital provider assessment on inpatient services is set at the rate of $218.38 multiplied by the difference of the hospital's occupied bed days less the hospital's Medicare bed days. The outpatient services assessment is imposed on each hospital provider in an amount equal to 0.008766 multiplied by the hospital's outpatient gross revenue. (305 ILCS 5/5A-2)

Exemptions: There is an exemption from the hospital provider fund assessment for any hospital provider, as described in Sec. 1903(w)(3)(F) of the federal Social Security Act, that is any of the following (305 ILCS 5/5A-3(b) and (b-2)):

— a state agency,

— a state university,

— a county, or

— any local government unit.

Payment and administration: Payment of the fees is due on the 14th day of each month and each payment should equal 1/12 of the annual assessment (305 ILCS 5/5A-4(a)).

The Illinois Department of Public Aid is charged with administering and enforcing the hospital provider fund assessment law. It also must collect the assessments and penalty assessments (305 ILCS 5/5A-7(a)). However, the Department must initiate administrative and/or judicial proceedings within three years after the due date of the assessment (305 ILCS 5/5A-7(a)(2)).

¶2214 Hydraulic Fracturing Tax

Law: Illinois Hydraulic Fracturing Tax Act, Sec. 1-5 *et seq.*[35 ILCS 450/1-1, *et seq.*] (CCH ILLINOIS TAX REPORTS, ¶ 37-301).

Beginning July 1, 2013, the Illinois hydraulic fracturing tax is imposed on the severance and production of oil or gas from a well on a production unit required to be permitted under the Illinois Hydraulic Fracturing Regulatory Act (35 ILCS 450/2-5 *et seq.*,). The tax applies equally to all portions of the value of each barrel of oil severed and the value of gas severed (35 ILCS 450/2-15(a)). Liability for the tax accrues at the time the oil or gas is removed from the production unit (35 ILCS 450/2-15(f)). Generally, the tax is upon the producers of such oil or gas in proportion to their respective beneficial interests at the time of severance.

Rates: For a period of 24 months from the month in which oil or gas was first produced from a well, the rate of tax is 3% of the value of the oil or gas severed from the earth or water in the state. Thereafter, the rate will be 6% of the value of gas severed, and the rate on oil severed will be based on each well's average daily production (ADP) each month, as follows (35 ILCS 450/2-15(a)(1)):

— if the ADP is less than 25 barrels, the rate is 3% of the oil's value;

— if the ADP is at least 25 barrels but less than 50 barrels, the rate is 4% of the oil's value;

— if the ADP at least 50 barrels but less than 100 barrels, the rate is 5% of the oil's value; and

— if the ADP is at least 100 barrels, the rate is 6% of the oil's value.

Exemptions: Oil produced from a well whose ADP is 15 barrels or less for the 12-month period immediately preceding the production is exempt from the tax (35 ILCS 450/2-15(b))

Severance and production of gas is exempt for gas that is (35 ILCS 450/2-15(d)):

— injected into the earth for the purpose of lifting oil, recycling, or repressuring;

— used for fuel in connection with the operation and development for, or production of, oil or gas in the production unit;

— lawfully vented or flared; or

— inadvertently lost on the production unit by reason of leaks, blowouts, or other accidental losses.

Local work force tax rate reduction: The rate of tax imposed on working interest owners of a well will be reduced by 0.25% for the life of the well when a minimum of 50% of the total work force hours on the well site are performed by Illinois construction workers being paid wages equal to or exceeding the general prevailing rate of hourly wages (35 ILCS 450/2-17(a)). When more than one well is drilled on a well site, total work force hours are determined on a well-by-well basis (35 ILCS 450/2-17(b)). The operator must obtain and retain any other records the Illinois Department of Revenue (IDOR) determines are necessary to verify a claim for a reduction in the tax and must make the records available to the IDOR upon request (35 ILCS 450/2-17(c)).

Withholding: Any purchaser who makes a monetary payment to a producer for his or her portion of the value of products from a production unit must withhold from such payment the amount of tax due from the producer. Any purchaser who pays any tax due from a producer shall be entitled to reimbursement from the producer for the tax so paid and may take credit for that amount from any monetary payment to the producer for the value of products. To the extent that a purchaser required to collect the tax has actually done so, that tax is held in trust for the benefit of the state. (35 ILCS 450/2-25)

Purchaser returns: Each purchaser must make a return to the IDOR showing the quantity of oil or gas purchased during the month for which the return is filed; the price paid therefor; the total value; the name and address of the operator or other person from whom the oil or gas was purchased; a description of the production unit from which the oil or gas was severed; and the amount of tax due from each production unit for each calendar month. All taxes due, or to be remitted, by the purchaser must accompany the return, which is due on or before the last day of the month after the calendar month for which the return is required. (35 ILCS 450/2-45)

Operator returns: The operator is responsible for remitting the tax on or before the last day of the month following the end of the calendar month in which the oil and gas was "removed" from the production unit by being:

(1) transported off the production unit by the operator,

(2) used on the production unit, or

(3) manufactured and converted into refined products on the production unit.

The payment must be accompanied by a return to the Department showing the gross quantity of oil or gas removed during the month for which the return is filed, the price paid therefore, and if no price is paid therefore, the value of the oil and gas, a description of the production unit from which such oil or gas was severed, and the amount of tax (35 ILCS 450/2-50).

Filing and payment: Generally, purchasers and operators must file all returns electronically and make payment by electronic funds transfer (EFT). Returns must be accompanied by an appropriate computer-generated magnetic media supporting schedule in a format prescribed by the IDOR. (35 ILCS 450/2-45 and 35 ILCS 450/2-50(b))

PART IX
LOCAL TAXES
CHAPTER 23
CHICAGO TAXES

¶2301 Scope of Chapter

This chapter deals with the Chicago employers' expense (head) tax, the transaction taxes, the Chicago sales and use taxes and service tax, and several other Chicago taxes. Additional discussion of Chicago taxes may be found in the "Licenses, Miscellaneous" division of the CCH ILLINOIS TAX REPORTS, at ¶31-001 and following.

CCH Advisory: Electronic Filing and Payment

Beginning in 2016, the City of Chicago requires most taxpayers and tax collectors to file and pay their taxes through the city's online filing program, Webtax. For additional information, see ¶2313.

¶2302 Employers' Expense Tax

Law: Chicago Munic. Code, Secs. 3-20-010—3-20-140 (CCH ILLINOIS TAX REPORTS, ¶17-351).

Forms: Form 7540.

Employers doing business in Chicago and having 50 or more full-time employees who earn at least $4,300 in a calendar quarter, including commission merchants, are subject to the tax (Chicago Munic. Code, Sec. 3-20-020). Employers are required to register with the Chicago Department of Revenue (Chicago Munic. Code, Sec. 3-20-080).

An employer is doing business within Chicago if it engages at least one individual to work in whole or in part within Chicago, and if the employer or the employee or commission merchant does any of the following:

— maintains a fixed place of business in Chicago;

— maintains a regular stock of tangible personal property in Chicago for sale in the ordinary course of business;

— owns or leases real property in Chicago for business purposes; or

— continuously solicits business within Chicago (Chicago Munic. Code, Sec. 3-20-040).

A ruling by the Chicago Department of Revenue provides definitions of "business," "employee," and "unitary business group." The ruling is intended to clarify, rather than change, existing law (*Employer's Expense Tax Ruling #2*, City of Chicago Department of Revenue, August 29, 2005, CCH ILLINOIS TAX REPORTS, ¶401-565).

The Chicago Department of Revenue properly combined the employees of commonly owned though separately incorporated restaurants for purposes of the employers' expense tax. The court held that the plain language of the Chicago code was compatible with an intent to tax every employer who has 50 or more full-time employees in the employer's business. The term "business" is broadly defined in the ordinance as "any activity, enterprise, profession, trade or undertaking of any nature conducted... with the object of gain... whether direct or indirect, to the employer." A business includes "entities which are subsidiary or independent." (*DTCT, Inc. et al. v. City of Chicago*, Appellate Court of Illinois, First District, Nos. 1-09-2272, 1-09-2274, & 1-09-2275, February 18, 2011, CCH ILLINOIS TAX REPORTS, ¶402-284)

Practitioner Comment: The Chicago "Head Tax" Cases

In DTCT, Inc, et al v. City of Chicago Department of Revenue, the Court went beyond the face of the ordinance and employed the income tax concept of "unitary business group" to a non-income based tax. During oral argument, the Chief Justice challenged the Department's ability to consolidate the corporate entities when "business" was defined by the ordinance and the Department had previously interpreted this ordinance in two separate rulings accordance with the definition provided by ordinance which was in contradiction to the definition it proffered in this matter. Chief Justice Cahill argued that if the Department wanted to enforce the ordinance to contain the "unitary group" definition of "business" then it needed to do so through City Council and not the Court system. However, at the end of the day the Chief Justice's objections were defeated and the decision came down 2-1 in favor of the Department.

Breen M. Schiller, Esq., Horwood Marcus & Berk Chartered

Practitioner Comment: Computation of Tax

In *Kayla Enterprises, Inc. v. Chicago Dep't of Revenue*, No. 05 TX 0531, Administrative Hearing, October 8, 2008 (Appeal Pending) an Illinois Administrative Law Judge ("ALJ") ruled in favor of the Chicago Department of Revenue, holding that the head tax liability of related entities is to be determined on a consolidated (unitary) basis. The taxpayer argued that the head tax should be imposed on each separate employer because the statute stated that the tax was imposed on "every employer," and defined "employer" as "any person." However, the ALJ's interpretation focused on the statute's definition of "business" because the statute imposed a head tax "upon every employer who, in connection with the employer's business . . . contracts with 50 or more individuals . . . " Under the statute, the definition of "business" includes "entities which are subsidiary or independent." Therefore, because the word "entities" is plural, the judge found that the law contemplated the possibility of multiple entities. The ALJ also held that even if the statute was ambiguous, the outcome would be the same because the Department's 2005 tax ruling regarding unitary business would be considered to help resolve the ambiguity. The ALJ then found that the companies were unitary.

Marilyn A. Wethekam, Esq., Horwood Marcus & Berk Chartered

Exemptions: In addition to those who employ fewer than 50 full-time employees, government agencies are exempt as are, in general, federally tax-exempt organizations. Also, in *The Prudential Insurance Co. of America et al. v. The City of Chicago et al.* (1977, SCt), 362 NE2d 1021; CCH ILLINOIS TAX REPORTS, ¶200-892, the Illinois Supreme Court held that insurance companies are exempt from the head tax.

Basis and rate: The tax is calculated on the number of employees or commission merchants who perform 50% or more of their work during a calendar quarter in Chicago. The tax rate is $4 per month per employee (Chicago Munic. Code, Sec. 3-20-030).

Returns and payment: Tax returns and payments are delinquent if not filed on or before the 15th day of the month following the close of each calendar quarter (Chicago Munic. Code, Sec. 3-20-050).

Chicago requires most taxpayers and tax collectors to file and pay their taxes through the city's online filing program, Webtax. For additional information, see ¶2313.

¶2303 Occupation (Sales) Taxes

Law: Chicago Munic. Code, Secs. 3-40-010, 3-40-020; Chicago Munic. Code, Secs. 3-40-430, 3-40-440 (CCH ILLINOIS TAX REPORTS, ¶61-730).

Chicago imposes a municipal retailers' occupation tax on persons engaged in the business of selling tangible personal property (except property titled or registered with a state agency) at retail in Chicago (Chicago Munic. Code, Sec. 3-40-010). In addition, a municipal service occupation tax is imposed on persons engaged in Chicago in the business of making sales of service. (Chicago Munic. Code, Sec. 3-40-430) A complementary use tax is discussed at ¶2305.

Exemptions: The taxes are not imposed on the following: (1) food for human consumption that is to be consumed off the premises where it is sold, except for alcoholic beverages, soft drinks, candy, and food that has been prepared for immediate consumption; and (2) medicines, drugs, medical appliances, and insulin, urine testing materials, syringes, and needles used by diabetics (Chicago Munic. Code, Sec. 3-40-010; Chicago Munic. Code, Sec. 3-40-430).

Basis and rate: In the case of sellers of personal property, the tax is imposed at the rate of 1.25% of the seller's gross receipts. In the case of sellers of service, the tax is imposed at the rate of 1.25% of the selling price of tangible personal property transferred incident to the sale of service (Chicago Munic. Code, Sec. 3-40-010; Chicago Munic. Code, Sec. 3-40-430).

Sourcing: Sourcing of local taxes is discussed at ¶1518.

Administration: The Illinois Department of Revenue collects the home rule sales tax, imposed on the same general merchandise base as the state sales tax, excluding titled or registered tangible personal property (such as vehicles, watercraft, aircraft, trailers, and mobile homes), and qualifying food, drugs, and medical appliances. In addition, the Department of Revenue administers the Chicago home rule use tax on automobiles and other titled or registered items that will be registered to an address within the corporate limits of Chicago (¶2306).

Chicago requires most taxpayers and tax collectors to file and pay their taxes through the city's online filing program, Webtax. For additional information, see ¶2313.

¶2304 Lease Transaction Tax

Law: Chicago Munic. Code, Secs. 3-32-030—3-32-050, 3-33-020—3-33-150 (CCH ILLINOIS TAX REPORTS, ¶ 60-460, 61-730).

Forms: Form 7550 (personal property); Form 7551 (real property).

A transaction tax is imposed on the lease or rental in the city of personal property or on the privilege of using in the city personal property that is leased or rented outside the city (Chicago Munic. Code, Sec. 3-32-030).

Practitioner Comment: Enterprise Leasing Co. v. City of Chicago, No. 11 L 50840

The Cook County Circuit Court held that a ruling issued by the Chicago Department of Revenue extending the reach of the city's personal property lease transaction tax to include car rental companies outside the city limits was impermissible. Issued on April 1, 2011, Chicago Personal Property Lease Transaction Tax Ruling #11 proposed to make car rental companies within three miles of the Chicago city limits subject to the record keeping requirements of the city's Personal Property Lease Transaction Tax. Defendants argued that because the plaintiff has locations in the city and it is likely that Chicago residents renting cars within three miles of the city will use the car in Chicago, Defendants have jurisdiction over the transaction. The court disagreed, finding that defendants have no jurisdiction over transactions occurring outside the city and therefore imposing such a tax is an impermissible extraterritorial exercise of power. Second, the court ruled that Ruling 11 exceeded the scope of the Personal Property Lease Transaction Tax. The court noted that a ruling extending the city's taxing jurisdiction beyond the city limits improperly broadens the tax beyond the scope of the municipal code. Finally, the court held that Ruling 11 unconstitutionally violated the Due Process Clause and the Commerce Clause of the United States Constitution as the taxing zone created by Ruling 11 included portions of Indiana and defendants lacked sufficient connection with those transactions. Based on these findings, the court ruled in favor of the plaintiffs, finding Ruling 11 to be an impermissible exercise of the city's taxing authority.

Breen M. Schiller, Esq., Horwood Marcus & Berk, Chartered

The Chicago real property transfer tax is imposed on transfers of title to, or beneficial interests in, real estate where the transaction is consummated in Chicago. The ultimate incidence of the tax falls on the consumer (the grantee in the case of realty transfers) (Chicago Munic. Code, Sec. 3-33-030).

The sale or purchase of Chicago real estate with wireless antennae and network communications equipment (cell sites) on it may be subject to the city real estate transfer tax if any consideration was given for an easement or a cell site was purchased. Because an easement is an interest in real property, any money or other property transferred for an easement would be taxable. (*Informational Bulletin*, Vol. 2009 No. 4, Chicago Department of Revenue, May 2009, CCH ILLINOIS TAX REPORTS, ¶ 401-975)

Exemptions: A lessee that is a governmental agency or an organization organized or operated for educational, charitable, or religious purposes is exempt from the transaction tax. (Chicago Munic. Code, Sec. 3-32-040) Transaction tax exemptions also include the nonpossessory lease of a computer in which the customer's use or control is *de minimis,* such as price quotation and news services, or in which the computer is used to effectuate the trade of securities, futures contracts, or the deposit, withdrawal, transfer, or loan of money or securities. Also exempt are leases and rentals of personal property between related parties and personal property primarily used outside the city (Chicago Munic. Code, Sec. 3-32-050).

Exempt realty transfers include transfers involving $500 or less; corrective deeds; transfers between certain affiliated companies; transfers involving an actual exchange of property, and a partial exemption for certain residential transfers (see below) (Chicago Munic. Code, Sec. 3-33-060).

Basis and rates: The tax rate on rentals and leases of personal property is 9% of the transfer price (Chicago Munic. Code, Sec. 3-32-030).

Effective January 1, 2016, the tax rate imposed on nonposessory computer leases of computers primarily used by customers to input, modify or retrieve data or information supplied by the customer is 5.25% of the lease or rental price, effective January 1, 2016 (Chicago Munic. Code, Sec. 3-32-030(B)). Previously, the rate was 9%. However, a "small new business", as defined, is not required to collect the tax or pay the tax when it is a lessor or lessee of a nonpossessory computer lease (Chicago Munic. Code, Sec. 3-32-030(B.1)).

Effective October 28, 2015, when a customer accesses a provider's computer under a nonpossessory computer lease, the Illinois Mobile Telecommunications Sourcing Conformity Act rules may be used to determine which customers and charges are subject to the personal property lease transaction tax.

The tax on realty transfers is $5.25 per $500 of the transfer price (Chicago Munic. Code, Sec. 3-33-030). An effective tax rate of $3.75 applies to transfers in which (1) the transfer price is less than $250,000 and (2) the transferee is a person at least 65 years old who will occupy the property as a principal dwelling for at least one year following the transfer. However, the reduced rate is in the form of a refund, which must be applied for within three years of the transfer. For additional details on the refund, see *Release,* Chicago Department of Revenue, March 21, 2008, CCH ILLINOIS TAX REPORTS, ¶ 401-871; *Notice,* Chicago Department of Revenue, March 2008, CCH ILLINOIS TAX REPORTS, ¶ 401-872; and *Release,* Chicago Department of Revenue, March 2008, CCH ILLINOIS TAX REPORTS, ¶ 401-873.

Returns and payment: Remittance returns are required to be filed with the Chicago Department of Revenue by the 15th day of each month, reflecting lease payments received during the immediately preceding month. An annual return must be filed on or before August 15 of each year to report tax liabilities for the preceding 12-month period (Chicago Munic. Code, Sec. 3-32-080). Beginning in 2016, all transfer tax declarations must be made through MyDec (**https://mytax.illinois.gov/MyDec/_/**). See ¶ 2313 for more details.

Payment of the real property transfer tax is evidenced by affixing stamps purchased from the Chicago Department of Revenue to the required document (Chicago Munic. Code, Sec. 3-33-040).

Practitioner Comment: Scope of Lease Tax

Chicago imposes a transaction tax upon: (1) the lease or rental in the city of personal property, or (2) the privilege of using in the city personal property that is leased or rented outside the city. The incidence of the tax and the obligation to pay the tax are upon the lessee of the personal property; however, the lessor has the duty to collect and remit the tax. The tax rate is determined by applying a 6% tax rate to the lease or rental payment.

The term "lease/rental" is defined broadly to include "nonpossessory leases," whereby use, but not possession, is transferred (*e.g.,* coin-operated washers/dryers and copying machines, and leased time for use of a billboard). In addition, "lease/rental" includes "nonpossessory computer leases," which includes access to the provider's software to input, modify, or retrieve data or information. The location of the terminal or other device by which a user accesses the computer is deemed to be the place of the lease or rental.

The Illinois Appellate Court has upheld the Chicago transaction tax as applied to flat-fee charges billed for searches using online databases like Lexis and Westlaw, even though the charges were not based on usage time (*Meites v. City of Chicago,* 184 Ill. App.

3d 887, 540 NE2d 973, 1st District 1989, CCH ILLINOIS TAX REPORTS, ¶ 400-390). However, the Illinois Appellate Court held that Chicago was prohibited from imposing the transaction tax on coin-operated self-service car washes, while exempting automatic and tunnel car washes, as the distinction violated the Uniformity Clause of the Illinois Constitution (*National Pride of Chicago, Inc. v. City of Chicago*, 206 Ill. App. 3d 1090, 565 NE2d 563, 1st Dist. 1990, CCH ILLINOIS TAX REPORTS, ¶ 400-477).

Horwood Marcus & Berk Chartered

Practitioner Comment: Computer-Related Transactions

City of Chicago Personal Property Lease Transaction Tax Ruling #12, effective January 1, 2016, interprets the Personal Property Lease Transaction Tax ("lease tax") to apply charges paid pursuant to a nonpossessory computer lease, unless the charges are otherwise exempt.

Examples of taxable transactions include charges incurred:

(1) to perform legal research or similar on-line database searches;

(2) to obtain consumer credit reports;

(3) to obtain real estate listings and prices, car prices, stock prices, economic statistics, and similar information or data that has been compiled, entered, and stored on the provider's computer; and

(4) to perform functions such as word processing, calculations, data processing, and other applications available to a customer through access to a provider's computer and its software.

The ruling also explains that charges for storage of information are not subject to tax, nor are nonpossessory leases of a computer if:

(a) the customer's use or control of the provider's computer is *de minimis* and

(b) the related charge is predominantly for information transferred to the customer rather than for the customer's use or control of the computer.

These exempt uses may be demonstrated either:

(1) by access to information or data that is entirely passive (such as streaming data), without interactive use, or in other cases; or

(2) by access to materials that are primarily proprietary, such as copyrighted newspapers, newsletters, or magazines.

In addition to explaining what types of transactions are taxable, Ruling #12 also provides that when a customer enters into a transaction subject to the transaction tax but uses the service within and without Chicago, the tax should be apportioned.

See also the discussion of whether the transaction tax or the amusement tax applies at ¶ 2307.

Horwood Marcus & Berk, Chartered

The Chicago Department of Finance has issued a bulletin discussing the application of the personal property lease transaction tax to nonpossessory computer leases, addressing recent amendments to lease tax ordinances, including a lower tax rate of 5.25% for certain cloud products and an exemption for small new businesses. The bulletin addresses changes in technology and the reasoning behind the issuance of Personal Property Lease Transaction Tax Ruling #12, as well as voluntary disclosure offers. Finally, the bulletin includes FAQ regarding the application of the lease tax. (*Information Bulletin: Nonpossessory Computer Leases*, Chicago Department of Finance, November 2015, CCH ILLINOIS TAX REPORTS, ¶ 403-049)

¶2304

Practitioner Comment: *Hertz Corp. v. City of Chicago, 2017 IL 119945*

The Illinois Supreme Court struck down a City of Chicago Revenue Ruling where the City of Chicago sought to impose its lease transaction tax on transactions occurring at vehicle rental locations located outside Chicago city limits. Under Chicago Rule 11, rental companies that were located within three miles of the city limits were presumed to be renting vehicles for use within the City of Chicago if the rentee had a Chicago's driver's license. Alternatively, the rentee could provide an affidavit that she was not going to use the vehicle in Chicago.

In striking down Rule 11, the Illinois Supreme Court held that the city's rule violated principles of extraterritorial taxation by improperly extending its home rule authority to tax beyond its borders. The Court found that the transactions entered into outside Chicago limits had no connection to the city and relied on the fact that delivery of the taxed items occurred outside Chicago and there was no sale or lease of a taxed item within the city of Chicago. For the tax to be proper, there had to be actual usage in the city to justify the tax, and not merely intent to use the vehicle in the city.

This case lends support for those taxpayers opposing a local jurisdiction's imposition of tax on activity occurring beyond its borders. This case may be particularly beneficial for taxpayers who are using or leasing mobile property and/or taxpayers in the cloud computing industry where property is moving in and out of a jurisdiction, or where property is used in multiple jurisdictions. This case signifies that a jurisdiction can only tax what occurs within its jurisdiction, and it can't make assumptions based on the billing address of the customer.

Another worthy point in the context of the Chicago Personal Property Lease Transaction Tax is that a key driver for taxability is the location of the property at lease inception. In Hertz, the lease was negotiated and signed outside of Chicago and the vehicles were delivered to a location outside Chicago. As such, the Court found none of the transaction occurred within Chicago. An open question is whether this analysis would change if the jurisdiction had proof that property was re-located into Chicago mid-lease. According to Hertz, however, a persuasive argument exists that the incidence of taxability occurs at the onset of the lease transaction and that such transaction would not come within the purview of the Chicago Lease Transaction Tax.

David W. Machemer, Esq., Horwood Marcus & Berk Chartered

¶2305 Use Tax on Nontitled Personal Property

Law: Chicago Munic. Code, Secs. 3-27-010—3-27-120 (CCH ILLINOIS TAX REPORTS, ¶61-730).

Forms: Form 8402; Form 8402CO (contractors); Form 8402IN (individuals); Form 8403 (retailers voluntarily collecting tax).

The Chicago use tax for nontitled personal property is imposed on the privilege of using in Chicago nontitled tangible personal property that is purchased at retail from a retailer located outside Chicago. The tax is imposed on the purchaser or user of the property. It may be voluntarily collected by the seller after receiving permission from the Chicago Department of Revenue, otherwise, the purchaser pays the tax directly to the Department (Chicago Munic. Code, Sec. 3-27-030).

Beginning in 2016, the City of Chicago requires most taxpayers and tax collectors to file and pay their taxes through the city's online filing program, Webtax. For additional information, see ¶2313.

• *Cook County tax invalidated*

The Illinois Appellate Court affirmed the circuit court, striking down the Cook County Non-Titled Personal Property Use Tax in violation of section 5-1009 of the Counties Code. The County had enacted the tax as a use tax on non-titled personal property to be measured by the "value" of property brought into the County. The County's sales tax, however, was measured by gross receipts or purchase price. The circuit court had concluded that not only did the tax violate Sec. 5-1009 of the Counties Code, which prohibits a home rule county use tax on non-titled personal property measured by gross receipts or purchase price, but also that the tax violated the United State Constitution's Commerce Clause and the Illinois Constitution's prohibition on ad valorem taxes. The Appellate Court did not reach the constitutional questions because it concluded that the issue could be resolved solely by reference to the Counties Code.

The Court held that the distinction provided by the County between the tax being measured by "value" rather than "purchase price" was insufficient, and that the tax was effectively based on "purchase price," thus rendering the tax invalid under the Counties Code. (*Reed Smith LLP and Horwood Marcus & Berk, Chtd. v. Cook County Department of Revenue*, 2014 IL App (1st) 132646-U, August 4, 2014; CCH ILLINOIS TAX REPORTS, ¶ 402-831)

Practitioner Comment: Tax Invalidated on Statutory Grounds

The Cook County Circuit Court invalidated the Non-Titled Personal Property Use Tax on three bases: the tax violated the Commerce Clause of the United States Constitution, the tax was unconstitutional under the Illinois Constitution as an ad valorem tax, and the tax was prohibited by section 5-1009. The Appellate Court, however, avoided the constitutional questions, as it could dispose of the tax simply by concluding that the tax was prohibited by section 5-1009. Although the Appellate Court did not cite to it, the decision reiterates the ruling in *Hornof v. the Kroger Co.*, 35 Ill. 2d 125 (1966), CCH ILLINOIS TAX REPORTS,¶ 200-404, which concluded that without any other measurable difference, "retail value" is the same as "gross receipts" from sales of personal property. Finally, the opinion is marked as a Rule 23 opinion, meaning that it cannot be cited as precedent.

Christopher T. Lutz, Esq., Horwood Marcus & Berk, Chartered

¶2306 Use Tax on Titled Property

Law: Chicago Munic. Code, Secs. 3-28-010—3-28-110 (CCH ILLINOIS TAX REPORTS, ¶ 61-730).

Forms: Form 8400 (use tax); Form BC11 (wheel tax).

The Chicago use tax for titled personal property is imposed upon users of titled personal property that is purchased through a sale at retail from a retailer. The tax is imposed upon the user for the privilege of using the property in the city and is collected by the retailer maintaining a place of business in the city who remits it to the Chicago Department of Revenue (Chicago Munic. Code, Sec. 3-28-030).

In addition to the use tax, a flat-rate wheel tax is imposed on automobiles (see below).

Exemptions: The Chicago use tax does not apply to titled personal property that is used:

— by any corporation, association, foundation, or institution organized and operated exclusively for charitable, religious, or educational purposes or by a governmental body;

— by interstate carriers for hire as rolling stock moving in interstate commerce or by lessors under leases of one year or longer that were in effect at the time of purchase for such use; or

— in Chicago after being acquired outside Illinois and upon which a tax was paid to another state that exceeds an amount allowed as a credit against the Illinois use tax.

Use tax is also not imposed on the use of a motor vehicle by a lessor when the vehicle is to be used for leasing to lessees on a daily or weekly basis for which the lessor is required to pay the Chicago motor vehicle lessor tax.

Basis and rate: The amount of the tax is equal to 1.25% of the "selling price" of property purchased at retail. The definition of "selling price" for Chicago sales tax purposes is substantially similar to the Illinois sales tax definition (¶1605) (Chicago Munic. Code, Sec. 3-28-020).

Definitions: "Retailer" means a person engaged in the business of making retail sales of property titled or registered with a state agency. "Retailer subject to city tax enforcement" means (Chicago Munic. Code, Sec. 3-28-020):

(1) having or maintaining within the city, an office, distribution house, sales house, warehouse, or other place of business or any agent or other representative operating in the city under the retailer's authority;

(2) engaging in soliciting orders in the city by catalogs, advertising, and other means regardless of whether the orders are received or accepted in the city;

(3) a retailer owned or controlled by a person that owns or controls other retailers that are engaged in the same or a similar business in the city; or

(4) owning or possessing real or personal property located or used in the city.

Licensing, returns, and payment: Retailers maintaining a place of business in the city must apply for registration certificates from the Chicago Department of Revenue no later than 30 days after incurring $1,000 or more of tax liability during the immediately preceding 12 months (Chicago Munic. Code, Sec. 3-28-070).

Generally, retailers required or authorized to collect the tax file monthly returns and make payments before the end of each calendar month for transactions occurring the preceding month. Annual returns are required by August 15 reflecting transactions for the 12 months ending or the preceding June 30. (See ¶2313 for more details). A retailer who discontinues business must file a final return no more than one month after discontinuing business. A collection discount of 2% of the amount of tax due is allowed to retailers who timely file returns and make payment (Chicago Munic. Code, Sec. 3-28-050). Provisions concerning quarter-monthly reporting are similar to state use tax provisions (see ¶1802). Purchasers or users who fail to pay the city use tax to a retailer must remit the tax directly to the Department of Revenue. (Chicago Munic. Code, Sec. 3-28-060). The Illinois Department of Revenue has the duty to collect the tax from retailers in Cook, DuPage, Lake, Kane, McHenry, or Will counties (Chicago Munic. Code, Sec. 3-28-036). Other retailers must remit the tax to the Chicago Department of Revenue (Chicago Munic. Code, Sec. 3-28-038).

Beginning in 2016, the City of Chicago requires most taxpayers and tax collectors to file and pay their taxes through the city's online filing program, Webtax. For additional information, see ¶2313.

• *Wheel tax*

Persons who use or register automobiles or other vehicles in Chicago are subject to a wheel tax. Rates include $75 per small automobile, $120 per larger passenger automobiles, $30 per antique automobile, or $45 per motorbicycle, tricycle, or moped (Chicago Munic. Code, Sec. 3-56-050).

¶2307 Amusement Tax

Law: Chicago Munic. Code Secs. 4-156-010—4-156-035, 4-156-060 (CCH ILLINOIS TAX REPORTS, ¶60-230, 61-730).

Forms: Form 7510; Form 7511 (subscribers to paid TV programming); Form 2221 (gambling format amusement machines); Form 2222 (nongambling format amusement machines).

Chicago imposes an amusement tax upon the patrons of any amusements within the city in the amount of 9% of the admission fees or other charges to witness, to view, or to participate in such amusement, where separate fees and charges are imposed for each witnessing, viewing or participation. The basis of the tax excludes federal and state taxes (Chicago Munic. Code, Sec. 4-156-020). The tax includes charges for paid television programming (Chicago Munic. Code, Sec. 4-156-010). A similar 3% tax is imposed by Cook County.

City of Chicago Amusement Tax Ruling #5, effective September 1, 2015, applies the amusement tax to charges paid for the privilege to witness, view or participate in amusements that are delivered electronically. Ruling #5 clarifies that charges paid for the privilege of watching electronically delivered television shows, movies or videos, listening to electronically delivered music, and participating in games online are subject to amusement tax if the shows, movies, videos, music, or games are delivered to a customer in Chicago. Finally, Ruling #5 clarifies that charges apply only to rentals (normally accomplished by streaming or a "temporary" download), not sales.

Mobile devices: Effective October 28, 2015, for the electronic delivery of amusements to mobile devices, such as video streaming, audio streaming and online games, the Illinois Mobile Telecommunications Sourcing Conformity Act rules may be used to determine which customers and charges are subject to the amusement tax. This is stated to be a clarification of existing ordinance rules and not a change in the law. (Chicago Munic. Code, Sec. 4-156-020(G.1))

Practitioner Comment: Amusement Tax or Transaction Tax?

Viewed together, the two rulings, Personal Property Lease Transaction Tax Ruling #12 (discussed at ¶2304) and Amusement Tax Ruling #5, attempt to delineate the contours of when the amusement tax will apply to a certain transaction, and when the transaction tax will apply. The Chicago Department of Revenue (CDOR) has recently attempted to explain when "nonpossessory computer leases" are subject to the Transaction Tax, but Rulings #12 and #5 certainly go further than the CDOR has previously ventured in its explanations.

One issue that remains unclear in the wake of these two new rulings is the extent to which the CDOR will find nexus to exist for a provider that is not located within Chicago. Each of the taxes is technically imposed upon the customer. To the extent a customer located in Chicago enters into transactions subject to either the amusement or transaction taxes, the tax will apply. However, whether the provider will be required to collect remains an open question. The rulings both specifically state that the issue of nexus is beyond the scope of the rulings.

Another obvious issue between these two taxes is which will apply to a particular transaction. Given the significant overlap between the applicability of the transaction tax and the amusement tax to online software and cloud computing services, taxpayers are likely to face confusion over which tax to apply.

In light of these and other concerns, a challenge to the recent rulings is anticipated.

At a minimum, the City of Chicago is expected to institute a *de minimis* exception, largely anticipated to exempt small businesses and start-ups from the ruling.

Christopher T. Lutz, Esq., Horwood Marcus & Berk, Chartered

Reduced rate: The rate of tax is reduced to 5% on tickets for live theatrical, musical, or other live cultural performances at a place in Chicago whose maximum capacity is more than 750 persons. There is no tax for live theatrical, musical, or cultural performances if the capacity is 750 or fewer (Chicago Munic. Code, Sec. 4-156-020).

¶2307

CCH Advisory: Disparate Tax Treatment of Adult Entertainment Cabaret is Lawful

The Illinois Supreme Court held that denying an exemption from the amusement tax imposed by the City of Chicago and Cook County for adult entertainment cabaret, while granting an exemption to other producers of live performances that offer theatrical, musical or cultural enrichment in a space with a maximum capacity of not more than 750 people (small venue exemption), was lawful. See *Pooh-Bah Enterprises, Inc., d/b/a Crazy Horse Too v. County of Cook*, 232 Ill.2d 463 4, March 19, 2009; CCH ILLINOIS TAX REPORTS, ¶401-954.

The taxpayer had alleged that the denial of the exemption violated the First Amendment of the United States Constitution and the free speech clause of the Illinois Constitution. The court disagreed and reasoned that the government may make content-based distinctions when it subsidizes speech. However, once it has chosen to fund an activity, it cannot discriminate based on a viewpoint. Here, despite the small venue exemption, the tax still applied to a wide variety of events. The court found it permissible for the city and county to encourage fine arts at small venues, while excluding adult entertainment from its goal. The court held that an amusement tax that exempts small venue performances — except those defined as adult entertainment cabaret — does not violate the First Amendment because the city and county can make content-based distinctions when it subsidizes speech through tax exemptions.

Ticket brokers and resellers: An additional tax is imposed on persons who sell tickets for theatrics, shows, exhibitions, athletic events and other amusements within Chicago at a place other than the theater or location where the amusement is given or exhibited. The rate of tax is 9% of any service fees or similar charges received by the seller (Chicago Munic. Code, Sec. 4-156-033).

A reseller of tickets is required to collect and remit tax only on the portion of the ticket price that exceeds the original or face amount of the tickets. A ticket reseller is not required to collect and remit amusement tax if the purchaser of such tickets will in turn act as a reseller of the same tickets, provided that the purchaser supplies to the reseller (1) a written verification that the purchaser intends to resell the tickets and (2) the tax registration number issued to the purchaser by the Department of Revenue (Chicago Munic. Code, Sec. 4-156-030).

Permanent seat licenses: The Illinois Appellate Court held that permanent seat licenses (PSL) sold to Chicago Bears fans are subject to the city of Chicago's amusement tax. The court first reasoned that PSLs are part of the total charges that allow the season ticket holder to enter the stadium and to sit in a specific seat. According to the court, acquiring a PSL is effectively an "additional step" to obtain the right to purchase Bears season tickets, and is therefore a personal privilege that carries no vested property rights. In determining whether the sale or purchase of a PSL involves tangible personal property, the court applied an "essence of the transaction" test to determine, and found that the purchase of a PSL is an actual and necessary part of obtaining season tickets. Moreover, the court found that a PSL is inseparable from the privilege of viewing a Bears game as the only intrinsic purpose of purchasing a PSL is to purchase the right to see the game. The court determined that owning a PSL is a prerequisite to purchasing a ticket for a PSL seat. Therefore, admission fees" and "other charges" paid to view the Bears game from that seat shall include both the season ticket price and the PSL fee. (*Stasko v. City of Chicago*, 2013 IL App (1st) 120265, 997 N.E.2d 975 appeal denied, 116848, 2014 WL 487479; CCH ILLINOIS TAX REPORTS, ¶ 402-713)

Mobile TV: Charges for mobile TV service, which allows users to view paid television programming on wireless phones, are subject to the Chicago amusement tax. Users are responsible for paying the tax to their wireless phone service providers, and the providers are responsible for collecting and remitting the tax to the Chicago Department of Revenue. Typically, users are charged a monthly fee for mobile TV service on their wireless phone bill.

The tax is to be remitted monthly with taxes collected in one month payable by the 15th day of the subsequent month. An annual return for the period commencing July 1 and ending June 30 of the subsequent year is due by August 15. Returns and payments can be made by mail, in person, or online.

The Mobile Telecommunications Sourcing Conformity Act, 35 ILCS 638, may be used as the basis for determining which mobile TV customers are subject to the city's amusement tax. This is the same rule used to determine which wireless phone service customers are subject to the city's simplified telecommunications tax. Therefore, customers who are subject to the city's telecommunications tax on their wireless phone service charges are also subject to the city's amusement tax on any charges for mobile TV. (*Informational Bulletin—Chicago Amusement Tax*, Chicago Department of Revenue, March 2009)

On-line auction and consignment websites: Illinois municipalities may not require an Internet auction listing service that resells tickets to entertainment events to collect and remit amusement taxes on resold tickets. The Illinois Supreme Court held that the state has a greater interest than any municipality in regulating this emerging business model and protecting consumers and concluded that municipalities may not require electronic intermediaries to collect and remit amusement taxes on resold tickets. (*City of Chicago v. StubHub*, Illinois Supreme Court, No. 111127, October 6, 2011, CCH ILLINOIS TAX REPORTS,¶ 402-415; affirmed, *City of Chicago v. StubHub, Inc.*, U.S. Court of Appeals, 7th Cir., No. 19-3432, November 23, 2011; *City of Chicago v. eBay, Inc.*, U.S. Court of Appeals, 7th Cir., No. 10-1144, November 23, 2011; CCH ILLINOIS TAX REPORTS,¶ 402-491). The opinion was modified upon rehearing, the Illinois Supreme Court concluding that municipalities may not require electronic intermediaries to collect and remit amusement taxes on resold tickets, because the state of Illinois has a vital interest in regulating online auctioneers and protecting consumers, resulting in Illinois having a greater interest than Chicago in local tax collection by Internet auction services (*City of Chicago v. StubHub, Inc.*, Illinois Supreme Court, No. 111127, November 26, 2012, CCH ILLINOIS TAX REPORTS, ¶ 402-583).

Exemptions: The amusement tax does not apply to patrons of automatic amusement machines, stock shows, business shows not open to the general public, and to any amusement that is sponsored or conducted by, and the proceeds inure exclusively to the benefit of the following (Chicago Munic. Code, Sec. 4-156-020):

(1) religious, educational, and charitable institutions, societies, and organizations;

(2) societies or organizations for the prevention of cruelty to children or animals;

(3) civic improvement societies or organizations;

(4) fraternal organizations, legion posts, social, and political groups sponsored occasionally but not more often than twice a year for no longer than 30 days;

(5) organizations or persons in the armed services of the United States, National Guard, reserve officers' association, or organizations or posts of war veterans, or auxiliary units or societies of such posts if they are organized in Illinois and no part of their earnings benefit any private shareholder or person;

(6) organizations or associations created to benefit the members, dependents, or heirs of members of the police or fire departments of any political subdivision of the state of Illinois; and

(7) symphony orchestras, opera performances, and artistic presentations.

Generally, applications for exemption from the amusement tax must be filed with the Chicago Department of Revenue at least 30 calendar days prior to the amusement or 15 calendar days prior to the date that admission tickets to the amusement are first made available for sale, whichever is earlier (Chicago Munic. Code, Sec. 4-156-020).

An exemption applies to certain amateur events if (1) the amateur event takes place primarily on the public way or other public property, (2) any required permits are obtained, (3) the event, or the organization conducting the event, is open to the public, (4) at least 100 individuals pay to participate in the event, and (5) the event will promote or celebrate the city, its civic institutions, or public activities or events in the city, and will promote the interests and welfare of the city (Sec. 4-156-020(b)(4.1), Chicago Amusement Tax Ordinance).

Returns and payment: Returns for the Chicago amusement tax must be filed annually. Taxpayers or tax collectors must pay or remit the actual amount of tax due on or before the 15th day of the month following the monthly (or quarterly, if applicable) tax period in which the tax liability was incurred (Chicago Munic. Code, Sec. 4-156-030). Certain taxpayers and tax collectors may make estimated payments in lieu of paying or remitting actual amounts due (see below for more details).

Taxpayers or tax collectors with annual tax liabilities of $1,200 or less for the 12-month period immediately preceding must file an annual return and pay or remit the total tax liability for the year with the return, without penalties or interest (Chicago Munic. Code, Sec. 3-4-187).

Beginning in 2016, the City of Chicago requires most taxpayers and tax collectors to file and pay their taxes through the city's online filing program, Webtax. For additional information, see ¶ 2313.

Estimated tax payment option: A taxpayer or tax collector may pay or remit estimated tax amounts for any annual tax return equal to $1/12$th ($1/4$th where applicable) of the taxpayer's or tax collector's total liability for the 12-month period immediately preceding the current annual tax year, and the amount paid needs to be accompanied by a payment or remittance coupon. However, a taxpayer or tax collector may make estimated tax payments only if (Chicago Munic. Code, Sec. 3-4-188):

(1) coupons or returns have been filed and amounts due for the annual return tax have been paid or remitted for the entire 12-month period immediately preceding the applicable annual tax year;

(2) the total tax liability for the immediately preceding annual tax year was less than or equal to $2 million; and

(3) actual liability during any three consecutive calendar months for the 12-month period immediately preceding the annual tax year was less than or equal to 50% of the total annual liability for the entire 12-month period.

Collection, payment, and administration: Tax is collected by ticket sellers and resellers at the time of sale, and must be remitted monthly to the Chicago Department of Revenue, City Hall, 121 North LaSalle Street, Chicago, IL 60602; telephone 312-747-9723.

- *Amusement devices*

The city of Chicago also imposes an annual tax on automatic amusement devices. The annual rate of tax is $150 for nongambling-type automatic amusement devices, and $225 for gambling-type automatic amusement devices (Chicago Munic. Code, Sec. 4-156-160).

¶2308 Alcoholic Beverage, Cigarette, Other Tobacco Products, Soft Drink, and Bottled Water Taxes

Law: Chicago Munic. Code Secs. 3-4-186, 3-4-189, 3-42-020, 3-43-010—3-43-140, 3-44-030, 3-45-010—3-45-140 (CCH Illinois Tax Reports, ¶ 35-008, 60-390, 61-730).

Forms: ST-14; Form 7590 (fountain soft drink tax).

Beginning in 2016, the City of Chicago requires most taxpayers and tax collectors to file and pay their taxes through the city's online filing program, Webtax. For additional information, see ¶ 2313.

• *Liquor tax*

Chicago imposes a liquor tax of (Chicago Municipal Code, Sec. 3-44-030):

— 29¢ per gallon of beer;

— 36¢ per gallon of liquor containing 14% or less alcohol by volume;

— 89¢ per gallon for liquor containing from 14% up to 20% of alcohol by volume; and

— $2.68 per gallon for liquor containing 20% or more alcohol by volume.

Returns: Returns for the Chicago liquor tax must be filed on an "annual return" basis (Chicago Munic. Code Sec. 3-4-186). Taxpayers or tax collectors of these taxes must pay or remit the actual amount of tax due on or before the 15th day of the month following the monthly (or quarterly, if applicable) tax period in which the tax liability was incurred. Certain taxpayers and tax collectors may make estimated payments in lieu of paying or remitting actual amounts due. Taxpayers or tax collectors with annual tax liabilities of $1,200 or less for the 12-month period immediately preceding must file an annual return and pay or remit the total tax liability for the year with the return, without penalties or interest.

Taxpayers and tax collectors that have multiple business sites are required to file a single annual consolidated return for each annual return tax, accompanied by a schedule that reports each business site's tax liability, and a single coupon covering all business sites should be used when paying or remitting taxes (Chicago Munic. Code Sec. 3-4-189).

• *Cigarette tax*

Chicago imposes a cigarette tax at the rate of $.059 per cigarette ($1.18 per pack of 20) (Chicago Municipal Code, Sec. 3-42-020(a)).

Tax on liquid nicotine: Effective January 1, 2016, Chicago imposes a tax on liquid nicotine products, at a rate of $1.25 per product unit, plus an additional 25 cents per fluid milliliter of consumable liquid, gel, or other solution contained in the product. Purchasers are liable for the tax (Chicago Municipal Code, Sec. 3-47-010 *et seq.*).

• *Other tobacco products tax*

Chicago imposes an other tobacco products tax at various rates, as follows:

(1) smoking tobacco, $1.80 per ounce;

(2) smokeless tobacco, $1.80 per ounce;

(3) pipe tobacco, $0.60 per ounce;

(4) little cigars, $0.20 per cigar; and

(5) large cigars, $0.20 per cigar.

(Chicago Municipal Code, Sec. 3-49-030).

On January 20, 2017, the Circuit Court of Cook County found the Chicago Other Tobacco Products Tax was preempted by state law. As of July 1, 1993, the City of Chicago (the "City") imposed taxes on cigarettes but not other tobacco products. On

March 8, 2013, the Illinois General Assembly enacted 65 ILCS 5/8-11-6a(2), which provides that home rule municipalities that had not imposed a tax "based on the number of units of cigarettes or other tobacco products" before July 1, 1993, could not impose "such a tax" after that date. The City enacted the "Chicago Other Tobacco Products Tax" on March 16, 2016, and the taxpayer challenged the ordinance on the basis that it was preempted by state law. (Chi. Mun. Code Ch. 3-49, Sec. 3-49-010, *et seq.*)

The City claimed that the plain language of Section 6a(2) should be read as grandfathering in all tobacco products taxes, not just taxes on cigarettes, because the City imposed a cigarette tax before 1993. However, the court determined that the language "such a tax" is singular because it modifies both "a" cigarette and "a" tobacco tax, separately. As a result, the Circuit Court held that the City's home rule authority to tax other tobacco products is preempted and the Chicago Other Tobacco Products Tax is invalid. (*Ries v. City of Chicago*, Circuit Court of Cook County, No. 2016-L-050356, January 20, 2017)

• *Soft drink tax*

Businesses that sell soft drinks at retail in Chicago must collect and pay the Chicago soft drink tax. The tax is imposed at the rate of 3% of the gross receipts from sales of soft drinks other than fountain soft drinks (Chicago Munic. Code, Sec. 3-45-040; see also *Publication 116*, Illinois Department of Revenue, December 2009, CCH ILLINOIS TAX REPORTS, ¶ 402-125).

"Soft drink" is defined as a non-alcoholic beverage that contains natural or artificial sweeteners. However, the term does not include beverages that contain milk or milk products, soy, rice or similar milk substitutes, or greater than 50% of vegetable or fruit juice by volume. (Chicago Munic. Code, Sec. 3-45-020; *Informational Bulletin FY 2010-01*, Illinois Department of Revenue, July 2009, CCH ILLINOIS TAX REPORTS, ¶ 401-995).

Every soft drink supplier must add the tax to the selling price.

Returns and payment: Retailers who are subject to the tax must file Illinois Form ST-14, Chicago Soft Drink Tax Return, and pay taxes due at the time they file with the Illinois Department of Revenue. The return is due on or before the 20th day of the month following the end of the liability period. Due dates are printed on the return.

Returns must be filed with the Chicago Department of Revenue on an annual basis on or before August 15 of each year.

Fountain soft drinks: There is also a fountain soft drink tax, imposed at the rate of 9% of the cost of syrup. Returns are filed directly with the Chicago Department of Finance (Chicago Munic. Code, Sec. 3-45-060).

• *Bottled water tax*

A tax on the retail sale of bottled water is imposed at the rate of 5¢ per bottle, regardless of the capacity of the bottle. The tax is paid by the purchaser, and it expressly is not a tax on the occupation of retail or wholesale bottled water dealer. The tax is to be collected and remitted by each wholesale bottled water dealer who sells bottles of water to a retail bottled water dealer located in the city (Chicago Munic. Code, Sec. 3-43-010, et seq.).

An Illinois Appellate Court has ruled that Chicago's tax on bottled water is a sales tax on tangible personal property, not an unauthorized home rule unit occupation tax that would violate the Illinois Constitution (*American Beverage Association v. The City of Chicago*, Illinois Appellate Court, No. 1-09-1511, September 23, 2010; CCH ILLINOIS TAX REPORTS, ¶ 402-222).

¶2309 Telecommunications Tax

Law: Chicago Munic. Code Secs. 3-73-010—3-73-140 (CCH ILLINOIS TAX REPORTS, ¶60-720, 61-730).

Forms: Form 7501; Form 7512 (reduced rate); Form 7508 (telecommunications infrastructure maintenance fee).

The Chicago Simplified Telecommunications Tax is imposed upon the act or privilege of originating in Chicago, or receiving in Chicago, intrastate and interstate telecommunications by a person. "Telecommunications" includes, but is not limited to, messages or information transmitted through use of local, toll and wide area telephone service, private line services, channel services, telegraph services, teletypewriter service, computer exchange services, cellular mobile telecommunications services, paging service or any other form of mobile and portable one-way or two-way communications, or any other transmission of messages or information by electronic or similar means, between or among points by wire, cable, fiber optics, laser, microwave, radio, satellite or similar facilities (Chicago Munic. Code, Sec. 3-73-020).

The tax is collected by persons engaged in the business of transmitting, supplying or furnishing telecommunications. The Chicago simplified telecommunications tax does not apply to prepaid calling arrangements.

Termination charges: If a term in a telecommunications service contract obligates the customer to pay a charge in the event of early termination of the contract, that early termination charge is included in the taxable gross charges. The charge is a part of what the customer agrees to pay the retailer in return for the privilege of originating or receiving telecommunications. (*Simplified Telecommunications Tax Ruling* #2, Chicago Department of Revenue, effective May 1, 2009)

Internet access: Digital subscriber line (DSL) services purchased, used, or sold by a provider of Internet access to provide Internet access are not subject to the Chicago telecommunications tax because of preemption by the federal Internet Tax Freedom Act Amendments Act of 2007. DSL services are also no longer subject to the Illinois Telecommunications Tax. However, DSL services purchased, used, or sold by a nonprovider of Internet access will remain subject to Chicago telecommunications tax. (*Information Bulletin No. 3*, Chicago Department of Revenue, July 2008)

Rate of tax: The tax rate is 7% of the gross charges for telecommunications service purchased at retail (Chicago Munic. Code, Sec. 3-73-030).

The E911 surcharge on telecommunications services is $3.90 per line, effective September 1, 2014. The E911 surcharge on sales of prepaid wireless telecommunications services is 7% until December 31, 2020. (*Informational Bulletin FY 2017-19*, Illinois Department of Revenue, July 2017; *Notice of E911 Surcharge Increase*, City of Chicago, July 2014)

Returns and payment: Returns are filed with the Chicago Department of Finance by retailers of telecommunication services on an annual basis, due on or before August 15 of each year.

Retailers may retain a collection allowance of 1% of the collected telecommunications tax (Chicago Munic. Code, Sec. 3-73-040).

Beginning in 2016, the City of Chicago requires most taxpayers and tax collectors to file and pay their taxes through the city's online filing program, Webtax. For additional information, see ¶2313.

Practitioner Comment: Chicago's Franchise Fee on Cable Modem Service is Illegal

The Illinois Supreme Court declared that the City of Chicago's 5% franchise fee on cable modem service was preempted by the Federal Cable Communications Policy Act. *City of Chicago v. Comcast Cable Holdings LLC*, 231 Ill.2d 399 (2008), CCH ILLINOIS TAX REPORTS, ¶401-922.

Prior to 2002, Comcast Cable Holdings LLC and several other cable television providers entered into franchise renewal agreements with the City of Chicago that imposed a 5% franchise fee on the providers' annual gross revenues from cable modem services. In March 2002, the Federal Communications Commission ("FCC") classified cable modem services as an information service, rather than as a cable service. As such, Comcast discontinued the payment of its franchise fee.

The City of Chicago filed suit against Comcast. The Illinois Supreme Court held that the FCC ruling preempts the portion of the parties' agreement the City relies upon to impose a 5% franchise fee on cable operators' cable modem service revenues.

Horwood Marcus & Berk, Chartered

¶2310 Motor Vehicle Lessor Tax

Law: Chicago Munic. Code Secs. 3-48-010—3-48-150 (CCH ILLINOIS TAX REPORTS, ¶60-570, 61-730).

Forms: Form 7575.

A motor vehicle lessor tax is imposed by Chicago on the privilege of leasing motor vehicles within Chicago on a daily or weekly basis. The tax rate is $2.75 per vehicle, per lease transaction. Although the company leasing the vehicle is liable for the tax, the tax may be passed on to the firm's customers as a separate charge on the rental bill or invoice. (Chicago Munic. Code, Sec. 3-48-030)

Payments and returns are due by the 15th day of the month following the month in which the vehicles are leased, and must be physically received by the Chicago Department of Revenue by the due date. Tax returns are also due on an annual basis.

Beginning in 2016, the City of Chicago requires most taxpayers and tax collectors to file and pay their taxes through the city's online filing program, Webtax. For additional information, see ¶2313.

Suburban lessors: Each suburban lessor doing business in Chicago is required, when renting from a location within three miles outside Chicago to a customer who will use the vehicle in the city, either to collect the city lease tax from the customer or to maintain written records supporting the exemption allowed for personal property used primarily (more than 50%) outside the city.

"Doing business" in the city includes, for example, having a location in the city or regularly renting vehicles that are used in the city, such that the company is subject to audit by the Department under state and federal law. Any company unsure as to whether its operations constitute "doing business" in the city may contact the Department for an opinion. (*Personal Property Lease Transaction Tax Ruling #11*, Chicago Department of Revenue, effective July 15, 2009).

Practitioner Comment: Suburban Tax Collection Requirement Upheld

The Illinois Appellate Court reversed the Circuit Court decision in *Hertz v. City of Chicago (formerly, Enterprise Leasing Co of Chicago, LLC v City of Chicago)*, 11 L 50804, Sept. 27, 2012, CCH ILLINOIS TAX REPORTS, ¶402-595, in which the Circuit Court concluded that the city could not require lessors located outside Chicago to collect Chicago tax on leased vehicles when the lessee was a Chicago resident. As part of the City of Chicago's Personal Property Lease Transaction Tax, the city enacted Rule 11 which required lessors located within 3 miles of Chicago's border to collect lease transaction tax when a lessee was a Chicago resident. The ruling provided an exemption for those that would use the vehicle more than 50% outside the city.

In reversing the Circuit Court and upholding Rule 11, the Appellate Court concluded that the treatment was within Chicago's home rule authority, did not exceed the scope of the Ordinance as an extraterritorial tax, and did not implicate the United States Constitution. As of the publication date, the case is pending on appeal with the Illinois Supreme Court. (*Hertz v. City of Chicago*, Appellate Court of Illinois, First District, No. 1-12-3210, 1-12-3211, 41 N.E.3d 574, September 22, 2015, CCH ILLINOIS TAX REPORTS, ¶403-065)

Practitioner Comment: The *Hertz* decision highlights how expansive the City of Chicago's home rule authority is. The appellate court's decision ultimately rested on the conclusion that the City exercised reasonable discretion in enforcing the Transaction Tax when vehicle leases were initiated outside the City. Because the activity in *Hertz* was entirely intrastate in nature, the protections provided by the United States Commerce Clause with respect to interstate transactions were not applicable.

However, notwithstanding the *Hertz* decision, Illinois law remains clear that a locality may not impose an extraterritorial tax. In *City of Carbondale v. Van Natta,* 61 Ill. 2d 483 (1976), for instance, the Illinois Supreme Court explained that the legislative history of the Sixth Illinois Constitutional Convention showed that "the intention was not to confer extraterritorial sovereign or governmental powers directly on home-rule units." (*City of Carbondale,* 61 Ill. 2d at 485)

In *Commercial Nat'l Bank v. Chicago,* 89 Ill. 2d 45 (1981), the Illinois Supreme Court confirmed that the limitation on home rule governmental powers extended to tax, and that the City of Chicago's attempt to tax all receipts associated with the performance of a service when only 50% of the service occurred in Chicago constituted an unlawful "attempt by the city of Chicago to give extraterritorial effect to its ordinance and to tax services that had no connection with the taxing city." (*Commercial Nat'l Bank,* 89 Ill. 2d at 77)

Depending on the outcome of the *Hertz* appeal, while the limit on home rule jurisdictions' authority to impose tax extraterritorially will remain good law, *Hertz* may stand for the proposition that the limitation is not categorical, and that a home rule unit's extraterritorial reach may be valid when it is reasonably calculated to tax transactions that have an apparent connection to the City. Just how meaningful that "reasonableness" limitation will be, however, will likely remain subject to speculation.

Christopher T. Lutz, Esq., Horwood Marcus & Berk Chartered

¶2311 Parking Lot and Boat Mooring Taxes

Law: Chicago Munic. Code Secs. 3-16-030—3-16-040, 4-236-010—4-236-120 (CCH ILLINOIS TAX REPORTS, ¶ 60-570, 61-730).

Forms: Form 7530.

Effective July 1, 2013, Chicago imposes a 20% tax on daily, weekly or monthly charges or fees paid for parking (Chicago Munic. Code, Sec. 4-236-020(d); *Information Bulletin: Chicago Parking Tax,* Chicago Department of Finance, June 2013, CCH ILLINOIS TAX REPORTS,¶ 402-691). The tax on daily parking is reduced to 18% for parking on Saturdays and Sundays. Previously, the parking tax rates were set at $5 per day, $25 per week, and $100 per month. (Chicago Munic. Code, Sec. 4-236-020)

A "charge or fee paid for parking" means the gross amount of consideration for the use or privilege of parking a motor vehicle in or upon any parking lot or garage in Chicago, valued in money, whether received in money or otherwise, including cash, credits, property and services, determined without any deduction for costs or expenses. A "charge or fee paid for parking" does not include parking or other taxes, and specifically excludes separately stated charges that are not for the use or privilege of parking. A separately stated charge that is not optional will be presumed to be part of the parking charge, unless proved otherwise. (Chicago Munic. Code, Sec. 4-236-010)

Effective January 1, 2016, the parking tax does not apply to parking by hospital employees in hospital-owned or operated parking facilities or parking in a lot or garage operated by a person who does not act as the operator of more than three parking spaces in Chicago (Chicago Munic. Code, Sec. 4-236-020(c)). Also, the four vehicle minimum in the definition of "parking lot" and "garage" in the parking tax ordinance is removed.

The tax is collected by parking lot owners and remitted to the city of Chicago by the 30th day of the month following the quarter for which the tax was collected. Returns are due quarterly with payment of the tax. Annual returns must be filed on or before August 15 of each year.

Beginning in 2016, the City of Chicago requires most taxpayers and tax collectors to file and pay their taxes through the city's online filing program, Webtax. For additional information, see ¶2313.

Cook County: The tax rates imposed on daily parking fees in excess of $3 range from 50¢ to $1, the tax rates on weekly parking fees in excess of $15 range from $2.50 to $5, and the tax rates on monthly parking fees in excess of $60 range from $10 to $20. The rate of tax is computed exclusive of any federal, state, or municipal taxes imposed (Cook County Parking Lot and Garage Operations Tax Ordinance Sec. 3).

• *Chicago boat mooring tax*

A tax is imposed on the mooring or docking of any watercraft for a fee in, or on, a harbor, river, or other body of water within the corporate limits or jurisdiction of the city. The person who pays the mooring or docking fee is liable for the boat mooring tax. The rate of tax is 7% of the mooring or docking fee (Chicago Munic. Code, Sec. 3-16-030). All Chicago mooring and docking facilities are responsible for collecting and remitting the tax to the Department (*Informational Bulletin, Vol. 9, No. 1,* Chicago Department of Revenue, March 2006, CCH ILLINOIS TAX REPORTS, ¶401-655).

Beginning in 2016, the City of Chicago requires most taxpayers and tax collectors to file and pay their taxes through the city's online filing program, Webtax. For additional information, see ¶2313.

The tax does not apply to the mooring or docking of any watercraft owned by a governmental body or any person, activity, or privilege that may not be taxed by Chicago under the constitution of the United States or Illinois (generally, watercraft engaged in interstate commerce). (Chicago Munic. Code, Sec. 3-16-040).

¶2312 Airport Departure and Ground Transportation Taxes

Law: 70 ILCS 210/13; Chicago Munic. Code Secs. 3-46-010—3-46-110 (CCH ILLINOIS TAX REPORTS, ¶60-740, 61-730).

Forms: Form 8500 (airport departure); Form 7595 (ground transportation).

The Metropolitan Pier and Exposition Authority is authorized to impose a tax upon all persons, other than a governmental agency, engaged in the business of providing ground transportation for hire to airline passengers in the Chicago metropolitan area. The rate is $4 per taxi or livery vehicle departure with passengers for hire from commercial service airports in the metropolitan area. For each departure with passengers for hire from a commercial service airport in the metropolitan area in a bus or van operated by a person other than a person regulated by the Illinois Commerce Commission, the rates are as follows (70 ILCS 210/13):

1—12 passengers	$18
13—24 passengers	36
25 and more passengers	54

For each departure with passengers for hire from a commercial service airport in the metropolitan area in a bus or van operated by a person regulated by the Interstate Commerce Commission or Illinois Commerce Commission, operating scheduled service from the airport and charging fares on a per passenger basis, the rate of tax is $1 per passenger for hire in each bus or van. "Commercial service airports" means those airports receiving scheduled passenger service and enplaning more than 100,000 passengers per year (70 ILCS 210/13).

Chicago also imposes a tax on all persons engaged in the occupation of providing ground-transportation vehicles for use in Chicago. The incidence of the tax and the obligation to pay the tax are on the license holder of the vehicle. The rates are as follows (Chicago Munic. Code, Sec. 3-46-030):

Ground-transportation vehicles	Per day
Taxicabs	$3.00
Vehicles other than taxicabs (seating 1 to 10)	3.50
Vehicles other than taxicabs (seating 11 to 24)	6.00
Vehicles other than taxicabs (seating more than 24)	9.00

Persons who are subject to this tax and are either the lessor or lessee of a ground-transportation vehicle are not subject to the motor vehicle lessor tax (¶ 2310). Persons who lease a ground-transportation vehicle from a license holder who is subject to this tax are exempt from the Chicago personal property lease transaction tax. (¶ 2304)

The following uses of a ground-transportation vehicle are exempt from the tax (Chicago Munic. Code, Sec. 3-46-060):

(1) the transportation of students to or from school-related activities or events;

(2) use by a nonprofit organization to the extent that the vehicle is used solely for the purposes for which the organization is dedicated;

(3) use of a vehicle that is provided by a person to a nonprofit organization or a governmental body to the extent the vehicle is used solely for nonprofit or governmental purposes and the applicable consideration is billed to and paid directly by the nonprofit or governmental body and not by any of the passengers;

(4) use of a vehicle in a ridesharing arrangement; and

(5) use of a vehicle that may not be taxed pursuant to the federal ICC Termination Act of 1995 (P.L. 104-88, Sec. 14505, 109 Stat 803, 904).

Practitioner Comment: Interstate Passengers

The Illinois Appellate Court upheld the constitutionality of the airport transit tax on ground transportation even when such transportation services are provided to passengers with destinations outside Illinois (*Tri-State Coach Lines, Inc. v. Metropolitan Pier and Exposition Authority*, 315 Ill. App. 3d 179 (2000), CCH ILLINOIS TAX REPORTS, ¶ 401-155).

Horwood Marcus & Berk Chartered

Returns and payment: Returns are filed on an annual basis, on or before August 15 of each year. Taxpayers or tax collectors must pay or remit the actual amount of tax due on or before the 15th day of the month following the monthly (or quarterly, if applicable) tax period in which the tax liability was incurred. Certain taxpayers and tax collectors may make estimated payments in lieu of paying or remitting actual amounts due.

Beginning in 2016, the City of Chicago requires most taxpayers and tax collectors to file and pay their taxes through the city's online filing program, Webtax. For additional information, see ¶ 2313.

¶ 2313 Administration of Chicago Taxes

Law: Chicago Munic. Code Secs. 3-4-100, 3-4-151, 3-4-152, 3-4-186—3-4-190, 3-4-265, 3-4-300, 3-4-305 (CCH ILLINOIS TAX REPORTS, ¶ 61-740).

Chicago taxes are administered by the Chicago Department of Revenue, City Hall, 121 North LaSalle Street, Chicago, IL 60602. The Department may be reached by telephone at 312-747-9723 (TTY 312-744-2975). The Department also maintains a website at **http:/www.cityofchicago.org/Revenue**.

The Chicago business taxpayers assistance ordinance prescribes procedures applicable to Chicago taxes and requires that the Chicago Department of Revenue provide certain information to taxpayers.

Taxpayers' rights: The Chicago Department of Revenue must furnish a written statement of rights to every taxpayer or tax collector issued a notice of tax assessment and determination, tax bill, or denial of a claim for credit and a brief written explanation of all tax liabilities and penalties on or with every tax notice issued (Chicago Munic. Code, Sec. 3-4-151). The Department must also maintain a Problems Resolution Committee, designed to resolve complex administrative problems, expedite matters when unreasonable delays have occurred, ensure that taxpayers' rights are protected, and give priority to time-sensitive inquiries or cases of an urgent nature. In addition, the Department has established a Financial Hardship Committee to consider abatements of tax, interest, or penalties in certain cases (Chicago Munic. Code, Sec. 3-4-152).

Voluntary disclosure program: The Department must make available written guidelines setting forth the terms and conditions of its voluntary disclosure program, which allows taxpayers and tax collectors to self-assess and pay outstanding tax liabilities in exchange for a waiver of penalties (Chicago Munic. Code, Sec. 3-4-265).

Right to protest: A written protest must be filed within 35 days after issuance of the tax determination and assessment. However, if a written protest is not filed within 35 days, the taxpayer may nonetheless obtain a hearing if the taxpayer pays, under protest, the tax and interest stated in the assessment and files a written protest within 30 days after the Department has issued to the taxpayer a written notice that the 35-day period has expired (Chicago Munic. Code, Sec. 3-4-330).

Liens: To secure payment of any final assessment of any tax, interest, or penalty due from a final assessee, a lien may be imposed upon all the assessee's real and personal property located or found within the city of Chicago, including all real or personal property acquired after the date on which any final assessment was issued; however, no city tax lien is effective against any bona fide purchaser for value of an item purchased in the usual and ordinary course of business from a person's stock in trade (Chicago Munic. Code, Sec. 3-4-300).

Liens, filed upon the property to be encumbered, are filed as follows (Chicago Munic. Code, Sec. 3-4-300):

(a) For real property, with the Registrar of Titles or the Recorder of Deeds of Cook County;

(b) For personal property, with the Recorder of Deeds of Cook County and with the Secretary of State of the State of Illinois.

At least 10 days prior to filing a lien, the Chicago Department of Revenue must give notice of its intent to file the lien. Any liens improperly recorded by the Department must be removed, and the Department must make every reasonable effort to correct the affected party's credit record. If a taxpayer or tax collector demonstrates reasonable reliance upon erroneous written information or advice from the Department or corporation counsel, the Director must abate any taxes, interest, or penalties resulting from the erroneous information or advice.

Statute of limitations: A six-year statute of limitations has been established for those taxpayers who fail to file a return or fail to pay at least 75% of the tax due (Chicago Munic. Code, Sec. 3-4-120). A three-year statute of limitations applies to responsible officer and employee liability. (Chicago Munic. Code, Sec. 3-4-270) A four-year period for refund applications applies, unless the specific tax ordinance provides otherwise (*i.e.,* the Chicago amusement tax provides for a one-year period). (Chicago Munic. Code, Sec. 3-4-120).

Application of payments: Payments for a tax period are applied first to the interest due for that period, then to the tax due for the period, and then to the penalties for the period. Any excess (monthly or quarterly) payments will be applied to any future liabilities that may become due during the annual tax year.

Annual returns: Annual return taxes must be paid on or before the 15th day following the end of the monthly or quarterly tax period in which the tax liability arose. For taxpayers that pay Chicago annual return taxes using the estimated tax payment option, the estimated taxes must be paid on or before the 15th day following the end of each calendar month. (Chicago Munic. Code Secs. 3-4-187 and 3-4-188)

Taxpayers or tax collectors with annual tax liabilities of $1,200 or less for the 12-month period immediately preceding must file an annual return and pay or remit the total tax liability for the year with the return, without penalties or interest. An annual return for Chicago local taxes must be filed on or before August 15 of each year, covering the 12-month period ending the immediately preceding June 30. The local taxes include: amusement tax, distribution of electricity tax, distribution of gas tax, electricity use tax, electricity infrastructure maintenance fee, emergency telephone system surcharge, emergency telephone fee (wireless), employers' expense tax, fountain soft drink tax, bottled water tax, ground transportation tax, hotel accommodation tax, liquor tax, motor vehicle lessor tax, parking lot and garage operations tax, personal property lease transactions tax, telecommunications tax, and telecommunications infrastructure maintenance fee.

Certain taxpayers and tax collectors may make estimated payments in lieu of paying or remitting actual amounts due (see below for more details).

CCH Advisory: Online Filing

Effective January 1, 2016, for taxes administered by the Chicago Department of Finance, tax collectors and taxpayers generally must file their tax returns through the department's website (https://webapps.cityofchicago.org/TaxWeb/), and all transfer tax declarations must be made through MyDec (https://mytax.illinois.gov/MyDec/_/).

The mandate does not apply to the sale of stamps, stickers, and decals; the automatic amusement device tax; or the cigarette tax. In relation to the electronic filing mandate, the department discusses web-based applications for real property transfer declarations and other city taxes; use of city computers; late filing and payment penalties; and waiver of the mandatory web filing requirement. (*Uniform Revenue Procedures Ordinance Ruling #5*, Chicago Department of Finance, December 8, 2015, CCH ILLINOIS TAX REPORTS, ¶ 403-074)

Consolidated returns and payments: Taxpayers and tax collectors that have multiple business sites are required to file a single annual consolidated return for each annual return tax, accompanied by a schedule that reports each business site's tax liability, and a single coupon covering all business sites should be used when paying or remitting taxes.

Penalties and interest: The late filing or late payment penalties are 5%. However, if a taxpayer or tax collector fails to file an annual return within the time or in the manner required by the annual return ordinance, then a late filing penalty will apply and be equal to the greater of 1% of the total tax due, up to a maximum of $5,000, for the applicable annual tax year or 5% of any amount payable with the annual return. An additional 25% penalty is imposed if the taxpayer or tax collector negligently or willfully failed to pay or remit the tax. Further, an additional 50% penalty is imposed for failure to remit tax collected by a business from its patrons but not remitted by the due date to the city of Chicago.

The late-filing penalty applies to incomplete returns, even if they are filed by the due date. However, the penalty can be waived for an amended return that was incomplete due only to a lack of a signature if the taxpayer provides a signature within 30 days.

¶2313

A penalty of 12% per year in interest applies to all late or insufficient payments made for taxes due and owing. Interest, at the rate of 1% per month, continues to accrue until all payments are made in full.

Estimated tax payment option: A taxpayer or tax collector may pay or remit estimated tax amounts for any annual tax return equal to $1/12$th ($1/4$th where applicable) of the taxpayer's or tax collector's total liability for the 12-month period immediately preceding the current annual tax year, and the amount paid needs to be accompanied by a payment or remittance coupon. However, a taxpayer or tax collector may make estimated tax payments only if:

(1) coupons or returns have been filed and amounts due for the annual return tax have been paid or remitted for the entire 12-month period immediately preceding the applicable annual tax year;

(2) the total tax liability for the immediately preceding annual tax year was less than or equal to $2 million; and

(3) actual liability during any three consecutive calendar months for the 12-month period immediately preceding the annual tax year was less than or equal to 50% of the total annual liability for the entire 12-month period.

¶2314 Vehicle Fuel Tax and Tire Fee

Law: Chicago Munic. Code Secs. 3-52-020, 3-52-040, 11-4-142 (CCH ILLINOIS TAX REPORTS, ¶ 40-012, 60-570, 61-730).

Forms: Form 7577 (Vehicle Fuel Tax).

A tax is imposed by Chicago on the privilege of purchasing or using in Chicago vehicle fuel purchased at retail. The tax rate is 5¢ per gallon of vehicle fuel. The vehicle fuel tax is imposed upon the purchaser or user of vehicle fuel and is collected by each vehicle fuel distributor or dealer doing business in Chicago.

Registration: Every vehicle fuel distributor doing business in Chicago is required to register with the Chicago Department of Revenue within 30 days of starting business. Any retail dealer, purchaser, or user who is required to remit the tax directly to the city on a frequently recurring basis shall register with the Department.

CCH Advisory: Fuel for Use Outside of Chicago

An automobile manufacturer subjected itself to the Chicago fuel tax when it put gasoline or diesel fuel into the tanks of new automobiles in the city, even though most of the fuel was shipped to automobile dealers and was consumed outside the city. The city ordinance unambiguously defined a taxable "use" of fuel as including the receipt of vehicle fuel by any person into a fuel supply tank of a vehicle. Although the manufacturer was a registered fuel distributor under the terms of the ordinance, it was making "use" of the fuel, regardless of where or when the fuel was ultimately burned to operate the new vehicles or where or when the vehicles were delivered or sold to a dealership. The ordinance defined "sale at retail" in part as any sale to a person for that person's use or consumption and not for resale to another, and, consequently, the manufacturer participated in a series of sales at retail and became liable for the tax. The fact that it dispensed fuel into the individual vehicle tanks precluded claims by the manufacturer for exemptions from the tax. (*Ford Motor Co. v. Chicago Department of Revenue*, Appellate Court of Illinois, First District, No. 1-13-0597, June 27, 2014, CCH ILLINOIS TAX REPORTS, ¶ 402-817)

Exemptions: The following sales are exempt: (1) sales by a distributor to another distributor holding a valid registration certificate; (2) sales by a distributor to a distributor or retailer of vehicle fuel whose place of business is outside Chicago and who will use the fuel for purposes other than for propulsion or operation of a vehicle;

(3) the sale to or use by any "transportation agency" that is subsidized or operated by the Regional Transportation Authority or its Service Boards; and (4) the sale or use to the extent that the tax imposed would violate the Illinois or United States Constitution.

Air common carriers are exempt from the Chicago vehicle fuel tax for the sale or use of fuel purchased at retail for qualifying flights to a destination outside the United States (*Vehicle Fuel Tax Ruling #1*, Chicago Department of Finance, May 8, 2014, CCH Illinois Tax Reports,¶ 402-802).

Returns and payments: Returns are filed on an annual basis. Taxpayers or tax collectors must pay or remit the actual amount of tax due on or before the 15th day of the month following the monthly (or quarterly, if applicable) tax period in which the tax liability was incurred. Certain taxpayers and tax collectors may make estimated payments in lieu of paying or remitting actual amounts due. See ¶ 2313 for further details.

Beginning in 2016, the City of Chicago requires most taxpayers and tax collectors to file and pay their taxes through the city's online filing program, Webtax. For additional information, see ¶ 2313.

• *Chicago tire fee*

Persons selling new tires at retail or offering new tires for retail sale in the City of Chicago must collect from purchasers a Chicago tire fee (Chicago Munic. Code Sec. 11-4-142). The fee applies exclusively to tires to be used for vehicles, aircraft, special mobile equipment, and implements of husbandry. The fee is applicable in instances where tires are sold separately and not in conjunction with the sale of a motor vehicle (*Release*, Chicago Department of Revenue, August 2005, CCH Illinois Tax Reports, ¶ 401-563).

Rate: The fee is $1 per new tire. A collection allowance of 4¢ per tire may be retained by the seller.

Exemptions: The Chicago tire fee does not apply to (1) used tires, (2) reprocessed tires, or (3) mail order sales. A reprocessed tire is a tire that has been recapped, retreaded, or regrooved and that has not been placed on a wheel rim. If a tire is 100% replaced under a manufacturer's warranty or road hazard warranty, no fee is applied because such an exchange is not a sale at retail. However, a full fee applies in the case of a pro-rata replacement, because the customer pays something, making the transaction a sale at retail. Sales tax does not apply to the tire fee.

Returns: The Chicago tire fee must be remitted monthly and is due by the last day of the month following collection. An annual fee return for the period commencing July 1 and ending June 30 of the subsequent year is due by August 15 of each year.

¶2315 Hotel Accommodation Tax

Law: Chicago Munic. Code Secs. 3-24-010 *et seq.* (CCH Illinois Tax Reports, ¶ 60-480, 61-730).

Forms: Form 7520.

A tax of 4.5% is imposed on gross rental or lease charges made by a guest to a hotel, motel, inn, apartment hotel, lodging house, or dormitory for accommodations in the city of Chicago. A 4% shared housing surcharge will be imposed on vacation rentals or shared housing units in Chicago, effective July 1, 2016. The tax and surcharge are collected by the operator and paid over to the Chicago Department of Revenue on a monthly basis.

Exemptions: The tax does not apply to accommodations that provide fewer than 10 rooms.

An exemption is allowed for hotel accommodations that are a tenant's domicile and permanent residence.

Returns and payment: The tax is due on the 15th day of the calendar month following the month in which receipts are received. Returns are filed on an annual basis due on or before August 15.

Beginning in 2016, the City of Chicago requires most taxpayers and tax collectors to file and pay their taxes through the city's online filing program, Webtax. For additional information, see ¶2313.

Cook County: Effective May 1, 2016, Cook County imposes a tax on the use of any hotel accommodations in Cook County at the rate of 1% of the gross rental or leasing charges.

Practitioner Comment: City of Chicago v. Expedia, Inc., 2017 IL App (1st) 153402 (Ill. App. Ct. 1st Dist. Apr. 26, 2017) (vacated)

On April 26, 2017, the Illinois Appellate Court considered whether the convenience or service fees collected by online travel companies ("OTCs") such as Expedia are subject to the City of Chicago Hotel Accommodations Tax ("CHAT") as a "gross rental or leasing charge." (*City of Chicago v. Expedia, Inc.,* 2017 IL App (1st) 153402) The taxpayers charged a total price consisting of four elements: (1) net rate set by the hotel; (2) OTC's facilitation fee; (3) tax recovery charge; and (4) defendant's OTC's service or convenience fee. The Appellate Court entered an Opinion holding that the convenience fees the OTCs charged customers were not for "the right to occupy hotel rooms," and therefore did not constitute a gross rental or leasing charge.

On May 8, 2017, however, the parties filed a Joint Motion to Vacate Decision on the basis that the parties reached a final and binding settlement of the dispute on April 25, 2017, which was prior to the Appellate Court's decision. In accordance with the parties' Joint Motion, on May 16, 2017 the Appellate Court withdrew the Opinion.

Although the vacated Opinion is frustrating for OTCs because the decision is no longer binding precedent, there is a silver lining for taxpayers. The Appellate Court's Opinion sets forth the posture of the court if a similarly situated taxpayer were to bring forth a similar challenge to the tax. Further, although the Appellate Court's stance on convenience fees is set forth in the context of the CHAT, their rationale is likely applicable to other similarly structured Chicago ordinances, such as the Chicago Amusement Tax.

Samantha K. Breslow, Esq., Horwood Marcus & Berk Chartered

CCH Advisory: Fees Charged by Online Travel Companies Are Taxable

The U.S. District Court for the Northern District of Illinois held that a 7% hotel tax imposed by the village of Rosemont, Illinois, on the full room rental fees charged by online travel companies (OTCs) is a valid use tax, and it does not violate the dormant Commerce Clause of the U.S. Constitution. The court first found that the OTCs were "owners" for purposes of the local hotel tax ordinance because customers could not access their hotel rooms until paying the room charge to the OTCs, not the hotels. An "owner" includes a person who receives consideration for the rental of a hotel or motel room. The court then held that the full rental fees paid by the customers to the OTCs, not just the charges paid by the OTCs to the hotels, were taxable.

OTCs charged Rosemont customers a room rental fee that included (1) the amounts that the hotels charged the OTCs, and (2) the OTCs' markup on the hotels' charges. The ordinance intended to tax the amount paid by customers to occupy a hotel room in Rosemont. OTCs' customers paid the OTCs' charges for the right to occupy hotel rooms in Rosemont. The court held that the OTCs' facilitation of travel-related services was incidental to the rental of hotel rooms, and that the hotel tax was a use tax. Illinois law establishes that a tax on hotel room rentals is a use tax, not an impermissible sales (occupation) tax. Services generally are not subject to sales tax.

In response to an argument made by the OTCs, the court found that the hotel tax did not violate the dormant Commerce Clause. First, the OTCs had nexus with Illinois because:

(1) the tax was levied for the right to use a hotel room in Illinois,

(2) the tax was paid by the person who uses the room, and

(3) the OTCs entered into contracts with hotels in Illinois for the right to market, facilitate, and book reservations and they profit from such reservations.

Second, the tax was fairly apportioned because it is imposed on a use that can occur in only one place. Third, the tax does not discriminate against interstate commerce as it is applied at the same rate to every hotel reservation in Rosemont. Finally, the tax is related to Illinois services because the renting person has the advantage of the state's police and fire protection, for example, while staying in Illinois. (*The Village of Rosement v. Priceline.com, Inc.*, U.S. District Court, N.D. Illinois, No. 09 C 4438, October 14, 2011; CCH Illinois Tax Reports, ¶ 402-417)

For additional information, see *Village of Bedford Park v. Expedia, Inc.*, U.S. District Court, N.D. Illinois, No. 13 C 5633, June 20, 2016, CCH Illinois Tax Reports, ¶ 403-109.

Practitioner Comment: City of Chicago v. Hotels.com, No. 2005 L 051003

The Cook County Circuit Court ruled in favor of the City of Chicago, holding that online travel booking sites are required to collect Chicago Hotel Accommodation Tax ("CHAT") on the rental rate of a particular room, rather than the rate collected by a particular hotel. Defendants argued that because the rate they charged to customers included service fees, and other costs not necessarily related to the hotels, that the tax should be imposed on the lower "net rate." The City, however, contended that the tax should be imposed on the gross charge, which included the charges imposed by the websites facilitating the sale of hotel rooms.

Interpreting the language regarding "gross receipts," the court found that CHAT applies to the higher Room Rental Rate. The court noted that if CHAT applied only to the Net Rate, which is unknown to customers, they would be unaware of tax obligations. Next, the court found that pursuant to the statute the defendants are owners, operators, or managers of hotel accommodations, and are "tax collectors" for the purpose of CHAT. Noting its previous findings, the court held that because defendants had collected CHAT on the Net Rate and not the Room Rental Rate, they had failed to properly collect taxes under CHAT. Moreover, the defendants improperly combined travel service fees into one lump sum, thus making it impossible for the tax liability to be evident. The court concluded that such impropriety amounted to a breach of fiduciary duty to the taxpayers incapable of delineating their tax liability.

In recent years heated legal disputes have arisen between states and local jurisdictions and online travel companies ("OTCs") over the taxable base for the rental of hotel rooms. The focus of the debate is whether or not the OTCs are responsible for collecting local hotel occupancy taxes on the retail price OTCs charge their customers as opposed to the wholesale price the OTCs negotiate with hotels. The core of this dispute seems to turn on whether OTCs "rent, lease or let for consideration" hotel space and whether they are considered "the person receiving the consideration for the lease or rental," so that they would be covered by each respective ordinance or statute. OTCs claim that under the structure of the current laws, hotel taxes are only due on the "wholesale" rate that the OTCs pay hotels, not the higher marked-up "Retail rate" that they charge their customers. OTCs maintain that they are not renting rooms but rather are acting as "intermediaries" between the hotels and the consumers, so that the mark-up margin that they charge the consumer is more of a commission; and therefore, are not subject to the hotel or occupancy taxes. Amid the growing number of legal battles, the states and local municipalities believe that they are being short-changed on hotel occupancy taxes because they are working with outdated statutes and ordinances that have not evolved with e-business. States and local jurisdictions argue that they are working with pre-Internet law containing ambiguous definitions of "accommodations intermediaries," or "hotel operator." Despite this disconnect between the laws as they currently stand and the business models of the OTCs, states and local jurisdictions are still trying to force the business model of the OTCs into the old statutes and ordinances in order to force revenue generation into the old statutes. Given the current economic environment and the need to increase revenue both the states and local municipalities are becoming aggressive in their pursuit of OTCs. Chicago is another municipality that has been successful in its attempts.

Breen M. Schiller, Esq., Horwood Marcus & Berk, Chartered

¶2316 Electricity and Gas Use Taxes

Law: Chicago Munic. Code Secs. 3-53-020, 3-41-050 (CCH ILLINOIS TAX REPORTS, ¶61-730, 80-008).

Forms: Form 7574 (gas use tax); 7577 (electricity use tax).

The Chicago electricity use tax is imposed upon residential customers for the privilege of using or consuming electricity acquired in a purchase at retail and used or consumed in the city. The rate of tax varies with the number of kilowatt hours consumed.

Chicago also imposes a tax at the rate of 6.3¢ per therm on the use or consumption of gas that is purchased in a retail sale. The retail purchaser is responsible for paying the tax to a public utility designated as Chicago's collection agent. The gas use tax does not apply to the use or consumption of gas by a governmental body, a person purchasing the gas for use as vehicle fuel, or a public utility engaged in the business of distributing gas.

Returns and payment: The electricity and gas use taxes collected by public utilities are payable to the city of Chicago annually by August 15. For the gas use tax, a collection allowance may be retained in the amount of 3% of the tax collected. There is no collection allowance for the electricity use tax.

Beginning in 2016, the City of Chicago requires most taxpayers and tax collectors to file and pay their taxes through the city's online filing program, Webtax. For additional information, see ¶2313.

¶2317 Restaurant Tax

Law: Chicago Munic. Code Secs. 3-30-020—3-30-050 (CCH ILLINOIS TAX REPORTS, ¶60-390).

Chicago imposes a 0.25% tax on the selling price of food and beverages sold at retail by places for eating located in Chicago. A "place for eating" means any restaurant or other business, by whatever name, that is engaged in the sale of food prepared for immediate consumption and provides for on-premises consumption of the food it sells.

A bulletin clarifies which businesses and transactions are subject to the tax on restaurants and other places for eating. The bulletin discusses establishments subject to the tax, carry out and delivery orders, exempt sales, alcohol sales, and catering sales. (*Information Bulletin—Chicago Restaurant Tax*, Chicago Department of Revenue, Vol. 2009, No. 2, March 2009)

Exemptions: Chicago exempts all sales of food and beverage that are exempt from the Illinois Retailers' Occupation Tax (ROT).

Occasional or de minimis sales: A place for eating with an annual tax liability of $200 or less is not required to file a return or pay the restaurant tax. However, this exception is not available to places for eating that separately state and charge tax to customers during the tax year.

Returns and payment: Places for eating subject to the restaurant tax must pay or remit the actual amount of tax due on or before the 15th day of the month following the monthly (or quarterly, if applicable) tax period in which the tax liability was incurred. Certain taxpayers and tax collectors may make estimated payments in lieu of paying or remitting actual amounts due. Returns must be filed on an annual basis on or before August 15 of each year.

Beginning in 2016, the City of Chicago requires most taxpayers and tax collectors to file and pay their taxes through the city's online filing program, Webtax. For additional information, see ¶2313.

¶2318 Cook County Sweetened Beverage Tax

Law: Cook County Ordinance No. 16-5931 (CCH ILLINOIS TAX REPORTS, ¶60-390).

Cook County adopted the Sweetened Beverage Tax under Cook County Ordinance No. 16-5931 ("Ordinance"). The Ordinance is effective March 1, 2017 and levies the tax beginning on July 1, 2017. The tax is levied at a rate of $0.01 per ounce on the retail sale of all sweetened beverages in Cook County. (Cook County Code Sec. 74-852(a)). Although the "ultimate incidence of and liability for payment of the tax" is on the retailer purchaser of the sweetened beverage, distributors must collect the tax from the retailer when the distributor sells the sweetened beverages, syrup and/or powder to a retailer or purchaser in Cook County. (Cook County Code Sec. 74-852)

Practitioner Comment: Validity of tax questioned

On June 27, 2017 the Illinois Retail Merchants Association and other retailers in Cook County filed a lawsuit seeking injunctive relief and a declaratory judgment on the grounds that the tax violates the uniformity clause of the Illinois Constitution and is unconstitutionally vague in violation of the Due Process Clause of the Illinois Constitution. The Circuit Court of Cook County, Illinois issued a Temporary Restraining Order of the sweetened beverage tax on June 30, 2017. The Temporary Restraining Order, however, was dissolved effective July 28, 2017, and the tax was levied in Cook County beginning August 2, 2017. At the time of publication, the lawsuit is pending.

Justin B. Stone, Esq., Horwood Marcus & Berk Chartered

¶2319 Chicago Checkout Bag Tax

Law: Chicago Municipal Code Secs. 3-50-010-140

Effective February 1, 2017, the City of Chicago imposes the "Checkout Bag Tax" on the retail sale or use of checkout bags in Chicago at a rate of $0.07. A "checkout bag" means a paper carryout bag or a plastic carryout bag. The Checkout Bag Tax does not apply to bags that are intended to: (1) package loose bulk items, such as fruit, vegetables, nuts, grains, candy, cookies or small hardware items, (2) contain or wrap frozen foods; (3) contain or wrap flowers or other damp items; (4) segregate food or merchandise that could damage or contaminate other food or merchandise when placed together in a bag; (5) contain unwrapped prepared foods or bakery goods; (6) contain prescription drugs; or (7) contain food or drink provided by a dine-in or take-out restaurant.

The tax is to be paid to by the user, but is collected by the store where the bag is sold and remitted to the wholesale checkout bag dealer. In remitting the tax to a wholesaler, a store is allowed a credit of $0.02 per checkout bag. Additionally, the store must separately state the tax on the receipt provided to the customer at the time of sale as the "Checkout Bag Tax." All tax returns shall be filed with the Chicago Department of Finance an annual basis on or before August 15 of each year.

Practitioner Comment: Will tax burden fall to store owners?

Although the incidence of the tax is on the user or purchaser of the checkout bags, there is a concern that the store will ultimately bear the burden of the cost of bags that are defective or damaged. Although the ordinance allows for a $0.02 credit per checkout bag, it is possible that this allowance will not be sufficient to cover the full amount of the runoff. Accordingly, if the burden of the tax falls to the store owners, the tax may function as an impermissible tax on occupations that is worthy of a taxpayer challenge.

Samantha K. Breslow, Esq., Horwood Marcus & Berk Chartered

PART X
ADMINISTRATION AND PROCEDURE
CHAPTER 24
ILLINOIS ADMINISTRATION AND PROCEDURE

¶2401 Authority of Department of Revenue

Law: 20 ILCS 2505/65, 20 ILCS 2505/250, 20 ILCS 2505/275, 20 ILCS 2505/300, 20 ILCS 2505/305, 20 ILCS 2505/315, 20 ILCS 2505/500, 20 ILCS 2505/605, 20 ILCS 2505/620, 20 ILCS 2505/700, 20 ILCS 2505/705, 20 ILCS 2505/795, 20 ILCS 2520/1; 2 Ill. Adm. Code 1200.110—1200.130 (CCH ILLINOIS TAX REPORTS, ¶ 89-058, 89-060, 89-064).

Most Illinois taxes are administered and collected by the Department of Revenue. Taxes administered by the Department include the following:

• *Income taxes*
  — income tax;
  — personal property replacement tax; and
  — employers withholding income tax.

• *Sales and use taxes*
  — retailers' occupation tax;
  — service occupation tax;
  — use tax;
  — service use tax;
  — automobile renting occupation and use taxes;
  — replacement vehicle taxes;
  — tire user fee;
  — vehicle use tax; and
  — privilege tax on cultivation of medical cannabis.

• *Excise and utilities taxes*
  — cigarette and cigarette use tax;
  — dry-cleaning solvent taxes and license fees;
  — gaming taxes;
  — hotel operators' occupation tax;
  — liquor taxes;
  — motor fuel and motor fuel use taxes;
  — public utilities revenue tax; and
  — tobacco product tax.

• *Other taxes and programs*
  — Circuit breaker and pharmaceutical assistance;
  — coin-operated amusement device and redemption machine tax;
  — hydraulic fracturing tax;

— Compassionate Use of Medical Cannabis Pilot Program;

— property tax; and

— taxes collected for local governments.

• *Scope of authority*

In carrying out its responsibilities, the Department is authorized to do the following:

— require the production of books, papers, and documents pertinent to any tax assessment, levy, investigation, inquiry, or hearing;

— issue subpoenas, administer oaths, and take testimony;

— examine the records and documents in any public office of any taxing district of the state;

— exchange tax information with federal and state officials;

— exchange tax information with the Illinois Department of Public Aid for the enforcement of a child support order;

— recommend tax legislation;

— investigate the tax systems of other states;

— prosecute public officials or corporations for failure to comply with the tax laws;

— hire investigators to conduct searches and seizures;

— cancel uncollectible debts after 10 years;

— credit overpayments and interest against any final tax liability arising under taxes administered by it;

— assist local governments concerning the assessment and equalization of property taxes; and

— establish an informal assessment review prior to a formal hearing.

The Department has the power to make reasonable rules and regulations to effectively enforce its authorized powers.

• *Organization of the Department of Revenue*

The Department is headed by the Director of Revenue who is appointed by the Governor.

The functions of the Department are carried out by several offices and bureaus, with most of the units located in both Springfield and Chicago. The divisions are as follows: Board of Appeals, Policy and Communications, Legislative, Administrative Services, Information Services Administration, Account Processing Administration, Taxpayer Services Administration, Tax Enforcement Administration, and Audit Bureau.

• *Contact information*

The headquarters address of the Illinois Department of Revenue is:

Willard Ice Building
101 West Jefferson Street
Springfield, IL 62702

See Ch. 27 for contact information for the department, including regional offices. For taxpayer assistance, phone 1-800-732-8866.

The Department maintains a website at **http:/www.revenue.state.il.us**.

¶2401

• *Technical assistance*

The Department issues periodic publications and rulings in response to taxpayer inquiries.

Private letter rulings: The Department may issue private letter rulings in response to specific taxpayer inquiries concerning the application of a tax statute or rule to a particular fact situation. Letter rulings are binding on the Department only as to the taxpayer who has requested the ruling. Letter rulings cease to bind the Department if there is a pertinent change in the statutory law, case law, rules, or material facts. In certain instances, the Department can revoke a previously issued letter ruling. In such circumstances, the taxpayer will incur no liability for any tax, interest, or penalty as a result of reliance on a revoked ruling.

General information letters: The Department may respond to written inquiries from taxpayers, taxpayer representatives, business, trade, and industrial associations with general information letters. These letters contain general discussions of tax principals and applications, and are designed to provide background information to topics of interest. Information letters do not constitute statements of department policy and are not binding on the Department.

Practitioner Comment: Automatic Revocation

Beginning July 1, 2002, every letter ruling is revoked on the date that is ten years after the date of issuance of the ruling or July 1, 2002, whichever is later. No ruling may be cited or relied upon for any purpose after the date of its revocation, and the ruling will cease to bind the Department after the date of revocation. Taxpayers entitled to rely on the opinion contained in a particular letter ruling must apply for a new letter ruling prior to the aforementioned revocation date.

Horwood Marcus & Berk Chartered

Information bulletins: The Department publishes information bulletins, which are short explanations of changes in law, rules, procedures, or basic explanations of topics of interest. The bulletins are not binding on the Department and may not be cited as authority.

• *Administration of other taxes*

Taxes that are not administered or collected by the Department of Revenue include:

— business license and occupation taxes, corporate franchise tax, motor vehicle fees (Secretary of State) (¶1406);

— gross premiums tax on insurance companies (Director of Insurance) (¶2206);

— corporate franchise tax (Secretary of State);

— motor vehicle fees (Secretary of State);

— estate tax (Attorney General) (¶1909); and

— unemployment compensation tax (Department of Employment Security) (¶2101).

For contact information, see Chapter 27.

¶2402 Returns and Payments

Law: Statute on Statutes Act Secs. 1.11, 1.25 [5 ILCS 70/1.11, 1.25], 20 ILCS 605/605-320; 20 ILCS 2505/2505—200, 20 ILCS 2505/2505-210, 20 ILCS 2505/2505-255, 35 ILCS 5/601, 35 ILCS 5/605, 35 ILCS 5/1407; 86 Ill. Adm. Code Sec. 100.7300; 86 Ill. Adm. Code Sec. 700.350, 86 Ill. Adm. Code Sec. 750-300 (CCH ILLINOIS TAX REPORTS, ¶89-102—89-112).

Illinois tax filing and payment requirements vary with the tax involved. Specific information about forms, filing, and payment requirements is discussed under each tax.

The Department of Revenue (DOR) may extend the due date for payment of personal and corporate income taxes to a date that is no later than the due date for the payment of the Illinois income taxpayer's federal tax liability.

Practitioner Comment: Voluntary Disclosure

Illinois offers a voluntary disclosure program for taxpayers that owe back taxes to Illinois. The program allows businesses and individuals to disclose their activities in Illinois, and pay back taxes owed for the prior four-year period (the "look-back period") without criminal prosecution. Unpaid taxes beyond the look-back period are forgiven (except for collected trust taxes), and Illinois does not retain the right to audit beyond the look-back period. Taxpayers are eligible only if they have not previously filed tax returns in Illinois for the tax for which voluntary disclosure is sought and if they have not been contacted by the state or the Multistate Tax Commissioner regarding such tax.

Unlike most states in which taxpayers may request voluntary disclosure anonymously, taxpayers interested in participating in voluntary disclosure in Illinois must submit their request using the Department's form and must disclose their identity on such form. Unlike other states' voluntary disclosure programs, penalty abatement is not automatic.

Jennifer A. Zimmerman, Esq., Horwood Marcus & Berk Chartered

• *Estimated tax returns*

Some taxpayers must make periodic estimated tax payments. Depending on the type of tax and amount owed, the frequency and due dates vary. Specific information about estimated tax payment requirements is discussed under each tax.

• *Annual report by recipients of tax incentives*

An annual reporting requirement is imposed on Illinois taxpayers that receive corporate income tax credits, personal income tax credits, sales tax exemptions, or the abatement of property tax under the Economic Development for a Growing Economy Tax Credit Act, the River Edge Redevelopment Zone Act, or the Enterprise Zone Act, including the High Impact Business program. Recipients of such incentives must provide the Department of Commerce and Economic Opportunity the following (20 ILCS 605/605-320):

— a detailed list of the occupation or job classifications and number of new employees or retained employees to be hired in full-time, permanent jobs;

— a schedule of anticipated starting dates of the new hires and the actual average wage by occupation or job classification; and

— total payroll to be created as a result of the incentives.

• *Payment methods*

Taxes may be paid by check, money order, cashier's check, or other written order to pay money unless payment by electronic funds transfer is required. A $25 penalty may be assessed if a check is not honored by the financial institution.

For programs that allow Illinois taxpayers to file returns, pay tax liabilities, and look up account information on-line, go to **http://www.revenue.state.il.us/ ElectronicServices**.

Credit cards: The DOR may adopt rules and regulations for payment by credit card of any amount due only when the DOR is not required to pay a discount fee charged by the credit card issuer (20 ILCS 2505/2505-255).

¶2402

Electronic filing: The Illinois Department of Revenue (IDOR) and the Internal Revenue Service (IRS) have developed the Illinois Business Income Tax (BIT) Modernized e-File Program (MeF). MeF is a Federal/State program, allowing both the federal and state returns to be electronically filed to the IRS. Payments are also allowed as a part of MeF. For detailed information, see BTR-36, *Implementation Guide for Business Income Tax, Federal/State Electronic Filing Program,* Illinois Department of Revenue, December 2014, **http://tax.illinois.gov/TaxProfessionals/ElectronicFiling/ BTR-36.pdf.**

• *Electronic funds transfer (EFT)*

Taxpayers with an Illinois annual personal income tax, corporate income tax, use tax, service use tax, service occupation (sales) tax, retailers' occupation (sales) tax, or electricity excise tax liability of $20,000 or more, or $12,000 for withholding income tax, must make all payments to the Department of Revenue by electronic funds transfer. (20 ILCS 2505/2505-210)

Withholding: Employers who are required to file their federal withholding returns electronically are also required to file their Illinois withholding returns electronically. Additionally, employers who are required to file W-2 information electronically for federal purposes are also required to file their W-2 information with the state electronically. (86 Ill. Adm. Code Sec. 100.7300)

MyTax Illinois is a centralized location on the Department of Revenue's website where taxpayers may register a new business, electronically file tax returns, make payments, and manage their tax accounts (**https://mytax.illinois.gov/_/**).

• *Rounding to whole dollar amounts*

Any amount required to be reported that is not a whole dollar amount must be increased to the nearest whole dollar amount if the amount is 50¢ or more. The amount is decreased to the nearest whole dollar amount if the amount is less than 50¢ (35 ILCS 5/140).

• *Mailing rules and legal holidays*

Returns and payments transmitted by U.S. mail are deemed filed on the date shown by the postmark stamp. If the due date of a return falls on a Saturday, Sunday, or legal holiday, the return is timely if it is filed on the first day following the due date that is not a Saturday, Sunday, or legal holiday (5 ILCS 70/1.11; 5 ILCS 70/1.25).

¶2403 Recordkeeping Requirements; Confidentiality

Law: Income Tax Act Sec. 302 [35 ILCS 5/302], Income Tax Act Secs. 913, 917 [35 ILCS 5/913, 917], Motor Fuel Tax Law Sec. 14a [35/ILCS 505/14a], Retailers' Occupation Tax Act Sec. 7 [35 ILCS 120/7], Service Occupation Tax Act Sec. 11 [35 ILCS 115/11], Service Use Tax Act Sec. 11 [35 ILCS 110/11], Use Tax Act Sec. 11 [35 ILCS 105/11], Motor Fuel Tax Law, Sec. 12 [35 ILCS 505/12], Employee Classification Act [20 ILCS 2505/2505-750]; 86 Ill. Adm. Code Sec. 100.7300; 86 Ill. Adm. Code Sec. 100.9530; 86 Ill. Adm. Code Sec. 130.801; 86 Ill. Adm. Code Sec. 130.815; 86 Ill. Adm. Code Sec. 140.701; 86 Ill. Adm. Code Sec. 500.265 (CCH ILLINOIS TAX REPORTS, ¶ 89-142).

Specific provisions regarding record maintenance and production vary by the type of tax imposed.

• *Income tax*

Books and records must be available for inspection at all times during regular business hours if the Department requires such records to determine whether the taxpayer may have an income tax (corporate and personal) liability. (35 ILCS 5/913)

Electronic records: If a taxpayer uses electronic data interchange (EDI) processes and technology, the level of record detail, in combination with other records related to the transaction, must be equivalent to the level of detail contained in an acceptable paper record.

Storage: For purposes of storage and retention, taxpayers may convert hardcopy documents received or produced in the normal course of business to microfilm, microfiche or other storage-only imaging systems. The original hardcopy documents may then be discarded if certain requirements are met, as specified in 86 Ill. Adm. Code 100.9530.

Withholding: Employers required to report and pay withheld taxes on an annual basis must retain a copy of each wage and tax statement on a combined W-2 form and must maintain copies of the combined W-2 forms until January 31 of the fourth year following the calendar year. If an employer issues a corrected copy of a combined W-2 to an employee for a prior calendar year, a copy must be retained for a period of four years from the date fixed for filing the employer's return of tax withheld for the period ending December 31 of the year in which the correction is made, or for any period in the year for which the return is made as a final return. A statement explaining the corrections must also be retained. (86 Ill. Adm. Code 100.7300)

Payroll providers: Payroll providers who withhold Illinois income tax for employers during the year and who are required to file copies of W-2s on magnetic media under 26 CFR 301.6011-2 must file copies of the W-2's with the Illinois Department of Revenue using the same magnetic media used for their federal filing no later than March 31 of the year following the year of the withholding, unless a later due date is prescribed under federal law. (86 Ill. Adm. Code 100.7300)

• *Sales and use tax*

Illinois retailers, users, service providers, and suppliers are required to keep books and records relating to sales and purchases of tangible personal property for the time period within which the Department of Revenue may issue notices of tax liability (35 ILCS 105/110; 35 ILCS 110/11; 35 ILCS 115/11; 35 ILCS 120/7). Records that must be kept include invoices, bills of lading, sales records, copies of bills of sale, inventories, credit memos, debit memos, shipping records, summaries, recapitulations, totals, journal entries, ledger accounts, accounts receivables and payables, statements, and tax returns.

Additional information on recordkeeping requirements for sales and use tax is at ¶ 1803.

• *Motor fuels tax*

Every distributor and supplier must keep records and books of all purchases, receipts, losses, sales distributions, use of motor fuel, and products used for the purpose of blending motor fuel (35 ILCS 505/12). Distributors and suppliers are also required to maintain an accurate daily record of gallonage in bulk and supply tanks. The records must include the date of delivery, invoice number, manifest, location of receipt, seller's name and address, fuel type, and pipeline batch number. Records of all gallonage delivered to storage facilities must be available to Department of Revenue employees (86 Ill. Adm. Code 500.265).

• *Confidentiality*

Except as provided by law, all information contained in returns or investigations is confidential except for official purposes, including procedures to collect tax. Confidential information may be shared with Illinois state agencies concerned with public assistance, employment security, or licensing. (35 ILCS 5/917)

Persons bidding on or entering into a contract for goods or services with an Illinois state or local governmental agency must certify that they and their affiliates are collecting and remitting Illinois use tax as required by law. In connection with enforcing such certification, the Department of Revenue may disclose to the contracting agency whether the bidder, contractor, or affiliate has failed to collect or pay Illinois corporate income tax or personal income tax. In addition, the Director may disclose whether a bidder or contractor is an affiliate of a person who is not collecting and remitting Illinois use taxes (35 ILCS 5/917).

• *Information-sharing agreements*

The Department of Revenue has the authority to exchange information necessary for efficient tax administration, except where specifically prohibited, with any state, local subdivision of any state, and the federal government. The Department has the power to exchange information with the Illinois Department of Public Aid any information that may be necessary for the enforcement of child support orders. However, the Department is not liable for any information disclosed by the Department of Public Aid (20 ILCS 2505/2505-65, 320 ILCS 25/4.1).

Classification of employees: The Department and other state agencies must share information concerning any suspected misclassification of any employees as independent contractors by an employer or an entity. The other state agencies involved are the Department of Labor, the Department of Employment Security, the Office of the State Comptroller, and the Illinois Workers' Compensation Commission. If the Department of Revenue is notified by one of those agencies of any employee misclassification, the Department of Revenue must check the employer or entity's compliance with its laws using its own definitions, standards, and procedures. (20 ILCS 2505/2505-750; 820 ILCS 185/1 *et seq.*)

An individual performing services for a contractor is deemed to be an employee of the employer unless the individual (820 ILCS 185/10(b)):

— is free from the control or direction over performance of the service;

— performs services outside the usual course of services performed by the contractor; and

— engages in an independently established trade, occupation, profession, or division; or

— is a legitimate sole proprietor or partnership.

There are 12 criteria that determine whether an individual is a legitimate sole proprietor or partnership (820 ILCS 185/10(c)).

Federal/state agreement on abusive tax shelters: The Internal Revenue Service has signed agreements with most states, including Illinois, and the District of Columbia to share information on "abusive tax avoidance transactions" and those taxpayers who participate in them. Under the agreements, the IRS will exchange information about leads with participating states, allowing the IRS and the states to avoid duplication of effort and to piggyback on the results of each other's work. The IRS and the states also will share information on any resulting tax adjustments. For additional information, see ¶ 2502.

See ¶ 2601 for information on taxpayers' rights.

Multistate Tax Compact: Illinois is an associate member of the Multistate Tax Compact. The Compact seeks to provide solutions to the problems of state taxation of interstate commerce by state action, rather than by federal restriction of state taxing powers. The Multistate Tax Compact is a document to which states may subscribe in the interest of uniform taxation of multistate corporate income tax and sales and use tax. The Compact created the Multistate Tax Commission and established for member states a joint audit program for multistate taxpayers.

Sales and use: The Multistate Tax Compact provides a use tax credit for sales or use tax paid to another state, provides that when a vendor accepts in good faith a resale or exemption certificate, the vendor is relieved of liability for tax on the transaction and provides for interstate audits, arbitration of apportionment disputes, and continuing study of interstate taxation problems.

Corporate income: The Multistate Tax Compact adopts UDITPA as an optional method of apportionment in member states. The option is not significant in such states as Illinois that have adopted UDITPA as their apportionment law.

Uniform Division of Income for Tax Purposes Act (UDITPA): Illinois has provisions that substantially follow the Uniform Division of Income for Tax Purposes Act (UDITPA). UDITPA is a model act for the allocation and apportionment of income among states. UDITPA was drafted to remedy the diversity that existed among the states for determining their respective shares of a corporation's income. UDITPA has been adopted, in whole or in part, by the majority of states.

Income tax agreements: The Director of the Illinois Department of Revenue may enter into an agreement with the taxing authorities of any state that imposes an income tax to provide that compensation paid in that state to residents of Illinois will be exempt from tax. In that case, any compensation paid in Illinois to residents of the other state will not be allocated to Illinois (35 ILCS 5/302). See ¶ 605.

Motor fuel tax agreements: The Department of Revenue may enter into reciprocal agreements with the appropriate officials of any other state under which the DOR may waive all or any part of the requirements imposed by the laws of Illinois upon those who use or consume motor fuel in Illinois upon which a tax has been paid to such other state, provided that the officials of the other state grant equivalent privileges with respect to motor fuel used in the other state but upon which the tax has been paid to Illinois.

International Fuel Tax Agreement (IFTA): The Department has the authority to enter the International Fuel Tax Agreement or other multistate compacts or agreements to permit base state or base jurisdiction licensing of persons using motor fuel in Illinois. Those agreements may provide the exchanges of information, auditing and assessing of interstate carriers and suppliers, and any other activities necessary to further uniformity (35 ILCS 505/14a).

ADMINISTRATION AND PROCEDURE
CHAPTER 25
AUDITS, ASSESSMENT, AND COLLECTION OF TAX

¶2501 Audits and Assessments

Law: Income Tax Act Secs. 903, 905, 913 [35 ILCS 5/903, 905, 913], Motor Fuel Tax Law Secs. 12a, 16 [35 ILCS 505/12a, 16], Retailers' Occupation Tax Act Secs. 4, 8, 9, 10 [35 ILCS 120/4, 8, 9, 10], Service Occupation Tax Act Sec. 11 [35 ILCS 115/11], Service Use Tax Act Sec. 11 [35 ILCS 110/11], Use Tax Act Sec. 11 [35 ILCS 105/11] (CCH ILLINOIS TAX REPORTS, ¶¶ 89-132—89-148, 89-230).

The tax laws administered by the Department of Revenue (DOR) require taxpayers to self-assess the amount of tax they owe. The purpose of the Department audit program is to promote voluntary compliance, educate taxpayers to correctly file required returns, collect deficiencies, and facilitate refunds.

Illinois is an associate member of the Multistate Tax Compact, and participates in the joint audit program of the Multistate Tax Commission.

Illinois has specific audit provisions applicable to income tax (corporate and personal), sales and use tax, and motor fuels tax, as discussed below. The DOR has posted information on audits for some Illinois taxes that it administers. Topics discussed include how the department selects taxpayers for audit; normal audit methods and procedures; taxpayer records required; how long audits take; where audits take place; taxpayer representation during an audit; taxpayer rights; and options to resolve issues after an audit. (*Illinois Audit Information,* Illinois Department of Revenue, October 2013, CCH ILLINOIS TAX REPORTS, ¶ 402-754)

• *Income tax audits*

Books and records must be available for inspection by the Department during regular business hours (35 ILCS 5/913).

Electronic records: The Department may examine the integrity of an electronic recordkeeping system during an audit. Illinois Department of Revenue Publication 107 (CCH ILLINOIS TAX REPORTS, ¶ 89-710) provides details concerning the systems and controls the Department will examine during the audit process.

Adjustments of federal amounts: The DOR may adjust an item on a taxpayer's federal income tax return to cause the taxpayer's adjusted gross income, the starting point for computation of Illinois income tax, to be the amount properly reportable. (*Administrative Hearing Decision No. IT 14-05,* Illinois Department of Revenue, May 1, 2014, CCH ILLINOIS TAX REPORTS, ¶ 402-799)

• *Sales and use tax audits*

The Department of Revenue may hold investigations and hearings in order to administer and enforce the sales and use tax laws. Books, papers, records, or memoranda relating to the sale and use of tangible personal property or services may be examined at such investigations or hearings. Persons with knowledge of a business may be required to attend. The attendance of witnesses and the production of records may be compelled by the issuance of subpoenas or by an attachment for contempt issued by any circuit court. No person may be excused from testimony or the production of records because by doing so, the person will be subject to a criminal penalty; however, such person will not be prosecuted regarding any transaction about which the person testifies or produces evidence (35 ILCS 105/11; 35 ILCS 110/11; 35 ILCS 115/11; 35 ILCS 120/7; 35 ILCS 120/8).

• *Motor fuels tax audits*

The Director of Revenue or any designated employee may enter the premises of any manufacturer, vendor, dealer, distributor, supplier, or user of motor fuel during regular business hours to examine books, records, invoices, storage tanks, or any other equipment pertaining to motor fuel to determine whether the tax has been paid. (35 ILCS 505/12a) The Department may bring suit in circuit court for an injunction to restrain any person from acting as a blender, distributor, supplier, or bulk user who fails to comply with the provisions of the motor fuel tax laws. (35 ILCS 505/16)

• *Taxpayers' rights*

Information on taxpayers' rights is discussed at ¶2601.

• *Limitations period for assessments*

Illinois has specific limitations provisions for income and sales and use taxes.

Income taxes: An income (corporate and personal) tax deficiency may not be assessed for a tax year for which a return was filed unless the notice of deficiency was issued no later than three years after the return was filed. The limitation is extended to five years if the taxpayer omits from base income over 25% of base income stated in the return. A deficiency notice may be issued at any time if the taxpayer fails to file a return or fails to report a change that is treated as a deficiency for federal income tax purposes. (35 ILCS 5/905) For limitations on assessment periods and refunds related to net losses, see ¶801 and ¶1304.

Withholding tax: A six-year limitations period is established for any notice of deficiency that is issued to an employer for any period beginning on or after January 1, 2013, in connection with the understatement of Illinois personal income withholding tax that exceeds 25% of the total amount of withholding required to be reported on a return. (35 ILCS 5/905(b)(3))

Sales and use taxes: All sales and use tax returns are examined by the Department of Revenue. If the Department determines that the tax owed is greater than the amount stated on the return, a deficiency assessment is issued together with a 15% penalty. An additional penalty may be imposed if the deficiency is due to negligence or fraud. A deficiency assessment may also be issued to a taxpayer who files a return and does not pay the tax due. No deficiency notice will be issued on and after each July 1 and January 1 covering gross receipts received during any time period more than three years prior to the July 1 or January 1 when the notice was issued. (35 ILCS 120/4)

• *Protest of audit*

Illinois has no specific provisions concerning the protest of audits. See ¶2601 for a discussion of the protest and appeal of assessments.

¶2502 Collection of Tax

Law: Ill. Const. Art. IX, Sec. 8a, Income Tax Act, Secs. 502, 505, 803, 902, 903, 909, 911.2, 1002, 1102, 1103, 1108, 1405 [35 ILCS 5/502, 505, 803, 902, 903, 909, 1002, 1102, 1103, 1108, 1405], Use Tax Act, Secs. 9, 22 [35 ILCS 105/9, 22], Service Use Tax Act Secs. 9, 20 [35 ILCS 110/9, 20], Service Occupation Tax, Secs. 9, 20 [35 ILCS 115/9, 20], Retailers' Occupation Tax, Secs. 2a, 3, 5, 5a, 5e, 6b [35 ILCS 120/2a, 3, 5, 5a, 5e, 6b], Property Tax Code Secs. 21-30, 21-135 [35 ILCS 200/21-30, 21-135], Tax Collection Suit, Act Sec. 1 [35 ILCS 705/1]; 86 Ill. Adm. Code Sec. 130.105; 86 Ill. Adm. Code Sec. 210.115; 86 Ill. Adm. Code Sec. 700.500; 86 Ill. Adm. Code Sec. 710.10; 86 Ill. Adm. Code Sec. 710.20 (CCH ILLINOIS TAX REPORTS, ¶89-162—89-192).

The Department of Revenue must begin the collection process with an assessment of tax, providing notice to the taxpayer. If the tax is not timely paid, it becomes delinquent.

• *Assessment of delinquent tax*

Notice requirements vary according to the type of tax collected and the action taken.

Corporate income: Corporate income and replacement tax is delinquent if not paid on or before the 15th day of the third month following the close of the corporation's tax year. (35 ILCS 5/505)

Personal income: Individual, partnership, and fiduciary income tax is delinquent if not paid on or before April 15 of the year following the close of the tax year. (35 ILCS 5/505)

Estimated income: Payments of estimated tax for the calendar tax year are delinquent if not paid by April 15, June 15, September 15, and December 15 (the following January 15 for individuals). (35 ILCS 5/803)

Sales and use: Retailers and service providers generally must file returns on or before the 20th day of each calendar month covering the preceding calendar month. (35 ILCS 120/3)

Property: All real estate taxes are payable in two installments. In most counties, the first installment is delinquent if not paid on or before June 1. The second installment is delinquent if not paid on or before September 1. (35 ILCS 200/21-15)

In Cook County, the first installment is delinquent if not paid on or before March 1, or no later than June 1 by ordinance. The second installment is delinquent if not paid on or before August 1. (35 ILCS 200/21-20)

CCH Advisory: Collection Agency Fees

If a liability for state taxes is referred by the Department of Revenue to a collection agency, any fee charged to Illinois by the collection agency: (1) will be considered an additional state tax imposed on the taxpayer; (2) will be deemed assessed at the time that payment of the tax is made to the collection agency; and (3) must be separately stated in any statement or notice of liability issued by the collection agency to the taxpayer. (20 ILCS 2505/2505-400.)

• *Other parties liable for tax*

A purchaser or transferee of a taxpayer's property or business is liable for any unpaid tax of the seller or transferor to the extent of the value of the property sold or transferred. The term "transferee" includes a donee, heir, legatee, distributee, or bulk purchaser. (35 ILCS 5/902) If there is a delinquency caused by a mortgage lender, the interest will be charged against the lender who shall then take all necessary steps to have the lien removed. (35 ILCS 200/21-15)

Trustees, receivers, executors, or administrators that continue to operate, manage, or control a business are liable for retailers' occupation (sales) tax on retail sales made in the course of liquidation. (86 Ill. Adm. Code 130.105)

If a business is insolvent or a responsible corporate officer willfully fails to remit withholding tax, the responsible officer is held personally liable for the unpaid tax, interest, and penalties. (35 ILCS 5/1002)

Practitioner Comment: Personal Liability

The Illinois Court of Appeals, Second District, upheld a Department of Revenue notice of personal liability against an owner of a restaurant corporation despite the fact that he did not run the business. The Plaintiff testified that the business had a manager with a 25% ownership interest in the restaurant, whose duties consisted of hiring and firing, purchasing, paying bills and rent, selecting purveyors, and paying taxes. The manager, however, absconded after having avoided the restaurant's financial responsibilities for many months. Despite scant evidence, the court upheld the Administrative Law Judge's conclusions that the Plaintiff was both a "responsible officer" and willfully failed to pay the corporation's taxes. Consequently, the Plaintiff was personally liable for the taxes owed by the company. (*Cerone v. Dept of Revenue*, Dkt. 09 L 51032, (Ill. App. Ct. 1st Dist.) 110214 (6/26/12); CCH ILLINOIS TAX REPORTS,¶ 402-500)

Breen M. Schiller, Esq., Horwood Marcus & Berk, Chartered

• *Tax liens*

The Department of Revenue has a lien for tax, interest, and penalties due upon all real and personal property of any person who has been issued a final assessment or has filed a return without payment of tax owed. The lien attaches after the period for judicial review has expired or judicial proceedings have terminated.

Lien registry: Effective January 1, 2018, for taxes administered by the Department of Revenue (DOR), a state tax lien registration program has been established to provide a uniform statewide system for filing notices of tax liens that are in favor of or enforced by the DOR. The scope of the program is real property and personal property, tangible and intangible, of taxpayers or other persons against whom the DOR has liens pursuant to law for unpaid final tax liabilities.

If any person neglects or refuses to pay any final tax liability, the DOR may file in the registry a notice of tax lien within three years from the date of the final liability. The lien is perfected at the time of the filing and attaches to all after-acquired property of the debtor. The notice of lien is a lien for 20 years from the date of the filing unless the DOR files an earlier release of lien in the registry (35 ILCS 750/1-15).

Notice of lien: The lien expires unless a notice of lien is filed within three years from the termination of judicial proceedings or the expiration of the period for judicial review. If the lien arose from the filing of a return without payment, the lien expires unless a notice of lien is filed within three years from the date the return was filed.

The limitations period on the right of the Illinois Department of Revenue to file a notice of lien against taxpayers that refuse or neglect to pay corporate income tax, personal income tax, or sales tax does not run during the term of a repayment plan into which the taxpayer has entered with the department, so long as the taxpayer remains in compliance with the terms of the repayment plan. (35 ILCS 5/1101(d))

Lien priorities: The rights of a bona fide purchaser, holder of security interest, mechanics lienholder, mortgagee, or judgment lien creditor that arise before the filing of a notice of lien have priority over the Department of Revenue. Also, the Department's lien is inferior to a lien for general taxes, special assessments, or special taxes levied by a political subdivision.

Release of lien: The Department will issue a certificate of complete or partial release of lien to the extent that the fair market value of the attached property exceeds the lien amount plus the amount of prior liens, the lien becomes unenforceable, the lien and interest due are paid, the taxpayer furnishes a bond conditioned on payment of the lien, or if the assessment is reduced pursuant to a rehearing or Department review. (35 ILCS 5/911.3; 35 ILCS 5/1103; 35 ILCS 120/5a)

Lien filing fees: For personal income, corporate income, and retailers' occupation (sales) tax purposes, taxpayers are liable for the filing fees incurred by the Department of Revenue for filing an assessment lien and filing the release of the assessment lien (35 ILCS 120/5a).

• *Methods of collection*

The Department of Revenue has the following methods of collection available:

Jeopardy assessment: The Department of Revenue may demand the immediate payment of a tax if it finds that a taxpayer is about to depart from, or conceal property in, the state or do any other act rendering the normal collection procedures ineffective, or if the Department otherwise finds that collection will be jeopardized by delay. The Department must include with the demand notice the findings of fact supporting the jeopardy assessment (35 ILCS 5/1102).

Within 20 days after being notified of the filing of a jeopardy assessment, a taxpayer who protests the amount of the assessment or believes that no jeopardy to the revenue in fact exists may request a hearing (35 ILCS 5/1102).

Tax warrant: The Department of Revenue may demand payment of any delinquent tax. If the tax remains unpaid for 10 days after such demand, the Department may direct the sheriff or other officer by warrant to levy upon the taxpayer's property and property rights. The property levied upon may be seized and sold.

Sale of property: Real property may be sold for nonpayment of taxes or special assessments (Ill. Const. Art. IX, Sec. 8(a)). Notice of the impending sale must be sent to the last assessee by registered or certified mail and notice by publication to all other interested parties (35 ILCS 200/21-135).

Foreclosure: The Department may foreclose in circuit court any lien on real property provided that there are no hearings or review proceedings pending and the time for instituting such hearings or proceedings has expired. Foreclosure proceedings may not be instituted more than five years after the filing of a notice of lien for unpaid income tax and not more than 20 years after the filing of such notice for unpaid sales and use tax (35 ILCS 5/1108; 35 ILCS 120/5e).

Offset: The Department may credit the amount of any overpayments, including accrued interest, against any income tax liabilities owed, even if the statute of limitations has run for other collection procedures. Overpayments may also be offset against estimated tax due for subsequent years (35 ILCS 5/909).

The Department participates in the IRS federal offset program under which Illinois personal income tax debts may be offset against federal tax refunds.

In the case of an Illinois income tax overpayment by an Illinois taxpayer, the Department of Revenue may credit the amount of the overpayment and interest thereon against any of the taxpayer's federal tax liability.

Also, if an Illinois taxpayer is owed any Illinois income tax refund, but is identified by another state as owing taxes to that state, the Illinois Department of Revenue may withhold any refund to which the taxpayer is entitled upon certification of the Illinois taxpayer's delinquent income tax liability in the claimant state and a request by a tax officer of the claimant state to the Illinois Director of Revenue that the refund be withheld.

The priority in which overpayments of any tax administered by the Department of Revenue are applied is as follows (86 Ill. Adm. Code Sec. 700.500):

(1) the oldest final tax liability for a tax administered by the Department;

(2) the oldest unpaid final tax liability arising under any other act;

(3) certified past due child support;

(4) any debt to the state;

(5) any liability arising from Title 26 of the U.S. Code;

(6) any request made under Sec. 911.2 of the Illinois Income Tax Act; and

(7) certified past due fees owed to the Clerk of the Circuit Court.

Delinquent taxpayer posting: The Department publishes an annual list of delinquent taxpayers that includes the name, address, type of tax, and amount due regarding the delinquent account. Prior to disclosure, the taxpayer's final tax liability must be greater than $1,000, and at least six months must have passed from the time the liability became final (20 ILCS 2505/39b54).

The Department's statement on the listing and the instructions for viewing the list can be accessed at **https://www.revenue.state.il.us/app/idti/**.

• *Requirement to post bond or security*

Dealers required to collect sales and use taxes or motor fuel taxes are required to become licensed and to post a bond or security. For sales and use tax requirements, see ¶1801. For motor fuel tax requirements, see ¶2203.

¶2502

• *Civil action*

The Department of Revenue may file a civil action against a taxpayer to recover sales and use taxes, interest, and penalties owed within six years after the deficiency assessment becomes final. If a taxpayer dies or becomes legally disabled, the action may be filed against the taxpayer's estate. The statute of limitations for filing suit is suspended during the pendency of a restraining order, an automatic stay imposed as a result of the filing of a bankruptcy petition, or if the taxpayer departs from and remains out of Illinois. (35 ILCS 120/5)

Out-of-state suits: The Illinois Attorney General may bring a civil action in an out-of-state court to collect any tax legally due to Illinois or to any political subdivision on whose behalf Illinois acts to collect tax.

• *Reciprocal enforcement*

Illinois courts recognize and enforce on a reciprocal basis the liability for state and local taxes imposed by states that extend like comity to Illinois.

• *Agreements in compromise of tax*

A petition in the nature of an offer in compromise may be filed by the taxpayer after the tax liability has become final only if there is uncertainty as to collectibility of such liability. (86 Ill. Adm. Code 210.115)

• *Installment payments*

The Department may enter into installment payment agreements with registered retail vendors who are delinquent in paying sales or use taxes, if the vendor pays a percentage of the delinquent amount and waives in writing all limitations upon the Department for collection of the remaining amount owed. The execution of an installment agreement does not stop the accrual of interest. (35 ILCS 120/2a)

Installment agreements may also be available for income taxpayers. To request a payment arrangement, contact:

> Installment Contract Unit
> Illinois Department of Revenue
> State Office Building
> P.O. Box 19035
> Springfield, IL 62794-9035

• *Recovery of erroneous refund*

If there has been an erroneous refund of sales or use taxes, the Department of Revenue may issue a notice of tax liability within three years of making the refund or, if the refund was induced by fraud or misrepresentation of a material fact, within five years of making the refund. The proposed assessment amount is limited to the amount of the erroneous refund (35 ILCS 105/22; 35 ILCS 115/20; 35 ILCS 120/6).

See ¶2005 for information on erroneous refunds of property taxes.

• *Intergovernmental tax collection agreements*

There are a number of agreements among governmental agencies to provide for assistance in tax collection, both between the Internal Revenue Service and the states and among the states themselves. See ¶2403 for discussion of intergovernmental information-sharing agreements.

The DOR may enter into reciprocal collection agreements with states that have similar reciprocal agreement laws and have entered into an agreement with Illinois. Upon the request and certification by a claimant state, the DOR will collect the tax and deposit the amount collected into the reciprocal tax collection fund. Certification must include the following:

> — the full name and address of the taxpayer;
> — the taxpayer's Social Security number or federal employer identification number;

— the amount of tax due and a detailed statement of related tax, interest, and penalties;

— a statement whether a return was filed by the taxpayer and, if so, whether it was filed under protest; and

— a statement that all appropriate administrative and judicial remedies have been exhausted or have lapsed and that the amount requested is legally enforceable under the laws of the claimant state.

Taxpayers have 60 days from receipt of notice of the claim to protest the collection of all or a portion of the taxes by filing a written protest. If a protest is timely filed, the DOR must refrain from collecting the tax and forward the protest to the claimant state for determination of the protest on its merits. (Sec. 5-5, Reciprocal Tax Collection Act, P.A. 96-1383 (H.B. 5781), Laws 2010, effective January 1, 2011)

Agreement with IRS Abusive Tax Avoidance Transactions (ATAT) Memorandum of Understanding: The Small Business/Self-Employed Division of the Internal Revenue Service signed ATAT Memorandums of Understanding with 40 states, including Illinois, and the District of Columbia on September 16, 2003, which provide for information-sharing on abusive tax avoidance transactions (*Memorandum of Understanding,* Internal Revenue Service, CCH ILLINOIS TAX REPORTS, ¶ 401-437). The Memorandum authorizes the IRS and Illinois to:

— exchange tax returns and return information;

— share audit results from ATAT participant cases;

— exchange information on identified types of ATAT schemes; and

— share audit technique guides.

The IRS will provide states with a list of participants in a particular ATAT scheme on a semi-annual basis on July 31 and January 31. The IRS generally refers to an abusive tax shelter arrangement as the promise of tax benefits with no meaningful change in the taxpayer's control over or benefit from the taxpayer's income or assets.

Social Security numbers: Upon the request of the DOR, the Secretary of State can provide the DOR with Social Security numbers solely for use by the DOR in the collection of any tax or debt it is authorized to collect. The Social Security number cannot be disclosed to anyone outside the DOR. (P.A. 96-1383 (H.B. 5781), Laws 2010, effective January 1, 2011)

¶2503 Penalties and Interest

Law: Uniform Penalty and Interest Act, Secs. 3-2, 3-3 [35 ILCS 735/3-2, 3-3], Income Tax Act, Secs. 602, 1001, 1002, 1008, 1301, 1405.5 [35 ILCS 5/602, 1001, 1002, 1008, 1301, 1505.5], Retailers' Occupation Tax Act, Sec. 2a [35 ILCS 120/2a], Business Corporation Act, Sec. 16.05 [805 ILCS 5/16.05], Motor Fuel Tax Law Sec. 15 [35 ILCS 505/15], Property Tax Code, Sec. 21-15 [35 ILCS 200/21-15], Retailers' Occupation Tax Sec. 13 [35 ILCS 120/13], Insurance Code Sec. 412(4), 446 [215 ILCS 5/412(4), 446]; Sec. 10 [35 ILCS 745/10], Tax Delinquency Amnesty Act; 86 Ill. Adm. Code Sec. 100.5050; 86 Ill. Adm. Code Sec. 210.120; 86 Ill. Adm. Code Sec. 700.400 (CCH ILLINOIS TAX REPORTS, ¶ 89-202—89-210).

Illinois has adopted the Uniform Penalty and Interest Act (UPIA), which contains uniform provisions for assessing penalties and interest. The UPIA does not apply to taxes imposed under the Racing Privilege Tax Act, Property Tax Code, Real Estate Transfer Tax Act, Coin-Operated Amusement Device Tax, and Motor Fuel Tax Law.

The Illinois Department of Revenue has reissued its publication on penalties and interest for all state taxes except the Racing Privilege Tax Act, the Property Tax Code, and the Real Estate Transfer Tax Act. The updated version includes new information on penalties for tax avoidance transactions (*Publication 103, Penalties and Interest for Illinois Taxes,* Illinois Department of Revenue, October 2015, CCH ILLINOIS TAX REPORTS, ¶ 403-011).

• *Civil penalties*

Failure to file by due date: The penalty for late filing or nonfiling is imposed for failure to file a processable return by the due date or failure to file a corrected return within 30 days after notification of the penalty assessment (Sec. 35 ILCS 735/3-3(a-10)). The penalty is calculated at the rate of 2% of the tax due, after subtraction of any payments made or credits allowed, and cannot exceed $250. If any return is not filed within 30 days after notice of nonfiling, an additional penalty is imposed equal to the greater of $250 or 2% of the tax shown due on the return but not exceeding $5,000. If an unprocessable return is corrected and filed within 30 days after notice by the Department of Revenue, the late filing or nonfiling penalty does not apply. If a penalty for late filing or nonfiling is imposed in addition to a penalty for late payment, both penalties are due. If a tax return is required to be filed more frequently than annually and if the failure to file the tax return on or before the due date is nonfraudulent and has not occurred in the 2 years immediately preceding the failure to file on the prescribed due date, the late filing penalty must be abated.

Effective for taxable years beginning after 2013, any taxpayer who is required to file a joint Illinois personal income tax return and who is not included on that return and does not file a separate return is deemed to have failed to file a return. The taxpayer may be assessed for the amount of any increase in personal income tax liability that should have been reported on the joint Illinois return. (35 ILCS 5/905(c))

A penalty of $100 will be imposed for failure to file a transaction reporting return required by Sec. 3 of the Retailers' Occupation Tax Act or Sec. 9 of the Use Tax Act (concerning sales of motor vehicles, aircraft, watercraft, or trailers; see ¶ 1802) on or before the date a return is required to be filed (not later than 20 days after delivery of the property). This penalty is in addition to any other statutory penalties and will be imposed regardless of whether the return, when properly prepared and filed, would result in the imposition of a tax. (35 ILCS 735/3-3(a-15))

Failure to prepay or pay tax due without a return: For Illinois corporate and personal income, sales and use, and excise tax returns, a penalty is imposed for the failure to make payment of any amount of tax due that is required to be made prior to the filing of a return or without a return. The penalty will be 2% of any amount that is paid within 30 days after the due date and 10% of any amount that is paid later than 30 days after the due date (Sec. 35 ILCS 735/3-3(b-20)(1)).

Failure to pay tax shown or required to be shown due on a return: A penalty also is imposed for failure to pay the tax shown due or required to be shown due on a return on or before the due date prescribed for payment or in an amount that is reported in an amended return (except an amended return timely filed following federal changes as required by Sec. 35 ILCS 506(b)). The penalty is (Sec. 35 ILCS 735/3-3(b-20)(2)):

— 2% of any amount paid within 30 days after the due date;

— 10% of any amount that is paid later than 30 days after the due date and prior to the date the Department of Revenue has initiated an audit or investigation; and

— 20% of any amount paid after the date the Department has initiated an audit or investigation, except that the penalty is reduced to 15% if the entire amount due is paid within 30 days following an audit and the taxpayer does not seek to recover the amount paid by refund or credit.

¶2503

Practitioner Comment: Reduction of Penalty

Illinois' current penalty scheme provides that penalties are reduced to 15% from 20% if a taxpayer pays the entire amount due within 30 days after the Department completes its audit. However, the 15% rate is rescinded if the taxpayer "makes any claim for refund or credit of tax, penalties, or interest." 35 ILCS 735/3 3(b)(20)(2) As applied, if a taxpayer pays the entire amount due within 30 days and then files a Board of Appeals Petition (BOA-1), the Department will not increase the penalty to 20%. Furthermore, the phrase "entire amount due" encompasses tax only. Therefore, if a taxpayer pays the tax, the taxpayer will get the benefit of the 15% penalty rate and the taxpayer can then file a BOA-1 seeking penalty relief without first having to pay the penalty.

Horwood Marcus & Berk Chartered

Collection penalty: A collection penalty will be imposed if any liability for tax, penalties, or interest is not paid in full and received prior to the 31st day after a notice and demand, a notice of additional tax due, or a request for payment of a final liability is issued. The collection penalty is: (1) $30 if the unpaid liability is less than $1,000; or (2) $100 if the unpaid liability is $1,000 or more (Sec. 35 ILCS 735/3-4.5).

Frivolous return: An Illinois personal income tax return is considered frivolous, and the taxpayer is subject to a $500 penalty, if the return contains an assertion that no tax is due because, among other claims, an income tax is not allowed by the federal or state constitution, the tax filing or payment is voluntary, or compensation for personal services does not constitute "income" (Sec. 35 ILCS 5/1006). Taxpayers are also subject to the penalty if the declaration on the prescribed state form is altered or qualified in any way, the filing is not made on the prescribed form and its verification is not identical to the verification on the prescribed form, or the return indicates on its face that the filer has intentionally failed to sign the verification. The penalty may be imposed even if the filing is not a processable return, it is not filed on the prescribed state form, or it is insufficient to avoid imposition of the penalty for failure to file a return (86 Ill. Adm. Code 100.5050).

Reportable transaction disclosure requirements: Any material advisor required to file a return of a reportable transaction to register a tax shelter under IRC Sec. 6111 are required to file a duplicate with the Department not later than the due date for the federal return (35 ICS 5/1001; 35 ILCS 5/1405.5; 86 Ill. Adm. Code 100.5080).

Failure to properly disclose a reportable transaction to the Department results in a $15,000 penalty for each failure to comply ($30,000 for listed transactions), subject to abatement for reasonable cause (35 ILCS 5/1001(b)). In addition, if a taxpayer fails to include on any return any information with respect to a reportable transaction, the statute of limitations for issuing deficiency notices is extended from three years to six years (limited to the nondisclosed item). Further, an understatement of tax due to reportable transactions results in a 20% penalty (30% penalty if the transaction is not adequately disclosed).

A 100% interest penalty is imposed if a taxpayer has been contacted by the IRS or the Department regarding the use of a potential tax avoidance transaction with respect to a taxable year and has a deficiency with respect to such taxable year or years. However, for any notice of deficiency issued before the taxpayer is contacted by the IRS or the Department regarding a potential tax avoidance transaction, the taxpayer is subject to interest as otherwise provided by law, but with respect to any deficiency attributable to a potential tax avoidance transaction, the taxpayer is subject to interest at a rate of 150% of the otherwise applicable rate (35 ILCS 5/1005).

A $15,000 penalty ($100,000 for listed transactions) is imposed for failure to register a federal tax shelter or maintain a list of investors in a potentially abusive tax shelter (35 ILCS 5/1007). This penalty may be abated for reasonable cause. Penalties are also imposed for promoting tax shelters, and the penalty is the greater of $10,000 or 50% of the gross income received (or to be received) by the promoter (35 ILCS 5/1008).

Withholding tax: Employers who fail to file a return or pay withholding tax are subject to interest on the unpaid tax. Interest and any penalty due is paid by the employer and may not be passed through to employees. If a business is insolvent or a responsible corporate officer willfully fails to remit withholding tax, the responsible officer is held personally liable for the unpaid tax, interest, and penalties (35 ILCS 5/1002).

Information returns: The penalty is $5 for each return or statement that is not timely filed. This penalty may be assessed up to a total of $25,000 during any calendar year. If the return is filed within 60 days of the due date, the penalty may be reduced by 50%.

Franchise tax: Domestic and foreign corporations are subject to penalties of 10% of the amount of annual franchise tax for a failure to file any annual report or report of cumulative changes in paid-in capital and pay any tax by the due date (805 ILCS 5/16.05).

Negligence penalty: The penalty is 20% of the deficiency attributable to the negligent act.

Fraud penalty: The penalty is 50% of the deficiency attributable to the fraudulent act.

Bad check penalty: $25 for each dishonored check, in addition to any other penalty imposed.

Insurance tax: The penalty for failure to file a timely tax return is $400 or 10% of the tax, whichever is greater, for each month, not to exceed $2,000 or 50% of the tax due, whichever is greater (215 ILCS 5/412(2)).

Denial or revocation of registration: The DOR may refuse to issue a certificate of registration, license, or permit to any person who is or has been named as a corporate officer, a partner, a manager or member of a limited liability company, or the owner of the applicant that is in default only for amounts that are established as a final liability within the 20 years before the date of the DOR's notice of refusal. If the DOR's decision to revoke a certificate of registration has become final, it also has the authority to disallow the sales and use tax discount that is available to retailers and service providers for the purpose of offsetting tax collection and reporting costs. (35 ILCS 120/2a)

CCH Advisory: Business Licenses

The Illinois Department of Financial and Professional Regulation (DFPR) has adopted a rule under which the agency will deny, refuse to renew, or suspend the business license of any person who has not filed an appropriate return or paid a tax for any tax administered by the state Department of Revenue (DOR). The DFPR will implement the license actions following qualifying notice from the Illinois Department of Revenue that the person has failed to:

— file a return;

— pay a tax, penalty, or interest shown on a filed return; or

— pay a final assessment of tax, penalty, or interest.

(68 Ill. Adm. Code Sec. 1100.560)

¶2503

• *Criminal penalties*

The following criminal penalties will be assessed for violations of the tax provisions:

Income tax: A person who fails to file a return, files a fraudulent return, willfully attempts to evade tax, or any agent who knowingly enters false information on a taxpayer's return is guilty of a Class 4 felony for the first offense and a Class 3 felony for each subsequent offense. A taxpayer signing a fraudulent return is guilty of perjury. Failure to keep books and records constitutes a Class A misdemeanor. (35 ILCS 5/1301)

Personal income tax refund anticipation loans: A person who violates the disclosure requirements in connection with a refund anticipation loan is guilty of a petty offense and may be fined up to $500 for each offense. In addition, a loan facilitator may be liable to any aggrieved borrower in an amount three times the refund anticipation loan fee and attorney's fees.

Sales and use taxes: A retail vendor who fails to file a return, willfully fails to pay tax, or files a fraudulent return is guilty of a Class 4 felony if the amount due is under $300 and a Class 3 felony if the amount due is $300 or more. (35 ILCS 120/13(a))

Effective January 1, 2014, a person commits the offense of sales tax evasion when the person (35 ILCS 120/13(b)):

(1) knowingly attempts in any manner to evade or defeat the tax imposed on him or on any other person, and

(2) commits an affirmative act in furtherance of the evasion.

An "affirmative act in furtherance of the evasion" is an act designed in whole, or in part, to either:

— conceal, misrepresent, falsify, or manipulate any material fact, or

— tamper with or destroy documents or materials related to a person's tax liability.

Two or more acts of sales tax evasion may be charged as a single count. The amounts of the tax deficiencies may be aggregated to determine the amount of tax evaded or attempted to be evaded. The period between the first and last acts of evasion may be claimed as the date of the offense.

When the amount of tax evaded or attempted to be evaded is less than $500, a person is guilty of a Class 4 felony (35 ILCS 120/13(b)(1)). When the amount is $500 or more, but less than $10,000, a person is guilty of a Class 3 felony (35 ILCS 120/13(b)(2)). When the amount is $10,000 or more, but less than $100,000, a person is guilty of a Class 2 felony (35 ILCS 120/13(b)(3)). When the amount is $100,000 or more, a person is guilty of a Class 1 felony (35 ILCS 120/13(b)(4)).

A prosecution for any act for which criminal penalties may be imposed may be brought at any time within five years of the commission of the act (35 ILCS 120/13(c)).

Motor carriers and motor fuels tax: A distributor, supplier, or motor carrier who knowingly operates without a valid license, fails to file a return, or fails to pay tax is guilty of a Class 3 felony. A motor carrier who operates without a valid motor fuel use tax license or a valid single trip license is guilty of a Class A misdemeanor for the first offense and a Class 4 felony for each subsequent offense. A motor carrier who fails to carry a manifest is guilty of a Class A misdemeanor. A person who knowingly fails to keep records as required by the International Fuel Tax Agreement, files a fraudulent application, or violates any rules and regulations is guilty of a Class A misdemeanor. A person who knowingly enters false information on required documentation is guilty of a Class 3 felony. A person who knowingly attempts to evade any motor fuel tax is guilty of a Class 2 felony. A person who knowingly sells or attempts to sell dyed diesel fuel for highway use is guilty of a Class 4 felony (35 ILCS 505/15).

Insurance tax: Any violation of the Insurance Code for which a penalty is not provided is considered a petty offense (215 ILCS 5/446).

• *Interest*

Beginning in 2014, interest paid by the DOR to taxpayers and interest charged to taxpayers by the DOR is the same as the underpayment rate established under IRC Sec. 6621. This represents a return to the rate determination method used prior to 2004. In between those years, interest was charged at the short-term federal rate for the one-year period beginning with the overpayment or underpayment; following that period, interest was charged at the rate of the federal underpayment rate. The interest rate is adjusted semiannually based upon the underpayment rate or short-term federal rate in effect on January 1 or July 1. (35 ILCS 735/3-2)

This interest rate does not apply to taxes imposed under the Racing Privilege Tax Act, Property Tax Code, Real Estate Transfer Tax Act, Coin-Operated Amusement Device Tax, and Motor Fuel Tax Law. Also, it does not apply to estate taxes, which are administered by the Attorney General.

Current interest rates: For interest accruing July 1, 2017, through December 31, 2017, the rate charged on tax underpayments and payable on tax overpayments is 4% (*Interest Rates,* Illinois Department of Revenue, June 28, 2017).

For interest accruing January 1, 2014, through June 30, 2016, the rate charged on tax underpayments and payable on tax overpayments was 3%. Interest is calculated on the tax due from the day after the original due date of the return through the date the tax is paid.

Prior interest rates: For interest accruing January 1, 2012, through December, 2013, the rate charged on tax underpayments and payable on tax overpayments was 0% for the first year that the underpayment or overpayment accrued interest and 3% for the period after the first year of interest accrual. For the period July 1, 2009 through December 31, 2011, the interest rate was 1% for the first year that the underpayment or overpayment accrued interest and 4% for the period after the first year of interest accrual. For the period July 1, 2008, through June 30, 2009, the interest rate was 2% for the first year that the underpayment or overpayment accrues interest and 5% for the period after the first year of interest accrual. Interest is calculated on the tax due from the day after the original due date of the return through the date the tax is paid.

Interest rates for earlier periods may be found at ¶89-204, CCH ILLINOIS TAX REPORTS.

Property taxes: Interest on delinquent property taxes is imposed at the rate of 1.5% per month or portion of the month (35 ILCS 200/21-15).

Estate tax: See ¶1910.

Insurance taxes: Interest on delinquent insurance taxes is imposed at the rate of 12% per annum from the due date unless a higher rate is established under the provisions of IRC Sec. 6621(b). (215 ILCS 5/412)

• *Abatement or cancellation of penalties or interest*

A taxpayer may file a petition for abatement of a penalty or interest imposed due to delinquent tax if the late filing was due to reasonable cause, an unreasonable delay by the Department of Revenue, or a timely payment was made by a person other than the taxpayer liable for the tax (35 ILCS 735/3-8). Other provisions regarding abatement of penalties and interest by the Department of Revenue vary by the type of tax.

¶2503

Income tax: Taxpayers, who are members of the United States Armed Forces serving in a combat zone and granted a filing extension, are exempt from penalties and interest. (35 ILCS 5/602)

Property tax: See ¶2003.

Sales and Use: See "Certified Audits" at ¶2501.

Reasonable cause: Penalties for failure to file or pay tax, failure to file a correct information return, or negligence will not apply if the taxpayer establishes that such failure was due to reasonable cause. Reasonable cause is determined on a case by case basis. One factor is the extent to which the taxpayer made a good faith effort to determine the proper tax liability and to file and pay tax in a timely fashion. Good faith is shown if the taxpayer exercised ordinary business care and prudence. The taxpayer's filing history is considered when making a good faith determination. Isolated computational or transcriptional errors generally do not indicate a lack of good faith (35 ILCS 735/3-8).

In the case of *Hollinger International v. Bower*, 363 Ill. App. 3d 313 (2005), CCH ILLINOIS TAX REPORTS, ¶401-617, the court refused to abate estimated tax penalties even though the taxpayer relied on its long-time CPA firm to prepare the installment payments because the corporation itself had "sophisticated and experienced" employees.

Practitioner Comment: Reasonable Cause for Penalty Abatement

Penalties imposed for (1) failure to file or pay, (2) failure to file correct information returns, (3) negligence, and (4) issuing a bad check, do not apply if the taxpayer shows that the failure to file or pay tax at the required time was due to reasonable cause. Illinois statutes do not define the term "reasonable cause." However, the statutes state that "reasonable cause shall be determined in each situation in accordance with the rules and regulations promulgated by the Department."

In 1994, the Department adopted a regulation concerning "reasonable cause" (86 Ill. Adm. Code Sec. 700.400). The regulation provides that reliance on the advice of a professional does not necessarily establish reasonable cause. An Illinois court held that the Department's "reasonable cause" regulation does not apply to tax years prior to 1994 (*Tyson Foods, Inc. v. Dep't of Revenue*, 312 Ill. App. 3d 64 (1999), CCH ILLINOIS TAX REPORTS, ¶401-119).

Upon reviewing a penalty assessed for the 1988-1991 tax years, an Illinois court held that "reliance on the advice of a competent tax advisor constitutes reasonable cause justifying full abatement of penalties" (*Exxon Corp. v. Bower*, Doc. No. 1-01-3302 (Ill. App. Ct. May 21, 2004) (unpublished decision), CCH ILLINOIS TAX REPORTS, ¶401-477; see also *Du Mont Ventilation Co. v. Dep't of Revenue*, 99 Ill. App. 3d 263 (1981), CCH ILLINOIS TAX REPORTS, ¶201-196). In the *Exxon* case, the court did not cite to the regulation (86 Ill. Adm. Code Sec. 700.400).

Horwood Marcus & Berk Chartered

ADMINISTRATION AND PROCEDURE
CHAPTER 26
TAXPAYER REMEDIES

¶2601 Taxpayer Rights and Remedies

Law: Taxpayers' Bill of Rights Act, Sec. 1 [20 ILCS 2520/1], Local Government Taxpayers' Bill of Rights Act, Sec. 1 [50 ILCS 45/1], Administrative Review Law Secs. 3-102 *et seq.* [735 ILCS 5/3-102 *et seq.*], Illinois Independent Tax Tribunal Act, Sec. 1-5 *et seq.* [35 ILCS 1010/1-5 *et seq.*]; Income Tax Act, Secs. 904(d); 908(a), 911(a) [35 ILCS 5/904(d), 5/908(a), 911(a)], Property Tax Code, Sec. 16-170 [35 ILCS 200/16-170], State Officers and Employees Money Disposition Act Sec. 2a [30 ILCS 230/2a]; 86 Ill. Adm. Code Sec. 100.9000; 86 Ill. Adm. Code Sec. 100.9200; 86 Ill. Adm. Code Sec. 200.110; 86 Ill. Adm. Code Sec. 200.135; 86 Ill. Adm. Code Sec. 215.100 *et seq.* (CCH ILLINOIS TAX REPORTS, ¶ 89-222—89-240).

The Taxpayers' Bill of Rights guarantees that Illinois taxpayers' rights are protected during the assessment and collection of taxes. Under the Taxpayers' Bill of Rights, the Department of Revenue must:

— furnish each taxpayer with a written statement upon the taxpayer's receipt of a protestable notice, bill, claim, denial, or reduction regarding any tax explaining the rights of such person and the obligations of the Department during the audit, appeals, refund and collections processes;

— include on all tax notices an explanation of tax liabilities and penalties;

— abate taxes and penalties assessed based upon erroneous written information or advice given by the Department;

— not cancel any installment contracts unless the taxpayer fails to provide accurate financial information, fails to pay any tax, or does not respond to any Department request for additional financial information;

— place nonperishable property seized for taxes in escrow for safekeeping for a period of 20 days to permit the taxpayer to correct any Department error; if seized property is of a perishable nature and in danger of immediate waste or decay, such property need not be placed in escrow prior to sale;

— place seized taxpayer bank accounts in escrow with the bank for 20 days to permit the taxpayer to correct any Department error;

— adopt regulations setting standards for times and places for taxpayer interviews and to permit any taxpayer to record such interviews;

— pay interest to taxpayers who have made overpayments at the same rate as interest charged on underpayments;

— grant automatic extensions to taxpayers in filing income tax returns when a federal extension has been granted;

— annually identify areas of recurrent taxpayer noncompliances with rules or guidelines and to report findings and recommendations concerning such noncompliance to the General Assembly in an annual report; and

— provide a closing letter to an audited taxpayer if no violations are found (20 ILCS 2520/1).

Identity theft: The Illinois Department of Revenue must notify an individual if the Department discovers or reasonably suspects that another person has used that individual's social security number (20 ILCS 2505/2505-680).

Taxpayer suits: Taxpayers may sue the Department of Revenue if it intentionally or recklessly disregards tax laws or regulations in collecting taxes. The maximum recovery for damages in such a suit is $100,000. If a taxpayer's suit is determined by the court to be frivolous the court may impose a penalty on the taxpayer not to exceed $10,000 to be collected as a tax (20 ILCS 2520/5).

Mathematical errors: If tax is understated on a return due to a mathematical error, the Department will notify the taxpayer that the excess tax is due and has been assessed. This notice is not considered a notice of deficiency and the taxpayer has no right of protest. The term "mathematical error" includes not only errors in calculations and entries made on the wrong line but also includes the omission of supporting information and an attempt to claim, deduct, exclude, or improperly report any item of income, exemption, deduction, or credit in a manner directly contrary to the Income Tax Act and regulations (35 ILCS 5/1501).

Review of liens: The Department must establish an internal review process concerning liens against taxpayers and if a lien is determined to be improper the Department must publicly disclose this fact and correct the taxpayer's credit record (20 ILCS 2520/6).

Costs: Attorneys or accountants fees incurred in aiding a taxpayer in an administrative hearing relating to the tax liability or in court are be recoverable against the Department of Revenue if the taxpayer prevails in an action under the Administrative Review Law and the Department has made an assessment or denied a claim without reasonable cause (20 ILCS 2520/7).

Practitioner Comment: Attorney or Accountant Fees

A taxpayer may recover fees for an attorney or accountant to aid the taxpayer in an administrative hearing or in court if (1) the taxpayer prevails in an action under the Administrative Review Law, and (2) the Department has made an assessment or denied a claim without reasonable cause (20 ILCS 2520/7; see also Ill. S. Ct. Rule 137). The term "reasonable cause" is not defined in the Taxpayers' Bill of Rights. An Illinois court has construed "reasonable cause," as used in the Taxpayers' Bill of Rights, to be determined on a case-by-case basis in the context of the law and the facts. The court discussed, but did not decide, whether the term "reasonable cause" should be construed to mean "the exercise of ordinary business care," which is the standard for penalty abatement, or alternatively, to mean whether the Department's position was "substantially justified," which is the standard under the federal Omnibus Taxpayers' Bill of Rights Act, which was enacted in 1988, one year prior to the Illinois Act (*Hercules, Inc. v. Dep't of Revenue,* 347 Ill. App. 3d 657 (2004), CCH Illinois Tax Reports, ¶ 401-461).

Horwood Marcus & Berk Chartered

• *Local Government Taxpayers' Bill of Rights*

The Local Government Taxpayers' Bill of Rights was enacted to provide taxpayers with various rights with regard to the assessment and collection of local taxes within Illinois. Local governments are required to:

     — adopt a statute of limitations for the assessment of taxes (50 ILCS 45/30);

     — provide for the application of tax payments (50 ILCS 45/25); and

     — publish local tax ordinances (50 ILCS 45/90).

Procedures for credit and refund claims, proposed audits, and an appeals process are also required. Further, interest rates for underpayments, late filing penalties, and voluntary disclosure programs must be established.

• *Taxpayer conference*

Informal conferences are available before and after a notice of deficiency has been issued.

¶2601

Informal Conference Board (ICB): For the purpose of reviewing adjustments to Illinois tax returns prior to the issuance of a notice of tax liability, notice of deficiency, or notice of claim denial, the Informal Conference Board (ICB) has been established by regulation. The ICB allows taxpayers to resolve some disagreements with the Department of Revenue prior to formal protest procedures. The ICB does not have the authority to compromise tax and ICB decisions are not subject to administrative review.

At the conclusion of an audit, the Department will send a notice of proposed liability or notice of proposed claim denial to the taxpayer. This notice will contain the grounds for proposed tax deficiency or claim denial along with information regarding the taxpayer's right to an informal review or in-person conference. A request for hearing before the ICB must be filed within 60 days of the date of the notice, using the mailing date to commence the 60-day period.

A request for review must state the taxpayer's specific reasons for disagreeing with the proposed assessment. For additional information on how to request a review, what to do when a request is granted or denied, and the impact of the ICB process on a taxpayer's formal appeal rights, see *PIO-58, Informal Conference Board Review,* Illinois Department of Revenue, May 2015, available at **http://tax.illinois.gov/ Publications/PIOs/PIO-58.pdf**.

In-person conference: Either the taxpayer or the ICB may request an in-person conference to explore and raise issues regarding the proposed assessment. An in-person conference will be scheduled within 45 days of receipt of the taxpayer's request. If a taxpayer does not agree to an informal conference, then he or she may be denied relief due to lack of sufficient information.

Informal review conference: Upon filing a timely protest and request for hearing, the Department may designate an employee to conduct an informal review conference with the taxpayer within 30 days after the filing of the protest. A request for an informal review must include a list of all supporting documentation to be presented at the review conference. The taxpayer may be represented by any person of his or her choice, and the representative need not be an attorney.

Practitioner Comment: Preassessment Dispute Resolution

The Informal Conference Board (ICB) is a forum for resolving tax disputes before the issuance of a proposed deficiency or a proposed refund claim denial. The ICB is a separate division within the Department, and is not a unit of the audit bureau, the legal department, or the administrative hearing office. In all cases where the Department finds a deficiency, or proposes to deny all or part of a refund claim, the Department will issue a "Notice of Proposed Liability" or a "Notice of Proposed Claim Denial." The taxpayer then has sixty days to file a written request for review of the proposed assessment or claim denial.

The ICB has three members, consisting of the following individuals or their delegates: the Department's General Counsel, the Chairperson of the Board of Appeals, and a Department employee, designated by the Director of Revenue, who is not under the direct supervision of either of the Board's other members. The Director also appoints a Board administrator with extensive experience in audit or legal practice and procedures.

A taxpayer may submit a settlement proposal or request a penalty waiver, either as part of the initial ICB request for review or at any point during the ICB review process. The ICB will issue an "action decision" within ninety days after receipt of the taxpayer's request for review (the ninety-day period may be extended by mutual consent). Any ICB decision requires the approval of at least two Board members.

The documentation or other information a taxpayer gives the ICB may not become part of any formal record and may not be forwarded to any other administrative body or judicial forum for purposes of making a determination on the merits of any case.

Moreover, all information a taxpayer gives the ICB is covered by the confidentiality provisions of various Illinois tax laws. The final "action decisions" of the ICB are not subject to administrative review, but if the Board does not grant the relief requested and a proposed assessment or claim denial is issued, the taxpayer may then seek relief through the administrative hearing system or the circuit courts.

Horwood Marcus & Berk Chartered

• *Appeals*

After a notice of deficiency has been issued, a taxpayer may file a written protest and request for a hearing with the Department of Revenue within 60 days after the issuance of the deficiency notice (150 days if the taxpayer is outside the United States). (35 ILCS 120/4).

For information on property tax appeals, see ¶2010.

Small claims hearings: Illinois has no provision for small claims hearings.

• *Independent Tax Tribunal*

Illinois has established a tax tribunal independent of the state Department of Revenue (DOR) to resolve some tax disputes between the DOR and taxpayers prior to requiring the taxpayer to pay the amounts in issue (Illinois Independent Tax Tribunal Act, Sec. 1-5 (35 ILCS 1010/1-15)). The tribunal will provide administrative hearings in all tax matters except those matters reserved to the DOR or another entity by statute.

Commencement of jurisdiction: The tribunal exercises its jurisdiction beginning on January 1, 2014. However, administrative law judges (ALJs) appointed prior to that date were authorized to take any action prior to that date that is necessary to enable the tribunal to properly exercise its jurisdiction on and after that date. (35 ILCS 1010/1-15)

Taxpayers involved in a protest prior to July 1, 2013, that otherwise would be within the jurisdiction of the tribunal may make an irrevocable election to have the administrative procedure handled by the tribunal, so long as the election is made on or after January 1, 2014, but no later than February 1, 2014. (35 ILCS 1010/1-15)

Administrative Law Judges (ALJs): The Chief ALJ is appointed by the governor for a five-year term. Up to three other ALJs are appointed for staggered terms of no more than four years each. After the initial staggered terms are over, ALJs other than the Chief ALJ will be appointed to four-year terms. ALJs are eligible for reappointment. An ALJ must be a U.S. citizen; have been licensed to practice law in Illinois for eight years at the time of appointment; have substantial knowledge of state tax laws and the making of a record in a tax case; and with certain exceptions, cannot engage in any other gainful employment or business or hold a position of profit in a government office during the ALJ's term. (35 ILCS 1010/1-25)

The tribunal must maintain principal offices in both Sangamon County and Cook County (35 ILCS 1010/1-30). Taxpayers whose residence or place of business is more than 100 miles from either principal office may petition the Tax Tribunal for an alternate hearing location, with a view toward securing to taxpayers a reasonable opportunity to appear before the Tax Tribunal with as little inconvenience and expense as possible.

Scope of jurisdiction: With certain limitations, the tribunal will have original jurisdiction over all determinations of the DOR reflected on a notice of deficiency, notice of tax liability, notice of claim denial, or notice of penalty liability issued under specified taxes administered by the DOR (35 ILCS 1010/1-45). However, the jurisdiction is limited to notices where either the amount at issue in a notice or the aggregate amount in multiple notices issued for the same year or audit period exceeds $15,000.

Generally, no person can contest any matter within the jurisdiction of the tribunal in any action, suit, or proceeding in court in the state.

Prior to the initiation of a hearing, the parties to an action may jointly petition the tribunal for mediation (35 ILCS 1010/1-63).

The tribunal does not have jurisdiction over property tax issues; exemption determinations; proposed notices of tax liability or proposed deficiency or any notice of intent to take action; any action or determination of the DOR that has become finalized; informal administrative appeal functions of the DOR; or administrative subpoenas issued by the DOR. It may decide questions regarding the constitutionality of statutes and rules as applied to the taxpayer, but it may not determine that a statute or rule is unconstitutional on its face. (35 ILCS 1010/1-45)

Illinois tax laws to which the tribunal's jurisdiction applies are the Income Tax Act, the Use Tax Act, the Service Use Tax Act, the Service Occupation Tax Act, the Retailers' Occupation Tax Act, the Cigarette Tax Act, the Cigarette Use Tax Act, the Tobacco Products Tax Act of 1995, the Hotel Operators' Occupation Tax Act, the Motor Fuel Tax Law, the Automobile Renting Occupation and Use Tax Act, the Coin-Operated Amusement Device and Redemption Machine Tax Act, the Gas Revenue Tax Act, the Water Company Invested Capital Tax Act, the Telecommunications Excise Tax Act, the Telecommunications Infrastructure Maintenance Fee Act, the Public Utilities Revenue Act, the Electricity Excise Tax Law, the Aircraft Use Tax Law, the Watercraft Use Tax Law, the Gas Use Tax Law, and the Uniform Penalty and Interest Act. (35 ILCS 1010/1-45)

Hearings and decisions: A taxpayer may commence a proceeding in the Tax Tribunal by filing a petition protesting the Department's determination imposing a liability for tax, penalty, or interest, or denying a claim for refund or credit application. Taxpayers may be required to post a bond, and there is a $500 fee for filing a petition (35 ILCS 1010/1-55). The petition must be filed within the time permitted by the statute of limitations for filing a protest. The Department must file its answer no later than 30 days after its receipt of the Tax Tribunal's notification of the taxpayer's petition. (35 ILCS 1010/1-50)

Proceedings before the tribunal are tried *de novo,* and generally the tribunal will take evidence, conduct hearings, rule on motions, and issue final decisions. Hearings are open to the public, and rules of evidence and privilege as applied in civil cases in circuit courts are followed. Taxpayers have the burden of proof on issues of fact. (35 ILCS 1010/1-65)

The tribunal must render a decision in a case in writing no later than 90 days after submission of the last brief filed subsequent to completion of the hearing, with a 30-day extension option for good cause. The decision becomes final 35 days after issuance of notice of a decision. (35 ILCS 1010/1-70)

Practitioner Comment: Illinois Independent Tax Tribunal Act of 2012

Beginning January 1, 2014, a new Independent Tax Tribunal has jurisdiction to hear all protests of asserted tax or penalty liability or the denial of a refund, provided the amount at issue exceeds $15,000, not including penalties and interest. The Department of Revenue retains jurisdiction over:

(1) all protests falling below the tax threshold,

(2) all actions that pursue a collection action on liabilities that have become final by law,

(3) all property tax and entity exemptions,

(4) notices relating to proposed liabilities, deficiencies, and assessments, and

(5) proceedings of the Department's informal administrative appeals function.

The Tribunal consists of one Chief Administrative Law Judge who serves a five-year term, and up to three additional Administrative Law Judges serving staggered four-year terms.

To file a petition with the Tribunal, a taxpayer is required to pay a $500 filing fee and the Department may file a motion to require the posting of a bond equal to 25% of the amount at issue under limited circumstances (35 ILCS 1005/5).

In recent years there has been a legislative effort supported by the business community to move the tax appeals process from the various Departments of Revenue to independent tax tribunals. In the last two years six states have established or considered establishing independent tax tribunals. Illinois joined this growing trend of establishing an independent body to handle tax controversies when it adopted enabling legislation last fall. The enactment of P.A. 97-1129 (H.B. 5192), Laws 2012, provides for the full implementation of the new Tax Tribunal.

Jennifer A. Zimmerman, Esq., Horwood Marcus & Berk, Chartered

---

• *Judicial appeals*

The taxpayer and the DOR are entitled to judicial review of a final decision of the Independent Tax Tribunal in the Illinois Appellate Court (35 ILCS 1010/1-75). Before the Tax Tribunal became operational, various judicial remedies were available for disputing a tax liability. Taxpayers could either seek direct judicial review by paying the tax under protest or pursue an administrative remedy. However, a taxpayer had to elect a remedy and could not pursue both the payment under protest procedure and administrative review.

Practitioner Comment: Invalid Regulation—Attorney's Fees

A taxpayer may recover reasonable expenses of litigation, including reasonable attorney's fees, in any case in which it has an administrative rule invalidated by a court for any reason, including but not limited to the agency's exceeding its statutory authority or the agency's failure to follow statutory procedures in the adoption of the rule (5 ILCS 100/10-55(c)). A Department regulation is invalid if, in adopting it, the Department fails to comply with the public notice and comment requirements set forth in the Illinois Administrative Procedure Act.

An Illinois court held that the Department did not violate the Illinois Administrative Procedure Act when it set forth its interpretation of a statute in a series of private letter rulings, rather than by adopting a regulation. The taxpayer had alleged that the Department's private letter rulings constituted a "rule" requiring compliance with the Act. However, the court found that the Department was interpreting a term in the context of a particular set of facts, rather than setting forth a policy of general applicability, and as such, was permitted to do so without enacting a regulation (*Ogden Chrysler Plymouth, Inc. v. Bower*, 348 Ill. App. 3d 944 (2004), CCH ILLINOIS TAX REPORTS, ¶401-467).

Horwood Marcus & Berk Chartered

• *Standing*

Practitioner Comment: Carr v. Koch, No. 113414

The Illinois Supreme Court affirmed the Appellate Court's finding that plaintiffs, as property owners, lacked standing because their alleged injury was not a direct result of the challenged statute. Plaintiffs brought suit to challenge the constitutionality of Illinois' public education funding system, arguing that the system caused taxpayers in property poor school districts to pay property taxes to fund local public schools at a higher rate than property owners in property-rich school districts.

The court noted that for a plaintiff to have standing, there must be an injury which is fairly traceable to the defendant's actions. Plaintiffs contended that the state's funding system, which creates classes of school districts, has the effect of forcing some to pay higher taxes and that enforcing this system is traceable to defendant's actions. The court disagreed. The court noted that the education funding statute is not a taxing statute and that the school districts, not the defendants, control the rate of taxes imposed. Based on these findings, the court held that the plaintiffs' alleged injury of property-poor districts paying a higher rate of property taxes is not a result of enforcing the educational funding statute or related to defendants enacting the statute and therefore plaintiffs lack standing necessary to bring this action. (*Carr v. Koch*, Supreme Court of Illinois, 2012 IL 113414, 981 N.E.2d 326, November 29, 2012; CCH ILLINOIS TAX REPORTS,¶402-587)

Breen M. Schiller, Esq., Horwood Marcus & Berk, Chartered

- *Qui tam actions*

    See discussion at ¶1605.

- *Protest Monies Act*

    The Protest Monies Act allows a taxpayer to seek a judicial determination of a disputed tax liability without exhausting administrative remedies. The disputed tax is paid under protest into the protest fund of the state. The taxpayer then has 30 days from the date of protest within which to file a complaint and obtain a temporary restraining order or preliminary injunction against the transfer of the protested payment to the appropriate state fund (735 ILCS 5/3-102).

    A taxpayer electing the payment under protest procedure rather than the administrative appeals process has the advantage of a remedy available for all taxes in dispute, an alternative to Departmental hearings, and the review court is not limited to the record made in the administrative review proceedings or to the Department decisions. The review court may try all issues and make an independent factual determination. Moreover, the applicable standard for judicial review is a preponderance of the evidence.

    Authorized payments from the protest fund bear interest at the rate of 6% per year from the date of deposit into the fund to the date of disbursement.

Practitioner Comment: Filing Suit under the Protest Monies Act

Illinois courts have addressed a number of issues concerning the Protest Monies Act, which allows taxpayers to litigate a tax dispute in circuit court (and bypass the Department's administrative hearing process) if the taxpayer first pays the disputed tax under protest and files a complaint in court. The Illinois Supreme Court has held that to have standing under the Act, a plaintiff-taxpayer must be considered the payer of the challenged tax, as opposed to a consumer who ultimately bore the economic burden of a higher tax levied on a manufacturer or distributor, which was passed along to retailers and then to consumers in the form of higher prices (*Wexler v. Wirtz Corp.*, 211 Ill. 2d 18 (2004), CCH ILLINOIS TAX REPORTS, ¶401-464).

Yet, if a plaintiff-taxpayer has standing to challenge a tax and the taxpayer prevails, the taxpayer may be barred from recovering the monies it paid under protest if the State challenges the taxpayer's entitlement a refund by raising the so-called pass-on defense, which states that in order for a plaintiff to be entitled to a tax refund, the plaintiff must show that it bore the burden of the tax and did not pass the tax along to its customers, thereby receiving a windfall (*Milwaukee Safeguard Ins. Co. v. Selcke*, 324 Ill. App. 3d 344 (2001), CCH ILLINOIS TAX REPORTS, ¶401-280).

An Illinois court has also held that a plaintiff-taxpayer's complaint was properly dismissed as moot where the Department had agreed to return the monies paid under protest by the taxpayer, even though the Department refused to concede the merits of the case (*Chicorp, Inc. v. Bower*, 336 Ill. App. 3d 132 (2002), CCH ILLINOIS TAX REPORTS, ¶401-379).

The Illinois Appellate Court has held that a taxpayer was permitted to file a protest monies action after it received a notice of proposed deficiency for income taxes, but before it received a notice of deficiency, without violating the ripeness doctrine. *National City Corporation v. Hamer*, Doc. No. 1-04-2907 (Ill. App. Ct. May 22, 2006), CCH ILLINOIS

TAX REPORTS, ¶401-672. In this case, the Department advised the taxpayer in a letter accompanying the notice of proposed deficiency to pay the disputed taxes under the Protest Monies Act before the tax amnesty period expired or face interest and penalties equal to 200% of normal interest and penalties if the assessment were ultimately upheld.

With Illinois' penalty scheme (*i.e.*, penalties are not automatically avoided if the tax is paid within 30 days after a notice of arithmetic error, notice and demand, or final assessment), taxpayers should consider paying disputed taxes under protest at the time they file their tax return to avoid such penalties. We would suggest that the complaint should be *ripe*, notwithstanding the fact that no notice of proposed deficiency has yet been issued, because the Protest Monies Act, on its face, does not require the Department to make an assessment as a condition to the Court having jurisdiction.

Horwood Marcus & Berk Chartered

Practitioner Comment: "Ripeness" Doctrine under the Protest Monies Act

In *National City Corp. v. Dept. of Revenue*, 366 Ill. App. 3d 37 (1st Dist. 2006), CCH ILLINOIS TAX REPORTS, ¶401-672, the Illinois Appellate Court held that the *ripeness* doctrine does not preclude a taxpayer from filing a protest monies action after it received a notice of proposed deficiency for income taxes from the Department, but before it received a notice of deficiency that would trigger its right to administrative protest and review.

The Court noted that the Protest Monies Act does not expressly require the person paying under protest to wait to file a lawsuit until the Department issues a final determination of tax liability. The Court rejected the Department's attempt to avoid the authority of *Chicago & Illinois Midland Ry. Co. v. Department of Revenue*, 359 N.E.2d 22 (1976), CCH ILLINOIS TAX REPORTS, ¶201-032, on the grounds that the Illinois Supreme Court there did not address the ripeness issue. According to the Appellate Court, the procedural posture at the time the taxpayer filed its cause of action in *Chicago & Illinois Midland Ry. Co.* was identical to the posture of this case when *National City* filed its complaint. Because the Supreme Court believed an informal notice provided by employees of the Department to the taxpayer regarding the deficiency determined on audit was sufficient to confer jurisdiction in *Chicago & Illinois Midland Ry. Co.*, the Court held that it must presume it is sufficient in this case.

As further support for its conclusion that the case was ripe for judicial review, the court pointed to the wording of the Department's letter, which called the asserted tax liability an "assessment" and told the taxpayer that it must act within a week to make a choice to pay or file suit. The Appellate Court found that for all practical purposes, the Department's use of this language is indicative "that the Department had concluded its audit investigation."

Marilyn A. Wethekam, Esq., Horwood Marcus & Berk Chartered

• *Administrative Review Law*

The Administrative Review Law (ARL) provides the statutory procedure for judicial review of the final decisions of Illinois administrative agencies. The ARL applies only to such final decisions. Rules, regulations, standards, and statements of policy are not administrative decisions (735 ILCS 5/3-102).

The ARL has been adopted in most of the revenue acts for which the Department of Revenue is the administrative agency.

Proceedings are commenced with the filing of a complaint and issuance of a summons within 35 days from the date that a copy of the decision sought to be reviewed was served upon the taxpayer. Service occurs at the time of personal service or on deposit of the decision in the U.S. mail in an envelope with postage prepaid. Filing suit is barred if a complaint is not filed within the 35-day period. The taxpayer must seek review under the ARL as a prerequisite to filing suit (735 ILCS 5/3-103).

Circuit courts have jurisdiction to review final administrative decisions. The proper venue for suit is generally prescribed in the individual tax acts. However, in the absence of a venue provision, suit is filed in the circuit court of any county where the administrative hearing was held, any part of the subject matter involved is situated, or any part of the transaction that gave rise to the proceedings occurred. Direct review to the Illinois appellate court is provided for certain administrative actions (735 ILCS 5/3-104).

Judicial review of a final administrative decision is confined to the record of the proceedings before the Department of Revenue. The findings and conclusions of the agency on questions of fact are prima facie true and correct. Findings will not be overturned unless they are contrary to the manifest weight of the evidence. A finding is against the manifest weight of the evidence only where an opposite conclusion is clearly evident (735 ILCS 5/3-110).

The circuit court may affirm or reverse the final decision in whole or in part, or remand the case for the taking of additional evidence (735 ILCS 5/3-111). Appeal from a circuit court decision in administrative review actions is filed in the same manner as other civil cases (735 ILCS 5/3-112).

• *Injunctions*

In cases challenging the validity of a tax assessment, the judicial remedies of injunction, mandamus, and certiorari are generally unavailable to taxpayers on the basis of the existence of an adequate legal remedy. An action for declaratory relief is generally denied because the statutory remedy of the payment under protest procedure is available.

Property taxes: Injunctive relief against the collection of property taxes is granted only when the tax is unauthorized by law or when the tax is levied on exempt property. Taxpayers must allege in complaints for injunctive relief a basis for equitable jurisdiction, such as fraudulently excessive assessment, and that an adequate remedy at law is not available. There is no requirement that taxes be paid in full before a suit for injunctive relief is instituted.

Mandamus is the remedy to compel a board of review to act and to review a claimed fraudulent assessment, or to assess omitted property.

A writ of certiorari may not be issued when another adequate legal remedy is available. Certiorari is considered necessary upon a showing that an administrative board has exceeded its jurisdiction or proceeded illegally.

• *Court action*

An assessment may be appealed to a federal court if there is a question involving the U.S. Constitution or a federal statute. However, the right to bring a federal suit is limited by the Tax Injunction Act and the fundamental principle of comity. The Tax Injunction Act prohibits injunctions in federal district courts against the assessment, levy, or collection of any state tax when there is a "plain, speedy, and efficient remedy" in state courts (28 U.S.C. § 1341). Because this federal provision has been the subject of considerable litigation, the case law interpreting this provision should be researched if a federal action is contemplated.

In addition, any appeal of a state tax case to a federal court is subject to established principles of federal jurisdiction and abstention.

Practitioner Comment: Appeals

An Illinois taxpayer confronted with either a notice of deficiency or notice of tax liability has three options:

     — file a written protest with the Department of Revenue;

     — pay the tax under protest and file suit in circuit court under the Protest Monies Act; or

     — pay the tax and file a subsequent refund claim.

Each of these options has advantages and disadvantages.

The primary advantage to filing a written protest is that it enables a taxpayer to challenge a proposed assessment without having to pay that assessment first. Interest, however, continues to accrue on the proposed assessment. Moreover, a taxpayer electing to file a written protest must first exhaust administrative remedies before obtaining judicial review.

Although the technical rules of evidence (hearsay is not considered a "technical" rule of evidence) do not apply at an administrative hearing before the Department of Revenue, litigation at the administrative level can still be costly and time-consuming. Unless a taxpayer's protest presents a pure legal issue, the Department will almost certainly engage in discovery, including written interrogatories, document production, and depositions. Additionally, the trier of fact at an administrative hearing is an administrative law judge employed by the Department of Revenue.

In light of this, many taxpayers opt to pay a proposed assessment under protest and file suit in circuit court pursuant to the Protest Monies Act, which has certain inherent advantages over a written protest. First, it insures that the taxpayer's case will be heard by an elected judge of the circuit court. Second, by paying the proposed assessment, the taxpayer prevents further accrual of interest. However, because the payment is deposited into a protest fund, not only will the taxpayer receive interest on any refund ordered by the court, but the fund itself guarantees that the money will be available for disbursement. Finally, a plaintiff taxpayer, like any other plaintiff in a civil action, must prove its case "by the preponderance of the evidence" as opposed to the higher "clearly erroneous" standard commonly applicable on administrative review of adverse Department decisions.

Any taxpayer electing the Protest Monies Act option must be certain to pay the entire proposed assessment within 60 days of the assessment notice. Payment of only part of the proposed assessment does not confer jurisdiction on the court. Moreover, as a general rule, a taxpayer may not elect to pursue administrative remedies and then "change its mind" by paying the proposed assessment under protest and filing suit in circuit court under the Protest Monies Act. Once a written protest is submitted to the Department, the taxpayer must pursue administrative remedies until they are exhausted. However, in certain instances, the circuit court has made exceptions to this general rule and allowed a taxpayer to withdraw its administrative protest and proceed under the Protest Monies Act. (See e.g., *Compuserve, Inc. v. Dep't of Revenue*, No. 03 L 51438 (Ill. Cir. Ct. Sept. 2, 2004); *Guardian Life Ins. Co. v. Dep't of Revenue*, No. 00 L 51119 (Ill. Cir. Ct. May 10, 2001), CCH ILLINOIS TAX REPORTS, ¶ 401-309; *but see Dover Corp. v. Zehnder*, No. 97 L 50559 (Ill. Cir. Ct. Dec. 4, 1997)).

Lastly, some taxpayers prefer to pay a proposed assessment and file a refund claim rather than a Protest Monies Act action. The advantages are twofold. First, interest no longer accrues on the deficiency. Second, the refund limitations periods for income tax (one year from date of payment) are significantly longer than the 30-day period by which a Protest Monies Act action must be filed. Accordingly, taxpayers are afforded additional time to monitor a case with similar facts or legal issues that might be pending either at the Department's administrative hearings division or in court. To the extent that the pending case impacts the taxpayer's case, paying the proposed assessment and filing a subsequent refund claim allows the taxpayer to await a decision in the pending case without having to incur the expenses of litigation.

David A. Hughes, Horwood Marcus & Berk Chartered

- *Representation of taxpayer*

At hearings and pretrial conferences before the Department of Revenue, a taxpayer may be represented by a licensed attorney (86 Ill. Adm. Code 200.110). However, a taxpayer may be represented by an accountant or any other person at an informal review conference or before the Informal Conference Board. A Power of Attorney (Form IL 2848) must be filed for all representatives (86 Ill. Adm. Code 200.135).

- *Limitations period for appeals*

For taxpayers seeking review of a tax liability after a notice of deficiency has been issued, the taxpayer must file a written protest and request for a hearing with the Department of Revenue within 60 days (150 days for taxpayers outside the United States) after the issuance of the deficiency notice. (35 ILCS 5/908(a); 35 ILCS 5/904(d); 86 Ill. Adm. Code Sec. 100.9200; 86 Ill. Adm. Code Sec. 100.9000)

Property Tax Appeals Board: An appeal before the Property Tax Appeals Board is commenced with the filing of a petition within 30 days after the date of the written decision of the local county board of review (25 ILCS 200/16-160).

• *Refund claims*

Credit or refund claims must be filed with the Department of Revenue within three years after the date the return was filed, estimated tax payments were paid or tax was withheld, or within one year of the date the tax was paid, whichever is later (35 ILCS 5/911).

ADMINISTRATION AND PROCEDURE
CHAPTER 27
ILLINOIS RESOURCES

Department of Revenue (DOR)
101 W. Jefferson St., Springfield, IL 62702 . . . . .800-732-8866 or 217-782-3336
Business Hot Line: 217-524-4772
Email: www.revenue.state.il/AboutIdor/ContactUs.htm
Internet: **http://www.revenue.state.il.us**
Regional offices: Addresses and telephone numbers for regional offices are
as follows:
Illinois
100 W. Randolph St. (concourse level), Chicago, IL 60601-3274 800-732-8866
9511 Harrison Ave., Des Plaines, IL 60016-1563 847-294-4200
15 Executive Dr., Ste. 2, Fairview Hts., IL 62208-1331 618-624-6773
2309 W. Main St., Suite 114, Marion, IL 62959-1196 618-993-7650
200 S. Wyman St., Rockford, IL 61101 815-987-5210

Department of Revenue—Forms
Telephone 800-356-6302
Internet: **http://www.revenue.state.il.us/AboutIdor/MailRoom.htm**

Department of Commerce & Economic Opportunity (DCEO)
500 E. Monroe St., Springfield, IL 62701 217-782-7500
TTY 800-785-6055
Director's Office: 100 W. Randolph St., Ste. 3-400, Chicago, IL 60601 312-814-7179
Internet: **www.ildceo.net**

Department of Employment Security
850 E. Madison St., Springfield, IL 62702-5603 800-244-5631
Chicago Office: 33 South State Street, Chicago, IL 60603 800-244-5631
Employer hotline 800-247-4984
TTY 866-212-8831
Internet: **www.ides.illinois.gov**

For nearest IDES office . . . . **http://www.ides.illinois.gov/**
Pages/Office_Locator.aspx
Department of Insurance
320 W. Washington St., Springfield, IL 62767 217-782-4515
Chicago office: 122 S. Michigan Ave., 19th Floor, Chicago, IL 60603 312-814-2420
Email: Director@ins.state.il.us
Internet: **insurance.illinois.gov**

Secretary of State
213 State Capitol, Springfield, IL 62756 800-252-8980
Business Services, 501 S. Second St., Room 350, Springfield, IL 62756 217-782-6961
Chicago Office: 69 W. Washington, Suite 1240, Chicago, IL 60602 312-793-3380
Internet: **www.cyberdriveillinois.com**

Attorney General
500 S. Second St., Springfield, IL 62701 217-782-1090
Chicago main office: 100 W. Randolph St., Chicago, IL 60601 312-814-3000
Carbondale main office: 601 South University Ave., Carbondale, IL 62901 618-529-6401
Internet: **www.illinoisattorneygeneral.gov**

Chicago Department of Finance
Tax Division: 333 S. State Street, Suite 300, Chicago, IL 60604 312-747-4747
Internet: **www.cityofchicago.org/city/en/depts/fin/provdrs/**
tax_division.html

PART XI
DOING BUSINESS IN ILLINOIS
CHAPTER 28
FEES AND TAXES

¶2801	Domestic Business Entities
¶2802	Foreign Business Entities

¶2801 Domestic Business Entities

Law: Business Corporation Act of 1983 [805 ILCS 5/1.01 *et seq.*], Secs. 5/1.17, 5/14.30(c), 5/14.30(d), 5/14.30(f),5/15.10, 5/15.15(a), 5/15/.15(b), 5/15.20, 5/15.25, 5/15.30, 5/15.35(a)—(d), 5/15.40, 5/15.45, 5/15.80, 5/16.05 (CCH ILLINOIS TAX REPORTS, ¶1-105, ¶5-001).

Illinois has several business-related enactments addressing the formation, operation, combination, and dissolution, etc. of for-profit domestic corporations and other domestic business entities. These corporate, limited liability company (LLC), and assorted partnership enactments provide significant information regarding the internal operations of a corporation, LLC, partnership, or other business entity, such as ownership rights, voting rules, director/manager obligations, and bylaw/agreement contents, etc. These enactments also address the service fees that are applicable to the various interactions between the state and the above domestic business entities. Business law resources and the location of applicable fee information are specifically noted below.

Corporate entities: The Illinois general corporation law provisions addressing domestic corporations are found within the Illinois Business Corporation Act of 1983 beginning at 805 ILCS 5/1.01.

All parties desiring to incorporate a for-profit domestic corporation in Illinois, that is, a corporation created under the laws of the state, must execute and file articles of incorporation with the Secretary of State. Among other items, such articles generally provide the name of the corporation, the number of shares that the corporation may issue, the address of the corporation's registered office in the state, and the name of its registered agent authorized to receive the service of process. The Illinois Secretary of State imposes and collects a service fee for this filing and for issuing a certificate of good standing. The Secretary also charges other related fees for assorted corporate filing activities. Such fees are generally payable at the time that the requisite documents are filed. For additional, specific information on the Secretary of State's publications, forms, and fees applicable to corporations, see **http://www.cyberdriveillinois.com/publications/business_services/dfc.html**.

Other business entities: In addition to forming and operating as a domestic corporation, among other choices, a business taxpayer can choose to form and operate as either a domestic LLC or as one of the varied domestic partnership formats. For additional information on pass-through entities, such as S corporations and limited liability entities, see Chapter 8.5. Noncorporate business entity choices are briefly addressed below.

LLCs.—The Illinois general LLC law provisions addressing domestic LLCs are found within the Illinois Limited Liability Company Act beginning at 805 ILCS 180/1-1.

All parties desiring to organize a for-profit domestic LLC in Illinois, that is, an LLC created under the laws of the state, must execute and file articles of organization with the Secretary of State. Among other items, such articles generally provide the name of the LLC, the address of the initial designated office, the name and address of the initial agent for service of process, and the name and address of each organizer. The Illinois Secretary of State imposes and collects a service fee for this filing and for issuing a certificate of good standing. The Secretary also charges other related fees for assorted LLC filing activities. Such fees are generally payable at the time that the requisite documents are filed. For additional, specific information on the Secretary of State's publications, forms, and fees applicable to LLCs, see **http:// www.cyberdriveillinois.com/publications/business_services/llc.html**.

Partnerships.—The Illinois general partnership law provisions addressing domestic partnerships are found within the Illinois Uniform Partnership Act, beginning at 805 ILCS 206/100. The Illinois Secretary of State imposes and collects a service fee for certain filings and for the issuance of specified instruments. Such fees are generally payable at the time that the requisite documents are filed. For additional, specific information on the Secretary of State's publications, forms, and fees applicable to limited partnerships and limited liability partnerships, see**http:// www.cyberdriveillinois.com/publications/business_services/home.html**.

Initial franchise tax: An initial franchise tax is payable at the time the first report of issuance of shares is filed. The basis for the initial franchise tax is the amount of paid-in capital as disclosed by the first report of the issuance of shares. The rate is $1.50 for each $1,000 of paid-in capital represented in Illinois. The minimum initial franchise tax is $25, which must be paid with the application. For discussion, see Chapter 14.

¶2802 Foreign Business Entities

Law: Business Corporation Act of 1983 [805 ILCS 5/1.01 *et seq.*], Secs. 5/1.17, 5/14.30(c), 5/14.30(d), 5/14.30(f), 5/15.10, 5/15.15(a), 5/15.15(b), 5/15.50(a)—(d), 5/15.55, 5/15.60, 5/15.65(a)—(d), 5/15.70, 5/15.75, 5/15.80, 5/16.05 (CCH ILLINOIS TAX REPORTS, ¶¶1-110, ¶5-001).

Illinois has several business-related enactments addressing the qualification and operation of for-profit foreign corporations and other foreign business entities. These corporate, limited liability company (LLC), and assorted partnership enactments provide significant information regarding the internal operations of a corporation, LLC, partnership, or other business entity, such as ownership rights, voting rules, director/manager obligations, and bylaw/agreement contents, etc. These enactments also address the service fees that are applicable to the various interactions between the state and the above foreign business entities. Business law resources and the location of applicable fee information are specifically noted below.

Corporate entities: Illinois general corporation law provisions addressing foreign corporations are found within the Illinois Business Corporation Act of 1983 beginning at 805 ILCS 5/1.01.

In the same manner that the incorporation of a domestic corporation and its ability to do business in Illinois is a privilege to be conferred only by law and upon such conditions and payments as the state sees fit, the exercise of the corporate franchise in Illinois and the transaction of business in the state by a business entity created and incorporated elsewhere is a privilege upon which conditions may be imposed and for which fees may be charged. No foreign corporation may engage in any business in Illinois until all applicable fees have been paid and the entity has procured a certificate of good standing from the Illinois Secretary of State to transact business in the state.

Upon the issuance of a certificate of good standing by the Secretary of State, the foreign corporation possesses rights, privileges, duties, and restrictions comparable to those of a domestic corporation incorporated in the state. A party desiring to qualify a foreign corporation in Illinois must apply for a certificate of good standing from the Secretary of State. Among other items, such an application must generally provide the name of the corporation, the place of incorporation, the address of its principal office, the number of shares that the corporation may issue, the address of the foreign corporation's registered office in the state, and the name of its registered agent authorized to receive the service of process.

A foreign corporation that transacts business in the state without a certificate of good standing is liable to the state for the years or parts thereof during which it engaged in business without a certificate of good standing. The charge will be an amount equal to all fees that would have been imposed upon the corporation had it applied for and received a certificate of good standing and filed all of the required reports, plus all penalties for the failure to pay the fees. The state's Attorney General will bring proceedings to recover all amounts due to the state.

The Illinois Secretary of State imposes and collects a service fee for reviewing the application for, and issuing, a certificate of good standing to a foreign corporation to "do business" (see below) in the state. The Secretary also charges other related fees for assorted corporate filing activities. Such fees are generally payable at the time that the requisite documents are filed. For additional, specific information on the Secretary of State's publications, forms, and fees applicable to corporations, see http://www.cyberdriveillinois.com/publications/business_services/dfc.html.

Other business entities: In addition to operating as a foreign corporation, among other choices, a business taxpayer can choose to operate as either a foreign LLC or as one of the varied foreign partnership formats. For additional information on pass-through entities, such as S corporations and limited liability entities, see Chapter 8.5. Noncorporate business entity choices are briefly addressed below.

LLCs.—Illinois's general LLC law provisions addressing foreign LLCs are found within the Illinois Limited Liability Company Act, beginning at 805 ILCS 180/1-1. All parties desiring to qualify a for-profit foreign LLC in Illinois must present the LLC's articles of organization and apply for a certificate of good standing from the Secretary of State. Among other items, the articles of organization generally provide the name of the LLC, the address of the initial designated office, the name and address of the initial agent for the service of process, and the name and address of each organizer.

The Illinois Secretary of State imposes and collects a service fee for reviewing the application for, and issuing, the certificate of good standing. The Secretary also charges other related fees for assorted LLC filing activities. Such fees are generally payable at the time that the requisite documents are filed. For additional, specific information on the Secretary of State's publications, forms, and fees applicable to LLCs, see http://www.cyberdriveillinois.com/publications/business_services/llc.html.

Partnerships.—Illinois's general partnership law provisions addressing foreign partnerships are found within the Illinois Uniform Partnership Act beginning at 805 ILCS 206/100. The Illinois Secretary of State imposes and collects a service fee for certain filings and for the issuance of specified instruments. Such fees are generally payable at the time that the requisite documents are filed. For additional, specific information on the Secretary of State's publications, forms, and fees applicable to limited partnerships and limited liability partnerships, seehttp://www.cyberdriveillinois.com/publications/business_services/home.html.

Initial franchise tax: Foreign corporations pay an initial franchise tax at the time the application for authority to do business is filed. The basis for the initial franchise tax is the amount of its paid-in capital represented in the state as disclosed by its application for authority. The minimum is $25, which must be paid with the application. For discussion, see Chapter 14.

• *Doing Business*

"Doing business," as far as a foreign business entity is concerned, refers to a link or connection that the entity establishes by its business operations or activities in a state. Whether a foreign business entity is doing business in a state is important in at least three areas of the law:

(1) whether the entity has subjected itself to a state's laws on qualification to transact business in the state;

(2) whether the entity is subject to the state's taxing power; and

(3) whether the entity is amenable to suit in the state.

The concept of "doing business", however, is not similarly defined in these three areas.

For additional, more specific information on this topic in the personal income tax context, see ¶103, in the corporate income tax context, see ¶904, and in the sales and use tax context, see ¶1512.

PART XII
UNCLAIMED PROPERTY

CHAPTER 29
UNCLAIMED PROPERTY

¶2901 Unclaimed Property

Generally, property that is unclaimed by its rightful owner is presumed abandoned after a specified period of years following the date upon which the owner may demand the property or the date upon which the obligation to pay or distribute the property arises, whichever comes first.

Compliance Alert: Revised Uniform Unclaimed Property Act adopted beginning in 2018

Effective January 1, 2018, the Revised Uniform Unclaimed Property Act will replace the current unclaimed property law. New types of property were specified, generally with a three-year dormancy period from some event related to the property. Examples include tax-deferred retirement accounts and custodial accounts for minors. In addition, from the time a property is presumed abandoned, any other property right or interest accrued or accruing from the property and not previously presumed abandoned is also presumed to be abandoned.

Among other items, the definition of "property" generally includes certain tangible property or a fixed and certain interest in intangible property. Specific items included in the definition are, among many others, "all income from or increments to the property," "virtual currency," and "an amount distributable from a trust or custodial fund established under a plan to provide health, welfare, pension, vacation, severance, retirement, death, stock purchase, profit-sharing, employee-savings, supplemental-unemployment insurance, or a similar benefit." "Property" specifically does not include game-related digital content, a loyalty card, or a gift card.

For purposes of the presumption of abandonment, the new law lists indicia of apparent owner interest in the property. Included among the indicia are:

— a record (i.e., certain electronic communications) communicated by the apparent owner;

— certain oral communications by the apparent owner in the property;

— presentment of a check or other instrument of payment with respect to an account;

— activity directed by an apparent owner on an account;

— deposits or withdrawals from an account at a banking organization, except for certain automatic deposits or withdrawals; and

— with qualifications, payment of an insurance premium.

Holders that fail to timely report, pay, or deliver property may be subject to interest charges and a civil penalty of $200 per day up to a maximum of $5,000. Holders that enter into contracts or other arrangements to evade an obligation under the law may be subject to a penalty of $1,000 per day up to a maximum of $25,000 plus 25% of the value of the property at issue. There are provisions for waiver of some of the interest and penalties.

(P.A. 100-22 (S.B. 9), Laws 2017, effective January 1, 2018)

What is unclaimed property?

"Unclaimed property" is all intangible personal property and any earnings thereon held by financial corporations, business associations, and life insurance companies that have remained unclaimed by the owner for five years and are presumed abandoned. (Instructions for Filing the Annual Report and the Annual Remittance Detail of Unclaimed Property, Office of the Illinois State Treasurer, Unclaimed Property Division)

Effective January 1, 2018, property generally is presumed abandoned if it is unclaimed by the apparent owner the earlier of:

— three years after the owner first has a right to demand the property or

— the obligation to pay arises.

In the event that the owner is deceased and the abandonment period is greater than two years, the property (other than an amount owed by certain life insurance policies and annuities) instead would be presumed abandoned two years from the date of the owner's last indication of interest in the property.

CCH Comment: Escheat

Escheat is an area of potential federal/state conflict. A federal statute may preempt state escheat provisions, as for instance Sec. 514(a) of the Employee Retirement Income Security Act of 1974 (ERISA). Pursuant to this provision, the Department of Labor and Workforce Development has been of the opinion that funds of missing participants in a qualified employee benefit plan must stay in the plan despite a state escheat provision because ERISA preempts application of the state escheat laws with respect to such funds (Advisory Opinion 94-41A, Department of Labor, Pension and Welfare Benefit Administration, Dec. 7, 1994). Some states have challenged the federal position on this and similar narrowly delineated situations. In the case of federal tax refunds, IRC Sec. 6408 disallows refunds if the refund would escheat to a state.

Practitioners are thus advised that a specific situation where federal and state policy cross on the issue of escheat may, at this time, be an area of unsettled law.

What are the dormancy periods for unclaimed property?

General rule. Unclaimed property is all intangible personal property and any earnings thereon held by business associations and life insurance companies that have remained unclaimed by the owner for five years (beginning January 1, 2018, three years) and are presumed abandoned.

Checks and drafts. Any sum payable on a check or written instruments (but not traveler's checks) on which a banking or financial organization is directly liable is presumed abandoned if it has been outstanding for more than five years after it was payable (or after its issuance, if the instrument is payable on demand).

Bank accounts. Any demand, savings, or matured time deposit with a banking organization, together with any interest or dividend thereon, excluding any charges that may lawfully be withheld, is presumed abandoned unless the owner has, within five years (beginning January 1, 2018, three years), acted in some way that indicates a lack of intent to abandon the property.

Property distributable in the course of demutualization or related reorganization of an insurance company. Funds or stock distributable in the course of a demutualization, rehabilitation, or related reorganization of an insurance company is considered abandoned two years (beginning January 1, 2018, three years) after the date of demutualization, rehabilitation, or reorganization.

Gift certificates, gift cards and credit memos. A five-year dormancy period applies only to gift certificates/cards that either have an expiration date or are subject to a post-sale charge/fee. Beginning January 1, 2018, gift cards and loyalty cards are not included in the term "property" for unclaimed property purposes. A three-year dormancy period will apply to stored-value cards as of that same date.

Stock and other intangibles. Stock or other intangible ownership interest in a business association is presumed abandoned five years (beginning January 1, 2018, three years) after the latest of the date:

of the most recent dividend, stock split, or other distribution claimed by the owner;

that a statement of account or other notification or communication concerning the stock or other equity interest was returned as undeliverable; or

that the holder of the stock or other equity interest discontinued mailings, notifications, or communications to the owner.

Other dormancy periods. Most states also have specified dormancy periods for:

Business association dissolutions/refunds,

Insurance policies,

IRAs/retirement funds,

Money orders,

Proceeds from class action suits,

Property held by fiduciaries,

Safe deposit boxes,

Shares in a financial institution,

Traveler's checks,

Utilities,

Wages/salaries, and

Property held by courts/public agencies.

Is there a business-to-business exemption for unclaimed property?

Any property due or owed by a business association to or for the benefit of another business association resulting from a transaction occurring in the normal and ordinary course of business is exempt from the Unclaimed Property Act.

What are the notice requirements for unclaimed property?

During the period of 120 days to 60 days before the deadline for filing the annual report, a holder must communicate with the owner at the owner's last known address, if any address is known to the holder, by way of a first class letter setting forth the provisions necessary to prevent abandonment from being presumed.

Effective January 1, 2018, for property with a value of at least $50, the notice period is not more than one year nor less than 60 days before filing the report.

What are the reporting requirements for unclaimed property?

General requirements. The reports are due before November 1, for property unclaimed as of the preceding June 30, from banking organizations, financial organizations, insurance corporations other than life insurance companies, and governmental entities. The reports are due before May 1, for property unclaimed as of the preceding December 31, from business associations, utilities, and life insurance corporations.

Effective January 1, 2018, the report generally is due November 1 of each year and must cover the 12 months preceding July 1 of that year. Reports for business associations, utilities, and life insurance companies must be filed before May 1 of each year for the immediately preceding calendar year.

Negative reporting. Negative reporting is required in Illinois. (Instructions for Filing the Annual Report and the Annual Remittance Detail of Unclaimed Property, Office of the Illinois Treasurer)

Minimum reporting. There are no minimum amount requirements for reporting.

Aggregate reporting. Unclaimed property with a value of less than $5 may be reported in the aggregate.

Electronic reporting. Holders with 10 or more owners to report must file the report electronically in the National Association of Unclaimed Property Administrators (NAUPA) standard.

Recordkeeping. Holders must retain records for five years beyond the period of abandonment. Effective January 1, 2018, a holder is required to retain records for 10 years after the later of the date the report was filed or the last date a timely report was due.

LAW AND REGULATION LOCATOR

This finding list shows where sections of Illinois statutory law and administrative regulations referred to in the *Guidebook* are discussed.

REGULATIONS

TOPICAL INDEX

»»→ *References are to paragraph (¶) numbers.*

EDU

ILL

IMP